P9-CMM-654

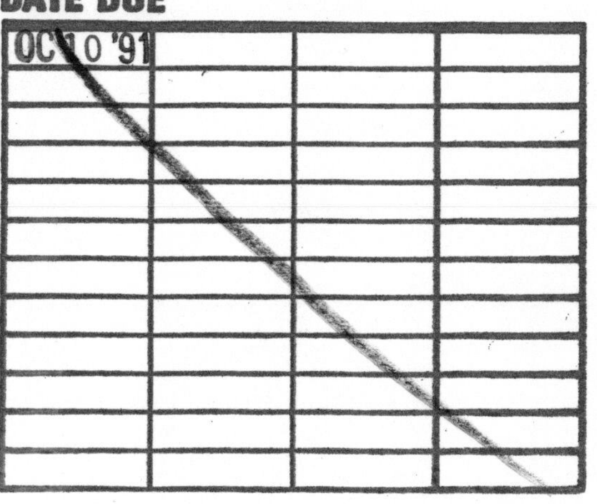
DATE DUE
OC 10 '91

American Higher Education in Decline

By KENNETH H. ASHWORTH

Foreword by LOGAN WILSON

Texas A&M University Press
COLLEGE STATION AND LONDON

Library of Congress Cataloging in Publication Data

Ashworth, Kenneth H.
American higher education in decline.

Includes bibliographical references.
1. Education, Higher—United States. I. Title.
LA227.3.A84 378.73 78-21780
ISBN 0-89096-074-7

Manufactured in the United States of America
FIRST EDITION

For Karen and Rodney

Contents

ideological views about desired social changes. Population growth, economic development, and other circumstances contributed to an enormous educational expansion. Rising egalitarianism and the trend to collectivism resulted in the politicization of institutions and a diminution of their traditional autonomy. Federal largesse was held out as an inducement to change, and the threat of withholding it became an important bureaucratic mode of getting compliance with directions from Washington.

Competition for students produced such outcomes, detailed in this book, as "the body-count game," relaxed entrance requirements, watered-down courses, easier grading standards and graduation regulations, the frauds inherent in external degrees, and other erosions of institutional integrity in altogether too many colleges and universities. Bureaucratic edicts and court orders set limits from the outside about who can be admitted, employed, promoted, or terminated. According to Ashworth, the regional accrediting associations have neglected their monitoring functions to the point of countenancing distortion in the institutional labeling of their wares and even the awarding of diplomas to the manifestly unqualified.

Responding to extremist egalitarian demands for equality of results as well as equality of opportunity, some professional educators have been so obsessed with the importance of leveling up the low achievers that they have forgotten the importance, at least equally great, of not leveling down the high achievers.

With a no-growth period immediately ahead in terms of sheer numbers of students, the author of *American Higher Education in Decline* sees an opportunity for better quality control. In his last three chapters, he goes beyond a diagnosis of higher education's current ills to highlight some prospects and predictions. He makes suggestions for shaping a system better suited to the needs of a postindustrial society in what will continue to be a highly competitive world and expresses the hope that higher education will exercise its proper role in elevating standards of human achievement and worth.

Kenneth Ashworth has written a provocative book, and I think it deserves the serious attention of all who want to know more about the shortcomings of American higher education and about what can and should be done to surmount them.

LOGAN WILSON
Former Chancellor, University of Texas System
President Emeritus, American Council on Education

Preface

THIS book is about the downside of higher education as I have seen it and worked with it. To those who see criticism of higher education as harmful, I say the means are at hand to address the criticisms. To those who say the book is not sufficiently documented and is full of personal opinions, I say it is my book, and I stand with Alice: in deciding whether quotation marks or I will be the master, I have indulged myself and elected the latter. The conditions and vignettes I describe are from real life; the views and interpretations belong to the prerogatives associated with authoring the book.

Higher education has a long record of solid achievements, social accomplishments, and forward strides that constitute an unsurpassable contribution to the public good. Higher education has probably had the most significant role in our society in the accumulation of the critical masses of trained individuals and scientific knowledge to feed the technological takeoff of the American industrial system. Our colleges and universities have contributed enormously to individuals through personal fulfillment and the enrichment of tastes, appreciation, and understanding. Higher education still offers the greatest promise for further human advancement and improved quality of life of any of our social institutions.

But it is time the higher-education community policed itself and addressed such abuses as dishonesty in packaging and labeling, the production of shoddy results, planned obsolescences, and living off government subsidies in pursuit of the profit motive, criticisms usually leveled at business corporations. If the ranks close and protect those abusing the noble reputation of higher education in the country, all colleges and universities will be the losers over time. Carl Shurz's often-quoted remark is rarely stated in its entirety: "My country right or wrong, when right, to be kept right, when wrong, to be put right."

In higher education I think there is much that needs to be put right. My purpose in writing this book is to stimulate the dialogue that will bring about a rethinking of some of the processes of higher learning. I am not suggesting uniformity or absolutism as a solution. But we need more educators to transcend their narrow, immediate assignments or interests and reconsider what is happening in higher education as a whole. We need to rethink the rationale of the higher educational endeavor and how we can go about carrying out its many purposes without having the various pieces compromise and burden each other, producing a dead-leveling of quality among all institutions. If I offend enough people on the one hand and outrage enough on the other, perhaps some things in higher education can be put right again.

In the chapters ahead I make my evaluations and judgments in the context of three cycles I see in American higher education. Those interested in cycles will have their own versions of those I propose. They will also note that I appear to be repeating part of Robert Hutchins's evaluation of higher education made in 1936. At that time John Dewey summed up Hutchins's diagnosis of disunity, discord, and disorder" in these words:

> Fundamentally, the ailment proceeds from too ready response of universities to immediate demands of the American public. This public is moved by love of money, and the higher learning responds to anything that promises to bring money to the college and university whether from donors, student fees, or state legislatures. The result is that these institutions become public service-stations. . . . Love of money results in demand for large numbers of students, and the presence of large numbers renders training even more indiscriminate in order to meet the demands of unselected heterogeneous groups. [*Documentary History*, p. 950]

But I do not plead with Hutchins for aloofness or seclusion for higher education. And I certainly do not argue for any prescribed or single form of higher learning.

1. Introduction

HISTORIANS tell us that to ignore the past is to risk repeating it. Social scientists warn us that we must recognize and understand our patterns of behavior before we can change them. Together they tell us that almost everything that happens is predictable; the *rare* event is the unpredictable occurrence brought about by conscious decisions to alter the flow of events from their predictable directions. Therefore, to learn what is probable or predictable is essential if we are to exert any free will in the control of our futures. As Marvin Harris has summed it up: "To change social life for the better, one must begin with the knowledge of why it usually changes for the worse" (*Cannibals and Kings,* p. xii).

It is ironic that our colleges and universities, the social institutions serving as the repositories for knowledge of history, the social sciences, behavior, and ways to predict the future, give so little attention to the study of their own past and the social processes at work upon them. The colleges and universities equally neglect consideration of their alternative futures. The university community probably spends less time studying itself than it does almost any other topic available for scholars to contemplate.

While not all changes in our colleges have been for the worse, we are permitting predictable courses of events to proceed unchecked to the detriment of quality in higher education. Continued deterioration of quality, in turn, will result in a loss of public support, upon which higher education is acutely dependent. When the public is fickle and higher education enters the courtship without principle, our colleges and universities are going to be used and taken advantage of and will end up with the reputation that they do not deserve respect.

Even in higher education, the past can tell us something about the future. Our colleges and universities are getting through the present by allowing themselves to drift through a series of familiar steps that are weakening their role as effective social institutions. By looking at our past, in which we have gone through similar series, we can identify and understand our predictable course. Our educational leaders can then make conscious decisions to control and direct events to achieve a better result than we are likely to get by continuing to drift.

American higher education has several times repeated a similar cycle of development. In this cycle, higher education first reaches out to serve a larger portion of our people or to serve the people in new ways. In the process, government increases its involvement in higher education. Eventually concern arises about the decline of quality, and the labels and titles whose prestige and meaning have accrued over generations become devalued. And in the current go-round, a new element, never felt to such an extent before, is likely to force even more severe accommodations in higher education. That new element is the prospect of no growth or even decline in enrollments and income.

But before addressing the consequences of the repeating cycle, I need to elaborate the cycle itself. It starts with a growing and recognized need in society and among some educators for a new or expanded role for higher education. This, in turn, results in external pressures on the colleges and universities, exerted principally by the federal government. As government has grown stronger and bureaucrats more confident that they know the answers to meeting social ills and needs, various agencies have increased their intervention into directing and redirecting higher education, its purposes, and its priorities. The public pressure and increased financial support from the government bring about expansion of capacity and growth in enrollments. Higher education, traditionally a nonprofit, at best break-even operation even with public and private subsidies,

Don K. Price perhaps best summed up the situation over a decade ago with a doggerel:

> There was a young lady from Kent
> Who said she knew what it meant
> When men took her to dine,
> Gave her cocktails and wine.
> She knew what it meant,
> But she went.

I will show that the repetitive cycle I have described does in fact exist in American higher education. After describing the current one in some detail, I will suggest some pressure points where educational leaders can take control to redirect or influence events just ahead. I will also present several alternative futures we should consider as we complete this cycle and get ready for the next one.

2. Aggies and Veterans

THE first contract for services between the federal government and an institution of higher education was executed in 1830 and was for research on the causes of explosions in steam boilers. Since the steam engine introduced the industrial revolution, it was fitting that the first contract between the government and an American school of higher learning should deal with steam boilers. This first encounter was only a simple contract for existing services and was in no way a federal effort to modify or redirect the purposes of an institution of higher education.

Not until near the time of the Civil War did the need for a different kind of higher education become evident enough to be felt in the political process. President Buchanan in 1859 vetoed the first Morrill Act to create land-grant agricultural colleges. Society's needs as articulated by some educators and political leaders had led to action by the U.S. Congress to alter the form of higher education or create a new form. The traditional colleges and universities, private and public, focused upon educating "gentlemen." They prepared their graduates for the ministry, the law, or the professions. Their curricula were based upon the assumptions that knowledge was finite, most of it already accumulated, and that a college's job was to cram as much of this knowledge as possible into the heads of undergraduate students. Consequently, the curricula were classical, that is, they consisted of languages, mathematics, history, literature, and some science. It was assumed that these subjects established mental discipline within the individual and developed his mind through the exercise of the intellect, just as repeated and prescribed use developed a muscle.

By the middle of the last century, the need for more practical and applied education had become apparent. Congress, undeterred by the veto of its land-grant program, passed again, and President Lincoln signed into law in 1862, the Morrill Act, which created colleges for the agricultural and mechanical arts. These schools were to be established and operated from interest on the income from the sale of public lands granted to each state that created at least one institution offering instruction in "agriculture and the mechanic arts without excluding other scientific and classical studies and including military tactics." Within eight years after the act was passed, thirty-seven states had agreed to establish the programs promoted by the federal legislation. But the new legislation did not accomplish the hoped-for objective right away. Some of the new schools and the established ones that added agricultural and mechanical courses still tended to track the curricula of the older colleges and so were seen as too impractical by the public they were intended to serve. In time, however, the Hatch Act of 1887, which created agricultural extension centers, and the second Morrill Act in 1890, spurred the agricultural and mechanical colleges to focus on utilitarian subjects and to serve the populist purposes of the federal legislation. The second Morrill Act provided for annual federal expenditures to support the land-grant colleges. It also stipulated that these federal funds could not be used to support the traditional scientific and classical studies from which the new institutions were being asked to change their direction. The additional federal funds provided for applied subjects stimulated the new schools to move ahead in teaching the practical arts.

These developments increased the colleges' capacity to enroll more students. Their new purpose, their geographic location, and their attitude toward a new student clientele extended educational opportunities to a large segment of the population not previously served.

Entrepreneurs got into the land-grant business, although not in the educational end of it. Swindling the states by speculating in the million out of a total population of 123 million; the annual awarding of degrees had grown to 140,000. But in that same year the total number of people holding college degrees in the United States was less than 1.5 million, or only about 2 percent of the population aged twenty to seventy. Compared with later generations, only a small portion of the population found higher education desirable or necessary.

Although some university research was funded by government contracts, even this aspect of higher education was carried out for the most part without government support. The era of defense research, applied research in science and technology, and the application of knowledge to social problems still lay ahead.

During World War II, the universities were in close step with the country as they turned their resources to support the war effort. They prepared the men, and some women, for service in the military branches. Education was for readying for war activities those who passed through the colleges' halls. The research done, the conversion of pure researchers to applied work, and the extension of earlier basic research to applied purposes were part of the war effort as well. Government made no effort to change permanently higher education's self-defined purposes and priorities. Most institutions of society did what they could for the war effort, but this was assumed to be a temporary arrangement by the colleges and universities for the duration of the war. No one expected them after the war to continue to prepare most male students for the officer corps or for technical positions in defense industries.

Society's next felt need concerned what to do with millions of veterans who would be discharged at the end of the war and dumped on the job market within a relatively short period. Postwar demobilization plans included efforts to keep the country from sinking back into the depression from which wartime industrial production had raised it. The Serviceman's Readjustment Act, the GI Bill, was a masterful solution. Veterans going to school would not be in the job market, and the country could show its gratitude to the fighting men by providing them support to attend college. The primary beneficiary was the veteran, but the colleges were aided as well. The government's GI Bill caused colleges and universities to expand enormously and, in absorbing more than 2.25 million veterans, to reach new groups of the population never previously served.

Concerns about quality were of course expressed. Standards presumably would decline. But most returning mature veterans were serious students. And the institutions, through their accrediting organizations, exerted quality control by working with the government to determine which institutions were eligible for the federal financial support to educate the veterans. A few hucksters and promoters saw this as a place to make a fast buck, but the abuses were relatively few except in some proprietary schools. The higher-education community stood together and worked with the federal government when the Veterans Readjustment Act of 1952 required the U.S. Commissioner of Education to publish a list of accrediting agencies he regarded as reliable to rule on schools' quality. This cooperation between the government and educators prevented any major erosion in excellence. Furthermore, the better schools did not need to lower standards to attract students, since the number of applicants exceeded the enrollment capacities of many colleges. Institutions could maintain admissions and performance standards, and some even raised them.

New forms of education did develop in order to address the vocational needs of some students. Also, technological advances, accelerated by the war, required more technical training. Men needed skills to take over some of the jobs filled during the war by women, many of whom were now stopping work to raise families. This need for technical training gave a strong push to the development of junior colleges, which could offer terminal programs in technical and vocational fields and also provide academic courses for transfer into the four-year colleges and universities.

Thus it became appropriate again to speak of the value of diversity in higher education. Private and public institutions alike were offering a wide range of programs. They could serve those interested in a liberal arts degree, whether for its own sake or as preparation for a graduate degree. They could serve those who desired a professional background in business, engineering, pharmacy, or whatever, with an appropriate mixture of general education. They could respond to those who wanted professional degrees in fields that were by that time affiliated with major universities, such as law and medicine. And they could respond to those wanting a one- or two-year program in a specific vocational or technical field. Admissions and performance standards varied. Wide choices were available in a diverse system of higher education.

With only slight modification, the approach followed after World War II was extended to the Korean veterans. This was done not so much, as before, to keep the new veterans out of the job market, as to reward those who had made a special sacrifice of time or body to the war. In addition, the GI Bill had been immensely successful; the program structure was in place, and the schools were ready to address the new group of veterans. The society benefited, and the lives and careers of individuals were enhanced. From a strictly fiscal point of view, the estimated increased tax revenues from higher incomes attributable to college education many times repaid the original government outlay for educating the veterans.

But the GI Bill was a desirable program for another reason. In the mid-1950's, the public came to recognize the advantages a college degree provided for chances of success in American society. This new appreciation for the practical and dollar values of a college diploma provided part of the drive that has been pushing American higher education through the third and current cycle, which is just now winding down — or more accurately, plateauing out.

The GI Bill's success and the increased importance of holding a college degree came in a decade, 1945 to 1955, during which the United States experienced a phenomenal expansion and conversion of industry. The industrial plant of most of the rest of the world had been laid waste by the war, leaving the United States industrially superior to every other nation. At that time many of our plants were new, and we were expanding into and discovering new processes. These circumstances required new scientists and technologists as well as technicians and managers. As the nation moved to industrial preeminence in the world, education propelled people upward in jobs and, beyond that, pump-primed new industries and contributed to further expansion. The circumstances promoted education, and education enhanced the circumstances. The stage was set for the next cycle.

Before leaving the two cycles described in this chapter, though, it is important to note that the federal government intruded relatively little into the internal affairs of higher education to entice the schools to respond to the social needs the government had identified. For one thing, there was not the sense of immediacy we face today. After passing the land-grant legislation in response to a perceived social need, the country could wait decades to let the changes take place.

Beyond that, though, the government's objectives were relatively simple compared with the kinds of social goals it now discovers for our colleges and universities. For example, educational assistance to veterans after World War II had a limited goal. Even if the consequences reached far beyond the original intentions, those original purposes were simple, as described above. Federal intrusion into college affairs was not necessary. Under the GI Bill, the government was using the colleges and universities to perform their usual services, as defined by the schools and not by the government, to reach a larger audience than had ever been touched before. The government provided the money to help the student, and the student's tuition in turn helped the schools. And except for monitoring the honest and legal use of the funds, the federal government had little concern with what took place within the schools so long as qualified educators attested to the quality of the offerings. The GI Bill was not intended as an instrument of social change, although it has served eminently in that capacity as well.

Then too, the government approached the simple objectives it did have quite directly. It was as though the government admitted the usefulness of what the colleges were already doing and felt that with some federal funds they could be assisted to do more of it. The form of the assistance, whether for agricultural, mechanical, and practical arts or for educating veterans, was general aid, which offered money as an enticement without providing, as current aid programs do, leverage to rearrange matters within the colleges. The difference, succinctly put, is that then the government believed the colleges were being useful to society simply by pursuing their own goals, while today government sees the colleges as most useful when they pursue government's own goals. The numerous categorical aid programs and the frequent intervention into institutional priorities, policies, and programs by federal agencies and the courts give evidence of this change in attitude.

Interestingly, left to choose whether to become involved in the federal programs for land-grant schools and for veterans, many colleges did participate. The principal intentions of the government — advancement of agriculture, extraction of natural resources, conquest of the frontiers, crossing and damming of rivers, and education for veterans — did have additional social consequences. But these were in many cases discovered and promoted not by federal officials but by the colleges. The programs were not created primarily to deal with social stratification, to correct social inequities, to bring new groups into the mainstream of American life, or to integrate the races (witness the land-grant act of 1890 permitting the creation of black agricultural and mechanical colleges). Yet the programs did unintentionally touch all these issues as well, due both to the nature of the programs and the change-agent role colleges assumed for themselves in administering the funds they received.

3. The Space Race and the Paper Chase

THE current cycle of federal involvement in higher education began when the Russians launched Sputnik. America was shocked. All the time we had thought that God was on our side, that righteousness would prevail, and now something serious had gone wrong in the organization of the universe.

The public consternation resulted in part from such a sudden disillusionment after a victorious war and a decade of unprecedented growth and increasing prosperity. The demonstration of greater Russian scientific advancement shattered the presumption of American superiority in all things. This was particularly frightening to a people who had just conducted with religious fervor a witch-hunt to root out the evils of communism. Where had we gone wrong? If right did not give us all might, what must we do to protect our way of life?

The American people needed someone to tell them what they must do, and President Eisenhower declared that education was their salvation. America had obviously ignored education if the Russians could get ahead of us in science. We had permitted the quality of teaching to slip behind that of our major rival. Congress and the people responded, declaring education the nation's first line of defense by quickly passing the National Defense Education Act and, later, many other measures. The government promoted the sciences, mathematics, languages, teacher education, and engineering through graduate fellowships, grants, and loans.

Over the next decade almost every committee of Congress and

every major agency of the executive branch would find ways to tie their programs to the colleges and universities. The Defense Department and the military services all found it beneficial to develop programs drawing upon higher education and promoting new strengths in selected universities. In time, still more government agencies turned to higher education for help on specific problems, both for research and for training people in the specialized fields required in an increasingly technological and international society. Government agencies promoted higher education's further involvement in health, natural resources, space, social problems, and the preparation of qualified administrators and specialists for government. The National Science Foundation and the Office of Education took on new and expanded responsibilities. The U.S. Office of Education especially, formerly staffed by monograph writers, statisticians, and educators, had to convert to an executive agency administering billions of dollars in grants and loans. The space race pushed the country into supporting education at all levels as it never had before.

Simultaneously, a major change that had been quietly underway for over a generation became palpably clear to all in business, industry, and government. Qualifications for advancement and hiring rose, making a college education not just desirable but a basic requirement. Coming up through the ranks no longer adequately prepared people to fill executive or even middle-management positions. The World War II veterans who had acquired college degrees upon returning from military duty were doing well. They were clear evidence of what an education could do for a career. They raised the standards and the expectations of employers, and, as they themselves became the employers and the supervisors and the executives, they expected better educated men and women around them. Connections still helped, but any boy from a modest or even poor economic background could rise to positions of increasing responsibility if he held a college degree. It was harder for women to rise through executive ranks even with a college degree, but without one a woman had little chance of substantial advancement.

By the sixties, the bulge on the population chart created by the baby boom after World War II moved into the college-going age-group. These students wanted a college education, and their parents, having seen and experienced what a degree could do for graduates in their generation, wanted them to have it. With the pressure of such large numbers of students, colleges and universities had to expand quickly, and they called for help. The federal government responded to the additional political pressure to assist higher education. The government provided grants and loans to the schools to construct dormitories and classrooms and laboratories and libraries and almost every type of facility needed for the crush of young people arriving on the campuses.

When students could not afford to attend college, the government overcame the economic barriers by providing more student grants, a work-study program, cooperative education programs, and direct and insured loans to students. The costs of such aid programs ran into the billions of dollars.

As it became clear that the colleges and universities could not find enough Ph. D.'s to fill the faculty ranks needed to teach all the new students, the government addressed that new bottleneck by injecting large amounts of funds to create additional graduate programs and to expand the existing ones. As other special needs became evident — such as the predominantly black schools, vocational schools, community junior colleges, the health and allied health professions, and engineering and research programs — they too received support.

Barriers of race, ethnic heritage, sex, and financial ability to pay for college all began to fall. The recommendations of the 1947 President's Commission on Higher Education "to make public education at all levels equally accessible to all, without regard to race, creed, sex or national origin" were finally becoming realizable. Anyone desiring to go to college and able to perform the required level of work, which varied over a wide range, should now be able to do so by finding a college appropriate to his or her educational needs. A college education, now available to almost all, was the key to upward mobility in income, to participation in society's decision-making activities, and to breaking out of or into or through classes of society. College credentials became more important to a successful adult than an inheritance, a sinecure, or a working spouse. There was room at the top, and the paper chase was the way to get there.

The higher-education community had never been so well off. The schools were in the midst of a seller's market for education. The student demand for a degree seemed insatiable. The colleges were the only social instruments available to respond to that demand. And the government was paying a large part of the costs. Despite the growth of public higher education, the private colleges and universities also fared well. There was enough for everybody in the education business. The value of the credential was beyond question; it was the ticket to a better life.

When the government starts disbursing large amounts of money and influences the issuance of tickets as important in society as college degrees, questions of distribution and the equity of the distribution system are certain to be raised. As changes occurred in the voting system to provide urban and minority populations a greater voice in government, the new voters were able to bring their concerns over educational equity into the political arena. The benefits large segments of the society received from college education had been largely denied members of minority groups. Concurrently with the expansion of educational programs, the idea grew that past injustices and deprivation in the larger society might be corrected through the educational institutions. Early efforts in this direction in the 1960's required that federal funds from the education-aid programs be provided only on the condition that all discrimination be removed from admissions policies, from hiring and recruitment policies, and even from contracts for construction of facilities.

During the period the government continued supporting higher education, the nation entered the long and unpopular Vietnam War. This war coincided with the period when the largest bulge of post–World War II babies reached college age, that is, war-fighting age. With hindsight, it is clear that all the conditions were set to cause this group of college students to become acutely concerned about our foreign and domestic policies. The numbers of students and the new diversity of young people admitted to colleges and universities would have sufficed to produce an unsettled time on the campuses. The tendency was intensified as more men went to college in order to avoid the draft. The greater freedom and permissiveness in these young people's upbringing also may have prepared them to rebel more against discipline and control than earlier generations. But the addition of an unpopular war, carried on under excessive governmental secrecy, guaranteed that, if the situation continued long enough, critics would emerge on the campuses. It is characteristic of our democracy that what government does in secret will always be challenged by some who want to know more about what is going on. The longer the secrecy continues, the more the critics insist on knowing what their government is hiding from the people. Government must eventually choose either to tell more or to discredit and suppress the critics. Because two American administrations chose the latter approach, the number of critics grew. And the higher-education community was in the vortex of the storm of criticism of government policy.

At the same time, the courts began to treat college students as adults, requiring college administrators to provide procedural due process in matters in which the colleges had traditionally acted as surrogate parents. The colleges were ordered to provide written rules and procedures for all kinds of matters a president or dean had traditionally resolved impromptu as he saw the situation and the facts at hand. Now they were told that such actions were capricious and arbitrary and that such offhand decisions by administrators would be overruled by the courts. If college rules did not exist or were inadequate, the courts would decide for the administrators how issues should be resolved. Then the people, through Congress and the state legislatures, acted to provide eighteen-year-old citizens the right to vote, and the colleges found that the young people they had treated as maturing children, or adolescents at best, were now adults legally. These young people quickly claimed the rights and privileges of autonomous adults. *In loco parentis* was almost as dead as the language in which it was written.

The years of student upheaval during the Vietnam War presented the colleges with difficult times, and the politicization of the campuses may never be completely removed. College administrators faced the challenges of maintaining freedom of expression for all points of view, guaranteeing procedural due process when imposing restrictions or discipline on one group or another, and trying to sustain some form of order, even in the face of protestors who cared nothing about civility, feelings, dignity, taste, or property. Morality was said to come out of the end of a gun. The colleges, which had been having it so good, were the focus for much of the violence and criticism. To play upon the argot of the day, the colleges provided the real estate for the war at home. Much of the luster the colleges had gained in the preceding few years faded as some students tried to use the campuses as sanctuaries from which to sally forth with impunity for attacks upon society and its policies and traditions.

Since a college education is now an accepted passport to success and advancement, it is no longer seen as a privilege but as something to which all citizens have a right. There must be unusually compelling reasons for depriving any citizen of an opportunity to obtain a college degree. In a time when inflation and increasing taxes make it more difficult for families to accumulate and pass on substantial estates, the best, and perhaps only, inheritance parents can pass on to their children is a college education. It is one of the few gifts that retain value for a lifetime and cannot be depreciated by inflation or lost in a depression or squandered in a moment of foolishness.

Given the view that a college education comes close to being a property right, the government next took the position that, in eliminating discriminatory practices, it was not enough for a college or university to adopt benign procedures, to abandon previous policies, and to prohibit past practices. By an Executive Order in 1965, the government adopted the policy that the schools must launch affirmative action programs to overcome the results of past discrimination, that is, they must take positive steps to correct past injustices. The government now examines schools to determine whether acceptable progress toward statistical ideals has been achieved. Goals now cover not just race and ethnic origin but sex and age and also require support and access for handicapped persons.

For example, the federal government appears to be on the verge of requiring all colleges and universities to make all buildings accessible to the physically handicapped, as new buildings already must be. Proposals that only some schools be required to make the conversions do not appear permissible, because they would deny equal access of all handicapped students to all campuses. No state permits every student interested in a Ph.D. program in any esoteric field to demand that such a program be placed on the campus of his or her choice. Ironically, society is permitted to deny the equal access of every citizen to every conceivable degree program on every campus. But the courts apparently consider it unreasonable for society to provide access to the handicapped only on certain campuses, even though the costs of converting physical plants to meet the needs of the handicapped have been estimated to be as high as several billion dollars.

Moreover, the courts have recently held that deaf students must be provided with interpreters at public expense. Another recent court order held that a deaf student excluded from a nursing program because of her handicap must be reconsidered for admission without consideration of her deafness. These two decisions show how little discretion remains to exclude any student from higher education, even if schools do not have funds to cover the extensive new costs associated with the needs of a particular student. Higher education is no longer a privilege for the few or even a privilege for the many; it is a right of all citizens regardless of special needs and the costs to society in duplicating access.

The major difficulties between government and higher education arise in two areas. First, some colleges and universities are very slow to respond to new social needs and, here and there, there still remain outright reluctance and opposition to providing greater equity to members of minority groups. The second major problem is that bureaucrats in the federal government are trying to substitute their judgments for those of the people responsible for the administration of the colleges and universities. The propensity of most bureaucrats is to standardize, quantify, refine, reduce, and make uniform. Then procedures and computations can be substituted for decisions and judgment. The apparent neatness is not only unworkable; in time it substitutes the rigidity of bureaucracy for the free-flowing adaptation necessary to stay in touch with reality. Bureaucrats tend to try to find simple, sometimes simplistic, solutions to complex questions. Furthermore, in the Washington atmosphere of expertise, solutions often turn on quantifiable data, resulting in the formulation of statistical models of perfection. It is instructive to look at the title of one project prepared for the Office of Civil Rights: "Algebraic Formulation of Elements of a Plan from Amended Criteria Specifying the Ingredients of Acceptable Plans to Desegregate State Systems of Public Higher Education (Revised Draft)." Additional updating of the project was promised. While data can help tell us where we need to make improvements, the use of statistics to describe perfection is an inadequate response to complex problems in social relations.

This criticism of bureaucracy is not to say that none of the federal government's objectives is desirable. And in view of the reluctance and resistance of some Americans to extending new opportunities to minorities, pressure from government is necessary. The point is that until recently the government has not used higher education as its arm in bringing about change in society. Rather, the government offered money in the form of block grants or assistance through the veterans for broadly defined programs. A school accepting the assistance was committed to those programs, but it did not expose itself to contingent requirements that other programs or unrelated institutional policies would be touched by the hand of government. To establish explicit conditions for receiving federal dollars for a specific program is one thing. To establish new conditions for continued federal support in one area in order to reach new areas or require new programs or policies or impose goals upon a school is a recent intrusion by government into setting the purposes and priorities of institutions of higher education.

There are several reasons why government's influence has increased. It may be partially due to the magnitude of federal support and higher education's dependence upon it. The increase in federal funding has been enormous, more than sixfold in less than twenty years. The temptation for higher education to give in to federal demands has never before been so great, for the largesse now totals nearly $7 billion per year, or approximately 17 percent of the total annual income to higher education.

Unfortunately, there are not many examples of resistance by higher education to federal incursions. One of the few occurred in 1977, when the government informed all medical schools that the continuation of capitation grants would depend upon each school's accepting the number of transferring foreign-educated American medical students decided upon by the Secretary of the Department of Health, Education, and Welfare (DHEW). The surprise was not that fifteen medical schools told the government they would not tolerate such interference with their admissions policies and the government could keep its money. Even in this case of resistance, the surprise was that every other medical school in the country was willing to accept such intrusion into its otherwise sacrosanct admissions policies as a price for receiving federal money.

Some colleges participating in the Comprehensive Employment Training Act (CETA) programs have been instructed that CETA students cannot be dismissed on grounds of not attending classes or failing their courses. Since the government has in effect placed the students on its payroll and is paying dependents' allowances, the school and the CETA courses are seen by some officials more as an employment program than as an educational or training activity. In the few fields in which graduates of CETA-sponsored programs must pass licensing examinations, the results of being unable to flunk or dismiss students have quickly shown up. Failure rates on the licensing exams have often been inordinately high. Any educational program handled in this way in a college is no more than a welfare activity. Even participating colleges that try to maintain sound educational standards and procedures have often lost control over CETA programs.

Under the *Adams* case, DHEW is presently trying to force certain states to give preference to placing all new degree programs in the predominantly black institutions. Many predominantly white colleges, however, are not on an equal par with the major universities in those states, either; most do not have doctoral programs or the full panoply of specialized studies supportable only in a few universities. States have very purposefully not made all colleges and universities of equal quality or with duplicate programs, but this diversity is now making the states vulnerable to criticism from DHEW. The department assumes that the predominantly black schools do not compare favorably with the major universities only because of discrimination, which has denied them degree programs that would have made them equal or nearly equal and thereby would have attracted enough white students to have desegregated them. Considerations of other factors that make a few universities great in contrast to others are not recognized. DHEW wants the states covered by the *Adams* case to agree to federal review of state decisions on the location of new degree programs. In other words, the state planning responsibility for higher education is being subjugated to federal government monitoring and interference.

It was precisely this kind of federal intervention in an area specifically left to the states in the U.S. Constitution that led President Buchanan to veto the Morrill Land-Grant College Bill of 1859. It does not have to turn out the way President Buchanan feared, but so far the trend toward federal control continues.

Part of the difficulty schools have in taking a vigorous position against federal pressures is that some of the government's general goals are worthy in their own right and are in the interest of a more just society. The institutions cannot make a case that the goals are all wrongheaded, for most schools have themselves been among the very first to recognize and acknowledge the just claims of the minorities. It is as though the college presidents, trustees, and faculty members would feel guilty if they resisted the damaging incursions by the government. They forget that in failing to stand firm they are permitting the government to injure the institutions that can do the most to redress the unfairness if they are left strong. But if they are damaged and weakened, their potential contributions will diminish. The reason the colleges and universities are so pressured now is that they have been recognized as a social institution that *can* make a difference. If the elements that make that so are compromised away, both the goals and the institutions will be lost.

To verify institutional compliance with federal expectations and rules, teams of investigators regularly visit the campuses to examine the bases of complaints by students, employees, or unsuccessful job applicants. The burden of proving themselves innocent rests upon the schools, and the government often refuses even to identify the parties accusing the institutions of real or imagined violations. Since almost any charge, however absurd, will be pursued, some investigations amount merely to a form of harassment.

Stories abound of the foolish, uninformed, simplistic, and inappropriate questions asked in some cases, which sometimes are pursued with the tenacity of a major criminal investigation. Schools have received court orders just days before Christmas or graduation or other peak-load activity to respond fully to a case within five days or be presumed to agree with the charges. Such requests have come after the government agency has sat on the complaints for months. Allegations of sex discrimination were relentlessly pursued for over a year in one case in which the unfortunate woman had been retired on full disability as a result of a stroke and had been found unemployable by the private insurance carrier and the state employment agency. In another case, one investigator asked a school official whether it was not true that the school had created the rank of assistant professor in order to discriminate against women and minorities.

When a federal agency can tell an institution of higher learning that government funds in one area of university activities will be cut off if the institution does not conform to government expectations in another, the entire university and almost everything it does become subject to government control. That major changes have occurred in the relationship between the federal government and higher education cannot be denied, and most of them, especially the increase in government's intrusion into the administration of higher education, have primarily come about in only the past two decades.

The question must be asked, what kind of system of higher

education will America have in another decade or two if we continue to allow the federal government to intrude as deeply and continuously as it has in recent years? If higher education does not remain autonomous, it cannot fulfill its unique function in society. The universities' roles of critic, observer, and evaluator of society and government require them not to become or be made dependent upon or creatures of the government.

The courts and the bureaucrats have brought higher education increasingly under federal control. There are signs here and there that the courts are beginning to see that they cannot continue to substitute their judgments for those of the educators and governing boards too frequently without having to take over running the schools. Unfortunately this understanding has not dawned on the bureaucrats. Very few career federal officials recognize the fragile nature of higher education and the harm that can be done by imposing outside decisions. Under legislation passed by the Congress, government officials develop rules and regulations that are largely insensitive to the delicate balance of forces that make an institution of higher learning either independent from or a creature of government. True, government should not permit colleges and universities to be irresponsible in fulfilling their role in society. But neither should federal officials simply assume that, unless the government makes decisions for educators or exerts leverage to influence what they do, they will act irresponsibly. Nor can colleges or universities be treated like "any other business." They are not like any other institution in society, and if, in the end, government controls make them over in the form of other organizations, true higher learning in America will have perished.

Since 1957, the colleges and universities have responded to new and expanded expectations held by society. The federal government has been the major instrument in bringing about the changes in higher education. During this period, physical plants and the capacity to enroll additional students have expanded enormously. Degrees awarded per year grew from 350,000 in 1955 to over 1.3 million in 1975. As stated earlier, higher education is now completing this third cycle of close involvement with the federal government. But the cycle has brought with it related ills that must be considered. The temporary profitability of higher education has attracted many new entrepreneurs, both inside and outside traditional postsecondary institutions. Partially as a result of their innovations, serious questions are being raised about quality and the large investments required by contemporary higher education. It is appropriate to turn now to those topics.

4. Nontraditional Education and Dwindling Quality

AT the same time that the public has recognized the benefits of a college degree and the federal government has discovered the need to make one or more degrees available to as many citizens as possible, individuals have found that there is money to be made in the field of higher education. Anything with an important social value can become a marketable item. The entrepreneurs have been attracted to the field of higher learning.

Diploma mills have long been a problem in higher education. For prices ranging from ten dollars to several hundred dollars, degrees can be ordered by mail. Operations dispensing such diplomas make no pretense to providing an education. They only sell the paper credentials and advertise in newspapers and some magazines. Most are run by individuals with access to a printing press; some operate out of small churches and issue degrees in religion or divinity. Degrees sold as credentials only are about as valuable as a Janizary University Ph.D. in military science or a Plenipotentiary College B.M. degree (Bachelor of Music) with a major in hemidemisemiquavers. But in some cases promoters will incur greater risk of legal repercussions by selling forgeries of degrees from well-recognized universities of national or international reputation.

The federal government tries to regulate such businesses when they involve mail fraud. The states usually deal with diploma mills more generally by passing legislation subjecting them to educational standards they cannot meet. As some states pass laws to regulate such activities, it is possible to trace the movement of these institutions to other states that do not have adequate laws. For example, some of these so-called schools forced out of Florida moved to Tennessee, from whence they moved to Texas or further west. When Texas tightened its law dealing with these institutions, one departing school wrote to the state agency forcing it out of business and said that God had found the school a better location in Arizona.

One step removed from the diploma mills is another group of schools undeserving to be classified as postsecondary institutions. But the one step removed is an important one. Some of these schools have existed for years; others are new and often dedicated to serving a small, special-interest clientele. In either case, the leaders of most of these schools are not profit-motivated promoters. They sincerely believe they are offering adequate education to award bachelor's, master's, and even doctoral degrees. They simply do not recognize what constitutes minimum standards for college-level education. They usually are not making money out of their educational operations and may even be subsidizing them from other activities. Nonetheless, they do recruit uninformed citizens into their programs. These consumers are being misled into thinking they are acquiring a bona fide college degree when they are not; this error may be an even greater disservice than that done by diploma mills in selling fraudulent degrees. At least those making an outright purchase of a degree can be under no misconception that they are acquiring an education. Consequently, steps need to be taken in all states to deal with the small, well-intentioned but inadequate schools offering credentials purported to be college degrees.

From fraudulent operations and the sincere but misguided little schools, it is a far cry to the colleges and universities that are offering so-called nontraditional or external degrees. These terms cover a wide range of structures, types, and programs. Unquestionably, certain degrees can be offered off an established campus. In some of these programs adequate quality can be maintained to justify labeling them college-level education. In many others practices are highly questionable. The liberal granting of credit for "life experience" or "work experience" is one common abuse — for example, granting nine hours' credit to a police officer for having held his job six years or granting six hours' credit in sociology to an urban minority student because he grew up in a slum ghetto. Granting thirty hours' credit for having served four or five years in a branch of the military service is still another case in point. Credits are liberally awarded for all sorts of activities; for instance, one school awarded nine hours' credit for a student's trip to Mexico City. At one school, students even requested, albeit unsuccessfully, college credit for completing psychotherapy treatment.

Not only have promoters entered this field by setting up new operations to make money, but some existing colleges that were in serious financial trouble have found ways to attract large sums of federal, state, and private money through off-campus programs. They have found that rather than having to attract students to their campuses, they can take their courses and programs to the students. They sometimes send faculty members out to the students, wherever they can be recruited, but they often hire local "pick-up" faculty to teach the courses. Favorite locations for such courses are the public schools, junior college campuses, military bases, and business firms. When federal or state grant funds, the GI Bill, local tax funds, or business subsidies can be used to pay all or part of the students' costs, it is even easier to make such programs attract enough students to produce a profit.

Administrators of these programs hold credentials ranging in respectability from quite high to very low. Regardless of credentials, however, most are promoter types rather than accepted members of the mainstream academic community. They pay a lot of lip service to academic quality, but their measurement of success is usually numbers, in terms of students, credit hours produced, numbers of courses or programs or sites, and ultimately dollars generated.

Horror stories grow out of the confluence of incentives that can occur in such situations. A local principal or school superintendent will teach a course for a distant university. He will register by mail the fifteen or twenty of his teachers whom he has directed to enroll in his course. To be certain the teachers cannot object to the costs of enrolling, he may arrange for a grant of local, state, or federal funds to cover their tuitions and fees. To placate their objections to taking the course, he may arrange to meet for a couple of hours one afternoon a week at which time he shows films. In response to the teachers' complaints about not having time to research and write a term paper, he may waive that requirement or ask for two pages on how each person's teaching has been helped by the course. For this course, he will be paid perhaps eight hundred to one thousand dollars by the university granting course credit to the teachers. The teachers, upon accruing six or nine hours of such graduate credit, often qualify for an automatic pay raise of at least several hundred dollars. The university, perhaps the instructor's alma mater, will collect several thousand dollars from the state for the students enrolled in the course.

The movement across the country to decentralize state agencies for elementary and secondary education has exacerbated the problem. These local service centers now offer workshops, orientation sessions, special conferences, and teacher-training programs for which they wish to grant college credit in order to help the teachers qualify for pay increases. The college credit also attracts more teachers for enrollment and justifies the existence of the field centers. The centers shop around until they can locate a university willing to grant college credit for such center activities. Since overhead costs to the colleges associated with such programs are low and since state funds pay for the enrollments and credit hours granted by the schools, it is frequently possible to find a school willing to grant college credit. One course for which graduate credit was granted was a five-day teacher conference at which the teachers voted on topics they wanted to discuss and elected teachers from among themselves to lead the discussions. In this case the university granting credit did not even have to pay a faculty salary out of the income it received for the enrollments in the "course."

Similar stories come out of the military services; retired officers, drawing upon past contacts across the nation and abroad to milk the military educational system, become promoters for mobile college offerings. One of the worst problems about military-base programs is the tendency to offer the least demanding program available, unless unusual steps are taken to ensure quality. The military bases are all dealing with accredited institutions, but they do not look behind the regional accrediting organizations' attestations to quality. There is a Gresham's law at work that often results in selecting the least rigorous program available. It could be looked upon as another form of accepting the lowest bid. If one school will eliminate the thesis requirement and waive the need for Graduate Record Examination scores or minimum grade-point averages for admission, other schools not willing to follow suit will be eliminated from consideration by some educational-service officers. The bidding continues on other components in order to find the schools willing to be most generous in granting credit for time in the military service, credit for service-school training, credit for on-the-job assignments. Residence requirements are bid out, once-a-week classes are bid in; requiring research or outside reading is out, acceptance of military officers or nearby retired officers as teachers is in. So long as the accrediting associations do not question such programs, military personnel assume they are adequate and do not question the quality of programs offered on U.S. government property and supported by U.S. government funds. Upon discharge or retirement, graduates of these programs will be able to add their degrees to their medals and say, "With these and fifty cents, I can get a cup of coffee anywhere in this land."

We cannot generalize from the horror stories that all nontraditional education is poor or is misrepresented to the public. Not every college or university involved in off-campus programs is out for the money to be made from students. Not every school involved in such teaching is doing it to maintain enrollments or garner enough income to support existing tenured faculty and faltering programs. But the good are not separated from the bad, the well-motivated, from the profit-makers, with enough severity. It does not take many abuses to bring into question the quality of every external degree program and every activity called a "university without walls."

The entry of promoters and recruiters and the introduction of the hard sell into higher education started during the period of rapid growth in the last decade. Since there were plenty of students to go around, the institutions maintaining the quality of their programs did not bother to raise strong objections to the minor infractions of some or the educational improprieties of others. Now that the competition for students is becoming more keen, the traditional institutions are finding that a large portion of their market is being served by inferior institutions, to which they previously had raised no objections. They are also learning that students who could not qualify for admission or were flunked out for not meeting performance standards are enrolled in off-campus programs offered in a nearby motel conference room or public-school facility. Traditional schools are further discovering that nontraditional institutions already have a substantial foothold in a number of locations, particularly on military bases. The admission of the new types of schools to accrediting associations in earlier years has also created a precedent. It is difficult to deny admission to similar nontraditional schools, which are now requesting accreditation. Now that students are growing scarce, requiring nontraditional schools to raise their quality as a condition for accreditation would appear self-serving on the part of the better schools, an appearance the traditionals are reluctant to risk. The response of some of the traditional institutions, instead, is to try to compete with these other types of institutions on the new terms, that is, by lowering their own standards.

The pool of applicants and students for higher education is no longer growing and may even be contracting. In the decade 1965 to 1975, enrollments nationwide grew by 88 percent, but projections for the decade to 1985 indicate the growth rate will be only about 2 percent. Schools in some areas of the country will face sharp declines in enrollments. In an enterprise where the money follows the student, through tuition or state funding, schools feel hard pressed to maintain their share of the enrollments. Competition will become very keen, and new activities described as nontraditional and innovative are already under way to attract and hold the students. The colleges and universities will be in the body-count game until at least the mid-1980's, and each one must find enough students in the intervening years to survive until then. The stage is set for continuing the decline in the quality of higher education.

5. The Body-Count Game

ONE way to obtain a higher body count in a college or university is to lower admissions standards. By making it easier for students to enter, institutions of higher education can reach out to a new clientele not previously eligible for admission. The junior colleges, which have always been open-door institutions, are finding that the senior colleges and universities are competing for some of the students heretofore exclusively within the community colleges' domain. The junior colleges, which had traditionally handled most remedial education, are finding that the public senior colleges are now introducing remedial and compensatory courses and requesting state support for them.

As the federal government pressures postsecondary schools to meet affirmative action goals, specific concern about the size of the minority enrollment exacerbates the lowering of standards caused by the general body-count game. Consider, for example, the following excerpt of a federal statement that tries to have it both ways on quality and the "opening" of admissions standards:

> . . . under these criteria and the goals they set, all applicants must be able to compete successfully. States' efforts under these criteria need not and should not lead to lowering academic standards. States may need to innovate in seeking out talented students who will profit from higher education. They may need to broaden definitions of potential; to discount the effects of early disadvantage on the development of academic competence; and to broaden the talents measured in admissions tests. But new and different yardsticks for measuring potential are not lower standards. They can be more valid measures of true potential and talent. Taken as a whole, these

criteria seek to preserve and protect academic standards of excellence. (Department of Health, Education and Welfare guidelines and criteria for states covered by the *Adams* case)

A second way to increase the body count in colleges and universities is to lower the performance standards. Lowering admissions standards for students only to flunk the students out promptly does not help raise the body count. Therefore, performance standards within the colleges and universities will have to be lowered in order to keep more students in school. The correlation between first-time-entering students and graduating classes four and five years later in the public senior colleges and universities over the past decade shows a progressive closing of the gap between the numbers of students admitted and the numbers graduated. While this is far from an exact longitudinal correlation of cohort groups, it is clearly one indication that it is much easier to graduate from college now than it was a decade or two ago. The earlier problem of high attrition rates has been handled in part by grade inflation and the reduction of the performance standards imposed on students.

A third approach to attracting more students is to embark upon active recruitment programs, which will include pirating of students from other institutions. Piracy leads to the fourth approach, reducing standards related to transfer policies. Colleges and universities interested in stealing students away from other institutions will make the transfer of credit easier by policies like the liberal awarding of credit for work and lifetime experiences, an approach referred to earlier. Students will then shop around for the best deal they can find on credits given for their unique living experiences.

The liberalization of transfer policies includes attempts by some senior colleges to recruit students away from the community colleges before the students have completed two years of work there. That is, they will, if permitted to do so, try to recruit students away from the junior colleges after only thirty or forty-five hours of work. But two can play at this game of competition between the senior colleges and the community colleges. If the senior colleges become too aggressive, the community colleges will prohibit their recruiters on campus and will begin to press more strongly for transferring up to ninety hours of junior-college credit into the senior colleges. In fact, rumors say that here and there a junior college has already indicated it will not advise students to attend certain four-year or upper-level institutions that do not accept up to ninety hours of credit from that junior college. Although it is possible that this type of competition between the junior and senior colleges would not dilute quality, turning the junior colleges into three-year institutions would substantially change the role and scope of those institutions, putting them only one year away from full four-year status. Such conversions would create additional headaches at a time when enrollments are stabilizing. Moreover, one year is not long enough for a senior college to make the discreet difference in a student's outlook and training that distinguishes the junior-college experience from the senior-college.

Some schools have gone so far in courting the students as to permit the students themselves to decide what constitutes a college degree and an educated person. Students at such institutions may devise their own curricula, courses, schedules of study, and standards to qualify for a degree. This approach is very close to the philosophy preached at some schools that the colleges should teach the students, not the subject matter. This is a way of saying, "Meet the level of the student, but do not set predetermined levels of performance." And although the related pass-fail grading system has its advantages in certain circumstances, its widespread use has led to lower performance standards in some institutions.

But of all the approaches to increasing the body count, the one most actively pursued at the present is the teaching of courses and programs at locations remote from the parent institution, often in newly created off-campus centers and branches. Increasingly these units are being set up in states other than that of the parent campus. Some schools have dozens of such centers, located hundreds or even thousands of miles from the home campus. A few schools have converted to, or have come into being as, almost exclusively branch-campus operations with only the administration and record keeping remaining on a central "campus." These are defended as being "universities without walls," a label legitimatized by early apologists for new, nontraditional structures for higher education. One such institution in Ohio operates a branch in Austin, Texas, which teaches "off-branch" courses in San Antonio and Mission, while all the Texas activities are supervised from the university's offices in San Francisco, California. Under present procedures neither the state nor the Southern Association of Colleges and Schools, the agency that accredits Texas institutions, has any jurisdiction over the branch, the parent campus, or the North Central Association, the accrediting agency that oversees the Ohio, Austin, San Antonio, Mission, and San Francisco operations of the institution. As evident from the case just cited, branches are often outside the geographic boundaries of the regional accrediting associations that monitor the home campuses.

Wayne Brown of the Tennessee Higher Education Commission holds a degree in astronomy. He says that he knows a secret about the static coming from outer space. The interterrestrial noise is the transmission of off-campus courses between planets.

The several approaches set out above to finding and enrolling more students are defended by various arguments. Some assert that admissions standards should be lowered in order to serve new audiences not previously given an opportunity for higher education. Others argue that admissions standards should be lowered to permit new chances for individuals who did not take advantage of higher education at an earlier day. This particularly applies to older citizens and those with established families and employment commitments. Another argument, condescending and patronizing though it is, holds that we need to lower standards in order to help minority groups.

On the question of lowering performance, some argue that we need to be more tolerant of new types of students and that we should not discourage students by giving them failing grades or any grade that might disappoint or discourage them. Some say that it is harmful to identify students' deficiencies because it hinders their social adjustment and scars their egos. In addition, we hear the argument that, if students are making failing grades, it is the teacher

With more than thirty universities from across the country teaching there, Washington, D.C., probably hosts more off-campus operations offering graduate-level degrees than any other city in the country. The motivations are often the same as listed earlier: for the school, take the program to the student to generate income; for the student, get another credential for promotion while on the job and find the easiest program available. Certainly Mr. Strangelove will go further with a doctorate.

The military services are jumping into this new area, too. Some military-base commanding officers are urging their education service officers (ESO's) to bring Ph.D. and other doctoral programs onto their bases. On-base degree programs help retain personnel in the voluntary armed services, and doctoral degrees would presumably help officers embark more easily on second careers upon retirement. At least one commanding officer has reportedly promised his education service officer an automatic grade increase if he can bring a doctoral program to the base. In at least one case, an ESO told local educators that, if they did not bring a doctoral program to the base, he would find an institution that would.

In one sense, the motivation for offering external degree programs begins with the person who thinks he needs a doctoral degree, whether it be a Doctor of Philosophy, Doctor of Education, Doctor of Business Administration, Doctor of Public Administration, Doctor of Science, Doctor of Engineering, or other doctorate. But there can be no question that the generation of income is the immediate spur for the universities to offer nontraditional doctorates. Public institutions can get state reimbursement for doctoral credit hours. Some private institutions offering such programs charge as much as $5,000 to $6,000 for a degree. But that is not excessive if the employer or school district will pay one-half or more of the tuition. The schools, by serving this new clientele, can collect income from the students, from employers, from local, state, and federal government payments for educational training, and from the Veterans Administration under the GI Bill.

Typically, the students in the new off-campus doctoral programs are described as different; they are the more "mature individuals," those working full time, those without geographic mobility, those who need more "flexible" requirements, and those who need a "different kind of content" for a degree program. Furthermore, these older, more mature students have had additional lifetime experiences for which nontraditional institutions give graduate credit, thereby reducing the time required to obtain a doctorate. The institutions offering off-campus degrees also state that, since their graduates are already working, their performance and thus the benefits of the education they receive can be measured on the job. Another group to whom these programs appeal is all-but-dissertation students ("ABD's"), that is, students who were not able to complete their degree requirements under traditional doctoral programs. By enrolling in the less demanding nontraditional programs, these students can now obtain the coveted degrees that previously eluded them.

One appeal of these nontraditional doctoral programs to the "special" student is that many such programs waive dissertation requirements in favor of projects related to the person's employment. That waiver is justified on the ground that doctorates are being acquired by such individuals to improve their job performance, not to embark on some new field of research or to demonstrate research competence. With the granting of credit for experience and the waiving of other requirements, the institutions can develop individually designed programs for each student, and students are thus not bound by what the nontraditional institutions call "inflexible and standardized requirements" for the doctorate.

Another attraction of nontraditional institutions' programs is that their doctorates can be completed in one or two years, or at most in three years, by students studying part time and holding full-time jobs. This contrasts with the average of six to seven years to complete a doctorate in a good traditional university. And in the longer programs the students typically spend full time in the institution in degree-related work. But perhaps less time is needed because the nontraditional student is, ostensibly, so unusually well qualified.

For the individually designed programs, faculty members are often hired only as needed to serve as preceptors, proctors, mentors, or faculty advisers for individual students. Since students are being educated individually under such guidance, regular classes are not required. Classes may meet once a week or even less frequently, and the faculty member or rotating lecturers are often from out of town or are otherwise inaccessible to students. But the advocates of the nontraditional doctorate contend that even this inaccessibility works to advantage. They claim that their programs more closely track the European approach than do traditional American programs; that is, the student works on his own with few required courses, and his faculty advisers control his examination. To deflect criticism regarding lack of exposure to other faculty members and other students, some programs require students to spend at least one month during a summer at some "campus." Typically faculty members teaching at such a site are employees at other universities who find such an arrangement more lucrative than working a summer term at their home campuses.

Sometimes the new institutions with nontraditional doctoral programs do contract with local faculty members of traditional schools to serve as preceptors and faculty advisers to the students. These faculty members are paid on a unit basis, that is, according to the number of students assisted or graduated. Such arrangements represent a kind of "fee for service" concept in higher education. The nontraditional doctoral-granting agency expects faculty members, whether local or long-distance, to supervise the work of the individual student, assist him with any problems he has with his program of study, keep him interested in the program and in moving toward completion of a degree, and help him find materials needed for his study. Moonlighting local faculty members are often even expected to arrange for library access at the faculty member's home campus for students not registered at that campus. They are also expected to arrange long-distance telephone conference calls at which the students defend their dissertations or projects when a requirement for an oral defense exists.

Some of these programs might be called freeze-dried education, for they travel light. They have no campuses, no libraries, no full-time regular faculties. Such requirements are "dysfunctional" to the educational purposes of these new and different institutions of higher learning. The innovators make up for the deficiencies of their freeze-dried programs by adding local water. Two parts credit for life experience, two parts credit for work experience, one part pick-up faculty, credit for a work-related project, a public-relations brochure, and, presto, a miracle degree program.

It seems absurd that such entities without campuses and without faculties should be offering doctoral degrees. But they are. Moreover, it seems incredible that they should be demanding recognition of the credentials they sell as fully equal to those traditional universities offer. But they are. And many educators are letting these nontraditional schools get away with these practices by acting as though the imposters did not exist. In addition, some educators, through their accrediting associations, are permitting such institutions to receive full recognition.

In fact, insistence on high standards usually leads to the charge that the supporters of traditional programs are advocating a form of elitism that deprives certain deserving students of a doctoral degree simply because they cannot follow the traditional mode. To the avid nontraditionalists promoting experiential learning, off-campus teaching, or whatever, anyone with the odd notion that a student's physical presence is necessary to acquire an education is an elitist. If, however, by *elitism* innovators mean the maintenance of demanding standards for the doctoral degree, then the label should not be considered pejorative. Elitism does, in fact, have an appropriate role in the conferring of doctorates, the awarding of those credentials which qualify individuals to become faculty members throughout our system of higher education.

Nontraditional institutions have been able to steal into the field of higher education because requirements of the degree have always been imprecisely defined. The loose definition of a doctorate has functioned well in the past because a core of full-time, committed, and dedicated faculty members has carefully screened admission to doctoral programs and closely supervised requirements for graduation. A loose definition was, indeed, needed to permit accommodation to individual needs. That inexactitude, however, now combined with the monetary value of the doctoral degree, has encouraged the proliferation of nontraditional institutions that award doctorates. That imprecision of definition and the competition for income have also led many traditional universities into the business of providing external master's and doctoral degrees.

Efforts by states to control the proliferation of such programs, and especially efforts to limit the ability of out-of-state institutions to offer nontraditional degrees, encounter strong resistance. The institutions that offer only nontraditional graduate degrees allege that such state efforts are being taken only to protect similar off-campus operations of in-state schools. Threats have been made to challenge — on constitutional grounds of interfering with interstate commerce — any efforts to keep out-of-state institutions from offering such programs. This willingness to resort to a legal response to state control makes clear just how lucrative the traffic in doctoral credentials has become.

It is almost possible to say that in America a college credential is now available to all, promising jobs, promotions, status, happiness, new opportunities, and advancement of minorities. For those who simply cannot meet the lowered admissions requirements or survive the lowered standards or obtain enough college credit by staying alive or holding a job, mail-order degrees are available. For those who cannot travel to a college, the courses and degrees will be brought to them.

We have created the perfect hallucinogen to fit contemporary needs: an educational system that provides immediate elevation in status with no permanent aftereffects and no mind-altering consequences. In a time of non-art, non-books, and non-music, as well as other nonsense, there seems to be a place for the nontraditional non-degree. The recognition of this need in society was established long ago. In *The Wizard of Oz,* the scarecrow traveled with Dorothy and her companions and shared their vicissitudes to request that he be granted a brain. But the Wizard did not give him a brain; he gave him what he needed more, a diploma.

6. The Potential for Quality Control

WHILE the caliber of American higher education has unquestionably declined in recent years, the potential to prevent further deterioration and in fact to recover some of the lost quality does exist. Stephen K. Bailey summed up the problem succinctly when he said: "On the one hand [higher education] is too valuable to be restricted to the elite; on the other hand, it is too important to have its standards bartered away by those who are more interested in selling credentials than knowledge."

The prostitution of credentials is precisely the problem in many of the nontraditional programs and is most pernicious at the doctoral level. The problem of maintaining quality in nontraditional programs turns on these schools' separation of the educational function from the credentialing function. Since the student "clientele" are often more interested in the credentials than they are in the education the credentials purportedly certify, very few students participating in mediocre or inferior programs ever voice any objection to them. Above all else, they want the pedigree and the related promotions and salary increases, so the quality of the education component is relegated to secondary or even lower importance.

Thus, the students themselves fail to exert any quality control. Employers, a real potential check on declining quality, also fail to use their influence, especially employers of doctoral-level personnel. Even if the credulity of some employers has been shaken by the declining dependability of undergraduate degrees, the doctorate still maintains its mystique and importance for most. If an employer does not himself hold a doctorate, how can he question someone who does, regardless of its source? A doctorate from any accredited institution is still accepted as signifying substantial educational attainment.

While controls over educational quality are generally weak today, controls in the nontraditional programs are especially limited. Full-time faculty members have always served as the major quality control in traditional doctoral programs; that is, they have applied to graduate students the standards of their institution as well as their personal measure of excellence and the standards of the field of specialization. The nontraditional institutions contend that they are following the same procedures as the traditional schools; their faculty members are applying their particular standards of what constitutes doctoral-level work. However, the nontraditional school, drawing faculty from many institutions, is not as likely to have a uniform standard of excellence or even of minimum performance. Also, without departments of faculties working together in a common location, there is no checking and sharing of standards among peers, an accepted procedure and safeguard among faculties in traditional universities.

The crucial matter, then, in the absence of collegiality, is the quality of the faculty members who supervise the students and the instructors' commitment to maintaining standards in the face of other enticements and pressures. The rhetoric of the nontraditional schools in defense of good teaching and student performance in their programs is voluminous; the proof is less available.

Traditional colleges and universities for which faculty members work could, if they chose, exert at least some minor control over the parasitic nontraditional doctoral programs by forbidding their faculty to moonlight for other institutions and by prohibiting the use of library and other facilities by people not registered as students there. Such measures, however, have been slow in coming.

Assuredly, any institution needs modifications and innovation if it is to continue to function effectively in a rapidly changing society. However, someone must control what flies under the guise of innovation. The burden of proof for innovative procedures should be placed in proper perspective. At present, the aggressive advocates of nontraditional programs have placed the traditional universities and educators on the defensive, demanding that they show cause why nontraditional degree programs should not receive equal recognition with the old-line degrees. The shoe is being placed on the wrong foot. Society has not changed so rapidly in the past decade that the experience of eight hundred years of higher education should be scuttled at the first threat from those who wish to appropriate the titles and good will associated with legitimate academic degree programs. Historically, those who recommend changes have usually borne the burden of proving them worthy or superior to existing, tested methods.

In 1937, Harry D. Gideonse summed it up in these words: "The University enjoys an enviable reputation as an institution not afraid to try the new. But this involves the correlated need to preserve such gains as have been made and not to give up known and tested practices until a reasonable chance exists that a superior practice is at hand to be tried. In education, as in everything else involving a change in social policy, the burden of proof is on the innovator. It is he who must show that what now is, is defective, and that what might and can be contains a reasonable probability of advance" (*Documentary History*, pp. 944–945).

Perhaps the real issue turns on truth in packaging. A nontraditional general educational development certificate (GED) is not confused with a high school diploma. We are not misled into thinking we are buying butter when we purchase oleomargarine, or that Dream Whip is whipped cream. The difficulty is that nontraditional institutions are passing off their nontraditional degrees as the equivalent of traditional degrees. Their degrees carry exactly the same labels. One major step to renew the significance of the traditional degrees would be to insist that nontraditional degrees be labeled differently.

The immediate argument of the advocates of nontraditional degrees is that much poor teaching occurs on the traditional campuses, so it is unfair to criticize nontraditional programs. These supporters offer to take such criticism seriously only when all inferior programs have been eliminated from the traditional institutions. However, no exemption to meeting high standards should be granted to the nontraditional programs just because some mediocre teaching exists in some traditional institutions. It is a poor program that would excuse its faults by pointing to the faults of others. Certainly no traditional institution justifies any low-quality program on a campus by pointing to substandard nontraditional offerings. Alexander Bickel summed it up this way, "No one will claim that the ideal university exists, or that all members of all faculties are intent on independent intellectual labors, but we approach no closer to the ideal by admitting nonprofessional and nonintellectual criteria" (*Morality of Consent*, pp. 127–128).

The principal responsibility for quality control lies with the traditional universities. No other social organization, no government agency or business enterprise can acquire the credibility or prestige that faculty members carry in assessing quality in academic programs. There is no one else to do the job. But if the universities do not do the job, someone else will seek to be designated to do it.

The recognized spokesmen for quality in higher education are the accrediting associations since they draw upon faculty members and college administrators to conduct evaluations of programs and schools. Under the American federal system, responsibility for education is left to the states. However, since the various states could not impose uniform higher-education standards among all states, voluntary accrediting associations came into being, covering the different regions of the country, to police and assist the colleges and universities in meeting minimum standards. The decisions of these associations have been accepted by society because they are based primarily upon assessments made by faculty members and administrators, those individuals in society who are best qualified to evaluate their peers and their mimics.

In recent years, the regional accrediting associations have relaxed their standards and have exerted very little control over the spread of nontraditional and off-campus degree programs. In fact, some have encouraged it. The increasing laxity in applying standards has come about for a number of reasons. The better universities have shown much less interest in the accrediting associations' work than in the past, leaving the field open to faculty representatives and administrators from lesser schools. Indeed, the better schools have largely abdicated their role of supervising the quality of other institutions. This has resulted in some infiltration by the promoters of off-campus programs into the accrediting associations and the visiting committees recommending on the granting of accreditation. The vigilance of the guards of quality in higher education has been relaxed. They will either reawaken to their charge or be replaced in that job.

At the moment, institutions awarding nontraditional degrees are staging a big drive for admission to the accrediting associations in order to gain full recognition of their programs. Some associations have begun to accede to these demands, admitting avowedly proprietary schools to membership. Accrediting agencies in this country originated as voluntary organizations, and the courts have held that they can establish their own conditions of membership, so long as their standards are not capricious or arbitrary. Recently, however, some institutions offering nontraditional programs have threatened legal action if they are not admitted to the accrediting bodies for traditional organizations. Scared by the original decision in the *Marjorie Webster* case, some regional associations have admitted nontraditional and proprietary schools and given them full accreditation.* In evaluating the new types of institutions for membership, associations have considered it necessary to find representatives of similar schools to be on the visiting committee that makes recommendations. The accrediting associations seem to overlook the conflict of interest they create by including as evaluators people whose

---

*Marjorie Webster Junior College, a proprietary school, applied for admission to the Middle States Association of Colleges and Schools, seeking accreditation equivalent to the other members in the organization. The association denied the school admission, on the grounds that it was created to provide a profit to owners and stockholders, in contrast to the purpose and organization of the other public and private college and university members. The lower court ordered the school's admission, but the appeals court reversed the decision and upheld the association's position of denying admission.

own salaries depend on the credibility of this kind of institution. However, the alternative seems little brighter: some nontraditional schools excluded from the association will pursue the issue in the courts because the monetary value of being accredited is substantial, since accreditation makes it feasible to charge higher tuition and fees.

Another threat nontraditional institutions are making is that they will create their own accrediting body if the regional associations do not admit them. This is really much less a threat than a solution to the problem they pose. The creation of such an accrediting agency seems entirely appropriate and in accord with the history of voluntarily organized accrediting bodies for traditional institutions. With the proviso that their degrees are differently designated or titled, the creation of a separate accrediting body would be a step toward establishing the appropriate distinction between traditional and nontraditional institutions and programs. In fact, the courts have suggested this as an appropriate approach: "Appellee [Marjorie Webster Junior College] . . . is free to join with other proprietary institutions in setting up an association for the accreditation of institutions of *such character;* and such an association, if recognized, could obtain for its members all the benefits of accreditation by appellant [Middle States Association] save, perhaps, prestige" (emphasis added).

The regional accrediting agencies should be like one of the Supreme Court justices, who said that, though he did not always understand art, he could recognize pornography when he saw it. Perhaps our accrediting associations cannot define fully what quality is, but they should be able to recognize fraud when they see it and then stand up and say no on admission to membership. The result of the justice's comment was that he received a lot of pornography to review. Our accrediting agencies should perhaps be reviewing a lot more fraud and labeling it for what they see.

The accrediting associations are reluctant to take on an adversarial relationship with their member schools or those seeking admission. They view themselves in their historical role of maintaining collegial and fraternal relations. From such a posture it is difficult to take tough positions on abuses and infractions of accepted educational practices. But when the field has its share of promoters and those out to make quick money off the situation, standards of excellence in education cannot safely be left to self-policing within the schools. Surely accreditors should not be reluctant to cry "Fraud" when necessary to keep higher education from being set back further. That standards are difficult to enforce does not permit the accrediting agencies to abandon them.

In the end, whether controls over quality are tightened will depend upon the expectations and desires of our people. When students and parents learn that the value of the degrees they invested in is not what they thought it was, they may begin to seek restitution, and as the word spreads, other students may then realize that such programs do not justify their time and money. A parent's suit against an accrediting agency for improperly admitting a school to membership or for letting quality collapse in a member institution without removing accreditation would provide a healthy counterstroke against the suits being threatened by some nontraditional schools to gain accreditation. Employers who hire graduates of inadequate programs and who find that they cannot perform will also become disenchanted. When enough segments of society become displeased with such programs, the educators will be expected to correct the situation. If the educators do not, legislators will confront the problem. And educators should have learned long ago that it is always risky to wait for lawmakers or the courts to resolve problems in education. Whether educators will take the initiative in addressing these matters, as they should, remains to be seen.

7. Squeezing the Melon

HIGHER education, in response to various forms of enticements and coercion from the government and from society, has changed and expanded. As in the previous cycles, this diversification had led to questions about the decline of quality. These questions have been raised by some educators for some time. Now increasing numbers of people outside higher education are posing them as well. The principal expression of this concern comes in pointing out how poorly prepared many new degree recipients are and how badly many of them perform on state and national tests and licensure examinations.

A major textbook publisher has requested its college-text authors to write at the tenth-grade reading level. This would seem absurd had not a recent test the Houston Independent School District administered to applicants for teaching positions revealed that half the applicants scored lower on the mathematics portion than the average eleventh-grade student in the United States. A third of the applicants scored lower on English than the average eleventh grader. And school districts, government agencies, and businesses all across the nation are revealing similarly poor performance on standard tests they use.

If the higher-education community is not aware that it is in trouble with the employers at all levels who hire college graduates, it is not paying attention to what is taking place. Major businesses are building their own facilities for postsecondary instruction. The Bureau of Labor Statistics (BLS) reported that "probably the largest proportion of occupational training for skilled and semiskilled jobs occurs in private industry." BLS wants more information on the types of training, time spent in training, characteristics of teachers, facilities, and costs. There are as yet no estimates of the expenditures by business and industry on higher-education activities within their organizations. But the costs are substantial and are growing, and businesses are not making these investments because they feel the colleges and universities are too rigorous in their education and training. Quite the contrary, in some cases they find that they have to provide the basic skills our colleges are not providing to or requiring of their graduates.

Firms, government agencies, and schools that cannot create their own institutions of postsecondary education to correct deficiencies, as well as those that still have faith in the work of the colleges and universities, continue to use traditional institutions' services even though they have to send some recently hired college graduates back to school. Or some hire selected faculty members on a consulting basis to bring appropriate courses, as prescribed and controlled by the hiring party, to their business offices and plants. This use of existing schools, however, is becoming more selective, for employers are recognizing that a college is not a college is not a college, to paraphrase Gertrude Stein.

It is the wise recruitment or personnel officer, in fact, who no longer automatically accepts at face value the academic credentials a job applicant brings to him. A prospective employee bearing a college degree used to be assumed to be prepared for employment, to be an educated man or woman, to be a person capable of writing and reasoning and performing basic computations. If he or she carried a specialized degree, it was fairly safe to assume that the college credentials certified at least entry-level competence in the field. But now the discerning hiring official must look behind the credentials and examine the applicant to determine his or her basic competencies. The personnel officers are beginning to grade the college diplomas.

There are a number of reasons why the quality of education has deteriorated in many of our colleges and universities, requiring every company and government agency to take a closer look at its job applicants. Many of our colleges have abdicated an important role they used to perform in society. They used to carry out the tasks of sorting, screening, selecting, classifying, training, and ranking, and college credentials attested to the probable performance of individuals in jobs upon graduation. The credentials the schools awarded certified that an educational experience of some rigor had been completed. Unfortunately, employers can no longer assume this; there are indicators that in many colleges and universities the role of granting credentials is becoming separated from the role of educating. And as pointed out earlier, trends in college enrollments in the next decade may lead to further deterioration in the quality of the education supposedly represented by a college degree.

Unless the colleges and universities uniformly begin to do a better job, business, industry, school districts, and government agencies seem to have no alternative but to devise their own screening and testing services. In fact, a place is fast developing in our economy for a centralized service industry that would identify and classify for all businesses those institutions whose degrees still signify quality education and those whose do not. However, the fees for such services probably would become exorbitant in order to cover the court costs that almost certainly would be incurred in defending the findings and reports. Invidious comparisons are not popular in an egalitarian and litigious society.

Business is not threatened so much by creeping socialism as it is by galloping mediocrity. Kurt Vonnegut summed it up by a businessman's outburst in *Cat's Cradle*: "Back in Chicago we don't make bicycles anymore. It's all human relations now. The eggheads sit around trying to find out new ways for everybody to be happy. Nobody can get fired, no matter what; and if somebody does accidentally make a bicycle, the union accuses us of cruel and inhuman practices and the government confiscates the bicycle for back taxes and gives it to a blind man in Afghanistan."

In the absence of uniform standards in higher education, employers are beginning to examine the academic credentials of every job applicant. Some of the questions they find they must ask are: What experience has the firm had with graduates of the applicant's school? Does the degree come from an accredited college or one licensed by the state in which it is located? If the field in which the applicant majored requires state licensure to practice, did he or she take the licensing examination? How did the applicant score on it? If there are national exams in the field, were they taken? What were the scores? Was the degree earned on the main campus or at a branch? How much of the credit was given for off-campus work? for life experience? for work experience? for military-base courses? If the college degree was earned under a nontraditional program, what did it entail educationally and how can it be assessed and measured? The personnel officer might request a transcript directly from the college registrar and ask that the transcript identify where the courses were taken. Employers would be well advised to squeeze the melon before they take it home.

And enough complaints about the quality of the product to the right parties might, over time, bring results. If the complaints are not effective, if educators do not reassert control over educational quality, American higher education's last vestiges of credibility will vanish.

8. Prospects and Predictions

THE integrity of our colleges and universities is under question. These times for higher education are not unlike the period in Roman history when questions arose about unethical practices that had become common in connection with building stones in construction. When stones were chipped or fractured in transit, the pieces were sometimes stuck back in place with wax. In time, the buildings constructed with such faulty materials collapsed, or pieces of stone flaked off and fell into the streets. It became necessary to require that stones be certified as sound by the imprint *sine cera*, "without wax." We are approaching the time in this country when we must find a way to validate educational credentials *sine cera*.

If the educational community does not take appropriate action, the consequences are not too difficult to imagine. One of the first, as discussed in the previous chapter, will be that the business community will begin selectively to freeze out the graduates of all but the few institutions whose alumni can be relied upon to be truly educated and prepared to assume positions of leadership and responsibility or positions requiring highly skilled technical or scientific proficiencies. Businesses will increasingly establish their own postsecondary institutions within their firms, and, having incurred these costs of education, they will be less generous with donations to colleges and universities and will begin to complain about the taxes going into a system of higher education that has become a useless appendage of society.

The Japanese have a saying which could be applied to this

condition in American higher education: "While crying, bee sting in the face."

A second prospect is that lowering standards for minorities will have a backlash effect. This will occur for two reasons. First, among the minorities themselves, there will be general disenchantment with mere certification for jobs for which they are not being hired because they are not adequately prepared. That is, there will be a reaction against the broad distribution of worthless pieces of sheepskin as a solution to a social problem of long standing. Printing more certificates without maintaining quality standards in education will have the same effect as printing more money and giving it to the poor: both the credentials and the money become devalued. Just as inflation steals from everyone, the broadcasting of educational credentials steals from every credentialed person.

Second, those members of minority groups who have not been excused from but have met the rigorous standards of competence will object to the lowering of standards for unqualified minority students. They will soon find that being a member of an easily recognizable minority group will have the additional disadvantage of being presumed to be unqualified for the educational credentials they hold. Every capable and well-educated minority person will be hurt by the lowered standards and requirements permitted for other members of the same group. Those who do the hiring and promoting but who never wanted to hire and promote minorities anyway will then have the excuse they want; they will be able to say that none of the minorities are qualified because so many are found not to be. And the illusory progress for those *given* their *credentials* will be a real loss to those who have *worked for* an *education.*

Another prospect if quality continues to deteriorate is a growing dissatisfaction with the accrediting associations. Within those associations, conflicts are emerging that may altogether destroy voluntary accreditation. For one thing, the standards some accrediting associations are applying fall below the modest minimum requirements some states set for licensing nonaccredited colleges. Nonetheless, such agencies may continue to do very little about tightening their standards for accreditation and still drift along for a while until they eventually become meaningless organizations. However, they face an immediate issue that may doom them to collapse within a much shorter period, perhaps within the next couple of years. This is the issue of how to handle accreditation of the unconventional institutions offering degrees with the same titles as those offered by the traditional universities. As stated earlier, the new, nontraditional entities call themselves universities. They describe as "dysfunctional" to their purposes and objectives the accrediting standards that require a physical plant, a student body, and the other accoutrements of a traditional university. On the other hand, they often are outstanding in administrative structure, the number of top staff positions, and the salaries paid to top administrators. They usually excel in keeping student records, and most can meet the requirements for financial stability.

If the accrediting associations admit such organizations to full membership, their degrees, which bear the same titles as those from the traditional universities, and the institutions themselves, which call themselves universities, will acquire the same imprimatur of academic validity that the associations now grant to their long-standing traditional members. There comes the rub; why should any traditional university pay the dues, incur the costs of self-studies, pay the expenses of visiting committees, spend money to respond to recommendations for library acquisitions or additional faculty, for example, and file periodic reports to show how the university is working to meet the standards of the accrediting association, when new schools admitted to full and equal membership are exempted from meeting these same, long-imposed standards? Either an accrediting association has standards of excellence or it does not. It cannot have two sets of standards to apply to different types of schools and then classify the two groups as equal and permit them to compete with each other. To do so is particularly intolerable when the nontraditional type, which cannot meet the normal standards, gets a hunting license to come into the service areas of established universities and compete for their students or perhaps even hire their faculty on a part-time basis and use their library facilities. If the accrediting associations admit such nontraditional schools to accreditation, the larger and better universities, those needed most by the accrediting associations to give them credibility, prestige, and financial support, will withdraw from membership. That will bring about a quick end of voluntary accreditation.

This brings us to the next prospect for higher education. Whether the accrediting associations continue to atrophy and finally fade away or whether they suddenly commit suicide by admitting the nonstandard entities of higher education to full membership, the result will likely be the same. The states will attempt to take over accreditation controls for a while. But this will not work; standards need to be applied across state boundaries as well as within each state. Moreover, the individual states are not prepared to evaluate and control the quality of public and private colleges and universities within their boundaries. If for no other reasons, state agency accreditation will fail because a state agency has a built-in conflict of interest in measuring the quality of public institutions that the state itself funds. Either such a state agency will be reluctant to identify deficiencies and recommend costly corrective actions, or, if it insists upon more funding for the institutions it is supposed to be supervising, the agency will be presumed to have become a mouthpiece on behalf of higher education. Also, state-agency accreditation provides no independent leverage on the state government to protect the free speech and other rights of faculty or to prevent political intervention in higher education, activities that the accrediting associations on occasion have had to address.

Consequently, the state governments would fail to establish quality control in higher education, and a ministry of education in Washington would have to take over the accreditation function. And this is probably no pie-in-the-sky speculation. In recent years some in Washington have suggested that the noble bureaucrats stand ready to take on this duty if the accrediting associations cannot do a better job of responding to public needs and if they continue to be serve the self-interests of the member colleges, universities, and professions. If the proposed Department of Education is established, it can easily become a European-style ministry of education without even a change in name.

And if anyone in higher education thinks that hints by the U.S. Office of Education about taking over the accrediting function are idle threats, he should consider the current situation with the Community College of the Air Force (CCAF). When the Southern Association of Colleges and Schools reviewed that operation and expressed concerns and reservations about granting accreditation, CCAF representatives made known that other regional associations had been contacted until at least one had been found that would grant accreditation with no questions asked. The Southern Association has been told that, if it does not grant accreditation, CCAF may relocate to another region. Another option has been laid out as well: if regional accreditation for this federal entity is not granted, CCAF may go to the Council on Postsecondary Accreditation for special accreditation. And if that fails, the Office of Education and the Department of the Air Force may go to Congress to seek special accreditation by federal legislation. Perhaps this is all bluff, but it does show how far the federal government will go in pushing around the only agencies we have to certify quality in higher education.

There are some who see a move toward accreditation by the federal government as necessary in order to obtain more neatness in the entire structure of higher education in this country. Anyone who believes that the federal hand in higher education will improve the situation should not forget the experience of one major university after it had conducted an international search for a new dean. After the appointment of a Canadian was agreed upon by the university's faculty, administration, and governing board, the Labor Department held up the man's work papers on the grounds that there were numerous qualified U.S. citizens available to fill the job.

Even if the American system of voluntary accreditation does not collapse but continues to muddle along, permitting the educational institutions to deteriorate further or stagger on in their present state, government controls over higher education will grow stronger. With increasing costs and growing taxpayer resistance, governments will demand greater accountability. Justifications and explanations of what higher education is doing will require more reporting, more data collection, more inquiries.

Already there are very few college administrators who have not felt the strong arm of the federal government. Sometimes after weighing the costs of resistance, the time required if one is to stand on principle, and the possibility that a court or administrative ruling would reach into new and unknown areas of the university, a president will decide not to fight. The legal costs alone can be staggering for a college budget, not to mention the costs of time and in-house studies. It is particularly difficult to resist when an applicant or unhappy employee is pursuing three or four different legal and administrative channels at the same time. When Columbia University rejected a woman for a faculty position recently and she filed a protest, the legal costs for the university to defend itself were $125,000. Sometimes an institution cannot even afford the cost of winning. But as long as the colleges and universities do not demonstrate that they can set priorities, make hard choices, and otherwise put their houses in order, governments will insist on reviewing proposed changes and plans to expand. Once that habit is established and bureaucracies are created to exert close supervision over colleges and universities, reversing government control will be difficult.

The consequences of continuing deterioration in educational quality are not confined to the higher-education community, though. They are society-wide. William James once said that the wealth of a nation lies largely in "the number of superior men it harbors." No significant society has long been able to retain its independence or to progress unless it has found ways to identify its brighter members and prepare them for the important roles of the community. In a completely egalitarian society this is not possible. A nation cannot be completely equal and excellent too if equality is extended to include intellectual endowments. If a demand for equality in the *results* of education replaces equality in *opportunity* for education, egalitarianism will have eliminated all possibility of making distinctions. Without distinctions we may have become equal, but we can no longer have excellence in performance. Under such conditions the United States would begin to lose its place among the nations of the world. By our own standards, it may be an understatement to say that the United States is a long way from overdoing equality. But the United States is nonetheless moving away from excellence.

There is one bright prospect. It appears that public and student disenchantment will soon reduce enrollments in schools with declining quality. As funding shortages become more acute and as the competition for students becomes more ruthless, many of the entrepreneurs and promoters will find it advantageous to leave higher education for more profitable fields. This trend will be accelerated if the schools most concerned about quality will act through their accrediting bodies and state governments to see that standards of excellence are reinstituted.

The current cycle, which started with the launching of Sputnik, will be completed as the educators begin to face the concerns about quality expressed by the public and by some within the higher-education community. Fads will fall, abuses will appear for what they are, and higher education will clean up its act. And as before, educators will again turn to diversity, in part to explain away some of the changes and in part to answer legitimately the question of how we can obtain more equality while we also protect some places of excellence.

Now that the United States has lost its unique but temporary international superiority in resources and production techniques, we face a new competition for intellectual superiority. This is why the maintenance of quality in all of education is so important at this particular time in American history. When the margin of production superiority is comfortable, as it was for America following World War II, there is a lot of room for error in techniques and in knowledge. But when the margin is gone or has shifted in favor of others, the risks from error are much higher.

The universe is neutral to the place of the United States in world history; only we can make and sustain that place. The launching of Sputnik should have taught us that. Good fortune and a dozen other things have helped us to be the nation we are. Hereafter luck will play much less a role, if any at all, in our fortunes. In the long run, the Soviet Union has far more resources within its land area than the United States. If we do not maintain high quality in education, we will be giving away our place of leadership and the position of privilege our people presently enjoy. At no time in our history have we had to run so hard merely to stay where we are. And difficult as it may seem, we must come to realize that this will now be a permanent condition for every succeeding generation.

But even while competing internationally for intellectual excellence, we must continue to extend equal rights, privileges, and opportunities. We need the very best individuals from every class and ethnic group at all levels of all organizations making up our society. Consequently, to defend diversity within our system of higher education is not sophistry. But the nature of that diversity must be modified for the new times. We will need more diversity *among* different kinds of institutions, but less diversity *within* a given type of school. As a result, the prospect is that we will have some schools where quality absolutely will not be compromised, and some where the opportunity for all, over a much wider spectrum of intelligence and preparation, comes ahead of a goal of intellectual perfection. And there will be a considerable number of schools in the middle, trying to go both ways and doing neither very well.

9. To Stop the Decline

IN order to deal with increased federal intervention, the colleges and universities need to do a number of things. Clearly, the answer is not to refuse all further federal assistance. The substantial federal support in the past three decades has contributed significantly to the improvement of higher education through the GI Bill and other student-aid programs and through general and categorical grants and contract programs. Despite the imposition of federal controls and the enticement of schools to abandon some standards, federal financial aid has probably helped more than the controls have hurt, if taken in total. More schools are stronger and more students from broader segments of society are served and, for the most part, served well. To withdraw from federal programs is an option every school should be able to exercise if it becomes necessary. However, that option should be used only if the problems of dealing with federal controls cannot be handled otherwise.

One of the biggest sources of federal threat to the schools lies in civil-service employees' lack of understanding of what a university is and how it works. Federal workers need to know how institutions of higher learning differ from other institutions in society and where education's mission can be damaged by inappropriate procedures and pressures from government. Our universities would do well to remember Edmund Burke's observation that however government is constituted, its performance rests largely on discretionary powers left "to the prudence and uprightness of ministers of state." Thus, one step educators could take would be to give rotating assignments of a year or more to personnel of the universities and the principal federal agencies touching higher education. The problem federal bureaucrats have is not just one of communications but of perspective, perception, and empathy. To work on communications alone may result only in a better recognition of the differences between the parties and no improvement in understanding the differing points of view. The bureaucrats need to learn how institutions of higher learning work by being inside them. And the educators, while working within government in Washington or in a regional education office, could do much to enlarge the understanding of higher education among those working around them there.

Federal officials need to learn what is unique about faculty members, not that they are necessarily smarter than others in our society nor even that they have more wisdom. Rather, bureaucrats need to learn firsthand what it is to be a person who has devoted his life to acquiring ever more knowledge, to learning how to evaluate information systematically, and to discovering how to apply techniques to analyze information, views, opinions, and statements. They need to learn that a faculty member knows and respects proven rules of procedure and is specifically trained to apply standards more effectively than other people to determine what is true in his field of study.

The second thing a bureaucrat needs to know is that teaching is not just a way to make a living; a dedicated faculty member is committed to the fundamental truth of what he knows about his field of study. If this were not the case, he would be no more than a semiskilled worker passing on bits of information in order to earn his salary. But a truly committed faculty member is a professional, dedicated to extending his knowledge of what is known in his field and to communicating this to students and to those in society who can use it. If he has the competence, he will also devote energy and time to extending the frontiers of knowledge in his field. It is this commitment to the validity of the processes and the knowledge of his field that makes him a professional.

And while faculty members have knowledge and pass on knowledge through teaching, they do not usually spend much of their time applying knowledge. They teach what is known and how to go about learning more. They teach how to think, how to interpret, how to discover, and how to use knowledge. They teach the logic of reasoning and rules of evidence and systematic procedures to students to prepare them to cope with the changing world they will encounter during their lifetimes.

The government administrator needs to understand that in view of faculty members' superior knowledge of their fields and the professional commitment they have to protect their fields against error and adulteration, and in view of their professional commitment to the methodology of discovery and the establishment of truth, faculty members must determine academic matters. They must retain primary control over faculty appointments and promotions, admission and performance standards, the examination and grading of students, the development and content of curriculum, and the freedom of expression and thought on their campuses. These must be controlled by faculty rather than by the public, the politicians, the laymen, the bureaucrats, or even the students because of one thing: the faculty's superior knowledge of their fields of scholarship.

The federal government itself could take some important steps to reverse the decline in educational quality. Specifically, the government should make it possible for independent colleges and universities to raise standards and maintain high academic requirements. The government should remove pressures on private foundations to fund activities popular with federal administrators and should leave the foundations as free of federal directives as possible. Government should also establish or encourage programs to increase students' freedom of choice to attend private rather than public colleges and universities despite the higher costs to students.

But it will not be enough for the federal government merely to remove pressures for schools to lower standards, although that would help. In addition the government needs to provide incentives for some schools to raise standards, to require greater achievement for admission, and to establish higher levels of performance. These are difficult steps to take in a democratic society committed to egalitarianism. And the government probably cannot do these things to any great extent. Thus it is even more important that the government at least stay out of the way of private efforts to do them.

If it seems that government pressure is the reason schools are becoming more alike, this is only partly true. The rest of the blame for the movement toward uniformity among schools rests with the schools themselves. Colleges and universities need to be more selective about which government programs they will participate in. Any liberal arts college, for example, that is committed to maintaining excellence in its general education programs but that accepts federal funds to support technical and vocational programs requiring a reduction in general admission standards cannot blame the federal government for having lowered the school's standards.

The private liberal arts colleges face a special problem in the next decade. They have historically been residential colleges focusing upon educating the recent high school graduate. Their students attend full time and do not seek specific vocational skills. However, the decline in the birthrate has resulted in a significant shrinking of the college-age population. The 14 – 17 age-group will decline from 16.9 million in 1974 to 14.4 million in 1985, a drop of 2.5 million persons. By the mid-1980's, the number of high school diplomas awarded will drop by half a million from over 3 million in 1978. Each year of the next decade, the pool of students traditionally recruited to the private institutions, and the public ones as well, will shrink. With the keen competition for these students, the independent liberal arts colleges face a serious dilemma. Will they convert their curricula to copy those of the public colleges and universities to compete more directly with them for students? Or will they try to maintain their traditional role of providing superior liberal arts education and hope thereby to continue to attract enough students to avoid financial collapse? If they choose the former, they will be offering a duplicate of what the subsidized public institutions already provide the students at a much lower cost. If they follow the latter approach, how can they hope to attract enough students to stay in business? It is a gamble either way, and it seems in the public's interest for the state and federal governments to assist those private schools which will be committed to maintaining high-caliber instruction in the liberal arts.

But if the situation facing the more selective private liberal arts colleges is bleak, the nonselective private colleges' prospects for the future are much more dismal. Such institutions will either have to raise their standards or they will find themselves in direct competition with public institutions that offer the same types of programs at much lower student costs. And raising standards at a time of declining student numbers appears to be sure suicide.

The competition of public institutions for private schools' students has already started, since much of the off-campus teaching takes away students who would otherwise attend private colleges. Some public schools have become ruthless about this competition. They claim that since they can offer the off-campus courses cheaper than the nearby private colleges, they can save money for area students and even reach other students who cannot afford to attend the private schools at all.

But the real motivation behind much off-campus teaching is that such courses offered by public colleges and universities are financed by state governments at the same rates they would be if taught on the main campus. This results in a profit on such courses, which can be used on the home campus. If the states reduced the financing of such courses to a break-even level, they would eliminate much of the unfair competition with the private schools. This would also ensure that those off-campus courses which were taught were responding to bona fide needs rather than "needs" created by profit-motivated marketing activities. The decision to offer such courses would then focus on the student who needs the course rather than on the income generated by the student. Of course, other controls need to be instituted as well to monitor the standards of these courses. This is primarily a state problem, except when federal funds pay the tuition and fees for students taking off-campus courses. Efforts should be made to determine whether the public offerings supported by federal funds are damaging nearby private institutions or even whether some government-supported private schools are hurting other private institutions.

One reason the off-campus activities have become so popular with the entrepreneurs and promoters is that some of the accrediting associations have been failing in their responsibilities for overseeing quality. Some staff members of the regional associations feel that additional supervision would impose an unnecessary burden on off-campus programs, the good as well as the bad. They feel that prior approvals and reviews of such programs should not be required since, they say, such monitoring would inhibit the good schools from extending instructional activities into the field. In the meantime, no adequate supervision of the poor programs is being exercised. And these inferior programs, the horror stories, are giving all higher education a bad name everywhere. Only the regional accrediting associations can remedy this presently, and some are busier looking for excuses than for abuses.

The Council on Postsecondary Accreditation (COPA) attempts to oversee the accrediting agencies. However, the accrediting associations seem at times to put up with COPA only under sufferance. COPA must work through persuasion and consensus and has very little authority to require the associations to improve their procedures or raise their standards. Part of the problem is that the accrediting agencies are too heavily represented on COPA's board. The logrolling tactics of accrediting agencies on the board cannot be criticized; they are an accepted practice in a political setting. But agencies' support of each other could be reduced if the associations' representation were diluted. Also, because of the extremely intense concerns of the accrediting representatives for issues touching their special areas of business, in contrast to the more general views of the public members, it is difficult for even the public's spokesmen to vote against the anguished accrediting representatives. Under the best of circumstances, it is a tough job to try to develop and impose stiffer standards on the associations. But continuing the overrepresentation of the accrediting associations on the COPA board is like asking the foxes to design the henhouse they will guard.

However, no mandates from COPA would go very far in raising the standards applied by the accrediting associations. What is needed more is an internal strengthening of the associations. Many of the more prestigious universities maintain only nominal membership in the associations, pay their dues, and reluctantly and at times resentfully undergo the reaccreditation reviews. But they do not encourage their own administrators or faculty members to become actively involved in the regional accrediting associations. If the regional associations are to show more concern for excellence in higher education, the nation's major universities must become involved in the issues those associations are addressing.

Not only the outstanding institutions are silent; so are the outstanding leaders. Any long shadows in higher education today mean only it is late in the day, not that we have any towering figures among us. One might ask, where are the Tappans, Eliots, Gilmans, Harpers, Kirklands when we really need them? Perhaps they are among us and not speaking up. Perhaps the formulas imposed upon decision makers have driven them out of higher education. Perhaps they are keeping a low profile in a time when creativity and the exercise of discretion get administrators into difficulty.

There is no question that most of the fun has disappeared from the job of a college president or administrator. Administrative guidelines and court decisions have so hamstrung the presidents that at times it seems it is assumed they will act wrongly unless someone in the government heirarchy provides them a formula for proper behavior. The presumption seems to be that since a person who has the latitude to act has the latitude to do wrong, the danger of independent decisions must be removed.

The depressing effect of replacing personalized style and individual discretion with set formulas may be part of the reason there are so few sharp voices or independent styles in higher education today. Laws, regulations, and court decisions prescribe uniform procedures and common solutions for all issues. And each and every one of these legal, standardized approaches eats up precious days and months of life, energy, and creativity with stultifying paperwork. Like Pavlov's dogs, administrators bit by bit are being conditioned to stay within very limited and well-trodden paths by shocks, commands, intimidations, and orders.

Perhaps Mark Twain was right, every dog should have a few

fleas to keep him from forgetting he is a dog, but the education-dog is becoming too flea-bitten. Every administrator has faced, as well he should, the jeopardy of having his decisions challenged as granting special privilege or misusing his power or being capricious, arbitrary, or just plain stupid. He has been proscribed from committing certain specific reprehensible or undesirable deeds. But until recently he was not bound by prescriptions on how he must handle or resolve nearly every issue facing him. Incremental change and compromise are suspect solutions now; the academic administrator is faced with the expectation of total solutions within fixed deadlines. College presidents and their subordinates are spending so much time scratching fleas they hardly have time to live the dogs' lives they are being conditioned to accept.

The overmanagement of higher education by all branches of government was in part what Alexander Solzhenitsyn was referring to in his Harvard graduation talk of 1978. He said: "I have spent all my life under a communist regime and I will tell you that a society without any objective legal scale is a terrible one indeed. But a society with no other scale but the legal one is not quite worthy of man either."

To improve the quality of higher education, then, the higher-education community must fight to reclaim some of its lost independence. Further, Congress, the executive branch, and the courts should undertake special efforts to return more autonomy to the colleges and universities.

One of the most effective ways for higher education to resist further government encroachment into its business is to oppose the creation of a federal Department of Education in the executive branch. Even were the new department not to become a full-blown ministry of education, in time it would become well enough organized to exert additional controls over all higher education. The people themselves as well as our colleges and universities are better served by a federal government that does not have a central mind to oversee and direct all of academia. The resulting inefficiency and lack of coordination in federal higher-education programs give greater benefit and less threat to the independence of higher learning than a centralized agency responsible for all of education.

Sometimes federal agencies' working at cross-purposes allows dissenting views to develop and provide some check on interference in education. For example, while the U.S. Office of Education makes grants to encourage off-campus teaching and the Labor Department objects to rigorous attendance or grading standards in the CETA program, the Department of Defense has shown some incipient concern about the issues described above and has pressed the accrediting associations to raise their standards and improve their review procedures for on-base programs. This action illustrates one value of keeping education fragmented within the federal government.

Moreover, the sum higher education gets from the various governmental departments is more than it would receive from the sum of the parts brought together in a single department. At present, different congressional committees oversee and consider programs aiding various segments of higher education. The fragmentation of such congressional interest in higher education means that almost every congressman has some say over funds of concern to educators in his constituency and therefore has an incentive to be generous toward higher education. This broad base of congressional interest and support might be lost if higher-education programs were centralized under one department, which would be reviewed by fewer congressional committees. Furthermore, the existing fragmentation gives Congress less chance to make any "sense" out of its programs for higher education. This confusion will prevent Congress's imposing additional controls. Not only is standardization prevented by the sheer technical difficulties posed by fragmentation, but it is also stymied by the possessiveness of committees concerned about whose turf is being walked on in educational policy. Since almost every committee has special interest in some program dealing with higher education, each one looks after something benefiting at least some colleges, and each blocks attempts by other committees to extend standardized measures to that area. Thus, no comprehensive congressional policy on higher education can emerge under the present fragmented arrangement, and the nation benefits from the situation.

Consequently, it will promote the health and welfare of education for Health, Education, and Welfare to remain consolidated. Under a separate department, education will not get more attention from the White House, nor will policies on higher education be better coordinated with other government programs. All of education across the nation will merely face a stronger, more autonomous administration without anyone above the education secretary to appeal to. Presently, appeals can be made over the education commissioner's head to the secretary of the larger department. In the proposed arrangement, the only appeal would be from the secretary of education to the president, and he already has too many people reporting to him, as Secretary Joseph Califano eloquently pointed out in a book he wrote before he took his present position. If a Department of Education is to be created, at a minimum the executive branch should be required to prepare a presidential powers impact statement, as Secretary Califano suggested in his book.

In short, there are many reasons to oppose the creation of a Department of Education in Washington. The overriding one is to preclude the government from enlarging its education-related bureaucracy and from making that bureaucracy more independent in applying its policies over the private and state education systems. With a stronger federal agency to oversee education, there would be an increased chance that an aggressive secretary could go a long way toward coercing the educational system to fit his particular vision of national needs before proper constraints could be brought into effect. The present organizational structure offers less opportunity for that to occur. What the Constitution reserved to the states in education has been nibbled away since Buchanan's veto of the Land Grant College Act in 1859. A federal Department of Education would not bode well for the little bit of state power remaining.

10. The Next Cycle: Riding Out the Curve

AS we approach the end of the third cycle of increased government involvement in American higher education, we should take note of our past experiences and plan to handle the next time around more effectively. Perhaps we can learn where to exert efforts to avoid the bad aspects of the next cycle, which in some respects has already begun. With the next perceived public need to alter higher education by government, we can pay more attention to protecting quality. Where new constituencies must be served, we can learn to apply the genius of diversity more discretely, maintaining centers of true excellence for some and supporting other schools to extend learning to new audiences, without melding the two and sinking to the lowest common denominator. We can be alert for the entrepreneurs who will try to enter the field if higher education ever becomes profitable again. And we can be more vigilant against the further extension of government controls over the internal processes and priorities of institutions of higher learning. If we are wise, we may even be able to influence some of the things government will emphasize in the next cycle.

The world has recently been shocked into realizing that there are limits to the amounts of energy, minerals, water, and food available. Some have even conceded that there may be levels of pollution that can severely damage the "ecolibrium" that supports life as we know it. But most are eager to deny these limitations on growth and the dismal prospects that then follow for economic systems and nations and individuals. They prefer to choose the optimistic belief that another round of scientific and technological advancement will ensure continued expansion.

But even if these hopes of continued growth are correct, new technology will only postpone the inevitable climax of man's consuming and poisoning his own planet. It is very likely that the recent handwriting on the wall is not a forgery; that we will, in not more than a generation or two, arrive at this planet's maximum, and probably even unsustainable, level of population and material production. Even now, in our present advanced state of civilization, more people are starving to death than at any time in the history of man. In less than one hundred years we have consumed so much of the stored energy put in place over hundreds of millions of years, and we have established such a curve of increasing use, that, as we finally have recognized, energy is running out. We have so peopled and polluted the earth that not an estuary remains from which an informed scientist would dare eat a raw oyster. Areas of the world that were once health centers for tuberculosis patients now issue regular warnings to stay indoors, because the air outside is too poisoned for even the healthy to breathe safely.

We must face the fact that it is impossible to imagine that any nation will voluntarily slow its growth rate. Certainly the United States will apply every scientific, technological, and political device possible to maintain the status quo, that is, continued growth and increasing consumption. If this seems a harsh judgment, it is only based on man's performance to date; despite many efforts, effective limits have not been placed on population growth, material production, or energy consumption.

When curbing growth finally does become necessary, violence aimed at forcing or preventing the redistribution of wealth and resources is likely to occur between classes and among nations. Only so long as growth continues will no real redistribution of income among classes be necessary. Until expansion stops, we can continue to distribute a portion of the increased income from growing productivity to make the poor better off without having to make the rich and middle classes worse off. Since 1900, the actual increase in industrial productivity per worker in the United States has increased by thirteen times, due largely to the use of cheap energy. The sharing of the wealth created by this increased productivity has greatly benefited the workers as well as those dependent upon society for support.

However, once production is forced to decline, net investments will shrink and profits will fall off. Falling profits will further reduce investments, and this will still further reduce profits, a set of circumstances last played out to its ultimate conclusion in the Great Depression. The prospects of class conflict and depression alone are sufficient to keep any nation pushing upward on the growth curve. But the urgent question is what to do if there is no choice and stabilization is forced upon us. Kenneth Boulding says that we know next to nothing about what we should or might do, for the western world has been operating in a growth situation almost without major disruption since the Black Plague. Decline in growth under present conditions will deprive the poor of their accustomed or expected standard of living, and it will deprive investors of the incentive to invest, causing a downward spiraling of the economy. Violence may be counterpoised by repression, as those who want more can get it only by taking from the privileged classes and as the privileged classes resist redistribution of wealth. Under such circumstances, the challenge to politics to hold the fabric of society together will be greater than ever before, and throughout the world governments will fall or undergo severe changes.

The distribution question will apply among nations as well as within nations. International relations will worsen at the very time internal strife begins to grow. Military strength in most nations will become more important both internationally, to resist attacks or initiate aggression, and at home, to control the social and economic turmoil.

Thus, the prospects of a no-growth world are dismal indeed. There will likely be an increase in the centralization of political power and in coercion, insularity, international blackmail, callousness, and wars of protection and acquisition. Sharing with and caring for the less fortunate will diminish as the haves try to deny the have-nots, both within and among nations. The probability, based on what man has done rather than what he has preached and theorized throughout history, is that the human condition, man's efforts to realize his distinction from the animals, will worsen.

But all this is for the long run. More immediately, we will move into a postindustrial era in America, the western world, Russia, and Japan. Those societies will mobilize science and technology to overcome a plateau caused by depletion and inefficiency in systems of production. In America we will rise to new heights of production and consumption.

Even without problems of scarcity, many difficulties will arise in moving into a postindustrial society, which is more dependent upon services, information, and knowledge. We will not consume diminishing amounts of resources or poison our world less. Postindustrial society will not have transcended the industrial or preindustrial societies. Rather, such a society must merely ride upon the manufacturing and fabricating production of the industrial society, which, in turn, is completely dependent upon the extractive and mining processes of the preindustrial world. Services and knowledge industries are supported by the economic surpluses of the production industries and the extractive processes. Moreover, postindustrial society is more inflation-prone than the eras upon which it rides, because it is a drag on productivity and growth. Since government, the greatest provider of services and the principal source of funds for many other forms of services, needs money, it will stimulate growth and inflation in order to extract a share of the real and the apparent increased gross national product in order to pay for its services. The question of how government will spend its limited resources will give rise to intense competition among special-interest groups in the society, not a new process at all but one that will become more intense in the postindustrial setting.

We find no shortage of dismal prospects, if one wishes to take that view, or of new challenges, if one wishes another. For on the one hand, the world will be forced into a slowdown in growth with all the attendant problems that prospect entails. On the other hand, the world will not immediately have to face total breakdown in productivity and consumption, so at least part of the world's civilization will move on into the postindustrial society with all its problems. Without doubt, the next cycle of felt social need for a new role for higher education will focus on *both* these sets of prospects: low or no growth and postindustrial society. The universities will be expected to play many roles as society begins to deal meaningfully with the practical problems associated with growth and limitations of growth. The world is fortunate that we have some time to continue our old habits, for we will need every bit of time we can buy to prepare for the winding down that must begin twenty or thirty years, certainly not more than forty years, from now.

Higher education will have two overriding tasks, both of which are merely intensifications of activities already underway. The first will be to focus science and technology on ways to continue our growth despite the undeniable constraints on resources and the low tolerance of the environment to additional abuse. It will be through the success of such scientific and technological advances that the universities may gain the time to obtain results from their second task, to which we will turn later.

The first, formidable task of increasing productivity and efficiency in our economy, while the supply of resources goes down and the prices up and while environmental costs climb, needs to proceed on two fronts simultaneously. Those in charge of allocating funds to higher education must be brought to understand the need for supporting both applied and basic research. If only applied research were funded, there would be very limited advancement of knowledge, and the applied benefits of past basic research would soon be exhausted. Certainly it is unfortunate that we cannot identify in advance which basic research will have beneficial returns; then we could select which projects to fund and which to leave undone. But, of course, research about the unknown, to be applied in an undefined future to uncertain needs, does not permit such selective support. Consequently, basic research over broad fields is essential in a society as dependent as ours is upon scientific and technological advances to save us from economic and social collapse before we have any idea how to deal with the new circumstances.

Nonetheless, as society again draws upon higher education,

there will be the danger of increasing government controls. In order to reduce the large costs of basic research and to justify funding those projects which are supported, the government will be increasingly prone to select and direct. Rather than permit scientists to pursue knowledge by the random approach that appears to be their wont, government will view higher education as an instrument to solve certain specific problems as defined by government itself. It will appear at times that science can be focused on a problem better if peripheral issues are left unpursued, that is, not funded. The danger is clear: higher education research could become subjugated to government control and direction. Yet universities need large increases in funding for basic research rather than the reductions we are currently observing. And those increases will almost certainly have to come from the federal government since the state legislatures provide relatively little research funding, and even that is given grudgingly. Since the need for basic-research funds is both immediate and continuing and the federal government will be the major source of such funds, the universities will always face the possibility of being made into research instruments of the government and losing their role as unfettered searchers for new knowledge for the sake of knowledge. Karl Jaspers summed up the situation on behalf of university research at the celebration of the five-hundredth year of existence of the University of Basel when he said:

> Scientific research, performance of technological service, recollection of the past, formative participation in what is handed down, all this is excellent, but it is not enough. For the calm that is allowed at the university exists so that we may experience the storm of world events in our hearts and thoughts in order to understand it. The university ought to be the place where there is the clearest consciousness of the age, where that which is uttermost attains clarity, be it that in one spot, at least, full consciousness of what is taking place is achieved, be it that this clarity, working out into the world, shall provide assistance. ["Truth and Science," p. 40]

The universities' second task is the more difficult, more important, and more necessary of the two it faces. Since stabilization, or even decline in growth, is inevitable, higher education must turn to a host of questions. The universities must serve as the central mind for modeling, theorizing, and discussing the impact of no-growth on economic systems and how we must prepare for adjustments and accommodations. The institutions of higher learning will need to do the same in the field of international relations. They should also study carefully the probable impact and effect of no-growth on governments. And above all, they should think far ahead to the problems of how a people can maintain a system of self-governance in the face of the turmoil and change that a no-growth setting will present. This, the universities' second task after helping to buy time through another surge of scientific and technological advancement, is nothing less than to discover how a stable, good, and improving society can be built and sustained in the face of the problems the world is certain to encounter within this generation or the next.

In looking at the future and trying to predict broad social, economic, and political consequences of alternative conditions or policies, there is a need for theorizing, model building, and guessing. This work will be called visionary, futuristic, and currently impractical, which, of course, it will be by its very nature. Much of this work will be unpopular and will be seen as subversive to the present circumstances. The second part of this task will be more immediate, for scholars will have to look closely at the upcoming periods of transition. The dangers to stable, just societies arise in times of such change. It is then that violence and repression challenge peaceful transition and revolution succeeds evolution. In a sense this problem is one of applied social science. For if peaceful accommodation cannot be made to succeed and representative government does not survive the transitions, there will be little need to theorize about the more distant future. Consequently, much attention needs to be given to the characteristics of the changes likely to occur, how people will react, what conditions and processes can be manipulated, and the kinds of accommodations and alternative courses of political action that will be possible. And perhaps the most important test to be repeated in each crisis or time of transition will be whether the people are sufficiently educated to grasp what is happening to all mankind and to show the wisdom and restraint necessary to hold representative government together.

And this unanswerable question is dependent to a very large extent upon the functioning and effectiveness of our institutions of higher learning.

To accomplish these two tasks, technological research and social understanding, the universities must not only survive; they must also prosper. To the extent that they solve immediate scientific and technological problems, they will fare well. But the prospects for adequate funding for basic research are not as good. Even less bright is the likelihood that the government will look favorably on funding social and political studies that predict severe changes in our way of life. With higher education serving at the least as a gratuitous commentator on society and often as an outright critic, substantial public support will be difficult to maintain.

The charges of low productivity in higher education will continue. It is hard to convince legislators that there is no way to shorten by very much the time required to produce a highly qualified expert mind in anything. In institutions where quality is maintained, compromises in educational processes are not tolerated, and the result is that higher education is labor-intensive, low in productivity, and costly. The better the quality, the higher the cost. Yet those institutions maintaining quality programs know too that ultimately public disenchantment will follow initial infatuation with easy forms of so-called education.

The cycle of higher education we are currently ending saw government making new demands on the teaching end of institutions: new students, new, less traditional curricula. The cycle we are now entering will see government's concern shift from the teaching to the research function of universities, as the government requests both technological and social research. With the next round of government money, the new entrepreneurs will probably be found in quasipublic and nonprofit research organizations, which will be willing to undertake government-directed research without balking at government dictates and interference in the processes for discovering new knowledge. Such research organizations will appear more efficient, short-term, and that is what interests politicians, the quick payoff on public investments. As Roland Eggers once said to an audience at Syracuse University, we are dealing with twenty-year problems with five-year plans funded by one-year appropriations. The universities will be on the defensive in facing the new "nontraditional delivery systems" for research, as they have been during the current cycle in facing nontraditional teaching systems. The schools will complain a lot, but in many cases they will modify their relations and attitudes in order to get their share of the research money, even if it means underbidding their competitors and abandoning the traditional, unfettered, and objective research methods of the past. Questions of quality in research and standards in the institutions of higher education will again arise, as in past cycles, and new forms of evaluating or prequalifying research organizations and universities will probably develop.

In the coming time of despair, disillusionment, deprivation, and depression there will be one more felt need to which the universities may respond. That will be the need to renew our faith in the dignity and meaning of human life. Much of human history has advanced without increasing material consumption, and that may become necessary again. The losses we will suffer need not paralyze us. Edith Hamilton reminds us that suffering without true feeling is mere pathos or agony without understanding. Speaking of tragic poetry and drama, Dame Hamilton said, "To answer the question, what makes a tragedy, is to answer the question of wherein lies the essential significance of life, what the dignity of humanity depends upon in the last analysis . . . . a deeper and more ultimate reality than that in which our lives are lived" (*The Greek Way*, pp. 169 and 172).

Daniel Bell points out that people and social institutions (such as universities) can be used for various purposes, depending upon the values of the society. He reminds us of the bestiality we have witnessed in this century as instruments of society were turned to inhumane purposes when values were driven to their lowest level. If a decline in material well-being results in compromising human decency, in the loss of representative government, in closing the open processes for resolving differences and conflicts, in debasing human beings, we will have failed in the challenge to the human race we are about to encounter. We will have become in times of trouble the beast we abhor in man in times of plenty and contentment. We will have turned all of civilization to maintaining an uncivilized existence.

We live in exciting times, either near the end of two centuries of uncontrolled exploitation of the earth or in the beginning of the transition to a slowdown and a decline in standards of living. The hedonism of consumption and growth can continue for only a little longer, and then we face major adjustments. In the end we can bear the adjustments and the suffering that will occur in the troubled times ahead if we choose to impart to our lives the important responsibility to pass on a society that is stable, peaceful, just, and getting better and a world that is tolerably clean and will provide the basic material support for health and life for the generations to come. It is unlikely that very many will develop what Dame Hamilton calls "a passion" for the suffering to come, but perhaps a tolerance of pain and disappointment and sacrifice, coming out of an understanding of the human condition, is not beyond our reach.

It is in this exciting and dangerous time that higher education will be asked to perform new services for government, and a new cycle for American higher education will begin. During that cycle the institutions will again face government intervention into internal processes and priorities, on behalf of an urgent public demand for the unique services of academia. Educators must then, in the face of government pressures, hold firm to their deepest raison d'être. To transmit the experience of man, to locate us in time and space, to recognize what is possible and accept what is impossible, to improve the quality of life through the mind, to raise us above the other animals — these are the purposes of higher education. If we fail in these, civilization as we know it will pass away.

Bibliographic Notes

Preface

Dewey's quotation is from "President Hutchins' Proposals to Remake Higher Education" from the January, 1937, *The Social Frontier*. The article is reproduced in Richard Hofstadter and Wilson Smith's *American Higher Education Documentary History* (Chicago: University of Chicago Press, 1961).

1. *Introduction*

The references here and elsewhere in the book are to Marvin Harris's *Cannibals and Kings: The Origins of Culture* (New York: Random House, 1977).

2. *Aggies and Veterans*

As general background for this chapter and the preceding and succeeding chapters, see Allan Nevins, *The State Universities and Democracy* (Urbana: The University of Illinois Press, 1962); Frederick Rudolph, *The American College and University* (New York: Knopf, 1962); and Richard Hofstadter and C. Dewitt Hardy, *The Development and Scope of Higher Education in the United States* (New York: Columbia University Press, 1962).

3. *The Space Race and the Paper Chase*

Recommendations of the President's Commission on Higher Education are reported in *Higher Education for American Democracy* (New York: Harper, 1948). The quote is from an excerpt of that report in *The History of American Education through Readings* (Boston: Heath and Co., 1964), p. 481. The Executive Order requiring affirmative action programs is Executive Order 11246, issued September 28, 1965, as amended by Executive Order 11375, issued October 17, 1967. The court case referred to is *Adams* v. *Califano*, originally *Adams* v. *Richardson* 480 F 2d 1159 (1973).

4. *Nontraditional Education and Dwindling Quality*

For more background the reader may wish to consult Lee Porter, *Degrees for Sale* (New York: Arco, 1972); my article, coauthored with William C. Lindley, in *Change* (February, 1977), entitled, "The Disgrace of Military Base Programs"; and my article in the Proceedings of the 26th Southern Regional Education Board Legislative Work Conference (1977), *Stability and Change — Postsecondary Education's Future*, "View from State Higher Education Agency."

5. *The Body-Count Game*

The guidelines for the *Adams* case appeared in the *Federal Register* vol. 43, no. 32, February 15, 1978.

The classification of the intelligence of one hundred Americans is from John Fischer's "The Editor's Easy Chair" in *Harper's Magazine*. His September, 1962, topic was "The Stupidity Problem," in which he summarized psychologists' findings that intelligence is distributed in a fairly consistent pattern. He appropriately footnoted this classification to acknowledge the reservations concerning IQ testing: that it includes bias, that the IQ of a person is not fixed, and that the testing is subject to other deficiencies and limitations.

Also the reader may wish to consult my article in the November, 1978, *Phi Delta Kappan*, entitled, "The Nontraditional Doctorate: Time for *Sine Cera*?" and in that same issue the article "The External Degree in Education: Growing Criticism and Crisis" by H. G. Vonk and Robert G. Brown. Additional readings include: Richard B. Morland, "The External Doctorate in Education: Blessing or Blasphemy?" in the November, 1973, *Phi Delta Kappan; Explorations in Non-traditional Study*, edited by Samuel G. Gould and Patricia Cross (San Francisco: Jossey-Bass, 1972); *The External Degree* by Cyril O. Houle (San Francisco: Jossey-Bass, 1973); *Independent Study* by Paul Dressel and Mary M. Thompson (San Francisco: Jossey-Bass, 1973); *Planning Non-traditional Programs* by K. Patricia Cross, John R. Valley, and Associates (San Francisco: Jossey-Bass, 1974); *Non-traditional Study: Threat, Promise, or Necessity?* Conferences on Non-traditional Study, Series No. 2 (Des Moines: Drake University, 1975); and Conference Report, *Exploring the External Degree*, Council on Higher Education (Seattle: University of Washington, 1975).

6. *The Potential for Quality Control*

The quotation by Bailey is from his remarks at the Army Continuing Education Services Conference at Fort Bliss, April 11, 1978.

The Gideonse quotation is from his *The Higher Learning in a Democracy* as excerpted in Hofstadter and Smith's *Documentary History* cited above.

Quotations here and elsewhere from Bickel are from his *The Morality of Consent* (New Haven and London: Yale University Press, 1975).

The full citation for the case quoted is: *Marjorie Webster Junior College Inc.*, v. *Middle States Association of Colleges and Secondary Schools, Inc.* 302 F. Supp 459 (Dist. Crt. D.C., 1969) and 432 F 2d 650 (Crt. of Appeals, D.C., 1970).

See also my article entitled "State Coordination and External Degree Programs," to be printed in the April, 1979, issue of *Peabody Journal of Education*.

9. *To Stop the Decline*

Joseph A. Califano's book referred to is *A Presidential Nation* (New York: Norton, 1975).

10. *The Next Cycle: Riding Out the Curve*

I have drawn on a number of books for this discussion, including Daniel Bell's *The Coming of Post-Industrial Society* (New York: Basic Books, 1973); Harrison Brown's *The Human Future Revisited* (New York: Norton, 1978); John K. Galbraith's *The Great Crash* (Boston: Houghton Mifflin, 1954); Robert I. Heilbroner's *An Inquiry into the Human Prospect* (New York: Norton, 1975); Kenneth Boulding's *Beyond Economics* (Ann Arbor: University of Michigan Press, 1970); and his article "The Liberal Arts Amid a Culture in Crisis" from *Liberal Education* 63 (March, 1972), published by the Association of American Colleges; and Burton J. Bledstein's *The Culture of Professionalism* (New York: Norton, 1976). The quotation by Jaspers is from "Truth and Science," *The Graduate Journal* (Spring, 1962), published by the University of Texas at Austin.

The statements on tragedy are from Edith Hamilton's *The Greek Way* (New York: Norton, 1930).

The apt word "ecolibrium" I acquired from Athelstan Spilhaus.

Acknowledgments

Although they are not responsible for any of the views expressed in the previous pages, there are several individuals whose advice and assistance I wish to recognize. They are Dr. Lois DeBakey of Baylor College of Medicine, Dr. B. S. Raj Thyagarajan of The University of Texas at San Antonio, and Dr. Jack K. Williams, former president and chancellor of The Texas A&M University System.

I am much indebted to Mrs. Mary Allen for preparing the manuscript in its several drafts.

KELLER: What do you want me to do? You're old enough to know your own mind.

CHRIS, *asking, annoyed:* Then it's all right, I'll go ahead with it?

KELLER: Well, you want to be sure Mother isn't going to—

CHRIS: Then it isn't just my business.

KELLER: I'm just sayin'—

CHRIS: Sometimes you infuriate me, you know that? Isn't it your business, too, if I tell this to Mother and she throws a fit about it? You have such a talent for ignoring things.

KELLER: I ignore what I gotta ignore. The girl is Larry's girl.

CHRIS: She's not Larry's girl.

KELLER: From Mother's point of view he is not dead and you have no right to take his girl. *Slight pause.* Now you can go on from there if you know where to go, but I'm tellin' you I don't know where to go. See? I don't know. Now what can I do for you?

CHRIS: I don't know why it is, but every time I reach out for something I want, I have to pull back because other people will suffer. My whole bloody life, time after time after time.

KELLER: You're a considerate fella, there's nothing wrong in that.

CHRIS: To hell with that.

KELLER: Did you ask Annie yet?

CHRIS: I wanted to get this settled first.

KELLER: How do you know she'll marry you? Maybe she feels the same way Mother does?

CHRIS: Well, if she does, then that's the end of it. From her letters I think she's forgotten him. I'll find out. And then we'll thrash it out with Mother? Right? Dad, don't avoid me.

KELLER: The trouble is, you don't see enough women. You never did.

CHRIS: So what? I'm not fast with women.

KELLER: I don't see why it has to be Annie.

CHRIS: Because it is.

KELLER: That's a good answer, but it don't answer anything. You haven't seen her since you went to war. It's five years.

CHRIS: I can't help it. I know her best. I was brought up next door to her. These years when I think of someone for my wife, I think of Annie. What do you want, a diagram?

KELLER: I don't want a diagram . . . I—I'm— She thinks he's coming back, Chris. You marry that girl and you're

pronouncing him dead. Now what's going to happen to Mother? Do you know? I don't! *Pause.*

CHRIS: All right, then, Dad.

KELLER, *thinking Chris has retreated:* Give it some more thought.

CHRIS: I've given it three years of thought. I'd hoped that if I waited, Mother would forget Larry and then we'd have a regular wedding and everything happy. But if that can't happen here, then I'll have to get out.

KELLER: What the hell is *this*?

CHRIS: I'll get out. I'll get married and live some place else. Maybe in New York.

KELLER: Are you crazy?

CHRIS: I've been a good son too long, a good sucker. I'm through with it.

KELLER: You've got a business here, what the hell is this?

CHRIS: The business! The business doesn't inspire me.

KELLER: Must you be inspired?

CHRIS: Yes. I like it an hour a day. If I have to grub for money all day long at least at evening I want it beautiful. I want a family, I want some kids, I want to build something I can give myself to. Annie is in the middle of that. Now . . . where do I find it?

KELLER: You mean— *Goes to him.* Tell me something, you mean you'd leave the business?

CHRIS: Yes. On this I would.

KELLER, *after a pause:* Well . . . you don't want to think like that.

CHRIS: Then help me stay here.

KELLER: All right, but—but don't think like that. Because what the hell did I work for? That's only for you, Chris, the whole shootin' match is for you!

CHRIS: I know that, Dad. Just you help me stay here.

KELLER, *putting a fist up to Chris's jaw:* But don't think that way, you hear me?

CHRIS: I am thinking that way.

KELLER, *lowering his hand:* I don't understand you, do I?

CHRIS: No, you don't. I'm a pretty tough guy.

KELLER: Yeah. I can see that.

Mother appears on porch. She is in her early fifties, a woman of uncontrolled inspirations and an overwhelming capacity for love.

MOTHER: Joe?

CHRIS, *going toward porch:* Hello, Mom.

MOTHER, *indicating house behind her; to Keller:* Did you take a bag from under the sink?

KELLER: Yeah, I put it in the pail.

MOTHER: Well, get it out of the pail. That's my potatoes.

Chris bursts out laughing—goes up into alley.

KELLER, *laughing:* I thought it was garbage.

MOTHER: Will you do me a favor, Joe? Don't be helpful.

KELLER: I can afford another bag of potatoes.

MOTHER: Minnie scoured that pail in boiling water last night. It's cleaner than your teeth.

KELLER: And I don't understand why, after I worked forty years and I got a maid, why I have to take out the garbage.

MOTHER: If you would make up your mind that every bag in the kitchen isn't full of garbage you wouldn't be throwing out my vegetables. Last time it was the onions.

Chris comes on, hands her bag.

KELLER: I don't like garbage in the house.

MOTHER: Then don't eat. *She goes into the kitchen with bag.*

CHRIS: That settles you for today.

KELLER: Yeah, I'm in last place again. I don't know, once upon a time I used to think that when I got money again I would have a maid and my wife would take it easy. Now I got money, and I got a maid, and my wife is workin' for the maid. *He sits in one of the chairs.*

Mother comes out on last line. She carries a pot of string beans.

MOTHER: It's her day off, what are you crabbing about?

CHRIS, *to Mother:* Isn't Annie finished eating?

MOTHER, *looking around preoccupiedly at yard:* She'll be right out. *Moves.* That wind did some job on this place. *Of the tree:* So much for that, thank God.

KELLER, *indicating chair beside him:* Sit down, take it easy.

MOTHER, *pressing her hand to top of her head:* I've got such a funny pain on the top of my head.

CHRIS: Can I get you an aspirin?

Mother picks a few petals off ground, stands there smelling them in her hand, then sprinkles them over plants.

MOTHER: No more roses. It's so funny . . . everything decides to happen at the same time. This month is his birthday; his tree blows down, Annie comes. Everything that happened seems to be coming back. I was just down the cellar, and what do I stumble over? His baseball glove. I haven't seen it in a century.

CHRIS: Don't you think Annie looks well?

MOTHER: Fine. There's no question about it. She's a beauty . . . I still don't know what brought her here. Not that I'm not glad to see her, but—

CHRIS: I just thought we'd all like to see each other again. *Mother just looks at him, nodding ever so slightly—almost as though admitting something.* And I wanted to see her myself.

MOTHER, *as her nods halt, to Keller:* The only thing is I think her nose got longer. But I'll always love that girl. She's one that didn't jump into bed with somebody else as soon as it happened with her fella.

KELLER, *as though that were impossible for Annie:* Oh, what're you—?

MOTHER: Never mind. Most of them didn't wait till the telegrams were opened. I'm just glad she came, so you can see I'm not *completely* out of my mind. *Sits, and rapidly breaks string beans in the pot.*

CHRIS: Just because she isn't married doesn't mean she's been mourning Larry.

MOTHER, *with an undercurrent of observation:* Why then isn't she?

CHRIS, *a little flustered:* Well . . . it could've been any number of things.

MOTHER, *directly at him:* Like what, for instance?

CHRIS, *embarrassed, but standing his ground:* I don't know. Whatever it is. Can I get you an aspirin?

Mother puts her hand to her head. She gets up and goes aimlessly toward the trees on rising.

MOTHER: It's not like a headache.

KELLER: You don't sleep, that's why. She's wearing out more bedroom slippers than shoes.

MOTHER: I had a terrible night. *She stops moving.* I never had a night like that.

CHRIS, *looking at Keller:* What was it, Mom? Did you dream?

MOTHER: More, more than a dream.

CHRIS, *hesitantly:* About Larry?

MOTHER: I was fast asleep, and— *Raising her arm over the audience:* Remember the way he used to fly low past the house when he was in training? When we used to see his face in the cockpit going by? That's the way I saw him. Only high up. Way, way up, where the clouds are. He was so real I could reach out and touch him. And suddenly he started to fall. And crying, crying to me . . . Mom, Mom! I could hear him like he was in the room. Mom! . . . it was his voice! If I could touch him I knew I could stop him, if I could only— *Breaks off, allowing her outstretched hand to fall.* I woke up and it was so funny— The wind . . . it was like the roaring of his engine. I came out here . . . I must've still been half asleep. I could hear that roaring like he was going by. The tree snapped right in front of me—and I like—came awake. *She is looking at tree. She suddenly realizes something, turns with a reprimanding finger shaking slightly at Keller.* See? We should never have planted that tree. I said so in the first place; it was too soon to plant a tree for him.

CHRIS, *alarmed:* Too soon!

MOTHER, *angering:* We rushed into it. Everybody was in such a hurry to bury him. I *said* not to plant it yet. *To Keller:* I *told* you to—!

CHRIS: Mother, Mother! *She looks into his face.* The wind blew it down. What significance has that got? What are you talking about? Mother, please . . . Don't go through it all again, will you? It's no good, it doesn't accomplish anything. I've been thinking, y'know?—maybe we ought to put our minds to forgetting him?

MOTHER: That's the third time you've said that this week.

CHRIS: Because it's not right; we never took up our lives again. We're like at a railroad station waiting for a train that never comes in.

MOTHER, *pressing top of her head:* Get me an aspirin, heh?

CHRIS: Sure, and let's break out of this, heh, Mom? I thought the four of us might go out to dinner a couple of nights, maybe go dancing out at the shore.

MOTHER: Fine. *To Keller:* We can do it tonight.

KELLER: Swell with me!

CHRIS: Sure, let's have some fun. *To Mother:* You'll start with this aspirin. *He goes up and into house with new spirit. Her smile vanishes.*

MOTHER, *with an accusing undertone:* Why did he invite her here?

KELLER: Why does that bother you?

MOTHER: She's been in New York three and a half years, why all of a sudden—?

KELLER: Well, maybe—maybe he just wanted to see her.

MOTHER: Nobody comes seven hundred miles "just to see."

KELLER: What do you mean? He lived next door to the girl all his life, why shouldn't he want to see her again? *Mother looks at him critically.* Don't look at me like that, he didn't tell me any more than he told you.

MOTHER—*a warning and a question:* He's not going to marry her.

KELLER: How do you know he's even thinking of it?

MOTHER: It's got that about it.

KELLER, *sharply watching her reaction:* Well? So what?

MOTHER, *alarmed:* What's going on here, Joe?

KELLER: Now listen, kid—

MOTHER, *avoiding contact with him:* She's not his girl, Joe; she knows she's not.

KELLER: You can't read her mind.

MOTHER: Then why is she still single? New York is full of men, why isn't she married? *Pause.* Probably a hundred people told her she's foolish, but she's waited.

KELLER: How do you know why she waited?

MOTHER: She knows what I know, that's why. She's faithful as

a rock. In my worst moments, I think of her waiting, and I know again that I'm right.

KELLER: Look, it's a nice day. What are we arguing for?

MOTHER, *warningly:* Nobody in this house dast take her faith away, Joe. Strangers might. But not his father, not his brother.

KELLER, *exasperated:* What do you want me to do? What do you want?

MOTHER: I want you to act like he's coming back. Both of you. Don't think I haven't noticed you since Chris invited her. I won't stand for any nonsense.

KELLER: But, Kate—

MOTHER: Because if he's not coming back, then I'll kill myself! Laugh. Laugh at me. *She points to tree.* But why did that happen the very night she came back? Laugh, but there are meanings in such things. She goes to sleep in his room and his memorial breaks in pieces. Look at it; look. *She sits on bench.* Joe—

KELLER: Calm yourself.

MOTHER: Believe with me, Joe. I can't stand all alone.

KELLER: Calm yourself.

MOTHER: Only last week a man turned up in Detroit, missing longer than Larry. You read it yourself.

KELLER: All right, all right, calm yourself.

MOTHER: You above all have got to believe, you—

KELLER, *rising:* Why me above all?

MOTHER: Just don't stop believing.

KELLER: What does that mean, me above all?

Bert comes rushing on.

BERT: Mr. Keller! Say, Mr. Keller . . . *Pointing up driveway:* Tommy just said it again!

KELLER, *not remembering any of it:* Said what? Who?

BERT: The dirty word.

KELLER: Oh. Well—

BERT: Gee, aren't you going to arrest him? I warned him.

MOTHER, *with suddenness:* Stop that, Bert. Go home. *Bert backs up, as she advances.* There's no jail here.

KELLER, *as though to say, "Oh-what-the-hell-let-him-believe-there-is":* Kate—

MOTHER, *turning on Keller furiously:* There's no jail here! I want you to stop that jail business! *He turns, shamed, but peeved.*

BERT, *past her to Keller:* He's right across the street.

MOTHER: Go home, Bert. *Bert turns around and goes up driveway. She is shaken. Her speech is bitten off, extremely urgent.* I want you to stop that, Joe. That whole jail business!

KELLER, *alarmed, therefore angered:* Look at you, look at you shaking.

MOTHER, *trying to control herself, moving about clasping her hands:* I can't help it.

KELLER: What have I got to hide? What the hell is the matter with you, Kate?

MOTHER: I didn't say you had anything to hide, I'm just telling you to stop it! Now stop it! *As Ann and Chris appear on porch. Ann is twenty-six, gentle but despite herself capable of holding fast to what she knows. Chris opens door for her.*

ANN: Hya, Joe! *She leads off a general laugh that is not self-conscious because they know one another too well.*

CHRIS, *bringing Ann down, with an outstretched, chivalric arm:* Take a breath of that air, kid. You never get air like that in New York.

MOTHER, *genuinely overcome with it:* Annie, where did you get that dress!

ANN: I couldn't resist. I'm taking it right off before I ruin it. *Swings around.* How's that for three weeks' salary?

MOTHER, *to Keller:* Isn't she the most—? *To Ann:* It's gorgeous, simply gor—

CHRIS, *to Mother:* No kidding, now, isn't she the prettiest gal you ever saw?

MOTHER, *caught short by his obvious admiration, she finds herself reaching out for a glass of water and aspirin in his hand, and—:* You gained a little weight, didn't you, darling? *She gulps pill and drinks.*

ANN: It comes and goes.

KELLER: Look how nice her legs turned out!

ANN, *as she runs to fence:* Boy, the poplars got thick, didn't they?

Keller moves to settee and sits.

KELLER: Well, it's three years, Annie. We're gettin' old, kid.
MOTHER: How does Mom like New York? *Ann keeps looking through trees.*
ANN, *a little hurt:* Why'd they take our hammock away?
KELLER: Oh, no, it broke. Couple of years ago.
MOTHER: What broke? He had one of his light lunches and flopped into it.
ANN *laughs and turns back toward Jim's yard:* Oh, excuse me!

Jim has come to fence and is looking over it. He is smoking a cigar. As she cries out, he comes on around on stage.

JIM: How do you do. *To Chris:* She looks very intelligent!
CHRIS: Ann, this is Jim—Doctor Bayliss.
ANN, *shaking Jim's hand:* Oh, sure, he writes a lot about you.
JIM: Don't you believe it. He likes everybody. In the battalion he was known as Mother McKeller.
ANN: I can believe it. You know—? *To Mother:* It's so strange seeing him come out of that yard. *To Chris:* I guess I never grew up. It almost seems that Mom and Pop are in there now. And you and my brother doing algebra, and Larry trying to copy my home-work. Gosh, those dear dead days beyond recall.
JIM: Well, I hope that doesn't mean you want me to move out?
SUE, *calling from offstage:* Jim, come in here! Mr. Hubbard is on the phone!
JIM: I told you I don't want—
SUE, *commandingly sweet:* Please, dear! Please!
JIM, *resigned:* All right, Susie. *Trailing off:* All right, all right . . . *To Ann:* I've only met you, Ann, but if I may offer you a piece of advice— When you marry, never—even in your mind—never count your husband's money.
SUE, *from offstage:* Jim?
JIM: At once! *Turns and goes off:* At once. *He exits.*
MOTHER—*Ann is looking at her. She speaks meaningfully:* I told her to take up the guitar. It'd be a common interest for them. *They laugh:* Well, he loves the guitar!

Ann, as though to overcome Mother, becomes suddenly lively, crosses to Keller on settee, sits on his lap.

ANN: Let's eat at the shore tonight! Raise some hell around here, like we used to before Larry went!

MOTHER, *emotionally:* You think of him! You see? *Triumphantly:* She thinks of him!

ANN, *with an uncomprehending smile:* What do you mean, Kate?

MOTHER: Nothing. Just that you—remember him, he's in your thoughts.

ANN: That's a funny thing to say; how could I help remembering him?

MOTHER—*it is drawing to a head the wrong way for her; she starts anew. She rises and comes to Ann:* Did you hang up your things?

ANN: Yeah . . . *To Chris:* Say, you've sure gone in for clothes. I could hardly find room in the closet.

MOTHER: No, don't you remember? That's Larry's room.

ANN: You mean . . . they're Larry's?

MOTHER: Didn't you recognize them?

ANN, *slowly rising, a little embarrassed:* Well, it never occurred to me that you'd— I mean the shoes are all shined.

MOTHER: Yes, dear. *Slight pause. Ann can't stop staring at her. Mother breaks it by speaking with the relish of gossip, putting her arm around Ann and walking with her.* For so long I've been aching for a nice conversation with you, Annie. Tell me something.

ANN: What?

MOTHER: I don't know. Something nice.

CHRIS, *wryly:* She means do you go out much?

MOTHER: Oh, shut up.

KELLER: And are any of them serious?

MOTHER, *laughing, sits in her chair:* Why don't you both choke?

KELLER: Annie, you can't go into a restaurant with that woman any more. In five minutes thirty-nine strange people are sitting at the table telling her their life story.

MOTHER: If I can't ask Annie a personal question—

KELLER: Askin' is all right, but don't beat her over the head. You're beatin' her, you're beatin' her. *They are laughing.*

Ann takes pan of beans off stool, puts them on floor under chair and sits.

ANN, *to Mother:* Don't let them bulldoze you. Ask me anything you like. What do you want to know, Kate? Come on, let's gossip.

MOTHER, *to Chris and Keller:* She's the only one is got any sense. *To Ann:* Your mother—she's not getting a divorce, heh?

ANN: No, she's calmed down about it now. I think when he gets out they'll probably live together. In New York, of course.

MOTHER: That's fine. Because your father is still—I mean he's a decent man after all is said and done.

ANN: I don't care. She can take him back if she likes.

MOTHER: And you? You—*shakes her head negatively*—go out much? *Slight pause.*

ANN, *delicately:* You mean am I still waiting for him?

MOTHER: Well, no. I don't expect you to wait for him but—

ANN, *kindly:* But that's what you mean, isn't it?

MOTHER: Well . . . yes.

ANN: Well, I'm not, Kate.

MOTHER, *faintly:* You're not?

ANN: Isn't it ridiculous? You don't really imagine he's—?

MOTHER: I know, dear, but don't say it's ridiculous, because the papers were full of it; I don't know about New York, but there was half a page about a man missing even longer than Larry, and he turned up from Burma.

CHRIS, *coming to Ann:* He couldn't have wanted to come home very badly, Mom.

MOTHER: Don't be so smart.

CHRIS: You can have a helluva time in Burma.

ANN *rises and swings around in back of Chris:* So I've heard.

CHRIS: Mother, I'll bet you money that you're the only woman in the country who after three years is still—

MOTHER: You're sure?

CHRIS: Yes, I am.

MOTHER: Well, if you're sure then you're sure. *She turns her head away an instant.* They don't say it on the radio but I'm sure that in the dark at night they're still waiting for their sons.

CHRIS: Mother, you're absolutely—

MOTHER, *waving him off:* Don't be so damned smart! Now stop it! *Slight pause.* There are just a few things you *don't*

know. All of you. And I'll tell you one of them, Annie. Deep, deep in your heart you've always been waiting for him.

ANN, *resolutely:* No, Kate.

MOTHER, *with increasing demand:* But deep in your heart, Annie!

CHRIS: She ought to know, shouldn't she?

MOTHER: Don't let them tell you what to think. Listen to your heart. Only your heart.

ANN: Why does your heart tell you he's alive?

MOTHER: Because he has to be.

ANN: But why, Kate?

MOTHER, *going to her:* Because certain things have to be, and certain things can never be. Like the sun has to rise, it has to be. That's why there's God. Otherwise anything could happen. But there's God, so certain things can never happen. I would know, Annie—just like I knew the day he—*indicates Chris*—went into that terrible battle. Did he write me? Was it in the papers? No, but that morning I couldn't raise my head off the pillow. Ask Joe. Suddenly, I knew. I knew! And he was nearly killed that day. Ann, you *know* I'm right!

Ann stands there in silence, then turns trembling, going upstage.

ANN: No, Kate.

MOTHER: I have to have some tea.

Frank appears, carrying ladder.

FRANK: Annie! *Coming down:* How are you, gee whiz!

ANN, *taking his hand:* Why, Frank, you're losing your hair.

KELLER: He's got responsibility.

FRANK: Gee whiz!

KELLER: Without Frank the stars wouldn't know when to come out.

FRANK *laughs; to Ann:* You look more womanly. You've matured. You—

KELLER: Take it easy, Frank, you're a married man.

ANN, *as they laugh:* You still haberdashering?

FRANK: Why not? Maybe I too can get to be president. How's your brother? Got his degree, I hear.

ANN: Oh, George has his own office now!

FRANK: Don't say! *Funereally:* And your dad? Is he—?

ANN, *abruptly:* Fine. I'll be in to see Lydia.

FRANK, *sympathetically:* How about it, does Dad expect a parole soon?

ANN, *with growing ill-ease:* I really don't know, I—

FRANK, *staunchly defending her father for her sake:* I mean because I feel, y'know, that if an intelligent man like your father is put in prison, there ought to be a law that says either you execute him, or let him go after a year.

CHRIS, *interrupting:* Want a hand with that ladder, Frank?

FRANK, *taking cue:* That's all right, I'll— *Picks up ladder.* I'll finish the horoscope tonight, Kate. *Embarrassed:* See you later, Ann, you look wonderful. *He exits. They look at Ann.*

ANN *to Chris, as she sits slowly on stool:* Haven't they stopped talking about Dad?

CHRIS *comes down and sits on arm of chair:* Nobody talks about him any more.

KELLER *rises and comes to her:* Gone and forgotten, kid.

ANN: Tell me. Because I don't want to meet anybody on the block if they're going to—

CHRIS: I don't want you to worry about it.

ANN, *to Keller:* Do they still remember the case, Joe? Do they talk about you?

KELLER: The only one still talks about it is my wife.

MOTHER: That's because you keep on playing policeman with the kids. All their parents hear out of you is jail, jail, jail.

KELLER: Actually what happened was that when I got home from the penitentiary the kids got very interested in me. You know kids. I was—*Laughs*—like the expert on the jail situation. And as time passed they got it confused and . . . I ended up a detective. *Laughs.*

MOTHER: Except that *they* didn't get it confused. *To Ann:* He hands out police badges from the Post Toasties boxes. *They laugh.*

Ann rises and comes to Keller, putting her arm around his shoulder.

ANN, *wondrously at them, happy:* Gosh, it's wonderful to hear you laughing about it.

CHRIS: Why, what'd you expect?

ANN: The last thing I remember on this block was one word —"Murderers!" Remember that, Kate?—Mrs. Hammond standing in front of our house and yelling that word? She's still around, I suppose?

MOTHER: They're all still around.

KELLER: Don't listen to her. Every Saturday night the whole gang is playin' poker in this arbor. All the ones who yelled murderer takin' my money now.

MOTHER: Don't, Joe; she's a sensitive girl, don't fool her. *To Ann:* They still remember about Dad. It's different with him. *Indicates Joe.* He was exonerated, your father's still there. That's why I wasn't so enthusiastic about your coming. Honestly, I know how sensitive you are, and I told Chris, I said—

KELLER: Listen, you do like I did and you'll be all right. The day I come home, I got out of my car—but not in front of the house . . . on the corner. You should've been here, Annie, and you too, Chris; you'd-a seen something. Everybody knew I was getting out that day; the porches were loaded. Picture it now; none of them believed I was innocent. The story was, I pulled a fast one getting myself exonerated. So I get out of my car, and I walk down the street. But very slow. And with a smile. The beast! I was the beast; the guy who sold cracked cylinder heads to the Army Air Force; the guy who made twenty-one P-40s crash in Australia. Kid, walkin' down the street that day I was guilty as hell. Except I wasn't, and there was a court paper in my pocket to prove I wasn't, and I walked . . . past . . . the porches. Result? Fourteen months later I had one of the best shops in the state again, a respected man again; bigger than ever.

CHRIS, *with admiration:* Joe McGuts.

KELLER, *now with great force:* That's the only way you lick 'em is guts! *To Ann:* The worst thing you did was to move away from here. You made it tough for your father when he gets out. That's why I tell you, I like to see him move back right on this block.

MOTHER, *pained:* How could they move back?

KELLER: It ain't gonna end *till* they move back! *To Ann:* Till people play cards with him again, and talk with him, and

smile with him—you play cards with a man you know he can't be a murderer. And the next time you write him I like you to tell him just what I said. *Ann simply stares at him.* You hear me?

ANN, *surprised:* Don't you hold anything against him?

KELLER: Annie, I never believed in crucifying people.

ANN, *mystified:* But he was your partner, he dragged you through the mud.

KELLER: Well, he ain't my sweetheart, but you gotta forgive, don't you?

ANN: You, either, Kate? Don't you feel any—?

KELLER, *to Ann:* The next time you write Dad—

ANN: I don't write him.

KELLER, *struck:* Well, every now and then you—

ANN, *a little shamed, but determined:* No, I've *never* written to him. Neither has my brother. *To Chris:* Say, do you feel this way, too?

CHRIS: He murdered twenty-one pilots.

KELLER: What the hell kinda talk is that?

MOTHER: That's not a thing to say about a man.

ANN: What else can you say? When they took him away I followed him, went to him every visiting day. I was crying all the time. Until the news came about Larry. Then I realized. It's wrong to pity a man like that. Father or no father, there's only one way to look at him. He knowingly shipped out parts that would crash an airplane. And how do you know Larry wasn't one of them?

MOTHER: I was waiting for that. *Going to her:* As long as you're here, Annie, I want to ask you never to say that again.

ANN: You surprise me. I thought you'd be mad at him.

MOTHER: What your father did had nothing to do with Larry. Nothing.

ANN: But we can't know that.

MOTHER, *striving for control:* As long as you're here!

ANN, *perplexed:* But, Kate—

MOTHER: Put that out of your head!

KELLER: Because—

MOTHER, *quickly to Keller:* That's all, that's enough. *Places her hand on her head:* Come inside now, and have some tea with me. *She turns and goes up steps.*

KELLER, *to Ann:* The one thing you—

MOTHER, *sharply:* He's not dead, so there's no argument! Now come!

KELLER, *angrily:* In a minute! *Mother turns and goes into house.* Now look, Annie—

CHRIS: All right, Dad, forget it.

KELLER: No, she dasn't feel that way. Annie—

CHRIS: I'm sick of the whole subject, now cut it out.

KELLER: You want her to go on like this? *To Ann:* Those cylinder heads went into P-40s only. What's the matter with you? You know Larry never flew a P-40.

CHRIS: So who flew those P-40s, pigs?

KELLER: The man was a fool, but don't make a murderer out of him. You got no sense? Look what it does to her! *To Ann:* Listen, you gotta appreciate what was doin' in that shop in the war. The both of you! It was a madhouse. Every half hour the Major callin' for cylinder heads, they were whippin' us with the telephone. The trucks were hauling them away hot, damn near. I mean just try to see it human, see it human. All of a sudden a batch comes out with a crack. That happens, that's the business. A fine, hairline crack. All right, so—so he's a little man, your father, always scared of loud voices. What'll the Major say?—Half a day's production shot. . . . What'll I say? You know what I mean? Human. *He pauses.* So he takes out his tools and he—covers over the cracks. All right—that's bad, it's wrong, but that's what a little man does. If I could have gone in that day I'd a told him—junk 'em, Steve, we can afford it. But alone he was afraid. But I know he meant no harm. He believed they'd hold up a hundred per cent. That's a mistake, but it ain't murder. You mustn't feel that way about him. You understand me? It ain't right.

ANN, *she regards him a moment:* Joe, let's forget it.

KELLER: Annie, the day the news came about Larry he was in the next cell to mine—Dad. And he cried, Annie—he cried half the night.

ANN, *touched:* He shoulda cried all night. *Slight pause.*

KELLER, *almost angered:* Annie, I do not understand why you—!

CHRIS, *breaking in—with nervous urgency:* Are you going to stop it?

ANN: Don't yell at him. He just wants everybody happy.

KELLER, *clasps her around waist, smiling:* That's my sentiments. Can you stand steak?

CHRIS: And champagne!

KELLER: Now you're operatin'! I'll call Swanson's for a table! Big time tonight, Annie!

ANN: Can't scare me.

KELLER, *to Chris, pointing at Ann:* I like that girl. Wrap her up. *They laugh. Goes up porch.* You got nice legs, Annie! . . . I want to see everybody drunk tonight. *Pointing to Chris:* Look at him, he's blushin'! *He exits, laughing, into house.*

CHRIS, *calling after him:* Drink your tea, Casanova. *He turns to Ann:* Isn't he a great guy?

ANN: You're the only one I know who loves his parents.

CHRIS: I know. It went out of style, didn't it?

ANN, *with a sudden touch of sadness:* It's all right. It's a good thing. *She looks about.* You know? It's lovely here. The air is sweet.

CHRIS, *hopefully:* You're not sorry you came?

ANN: Not sorry, no. But I'm—not going to stay.

CHRIS: Why?

ANN: In the first place, your mother as much as told me to go.

CHRIS: Well—

ANN: You saw that—and then you—you've been kind of—

CHRIS: What?

ANN: Well . . . kind of embarrassed ever since I got here.

CHRIS: The trouble is I planned on kind of sneaking up on you over a period of a week or so. But they take it for granted that we're all set.

ANN: I knew they would. Your mother anyway.

CHRIS: How did you know?

ANN: From *her* point of view, why else would I come?

CHRIS: Well . . . would you want to? *Ann still studies him.* I guess you know this is why I asked you to come.

ANN: I guess this is why I came.

CHRIS: Ann, I love you. I love you a great deal. *Finally:* I love you. *Pause. She waits.* I have no imagination . . . that's all I

know to tell you. *Ann is waiting, ready.* I'm embarrassing you. I didn't want to tell it to you here. I wanted some place we'd never been; a place where we'd be brand new to each other. . . . You feel it's wrong here, don't you? This yard, this chair? I want you to be ready for me. I don't want to win you away from anything.

ANN, *putting her arms around him:* Oh, Chris, I've been ready a long, long time!

CHRIS: Then he's gone forever. You're sure.

ANN: I almost got married two years ago.

CHRIS: Why didn't you?

ANN: You started to write to me— *Slight pause.*

CHRIS: You felt something that far back?

ANN: Every day since!

CHRIS: Ann, why didn't you let me know?

ANN: I was waiting for you, Chris. Till then you never wrote. And when you did, what did you say? You sure can be ambiguous, you know.

CHRIS *looks toward house, then at her, trembling:* Give me a kiss, Ann. Give me a— *They kiss.* God, I kissed you, Annie, I kissed Annie. How long, how long I've been waiting to kiss you!

ANN: I'll never forgive you. Why did you wait all these years? All I've done is sit and wonder if I was crazy for thinking of you.

CHRIS: Annie, we're going to live now! I'm going to make you so happy. *He kisses her, but without their bodies touching.*

ANN, *a little embarrassed:* Not like that you're not.

CHRIS: I kissed you . . .

ANN: Like Larry's brother. Do it like you, Chris. *He breaks away from her abruptly.* What is it, Chris?

CHRIS: Let's drive some place . . . I want to be alone with you.

ANN: No . . . what is it, Chris, your mother?

CHRIS: No—nothing like that.

ANN: Then what's wrong? Even in your letters, there was something ashamed.

CHRIS: Yes. I suppose I have been. But it's going from me.

ANN: You've got to tell me—

CHRIS: I don't know how to start. *He takes her hand.*

ANN: It wouldn't work this way. *Slight pause.*

CHRIS *speaks quietly, factually at first:* It's all mixed up with so many other things. . . . You remember, overseas, I was in command of a company?

ANN: Yeah, sure.

CHRIS: Well, I lost them.

ANN: How many?

CHRIS: Just about all.

ANN: Oh, gee!

CHRIS: It takes a little time to toss that off. Because they weren't just men. For instance, one time it'd been raining several days and this kid came to me, and gave me his last pair of dry socks. Put them in my pocket. That's only a little thing—but . . . that's the kind of guys I had. They didn't die; they killed themselves for each other. I mean that exactly; a little more selfish and they'd 've been here today. And I got an idea—watching them go down. Everything was being destroyed, see, but it seemed to me that one new thing was made. A kind of—responsibility. Man for man. You understand me?—To show that, to bring that onto the earth again like some kind of a monument and everyone would feel it standing there, behind him, and it would make a difference to him. *Pause.* And then I came home and it was incredible. I—there was no meaning in it here; the whole thing to them was a kind of a—bus accident. I went to work with Dad, and that rat-race again. I felt—what you said—ashamed somehow. Because nobody was changed at all. It seemed to make suckers out of a lot of guys. I felt wrong to be alive, to open the bank-book, to drive the new car, to see the new refrigerator. I mean you can take those things out of a war, but when you drive that car you've got to know that it came out of the love a man can have for a man, you've got to be a little better because of that. Otherwise what you have is really loot, and there's blood on it. I didn't want to take any of it. And I guess that included you.

ANN: And you still feel that way?

CHRIS: I want you now, Annie.

ANN: Because you mustn't feel that way any more. Because you have a right to whatever you have. Everything, Chris, understand that? To me, too . . . And the money, there's nothing wrong in your money. Your father put hundreds of

planes in the air, you should be proud. A man should be paid for that . . .

CHRIS: Oh Annie, Annie . . . I'm going to make a fortune for you!

KELLER, *offstage:* Hello . . . Yes. Sure.

ANN, *laughing softly:* What'll I do with a fortune?

They kiss. Keller enters from house.

KELLER, *thumbing toward house:* Hey, Ann, your brother— *They step apart shyly. Keller comes down, and wryly:* What is this, Labor Day?

CHRIS, *waving him away, knowing the kidding will be endless:* All right, all right.

ANN: You shouldn't burst out like that.

KELLER: Well, nobody told me it was Labor Day. *Looks around.* Where's the hot dogs?

CHRIS, *loving it:* All right. You said it once.

KELLER: Well, as long as I know it's Labor Day from now on, I'll wear a bell around my neck.

ANN, *affectionately:* He's so subtle!

CHRIS: George Bernard Shaw as an elephant.

KELLER: George!—hey, you kissed it out of my head—your brother's on the phone.

ANN, *surprised:* My brother?

KELLER: Yeah, George. Long distance.

ANN: What's the matter, is anything wrong?

KELLER: I don't know, Kate's talking to him. Hurry up, she'll cost him five dollars.

ANN *takes a step upstage, then comes down toward Chris:* I wonder if we ought to tell your mother yet? I mean I'm not very good in an argument.

CHRIS: We'll wait till tonight. After dinner. Now don't get tense, just leave it to me.

KELLER: What're you telling her?

CHRIS: Go ahead, Ann. *With misgivings, Ann goes up and into house.* We're getting married, Dad. *Keller nods indecisively.* Well, don't you say anything?

KELLER, *distracted:* I'm glad, Chris, I'm just—George is calling from Columbus.

CHRIS: Columbus!

KELLER: Did Annie tell you he was going to see his father today?

CHRIS: No, I don't think she knew anything about it.

KELLER, *asking uncomfortably:* Chris! You—you think you know her pretty good?

CHRIS, *hurt and apprehensive:* What kind of a question?

KELLER: I'm just wondering. All these years George don't go to see his father. Suddenly he goes . . . and she comes here.

CHRIS: Well, what about it?

KELLER: It's crazy, but it comes to my mind. She don't hold nothin' against me, does she?

CHRIS, *angry:* I don't know what you're talking about.

KELLER, *a little more combatively:* I'm just talkin'. To his last day in court the man blamed it all on me; and this is his daughter. I mean if she was sent here to find out something?

CHRIS, *angered:* Why? What is there to find out?

ANN, *on phone, offstage:* Why are you so excited, George? What happened there?

KELLER: I mean if they want to open up the case again, for the nuisance value, to hurt us?

CHRIS: Dad . . . how could you think that of her?
ANN, *still on phone:* But what did he say to you, for God's sake?
} *Together*

KELLER: It couldn't be, heh. You know.

CHRIS: Dad, you amaze me . . .

KELLER, *breaking in:* All right, forget it, forget it. *With great force, moving about.* I want a clean start for you, Chris. I want a new sign over the plant—Christopher Keller, Incorporated.

CHRIS, *a little uneasily:* J. O. Keller is good enough.

KELLER: We'll talk about it. I'm going to build you a house, stone, with a driveway from the road. I want you to spread out, Chris, I want you to use what I made for you. *He is close to him now.* I mean, with joy, Chris, without shame . . . with joy.

CHRIS, *touched:* I will, Dad.

KELLER, *with deep emotion:* Say it to me.

CHRIS: Why?

KELLER: Because sometimes I think you're . . . ashamed of the money.

CHRIS: No, don't feel that.

KELLER: Because it's good money, there's nothing wrong with that money.

CHRIS, *a little frightened:* Dad, you don't have to tell me this.

KELLER—*with overriding affection and self-confidence now. He grips Chris by the back of the neck, and with laughter between his determined jaws:* Look, Chris, I'll go to work on Mother for you. We'll get her so drunk tonight we'll all get married! *Steps away, with a wide gesture of his arm.* There's gonna be a wedding, kid, like there never was seen! Champagne, tuxedos—!

He breaks off as Ann's voice comes out loud from the house where she is still talking on phone.

ANN: Simply because when you get excited you don't control yourself. . . . *Mother comes out of house.* Well, what did he tell you for God's sake? *Pause.* All right, come then. *Pause.* Yes, they'll all be here. Nobody's running away from you. And try to get hold of yourself, will you? *Pause.* All right, all right. Good-by. *There is a brief pause as Ann hangs up receiver, then comes out of kitchen.*

CHRIS: Something happen?

KELLER: He's coming here?

ANN: On the seven o'clock. He's in Columbus. *To Mother:* I told him it would be all right.

KELLER: Sure, fine! Your father took sick?

ANN, *mystified:* No, George didn't say he was sick. I— *Shaking it off:* I don't know, I suppose it's something stupid, you know my brother— *She comes to Chris.* Let's go for a drive, or something . . .

CHRIS: Sure. Give me the keys, Dad.

MOTHER: Drive through the park. It's beautiful now.

CHRIS: Come on, Ann. *To them:* Be back right away.

ANN, *as she and Chris exit up driveway:* See you.

Mother comes down toward Keller, her eyes fixed on him.

KELLER: Take your time. *To Mother:* What does George want?

MOTHER: He's been in Columbus since this morning with Steve. He's gotta see Annie right away, he says.

KELLER: What for?

MOTHER: I don't know. *She speaks with warning:* He's a lawyer

now, Joe. George is a lawyer. All these years he never even sent a postcard to Steve. Since he got back from the war, not a postcard.

KELLER: So what?

MOTHER, *her tension breaking out:* Suddenly he takes an airplane from New York to see him. An airplane!

KELLER: Well? So?

MOTHER, *trembling:* Why?

KELLER: I don't read minds. Do you?

MOTHER: Why, Joe? What has Steve suddenly got to tell him that he takes an airplane to see him?

KELLER: What do I care what Steve's got to tell him?

MOTHER: You're sure, Joe?

KELLER, *frightened, but angry:* Yes, I'm sure.

MOTHER, *sits stiffly in a chair:* Be smart now, Joe. The boy is coming. Be smart.

KELLER, *desperately:* Once and for all, did you hear what I said? I said I'm sure!

MOTHER *nods weakly:* All right, Joe. *He straightens up.* Just . . . be smart.

Keller, in hopeless fury, looks at her, turns around, goes up to porch and into house, slamming screen door violently behind him. Mother sits in chair downstage, stiffly, staring, seeing.

CURTAIN

ACT TWO

As twilight falls, that evening.

On the rise, Chris is discovered sawing the broken-off tree, leaving stump standing alone. He is dressed in good pants, white shoes, but without a shirt. He disappears with tree up the alley when Mother appears on porch. She comes down and stands watching him. She has on a dressing gown, carries a tray of grape-juice drink in a pitcher, and glasses with sprigs of mint in them.

MOTHER, *calling up alley:* Did you have to put on good pants to do that? *She comes downstage and puts tray on table in the arbor. Then looks around uneasily, then feels pitcher for coolness. Chris enters from alley brushing off his hands:* You notice there's more light with that thing gone?

CHRIS: Why aren't you dressing?

MOTHER: It's suffocating upstairs. I made a grape drink for Georgie. He always liked grape. Come and have some.

CHRIS, *impatiently:* Well, come on, get dressed. And what's Dad sleeping so much for? *He goes to table and pours a glass of juice.*

MOTHER: He's worried. When he's worried he sleeps. *Pauses. Looks into his eyes.* We're dumb, Chris. Dad and I are stupid people. We don't know anything. You've got to protect us.

CHRIS: You're silly; what's there to be afraid of?

MOTHER: To his last day in court Steve never gave up the idea that Dad made him do it. If they're going to open the case again I won't live through it.

CHRIS: George is just a damn fool, Mother. How can you take him seriously?

MOTHER: That family hates us. Maybe even Annie—

CHRIS: Oh, now, Mother . . .

MOTHER: You think just because you like everybody, they like you!

CHRIS: All right, stop working yourself up. Just leave everything to me.

MOTHER: When George goes home tell her to go with him.

CHRIS, *noncommittally:* Don't worry about Annie.
MOTHER: Steve is her father, too.
CHRIS: Are you going to cut it out? Now, come.
MOTHER, *going upstage with him:* You don't realize how people can hate, Chris, they can hate so much they'll tear the world to pieces.

Ann, dressed up, appears on porch.

CHRIS: Look! She's dressed already. *As he and Mother mount porch:* I've just got to put on a shirt.
ANN, *in a preoccupied way:* Are you feeling well, Kate?
MOTHER: What's the difference, dear. There are certain people, y'know, the sicker they get the longer they live. *She goes into house.*
CHRIS: You look nice.
ANN: We're going to tell her tonight.
CHRIS: Absolutely, don't worry about it.
ANN: I wish we could tell her now. I can't stand scheming. My stomach gets hard.
CHRIS: It's not scheming, we'll just get her in a better mood.
MOTHER, *offstage, in the house:* Joe, are you going to sleep all day!
ANN, *laughing:* The only one who's relaxed is your father. He's fast asleep.
CHRIS: I'm relaxed.
ANN: Are you?
CHRIS: Look. *He holds out his hand and makes it shake.* Let me know when George gets here.

He goes into the house. Ann moves aimlessly, and then is drawn toward tree stump. She goes to it, hesitantly touches broken top in the hush of her thoughts. Offstage Lydia calls, "Johnny! Come get your supper!" Sue enters, and halts, seeing Ann.

SUE: Is my husband—?
ANN, *turns, startled:* Oh!
SUE: I'm terribly sorry.
ANN: It's all right, I—I'm a little silly about the dark.
SUE, *looks about:* It is getting dark.
ANN: Are you looking for your husband?

SUE: As usual. *Laughs tiredly.* He spends so much time here, they'll be charging him rent.
ANN: Nobody was dressed so he drove over to the depot to pick up my brother.
SUE: Oh, your brother's in?
ANN: Yeah, they ought to be here any minute now. Will you have a cold drink?
SUE: I will, thanks. *Ann goes to table and pours.* My husband. Too hot to drive me to beach. Men are like little boys; for the neighbors they'll always cut the grass.
ANN: People like to do things for the Kellers. Been that way since I can remember.
SUE: It's amazing. I guess your brother's coming to give you away, heh?
ANN, *giving her drink:* I don't know. I suppose.
SUE: You must be all nerved up.
ANN: It's always a problem getting yourself married, isn't it?
SUE: That depends on your shape, of course. I don't see why you should have had a problem.
ANN: I've had chances—
SUE: I'll bet. It's romantic . . . it's very unusual to me, marrying the brother of your sweetheart.
ANN: I don't know. I think it's mostly that whenever I need somebody to tell me the truth I've always thought of Chris. When he tells you something you know it's so. He relaxes me.
SUE: And he's got money. That's important, you know.
ANN: It wouldn't matter to me.
SUE: You'd be surprised. It makes all the difference. I married an intern. On my salary. And that was bad, because as soon as a woman supports a man he owes her something. You can never owe somebody without resenting them. *Ann laughs.* That's true, you know.
ANN: Underneath, I think the doctor is very devoted.
SUE: Oh, certainly. But it's bad when a man always sees the bars in front of him. Jim thinks he's in jail all the time.
ANN: Oh . . .
SUE: That's why I've been intending to ask you a small favor, Ann. It's something very important to me.
ANN: Certainly, if I can do it.

SUE: You can. When you take up housekeeping, try to find a place away from here.

ANN: Are you fooling?

SUE: I'm very serious. My husband is unhappy with Chris around.

ANN: How is that?

SUE: Jim's a successful doctor. But he's got an idea he'd like to do medical research. Discover things. You see?

ANN: Well, isn't that good?

SUE: Research pays twenty-five dollars a week minus laundering the hair shirt. You've got to give up your life to go into it.

ANN: How does Chris—

SUE, *with growing feeling:* Chris makes people want to be better than it's possible to be. He does that to people.

ANN: Is that bad?

SUE: My husband has a family, dear. Every time he has a session with Chris he feels as though he's compromising by not giving up everything for research. As though Chris or anybody else isn't compromising. It happens with Jim every couple of years. He meets a man and makes a statue out of him.

ANN: Maybe he's right. I don't mean that Chris is a statue, but—

SUE: Now darling, you know he's not right.

ANN: I don't agree with you. Chris—

SUE: Let's face it, dear. Chris is working with his father, isn't he? He's taking money out of that business every week in the year.

ANN: What of it?

SUE: You ask me what of it?

ANN: I certainly do. *She seems about to burst out.* You oughtn't cast aspersions like that, I'm surprised at you.

SUE: You're surprised at me!

ANN: He'd never take five cents out of that plant if there was anything wrong with it.

SUE: You know that.

ANN: I know it. I resent everything you've said.

SUE, *moving toward her:* You know what I resent, dear?

ANN: Please, I don't want to argue.

SUE: I resent living next door to the Holy Family. It makes me look like a bum, you understand?

ANN: I can't do anything about that.

SUE: Who is he to ruin a man's life? Everybody knows Joe pulled a fast one to get out of jail.

ANN: That's not true!

SUE: Then why don't you go out and talk to people? Go on, talk to them. There's not a person on the block who doesn't know the truth.

ANN: That's a lie. People come here all the time for cards and—

SUE: So what? They give him credit for being smart. I do, too, I've got nothing against Joe. But if Chris wants people to put on the hair shirt let him take off his broadcloth. He's driving my husband crazy with that phony idealism of his, and I'm at the end of my rope on it! *Chris enters on porch, wearing shirt and tie now. She turns quickly, hearing. With a smile:* Hello, darling. How's Mother?

CHRIS: I thought George came.

SUE: No, it was just us.

CHRIS, *coming down to them:* Susie, do me a favor, heh? Go up to Mother and see if you can calm her. She's all worked up.

SUE: She still doesn't know about you two?

CHRIS, *laughs a little:* Well, she senses it, I guess. You know my mother.

SUE, *going up to porch:* Oh, yeah, she's psychic.

CHRIS: Maybe there's something in the medicine chest.

SUE: I'll give her one of everything. *On porch:* Don't worry about Kate; couple of drinks, dance her around a little . . . She'll love Ann. *To Ann:* Because you're the female version of him. *Chris laughs.* Don't be alarmed, I said version. *She goes into house.*

CHRIS: Interesting woman, isn't she?

ANN: Yeah, she's very interesting.

CHRIS: She's a great nurse, you know, she—

ANN, *in tension, but trying to control it:* Are you still doing that?

CHRIS, *sensing something wrong, but still smiling:* Doing what?

ANN: As soon as you get to know somebody you find a distinction for them. How do you know she's a great nurse?

CHRIS: What's the matter, Ann?

ANN: The woman hates you. She despises you!
CHRIS: Hey . . . What's hit you?
ANN: Gee, Chris—
CHRIS: What happened here?
ANN: You never— Why didn't you tell me?
CHRIS: Tell you what?
ANN: She says they think Joe is guilty.
CHRIS: What difference does it make what they think?
ANN: I don't care what they think, I just don't understand why you took the trouble to deny it. You said it was all forgotten.
CHRIS: I didn't want you to feel there was anything wrong in you coming here, that's all. I know a lot of people think my father was guilty, and I assumed there might be some question in your mind.
ANN: But I never once said I suspected him.
CHRIS: Nobody says it.
ANN: Chris, I know how much you love him, but it could never—
CHRIS: Do you think I could forgive him if he'd done that thing?
ANN: I'm not here out of a blue sky, Chris. I turned my back on my father, if there's anything wrong here now—
CHRIS: I know that, Ann.
ANN: George is coming from Dad, and I don't think it's with a blessing.
CHRIS: He's welcome here. You've got nothing to fear from George.
ANN: Tell me that . . . Just tell me that.
CHRIS: The man is innocent, Ann. Remember he was falsely accused once and it put him through hell. How would you behave if you were faced with the same thing again? Annie, believe me, there's nothing wrong for you here, believe me, kid.
ANN: All right, Chris, all right. *They embrace as Keller appears quietly on porch. Ann simply studies him.*
KELLER: Every time I come out here it looks like Playland! *They break and laugh in embarrassment.*
CHRIS: I thought you were going to shave?
KELLER, *sitting on bench:* In a minute. I just woke up, I can't see nothin'.

ANN: You look shaved.

KELLER: Oh, no. *Massages his jaw.* Gotta be extra special tonight. Big night, Annie. So how's it feel to be a married woman?

ANN *laughs:* I don't know, yet.

KELLER, *to Chris:* What's the matter, you slippin'? *He takes a little box of apples from under the bench as they talk.*

CHRIS: The great roué!

KELLER: What is that, roué?

CHRIS: It's French.

KELLER: Don't talk dirty. *They laugh.*

CHRIS, *to Ann:* You ever meet a bigger ignoramus?

KELLER: Well, somebody's got to make a living.

ANN, *as they laugh:* That's telling him.

KELLER: I don't know, everybody's gettin' so Goddam educated in this country there'll be nobody to take away the garbage. *They laugh.* It's gettin' so the only dumb ones left are the bosses.

ANN: You're not so dumb, Joe.

KELLER: I know, but you go into our plant, for instance. I got so many lieutenants, majors and colonels that I'm ashamed to ask somebody to sweep the floor. I gotta be careful I'll insult somebody. No kiddin'. It's a tragedy: you stand on the street today and spit, you're gonna hit a college man.

CHRIS: Well, don't spit.

KELLER *breaks apple in half, passing it to Ann and Chris:* I mean to say, it's comin' to a pass. *He takes a breath.* I been thinkin', Annie . . . your brother, George. I been thinkin' about your brother George. When he comes I like you to *brooch* something to him.

CHRIS: Broach.

KELLER: What's the matter with brooch?

CHRIS, *smiling:* It's not English.

KELLER: When I went to night school it was brooch.

ANN, *laughing:* Well, in day school it's broach.

KELLER: Don't surround me, will you? Seriously, Ann . . . You say he's not well. George, I been thinkin', why should he knock himself out in New York with that cut-throat competition, when I got so many friends here; I'm very

friendly with some big lawyers in town. I could set George up here.

ANN: That's awfully nice of you, Joe.

KELLER: No, kid, it ain't nice of me. I want you to understand me. I'm thinking of Chris. *Slight pause.* See . . . this is what I mean. You get older, you want to feel that you—accomplished something. My only accomplishment is my son. I ain't brainy. That's all I accomplished. Now, a year, eighteen months, your father'll be a free man. Who is he going to come to, Annie? His baby. You. He'll come, old, mad, into your house.

ANN: That can't matter any more, Joe.

KELLER: I don't want that to come between us. *Gestures between Chris and himself.*

ANN: I can only tell you that that could never happen.

KELLER: You're in love now, Annie, but believe me, I'm older than you and I know—a daughter is a daughter, and a father is a father. And it could happen. *He pauses.* I like you and George to go to him in prison and tell him . . . "Dad, Joe wants to bring you into the business when you get out."

ANN, *surprised, even shocked:* You'd have him as a partner?

KELLER: No, no partner. A good job. *Pause. He sees she is shocked, a little mystified. He gets up, speaks more nervously.* I want him to know, Annie . . . while he's sitting there I want him to know that when he gets out he's got a place waitin' for him. It'll take his bitterness away. To know you got a place . . . it sweetens you.

ANN: Joe, you owe him nothing.

KELLER: I owe him a good kick in the teeth, but he's your father.

CHRIS: Then kick him in the teeth! I don't want him in the plant, so that's that! You understand? And besides, don't talk about him like that. People misunderstand you!

KELLER: And I don't understand why she has to crucify the man.

CHRIS: Well, it's her father, if she feels—

KELLER: No, no.

CHRIS, *almost angrily:* What's it to you? Why—?

KELLER—*a commanding outburst in high nervousness:* A father

is a father! *As though the outburst had revealed him, he looks about, wanting to retract it. His hand goes to his cheek.* I better—I better shave. *He turns and a smile is on his face. To Ann:* I didn't mean to yell at you, Annie.

ANN: Let's forget the whole thing, Joe.

KELLER: Right. *To Chris:* She's likeable.

CHRIS, *a little peeved at the man's stupidity:* Shave, will you?

KELLER: Right again.

As he turns to porch Lydia comes hurrying from her house.

LYDIA: I forgot all about it. *Seeing Chris and Ann:* Hya. *To Joe:* I promised to fix Kate's hair for tonight. Did she comb it yet?

KELLER: Always a smile, hey, Lydia?

LYDIA: Sure, why not?

KELLER, *going up on porch:* Come on up and comb my Katie's hair. *Lydia goes up on porch:* She's got a big night, make her beautiful.

LYDIA: I will.

KELLER *holds door open for her and she goes into kitchen. To Chris and Ann:* Hey, that could be a song. *He sings softly:*

"Come on up and comb my Katie's hair . . .
Oh, come on up, 'cause she's my lady fair—"

To Ann: How's that for one year of night school? *He continues singing as he goes into kitchen.*

"Oh, come on up, come on up, and comb my lady's hair—"

Jim Bayliss rounds corner of driveway, walking rapidly. Jim crosses to Chris, motions him and pulls him down excitedly. Keller stands just inside kitchen door, watching them.

CHRIS: What's the matter? Where is he?

JIM: Where's your mother?

CHRIS: Upstairs, dressing.

ANN, *crossing to them rapidly:* What happened to George?

JIM: I asked him to wait in the car. Listen to me now. Can you take some advice? *They wait.* Don't bring him in here.

ANN: Why?

JIM: Kate is in bad shape, you can't explode this in front of her.

ANN: Explode what?

JIM: You know why he's here, don't try to kid it away. There's blood in his eye; drive him somewhere and talk to him alone.

Ann turns to go up drive, takes a couple of steps, sees Keller, and stops. He goes quietly on into house.

CHRIS, *shaken, and therefore angered:* Don't be an old lady.

JIM: He's come to take her home. What does that mean? *To Ann:* You know what that means. Fight it out with him some place else.

ANN *comes back down toward Chris:* I'll drive . . . him somewhere.

CHRIS *goes to her:* No.

JIM: Will you stop being an idiot?

CHRIS: Nobody's afraid of him here. Cut that out!

He starts for driveway, but is brought up short by George, who enters there. George is Chris's age, but a paler man, now on the edge of his self-restraint. He speaks quietly, as though afraid to find himself screaming. An instant's hesitation and Chris steps up to him, hand extended, smiling.

CHRIS: Helluva way to do; what're you sitting out there for?

GEORGE: Doctor said your mother isn't well, I—

CHRIS: So what? She'd want to see you, wouldn't she? We've been waiting for you all afternoon. *He puts his hand on George's arm, but George pulls away, coming across toward Ann.*

ANN, *touching his collar:* This is filthy, didn't you bring another shirt?

George breaks away from her, and moves down, examining the yard. Door opens, and he turns rapidly, thinking it is Kate, but it's Sue. She looks at him; he turns away and moves to fence. He looks over it at his former home. Sue comes downstage.

SUE, *annoyed:* How about the beach, Jim?

JIM: Oh, it's too hot to drive.

SUE: How'd you get to the station—Zeppelin?

CHRIS: This is Mrs. Bayliss, George. *Calling, as George pays no attention, staring at house:* George! *George turns.* Mrs. Bayliss.

SUE: How do you do.

GEORGE, *removing his hat:* You're the people who bought our house, aren't you?

SUE: That's right. Come and see what we did with it before you leave.

GEORGE *walks down and away from her:* I liked it the way it was.

SUE, *after a brief pause:* He's frank, isn't he?

JIM, *pulling her off:* See you later. . . . Take it easy, fella. *They exit.*

CHRIS, *calling after them:* Thanks for driving him! *Turning to George:* How about some grape juice? Mother made it especially for you.

GEORGE, *with forced appreciation:* Good old Kate, remembered my grape juice.

CHRIS: You drank enough of it in this house. How've you been, George?—Sit down.

GEORGE *keeps moving:* It takes me a minute. *Looking around:* It seems impossible.

CHRIS: What?

GEORGE: I'm back here.

CHRIS: Say, you've gotten a little nervous, haven't you?

GEORGE: Yeah, toward the end of the day. What're you, big executive now?

CHRIS: Just kind of medium. How's the law?

GEORGE: I don't know. When I was studying in the hospital it seemed sensible, but outside there doesn't seem to be much of a law. The trees got thick, didn't they? *Points to stump:* What's that?

CHRIS: Blew down last night. We had it there for Larry. You know.

GEORGE: Why, afraid you'll forget him?

CHRIS *starts for George:* Kind of a remark is that?

ANN, *breaking in, putting a restraining hand on Chris:* When did you start wearing a hat?

GEORGE *discovers hat in his hand:* Today. From now on I decided to look like a lawyer, anyway. *He holds it up to her:* Don't you recognize it?

ANN: Why? Where—?

GEORGE: Your father's— He asked me to wear it.

ANN: How is he?

GEORGE: He got smaller.

ANN: Smaller?

GEORGE: Yeah, little. *Holds out his hand to measure:* He's a little man. That's what happens to suckers, you know. It's good I went to him in time—another year there'd be nothing left but his smell.

CHRIS: What's the matter, George, what's the trouble?

GEORGE: The trouble? The trouble is when you make suckers out of people once, you shouldn't try to do it twice.

CHRIS: What does that mean?

GEORGE, *to Ann:* You're not married yet, are you?

ANN: George, will you sit down and stop—?

GEORGE: Are you married yet?

ANN: No, I'm not married yet.

GEORGE: You're not going to marry him.

ANN: Why am I not going to marry him?

GEORGE: Because his father destroyed your family.

CHRIS: Now look, George . . .

GEORGE: Cut it short, Chris. Tell her to come home with me. Let's not argue, you know what I've got to say.

CHRIS: George, you don't want to be the voice of God, do you?

GEORGE: I'm—

CHRIS: That's been your trouble all your life, George, you dive into things. What kind of a statement is that to make? You're a big boy now.

GEORGE: I'm a big boy now.

CHRIS: Don't come bulling in here. If you've got something to say, be civilized about it.

GEORGE: Don't civilize me!

ANN: Shhh!

CHRIS, *ready to hit him:* Are you going to talk like a grown man or aren't you?

ANN, *quickly, to forestall an outburst:* Sit down, dear. Don't be angry, what's the matter? *He allows her to seat him, looking at her.* Now what happened? You kissed me when I left, now you—

GEORGE, *breathlessly:* My life turned upside down since then. I couldn't go back to work when you left. I wanted to go to Dad and tell him you were going to be married. It seemed impossible not to tell him. He loved you so much. *He pauses.* Annie—we did a terrible thing. We can never be forgiven.

Not even to send him a card at Christmas. I didn't see him once since I got home from the war! Annie, you don't know what was done to that man. You don't know what happened.

ANN, *afraid:* Of course I know.

GEORGE: You can't know, you wouldn't be here. Dad came to work that day. The night foreman came to him and showed him the cylinder heads . . . they were coming out of the process with defects. There was something wrong with the process. So Dad went directly to the phone and called here and told Joe to come down right away. But the morning passed. No sign of Joe. So Dad called again. By this time he had over a hundred defectives. The Army was screaming for stuff and Dad didn't have anything to ship. So Joe told him . . . on the phone he told him to weld, cover up the cracks in any way he could, and ship them out.

CHRIS: Are you through now?

GEORGE, *surging up at him:* I'm not through now! *Back to Ann:* Dad was afraid. He wanted Joe there if he was going to do it. But Joe can't come down . . . He's sick. Sick! He suddenly gets the flu! Suddenly! But he promised to take responsibility. Do you understand what I'm saying? On the telephone you can't have responsibility! In a court you can always deny a phone call and that's exactly what he did. They knew he was a liar the first time, but in the appeal they believed that rotten lie and now Joe is a big shot and your father is the patsy. *He gets up.* Now what're you going to do? Eat his food, sleep in his bed? Answer me; what're you going to do?

CHRIS: What're you going to do, George?

GEORGE: He's too smart for me, I can't prove a phone call.

CHRIS: Then how dare you come in here with that rot?

ANN: George, the court—

GEORGE: The court didn't know your father! But you know him. You know in your heart Joe did it.

CHRIS, *whirling him around:* Lower your voice or I'll throw you out of here!

GEORGE: She knows. She knows.

CHRIS, *to Ann:* Get him out of here, Ann. Get him out of here.

ANN: George, I know everything you've said. Dad told that whole thing in court, and they—

GEORGE—*almost a scream:* The court did not know him, Annie!

ANN: Shhh!—But he'll say anything, George. You know how quick he can lie.

GEORGE, *turning to Chris, with deliberation:* I'll ask you something, and look me in the eye when you answer me.

CHRIS: I'll look you in the eye.

GEORGE: You know your father—

CHRIS: I know him well.

GEORGE: And he's the kind of boss to let a hundred and twenty-one cylinder heads be repaired and shipped out of his shop without even knowing about it?

CHRIS: He's that kind of boss.

GEORGE: And that's the same Joe Keller who never left his shop without first going around to see that all the lights were out.

CHRIS, *with growing anger:* The same Joe Keller.

GEORGE: The same man who knows how many minutes a day his workers spend in the toilet.

CHRIS: The same man.

GEORGE: And my father, that frightened mouse who'd never buy a shirt without somebody along—that man would dare do such a thing on his own?

CHRIS: On his own. And because he's a frightened mouse this is another thing he'd do—throw the blame on somebody else because he's not man enough to take it himself. He tried it in court but it didn't work, but with a fool like you it works!

GEORGE: Oh, Chris, you're a liar to yourself!

ANN, *deeply shaken:* Don't talk like that!

CHRIS *sits facing George:* Tell me, George. What happened? The court record was good enough for you all these years, why isn't it good now? Why did you believe it all these years?

GEORGE, *after a slight pause:* Because you believed it. . . . That's the truth, Chris. I believed everything, because I thought you did. But today I heard it from his mouth. From his mouth it's altogether different than the record. Anyone who knows him, and knows your father, will believe it from his mouth. Your Dad took everything we have. I can't beat

that. But she's one item he's not going to grab. *He turns to Ann.* Get your things. Everything they have is covered with blood. You're not the kind of a girl who can live with that. Get your things.

CHRIS: Ann . . . you're not going to believe that, are you?

ANN *goes to him:* You know it's not true, don't you?

GEORGE: How can he tell you? It's his father. *To Chris:* None of these things ever even cross your mind?

CHRIS: Yes, they crossed my mind. Anything can cross your mind!

GEORGE: *He knows,* Annie. He knows!

CHRIS: The voice of God!

GEORGE: Then why isn't your name on the business? Explain that to her!

CHRIS: What the hell has that got to do with—?

GEORGE: Annie, why isn't his name on it?

CHRIS: Even when I don't own it!

GEORGE: Who're you kidding? Who gets it when he dies? *To Ann:* Open your eyes, you know the both of them, isn't that the first thing they'd do, the way they love each other?— J. O. Keller and Son? *Pause. Ann looks from him to Chris.* I'll settle it. Do you want to settle it, or are you afraid to?

CHRIS: What do you mean?

GEORGE: Let me go up and talk to your father. In ten minutes you'll have the answer. Or are you afraid of the answer?

CHRIS: I'm not afraid of the answer. I know the answer. But my mother isn't well and I don't want a fight here now.

GEORGE: Let me go to him.

CHRIS: You're not going to start a fight here now.

GEORGE, *to Ann:* What more do you want! *There is a sound of footsteps in the house.*

ANN *turns her head suddenly toward house:* Someone's coming.

CHRIS, *to George, quietly:* You won't say anything now.

ANN: You'll go soon. I'll call a cab.

GEORGE: You're coming with me.

ANN: And don't mention marriage, because we haven't told her yet.

GEORGE: You're coming with me.

ANN: You understand? Don't— George, you're not going to start anything now! *She hears footsteps.* Shsh!

Mother enters on porch. She is dressed almost formally; her hair is fixed. They are all turned toward her. On seeing George she raises both hands, comes down toward him.

MOTHER: Georgie, Georgie.

GEORGE—*he has always liked her:* Hello, Kate.

MOTHER *cups his face in her hands:* They made an old man out of you. *Touches his hair.* Look, you're gray.

GEORGE—*her pity, open and unabashed, reaches into him, and he smiles sadly:* I know, I—

MOTHER: I told you when you went away, don't try for medals.

GEORGE *laughs, tiredly:* I didn't try, Kate. They made it very easy for me.

MOTHER, *actually angry:* Go on. You're all alike. *To Ann:* Look at him, why did you say he's fine? He looks like a ghost.

GEORGE, *relishing her solicitude:* I feel all right.

MOTHER: I'm sick to look at you. What's the matter with your mother, why don't she feed you?

ANN: He just hasn't any appetite.

MOTHER: If he ate in my house he'd have an appetite. *To Ann:* I pity your husband! *To George:* Sit down. I'll make you a sandwich.

GEORGE—*sits with an embarrassed laugh:* I'm really not hungry.

MOTHER: Honest to God, it breaks my heart to see what happened to all the children. How we worked and planned for you, and you end up no better than us.

GEORGE, *with deep feeling for her:* You . . . you haven't changed at all, you know that, Kate?

MOTHER: None of us changed, Georgie. We all love you. Joe was just talking about the day you were born and the water got shut off. People were carrying basins from a block away—a stranger would have thought the whole neighborhood was on fire! *They laugh. She sees the juice. To Ann:* Why didn't you give him some juice!

ANN, *defensively:* I offered it to him.

MOTHER, *scoffingly:* You offered it to him! *Thrusting glass into George's hand:* Give it to him! *To George, who is laughing:* And now you're going to sit here and drink some juice . . . and look like something!

GEORGE, *sitting:* Kate, I feel hungry already.

CHRIS, *proudly:* She could turn Mahatma Ghandi into a heavy-weight!

MOTHER, *to Chris, with great energy:* Listen, to hell with the restaurant! I got a ham in the icebox, and frozen strawberries, and avocados, and—

ANN: Swell, I'll help you!

GEORGE: The train leaves at eight-thirty, Ann.

MOTHER, *to Ann:* You're leaving?

CHRIS: No, Mother, she's not—

ANN, *breaking through it, going to George:* You hardly got here; give yourself a chance to get acquainted again.

CHRIS: Sure, you don't even know us any more.

MOTHER: Well, Chris, if they can't stay, don't—

CHRIS: No, it's just a question of George, Mother, he planned on—

GEORGE *gets up politely, nicely, for Kate's sake:* Now wait a minute, Chris . . .

CHRIS, *smiling and full of command, cutting him off:* If you want to go, I'll drive you to the station now, but if you're staying, no arguments while you're here.

MOTHER, *at last confessing the tension:* Why should he argue? *She goes to him. With desperation and compassion, stroking his hair:* Georgie and us have no argument. How could we have an argument, Georgie? We all got hit by the same lightning, how can you—? Did you see what happened to Larry's tree, Georgie? *She has taken his arm, and unwillingly he moves across stage with her.* Imagine? While I was dreaming of him in the middle of the night, the wind came along and—

Lydia enters on porch. As soon as she sees him:

LYDIA: Hey, Georgie! Georgie! Georgie! Georgie! Georgie! *She comes down to him eagerly. She has a flowered hat in her hand, which Kate takes from her as she goes to George.*

GEORGE, *as they shake hands eagerly, warmly:* Hello, Laughy. What'd you do, grow?

LYDIA: I'm a big girl now.

MOTHER: Look what she can do to a hat!

ANN, *to Lydia, admiring the hat:* Did you make that?

MOTHER: In ten minutes! *She puts it on.*

LYDIA, *fixing it on her head:* I only rearranged it.

GEORGE: You still make your own clothes?

CHRIS, *of Mother:* Ain't she classy! All she needs now is a Russian wolfhound.

MOTHER, *moving her head:* It feels like somebody is sitting on my head.

ANN: No, it's beautiful, Kate.

MOTHER *kisses Lydia. To George:* She's a genius! You should've married her. *They laugh.* This one can feed you!

LYDIA, *strangely embarrassed:* Oh, stop that, Kate.

GEORGE, *to Lydia:* Didn't I hear you had a baby?

MOTHER: You don't hear so good. She's got three babies.

GEORGE, *a little hurt by it—to Lydia:* No kidding, three?

LYDIA: Yeah, it was one, two, three— You've been away a long time, Georgie.

GEORGE: I'm beginning to realize.

MOTHER, *to Chris and George:* The trouble with you kids is you *think* too much.

LYDIA: Well, we think, too.

MOTHER: Yes, but not all the time.

GEORGE, *with almost obvious envy:* They never took Frank, heh?

LYDIA, *a little apologetically:* No, he was always one year ahead of the draft.

MOTHER: It's amazing. When they were calling boys twenty-seven Frank was just twenty-eight, when they made it twenty-eight he was just twenty-nine. That's why he took up astrology. It's all in when you were born, it just goes to show.

CHRIS: What does it go to show?

MOTHER, *to Chris:* Don't be so intelligent. Some superstitions are very nice! *To Lydia:* Did he finish Larry's horoscope?

LYDIA: I'll ask him now, I'm going in. *To George, a little sadly, almost embarrassed:* Would you like to see my babies? Come on.

GEORGE: I don't think so, Lydia.

LYDIA, *understanding:* All right. Good luck to you, George.

GEORGE: Thanks. And to you . . . And Frank. *She smiles at him, turns and goes off to her house. George stands staring after her.*

LYDIA, *as she runs off:* Oh, Frank!

MOTHER, *reading his thoughts:* She got pretty, heh?

GEORGE, *sadly:* Very pretty.

MOTHER, *as a reprimand:* She's beautiful, you damned fool!

GEORGE *looks around longingly; and softly, with a catch in his throat:* She makes it seem so nice around here.

MOTHER, *shaking her finger at him:* Look what happened to you because you wouldn't listen to me! I told you to marry that girl and stay out of the war!

GEORGE *laughs at himself:* She used to laugh too much.

MOTHER: And you didn't laugh enough. While you were getting mad about Fascism Frank was getting into her bed.

GEORGE, *to Chris:* He won the war, Frank.

CHRIS: All the battles.

MOTHER, *in pursuit of this mood:* The day they started the draft, Georgie, I told you you loved that girl.

CHRIS *laughs:* And truer love hath no man!

MOTHER: I'm smarter than any of you.

GEORGIE, *laughing:* She's wonderful!

MOTHER: And now you're going to listen to me, George. You had big principles, Eagle Scouts the three of you; so now I got a tree, and this one—*Indicating Chris*—when the weather gets bad he can't stand on his feet; and that big dope—*Pointing to Lydia's house*—next door who never reads anything but Andy Gump has three children and his house paid off. Stop being a philosopher, and look after yourself. Like Joe was just saying—you move back here, he'll help you get set, and I'll find you a girl and put a smile on your face.

GEORGE: Joe? Joe wants me here?

ANN, *eagerly:* He asked me to tell you, and I think it's a good idea.

MOTHER: Certainly. Why must you make believe you hate us? Is that another principle?—that you have to hate us? You don't hate us, George, I know you, you can't fool me, I diapered you. *Suddenly, to Ann:* You remember Mr. Marcy's daughter?

ANN, *laughing, to George:* She's got you hooked already! *George laughs, is excited.*

MOTHER: You look her over, George; you'll see she's the most beautiful—

CHRIS: She's got warts, George.

MOTHER, *to Chris:* She hasn't got warts! *To George:* So the girl has a little beauty mark on her chin—

CHRIS: And two on her nose.

MOTHER: You remember. Her father's the retired police inspector.

CHRIS: Sergeant, George.

MOTHER: He's a very kind man!

CHRIS: He looks like a gorilla.

MOTHER, *to George:* He never shot anybody.

They all burst out laughing, as Keller appears in doorway. George rises abruptly and stares at Keller, who comes rapidly down to him.

KELLER—*the laughter stops. With strained joviality:* Well! Look who's here! *Extending his hand:* Georgie, good to see ya.

GEORGE, *shaking hands—somberly:* How're you, Joe?

KELLER: So-so. Gettin' old. You comin' out to dinner with us?

GEORGE: No, got to be back in New York.

ANN: I'll call a cab for you. *She goes up into the house.*

KELLER: Too bad you can't stay, George. Sit down. *To Mother:* He looks fine.

MOTHER: He looks terrible.

KELLER: That's what I said, you look terrible, George. *They laugh.* I wear the pants and she beats me with the belt.

GEORGE: I saw your factory on the way from the station. It looks like General Motors.

KELLER: I wish it was General Motors, but it ain't. Sit down, George. Sit down. *Takes cigar out of his pocket.* So you finally went to see your father, I hear?

GEORGE: Yes, this morning. What kind of stuff do you make now?

KELLER: Oh, little of everything. Pressure cookers, an assembly for washing machines. Got a nice, flexible plant now. So how'd you find Dad? Feel all right?

GEORGE, *searching Keller, speaking indecisively:* No, he's not well, Joe.

KELLER, *lighting his cigar:* Not his heart again, is it?

GEORGE: It's everything, Joe. It's his soul.

KELLER, *blowing out smoke:* Uh huh—

CHRIS: How about seeing what they did with your house?
KELLER: Leave him be.
GEORGE, *to Chris, indicating Keller:* I'd like to talk to him.
KELLER: Sure, he just got here. That's the way they do, George. A little man makes a mistake and they hang him by the thumbs; the big ones become ambassadors. I wish you'd-a told me you were going to see Dad.
GEORGE, *studying him:* I didn't know you were interested.
KELLER: In a way, I am. I would like him to know, George, that as far as I'm concerned, any time he wants, he's got a place with me. I would like him to know that.
GEORGE: He hates your guts, Joe. Don't you know that?
KELLER: I imagined it. But that can change, too.
MOTHER: Steve was never like that.
GEORGE: He's like that now. He'd like to take every man who made money in the war and put him up against a wall.
CHRIS: He'll need a lot of bullets.
GEORGE: And he'd better not get any.
KELLER: That's a sad thing to hear.
GEORGE, *with bitterness dominant:* Why? What'd you expect him to think of you?
KELLER—*the force of his nature rising, but under control:* I'm sad to see he hasn't changed. As long as I know him, twenty-five years, the man never learned how to take the blame. You know that, George.
GEORGE—*he does:* Well, I—
KELLER: But you do know it. Because the way you come in here you don't look like you remember it. I mean like in nineteen thirty-seven when we had the shop on Flood Street. And he damn near blew us all up with that heater he left burning for two days without water. He wouldn't admit that was his fault, either. I had to fire a mechanic to save his face. You remember that.
GEORGE: Yes, but—
KELLER: I'm just mentioning it, George. Because this is just another one of a lot of things. Like when he gave Frank that money to invest in oil stock.
GEORGE, *distressed:* I know that, I—
KELLER, *driving in, but restrained:* But it's good to remember those things, kid. The way he cursed Frank because the stock

went down. Was that Frank's fault? To listen to him Frank was a swindler. And all the man did was give him a bad tip.

GEORGE *gets up, moves away:* I know those things . . .

KELLER: Then remember them, remember them. *Ann comes out of house.* There are certain men in the world who rather see everybody hung before they'll take blame. You understand me, George?

They stand facing each other, George trying to judge him.

ANN, *coming downstage:* The cab's on its way. Would you like to wash?

MOTHER, *with the thrust of hope:* Why must he go? Make the midnight, George.

KELLER: Sure, you'll have dinner with us!

ANN: How about it? Why not? We're eating at the lake, we could have a swell time.

A long pause, as George looks at Ann, Chris, Keller, then back to her.

GEORGE: All right.

MOTHER: Now you're talking.

CHRIS: I've got a shirt that'll go right with that suit.

MOTHER: Size fifteen and a half, right, George?

GEORGE: Is Lydia—? I mean—Frank and Lydia coming?

MOTHER: I'll get you a date that'll make her look like a— *She starts upstage.*

GEORGE, *laughing:* No, I don't want a date.

CHRIS: I know somebody just for you! Charlotte Tanner! *He starts for the house.*

KELLER: Call Charlotte, that's right.

MOTHER: Sure, call her up. *Chris goes into house.*

ANN: You go up and pick out a shirt and tie.

GEORGE *stops, looks around at them and the place:* I never felt at home anywhere but here. I feel so— *He nearly laughs, and turns away from them.* Kate, you look so young, you know? You didn't change at all. It . . . rings an old bell. *Turns to Keller.* You too, Joe, you're amazingly the same. The whole atmosphere is.

KELLER: Say, I ain't got time to get sick.

MOTHER: He hasn't been laid up in fifteen years.

KELLER: Except my flu during the war.
MOTHER: Huhh?
KELLER: My flu, when I was sick during . . . the war.
MOTHER: Well, sure . . . *To George:* I mean except for that flu. *George stands perfectly still.* Well, it slipped my mind, don't look at me that way. He wanted to go to the shop but he couldn't lift himself off the bed. I thought he had pneumonia.
GEORGE: Why did you say he's never—?
KELLER: I know how you feel, kid, I'll never forgive myself. If I could've gone in that day I'd never allow Dad to touch those heads.
GEORGE: She said you've never been sick.
MOTHER: I said he was sick, George.
GEORGE, *going to Ann:* Ann, didn't you hear her say—?
MOTHER: Do you remember every time you were sick?
GEORGE: I'd remember pneumonia. Especially if I got it just the day my partner was going to patch up cylinder heads . . . What happened that day, Joe?

Frank enters briskly from driveway, holding Larry's horoscope in his hand. He comes to Kate.

FRANK: Kate! Kate!
MOTHER: Frank, did you see George?
FRANK, *extending his hand:* Lydia told me, I'm glad to . . . you'll have to pardon me. *Pulling Mother over:* I've got something amazing for you, Kate, I finished Larry's horoscope.
MOTHER: You'd be interested in this, George. It's wonderful the way he can understand the—
CHRIS, *entering from house:* George, the girl's on the phone—
MOTHER, *desperately:* He finished Larry's horoscope!
CHRIS: Frank, can't you pick a better time than this?
FRANK: The greatest men who ever lived believed in the stars!
CHRIS: Stop filling her head with that junk!
FRANK: Is it junk to feel that there's a greater power than ourselves? I've studied the stars of his life! I won't argue with you, I'm telling you. Somewhere in this world your brother is alive!
MOTHER, *instantly to Chris:* Why isn't it possible?
CHRIS: Because it's insane.

FRANK: Just a minute now. I'll tell you something and you can do as you please. Just let me say it. He was supposed to have died on November twenty-fifth. But November twenty-fifth was his favorable day.

CHRIS: Mother!

MOTHER: Listen to him!

FRANK: It was a day when everything good was shining on him, the kind of day he should've married on. You can laugh at a lot of it, I can understand you laughing. But the odds are a million to one that a man won't die on his favorable day. That's known, that's known, Chris!

MOTHER: Why isn't it possible, why isn't it possible, Chris!

GEORGE, *to Ann:* Don't you understand what she's saying? She just told you to go. What are you waiting for now?

CHRIS: Nobody can tell her to go. *A car horn is heard.*

MOTHER, *to Frank:* Thank you, darling, for your trouble. Will you tell him to wait, Frank?

FRANK, *as he goes:* Sure thing.

MOTHER, *calling out:* They'll be right out, driver!

CHRIS: She's not leaving, Mother.

GEORGE: You heard her say it, he's never been sick!

MOTHER: He misunderstood me, Chris! *Chris looks at her, struck.*

GEORGE, *to Ann:* He simply told your father to kill pilots, and covered himself in bed!

CHRIS: You'd better answer him, Annie. Answer him.

MOTHER: I packed your bag, darling.

CHRIS: What?

MOTHER: I packed your bag. All you've got to do is close it.

ANN: I'm not closing anything. He asked me here and I'm staying till he tells me to go. *To George:* Till Chris tells me!

CHRIS: That's all! Now get out of here, George!

MOTHER, *to Chris:* But if that's how he feels—

CHRIS: That's all, nothing more till Christ comes, about the case or Larry as long as I'm here! *To George:* Now get out of here, George!

GEORGE, *to Ann:* You tell me. I want to hear you tell me.

ANN: Go, George!

They disappear up the driveway, Ann saying, "Don't take it that way, Georgie! Please don't take it that way."

CHRIS, *turning to his mother:* What do you mean, you packed her bag? How dare you pack her bag?

MOTHER: Chris—

CHRIS: How dare you pack her bag?

MOTHER: She doesn't belong here.

CHRIS: Then I don't belong here.

MOTHER: She's Larry's girl.

CHRIS: And I'm his brother and he's dead, and I'm marrying his girl.

MOTHER: Never, never in this world!

KELLER: You lost your mind?

MOTHER: You have nothing to say!

KELLER, *cruelly:* I got plenty to say. Three and a half years you been talking like a maniac—

Mother smashes him across the face.

MOTHER: Nothing. You have nothing to say. Now I say. He's coming back, and everybody has got to wait.

CHRIS: Mother, Mother—

MOTHER: Wait, wait—

CHRIS: How long? How long?

MOTHER, *rolling out of her:* Till he comes; forever and ever till he comes!

CHRIS, *as an ultimatum:* Mother, I'm going ahead with it.

MOTHER: Chris, I've never said no to you in my life, now I say no!

CHRIS: You'll never let him go till I do it.

MOTHER: I'll never let him go and you'll never let him go!

CHRIS: I've let him go. I've let him go a long—

MOTHER, *with no less force, but turning from him:* Then let your father go. *Pause. Chris stands transfixed.*

KELLER: She's out of her mind.

MOTHER: Altogether! *To Chris, but not facing them:* Your brother's alive, darling, because if he's dead, your father killed him. Do you understand me now? As long as you live, that boy is alive. God does not let a son be killed by his father. Now you see, don't you? Now you see. *Beyond control, she hurries up and into house.*

KELLER—*Chris has not moved. He speaks insinuatingly, questioningly:* She's out of her mind.
CHRIS *in a broken whisper:* Then . . . you did it?
KELLER, *with the beginning of plea in his voice:* He never flew a P-40—
CHRIS, *struck; deadly:* But the others.
KELLER, *insistently:* She's out of her mind. *He takes a step toward Chris, pleadingly.*
CHRIS, *unyielding:* Dad . . . you did it?
KELLER: He never flew a P-40, what's the matter with you?
CHRIS, *still asking, and saying:* Then you did it. To the others.

Both hold their voices down.

KELLER, *afraid of him, his deadly insistence:* What's the matter with you? What the hell is the matter with you?
CHRIS, *quietly, incredibly:* How could you do that? How?
KELLER: What's the matter with you!
CHRIS: Dad . . . Dad, you killed twenty-one men!
KELLER: What, killed?
CHRIS: You killed them, you murdered them.
KELLER, *as though throwing his whole nature open before Chris:* How could I kill anybody?
CHRIS: Dad! Dad!
KELLER, *trying to hush him:* I didn't kill anybody!
CHRIS: Then explain it to me. What did you do? Explain it to me or I'll tear you to pieces!
KELLER, *horrified at his overwhelming fury:* Don't, Chris, don't—
CHRIS: I want to know what you did, now what did you do? You had a hundred and twenty cracked engine-heads, now what did you do?
KELLER: If you're going to hang me then I—
CHRIS: I'm listening. God Almighty, I'm listening!
KELLER—*their movements now are those of subtle pursuit and escape. Keller keeps a step out of Chris's range as he talks:* You're a boy, what could I do! I'm in business, a man is in business; a hundred and twenty cracked, you're out of business; you got a process, the process don't work you're out of business; you don't know how to operate, your stuff is no good; they

close you up, they tear up your contracts, what the hell's it to them? You lay forty years into a business and they knock you out in five minutes, what could I do, let them take forty years, let them take my life away? *His voice cracking:* I never thought they'd install them. I swear to God. I thought they'd stop 'em before anybody took off.

CHRIS: Then why'd you ship them out?

KELLER: By the time they could spot them I thought I'd have the process going again, and I could show them they needed me and they'd let it go by. But weeks passed and I got no kick-back, so I was going to tell them.

CHRIS: Then why didn't you tell them?

KELLER: It was too late. The paper, it was all over the front page, twenty-one went down, it was too late. They came with handcuffs into the shop, what could I do? *He sits on bench.* Chris . . . Chris, I did it for you, it was a chance and I took it for you. I'm sixty-one years old, when would I have another chance to make something for you? Sixty-one years old you don't get another chance, do ya?

CHRIS: You even knew they wouldn't hold up in the air.

KELLER: I didn't say that.

CHRIS: But you were going to warn them not to use them—

KELLER: But that don't mean—

CHRIS: It means you knew they'd crash.

KELLER: It don't mean that.

CHRIS: Then you *thought* they'd crash.

KELLER: I was afraid maybe—

CHRIS: You were afraid maybe! God in heaven, what kind of a man are you? Kids were hanging in the air by those heads. You knew that!

KELLER: For you, a business for you!

CHRIS, *with burning fury:* For me! Where do you live, where have you come from? For me!—I was dying every day and you were killing my boys and you did it for me? What the hell do you think I was thinking of, the Goddam business? Is that as far as your mind can see, the business? What is that, the world—the business? What the hell do you mean, you did it for me? Don't you have a country? Don't you live in the world? What the hell are you? You're not even an

animal, no animal kills his own, what are you? What must I do to you? I ought to tear the tongue out of your mouth, what must I do? *With his fist he pounds down upon his father's shoulder. He stumbles away, covering his face as he weeps.* What must I do, Jesus God, what must I do?

KELLER: Chris . . . My Chris . . .

CURTAIN

ACT THREE

Two o'clock the following morning, Mother is discovered on the rise, rocking ceaselessly in a chair, staring at her thoughts. It is an intense, slight, sort of rocking. A light shows from upstairs bedroom, lower floor windows being dark. The moon is strong and casts its bluish light.

Presently Jim, dressed in jacket and hat, appears, and seeing her, goes up beside her.

JIM: Any news?

MOTHER: No news.

JIM, *gently:* You can't sit up all night, dear, why don't you go to bed?

MOTHER: I'm waiting for Chris. Don't worry about me, Jim, I'm perfectly all right.

JIM: But it's almost two o'clock.

MOTHER: I can't sleep. *Slight pause.* You had an emergency?

JIM, *tiredly:* Somebody had a headache and thought he was dying. *Slight pause.* Half of my patients are quite mad. Nobody realizes how many people are walking around loose, and they're cracked as coconuts. Money. Money-money-money-money. You say it long enough it doesn't mean anything. *She smiles, makes a silent laugh.* Oh, how I'd love to be around when that happens!

MOTHER, *shaking her head:* You're so childish, Jim! Sometimes you are.

JIM *looks at her a moment:* Kate. *Pause.* What happened?

MOTHER: I told you. He had an argument with Joe. Then he got in the car and drove away.

JIM: What kind of an argument?

MOTHER: An argument, Joe . . . He was crying like a child, before.

JIM: They argued about Ann?

MOTHER, *after slight hesitation:* No, not Ann. Imagine? *Indicates lighted window above.* She hasn't come out of that room since he left. All night in that room.

JIM *looks at window, then at her:* What'd Joe do, tell him?

MOTHER *stops rocking:* Tell him what?

JIM: Don't be afraid, Kate, I know. I've always known.

MOTHER: How?

JIM: It occurred to me a long time ago.

MOTHER: I always had the feeling that in the back of his head, Chris . . . . almost knew. I didn't think it would be such a shock.

JIM *gets up:* Chris would never know how to live with a thing like that. It takes a certain talent—for lying. You have it, and I do. But not him.

MOTHER: What do you mean . . . . He's not coming back?

JIM: Oh, no, he'll come back. We all come back, Kate. These private little revolutions always die. The compromise is always made. In a peculiar way. Frank is right—every man does have a star. The star of one's honesty. And you spend your life groping for it, but once it's out it never lights again. I don't think he went very far. He probably just wanted to be alone to watch his star go out.

MOTHER: Just as long as he comes back.

JIM: I wish he wouldn't, Kate. One year I simply took off, went to New Orleans; for two months I lived on bananas and milk, and studied a certain disease. It was beautiful. And then she came, and she cried. And I went back home with her. And now I live in the usual darkness; I can't find myself; it's even hard sometimes to remember the kind of man I wanted to be. I'm a good husband; Chris is a good son—he'll come back.

Keller comes out on porch in dressing gown and slippers. He goes upstage—to alley. Jim goes to him.

JIM: I have a feeling he's in the park. I'll look around for him. Put her to bed, Joe; this is no good for what she's got. *Jim exits up driveway.*

KELLER, *coming down:* What does he want here?

MOTHER: His friend is not home.

KELLER *comes down to her. His voice is husky:* I don't like him mixing in so much.

MOTHER: It's too late, Joe. He knows.

KELLER, *apprehensively:* How does he know?

MOTHER: He guessed a long time ago.

KELLER: I don't like that.

MOTHER *laughs dangerously, quietly into the line:* What you don't like.

KELLER: Yeah, what I don't like.

MOTHER: You can't bull yourself through this one, Joe, you better be smart now. This thing—this thing is not over yet.

KELLER, *indicating lighted window above:* And what is she doing up there? She don't come out of the room.

MOTHER: I don't know, what is she doing? Sit down, stop being mad. You want to live? You better figure out your life.

KELLER: She don't know, does she?

MOTHER: She saw Chris storming out of here. It's one and one —she knows how to add.

KELLER: Maybe I ought to talk to her?

MOTHER: Don't ask me, Joe.

KELLER—*almost an outburst:* Then who do I ask? But I don't think she'll do anything about it.

MOTHER: You're asking me again.

KELLER: I'm askin' you. What am I, a stranger? I thought I had a family here. What happened to my family?

MOTHER: You've got a family. I'm simply telling you that I have no strength to think any more.

KELLER: You have no strength. The minute there's trouble you have no strength.

MOTHER: Joe, you're doing the same thing again; all your life whenever there's trouble you yell at me and you think that settles it.

KELLER: Then what do I do? Tell me, talk to me, what do I do?

MOTHER: Joe . . . I've been thinking this way. If he comes back—

KELLER: What do you mean "if"? He's comin' back!

MOTHER: I think if you sit him down and you—explain yourself. I mean you ought to make it clear to him that you know you did a terrible thing. *Not looking into his eyes:* I mean if he saw that you realize what you did. You see?

KELLER: What ice does that cut?

MOTHER, *a little fearfully:* I mean if you told him that you want to pay for what you did.

KELLER, *sensing . . . quietly:* How can I pay?

MOTHER: Tell him—you're willing to go to prison. *Pause.*

KELLER, *struck, amazed:* I'm willing to—?

MOTHER, *quickly:* You wouldn't go, he wouldn't ask you to go. But if you told him you wanted to, if he could feel that you wanted to pay, maybe he would forgive you.

KELLER: He would forgive me! For what?

MOTHER: Joe, you know what I mean.

KELLER: I don't know what you mean! You wanted money, so I made money. What must I be forgiven? You wanted money, didn't you?

MOTHER: I didn't want it that way.

KELLER: I didn't want it that way, either! What difference is it what you want? I spoiled the both of you. I should've put him out when he was ten like I was put out, and make him earn his keep. Then he'd know how a buck is made in this world. Forgiven! I could live on a quarter a day myself, but I got a family so I—

MOTHER: Joe, Joe . . . It don't excuse it that you did it for the family.

KELLER: It's got to excuse it!

MOTHER: There's something bigger than the family to him.

KELLER: Nothin' is bigger!

MOTHER: There is to him.

KELLER: There's nothin' he could do that I wouldn't forgive. Because he's my son. Because I'm his father and he's my son.

MOTHER: Joe, I tell you—

KELLER: Nothin's bigger than that. And you're goin' to tell him, you understand? I'm his father and he's my son, and if there's something bigger than that I'll put a bullet in my head!

MOTHER: You stop that!

KELLER: You heard me. Now you know what to tell him. *Pause. He moves from her—halts.* But he wouldn't put me away though . . . He wouldn't do that . . . Would he?

MOTHER: He loved you, Joe, you broke his heart.

KELLER: But to put me away . . .

MOTHER: I don't know. I'm beginning to think we don't really know him. They say in the war he was such a killer. Here he was always afraid of mice. I don't know him. I don't know what he'll do.

KELLER: Goddam, if Larry was alive he wouldn't act like this. He understood the way the world is made. He listened to

me. To him
building line. rld had a forty-foot fr
deal, overchargne, everything bothers at the
understand money cents, and his hair fall nake a
That was a boy ... easy, it came too easy. don't
front of her. What ... Larry. Larry. *He slump* arry.
MOTHER: Joe, Joe, pl ... nna do, Kate? ... *r in*
going to happen. ... You'll be all right, ... is
KELLER, *desperately, lost:* Fo...
all I ever lived for . . . Kate, for both of you, ... s
MOTHER: I know, darling, I know. ... *enters from house.* ...
say nothing, waiting for her to spea...
ANN: Why do you stay up? I'll tell you when ... comes.
KELLER *rises, goes to her:* You didn't eat suppe... did you? *To Mother:* Why don't you make her something?
MOTHER: Sure, I'll—
ANN: Never mind, Kate, I'm all right. *They are unable to speak to each other.* There's something I want to tell you. *She starts, then halts.* I'm not going to do anything about it.
MOTHER: She's a good girl! *To Keller:* You see? She's a—
ANN: I'll do nothing about Joe, but you're going to do something for me. *Directly to Mother:* You made Chris feel guilty with me. Whether you wanted to or not, you've crippled him in front of me. I'd like you to tell him that Larry is dead and that you know it. You understand me? I'm not going out of here alone. There's no life for me that way. I want you to set him free. And then I promise you, everything will end, and we'll go away, and that's all.
KELLER: You'll do that. You'll tell him.
ANN: I know what I'm asking, Kate. You had two sons. But you've only got one now.
KELLER: You'll tell him.
ANN: And you've got to say it to him so he knows you mean it.
MOTHER: My dear, if the boy was dead, it wouldn't depend on my words to make Chris know it. . . . The night he gets into your bed, his heart will dry up. Because he knows and you know. To his dying day he'll wait for his brother! No, my dear, no such thing. You're going in the morning, and you're going alone. That's your life, that's your lonely life. *She goes to porch, and starts in.*

ANN: Larry is dead, Kate.

MOTHER—*she stops:* Don't speak to me.

ANN: I said he's dead. I know! He crashed off the coast of China November twenty-fifth! His engine didn't fail him. But he died. I know . . .

MOTHER: How did he die? You're lying to me. If you know, how did he die?

ANN: I loved him. You know I loved him. Would I have looked at anyone else if I wasn't sure? That's enough for you.

MOTHER, *moving on her:* What's enough for me? What're you talking about? *She grasps Ann's wrists.*

ANN: You're hurting my wrists.

MOTHER: What are you talking about! *Pause. She stares at Ann a moment, then turns and goes to Keller.*

ANN: Joe, go in the house.

KELLER: Why should I—

ANN: Please go.

KELLER: Lemme know when he comes. *Keller goes into house.*

MOTHER, *as she sees Ann taking a letter from her pocket:* What's that?

ANN: Sit down. *Mother moves left to chair, but does not sit.* First you've got to understand. When I came, I didn't have any idea that Joe—I had nothing against him or you. I came to get married. I hoped . . . So I didn't bring this to hurt you. I thought I'd show it to you only if there was no other way to settle Larry in your mind.

MOTHER: Larry? *Snatches letter from Ann's hand.*

ANN: He wrote it to me just before he— *Mother opens and begins to read letter.* I'm not trying to hurt you, Kate. You're making me do this, now remember you're— Remember. I've been so lonely, Kate . . . I can't leave here alone again. *A long, low moan comes from Mother's throat as she reads.* You made me show it to you. You wouldn't believe me. I told you a hundred times, why wouldn't you believe me!

MOTHER: Oh, my God . . .

ANN, *with pity and fear:* Kate, please, please . . .

MOTHER: My God, my God . . .

ANN: Kate, dear, I'm so sorry . . . I'm so sorry.

Chris enters from driveway. He seems exhausted.

CHRIS: What's the matter—?

ANN: Where were you? . . . You're all perspired. *Mother doesn't move.* Where were you?

CHRIS: Just drove around a little. I thought you'd be gone.

ANN: Where do I go? I have nowhere to go.

CHRIS, *to Mother:* Where's Dad?

ANN: Inside lying down.

CHRIS: Sit down, both of you. I'll say what there is to say.

MOTHER: I didn't hear the car . . .

CHRIS: I left it in the garage.

MOTHER: Jim is out looking for you.

CHRIS: Mother . . . I'm going away. There are a couple of firms in Cleveland, I think I can get a place. I mean, I'm going away for good. *To Ann alone:* I know what you're thinking, Annie. It's true. I'm yellow. I was made yellow in this house because I suspected my father and I did nothing about it, but if I knew that night when I came home what I know now, he'd be in the district attorney's office by this time, and I'd have brought him there. Now if I look at him, all I'm able to do is cry.

MOTHER: What are you talking about? What else can you do?

CHRIS: I could jail him! I could jail him, if I were human any more. But I'm like everybody else now. I'm practical now. You made me practical.

MOTHER: But you have to be.

CHRIS: The cats in that alley are practical, the bums who ran away when we were fighting were practical. Only the dead ones weren't practical. But now I'm practical, and I spit on myself. I'm going away. I'm going now.

ANN, *going up to him:* I'm coming with you.

CHRIS: No, Ann.

ANN: Chris, I don't ask you to do anything about Joe.

CHRIS: You do, you do.

ANN: I swear I never will.

CHRIS: In your heart you always will.

ANN: Then do what you have to do!

CHRIS: Do what? What is there to do? I've looked all night for a reason to make him suffer.

ANN: There's reason, there's reason!

CHRIS: What? Do I raise the dead when I put him behind bars?

Then what'll I do it for? We used to shoot a man who acted like a dog, but honor was real there, you were protecting something. But here? This is the land of the great big dogs, you don't love a man here, you eat him! That's the principle; the only one we live by—it just happened to kill a few people this time, that's all. The world's that way, how can I take it out on him? What sense does that make? This is a zoo, a zoo!

ANN, *to Mother:* You know what he's got to do! Tell him!

MOTHER: Let him go.

ANN: I won't let him go. You'll tell him what he's got to do . . .

MOTHER: Annie!

ANN: Then I will!

Keller enters from house. Chris sees him, goes down near arbor.

KELLER: What's the matter with you? I want to talk to you.

CHRIS: I've got nothing to say to you.

KELLER, *taking his arm:* I want to talk to you!

CHRIS, *pulling violently away from him:* Don't do that, Dad. I'm going to hurt you if you do that. There's nothing to say, so say it quick.

KELLER: Exactly what's the matter? What's the matter? You got too much money? Is that what bothers you?

CHRIS, *with an edge of sarcasm:* It bothers me.

KELLER: If you can't get used to it, then throw it away. You hear me? Take every cent and give it to charity, throw it in the sewer. Does that settle it? In the sewer, that's all. You think I'm kidding? I'm tellin' you what to do, if it's dirty then burn it. It's your money, that's not my money. I'm a dead man, I'm an old dead man, nothing's mine. Well, talk to me! What do you want to do!

CHRIS: It's not what I want to do. It's what you want to do.

KELLER: What should I want to do? *Chris is silent.* Jail? You want me to go to jail? If you want me to go, say so! Is that where I belong? Then tell me so! *Slight pause.* What's the matter, why can't you tell me? *Furiously.* You say everything else to me, say that! *Slight pause.* I'll tell you why you can't say it. Because you know I don't belong there. Because you know! *With growing emphasis and passion, and a persistent*

tone of desperation: Who worked for nothin' in that war? When they work for nothin', I'll work for nothin'. Did they ship a gun or a truck outa Detroit before they got their price? Is that clean? It's dollars and cents, nickels and dimes; war and peace, it's nickels and dimes, what's clean? Half the Goddam country is gotta go if I go! That's why you can't tell me.

CHRIS: That's exactly why.

KELLER: Then . . . why am *I* bad?

CHRIS: *I* know you're no worse than most men but I thought you were better. I never saw you as a man. I saw you as my father. *Almost breaking:* I can't look at you this way, I can't look at myself!

He turns away, unable to face Keller. Ann goes quickly to Mother, takes letter from her and starts for Chris. Mother instantly rushes to intercept her.

MOTHER: Give me that!

ANN: He's going to read it! *She thrusts letter into Chris's hand.* Larry. He wrote it to me the day he died.

KELLER: Larry!

MOTHER: Chris, it's not for you. *He starts to read.* Joe . . . go away . . .

KELLER, *mystified, frightened:* Why'd she say, Larry, what—?

MOTHER *desperately pushes him toward alley, glancing at Chris:* Go to the street, Joe, go to the street! *She comes down beside Keller.* Don't, Chris . . . *Pleading from her whole soul:* Don't tell him.

CHRIS, *quietly:* Three and one half years . . . talking, talking. Now you tell me what you must do. . . . This is how he died, now tell me where you belong.

KELLER, *pleading:* Chris, a man can't be a Jesus in this world!

CHRIS: I know all about the world. I know the whole crap story. Now listen to this, and tell me what a man's got to be! *Reads:* "My dear Ann: . . ." You listening? He wrote this the day he died. Listen, don't cry. . . . Listen! "My dear Ann: It is impossible to put down the things I feel. But I've got to tell you something. Yesterday they flew in a load of papers from the States and I read about Dad and your father

being convicted. I can't express myself. I can't tell you how I feel—I can't bear to live any more. Last night I circled the base for twenty minutes before I could bring myself in. How could he have done that? Every day three or four men never come back and he sits back there doing business. . . . I don't know how to tell you what I feel. . . . I can't face anybody. . . . I'm going out on a mission in a few minutes. They'll probably report me missing. If they do, I want you to know that you mustn't wait for me. I tell you, Ann, if I had him there now I could kill him—" *Keller grabs letter from Chris's hand and reads it. After a long pause:* Now blame the world. Do you understand that letter?

KELLER, *speaking almost inaudibly:* I think I do. Get the car. I'll put on my jacket. *He turns and starts slowly for the house. Mother rushes to intercept him.*

MOTHER: Why are you going? You'll sleep, why are you going?

KELLER: I can't sleep here. I'll feel better if I go.

MOTHER: You're so foolish. Larry was your son too, wasn't he? You know he'd never tell you to do this.

KELLER, *looking at letter in his hand:* Then what is this if it isn't telling me? Sure, he was my son. But I think to him they were all my sons. And I guess they were, I guess they were. I'll be right down. *Exits into house.*

MOTHER, *to Chris, with determination:* You're not going to take him!

CHRIS: I'm taking him.

MOTHER: It's up to you, if you tell him to stay he'll stay. Go and tell him!

CHRIS: Nobody could stop him now.

MOTHER: You'll stop him! How long will he live in prison? Are you trying to kill him?

CHRIS, *holding out letter:* I thought you read this!

MOTHER, *of Larry, the letter:* The war is over! Didn't you hear? It's over!

CHRIS: Then what was Larry to you? A stone that fell into the water? It's not enough for him to be sorry. Larry didn't kill himself to make you and Dad sorry.

MOTHER: What more can we be!

CHRIS: You can be better! Once and for all you can know

there's a universe of people outside and you're responsible to it, and unless you know that, you threw away your son because that's why he died.

A shot is heard in the house. They stand frozen for a brief second. Chris starts for porch, pauses at step, turns to Ann.

CHRIS: Find Jim! *He goes on into the house and Ann runs up driveway. Mother stands alone, transfixed.*

MOTHER, *softly, almost moaning:* Joe . . . Joe . . . Joe . . . Joe . . . *Chris comes out of house, down to Mother's arms.*

CHRIS, *almost crying:* Mother, I didn't mean to—

MOTHER: Don't dear. Don't take it on yourself. Forget now. Live. *Chris stirs as if to answer.* Shhh . . . *She puts his arms down gently and moves toward porch.* Shhh . . . *As she reaches porch steps she begins sobbing.*

CURTAIN

DEATH OF A SALESMAN

Certain Private Conversations
in Two Acts and a Requiem

THE CHARACTERS:

WILLY LOMAN
LINDA
BIFF
HAPPY
BERNARD
THE WOMAN
CHARLEY
UNCLE BEN
HOWARD WAGNER
JENNY
STANLEY
MISS FORSYTHE
LETTA

The action takes place in Willy Loman's house and yard and in various places he visits in the New York and Boston of today.

ACT ONE

A melody is heard, played upon a flute. It is small and fine, telling of grass and trees and the horizon. The curtain rises.

Before us is the Salesman's house. We are aware of towering, angular shapes behind it, surrounding it on all sides. Only the blue light of the sky falls upon the house and forestage; the surrounding area shows an angry glow of orange. As more light appears, we see a solid vault of apartment houses around the small, fragile-seeming home. An air of the dream clings to the place, a dream rising out of reality. The kitchen at center seems actual enough, for there is a kitchen table with three chairs, and a refrigerator. But no other fixtures are seen. At the back of the kitchen there is a draped entrance, which leads to the living-room. To the right of the kitchen, on a level raised two feet, is a bedroom furnished only with a brass bedstead and a straight chair. On a shelf over the bed a silver athletic trophy stands. A window opens onto the apartment house at the side.

Behind the kitchen, on a level raised six and a half feet, is the boys' bedroom, at present barely visible. Two beds are dimly seen, and at the back of the room a dormer window. (This bedroom is above the unseen living-room.) At the left a stairway curves up to it from the kitchen.

The entire setting is wholly or, in some places, partially transparent. The roof-line of the house is one-dimensional; under and over it we see the apartment buildings. Before the house lies an apron, curving beyond the forestage into the orchestra. This forward area serves as the back yard as well as the locale of all Willy's imaginings and of his city scenes. Whenever the action is in the present the actors observe the imaginary wall-lines, entering the house only through its door at the left. But in the scenes of the past these boundaries are broken, and characters enter or leave a room by stepping "through" a wall onto the forestage.

From the right, Willy Loman, the Salesman, enters, carrying two large sample cases. The flute plays on. He hears but is not aware of it. He is past sixty years of age, dressed quietly. Even as he crosses the stage to the doorway of the house, his exhaustion is apparent. He unlocks the door, comes into the kitchen, and

thankfully lets his burden down, feeling the soreness of his palms. A word-sigh escapes his lips—it might be "Oh, boy, oh, boy." He closes the door, then carries his cases out into the living-room, through the draped kitchen doorway.

Linda, his wife, has stirred in her bed at the right. She gets out and puts on a robe, listening. Most often jovial, she has developed an iron repression of her exceptions to Willy's behavior—she more than loves him, she admires him, as though his mercurial nature, his temper, his massive dreams and little cruelties, served her only as sharp reminders of the turbulent longings within him, longings which she shares but lacks the temperament to utter and follow to their end.

LINDA, *hearing Willy outside the bedroom, calls with some trepidation:* Willy!

WILLY: It's all right. I came back.

LINDA: Why? What happened? *Slight pause.* Did something happen, Willy?

WILLY: No, nothing happened.

LINDA: You didn't smash the car, did you?

WILLY, *with casual irritation:* I said nothing happened. Didn't you hear me?

LINDA: Don't you feel well?

WILLY: I'm tired to the death. *The flute has faded away. He sits on the bed beside her, a little numb.* I couldn't make it. I just couldn't make it, Linda.

LINDA, *very carefully, delicately:* Where were you all day? You look terrible.

WILLY: I got as far as a little above Yonkers. I stopped for a cup of coffee. Maybe it was the coffee.

LINDA: What?

WILLY, *after a pause:* I suddenly couldn't drive any more. The car kept going off onto the shoulder, y'know?

LINDA, *helpfully:* Oh. Maybe it was the steering again. I don't think Angelo knows the Studebaker.

WILLY: No, it's me, it's me. Suddenly I realize I'm goin' sixty miles an hour and I don't remember the last five minutes. I'm—I can't seem to—keep my mind to it.

LINDA: Maybe it's your glasses. You never went for your new glasses.

WILLY: No, I see everything. I came back ten miles an hour. It took me nearly four hours from Yonkers.

LINDA, *resigned:* Well, you'll just have to take a rest, Willy, you can't continue this way.

WILLY: I just got back from Florida.

LINDA: But you didn't rest your mind. Your mind is overactive, and the mind is what counts, dear.

WILLY: I'll start out in the morning. Maybe I'll feel better in the morning. *She is taking off his shoes.* These goddam arch supports are killing me.

LINDA: Take an aspirin. Should I get you an aspirin? It'll soothe you.

WILLY, *with wonder:* I was driving along, you understand? And I was fine. I was even observing the scenery. You can imagine, me looking at scenery, on the road every week of my life. But it's so beautiful up there, Linda, the trees are so thick, and the sun is warm. I opened the windshield and just let the warm air bathe over me. And then all of a sudden I'm goin' off the road! I'm tellin' ya, I absolutely forgot I was driving. If I'd've gone the other way over the white line I might've killed somebody. So I went on again—and five minutes later I'm dreamin' again, and I nearly— *He presses two fingers against his eyes.* I have such thoughts, I have such strange thoughts.

LINDA: Willy, dear. Talk to them again. There's no reason why you can't work in New York.

WILLY: They don't need me in New York. I'm the New England man. I'm vital in New England.

LINDA: But you're sixty years old. They can't expect you to keep traveling every week.

WILLY: I'll have to send a wire to Portland. I'm supposed to see Brown and Morrison tomorrow morning at ten o'clock to show the line. Goddammit, I could sell them! *He starts putting on his jacket.*

LINDA, *taking the jacket from him:* Why don't you go down to the place tomorrow and tell Howard you've simply got to work in New York? You're too accommodating, dear.

WILLY: If old man Wagner was alive I'd a been in charge of New York now! That man was a prince, he was a masterful man. But that boy of his, that Howard, he don't appreciate.

When I went north the first time, the Wagner Company didn't know where New England was!

LINDA: Why don't you tell those things to Howard, dear?

WILLY, *encouraged:* I will, I definitely will. Is there any cheese?

LINDA: I'll make you a sandwich.

WILLY: No, go to sleep. I'll take some milk. I'll be up right away. The boys in?

LINDA: They're sleeping. Happy took Biff on a date tonight.

WILLY, *interested:* That so?

LINDA: It was so nice to see them shaving together, one behind the other, in the bathroom. And going out together. You notice? The whole house smells of shaving lotion.

WILLY: Figure it out. Work a lifetime to pay off a house. You finally own it, and there's nobody to live in it.

LINDA: Well, dear, life is a casting off. It's always that way.

WILLY: No, no, some people—some people accomplish something. Did Biff say anything after I went this morning?

LINDA: You shouldn't have criticized him, Willy, especially after he just got off the train. You mustn't lose your temper with him.

WILLY: When the hell did I lose my temper? I simply asked him if he was making any money. Is that a criticism?

LINDA: But, dear, how could he make any money?

WILLY, *worried and angered:* There's such an undercurrent in him. He became a moody man. Did he apologize when I left this morning?

LINDA: He was crestfallen, Willy. You know how he admires you. I think if he finds himself, then you'll both be happier and not fight any more.

WILLY: How can he find himself on a farm? Is that a life? A farmhand? In the beginning, when he was young, I thought, well, a young man, it's good for him to tramp around, take a lot of different jobs. But it's more than ten years now and he has yet to make thirty-five dollars a week!

LINDA: He's finding himself, Willy.

WILLY: Not finding yourself at the age of thirty-four is a disgrace!

LINDA: Shh!

WILLY: The trouble is he's lazy, goddammit!

LINDA: Willy, please!

WILLY: Biff is a lazy bum!

LINDA: They're sleeping. Get something to eat. Go on down.

WILLY: Why did he come home? I would like to know what brought him home.

LINDA: I don't know. I think he's still lost, Willy. I think he's very lost.

WILLY: Biff Loman is lost. In the greatest country in the world a young man with such—personal attractiveness, gets lost. And such a hard worker. There's one thing about Biff—he's not lazy.

LINDA: Never.

WILLY, *with pity and resolve:* I'll see him in the morning; I'll have a nice talk with him. I'll get him a job selling. He could be big in no time. My God! Remember how they used to follow him around in high school? When he smiled at one of them their faces lit up. When he walked down the street . . . *He loses himself in reminiscences.*

LINDA, *trying to bring him out of it:* Willy, dear, I got a new kind of American-type cheese today. It's whipped.

WILLY: Why do you get American when I like Swiss?

LINDA: I just thought you'd like a change—

WILLY: I don't want a change! I want Swiss cheese. Why am I always being contradicted?

LINDA, *with a covering laugh:* I thought it would be a surprise.

WILLY: Why don't you open a window in here, for God's sake?

LINDA, *with infinite patience:* They're all open, dear.

WILLY: The way they boxed us in here. Bricks and windows, windows and bricks.

LINDA: We should've bought the land next door.

WILLY: The street is lined with cars. There's not a breath of fresh air in the neighborhood. The grass don't grow any more, you can't raise a carrot in the back yard. They should've had a law against apartment houses. Remember those two beautiful elm trees out there? When I and Biff hung the swing between them?

LINDA: Yeah, like being a million miles from the city.

WILLY: They should've arrested the builder for cutting those down. They massacred the neighborhood. *Lost:* More and

more I think of those days, Linda. This time of year it was lilac and wisteria. And then the peonies would come out, and the daffodils. What fragrance in this room!

LINDA: Well, after all, people had to move somewhere.

WILLY: No, there's more people now.

LINDA: I don't think there's more people. I think—

WILLY: There's more people! That's what ruining this country! Population is getting out of control. The competition is maddening! Smell the stink from that apartment house! And another one on the other side . . . How can they whip cheese?

On Willy's last line, Biff and Happy raise themselves up in their beds, listening.

LINDA: Go down, try it. And be quiet.

WILLY, *turning to Linda, guiltily:* You're not worried about me, are you, sweetheart?

BIFF: What's the matter?

HAPPY: Listen!

LINDA: You've got too much on the ball to worry about.

WILLY: You're my foundation and my support, Linda.

LINDA: Just try to relax, dear. You make mountains out of molehills.

WILLY: I won't fight with him any more. If he wants to go back to Texas, let him go.

LINDA: He'll find his way.

WILLY: Sure. Certain men just don't get started till later in life. Like Thomas Edison, I think. Or B. F. Goodrich. One of them was deaf. *He starts for the bedroom doorway.* I'll put my money on Biff.

LINDA: And Willy—if it's warm Sunday we'll drive in the country. And we'll open the windshield, and take lunch.

WILLY: No, the windshields don't open on the new cars.

LINDA: But you opened it today.

WILLY: Me? I didn't. *He stops.* Now isn't that peculiar! Isn't that a remarkable— *He breaks off in amazement and fright as the flute is heard distantly.*

LINDA: What, darling?

WILLY: That is the most remarkable thing.

LINDA: What, dear?

WILLY: I was thinking of the Chevvy. *Slight pause.* Nineteen twenty-eight . . . when I had that red Chevvy— *Breaks off.* That funny? I coulda sworn I was driving that Chevvy today.

LINDA: Well, that's nothing. Something must've reminded you.

WILLY: Remarkable. Ts. Remember those days? The way Biff used to simonize that car? The dealer refused to believe there was eighty thousand miles on it. *He shakes his head.* Heh! *To Linda:* Close your eyes, I'll be right up. *He walks out of the bedroom.*

HAPPY, *to Biff:* Jesus, maybe he smashed up the car again!

LINDA, *calling after Willy:* Be careful on the stairs, dear! The cheese is on the middle shelf! *She turns, goes over to the bed, takes his jacket, and goes out of the bedroom.*

Light has risen on the boys' room. Unseen, Willy is heard talking to himself, "Eighty thousand miles," and a little laugh. Biff gets out of bed, comes downstage a bit, and stands attentively. Biff is two years older than his brother Happy, well built, but in these days bears a worn air and seems less self-assured. He has succeeded less, and his dreams are stronger and less acceptable than Happy's. Happy is tall, powerfully made. Sexuality is like a visible color on him, or a scent that many women have discovered. He, like his brother, is lost, but in a different way, for he has never allowed himself to turn his face toward defeat and is thus more confused and hard-skinned, although seemingly more content.

HAPPY, *getting out of bed:* He's going to get his license taken away if he keeps that up. I'm getting nervous about him, y'know, Biff?

BIFF: His eyes are going.

HAPPY: No, I've driven with him. He sees all right. He just doesn't keep his mind on it. I drove into the city with him last week. He stops at a green light and then it turns red and he goes. *He laughs.*

BIFF: Maybe he's color-blind.

HAPPY: Pop? Why he's got the finest eye for color in the business. You know that.

BIFF, *sitting down on his bed:* I'm going to sleep.

HAPPY: You're not still sour on Dad, are you, Biff?

BIFF: He's all right, I guess.

WILLY, *underneath them, in the living-room:* Yes, sir, eighty thousand miles—eighty-two thousand!

BIFF: You smoking?

HAPPY, *holding out a pack of cigarettes:* Want one?

BIFF, *taking a cigarette:* I can never sleep when I smell it.

WILLY: What a simonizing job, heh!

HAPPY, *with deep sentiment:* Funny, Biff, y'know? Us sleeping in here again? The old beds. *He pats his bed affectionately.* All the talk that went across those two beds, huh? Our whole lives.

BIFF: Yeah. Lotta dreams and plans.

HAPPY, *with a deep and masculine laugh:* About five hundred women would like to know what was said in this room.

They share a soft laugh.

BIFF: Remember that big Betsy something—what the hell was her name—over on Bushwick Avenue?

HAPPY, *combing his hair:* With the collie dog!

BIFF: That's the one. I got you in there, remember?

HAPPY: Yeah, that was my first time—I think. Boy, there was a pig! *They laugh, almost crudely.* You taught me everything I know about women. Don't forget that.

BIFF: I bet you forgot how bashful you used to be. Especially with girls.

HAPPY: Oh, I still am, Biff.

BIFF: Oh, go on.

HAPPY: I just control it, that's all. I think I got less bashful and you got more so. What happened, Biff? Where's the old humor, the old confidence? *He shakes Biff's knee. Biff gets up and moves restlessly about the room.* What's the matter?

BIFF: Why does Dad mock me all the time?

HAPPY: He's not mocking you, he—

BIFF: Everything I say there's a twist of mockery on his face. I can't get near him.

HAPPY: He just wants you to make good, that's all. I wanted to talk to you about Dad for a long time, Biff. Something's —happening to him. He—talks to himself.

BIFF: I noticed that this morning. But he always mumbled.

HAPPY: But not so noticeable. It got so embarrassing I sent

him to Florida. And you know something? Most of the time he's talking to you.

BIFF: What's he say about me?

HAPPY: I can't make it out.

BIFF: What's he say about me?

HAPPY: I think the fact that you're not settled, that you're still kind of up in the air . . .

BIFF: There's one or two other things depressing him, Happy.

HAPPY: What do you mean?

BIFF: Never mind. Just don't lay it all to me.

HAPPY: But I think if you just got started—I mean—is there any future for you out there?

BIFF: I tell ya, Hap, I don't know what the future is. I don't know—what I'm supposed to want.

HAPPY: What do you mean?

BIFF: Well, I spent six or seven years after high school trying to work myself up. Shipping clerk, salesman, business of one kind or another. And it's a measly manner of existence. To get on that subway on the hot mornings in summer. To devote your whole life to keeping stock, or making phone calls, or selling or buying. To suffer fifty weeks of the year for the sake of a two-week vacation, when all you really desire is to be outdoors, with your shirt off. And always to have to get ahead of the next fella. And still—that's how you build a future.

HAPPY: Well, you really enjoy it on a farm? Are you content out there?

BIFF, *with rising agitation:* Hap, I've had twenty or thirty different kinds of jobs since I left home before the war, and it always turns out the same. I just realized it lately. In Nebraska when I herded cattle, and the Dakotas, and Arizona, and now in Texas. It's why I came home now, I guess, because I realized it. This farm I work on, it's spring there now, see? And they've got about fifteen new colts. There's nothing more inspiring or—beautiful than the sight of a mare and a new colt. And it's cool there now, see? Texas is cool now, and it's spring. And whenever spring comes to where I am, I suddenly get the feeling, my God, I'm not gettin' anywhere! What the hell am I doing, playing around with horses, twenty-eight dollars a week! I'm thirty-four years old, I

oughta be makin' my future. That's when I come running home. And now, I get here, and I don't know what to do with myself. *After a pause:* I've always made a point of not wasting my life, and everytime I come back here I know that all I've done is to waste my life.

HAPPY: You're a poet, you know that, Biff? You're a—you're an idealist!

BIFF: No, I'm mixed up very bad. Maybe I oughta get married. Maybe I oughta get stuck into something. Maybe that's my trouble. I'm like a boy. I'm not married, I'm not in business, I just—I'm like a boy. Are you content, Hap? You're a success, aren't you? Are you content?

HAPPY: Hell, no!

BIFF: Why? You're making money, aren't you?

HAPPY, *moving about with energy, expressiveness:* All I can do now is wait for the merchandise manager to die. And suppose I get to be merchandise manager? He's a good friend of mine, and he just built a terrific estate on Long Island. And he lived there about two months and sold it, and now he's building another one. He can't enjoy it once it's finished. And I know that's just what I would do. I don't know what the hell I'm workin' for. Sometimes I sit in my apartment—all alone. And I think of the rent I'm paying. And it's crazy. But then, it's what I always wanted. My own apartment, a car, and plenty of women. And still, goddammit, I'm lonely.

BIFF, *with enthusiasm:* Listen, why don't you come out West with me?

HAPPY: You and I, heh?

BIFF: Sure, maybe we could buy a ranch. Raise cattle, use our muscles. Men built like we are should be working out in the open.

HAPPY, *avidly:* The Loman Brothers, heh?

BIFF, *with vast affection:* Sure, we'd be known all over the counties!

HAPPY, *enthralled:* That's what I dream about, Biff. Sometimes I want to just rip my clothes off in the middle of the store and outbox that goddam merchandise manager. I mean I can outbox, outrun, and outlift anybody in that store, and I have to take orders from those common, petty sons-of-bitches till I can't stand it any more.

BIFF: I'm tellin' you, kid, if you were with me I'd be happy out there.

HAPPY, *enthused:* See, Biff, everybody around me is so false that I'm constantly lowering my ideals . . .

BIFF: Baby, together we'd stand up for one another, we'd have someone to trust.

HAPPY: If I were around you—

BIFF: Hap, the trouble is we weren't brought up to grub for money. I don't know how to do it.

HAPPY: Neither can I!

BIFF: Then let's go!

HAPPY: The only thing is—what can you make out there?

BIFF: But look at your friend. Builds an estate and then hasn't the peace of mind to live in it.

HAPPY: Yeah, but when he walks into the store the waves part in front of him. That's fifty-two thousand dollars a year coming through the revolving door, and I got more in my pinky finger than he's got in his head.

BIFF: Yeah, but you just said—

HAPPY: I gotta show some of those pompous, self-important executives over there that Hap Loman can make the grade. I want to walk into the store the way he walks in. Then I'll go with you, Biff. We'll be together yet, I swear. But take those two we had tonight. Now weren't they gorgeous creatures?

BIFF: Yeah, yeah, most gorgeous I've had in years.

HAPPY: I get that any time I want, Biff. Whenever I feel disgusted. The only trouble is, it gets like bowling or something. I just keep knockin' them over and it doesn't mean anything. You still run around a lot?

BIFF: Naa. I'd like to find a girl—steady, somebody with substance.

HAPPY: That's what I long for.

BIFF: Go on! You'd never come home.

HAPPY: I would! Somebody with character, with resistance! Like Mom, y'know? You're gonna call me a bastard when I tell you this. That girl Charlotte I was with tonight is engaged to be married in five weeks. *He tries on his new hat.*

BIFF: No kiddin'!

HAPPY: Sure, the guy's in line for the vice-presidency of the

store. I don't know what gets into me, maybe I just have an overdeveloped sense of competition or something, but I went and ruined her, and furthermore I can't get rid of her. And he's the third executive I've done that to. Isn't that a crummy characteristic? And to top it all, I go to their weddings! *Indignantly, but laughing:* Like I'm not supposed to take bribes. Manufacturers offer me a hundred-dollar bill now and then to throw an order their way. You know how honest I am, but it's like this girl, see. I hate myself for it. Because I don't want the girl, and, still, I take it and—I love it!

BIFF: Let's go to sleep.

HAPPY: I guess we didn't settle anything, heh?

BIFF: I just got one idea that I think I'm going to try.

HAPPY: What's that?

BIFF: Remember Bill Oliver?

HAPPY: Sure, Oliver is very big now. You want to work for him again?

BIFF: No, but when I quit he said something to me. He put his arm on my shoulder, and he said, "Biff, if you ever need anything, come to me."

HAPPY: I remember that. That sounds good.

BIFF: I think I'll go to see him. If I could get ten thousand or even seven or eight thousand dollars I could buy a beautiful ranch.

HAPPY: I bet he'd back you. 'Cause he thought highly of you, Biff. I mean, they all do. You're well liked, Biff. That's why I say to come back here, and we both have the apartment. And I'm tellin' you, Biff, any babe you want . . .

BIFF: No, with a ranch I could do the work I like and still be something. I just wonder though. I wonder if Oliver still thinks I stole that carton of basketballs.

HAPPY: Oh, he probably forgot that long ago. It's almost ten years. You're too sensitive. Anyway, he didn't really fire you.

BIFF: Well, I think he was going to. I think that's why I quit. I was never sure whether he knew or not. I know he thought the world of me, though. I was the only one he'd let lock up the place.

WILLY, *below:* You gonna wash the engine, Biff?

HAPPY: Shh!

Biff looks at Happy, who is gazing down, listening. Willy is mumbling in the parlor.

HAPPY: You hear that?

They listen. Willy laughs warmly.

BIFF, *growing angry:* Doesn't he know Mom can hear that?
WILLY: Don't get your sweater dirty, Biff!

A look of pain crosses Biff's face.

HAPPY: Isn't that terrible? Don't leave again, will you? You'll find a job here. You gotta stick around. I don't know what to do about him, it's getting embarrassing.
WILLY: What a simonizing job!
BIFF: Mom's hearing that!
WILLY: No kiddin', Biff, you got a date? Wonderful!
HAPPY: Go on to sleep. But talk to him in the morning, will you?
BIFF, *reluctantly getting into bed:* With her in the house. Brother!
HAPPY, *getting into bed:* I wish you'd have a good talk with him.

The light on their room begins to fade.

BIFF, *to himself in bed:* That selfish, stupid . . .
HAPPY: Sh . . . Sleep, Biff.

Their light is out. Well before they have finished speaking, Willy's form is dimly seen below in the darkened kitchen. He opens the refrigerator, searches in there, and takes out a bottle of milk. The apartment houses are fading out, and the entire house and surroundings become covered with leaves. Music insinuates itself as the leaves appear.

WILLY: Just wanna be careful with those girls, Biff, that's all. Don't make any promises. No promises of any kind. Because a girl, y'know, they always believe what you tell 'em, and you're very young, Biff, you're too young to be talking seriously to girls.

Light rises on the kitchen. Willy, talking, shuts the refrigerator door and comes downstage to the kitchen table. He pours milk into a glass. He is totally immersed in himself, smiling faintly.

WILLY: Too young entirely, Biff. You want to watch your schooling first. Then when you're all set, there'll be plenty of girls for a boy like you. *He smiles broadly at a kitchen chair.* That so? The girls pay for you? *He laughs.* Boy, you must really be makin' a hit.

Willy is gradually addressing—physically—a point offstage, speaking through the wall of the kitchen, and his voice has been rising in volume to that of a normal conversation.

WILLY: I been wondering why you polish the car so careful. Ha! Don't leave the hubcaps, boys. Get the chamois to the hubcaps. Happy, use newspaper on the windows, it's the easiest thing. Show him how to do it, Biff! You see, Happy? Pad it up, use it like a pad. That's it, that's it, good work. You're doin' all right, Hap. *He pauses, then nods in approbation for a few seconds, then looks upward.* Biff, first thing we gotta do when we get time is clip that big branch over the house. Afraid it's gonna fall in a storm and hit the roof. Tell you what. We get a rope and sling her around, and then we climb up there with a couple of saws and take her down. Soon as you finish the car, boys, I wanna see ya. I got a surprise for you, boys.

BIFF, *offstage:* Whatta ya got, Dad?

WILLY: No, you finish first. Never leave a job till you're finished —remember that. *Looking toward the "big trees":* Biff, up in Albany I saw a beautiful hammock. I think I'll buy it next trip, and we'll hang it right between those two elms. Wouldn't that be something? Just swingin' there under those branches. Boy, that would be . . .

Young Biff and Young Happy appear from the direction Willy was addressing. Happy carries rags and a pail of water. Biff, wearing a sweater with a block "S," carries a football.

BIFF, *pointing in the direction of the car offstage:* How's that, Pop, professional?

WILLY: Terrific. Terrific job, boys. Good work, Biff.

HAPPY: Where's the surprise, Pop?
WILLY: In the back seat of the car.
HAPPY: Boy! *He runs off.*
BIFF: What is it, Dad? Tell me, what'd you buy?
WILLY, *laughing, cuffs him:* Never mind, something I want you to have.
BIFF, *turns and starts off:* What is it, Hap?
HAPPY, *offstage:* It's a punching bag!
BIFF: Oh, Pop!
WILLY: It's got Gene Tunney's signature on it!

Happy runs onstage with a punching bag.

BIFF: Gee, how'd you know we wanted a punching bag?
WILLY: Well, it's the finest thing for the timing.
HAPPY, *lies down on his back and pedals with his feet:* I'm losing weight, you notice, Pop?
WILLY, *to Happy:* Jumping rope is good too.
BIFF: Did you see the new football I got?
WILLY, *examining the ball:* Where'd you get a new ball?
BIFF: The coach told me to practice my passing.
WILLY: That so? And he gave you the ball, heh?
BIFF: Well, I borrowed it from the locker room. *He laughs confidentially.*
WILLY, *laughing with him at the theft:* I want you to return that.
HAPPY: I told you he wouldn't like it!
BIFF, *angrily:* Well, I'm bringing it back!
WILLY, *stopping the incipient argument, to Happy:* Sure, he's gotta practice with a regulation ball, doesn't he? *To Biff:* Coach'll probably congratulate you on your initiative!
BIFF: Oh, he keeps congratulating my initiative all the time, Pop.
WILLY: That's because he likes you. If somebody else took that ball there'd be an uproar. So what's the report, boys, what's the report?
BIFF: Where'd you go this time, Dad? Gee we were lonesome for you.
WILLY, *pleased, puts an arm around each boy and they come down to the apron:* Lonesome, heh?
BIFF: Missed you every minute.

WILLY: Don't say? Tell you a secret, boys. Don't breathe it to a soul. Someday I'll have my own business, and I'll never have to leave home any more.

HAPPY: Like Uncle Charley, heh?

WILLY: Bigger than Uncle Charley! Because Charley is not—liked. He's liked, but he's not—well liked.

BIFF: Where'd you go this time, Dad?

WILLY: Well, I got on the road, and I went north to Providence. Met the Mayor.

BIFF: The Mayor of Providence!

WILLY: He was sitting in the hotel lobby.

BIFF: What'd he say?

WILLY: He said, "Morning!" And I said, "You got a fine city here, Mayor." And then he had coffee with me. And then I went to Waterbury. Waterbury is a fine city. Big clock city, the famous Waterbury clock. Sold a nice bill there. And then Boston—Boston is the cradle of the Revolution. A fine city. And a couple of other towns in Mass., and on to Portland and Bangor and straight home!

BIFF: Gee, I'd love to go with you sometime, Dad.

WILLY: Soon as summer comes.

HAPPY: Promise?

WILLY: You and Hap and I, and I'll show you all the towns. America is full of beautiful towns and fine, upstanding people. And they know me, boys, they know me up and down New England. The finest people. And when I bring you fellas up, there'll be open sesame for all of us, 'cause one thing, boys: I have friends. I can park my car in any street in New England, and the cops protect it like their own. This summer, heh?

BIFF and HAPPY, *together:* Yeah! You bet!

WILLY: We'll take our bathing suits.

HAPPY: We'll carry your bags, Pop!

WILLY: Oh, won't that be something! Me comin' into the Boston stores with you boys carryin' my bags. What a sensation!

Biff is prancing around, practicing passing the ball.

WILLY: You nervous, Biff, about the game?

BIFF: Not if you're gonna be there.

WILLY: What do they say about you in school, now that they made you captain?

HAPPY: There's a crowd of girls behind him everytime the classes change.

BIFF, *taking Willy's hand:* This Saturday, Pop, this Saturday—just for you, I'm going to break through for a touchdown.

HAPPY: You're supposed to pass.

BIFF: I'm takin' one play for Pop. You watch me, Pop, and when I take off my helmet, that means I'm breakin' out. Then you watch me crash through that line!

WILLY, *kisses Biff:* Oh, wait'll I tell this in Boston!

Bernard enters in knickers. He is younger than Biff, earnest and loyal, a worried boy.

BERNARD: Biff, where are you? You're supposed to study with me today.

WILLY: Hey, looka Bernard. What're you lookin' so anemic about, Bernard?

BERNARD: He's gotta study, Uncle Willy. He's got Regents next week.

HAPPY, *tauntingly, spinning Bernard around:* Let's box, Bernard!

BERNARD: Biff! *He gets away from Happy.* Listen, Biff, I heard Mr. Birnbaum say that if you don't start studyin' math he's gonna flunk you, and you won't graduate. I heard him!

WILLY: You better study with him, Biff. Go ahead now.

BERNARD: I heard him!

BIFF: Oh, Pop, you didn't see my sneakers! *He holds up a foot for Willy to look at.*

WILLY: Hey, that's a beautiful job of printing!

BERNARD, *wiping his glasses:* Just because he printed University of Virginia on his sneakers doesn't mean they've got to graduate him, Uncle Willy!

WILLY, *angrily:* What're you talking about? With scholarships to three universities they're gonna flunk him?

BERNARD: But I heard Mr. Birnbaum say—

WILLY: Don't be a pest, Bernard! *To his boys:* What an anemic!

BERNARD: Okay, I'm waiting for you in my house, Biff.

Bernard goes off. The Lomans laugh.

WILLY: Bernard is not well liked, is he?
BIFF: He's liked, but he's not well liked.
HAPPY: That's right, Pop.
WILLY: That's just what I mean. Bernard can get the best marks in school, y'understand, but when he gets out in the business world, y'understand, you are going to be five times ahead of him. That's why I thank Almighty God you're both built like Adonises. Because the man who makes an appearance in the business world, the man who creates personal interest, is the man who gets ahead. Be liked and you will never want. You take me, for instance. I never have to wait in line to see a buyer. "Willy Loman is here!" That's all they have to know, and I go right through.
BIFF: Did you knock them dead, Pop?
WILLY: Knocked 'em cold in Providence, slaughtered 'em in Boston.
HAPPY, *on his back, pedaling again:* I'm losing weight, you notice, Pop?

Linda enters, as of old, a ribbon in her hair, carrying a basket of washing.

LINDA, *with youthful energy:* Hello, dear!
WILLY: Sweetheart!
LINDA: How'd the Chevvy run?
WILLY: Chevrolet, Linda, is the greatest car ever built. *To the boys:* Since when do you let your mother carry wash up the stairs?
BIFF: Grab hold there, boy!
HAPPY: Where to, Mom?
LINDA: Hang them up on the line. And you better go down to your friends, Biff. The cellar is full of boys. They don't know what to do with themselves.
BIFF: Ah, when Pop comes home they can wait!
WILLY, *laughs appreciatively:* You better go down and tell them what to do, Biff.
BIFF: I think I'll have them sweep out the furnace room.
WILLY: Good work, Biff.
BIFF, *goes through wall-line of kitchen to doorway at back and calls down:* Fellas! Everybody sweep out the furnace room! I'll be right down!

VOICES: All right! Okay, Biff.

BIFF: George and Sam and Frank, come out back! We're hangin' up the wash! Come on, Hap, on the double! *He and Happy carry out the basket.*

LINDA: The way they obey him!

WILLY: Well, that's training, the training. I'm tellin' you, I was sellin' thousands and thousands, but I had to come home.

LINDA: Oh, the whole block'll be at that game. Did you sell anything?

WILLY: I did five hundred gross in Providence and seven hundred gross in Boston.

LINDA: No! Wait a minute, I've got a pencil. *She pulls pencil and paper out of her apron pocket.* That makes your commission . . . Two hundred—my God! Two hundred and twelve dollars!

WILLY: Well, I didn't figure it yet, but . . .

LINDA: How much did you do?

WILLY: Well, I—I did—about a hundred and eighty gross in Providence. Well, no—it came to—roughly two hundred gross on the whole trip.

LINDA, *without hesitation:* Two hundred gross. That's . . . *She figures.*

WILLY: The trouble was that three of the stores were half closed for inventory in Boston. Otherwise I woulda broke records.

LINDA: Well, it makes seventy dollars and some pennies. That's very good.

WILLY: What do we owe?

LINDA: Well, on the first there's sixteen dollars on the refrigerator—

WILLY: Why sixteen?

LINDA: Well, the fan belt broke, so it was a dollar eighty.

WILLY: But it's brand new.

LINDA: Well, the man said that's the way it is. Till they work themselves in, y'know.

They move through the wall-line into the kitchen.

WILLY: I hope we didn't get stuck on that machine.

LINDA: They got the biggest ads of any of them!

WILLY: I know, it's a fine machine. What else?

LINDA: Well, there's nine-sixty for the washing machine. And for the vacuum cleaner there's three and a half due on the fifteenth. Then the roof, you got twenty-one dollars remaining.

WILLY: It don't leak, does it?

LINDA: No, they did a wonderful job. Then you owe Frank for the carburetor.

WILLY: I'm not going to pay that man! That goddam Chevrolet, they ought to prohibit the manufacture of that car!

LINDA: Well, you owe him three and a half. And odds and ends, comes to around a hundred and twenty dollars by the fifteenth.

WILLY: A hundred and twenty dollars! My God, if business don't pick up I don't know what I'm gonna do!

LINDA: Well, next week you'll do better.

WILLY: Oh, I'll knock 'em dead next week. I'll go to Hartford. I'm very well liked in Hartford. You know, the trouble is, Linda, people don't seem to take to me.

They move onto the forestage.

LINDA: Oh, don't be foolish.

WILLY: I know it when I walk in. They seem to laugh at me.

LINDA: Why? Why would they laugh at you? Don't talk that way, Willy.

Willy moves to the edge of the stage. Linda goes into the kitchen and starts to darn stockings.

WILLY: I don't know the reason for it, but they just pass me by. I'm not noticed.

LINDA: But you're doing wonderful, dear. You're making seventy to a hundred dollars a week.

WILLY: But I gotta be at it ten, twelve hours a day. Other men —I don't know—they do it easier. I don't know why—I can't stop myself—I talk too much. A man oughta come in with a few words. One thing about Charley. He's a man of few words, and they respect him.

LINDA: You don't talk too much, you're just lively.

WILLY, *smiling:* Well, I figure, what the hell, life is short, a couple of jokes. *To himself:* I joke too much! *The smile goes.*

LINDA: Why? You're—

WILLY: I'm fat. I'm very—foolish to look at, Linda. I didn't

tell you, but Christmas time I happened to be calling on F. H. Stewarts, and a salesman I know, as I was going in to see the buyer I heard him say something about—walrus. And I—I cracked him right across the face. I won't take that. I simply will not take that. But they do laugh at me. I know that.

LINDA: Darling . . .

WILLY: I gotta overcome it. I know I gotta overcome it. I'm not dressing to advantage, maybe.

LINDA: Willy, darling, you're the handsomest man in the world—

WILLY: Oh, no, Linda.

LINDA: To me you are. *Slight pause.* The handsomest.

From the darkness is heard the laughter of a woman. Willy doesn't turn to it, but it continues through Linda's lines.

LINDA: And the boys, Willy. Few men are idolized by their children the way you are.

Music is heard as behind a scrim, to the left of the house, The Woman, dimly seen, is dressing.

WILLY, *with great feeling:* You're the best there is, Linda, you're a pal, you know that? On the road—on the road I want to grab you sometimes and just kiss the life outa you.

The laughter is loud now, and he moves into a brightening area at the left, where The Woman has come from behind the scrim and is standing, putting on her hat, looking into a "mirror" and laughing.

WILLY: 'Cause I get so lonely—especially when business is bad and there's nobody to talk to. I get the feeling that I'll never sell anything again, that I won't make a living for you, or a business, a business for the boys. *He talks through The Woman's subsiding laughter! The Woman primps at the "mirror."* There's so much I want to make for—

THE WOMAN: Me? You didn't make me, Willy. I picked you.

WILLY, *pleased:* You picked me?

THE WOMAN, *who is quite proper-looking, Willy's age:* I did. I've been sitting at that desk watching all the salesmen go by, day

in, day out. But you've got such a sense of humor, and we do have such a good time together, don't we?

WILLY: Sure, sure. *He takes her in his arms.* Why do you have to go now?

THE WOMAN: It's two o'clock . . .

WILLY: No, come on in! *He pulls her.*

THE WOMAN: . . . my sisters'll be scandalized. When'll you be back?

WILLY: Oh, two weeks about. Will you come up again?

THE WOMAN: Sure thing. You do make me laugh. It's good for me. *She squeezes his arm, kisses him.* And I think you're a wonderful man.

WILLY: You picked me, heh?

THE WOMAN: Sure. Because you're so sweet. And such a kidder.

WILLY: Well, I'll see you next time I'm in Boston.

THE WOMAN: I'll put you right through to the buyers.

WILLY, *slapping her bottom:* Right. Well, bottoms up!

THE WOMAN, *slaps him gently and laughs:* You just kill me, Willy. *He suddenly grabs her and kisses her roughly.* You kill me. And thanks for the stockings. I love a lot of stockings. Well, good night.

WILLY: Good night. And keep your pores open!

THE WOMAN: Oh, Willy!

The woman bursts out laughing, and Linda's laughter blends in. The Woman disappears into the dark. Now the area at the kitchen table brightens. Linda is sitting where she was at the kitchen table, but now is mending a pair of her silk stockings.

LINDA: You are, Willy. The handsomest man. You've got no reason to feel that—

WILLY, *coming out of The Woman's dimming area and going over to Linda:* I'll make it all up to you, Linda, I'll—

LINDA: There's nothing to make up, dear. You're doing fine, better than—

WILLY, *noticing her mending:* What's that?

LINDA: Just mending my stockings. They're so expensive—

WILLY, *angrily, taking them from her:* I won't have you mending stockings in this house! Now throw them out!

Linda puts the stockings in her pocket.

BERNARD, *entering on the run:* Where is he? If he doesn't study!

WILLY, *moving to the forestage, with great agitation:* You'll give him the answers!

BERNARD: I do, but I can't on a Regents! That's a state exam! They're liable to arrest me!

WILLY: Where is he? I'll whip him, I'll whip him!

LINDA: And he'd better give back that football, Willy, it's not nice.

WILLY: Biff! Where is he? Why is he taking everything?

LINDA: He's too rough with the girls, Willy. All the mothers are afraid of him!

WILLY: I'll whip him!

BERNARD: He's driving the car without a license!

The Woman's laugh is heard.

WILLY: Shut up!

LINDA: All the mothers—

WILLY: Shut up!

BERNARD, *backing quietly away and out:* Mr. Birnbaum says he's stuck up.

WILLY: Get outa here!

BERNARD: If he doesn't buckle down he'll flunk math! *He goes off.*

LINDA: He's right, Willy, you've gotta—

WILLY, *exploding at her:* There's nothing the matter with him! You want him to be a worm like Bernard? He's got spirit, personality . . .

As he speaks, Linda, almost in tears, exits into the living-room. Willy is alone in the kitchen, wilting and staring. The leaves are gone. It is night again, and the apartment houses look down from behind.

WILLY: Loaded with it. Loaded! What is he stealing? He's giving it back, isn't he? Why is he stealing? What did I tell him? I never in my life told him anything but decent things.

Happy in pajamas has come down the stairs; Willy suddenly becomes aware of Happy's presence.

HAPPY: Let's go now, come on.

WILLY, *sitting down at the kitchen table:* Huh! Why did she have

to wax the floors herself? Everytime she waxes the floors she keels over. She knows that!

HAPPY: Shh! Take it easy. What brought you back tonight?

WILLY: I got an awful scare. Nearly hit a kid in Yonkers. God! Why didn't I go to Alaska with my brother Ben that time! Ben! That man was a genius, that man was success incarnate! What a mistake! He begged me to go.

HAPPY: Well, there's no use in—

WILLY: You guys! There was a man started with the clothes on his back and ended up with diamond mines!

HAPPY: Boy, someday I'd like to know how he did it.

WILLY: What's the mystery? The man knew what he wanted and went out and got it! Walked into a jungle, and comes out, the age of twenty-one, and he's rich! The world is an oyster, but you don't crack it open on a mattress!

HAPPY: Pop, I told you I'm gonna retire you for life.

WILLY: You'll retire me for life on seventy goddam dollars a week? And your women and your car and your apartment, and you'll retire me for life! Christ's sake, I couldn't get past Yonkers today! Where are you guys, where are you? The woods are burning! I can't drive a car!

Charley has appeared in the doorway. He is a large man, slow of speech, laconic, immovable. In all he says, despite what he says, there is pity, and, now, trepidation. He has a robe over pajamas, slippers on his feet. He enters the kitchen.

CHARLEY: Everything all right?

HAPPY: Yeah, Charley, everything's . . .

WILLY: What's the matter?

CHARLEY: I heard some noise. I thought something happened. Can't we do something about the walls? You sneeze in here, and in my house hats blow off.

HAPPY: Let's go to bed, Dad. Come on.

Charley signals to Happy to go.

WILLY: You go ahead, I'm not tired at the moment.

HAPPY, *to Willy:* Take it easy, huh? *He exits.*

WILLY: What're you doin' up?

CHARLEY, *sitting down at the kitchen table opposite Willy:* Couldn't sleep good. I had a heartburn.

WILLY: Well, you don't know how to eat.
CHARLEY: I eat with my mouth.
WILLY: No, you're ignorant. You gotta know about vitamins and things like that.
CHARLEY: Come on, let's shoot. Tire you out a little.
WILLY, *hesitantly:* All right. You got cards?
CHARLEY, *taking a deck from his pocket:* Yeah, I got them. Someplace. What is it with those vitamins?
WILLY, *dealing:* They build up your bones. Chemistry.
CHARLEY: Yeah, but there's no bones in a heartburn.
WILLY: What are you talkin' about? Do you know the first thing about it?
CHARLEY: Don't get insulted.
WILLY: Don't talk about something you don't know anything about.

They are playing. Pause.

CHARLEY: What're you doin' home?
WILLY: A little trouble with the car.
CHARLEY: Oh. *Pause.* I'd like to take a trip to California.
WILLY: Don't say.
CHARLEY: You want a job?
WILLY: I got a job, I told you that. *After a slight pause:* What the hell are you offering me a job for?
CHARLEY: Don't get insulted.
WILLY: Don't insult me.
CHARLEY: I don't see no sense in it. You don't have to go on this way.
WILLY: I got a good job. *Slight pause.* What do you keep comin' in here for?
CHARLEY: You want me to go?
WILLY, *after a pause, withering:* I can't understand it. He's going back to Texas again. What the hell is that?
CHARLEY: Let him go.
WILLY: I got nothin' to give him, Charley, I'm clean, I'm clean.
CHARLEY: He won't starve. None a them starve. Forget about him.
WILLY: Then what have I got to remember?
CHARLEY: You take it too hard. To hell with it. When a deposit bottle is broken you don't get your nickel back.

WILLY: That's easy enough for you to say.
CHARLEY: That ain't easy for me to say.
WILLY: Did you see the ceiling I put up in the living-room?
CHARLEY: Yeah, that's a piece of work. To put up a ceiling is a mystery to me. How do you do it?
WILLY: What's the difference?
CHARLEY: Well, talk about it.
WILLY: You gonna put up a ceiling?
CHARLEY: How could I put up a ceiling?
WILLY: Then what the hell are you bothering me for?
CHARLEY: You're insulted again.
WILLY: A man who can't handle tools is not a man. You're disgusting.
CHARLEY: Don't call me disgusting, Willy.

Uncle Ben, carrying a valise and an umbrella, enters the forestage from around the right corner of the house. He is a stolid man, in his sixties, with a mustache and an authoritative air. He is utterly certain of his destiny, and there is an aura of far places about him. He enters exactly as Willy speaks.

WILLY: I'm getting awfully tired, Ben.

Ben's music is heard. Ben looks around at everything.

CHARLEY: Good, keep playing; you'll sleep better. Did you call me Ben?

Ben looks at his watch.

WILLY: That's funny. For a second there you reminded me of my brother Ben.
BEN: I only have a few minutes. *He strolls, inspecting the place. Willy and Charley continue playing.*
CHARLEY: You never heard from him again, heh? Since that time?
WILLY: Didn't Linda tell you? Couple of weeks ago we got a letter from his wife in Africa. He died.
CHARLEY: That so.
BEN, *chuckling:* So this is Brooklyn, eh?
CHARLEY: Maybe you're in for some of his money.
WILLY: Naa, he had seven sons. There's just one opportunity I had with that man . . .

BEN: I must make a train, William. There are several properties I'm looking at in Alaska.

WILLY: Sure, sure! If I'd gone with him to Alaska that time, everything would've been totally different.

CHARLEY: Go on, you'd froze to death up there.

WILLY: What're you talking about?

BEN: Opportunity is tremendous in Alaska, William. Surprised you're not up there.

WILLY: Sure, tremendous.

CHARLEY: Heh?

WILLY: There was the only man I ever met who knew the answers.

CHARLEY: Who?

BEN: How are you all?

WILLY, *taking a pot, smiling:* Fine, fine.

CHARLEY: Pretty sharp tonight.

BEN: Is Mother living with you?

WILLY: No, she died a long time ago.

CHARLEY: Who?

BEN: That's too bad. Fine specimen of a lady, Mother.

WILLY, *to Charley:* Heh?

BEN: I'd hoped to see the old girl.

CHARLEY: Who died?

BEN: Heard anything from Father, have you?

WILLY, *unnerved:* What do you mean, who died?

CHARLEY, *taking a pot:* What're you talkin' about?

BEN, *looking at his watch:* William, it's half-past eight!

WILLY, *as though to dispel his confusion he angrily stops Charley's hand:* That's my build!

CHARLEY: I put the ace—

WILLY: If you don't know how to play the game I'm not gonna throw my money away on you!

CHARLEY, *rising:* It was my ace, for God's sake!

WILLY: I'm through, I'm through!

BEN: When did Mother die?

WILLY: Long ago. Since the beginning you never knew how to play cards.

CHARLEY, *picks up the cards and goes to the door:* All right! Next time I'll bring a deck with five aces.

WILLY: I don't play that kind of game!

CHARLEY, *turning to him:* You ought to be ashamed of yourself!

WILLY: Yeah?

CHARLEY: Yeah! *He goes out.*

WILLY, *slamming the door after him:* Ignoramus!

BEN, *as Willy comes toward him through the wall-line of the kitchen:* So you're William.

WILLY, *shaking Ben's hand:* Ben! I've been waiting for you so long! What's the answer? How did you do it?

BEN: Oh, there's a story in that.

Linda enters the forestage, as of old, carrying the wash basket.

LINDA: Is this Ben?

BEN, *gallantly:* How do you do, my dear.

LINDA: Where've you been all these years? Willy's always wondered why you—

WILLY, *pulling Ben away from her impatiently:* Where is Dad? Didn't you follow him? How did you get started?

BEN: Well, I don't know how much you remember.

WILLY: Well, I was just a baby, of course, only three or four years old—

BEN: Three years and eleven months.

WILLY: What a memory, Ben!

BEN: I have many enterprises, William, and I have never kept books.

WILLY: I remember I was sitting under the wagon in—was it Nebraska?

BEN: It was South Dakota, and I gave you a bunch of wild flowers.

WILLY: I remember you walking away down some open road.

BEN, *laughing:* I was going to find Father in Alaska.

WILLY: Where is he?

BEN: At that age I had a very faulty view of geography, William. I discovered after a few days that I was heading due south, so instead of Alaska, I ended up in Africa.

LINDA: Africa!

WILLY: The Gold Coast!

BEN: Principally diamond mines.

LINDA: Diamond mines!

BEN: Yes, my dear. But I've only a few minutes—

WILLY: No! Boys! Boys! *Young Biff and Happy appear.* Listen to this. This is your Uncle Ben, a great man! Tell my boys, Ben!

BEN: Why, boys, when I was seventeen I walked into the jungle, and when I was twenty-one I walked out. *He laughs.* And by God I was rich.

WILLY, *to the boys:* You see what I been talking about? The greatest things can happen!

BEN, *glancing at his watch:* I have an appointment in Ketchikan Tuesday week.

WILLY: No, Ben! Please tell about Dad. I want my boys to hear. I want them to know the kind of stock they spring from. All I remember is a man with a big beard, and I was in Mamma's lap, sitting around a fire, and some kind of high music.

BEN: His flute. He played the flute.

WILLY: Sure, the flute, that's right!

New music is heard, a high, rollicking tune.

BEN: Father was a very great and a very wild-hearted man. We would start in Boston, and he'd toss the whole family into the wagon, and then he'd drive the team right across the country; through Ohio, and Indiana, Michigan, Illinois, and all the Western states. And we'd stop in the towns and sell the flutes that he'd made on the way. Great inventor, Father. With one gadget he made more in a week than a man like you could make in a lifetime.

WILLY: That's just the way I'm bringing them up, Ben—rugged, well liked, all-around.

BEN: Yeah? *To Biff:* Hit that, boy—hard as you can. *He pounds his stomach.*

BIFF: Oh, no, sir!

BEN, *taking boxing stance:* Come on, get to me! *He laughs.*

WILLY: Go to it, Biff! Go ahead, show him!

BIFF: Okay! *He cocks his fists and starts in.*

LINDA, *to Willy:* Why must he fight, dear?

BEN, *sparring with Biff:* Good boy! Good boy!

WILLY: How's that, Ben, heh?

HAPPY: Give him the left, Biff!

LINDA: Why are you fighting?

BEN: Good boy! *Suddenly comes in, trips Biff, and stands over him, the point of his umbrella poised over Biff's eye.*

LINDA: Look out, Biff!

BIFF: Gee!

BEN, *patting Biff's knee:* Never fight fair with a stranger, boy. You'll never get out of the jungle that way. *Taking Linda's hand and bowing:* It was an honor and a pleasure to meet you, Linda.

LINDA, *withdrawing her hand coldly, frightened:* Have a nice—trip.

BEN, *to Willy:* And good luck with your—what do you do?

WILLY: Selling.

BEN: Yes. Well . . . *He raises his hand in farewell to all.*

WILLY: No, Ben, I don't want you to think . . . *He takes Ben's arm to show him.* It's Brooklyn, I know, but we hunt too.

BEN: Really, now.

WILLY: Oh, sure, there's snakes and rabbits and—that's why I moved out here. Why, Biff can fell any one of these trees in no time! Boys! Go right over to where they're building the apartment house and get some sand. We're gonna rebuild the entire front stoop right now! Watch this, Ben!

BIFF: Yes, sir! On the double, Hap!

HAPPY, *as he and Biff run off:* I lost weight, Pop, you notice?

Charley enters in knickers, even before the boys are gone.

CHARLEY: Listen, if they steal any more from that building the watchman'll put the cops on them!

LINDA, *to Willy:* Don't let Biff . . .

Ben laughs lustily.

WILLY: You shoulda seen the lumber they brought home last week. At least a dozen six-by-tens worth all kinds a money.

CHARLEY: Listen, if that watchman—

WILLY: I gave them hell, understand. But I got a couple of fearless characters there.

CHARLEY: Willy, the jails are full of fearless characters.

BEN, *clapping Willy on the back, with a laugh at Charley:* And the stock exchange, friend!

WILLY, *joining in Ben's laughter:* Where are the rest of your pants?

CHARLEY: My wife bought them.

WILLY: Now all you need is a golf club and you can go upstairs and go to sleep. *To Ben:* Great athlete! Between him and his son Bernard they can't hammer a nail!

BERNARD, *rushing in:* The watchman's chasing Biff!

WILLY, *angrily:* Shut up! He's not stealing anything!

LINDA, *alarmed, hurrying off left:* Where is he? Biff, dear! *She exits.*

WILLY, *moving toward the left, away from Ben:* There's nothing wrong. What's the matter with you?

BEN: Nervy boy. Good!

WILLY, *laughing:* Oh, nerves of iron, that Biff!

CHARLEY: Don't know what it is. My New England man comes back and he's bleedin', they murdered him up there.

WILLY: It's contacts, Charley, I got important contacts!

CHARLEY, *sarcastically:* Glad to hear it, Willy. Come in later, we'll shoot a little casino. I'll take some of your Portland money. *He laughs at Willy and exits.*

WILLY, *turning to Ben:* Business is bad, it's murderous. But not for me, of course.

BEN: I'll stop by on my way back to Africa.

WILLY, *longingly:* Can't you stay a few days? You're just what I need, Ben, because I—I have a fine position here, but I—well, Dad left when I was such a baby and I never had a chance to talk to him and I still feel—kind of temporary about myself.

BEN: I'll be late for my train.

They are at opposite ends of the stage.

WILLY: Ben, my boys—can't we talk? They'd go into the jaws of hell for me, see, but I—

BEN: William, you're being first-rate with your boys. Outstanding, manly chaps!

WILLY, *hanging on to his words:* Oh, Ben, that's good to hear! Because sometimes I'm afraid that I'm not teaching them the right kind of— Ben, how should I teach them?

BEN, *giving great weight to each word, and with a certain vicious*

audacity: William, when I walked into the jungle, I was seventeen. When I walked out I was twenty-one. And, by God, I was rich! *He goes off into darkness around the right corner of the house.*

WILLY: . . . was rich! That's just the spirit I want to imbue them with! To walk into a jungle! I was right! I was right! I was right!

Ben is gone, but Willy is still speaking to him as Linda, in nightgown and robe, enters the kitchen, glances around for Willy, then goes to the door of the house, looks out and sees him. Comes down to his left. He looks at her.

LINDA: Willy, dear? Willy?

WILLY: I was right!

LINDA: Did you have some cheese? *He can't answer.* It's very late, darling. Come to bed, heh?

WILLY, *looking straight up:* Gotta break your neck to see a star in this yard.

LINDA: You coming in?

WILLY: Whatever happened to that diamond watch fob? Remember? When Ben came from Africa that time? Didn't he give me a watch fob with a diamond in it?

LINDA: You pawned it, dear. Twelve, thirteen years ago. For Biff's radio correspondence course.

WILLY: Gee, that was a beautiful thing. I'll take a walk.

LINDA: But you're in your slippers.

WILLY, *starting to go around the house at the left:* I was right! I was! *Half to Linda, as he goes, shaking his head:* What a man! There was a man worth talking to. I was right!

LINDA, *calling after Willy:* But in your slippers, Willy!

Willy is almost gone when Biff, in his pajamas, comes down the stairs and enters the kitchen.

BIFF: What is he doing out there?

LINDA: Sh!

BIFF: God Almighty, Mom, how long has he been doing this?

LINDA: Don't, he'll hear you.

BIFF: What the hell is the matter with him?

LINDA: It'll pass by morning.

BIFF: Shouldn't we do anything?

LINDA: Oh, my dear, you should do a lot of things, but there's nothing to do, so go to sleep.

Happy comes down the stair and sits on the steps.

HAPPY: I never heard him so loud, Mom.

LINDA: Well, come around more often; you'll hear him. *She sits down at the table and mends the lining of Willy's jacket.*

BIFF: Why didn't you ever write me about this, Mom?

LINDA: How would I write to you? For over three months you had no address.

BIFF: I was on the move. But you know I thought of you all the time. You know that, don't you, pal?

LINDA: I know, dear, I know. But he likes to have a letter. Just to know that there's still a possibility for better things.

BIFF: He's not like this all the time, is he?

LINDA: It's when you come home he's always the worst.

BIFF: When I come home?

LINDA: When you write you're coming, he's all smiles, and talks about the future, and—he's just wonderful. And then the closer you seem to come, the more shaky he gets, and then, by the time you get here, he's arguing, and he seems angry at you. I think it's just that maybe he can't bring himself to—to open up to you. Why are you so hateful to each other? Why is that?

BIFF, *evasively:* I'm not hateful, Mom.

LINDA: But you no sooner come in the door than you're fighting!

BIFF: I don't know why. I mean to change. I'm tryin', Mom, you understand?

LINDA: Are you home to stay now?

BIFF: I don't know. I want to look around, see what's doin'.

LINDA: Biff, you can't look around all your life, can you?

BIFF: I just can't take hold, Mom. I can't take hold of some kind of a life.

LINDA: Biff, a man is not a bird, to come and go with the springtime.

BIFF: Your hair . . . *He touches her hair.* Your hair got so gray.

LINDA: Oh, it's been gray since you were in high school. I just stopped dyeing it, that's all.

BIFF: Dye it again, will ya? I don't want my pal looking old. *He smiles.*

LINDA: You're such a boy! You think you can go away for a year and . . . You've got to get it into your head now that one day you'll knock on this door and there'll be strange people here—

BIFF: What are you talking about? You're not even sixty, Mom.

LINDA: But what about your father?

BIFF, *lamely:* Well, I meant him too.

HAPPY: He admires Pop.

LINDA: Biff, dear, if you don't have any feeling for him, then you can't have any feeling for me.

BIFF: Sure I can, Mom.

LINDA: No. You can't just come to see me, because I love him. *With a threat, but only a threat, of tears:* He's the dearest man in the world to me, and I won't have anyone making him feel unwanted and low and blue. You've got to make up your mind now, darling, there's no leeway any more. Either he's your father and you pay him that respect, or else you're not to come here. I know he's not easy to get along with—nobody knows that better than me—but . . .

WILLY, *from the left, with a laugh:* Hey, hey, Biffo!

BIFF, *starting to go out after Willy:* What the hell is the matter with him? *Happy stops him.*

LINDA: Don't—don't go near him!

BIFF: Stop making excuses for him! He always, always wiped the floor with you. Never had an ounce of respect for you.

HAPPY: He's always had respect for—

BIFF: What the hell do you know about it?

HAPPY, *surlily:* Just don't call him crazy!

BIFF: He's got no character— Charley wouldn't do this. Not in his own house—spewing out that vomit from his mind.

HAPPY: Charley never had to cope with what he's got to.

BIFF: People are worse off than Willy Loman. Believe me, I've seen them!

LINDA: Then make Charley your father, Biff. You can't do that, can you? I don't say he's a great man. Willy Loman never made a lot of money. His name was never in the paper. He's not the finest character that ever lived. But he's a human

being, and a terrible thing is happening to him. So attention must be paid. He's not to be allowed to fall into his grave like an old dog. Attention, attention must be finally paid to such a person. You called him crazy—

BIFF: I didn't mean—

LINDA: No, a lot of people think he's lost his—balance. But you don't have to be very smart to know what his trouble is. The man is exhausted.

HAPPY: Sure!

LINDA: A small man can be just as exhausted as a great man. He works for a company thirty-six years this March, opens up unheard-of territories to their trademark, and now in his old age they take his salary away.

HAPPY, *indignantly:* I didn't know that, Mom.

LINDA: You never asked, my dear! Now that you get your spending money someplace else you don't trouble your mind with him.

HAPPY: But I gave you money last—

LINDA: Christmas time, fifty dollars! To fix the hot water it cost ninety-seven fifty! For five weeks he's been on straight commission, like a beginner, an unknown!

BIFF: Those ungrateful bastards!

LINDA: Are they any worse than his sons? When he brought them business, when he was young, they were glad to see him. But now his old friends, the old buyers that loved him so and always found some order to hand him in a pinch—they're all dead, retired. He used to be able to make six, seven calls a day in Boston. Now he takes his valises out of the car and puts them back and takes them out again and he's exhausted. Instead of walking he talks now. He drives seven hundred miles, and when he gets there no one knows him any more, no one welcomes him. And what goes through a man's mind, driving seven hundred miles home without having earned a cent? Why shouldn't he talk to himself? Why? When he has to go to Charley and borrow fifty dollars a week and pretend to me that it's his pay? How long can that go on? How long? You see what I'm sitting here and waiting for? And you tell me he has no character? The man who never worked a day but for your benefit? When does he

get the medal for that? Is this his reward—to turn around at the age of sixty-three and find his sons, who he loved better than his life, one a philandering bum—

HAPPY: Mom!

LINDA: That's all you are, my baby! *To Biff:* And you! What happened to the love you had for him? You were such pals! How you used to talk to him on the phone every night! How lonely he was till he could come home to you!

BIFF: All right, Mom. I'll live here in my room, and I'll get a job. I'll keep away from him, that's all.

LINDA: No, Biff. You can't stay here and fight all the time.

BIFF: He threw me out of this house, remember that.

LINDA: Why did he do that? I never knew why.

BIFF: Because I know he's a fake and he doesn't like anybody around who knows!

LINDA: Why a fake? In what way? What do you mean?

BIFF: Just don't lay it all at my feet. It's between me and him—that's all I have to say. I'll chip in from now on. He'll settle for half my pay check. He'll be all right. I'm going to bed. *He starts for the stairs.*

LINDA: He won't be all right.

BIFF, *turning on the stairs, furiously:* I hate this city and I'll stay here. Now what do you want?

LINDA: He's dying, Biff.

Happy turns quickly to her, shocked.

BIFF, *after a pause:* Why is he dying?

LINDA: He's been trying to kill himself.

BIFF, *with great horror:* How?

LINDA: I live from day to day.

BIFF: What're you talking about?

LINDA: Remember I wrote you that he smashed up the car again? In February?

BIFF: Well?

LINDA: The insurance inspector came. He said that they have evidence. That all these accidents in the last year—weren't—weren't—accidents.

HAPPY: How can they tell that? That's a lie.

LINDA: It seems there's a woman . . . *She takes a breath as*

{ BIFF, *sharply but contained:* What woman?
{ LINDA, *simultaneously:* . . . and this woman . . .

LINDA: What?

BIFF: Nothing. Go ahead.

LINDA: What did you say?

BIFF: Nothing. I just said what woman?

HAPPY: What about her?

LINDA: Well, it seems she was walking down the road and saw his car. She says that he wasn't driving fast at all, and that he didn't skid. She says he came to that little bridge, and then deliberately smashed into the railing, and it was only the shallowness of the water that saved him.

BIFF: Oh, no, he probably just fell asleep again.

LINDA: I don't think he fell asleep.

BIFF: Why not?

LINDA: Last month . . . *With great difficulty:* Oh, boys, it's so hard to say a thing like this! He's just a big stupid man to you, but I tell you there's more good in him than in many other people. *She chokes, wipes her eyes.* I was looking for a fuse. The lights blew out, and I went down the cellar. And behind the fuse box—it happened to fall out—was a length of rubber pipe—just short.

HAPPY: No kidding?

LINDA: There's a little attachment on the end of it. I knew right away. And sure enough, on the bottom of the water heater there's a new little nipple on the gas pipe.

HAPPY, *angrily:* That—jerk.

BIFF: Did you have it taken off?

LINDA: I'm—I'm ashamed to. How can I mention it to him? Every day I go down and take away that little rubber pipe. But, when he comes home, I put it back where it was. How can I insult him that way? I don't know what to do. I live from day to day, boys. I tell you, I know every thought in his mind. It sounds so old-fashioned and silly, but I tell you he put his whole life into you and you've turned your backs on him. *She is bent over in the chair, weeping, her face in her hands.* Biff, I swear to God! Biff, his life is in your hands!

HAPPY, *to Biff:* How do you like that damned fool!

BIFF, *kissing her:* All right, pal, all right. It's all settled now. I've

been remiss. I know that, Mom. But now I'll stay, and I swear to you, I'll apply myself. *Kneeling in front of her, in a fever of self-reproach:* It's just—you see, Mom, I don't fit in business. Not that I won't try. I'll try, and I'll make good.

HAPPY: Sure you will. The trouble with you in business was you never tried to please people.

BIFF: I know, I—

HAPPY: Like when you worked for Harrison's. Bob Harrison said you were tops, and then you go and do some damn fool thing like whistling whole songs in the elevator like a comedian.

BIFF, *against Happy:* So what? I like to whistle sometimes.

HAPPY: You don't raise a guy to a responsible job who whistles in the elevator!

LINDA: Well, don't argue about it now.

HAPPY: Like when you'd go off and swim in the middle of the day instead of taking the line around.

BIFF, *his resentment rising:* Well, don't you run off? You take off sometimes, don't you? On a nice summer day?

HAPPY: Yeah, but I cover myself!

LINDA: Boys!

HAPPY: If I'm going to take a fade the boss can call any number where I'm supposed to be and they'll swear to him that I just left. I'll tell you something that I hate to say, Biff, but in the business world some of them think you're crazy.

BIFF, *angered:* Screw the business world!

HAPPY: All right, screw it! Great, but cover yourself!

LINDA: Hap, Hap!

BIFF: I don't care what they think! They've laughed at Dad for years, and you know why? Because we don't belong in this nuthouse of a city! We should be mixing cement on some open plain, or—or carpenters. A carpenter is allowed to whistle!

Willy walks in from the entrance of the house, at left.

WILLY: Even your grandfather was better than a carpenter. *Pause. They watch him.* You never grew up. Bernard does not whistle in the elevator, I assure you.

BIFF, *as though to laugh Willy out of it:* Yeah, but you do, Pop.

WILLY: I never in my life whistled in an elevator! And who in the business world thinks I'm crazy?

BIFF: I didn't mean it like that, Pop. Now don't make a whole thing out of it, will ya?

WILLY: Go back to the West! Be a carpenter, a cowboy, enjoy yourself!

LINDA: Willy, he was just saying—

WILLY: I heard what he said!

HAPPY, *trying to quiet Willy:* Hey, Pop, come on now . . .

WILLY, *continuing over Happy's line:* They laugh at me, heh? Go to Filene's, go to the Hub, go to Slattery's, Boston. Call out the name Willy Loman and see what happens! Big shot!

BIFF: All right, Pop.

WILLY: Big!

BIFF: All right!

WILLY: Why do you always insult me?

BIFF: I didn't say a word. *To Linda:* Did I say a word?

LINDA: He didn't say anything, Willy.

WILLY, *going to the doorway of the living-room:* All right, good night, good night.

LINDA: Willy, dear, he just decided . . .

WILLY, *to Biff:* If you get tired hanging around tomorrow, paint the ceiling I put up in the living-room.

BIFF: I'm leaving early tomorrow.

HAPPY: He's going to see Bill Oliver, Pop.

WILLY, *interestedly:* Oliver? For what?

BIFF, *with reserve, but trying, trying:* He always said he'd stake me. I'd like to go into business, so maybe I can take him up on it.

LINDA: Isn't that wonderful?

WILLY: Don't interrupt. What's wonderful about it? There's fifty men in the City of New York who'd stake him. *To Biff:* Sporting goods?

BIFF: I guess so. I know something about it and—

WILLY: He knows something about it! You know sporting goods better than Spalding, for God's sake! How much is he giving you?

BIFF: I don't know, I didn't even see him yet, but—

WILLY: Then what're you talkin' about?

BIFF, *getting angry:* Well, all I said was I'm gonna see him, that's all!

WILLY, *turning away:* Ah, you're counting your chickens again.

BIFF, *starting left for the stairs:* Oh, Jesus, I'm going to sleep!

WILLY, *calling after him:* Don't curse in this house!

BIFF, *turning:* Since when did you get so clean?

HAPPY, *trying to stop them:* Wait a . . .

WILLY: Don't use that language to me! I won't have it!

HAPPY, *grabbing Biff, shouts:* Wait a minute! I got an idea. I got a feasible idea. Come here, Biff, let's talk this over now, let's talk some sense here. When I was down in Florida last time, I thought of a great idea to sell sporting goods. It just came back to me. You and I, Biff—we have a line, the Loman Line. We train a couple of weeks, and put on a couple of exhibitions, see?

WILLY: That's an idea!

HAPPY: Wait! We form two basketball teams, see? Two water-polo teams. We play each other. It's a million dollars' worth of publicity. Two brothers, see? The Loman Brothers. Displays in the Royal Palms—all the hotels. And banners over the ring and the basketball court: "Loman Brothers." Baby, we could sell sporting goods!

WILLY: That is a one-million-dollar idea!

LINDA: Marvelous!

BIFF: I'm in great shape as far as that's concerned.

HAPPY: And the beauty of it is, Biff, it wouldn't be like a business. We'd be out playin' ball again . . .

BIFF, *enthused:* Yeah, that's . . .

WILLY: Million-dollar . . .

HAPPY: And you wouldn't get fed up with it, Biff. It'd be the family again. There'd be the old honor, and comradeship, and if you wanted to go off for a swim or somethin'—well, you'd do it! Without some smart cooky gettin' up ahead of you!

WILLY: Lick the world! You guys together could absolutely lick the civilized world.

BIFF: I'll see Oliver tomorrow. Hap, if we could work that out . . .

LINDA: Maybe things are beginning to—

WILLY, *wildly enthused, to Linda:* Stop interrupting! *To Biff:* But don't wear sport jacket and slacks when you see Oliver.

BIFF: No, I'll—

WILLY: A business suit, and talk as little as possible, and don't crack any jokes.

BIFF: He did like me. Always liked me.

LINDA: He loved you!

WILLY, *to Linda:* Will you stop! *To Biff:* Walk in very serious. You are not applying for a boy's job. Money is to pass. Be quiet, fine, and serious. Everybody likes a kidder, but nobody lends him money.

HAPPY: I'll try to get some myself, Biff. I'm sure I can.

WILLY: I see great things for you kids, I think your troubles are over. But remember, start big and you'll end big. Ask for fifteen. How much you gonna ask for?

BIFF: Gee, I don't know—

WILLY: And don't say "Gee." "Gee" is a boy's word. A man walking in for fifteen thousand dollars does not say "Gee!"

BIFF: Ten, I think, would be top though.

WILLY: Don't be so modest. You always started too low. Walk in with a big laugh. Don't look worried. Start off with a couple of your good stories to lighten things up. It's not what you say, it's how you say it—because personality always wins the day.

LINDA: Oliver always thought the highest of him—

WILLY: Will you let me talk?

BIFF: Don't yell at her, Pop, will ya?

WILLY, *angrily:* I was talking, wasn't I?

BIFF: I don't like you yelling at her all the time, and I'm tellin' you, that's all.

WILLY: What're you, takin' over this house?

LINDA: Willy—

WILLY, *turning on her:* Don't take his side all the time, goddammit!

BIFF, *furiously:* Stop yelling at her!

WILLY, *suddenly pulling on his cheek, beaten down, guilt ridden:* Give my best to Bill Oliver—he may remember me. *He exits through the living-room doorway.*

LINDA, *her voice subdued:* What'd you have to start that for?

Biff turns away. You see how sweet he was as soon as you talked hopefully? *She goes over to Biff.* Come up and say good night to him. Don't let him go to bed that way.

HAPPY: Come on, Biff, let's buck him up.

LINDA: Please, dear. Just say good night. It takes so little to make him happy. Come. *She goes through the living-room doorway, calling upstairs from within the living-room:* Your pajamas are hanging in the bathroom, Willy!

HAPPY, *looking toward where Linda went out:* What a woman! They broke the mold when they made her. You know that, Biff?

BIFF: He's off salary. My God, working on commission!

HAPPY: Well, let's face it: he's no hot-shot selling man. Except that sometimes, you have to admit, he's a sweet personality.

BIFF, *deciding:* Lend me ten bucks, will ya? I want to buy some new ties.

HAPPY: I'll take you to a place I know. Beautiful stuff. Wear one of my striped shirts tomorrow.

BIFF: She got gray. Mom got awful old. Gee, I'm gonna go in to Oliver tomorrow and knock him for a—

HAPPY: Come on up. Tell that to Dad. Let's give him a whirl. Come on.

BIFF, *steamed up:* You know, with ten thousand bucks, boy!

HAPPY, *as they go into the living-room:* That's the talk, Biff, that's the first time I've heard the old confidence out of you! *From within the living-room, fading off:* You're gonna live with me, kid, and any babe you want just say the word . . . *The last lines are hardly heard. They are mounting the stairs to their parents' bedroom.*

LINDA, *entering her bedroom and addressing Willy, who is in the bathroom. She is straightening the bed for him:* Can you do anything about the shower? It drips.

WILLY, *from the bathroom:* All of a sudden everything falls to pieces! Goddam plumbing, oughta be sued, those people. I hardly finished putting it in and the thing . . . *His words rumble off.*

LINDA: I'm just wondering if Oliver will remember him. You think he might?

WILLY, *coming out of the bathroom in his pajamas:* Remember him? What's the matter with you, you crazy? If he'd've

stayed with Oliver he'd be on top by now! Wait'll Oliver gets a look at him. You don't know the average caliber any more. The average young man today—*he is getting into bed*—is got a caliber of zero. Greatest thing in the world for him was to bum around.

Biff and Happy enter the bedroom. Slight pause.

WILLY, *stops short, looking at Biff:* Glad to hear it, boy.

HAPPY: He wanted to say good night to you, sport.

WILLY, *to Biff:* Yeah. Knock him dead, boy. What'd you want to tell me?

BIFF: Just take it easy, Pop. Good night. *He turns to go.*

WILLY, *unable to resist:* And if anything falls off the desk while you're talking to him—like a package or something—don't you pick it up. They have office boys for that.

LINDA: I'll make a big breakfast—

WILLY: Will you let me finish? *To Biff:* Tell him you were in the business in the West. Not farm work.

BIFF: All right, Dad.

LINDA: I think everything—

WILLY, *going right through her speech:* And don't undersell yourself. No less than fifteen thousand dollars.

BIFF, *unable to bear him:* Okay. Good night, Mom. *He starts moving.*

WILLY: Because you got a greatness in you, Biff, remember that. You got all kinds a greatness . . . *He lies back, exhausted. Biff walks out.*

LINDA, *calling after Biff:* Sleep well, darling!

HAPPY: I'm gonna get married, Mom. I wanted to tell you.

LINDA: Go to sleep, dear.

HAPPY, *going:* I just wanted to tell you.

WILLY: Keep up the good work. *Happy exits.* God . . . remember that Ebbets Field game? The championship of the city?

LINDA: Just rest. Should I sing to you?

WILLY: Yeah. Sing to me. *Linda hums a soft lullaby.* When that team came out—he was the tallest, remember?

LINDA: Oh, yes. And in gold.

Biff enters the darkened kitchen, takes a cigarette, and leaves the house. He comes downstage into a golden pool of light. He smokes, staring at the night.

WILLY: Like a young god. Hercules—something like that. And the sun, the sun all around him. Rememb[illegible] he waved to me? Right up from the field, with the representatives of three colleges standing by? And the buyers I brought, and the cheers when he came out—Loman, Loman, Loman! God Almighty, he'll be great yet. A star like that, magnificent, can never really fade away!

The light on Willy is fading. The gas heater begins to glow through the kitchen wall, near the stairs, a blue flame beneath red coils.

LINDA, *timidly:* Willy dear, what has he got against you?

WILLY: I'm so tired. Don't talk any more.

Biff slowly returns to the kitchen. He stops, stares toward the heater.

LINDA: Will you ask Howard to let you work in New York?

WILLY: First thing in the morning. Everything'll be all right.

Biff reaches behind the heater and draws out a length of rubber tubing. He is horrified and turns his head toward Willy's room, still dimly lit, from which the strains of Linda's desperate but monotonous humming rise.

WILLY, *staring through the window into the moonlight:* Gee, look at the moon moving between the buildings!

Biff wraps the tubing around his hand and quickly goes up the stairs.

CURTAIN

ACT TWO

Music is heard, gay and bright. The curtain rises as the music fades away. Willy, in shirt sleeves, is sitting at the kitchen table, sipping coffee, his hat in his lap. Linda is filling his cup when she can.

WILLY: Wonderful coffee. Meal in itself.
LINDA: Can I make you some eggs?
WILLY: No. Take a breath.
LINDA: You look so rested, dear.
WILLY: I slept like a dead one. First time in months. Imagine, sleeping till ten on a Tuesday morning. Boys left nice and early, heh?
LINDA: They were out of here by eight o'clock.
WILLY: Good work!
LINDA: It was so thrilling to see them leaving together. I can't get over the shaving lotion in this house!
WILLY, *smiling:* Mmm—
LINDA: Biff was very changed this morning. His whole attitude seemed to be hopeful. He couldn't wait to get downtown to see Oliver.
WILLY: He's heading for a change. There's no question, there simply are certain men that take longer to get—solidified. How did he dress?
LINDA: His blue suit. He's so handsome in that suit. He could be a—anything in that suit!

Willy gets up from the table. Linda holds his jacket for him.

WILLY: There's no question, no question at all. Gee, on the way home tonight I'd like to buy some seeds.
LINDA, *laughing:* That'd be wonderful. But not enough sun gets back there. Nothing'll grow any more.
WILLY: You wait, kid, before it's all over we're gonna get a little place out in the country, and I'll raise some vegetables, a couple of chickens . . .
LINDA: You'll do it yet, dear.

Willy walks out of his jacket. Linda follows him.

WILLY: And they'll get married, and come for a weekend. I'd build a little guest house. 'Cause I got so many fine tools, all I'd need would be a little lumber and some peace of mind.

LINDA, *joyfully:* I sewed the lining . . .

WILLY: I could build two guest houses, so they'd both come. Did he decide how much he's going to ask Oliver for?

LINDA, *getting him into the jacket:* He didn't mention it, but I imagine ten or fifteen thousand. You going to talk to Howard today?

WILLY: Yeah. I'll put it to him straight and simple. He'll just have to take me off the road.

LINDA: And Willy, don't forget to ask for a little advance, because we've got the insurance premium. It's the grace period now.

WILLY: That's a hundred . . . ?

LINDA: A hundred and eight, sixty-eight. Because we're a little short again.

WILLY: Why are we short?

LINDA: Well, you had the motor job on the car . . .

WILLY: That goddam Studebaker!

LINDA: And you got one more payment on the refrigerator . . .

WILLY: But it just broke again!

LINDA: Well, it's old, dear.

WILLY: I told you we should've bought a well-advertised machine. Charley bought a General Electric and it's twenty years old and it's still good, that son-of-a-bitch.

LINDA: But, Willy—

WILLY: Whoever heard of a Hastings refrigerator? Once in my life I would like to own something outright before it's broken! I'm always in a race with the junkyard! I just finished paying for the car and it's on its last legs. The refrigerator consumes belts like a goddam maniac. They time those things. They time them so when you finally paid for them, they're used up.

LINDA, *buttoning up his jacket as he unbuttons it:* All told, about two hundred dollars would carry us, dear. But that includes the last payment on the mortgage. After this payment, Willy, the house belongs to us.

WILLY: It's twenty-five years!

LINDA: Biff was nine years old when we bought it.

WILLY: Well, that's a great thing. To weather a twenty-five year mortgage is—

LINDA: It's an accomplishment.

WILLY: All the cement, the lumber, the reconstruction I put in this house! There ain't a crack to be found in it any more.

LINDA: Well, it served its purpose.

WILLY: What purpose? Some stranger'll come along, move in, and that's that. If only Biff would take this house, and raise a family . . . *He starts to go.* Good-by, I'm late.

LINDA, *suddenly remembering:* Oh, I forgot! You're supposed to meet them for dinner.

WILLY: Me?

LINDA: At Frank's Chop House on Forty-eighth near Sixth Avenue.

WILLY: Is that so! How about you?

LINDA: No, just the three of you. They're gonna blow you to a big meal!

WILLY: Don't say! Who thought of that?

LINDA: Biff came to me this morning, Willy, and he said, "Tell Dad, we want to blow him to a big meal." Be there six o'clock. You and your two boys are going to have dinner.

WILLY: Gee whiz! That's really somethin'. I'm gonna knock Howard for a loop, kid. I'll get an advance, and I'll come home with a New York job. Goddammit, now I'm gonna do it!

LINDA: Oh, that's the spirit, Willy!

WILLY: I will never get behind a wheel the rest of my life!

LINDA: It's changing, Willy, I can feel it changing!

WILLY: Beyond a question. G'by, I'm late. *He starts to go again.*

LINDA, *calling after him as she runs to the kitchen table for a handkerchief:* You got your glasses?

WILLY, *feels for them, then comes back in:* Yeah, yeah, got my glasses.

LINDA, *giving him the handkerchief:* And a handkerchief.

WILLY: Yeah, handkerchief.

LINDA: And your saccharine?

WILLY: Yeah, my saccharine.

LINDA: Be careful on the subway stairs.

She kisses him, and a silk stocking is seen hanging from her hand. Willy notices it.

WILLY: Will you stop mending stockings? At least while I'm in the house. It gets me nervous. I can't tell you. Please.

Linda hides the stocking in her hand as she follows Willy across the forestage in front of the house.

LINDA: Remember, Frank's Chop House.
WILLY, *passing the apron:* Maybe beets would grow out there.
LINDA, *laughing:* But you tried so many times.
WILLY: Yeah. Well, don't work hard today. *He disappears around the right corner of the house.*
LINDA: Be careful!

As Willy vanishes, Linda waves to him. Suddenly the phone rings. She runs across the stage and into the kitchen and lifts it.

LINDA: Hello? Oh, Biff! I'm so glad you called, I just . . . Yes, sure, I just told him. Yes, he'll be there for dinner at six o'clock, I didn't forget. Listen, I was just dying to tell you. You know that little rubber pipe I told you about? That he connected to the gas heater? I finally decided to go down the cellar this morning and take it away and destroy it. But it's gone! Imagine? He took it away himself, it isn't there! *She listens.* When? Oh, then you took it. Oh—nothing, it's just that I'd hoped he'd taken it away himself. Oh, I'm not worried, darling, because this morning he left in such high spirits, it was like the old days! I'm not afraid any more. Did Mr. Oliver see you? . . . Well, you wait there then. And make a nice impression on him, darling. Just don't perspire too much before you see him. And have a nice time with Dad. He may have big news too! . . . That's right, a New York job. And be sweet to him tonight, dear. Be loving to him. Because he's only a little boat looking for a harbor. *She is trembling with sorrow and joy.* Oh, that's wonderful, Biff, you'll save his life. Thanks, darling. Just put your arm around him when he comes into the restaurant. Give him a smile. That's the boy . . . Good-by, dear. . . . You got your comb? . . . That's fine. Good-by, Biff dear.

In the middle of her speech, Howard Wagner, thirty-six, wheels on a small typewriter table on which is a wire-recording machine and proceeds to plug it in. This is on the left forestage. Light slowly fades on Linda as it rises on Howard. Howard is intent on threading the machine and only glances over his shoulder as Willy appears.

WILLY: Pst! Pst!
HOWARD: Hello, Willy, come in.
WILLY: Like to have a little talk with you, Howard.
HOWARD: Sorry to keep you waiting. I'll be with you in a minute.
WILLY: What's that, Howard?
HOWARD: Didn't you ever see one of these? Wire recorder.
WILLY: Oh. Can we talk a minute?
HOWARD: Records things. Just got delivery yesterday. Been driving me crazy, the most terrific machine I ever saw in my life. I was up all night with it.
WILLY: What do you do with it?
HOWARD: I bought it for dictation, but you can do anything with it. Listen to this. I had it home last night. Listen to what I picked up. The first one is my daughter. Get this. *He flicks the switch and "Roll out the Barrel" is heard being whistled.* Listen to that kid whistle.
WILLY: That is lifelike, isn't it?
HOWARD: Seven years old. Get that tone.
WILLY: Ts, ts. Like to ask a little favor if you . . .

The whistling breaks off, and the voice of Howard's daughter is heard.

HIS DAUGHTER: "Now you, Daddy."
HOWARD: She's crazy for me! *Again the same song is whistled.* That's me! Ha! *He winks.*
WILLY: You're very good!

The whistling breaks off again. The machine runs silent for a moment.

HOWARD: Sh! Get this now, this is my son.
HIS SON: "The capital of Alabama is Montgomery; the capital of Arizona is Phoenix; the capital of Arkansas is Little

Rock; the capital of California is Sacramento . . ." *and on, and on.*

HOWARD, *holding up five fingers:* Five years old, Willy!

WILLY: He'll make an announcer some day!

HIS SON, *continuing:* "The capital . . ."

HOWARD: Get that—alphabetical order! *The machine breaks off suddenly.* Wait a minute. The maid kicked the plug out.

WILLY: It certainly is a—

HOWARD: Sh, for God's sake!

HIS SON: "It's nine o'clock, Bulova watch time. So I have to go to sleep."

WILLY: That really is—

HOWARD: Wait a minute! The next is my wife.

They wait.

HOWARD'S VOICE: "Go on, say something." *Pause.* "Well, you gonna talk?"

HIS WIFE: "I can't think of anything."

HOWARD'S VOICE: "Well, talk—it's turning."

HIS WIFE, *shyly, beaten:* "Hello." *Silence.* "Oh, Howard, I can't talk into this . . ."

HOWARD, *snapping the machine off:* That was my wife.

WILLY: That is a wonderful machine. Can we—

HOWARD: I tell you, Willy, I'm gonna take my camera, and my bandsaw, and all my hobbies, and out they go. This is the most fascinating relaxation I ever found.

WILLY: I think I'll get one myself.

HOWARD: Sure, they're only a hundred and a half. You can't do without it. Supposing you wanna hear Jack Benny, see? But you can't be at home at that hour. So you tell the maid to turn the radio on when Jack Benny comes on, and this automatically goes on with the radio . . .

WILLY: And when you come home you . . .

HOWARD: You can come home twelve o'clock, one o'clock, any time you like, and you get yourself a Coke and sit yourself down, throw the switch, and there's Jack Benny's program in the middle of the night!

WILLY: I'm definitely going to get one. Because lots of time I'm on the road, and I think to myself, what I must be missing on the radio!

HOWARD: Don't you have a radio in the car?
WILLY: Well, yeah, but who ever thinks of turning it on?
HOWARD: Say, aren't you supposed to be in Boston?
WILLY: That's what I want to talk to you about, Howard. You got a minute? *He draws a chair in from the wing.*
HOWARD: What happened? What're you doing here?
WILLY: Well . . .
HOWARD: You didn't crack up again, did you?
WILLY: Oh, no. No . . .
HOWARD: Geez, you had me worried there for a minute. What's the trouble?
WILLY: Well, tell you the truth, Howard. I've come to the decision that I'd rather not travel any more.
HOWARD: Not travel! Well, what'll you do?
WILLY: Remember, Christmas time, when you had the party here? You said you'd try to think of some spot for me here in town.
HOWARD: With us?
WILLY: Well, sure.
HOWARD: Oh, yeah, yeah. I remember. Well, I couldn't think of anything for you, Willy.
WILLY: I tell ya, Howard. The kids are all grown up, y'know. I don't need much any more. If I could take home—well, sixty-five dollars a week, I could swing it.
HOWARD: Yeah, but Willy, see I—
WILLY: I tell ya why, Howard. Speaking frankly and between the two of us, y'know—I'm just a little tired.
HOWARD: Oh, I could understand that, Willy. But you're a road man, Willy, and we do a road business. We've only got a half-dozen salesmen on the floor here.
WILLY: God knows, Howard, I never asked a favor of any man. But I was with the firm when your father used to carry you in here in his arms.
HOWARD: I know that, Willy, but—
WILLY: Your father came to me the day you were born and asked me what I thought of the name of Howard, may he rest in peace.
HOWARD: I appreciate that, Willy, but there just is no spot here for you. If I had a spot I'd slam you right in, but I just don't have a single solitary spot.

He looks for his lighter. Willy has picked it up and gives it to him. Pause.

WILLY, *with increasing anger:* Howard, all I need to set my table is fifty dollars a week.

HOWARD: But where am I going to put you, kid?

WILLY: Look, it isn't a question of whether I can sell merchandise, is it?

HOWARD: No, but it's a business, kid, and everybody's gotta pull his own weight.

WILLY, *desperately:* Just let me tell you a story, Howard—

HOWARD: 'Cause you gotta admit, business is business.

WILLY, *angrily:* Business is definitely business, but just listen for a minute. You don't understand this. When I was a boy —eighteen, nineteen—I was already on the road. And there was a question in my mind as to whether selling had a future for me. Because in those days I had a yearning to go to Alaska. See, there were three gold strikes in one month in Alaska, and I felt like going out. Just for the ride, you might say.

HOWARD, *barely interested:* Don't say.

WILLY: Oh, yeah, my father lived many years in Alaska. He was an adventurous man. We've got quite a little streak of self-reliance in our family. I thought I'd go out with my older brother and try to locate him, and maybe settle in the North with the old man. And I was almost decided to go, when I met a salesman in the Parker House. His name was Dave Singleman. And he was eighty-four years old, and he'd drummed merchandise in thirty-one states. And old Dave, he'd go up to his room, y'understand, put on his green velvet slippers—I'll never forget—and pick up his phone and call the buyers, and without ever leaving his room, at the age of eighty-four, he made his living. And when I saw that, I realized that selling was the greatest career a man could want. 'Cause what could be more satisfying than to be able to go, at the age of eighty-four, into twenty or thirty different cities, and pick up a phone, and be remembered and loved and helped by so many different people? Do you know? when he died—and by the way he died the death of a salesman, in his green velvet slippers in the smoker of the

New York, New Haven and Hartford, going into Boston—when he died, hundreds of salesmen and buyers were at his funeral. Things were sad on a lotta trains for months after that. *He stands up. Howard has not looked at him.* In those days there was personality in it, Howard. There was respect, and comradeship, and gratitude in it. Today, it's all cut and dried, and there's no chance for bringing friendship to bear—or personality. You see what I mean? They don't know me any more.

HOWARD, *moving away, toward the right:* That's just the thing, Willy.

WILLY: If I had forty dollars a week—that's all I'd need. Forty dollars, Howard.

HOWARD: Kid, I can't take blood from a stone, I—

WILLY, *desperation is on him now:* Howard, the year Al Smith was nominated, your father came to me and—

HOWARD, *starting to go off:* I've got to see some people, kid.

WILLY, *stopping him:* I'm talking about your father! There were promises made across this desk! You mustn't tell me you've got people to see—I put thirty-four years into this firm, Howard, and now I can't pay my insurance! You can't eat the orange and throw the peel away—a man is not a piece of fruit! *After a pause:* Now pay attention. Your father—in 1928 I had a big year. I averaged a hundred and seventy dollars a week in commissions.

HOWARD, *impatiently:* Now, Willy, you never averaged—

WILLY, *banging his hand on the desk:* I averaged a hundred and seventy dollars a week in the year of 1928! And your father came to me—or rather, I was in the office here—it was right over this desk—and he put his hand on my shoulder—

HOWARD, *getting up:* You'll have to excuse me, Willy, I gotta see some people. Pull yourself together. *Going out:* I'll be back in a little while.

On Howard's exit, the light on his chair grows very bright and strange.

WILLY: Pull myself together! What the hell did I say to him? My God, I was yelling at him! How could I! *Willy breaks off, staring at the light, which occupies the chair, animating it. He approaches this chair, standing across the desk from it.* Frank,

Frank, don't you remember what you told me that time? How you put your hand on my shoulder, and Frank . . . *He leans on the desk and as he speaks the dead man's name he accidentally switches on the recorder, and instantly*

HOWARD'S SON: ". . . of New York is Albany. The capital of Ohio is Cincinnati, the capital of Rhode Island is . . ." *The recitation continues.*

WILLY, *leaping away with fright, shouting:* Ha! Howard! Howard! Howard!

HOWARD, *rushing in:* What happened?

WILLY, *pointing at the machine, which continues nasally, childishly, with the capital cities:* Shut it off! Shut it off!

HOWARD, *pulling the plug out:* Look, Willy . . .

WILLY, *pressing his hands to his eyes:* I gotta get myself some coffee. I'll get some coffee . . .

Willy starts to walk out. Howard stops him.

HOWARD, *rolling up the cord:* Willy, look . . .

WILLY: I'll go to Boston.

HOWARD: Willy, you can't go to Boston for us.

WILLY: Why can't I go?

HOWARD: I don't want you to represent us. I've been meaning to tell you for a long time now.

WILLY: Howard, are you firing me?

HOWARD: I think you need a good long rest, Willy.

WILLY: Howard—

HOWARD: And when you feel better, come back, and we'll see if we can work something out.

WILLY: But I gotta earn money, Howard. I'm in no position to—

HOWARD: Where are your sons? Why don't your sons give you a hand?

WILLY: They're working on a very big deal.

HOWARD: This is no time for false pride, Willy. You go to your sons and you tell them that you're tired. You've got two great boys, haven't you?

WILLY: Oh, no question, no question, but in the meantime . . .

HOWARD: Then that's that, heh?

WILLY: All right, I'll go to Boston tomorrow.

HOWARD: No, no.

WILLY: I can't throw myself on my sons. I'm not a cripple!

HOWARD: Look, kid, I'm busy this morning.

WILLY, *grasping Howard's arm:* Howard, you've got to let me go to Boston!

HOWARD, *hard, keeping himself under control:* I've got a line of people to see this morning. Sit down, take five minutes, and pull yourself together, and then go home, will ya? I need the office, Willy. *He starts to go, turns, remembering the recorder, starts to push off the table holding the recorder.* Oh, yeah. Whenever you can this week, stop by and drop off the samples. You'll feel better, Willy, and then come back and we'll talk. Pull yourself together, kid, there's people outside.

Howard exits, pushing the table off left. Willy stares into space, exhausted. Now the music is heard—Ben's music—first distantly, then closer, closer. As Willy speaks, Ben enters from the right. He carries valise and umbrella.

WILLY: Oh, Ben, how did you do it? What is the answer? Did you wind up the Alaska deal already?

BEN: Doesn't take much time if you know what you're doing. Just a short business trip. Boarding ship in an hour. Wanted to say good-by.

WILLY: Ben, I've got to talk to you.

BEN, *glancing at his watch:* Haven't the time, William.

WILLY, *crossing the apron to Ben:* Ben, nothing's working out. I don't know what to do.

BEN: Now, look here, William. I've bought timberland in Alaska and I need a man to look after things for me.

WILLY: God, timberland! Me and my boys in those grand outdoors!

BEN: You've a new continent at your doorstep, William. Get out of these cities, they're full of talk and time payments and courts of law. Screw on your fists and you can fight for a fortune up there.

WILLY: Yes, yes! Linda, Linda!

Linda enters as of old, with the wash.

LINDA: Oh, you're back?

BEN: I haven't much time.

WILLY: No, wait! Linda, he's got a proposition for me in Alaska.

LINDA: But you've got— *To Ben:* He's got a beautiful job here.
WILLY: But in Alaska, kid, I could—
LINDA: You're doing well enough, Willy!
BEN, *to Linda:* Enough for what, my dear?
LINDA, *frightened of Ben and angry at him:* Don't say those things to him! Enough to be happy right here, right now. *To Willy, while Ben laughs:* Why must everybody conquer the world? You're well liked, and the boys love you, and someday—*to Ben*—why, old man Wagner told him just the other day that if he keeps it up he'll be a member of the firm, didn't he, Willy?
WILLY: Sure, sure. I am building something with this firm, Ben, and if a man is building something he must be on the right track, mustn't he?
BEN: What are you building? Lay your hand on it. Where is it?
WILLY, *hesitantly:* That's true, Linda, there's nothing.
LINDA: Why? *To Ben:* There's a man eighty-four years old—
WILLY: That's right, Ben, that's right. When I look at that man I say, what is there to worry about?
BEN: Bah!
WILLY: It's true, Ben. All he has to do is go into any city, pick up the phone, and he's making his living and you know why?
BEN, *picking up his valise:* I've got to go.
WILLY, *holding Ben back:* Look at this boy!

Biff, in his high school sweater, enters carrying suitcase. Happy carries Biff's shoulder guards, gold helmet, and football pants.

WILLY: Without a penny to his name, three great universities are begging for him, and from there the sky's the limit, because it's not what you do, Ben. It's who you know and the smile on your face! It's contacts, Ben, contacts! The whole wealth of Alaska passes over the lunch table at the Commodore Hotel, and that's the wonder, the wonder of this country, that a man can end with diamonds here on the basis of being liked! *He turns to Biff.* And that's why when you get out on that field today it's important. Because thousands of people will be rooting for you and loving you. *To Ben, who has again begun to leave:* And Ben! when he walks into a business office his name will sound out like a bell and

all the doors will open to him! I've seen it, Ben, I've seen it a thousand times! You can't feel it with your hand like timber, but it's there!

BEN: Good-by, William.

WILLY: Ben, am I right? Don't you think I'm right? I value your advice.

BEN: There's a new continent at your doorstep, William. You could walk out rich. Rich! *He is gone.*

WILLY: We'll do it here, Ben! You hear me? We're gonna do it here!

Young Bernard rushes in. The gay music of the Boys is heard.

BERNARD: Oh, gee, I was afraid you left aleady!

WILLY: Why? What time is it?

BERNARD: It's half-past one!

WILLY: Well, come on, everybody! Ebbets Field next stop! Where's the pennants? *He rushes through the wall-line of the kitchen and out into the living-room.*

LINDA, *to Biff:* Did you pack fresh underwear?

BIFF, *who has been limbering up:* I want to go!

BERNARD: Biff, I'm carrying your helmet, ain't I?

HAPPY: No, I'm carrying the helmet.

BERNARD: Oh, Biff, you promised me.

HAPPY: I'm carrying the helmet.

BERNARD: How am I going to get in the locker room?

LINDA: Let him carry the shoulder guards. *She puts her coat and hat on in the kitchen.*

BERNARD: Can I, Biff? 'Cause I told everybody I'm going to be in the locker room.

HAPPY: In Ebbets Field it's the clubhouse.

BERNARD: I meant the clubhouse. Biff!

HAPPY: Biff!

BIFF, *grandly, after a slight pause:* Let him carry the shoulder guards.

HAPPY, *as he gives Bernard the shoulder guards:* Stay close to us now.

Willy rushes in with the pennants.

WILLY, *handing them out:* Everybody wave when Biff comes out on the field. *Happy and Bernard run off.* You set now, boy?

The music has died away.

BIFF: Ready to go, Pop. Every muscle is ready.

WILLY, *at the edge of the apron:* You realize what this means?

BIFF: That's right, Pop.

WILLY, *feeling Biff's muscles:* You're comin' home this afternoon captain of the All-Scholastic Championship Team of the City of New York.

BIFF: I got it, Pop. And remember, pal, when I take off my helmet, that touchdown is for you.

WILLY: Let's go! *He is starting out, with his arm around Biff, when Charley enters, as of old, in knickers.* I got no room for you, Charley.

CHARLEY: Room? For what?

WILLY: In the car.

CHARLEY: You goin' for a ride? I wanted to shoot some casino.

WILLY, *furiously:* Casino! *Incredulously:* Don't you realize what today is?

LINDA: Oh, he knows, Willy. He's just kidding you.

WILLY: That's nothing to kid about!

CHARLEY: No, Linda, what's goin' on?

LINDA: He's playing in Ebbets Field.

CHARLEY: Baseball in this weather?

WILLY: Don't talk to him. Come on, come on! *He is pushing them out.*

CHARLEY: Wait a minute, didn't you hear the news?

WILLY: What?

CHARLEY: Don't you listen to the radio? Ebbets Field just blew up.

WILLY: You go to hell! *Charley laughs. Pushing them out:* Come on, come on! We're late.

CHARLEY, *as they go:* Knock a homer, Biff, knock a homer!

WILLY, *the last to leave, turning to Charley:* I don't think that was funny, Charley. This is the greatest day of his life.

CHARLEY: Willy, when are you going to grow up?

WILLY: Yeah, heh? When this game is over, Charley, you'll be laughing out of the other side of your face. They'll be calling him another Red Grange. Twenty-five thousand a year.

CHARLEY, *kidding:* Is that so?

WILLY: Yeah, that's so.

CHARLEY: Well, then, I'm sorry, Willy. But tell me something.
WILLY: What?
CHARLEY: Who is Red Grange?
WILLY: Put up your hands. Goddam you, put up your hands!

Charley, chuckling, shakes his head and walks away, around the left corner of the stage. Willy follows him. The music rises to a mocking frenzy.

WILLY: Who the hell do you think you are, better than everybody else? You don't know everything, you big, ignorant, stupid . . . Put up your hands!

Light rises, on the right side of the forestage, on a small table in the reception room of Charley's office. Traffic sounds are heard. Bernard, now mature, sits whistling to himself. A pair of tennis rackets and an overnight bag are on the floor beside him.

WILLY, *offstage:* What are you walking away for? Don't walk away! If you're going to say something say it to my face! I know you laugh at me behind my back. You'll laugh out of the other side of your goddam face after this game. Touchdown! Touchdown! Eighty thousand people! Touchdown! Right between the goal posts.

Bernard is a quiet, earnest, but self-assured young man. Willy's voice is coming from right upstage now. Bernard lowers his feet off the table and listens. Jenny, his father's secretary, enters.

JENNY, *distressed:* Say, Bernard, will you go out in the hall?
BERNARD: What is that noise? Who is it?
JENNY: Mr. Loman. He just got off the elevator.
BERNARD, *getting up:* Who's he arguing with?
JENNY: Nobody. There's nobody with him. I can't deal with him any more, and your father gets all upset everytime he comes. I've got a lot of typing to do, and your father's waiting to sign it. Will you see him?
WILLY, *entering:* Touchdown! Touch— *He sees Jenny.* Jenny, Jenny, good to see you. How're ya? Workin'? Or still honest?
JENNY: Fine. How've you been feeling?
WILLY: Not much any more, Jenny. Ha, ha! *He is surprised to see the rackets.*

BERNARD: Hello, Uncle Willy.

WILLY, *almost shocked:* Bernard! Well, look who's here! *He comes quickly, guiltily, to Bernard and warmly shakes his hand.*

BERNARD: How are you? Good to see you.

WILLY: What are you doing here?

BERNARD: Oh, just stopped by to see Pop. Get off my feet till my train leaves. I'm going to Washington in a few minutes.

WILLY: Is he in?

BERNARD: Yes, he's in his office with the accountant. Sit down.

WILLY, *sitting down:* What're you going to do in Washington?

BERNARD: Oh, just a case I've got there, Willy.

WILLY: That so? *Indicating the rackets:* You going to play tennis there?

BERNARD: I'm staying with a friend who's got a court.

WILLY: Don't say. His own tennis court. Must be fine people, I bet.

BERNARD: They are, very nice. Dad tells me Biff's in town.

WILLY, *with a big smile:* Yeah, Biff's in. Working on a very big deal, Bernard.

BERNARD: What's Biff doing?

WILLY: Well, he's been doing very big things in the West. But he decided to establish himself here. Very big. We're having dinner. Did I hear your wife had a boy?

BERNARD: That's right. Our second.

WILLY: Two boys! What do you know!

BERNARD: What kind of a deal has Biff got?

WILLY: Well, Bill Oliver—very big sporting-goods man—he wants Biff very badly. Called him in from the West. Long distance, carte blanche, special deliveries. Your friends have their own private tennis court?

BERNARD: You still with the old firm, Willy?

WILLY, *after a pause:* I'm—I'm overjoyed to see how you made the grade, Bernard, overjoyed. It's an encouraging thing to see a young man really—really— Looks very good for Biff—very— *He breaks off, then:* Bernard— *He is so full of emotion, he breaks off again.*

BERNARD: What is it, Willy?

WILLY, *small and alone:* What—what's the secret?

BERNARD: What secret?

WILLY: How—how did you? Why didn't he ever catch on?

BERNARD: I wouldn't know that, Willy.

WILLY, *confidentially, desperately:* You were his friend, his boyhood friend. There's something I don't understand about it. His life ended after that Ebbets Field game. From the age of seventeen nothing good ever happened to him.

BERNARD: He never trained himself for anything.

WILLY: But he did, he did. After high school he took so many correspondence courses. Radio mechanics; television; God knows what, and never made the slightest mark.

BERNARD, *taking off his glasses:* Willy, do you want to talk candidly?

WILLY, *rising, faces Bernard:* I regard you as a very brilliant man, Bernard. I value your advice.

BERNARD: Oh, the hell with the advice, Willy. I couldn't advise you. There's just one thing I've always wanted to ask you. When he was supposed to graduate, and the math teacher flunked him—

WILLY: Oh, that son-of-a-bitch ruined his life.

BERNARD: Yeah, but, Willy, all he had to do was go to summer school and make up that subject.

WILLY: That's right, that's right.

BERNARD: Did you tell him not to go to summer school?

WILLY: Me? I begged him to go. I ordered him to go!

BERNARD: Then why wouldn't he go?

WILLY: Why? Why! Bernard, that question has been trailing me like a ghost for the last fifteen years. He flunked the subject, and laid down and died like a hammer hit him!

BERNARD: Take it easy, kid.

WILLY: Let me talk to you—I got nobody to talk to. Bernard, Bernard, was it my fault? Y'see? It keeps going around in my mind, maybe I did something to him. I got nothing to give him.

BERNARD: Don't take it so hard.

WILLY: Why did he lay down? What is the story there? You were his friend!

BERNARD: Willy, I remember, it was June, and our grades came out. And he'd flunked math.

WILLY: That son-of-a-bitch!

BERNARD: No, it wasn't right then. Biff just got very angry, I remember, and he was ready to enroll in summer school.

WILLY, *surprised:* He was?

BERNARD: He wasn't beaten by it at all. But then, Willy, he disappeared from the block for almost a month. And I got the idea that he'd gone up to New England to see you. Did he have a talk with you then?

Willy stares in silence.

BERNARD: Willy?

WILLY, *with a strong edge of resentment in his voice:* Yeah, he came to Boston. What about it?

BERNARD: Well, just that when he came back—I'll never forget this, it always mystifies me. Because I'd thought so well of Biff, even though he'd always taken advantage of me. I loved him, Willy, y'know? And he came back after that month and took his sneakers—remember those sneakers with "University of Virginia" printed on them? He was so proud of those, wore them every day. And he took them down in the cellar, and burned them up in the furnace. We had a fist fight. It lasted at least half an hour. Just the two of us, punching each other down the cellar, and crying right through it. I've often thought of how strange it was that I knew he'd given up his life. What happened in Boston, Willy?

Willy looks at him as at an intruder.

BERNARD: I just bring it up because you asked me.

WILLY, *angrily:* Nothing. What do you mean, "What happened?" What's that got to do with anything?

BERNARD: Well, don't get sore.

WILLY: What are you trying to do, blame it on me? If a boy lays down is that my fault?

BERNARD: Now, Willy, don't get—

WILLY: Well, don't—don't talk to me that way! What does that mean, "What happened?"

Charley enters. He is in his vest, and he carries a bottle of bourbon.

CHARLEY: Hey, you're going to miss that train. *He waves the bottle.*

BERNARD: Yeah, I'm going. *He takes the bottle.* Thanks, Pop. *He*

picks up his rackets and bag. Good-by, Willy, and don't worry about it. You know, "If at first you don't succeed . . ."

WILLY: Yes, I believe in that.

BERNARD: But sometimes, Willy, it's better for a man just to walk away.

WILLY: Walk away?

BERNARD: That's right.

WILLY: But if you can't walk away?

BERNARD, *after a slight pause:* I guess that's when it's tough. *Extending his hand:* Good-by, Willy.

WILLY, *shaking Bernard's hand:* Good-by, boy.

CHARLEY, *an arm on Bernard's shoulder:* How do you like this kid? Gonna argue a case in front of the Supreme Court.

BERNARD, *protesting:* Pop!

WILLY, *genuinely shocked, pained, and happy:* No! The Supreme Court!

BERNARD: I gotta run. 'By, Dad!

CHARLEY: Knock 'em dead, Bernard!

Bernard goes off.

WILLY, *as Charley takes out his wallet:* The Supreme Court! And he didn't even mention it!

CHARLEY, *counting out money on the desk:* He don't have to—he's gonna do it.

WILLY: And you never told him what to do, did you? You never took any interest in him.

CHARLEY: My salvation is that I never took any interest in anything. There's some money—fifty dollars. I got an accountant inside.

WILLY: Charley, look . . . *With difficulty:* I got my insurance to pay. If you can manage it—I need a hundred and ten dollars.

Charley doesn't reply for a moment; merely stops moving.

WILLY: I'd draw it from my bank but Linda would know, and I . . .

CHARLEY: Sit down, Willy.

WILLY, *moving toward the chair:* I'm keeping an account of everything, remember. I'll pay every penny back. *He sits.*

CHARLEY: Now listen to me, Willy.

WILLY: I want you to know I appreciate . . .

CHARLEY, *sitting down on the table:* Willy, what're you doin'? What the hell is goin' on in your head?

WILLY: Why? I'm simply . . .

CHARLEY: I offered you a job. You can make fifty dollars a week. And I won't send you on the road.

WILLY: I've got a job.

CHARLEY: Without pay? What kind of a job is a job without pay? *He rises.* Now, look, kid, enough is enough. I'm no genius but I know when I'm being insulted.

WILLY: Insulted!

CHARLEY: Why don't you want to work for me?

WILLY: What's the matter with you? I've got a job.

CHARLEY: Then what're you walkin' in here every week for?

WILLY, *getting up:* Well, if you don't want me to walk in here—

CHARLEY: I am offering you a job.

WILLY: I don't want your goddam job!

CHARLEY: When the hell are you going to grow up?

WILLY, *furiously:* You big ignoramus, if you say that to me again I'll rap you one! I don't care how big you are! *He's ready to fight.*

Pause.

CHARLEY, *kindly, going to him:* How much do you need, Willy?

WILLY: Charley, I'm strapped, I'm strapped. I don't know what to do. I was just fired.

CHARLEY: Howard fired you?

WILLY: That snotnose. Imagine that? I named him. I named him Howard.

CHARLEY: Willy, when're you gonna realize that them things don't mean anything? You named him Howard, but you can't sell that. The only thing you got in this world is what you can sell. And the funny thing is that you're a salesman, and you don't know that.

WILLY: I've always tried to think otherwise, I guess. I always felt that if a man was impressive, and well liked, that nothing—

CHARLEY: Why must everybody like you? Who liked J. P. Morgan? Was he impressive? In a Turkish bath he'd look like a

butcher. But with his pockets on he was very well liked. Now listen, Willy, I know you don't like me, and nobody can say I'm in love with you, but I'll give you a job because—just for the hell of it, put it that way. Now what do you say?

WILLY: I—I just can't work for you, Charley.

CHARLEY: What're you, jealous of me?

WILLY: I can't work for you, that's all, don't ask me why.

CHARLEY, *angered, takes out more bills:* You been jealous of me all your life, you damned fool! Here, pay your insurance. *He puts the money in Willy's hand.*

WILLY: I'm keeping strict accounts.

CHARLEY: I've got some work to do. Take care of yourself. And pay your insurance.

WILLY, *moving to the right:* Funny, y'know? After all the highways, and the trains, and the appointments, and the years, you end up worth more dead than alive.

CHARLEY: Willy, nobody's worth nothin' dead. *After a slight pause:* Did you hear what I said?

Willy stands still, dreaming.

CHARLEY: Willy!

WILLY: Apologize to Bernard for me when you see him. I didn't mean to argue with him. He's a fine boy. They're all fine boys, and they'll end up big—all of them. Someday they'll all play tennis together. Wish me luck, Charley. He saw Bill Oliver today.

CHARLEY: Good luck.

WILLY, *on the verge of tears:* Charley, you're the only friend I got. Isn't that a remarkable thing? *He goes out.*

CHARLEY: Jesus!

Charley stares after him a moment and follows. All light blacks out. Suddenly raucous music is heard, and a red glow rises behind the screen at right. Stanley, a young waiter, appears, carrying a table, followed by Happy, who is carrying two chairs.

STANLEY, *putting the table down:* That's all right, Mr. Loman, I can handle it myself. *He turns and takes the chairs from Happy and places them at the table.*

HAPPY, *glancing around:* Oh, this is better.

STANLEY: Sure, in the front there you're in the middle of all kinds a noise. Whenever you got a party, Mr. Loman, you just tell me and I'll put you back here. Y'know, there's a lotta people they don't like it private, because when they go out they like to see a lotta action around them because they're sick and tired to stay in the house by theirself. But I know you, you ain't from Hackensack. You know what I mean?

HAPPY, *sitting down:* So how's it coming, Stanley?

STANLEY: Ah, it's a dog's life. I only wish during the war they'd a took me in the Army. I coulda been dead by now.

HAPPY: My brother's back, Stanley.

STANLEY: Oh, he come back, heh? From the Far West.

HAPPY: Yeah, big cattle man, my brother, so treat him right. And my father's coming too.

STANLEY: Oh, your father too!

HAPPY: You got a couple of nice lobsters?

STANLEY: Hundred per cent, big.

HAPPY: I want them with the claws.

STANLEY: Don't worry, I don't give you no mice. *Happy laughs.* How about some wine? It'll put a head on the meal.

HAPPY: No. You remember, Stanley, that recipe I brought you from overseas? With the champagne in it?

STANLEY: Oh, yeah, sure. I still got it tacked up yet in the kitchen. But that'll have to cost a buck apiece anyways.

HAPPY: That's all right.

STANLEY: What'd you, hit a number or somethin'?

HAPPY: No, it's a little celebration. My brother is—I think he pulled off a big deal today. I think we're going into business together.

STANLEY: Great! That's the best for you. Because a family business, you know what I mean?—that's the best.

HAPPY: That's what I think.

STANLEY: 'Cause what's the difference? Somebody steals? It's in the family. Know what I mean? *Sotto voce:* Like this bartender here. The boss is goin' crazy what kinda leak he's got in the cash register. You put it in but it don't come out.

HAPPY, *raising his head:* Sh!

STANLEY: What?

HAPPY: You notice I wasn't lookin' right or left, was I?

STANLEY: No.
HAPPY: And my eyes are closed.
STANLEY: So what's the—?
HAPPY: Strudel's comin'.
STANLEY, *catching on, looks around:* Ah, no, there's no—

He breaks off as a furred, lavishly dressed girl enters and sits at the next table. Both follow her with their eyes.

STANLEY: Geez, how'd ya know?
HAPPY: I got radar or something. *Staring directly at her profile:* Oooooooo . . . Stanley.
STANLEY: I think that's for you, Mr. Loman.
HAPPY: Look at that mouth. Oh, God. And the binoculars.
STANLEY: Geez, you got a life, Mr. Loman.
HAPPY: Wait on her.
STANLEY, *going to the girl's table:* Would you like a menu, ma'am?
GIRL: I'm expecting someone, but I'd like a—
HAPPY: Why don't you bring her—excuse me, miss, do you mind? I sell champagne, and I'd like you to try my brand. Bring her a champagne, Stanley.
GIRL: That's awfully nice of you.
HAPPY: Don't mention it. It's all company money. *He laughs.*
GIRL: That's a charming product to be selling, isn't it?
HAPPY: Oh, gets to be like everything else. Selling is selling, y'know.
GIRL: I suppose.
HAPPY: You don't happen to sell, do you?
GIRL: No, I don't sell.
HAPPY: Would you object to a compliment from a stranger? You ought to be on a magazine cover.
GIRL, *looking at him a little archly:* I have been.

Stanley comes in with a glass of champagne.

HAPPY: What'd I say before, Stanley? You see? She's a cover girl.
STANLEY: Oh, I could see, I could see.
HAPPY, *to the Girl:* What magazine?
GIRL: Oh, a lot of them. *She takes the drink.* Thank you.

HAPPY: You [illegible] what th[illegible]ay [illegible]rance, don't you? "Champagne is the drink [illegible] c[illegible]plexion"—Hya, Biff!

Biff has entered an[illegible] with Happy.

BIFF: Hello, kid. Sorry I'm late.
HAPPY: I just got here. Uh, Miss—?
GIRL: Forsythe.
HAPPY: Miss Forsythe, this is my brother.
BIFF: Is Dad here?
HAPPY: His name is Biff. You might've hear[illegible] him. Great football player.
GIRL: Really? What team?
HAPPY: Are you familiar with football?
GIRL: No, I'm afraid I'm not.
HAPPY: Biff is quarterback with the New Y[illegible]k Giants.
GIRL: Well, that is nice, isn't it? *She drink[illegible]*
HAPPY: Good health.
GIRL: I'm happy to meet you.
HAPPY: That's my name. Hap. It's real[illegible]y Harold, but at West Point they called me Happy.
GIRL, *now really impressed:* Oh, I see. How do you do? *She turns her profile.*
BIFF: Isn't Dad coming?
HAPPY: You want her?
BIFF: Oh, I could never make that.
HAPPY: I remember the time that idea would never come into your head. Where's the old confidence, Biff?
BIFF: I just saw Oliver—
HAPPY: Wait a minute. I've got to see that old confidence again. Do you want her? She's on call.
BIFF: Oh, no. *He turns to look at the Girl.*
HAPPY: I'm telling you. Watch this. *Turning to the Girl:* Honey? *She turns to him.* Are you busy?
GIRL: Well, I am . . . but I could make a phone call.
HAPPY: Do that, will you, honey? And see if you can get a friend. We'll be here for a while. Biff is one of the greatest football players in the country.
GIRL, *standing up:* Well, I'm certainly happy to meet you.
HAPPY: Come back soon.
GIRL: I'll try.

HAPPY: Don't try, honey, try hard.

The Girl exits. Stanley follows, shaking his head in bewildered admiration.

HAPPY: Isn't that a shame now? A beautiful girl like that? That's why I can't get married. There's not a good woman in a thousand. New York is loaded with them, kid!

BIFF: Hap, look—

HAPPY: I told you she was on call!

BIFF, *strangely unnerved:* Cut it out, will ya? I want to say something to you.

HAPPY: Did you see Oliver?

BIFF: I saw him all right. Now look, I want to tell Dad a couple of things and I want you to help me.

HAPPY: What? Is he going to back you?

BIFF: Are you crazy? You're out of your goddam head, you know that?

HAPPY: Why? What happened?

BIFF, *breathlessly:* I did a terrible thing today, Hap. It's been the strangest day I ever went through. I'm all numb, I swear.

HAPPY: You mean he wouldn't see you?

BIFF: Well, I waited six hours for him, see? All day. Kept sending my name in. Even tried to date his secretary so she'd get me to him, but no soap.

HAPPY: Because you're not showin' the old confidence, Biff. He remembered you, didn't he?

BIFF, *stopping Happy with a gesture:* Finally, about five o'clock, he comes out. Didn't remember who I was or anything. I felt like such an idiot, Hap.

HAPPY: Did you tell him my Florida idea?

BIFF: He walked away. I saw him for one minute. I got so mad I could've torn the walls down! How the hell did I ever get the idea I was a salesman there? I even believed myself that I'd been a salesman for him! And then he gave me one look and—I realized what a ridiculous lie my whole life has been! We've been talking in a dream for fifteen years. I was a shipping clerk.

HAPPY: What'd you do?

BIFF, *with great tension and wonder:* Well, he left, see. And the secretary went out. I was all alone in the waiting-room. I

don't know what came over me, Hap. The next thing I know I'm in his office—paneled walls, everything. I can't explain it. I—Hap, I took his fountain pen.

HAPPY: Geez, did he catch you?

BIFF: I ran out. I ran down all eleven flights. I ran and ran and ran.

HAPPY: That was an awful dumb—what'd you do that for?

BIFF, *agonized:* I don't know, I just—wanted to take something, I don't know. You gotta help me, Hap, I'm gonna tell Pop.

HAPPY: You crazy? What for?

BIFF: Hap, he's got to understand that I'm not the man somebody lends that kind of money to. He thinks I've been spiting him all these years and it's eating him up.

HAPPY: That's just it. You tell him something nice.

BIFF: I can't.

HAPPY: Say you got a lunch date with Oliver tomorrow.

BIFF: So what do I do tomorrow?

HAPPY: You leave the house tomorrow and come back at night and say Oliver is thinking it over. And he thinks it over for a couple of weeks, and gradually it fades away and nobody's the worse.

BIFF: But it'll go on forever!

HAPPY: Dad is never so happy as when he's looking forward to something!

Willy enters.

HAPPY: Hello, scout!

WILLY: Gee, I haven't been here in years!

Stanley has followed Willy in and sets a chair for him. Stanley starts off but Happy stops him.

HAPPY: Stanley!

Stanley stands by, waitng for an order.

BIFF, *going to Willy with guilt, as to an invalid:* Sit down, Pop. You want a drink?

WILLY: Sure, I don't mind.

BIFF: Let's get a load on.

WILLY: You look worried.

BIFF: N-no. *To Stanley:* Scotch all around. Make it doubles.
STANLEY: Doubles, right. *He goes.*
WILLY: You had a couple already, didn't you?
BIFF: Just a couple, yeah.
WILLY: Well, what happened, boy? *Nodding affirmatively, with a smile:* Everything go all right?
BIFF, *takes a breath, then reaches out and grasps Willy's hand:* Pal . . . *He is smiling bravely, and Willy is smiling too.* I had an experience today.
HAPPY: Terrific, Pop.
WILLY: That so? What happened?
BIFF, *high, slightly alcoholic, above the earth:* I'm going to tell you everything from first to last. It's been a strange day. *Silence. He looks around, composes himself as best he can, but his breath keeps breaking the rhythm of his voice.* I had to wait quite a while for him, and—
WILLY: Oliver?
BIFF: Yeah, Oliver. All day, as a matter of cold fact. And a lot of —instances—facts, Pop, facts about my life came back to me. Who was it, Pop? Who ever said I was a salesman with Oliver?
WILLY: Well, you were.
BIFF: No, Dad, I was a shipping clerk.
WILLY: But you were practically—
BIFF, *with determination:* Dad, I don't know who said it first, but I was never a salesman for Bill Oliver.
WILLY: What're you talking about?
BIFF: Let's hold on to the facts tonight, Pop. We're not going to get anywhere bullin' around. I was a shipping clerk.
WILLY, *angrily:* All right, now listen to me—
BIFF: Why don't you let me finish?
WILLY: I'm not interested in stories about the past or any crap of that kind because the woods are burning, boys, you understand? There's a big blaze going on all around. I was fired today.
BIFF, *shocked:* How could you be?
WILLY: I was fired, and I'm looking for a little good news to tell your mother, because the woman has waited and the woman has suffered. The gist of it is that I haven't got a story left in my head, Biff. So don't give me a lecture about

facts and aspects. I am not interested. Now what've you got to say to me?

Stanley enters with three drinks. They wait until he leaves.

WILLY: Did you see Oliver?

BIFF: Jesus, Dad!

WILLY: You mean you didn't go up there?

HAPPY: Sure he went up there.

BIFF: I did. I—saw him. How could they fire you?

WILLY, *on the edge of his chair:* What kind of a welcome did he give you?

BIFF: He won't even let you work on commission?

WILLY: I'm out! *Driving:* So tell me, he gave you a warm welcome?

HAPPY: Sure, Pop, sure!

BIFF, *driven:* Well, it was kind of—

WILLY: I was wondering if he'd remember you. *To Happy:* Imagine, man doesn't see him for ten, twelve years and gives him that kind of a welcome!

HAPPY: Damn right!

BIFF, *trying to return to the offensive:* Pop, look—

WILLY: You know why he remembered you, don't you? Because you impressed him in those days.

BIFF: Let's talk quietly and get this down to the facts, huh?

WILLY, *as though Biff had been interrupting:* Well, what happened? It's great news, Biff. Did he take you into his office or'd you talk in the waiting-room?

BIFF: Well, he came in, see, and—

WILLY, *with a big smile:* What'd he say? Betcha he threw his arm around you.

BIFF: Well, he kinda—

WILLY: He's a fine man. *To Happy:* Very hard man to see, y'know.

HAPPY, *agreeing:* Oh, I know.

WILLY, *to Biff:* Is that where you had the drinks?

BIFF: Yeah, he gave me a couple of—no, no!

HAPPY, *cutting in:* He told him my Florida idea.

WILLY: Don't interrupt. *To Biff:* How'd he react to the Florida idea?

BIFF: Dad, will you give me a minute to explain?

WILLY: I've been waiting for you to explain since I sat down here! What happened? He took you into his office and what?

BIFF: Well—I talked. And—and he listened, see.

WILLY: Famous for the way he listens, y'know. What was his answer?

BIFF: His answer was— *He breaks off, suddenly angry.* Dad, you're not letting me tell you what I want to tell you!

WILLY, *accusing, angered:* You didn't see him, did you?

BIFF: I did see him!

WILLY: What'd you insult him or something? You insulted him, didn't you?

BIFF: Listen, will you let me out of it, will you just let me out of it!

HAPPY: What the hell!

WILLY: Tell me what happened!

BIFF, *to Happy:* I can't talk to him!

A single trumpet note jars the ear. The light of green leaves stains the house, which holds the air of night and a dream. Young Bernard enters and knocks on the door of the house.

YOUNG BERNARD, *frantically:* Mrs. Loman, Mrs. Loman!

HAPPY: Tell him what happened!

BIFF, *to Happy:* Shut up and leave me alone!

WILLY: No, no! You had to go and flunk math!

BIFF: What math? What're you talking about?

YOUNG BERNARD: Mrs. Loman, Mrs. Loman!

Linda appears in the house, as of old.

WILLY, *wildly:* Math, math, math!

BIFF: Take it easy, Pop!

YOUNG BERNARD: Mrs. Loman!

WILLY, *furiously:* If you hadn't flunked you'd've been set by now!

BIFF: Now, look, I'm gonna tell you what happened, and you're going to listen to me.

YOUNG BERNARD: Mrs. Loman!

BIFF: I waited six hours—

HAPPY: What the hell are you saying?

BIFF: I kept sending in my name but he wouldn't see me. So finally he . . . *He continues unheard as light fades low on the restaurant.*

YOUNG BERNARD: Biff flunked math!

LINDA: No!

YOUNG BERNARD: Birnbaum flunked him! They won't graduate him!

LINDA: But they have to. He's gotta go to the university. Where is he? Biff! Biff!

YOUNG BERNARD: No, he left. He went to Grand Central.

LINDA: Grand— You mean he went to Boston!

YOUNG BERNARD: Is Uncle Willy in Boston?

LINDA: Oh, maybe Willy can talk to the teacher. Oh, the poor, poor boy!

Light on house area snaps out.

BIFF, *at the table, now audible, holding up a gold fountain pen:* . . . so I'm washed up with Oliver, you understand? Are you listening to me?

WILLY, *at a loss:* Yeah, sure. If you hadn't flunked—

BIFF: Flunked what? What're you talking about?

WILLY: Don't blame everything on me! I didn't flunk math—you did! What pen?

HAPPY: That was awful dumb, Biff, a pen like that is worth—

WILLY, *seeing the pen for the first time:* You took Oliver's pen?

BIFF, *weakening:* Dad, I just explained it to you.

WILLY: You stole Bill Oliver's fountain pen!

BIFF: I didn't exactly steal it! That's just what I've been explaining to you!

HAPPY: He had it in his hand and just then Oliver walked in, so he got nervous and stuck it in his pocket!

WILLY: My God, Biff!

BIFF: I never intended to do it, Dad!

OPERATOR'S VOICE: Standish Arms, good evening!

WILLY, *shouting:* I'm not in my room!

BIFF, *frightened:* Dad, what's the matter? *He and Happy stand up.*

OPERATOR: Ringing Mr. Loman for you!

WILLY: I'm not there, stop it!

BIFF, *horrified, gets down on one knee before Willy:* Dad, I'll make

good, I'll make good. *Willy tries to get to his feet. Biff holds him down.* Sit down now.

WILLY: No, you're no good, you're no good for anything.

BIFF: I am, Dad, I'll find something else, you understand? Now don't worry about anything. *He holds up Willy's face:* Talk to me, Dad.

OPERATOR: Mr. Loman does not answer. Shall I page him?

WILLY, *attempting to stand, as though to rush and silence the Operator:* No, no, no!

HAPPY: He'll strike something, Pop.

WILLY: No, no . . .

BIFF, *desperately, standing over Willy:* Pop, listen! Listen to me! I'm telling you something good. Oliver talked to his partner about the Florida idea. You listening? He—he talked to his partner, and he came to me . . . I'm going to be all right, you hear? Dad, listen to me, he said it was just a question of the amount!

WILLY: Then you . . . got it?

HAPPY: He's gonna be terrific, Pop!

WILLY, *trying to stand:* Then you got it, haven't you? You got it! You got it!

BIFF, *agonized, holds Willy down:* No, no. Look, Pop. I'm supposed to have lunch with them tomorrow. I'm just telling you this so you'll know that I can still make an impression, Pop. And I'll make good somewhere, but I can't go tomorrow, see?

WILLY: Why not? You simply—

BIFF: But the pen, Pop!

WILLY: You give it to him and tell him it was an oversight!

HAPPY: Sure, have lunch tomorrow!

BIFF: I can't say that—

WILLY: You were doing a crossword puzzle and accidentally used his pen!

BIFF: Listen, kid, I took those balls years ago, now I walk in with his fountain pen? That clinches it, don't you see? I can't face him like that! I'll try elsewhere.

PAGE'S VOICE: Paging Mr. Loman!

WILLY: Don't you want to be anything?

BIFF: Pop, how can I go back?

WILLY: You don't want to be anything, is that what's behind it?

BIFF, *now angry at Willy for not crediting his sympathy:* Don't take it that way! You think it was easy walking into that office after what I'd done to him? A team of horses couldn't have dragged me back to Bill Oliver!

WILLY: Then why'd you go?

BIFF: Why did I go? Why did I go! Look at you! Look at what's become of you!

Off left, The Woman laughs.

WILLY: Biff, you're going to go to that lunch tomorrow, or—

BIFF: I can't go. I've got no appointment!

HAPPY: Biff, for . . . !

WILLY: Are you spiting me?

BIFF: Don't take it that way! Goddammit!

WILLY, *strikes Biff and falters away from the table:* You rotten little louse! Are you spiting me?

THE WOMAN: Someone's at the door, Willy!

BIFF: I'm no good, can't you see what I am?

HAPPY, *separating them:* Hey, you're in a restaurant! Now cut it out, both of you? *The girls enter.* Hello, girls, sit down.

The Woman laughs, off left.

MISS FORSYTHE: I guess we might as well. This is Letta.

THE WOMAN: Willy, are you going to wake up?

BIFF, *ignoring Willy:* How're ya, miss, sit down. What do you drink?

MISS FORSYTHE: Letta might not be able to stay long.

LETTA: I gotta get up very early tomorrow. I got jury duty. I'm so excited! Were you fellows ever on a jury?

BIFF: No, but I been in front of them! *The girls laugh.* This is my father.

LETTA: Isn't he cute? Sit down with us, Pop.

HAPPY: Sit him down, Biff!

BIFF, *going to him:* Come on, slugger, drink us under the table. To hell with it! Come on, sit down, pal.

On Biff's last insistence, Willy is about to sit.

THE WOMAN, *now urgently:* Willy, are you going to answer the door!

The Woman's call pulls Willy back. He starts right, befuddled.

BIFF: Hey, where are you going?
WILLY: Open the door.
BIFF: The door?
WILLY: The washroom . . . the door . . . where's the door?
BIFF, *leading Willy to the left:* Just go straight down.

Willy moves left.

THE WOMAN: Willy, Willy, are you going to get up, get up, get up, get up?

Willy exits left.

LETTA: I think it's sweet you bring your daddy along.
MISS FORSYTHE: Oh, he isn't really your father!
BIFF, *at left, turning to her resentfully:* Miss Forsythe, you've just seen a prince walk by. A fine, troubled prince. A hard-working, unappreciated prince. A pal, you understand? A good companion. Always for his boys.
LETTA: That's so sweet.
HAPPY: Well, girls, what's the program? We're wasting time. Come on, Biff. Gather round. Where would you like to go?
BIFF: Why don't you do something for him?
HAPPY: Me!
BIFF: Don't you give a damn for him, Hap?
HAPPY: What're you talking about? I'm the one who—
BIFF: I sense it, you don't give a good goddam about him. *He takes the rolled-up hose from his pocket and puts it on the table in front of Happy.* Look what I found in the cellar, for Christ's sake. How can you bear to let it go on?
HAPPY: Me? Who goes away? Who runs off and—
BIFF: Yeah, but he doesn't mean anything to you. You could help him—I can't! Don't you understand what I'm talking about? He's going to kill himself, don't you know that?
HAPPY: Don't I know it! Me!
BIFF: Hap, help him! Jesus . . . help him . . . Help me, help me, I can't bear to look at his face! *Ready to weep, he hurries out, up right.*
HAPPY, *starting after him:* Where are you going?
MISS FORSYTHE: What's he so mad about?

HAPPY: Come on, girls, we'll catch up with him.

MISS FORSYTHE, *as Happy pushes her out:* Say, I don't like that temper of his!

HAPPY: He's just a little overstrung, he'll be all right!

WILLY, *off left, as The Woman laughs:* Don't answer! Don't answer!

LETTA: Don't you want to tell your father—

HAPPY: No, that's not my father. He's just a guy. Come on, we'll catch Biff, and, honey, we're going to paint this town! Stanley, where's the check! Hey, Stanley!

They exit. Stanley looks toward left.

STANLEY, *calling to Happy indignantly:* Mr. Loman! Mr. Loman!

Stanley picks up a chair and follows them off. Knocking is heard off left. The Woman enters, laughing. Willy follows her. She is in a black slip; he is buttoning his shirt. Raw, sensuous music accompanies their speech.

WILLY: Will you stop laughing? Will you stop?

THE WOMAN: Aren't you going to answer the door? He'll wake the whole hotel.

WILLY: I'm not expecting anybody.

THE WOMAN: Whyn't you have another drink, honey, and stop being so damn self-centered?

WILLY: I'm so lonely.

THE WOMAN: You know you ruined me, Willy? From now on, whenever you come to the office, I'll see that you go right through to the buyers. No waiting at my desk any more, Willy. You ruined me.

WILLY: That's nice of you to say that.

THE WOMAN: Gee, you are self-centered! Why so sad? You are the saddest, self-centeredest soul I ever did see-saw. *She laughs. He kisses her.* Come on inside, drummer boy. It's silly to be dressing in the middle of the night. *As knocking is heard:* Aren't you going to answer the door?

WILLY: They're knocking on the wrong door.

THE WOMAN: But I felt the knocking. And he heard us talking in here. Maybe the hotel's on fire!

WILLY, *his terror rising:* It's a mistake.

THE WOMAN: Then tell him to go away!

WILLY: There's nobody there.

THE WOMAN: It's getting on my nerves, Willy. There's somebody standing out there and it's getting on my nerves!

WILLY, *pushing her away from him:* All right, stay in the bathroom here, and don't come out. I think there's a law in Massachusetts about it, so don't come out. It may be that new room clerk. He looked very mean. So don't come out. It's a mistake, there's no fire.

The knocking is heard again. He takes a few steps away from her, and she vanishes into the wing. The light follows him, and now he is facing Young Biff, who carries a suitcase. Biff steps toward him. The music is gone.

BIFF: Why didn't you answer?

WILLY: Biff! What are you doing in Boston?

BIFF: Why didn't you answer? I've been knocking for five minutes, I called you on the phone—

WILLY: I just heard you. I was in the bathroom and had the door shut. Did anything happen home?

BIFF: Dad—I let you down.

WILLY: What do you mean?

BIFF: Dad . . .

WILLY: Biffo, what's this about? *Putting his arm around Biff:* Come on, let's go downstairs and get you a malted.

BIFF: Dad, I flunked math.

WILLY: Not for the term?

BIFF: The term. I haven't got enough credits to graduate.

WILLY: You mean to say Bernard wouldn't give you the answers?

BIFF: He did, he tried, but I only got a sixty-one.

WILLY: And they wouldn't give you four points?

BIFF: Birnbaum refused absolutely. I begged him, Pop, but he won't give me those points. You gotta talk to him before they close the school. Because if he saw the kind of man you are, and you just talked to him in your way, I'm sure he'd come through for me. The class came right before practice, see, and I didn't go enough. Would you talk to him? He'd like you, Pop. You know the way you could talk.

WILLY: You're on. We'll drive right back.

BIFF: Oh, Dad, good work! I'm sure he'll change it for you!

WILLY: Go downstairs and tell the clerk I'm checkin' out. Go right down.

BIFF: Yes, sir! See, the reason he hates me, Pop—one day he was late for class so I got up at the blackboard and imitated him. I crossed my eyes and talked with a lithp.

WILLY, *laughing:* You did? The kids like it?

BIFF: They nearly died laughing!

WILLY: Yeah? What'd you do?

BIFF: The thquare root of thixthy twee is . . . *Willy bursts out laughing; Biff joins him.* And in the middle of it he walked in!

Willy laughs and The Woman joins in offstage.

WILLY, *without hesitation:* Hurry downstairs and—

BIFF: Somebody in there?

WILLY: No, that was next door.

The Woman laughs offstage.

BIFF: Somebody got in your bathroom!

WILLY: No, it's the next room, there's a party—

THE WOMAN, *enters, laughing. She lisps this:* Can I come in? There's something in the bathtub, Willy, and it's moving!

Willy looks at Biff, who is staring open-mouthed and horrified at The Woman.

WILLY: Ah—you better go back to your room. They must be finished painting by now. They're painting her room so I let her take a shower here. Go back, go back . . . *He pushes her.*

THE WOMAN, *resisting:* But I've got to get dressed, Willy, I can't—

WILLY: Get out of here! Go back, go back . . . *Suddenly striving for the ordinary:* This is Miss Francis, Biff, she's a buyer. They're painting her room. Go back, Miss Francis, go back . . .

THE WOMAN: But my clothes, I can't go out naked in the hall!

WILLY, *pushing her offstage:* Get outa here! Go back, go back!

Biff slowly sits down on his suitcase as the argument continues offstage.

THE WOMAN: Where's my stockings? You promised me stockings, Willy!

WILLY: I have no stockings here!

THE WOMAN: You had two boxes of size nine sheers for me, and I want them!

WILLY: Here, for God's sake, will you get outa here!

THE WOMAN, *enters holding a box of stockings:* I just hope there's nobody in the hall. That's all I hope. *To Biff:* Are you football or baseball?

BIFF: Football.

THE WOMAN, *angry, humiliated:* That's me too. G'night. *She snatches her clothes from Willy, and walks out.*

WILLY, *after a pause:* Well, better get going. I want to get to the school first thing in the morning. Get my suits out of the closet. I'll get my valise. *Biff doesn't move.* What's the matter? *Biff remains motionless, tears falling.* She's a buyer. Buys for J. H. Simmons. She lives down the hall—they're painting. You don't imagine— *He breaks off. After a pause:* Now listen, pal, she's just a buyer. She sees merchandise in her room and they have to keep it looking just so . . . *Pause. Assuming command:* All right, get my suits. *Biff doesn't move.* Now stop crying and do as I say. I gave you an order. Biff, I gave you an order! Is that what you do when I give you an order? How dare you cry! *Putting his arm around Biff:* Now look, Biff, when you grow up you'll understand about these things. You mustn't—you mustn't overemphasize a thing like this. I'll see Birnbaum first thing in the morning.

BIFF: Never mind.

WILLY, *getting down beside Biff:* Never mind! He's going to give you those points. I'll see to it.

BIFF: He wouldn't listen to you.

WILLY: He certainly will listen to me. You need those points for the U. of Virginia.

BIFF: I'm not going there.

WILLY: Heh? If I can't get him to change that mark you'll make it up in summer school. You've got all summer to—

BIFF, *his weeping breaking from him:* Dad . . .

WILLY, *infected by it:* Oh, my boy . . .

BIFF: Dad . . .

WILLY: She's nothing to me, Biff. I was lonely, I was terribly lonely.

BIFF: You—you gave her Mama's stockings! *His tears break through and he rises to go.*

WILLY, *grabbing for Biff:* I gave you an order!

BIFF: Don't touch me, you—liar!

WILLY: Apologize for that!

BIFF: You fake! You phony little fake! You fake! *Overcome, he turns quickly and weeping fully goes out with his suitcase. Willy is left on the floor on his knees.*

WILLY: I gave you an order! Biff, come back here or I'll beat you! Come back here! I'll whip you!

Stanley comes quickly in from the right and stands in front of Willy.

WILLY, *shouts at Stanley:* I gave you an order . . .

STANLEY: Hey, let's pick it up, pick it up, Mr. Loman. *He helps Willy to his feet.* Your boys left with the chippies. They said they'll see you home.

A second waiter watches some distance away.

WILLY: But we were supposed to have dinner together.

Music is heard, Willy's theme.

STANLEY: Can you make it?

WILLY: I'll—sure, I can make it. *Suddenly concerned about his clothes:* Do I—I look all right?

STANLEY: Sure, you look all right. *He flicks a speck off Willy's lapel.*

WILLY: Here—here's a dollar.

STANLEY: Oh, your son paid me. It's all right.

WILLY, *putting it in Stanley's hand:* No, take it. You're a good boy.

STANLEY: Oh, no, you don't have to . . .

WILLY: Here—here's some more, I don't need it any more. *After a slight pause:* Tell me—is there a seed store in the neighborhood?

STANLEY: Seeds? You mean like to plant?

As Willy turns, Stanley slips the money back into his jacket pocket.

WILLY: Yes. Carrots, peas . . .

STANLEY: Well, there's hardware stores on Sixth Avenue, but it may be too late now.

WILLY, *anxiously:* Oh, I'd better hurry. I've got to get some seeds. *He starts off to the right.* I've got to get some seeds, right away. Nothing's planted. I don't have a thing in the ground.

Willy hurries out as the light goes down. Stanley moves over to the right after him, watches him off. The other waiter has been staring at Willy.

STANLEY, *to the waiter:* Well, whatta you looking at?

The waiter picks up the chairs and moves off right. Stanley takes the table and follows him. The light fades on this area. There is a long pause, the sound of the flute coming over. The light gradually rises on the kitchen, which is empty. Happy appears at the door of the house, followed by Biff. Happy is carrying a large bunch of long-stemmed roses. He enters the kitchen, looks around for Linda. Not seeing her, he turns to Biff, who is just outside the house door, and makes a gesture with his hands, indicating "Not here, I guess." He looks into the living-room and freezes. Inside, Linda, unseen, is seated, Willy's coat on her lap. She rises ominously and quietly and moves toward Happy, who backs up into the kitchen, afraid.

HAPPY: Hey, what're you doing up? *Linda says nothing but moves toward him implacably.* Where's Pop? *He keeps backing to the right, and now Linda is in full view in the doorway to the living-room.* Is he sleeping?

LINDA: Where were you?

HAPPY, *trying to laugh it off:* We met two girls, Mom, very fine types. Here, we brought you some flowers. *Offering them to her:* Put them in your room, Ma.

She knocks them to the floor at Biff's feet. He has now come inside and closed the door behind him. She stares at Biff, silent.

HAPPY: Now what'd you do that for? Mom, I want you to have some flowers—

LINDA, *cutting Happy off, violently to Biff:* Don't you care whether he lives or dies?

HAPPY, *going to the stairs:* Come upstairs, Biff.

BIFF, *with a flare of disgust, to Happy:* Go away from me! *To Linda:* What do you mean, lives or dies? Nobody's dying around here, pal.

LINDA: Get out of my sight! Get out of here!

BIFF: I wanna see the boss.

LINDA: You're not going near him!

BIFF: Where is he? *He moves into the living-room and Linda follows.*

LINDA, *shouting after Biff:* You invite him for dinner. He looks forward to it all day—*Biff appears in his parents' bedroom, looks around, and exits*—and then you desert him there. There's no stranger you'd do that to!

HAPPY: Why? He had a swell time with us. Listen, when I—*Linda comes back into the kitchen*—desert him I hope I don't outlive the day!

LINDA: Get out of here!

HAPPY: Now look, Mom . . .

LINDA: Did you have to go to women tonight? You and your lousy rotten whores!

Biff re-enters the kitchen.

HAPPY: Mom, all we did was follow Biff around trying to cheer him up! *To Biff:* Boy, what a night you gave me!

LINDA: Get out of here, both of you, and don't come back! I don't want you tormenting him any more. Go on now, get your things together! *To Biff:* You can sleep in his apartment. *She starts to pick up the flowers and stops herself.* Pick up this stuff, I'm not your maid any more. Pick it up, you bum, you!

Happy turns his back to her in refusal. Biff slowly moves over and gets down on his knees, picking up the flowers.

LINDA: You're a pair of animals! Not one, not another living soul would have had the cruelty to walk out on that man in a restaurant!

BIFF, *not looking at her:* Is that what he said?

LINDA: He didn't have to say anything. He was so humiliated he nearly limped when he came in.

HAPPY: But, Mom, he had a great time with us—

BIFF, *cutting him off violently:* Shut up!

Without another word, Happy goes upstairs.

LINDA: You! You didn't even go in to see if he was all right!
BIFF, *still on the floor in front of Linda, the flowers in his hand; with self-loathing:* No. Didn't. Didn't do a damned thing. How do you like that, heh? Left him babbling in a toilet.
LINDA: You louse. You . . .
BIFF: Now you hit it on the nose! *He gets up, throws the flowers in the wastebasket.* The scum of the earth, and you're looking at him!
LINDA: Get out of here!
BIFF: I gotta talk to the boss, Mom. Where is he?
LINDA: You're not going near him. Get out of this house!
BIFF, *with absolute assurance, determination:* No. We're gonna have an abrupt conversation, him and me.
LINDA: You're not talking to him!

Hammering is heard from outside the house, off right. Biff turns toward the noise.

LINDA, *suddenly pleading:* Will you please leave him alone?
BIFF: What's he doing out there?
LINDA: He's planting the garden!
BIFF, *quietly:* Now? Oh, my God!

Biff moves outside, Linda following. The light dies down on them and comes up on the center of the apron as Willy walks into it. He is carrying a flashlight, a hoe, and a handful of seed packets. He raps the top of the hoe sharply to fix it firmly, and then moves to the left, measuring off the distance with his foot. He holds the flashlight to look at the seed packets, reading off the instructions. He is in the blue of night.

WILLY: Carrots . . . quarter-inch apart. Rows . . . one-foot rows. *He measures it off.* One foot. *He puts down a package and measures off.* Beets. *He puts down another package and measures again.* Lettuce. *He reads the package, puts it down.* One foot— *He breaks off as Ben appears at the right and moves slowly down to him.* What a proposition, ts, ts. Terrific, terrific. 'Cause she's suffered, Ben, the woman has suffered. You understand me? A man can't go out the way he came in,

Ben, a man has got to add up to something. You can't, you can't— *Ben moves toward him as though to interrupt.* You gotta consider, now. Don't answer so quick. Remember, it's a guaranteed twenty-thousand-dollar proposition. Now look, Ben, I want you to go through the ins and outs of this thing with me. I've got nobody to talk to, Ben, and the woman has suffered, you hear me?

BEN, *standing still, considering:* What's the proposition?

WILLY: It's twenty thousand dollars on the barrelhead. Guaranteed, gilt-edged, you understand?

BEN: You don't want to make a fool of yourself. They might not honor the policy.

WILLY: How can they dare refuse? Didn't I work like a coolie to meet every premium on the nose? And now they don't pay off! Impossible!

BEN: It's called a cowardly thing, William.

WILLY: Why? Does it take more guts to stand here the rest of my life ringing up a zero?

BEN, *yielding:* That's a point, William. *He moves, thinking, turns.* And twenty thousand—that *is* something one can feel with the hand, it is there.

WILLY, *now assured, with rising power:* Oh, Ben, that's the whole beauty of it! I see it like a diamond, shining in the dark, hard and rough, that I can pick up and touch in my hand. Not like—like an appointment! This would not be another damned-fool appointment, Ben, and it changes all the aspects. Because he thinks I'm nothing, see, and so he spites me. But the funeral— *Straightening up:* Ben, that funeral will be massive! They'll come from Maine, Massachusetts, Vermont, New Hampshire! All the old-timers with the strange license plates—that boy will be thunder-struck, Ben, because he never realized—I am known! Rhode Island, New York, New Jersey—I am known, Ben, and he'll see it with his eyes once and for all. He'll see what I am, Ben! He's in for a shock, that boy!

BEN, *coming down to the edge of the garden:* He'll call you a coward.

WILLY, *suddenly fearful:* No, that would be terrible.

BEN: Yes. And a damned fool.

WILLY: No, no, he mustn't, I won't have that! *He is broken and desperate.*
BEN: He'll hate you, William.

The gay music of the Boys is heard.

WILLY: Oh, Ben, how do we get back to all the great times? Used to be so full of light, and comradeship, the sleigh-riding in winter, and the ruddiness on his cheeks. And always some kind of good news coming up, always something nice coming up ahead. And never even let me carry the valises in the house, and simonizing, simonizing that little red car! Why, why can't I give him something and not have him hate me?
BEN: Let me think about it. *He glances at his watch.* I still have a little time. Remarkable proposition, but you've got to be sure you're not making a fool of yourself.

Ben drifts off upstage and goes out of sight. Biff comes down from the left.

WILLY, *suddenly conscious of Biff, turns and looks up at him, then begins picking up the packages of seeds in confusion:* Where the hell is that seed? *Indignantly:* You can't see nothing out here! They boxed in the whole goddam neighborhood!
BIFF: There are people all around here. Don't you realize that?
WILLY: I'm busy. Don't bother me.
BIFF, *taking the hoe from Willy:* I'm saying good-by to you, Pop. *Willy looks at him, silent, unable to move.* I'm not coming back any more.
WILLY: You're not going to see Oliver tomorrow?
BIFF: I've got no appointment, Dad.
WILLY: He put his arm around you, and you've got no appointment?
BIFF: Pop, get this now, will you? Everytime I've left it's been a fight that sent me out of here. Today I realized something about myself and I tried to explain it to you and I—I think I'm just not smart enough to make any sense out of it for you. To hell with whose fault it is or anything like that. *He takes Willy's arm.* Let's just wrap it up, heh? Come on in, we'll tell Mom. *He gently tries to pull Willy to left.*

WILLY, *frozen, immobile, with guilt in his voice:* No, I don't want to see her.

BIFF: Come on! *He pulls again, and Willy tries to pull away.*

WILLY, *highly nervous:* No, no, I don't want to see her.

BIFF, *tries to look into Willy's face, as if to find the answer there:* Why don't you want to see her?

WILLY, *more harshly now:* Don't bother me, will you?

BIFF: What do you mean, you don't want to see her? You don't want them calling you yellow, do you? This isn't your fault; it's me, I'm a bum. Now come inside! *Willy strains to get away.* Did you hear what I said to you?

Willy pulls away and quickly goes by himself into the house. Biff follows.

LINDA, *to Willy:* Did you plant, dear?

BIFF, *at the door, to Linda:* All right, we had it out. I'm going and I'm not writing any more.

LINDA, *going to Willy in the kitchen:* I think that's the best way, dear. 'Cause there's no use drawing it out, you'll just never get along.

Willy doesn't respond.

BIFF: People ask where I am and what I'm doing, you don't know, and you don't care. That way it'll be off your mind and you can start brightening up again. All right? That clears it, doesn't it? *Willy is silent, and Biff goes to him.* You gonna wish me luck, scout? *He extends his hand.* What do you say?

LINDA: Shake his hand, Willy.

WILLY, *turning to her, seething with hurt:* There's no necessity to mention the pen at all, y'know.

BIFF, *gently:* I've got no appointment, Dad.

WILLY, *erupting fiercely:* He put his arm around . . . ?

BIFF: Dad, you're never going to see what I am, so what's the use of arguing? If I strike oil I'll send you a check. Meantime forget I'm alive.

WILLY, *to Linda:* Spite, see?

BIFF: Shake hands, Dad.

WILLY: Not my hand.

BIFF: I was hoping not to go this way.
WILLY: Well, this is the way you're going. Good-by.

Biff looks at him a moment, then turns sharply and goes to the stairs.

WILLY, *stops him with:* May you rot in hell if you leave this house!
BIFF, *turning:* Exactly what is it that you want from me?
WILLY: I want you to know, on the train, in the mountains, in the valleys, wherever you go, that you cut down your life for spite!
BIFF: No, no.
WILLY: Spite, spite, is the word of your undoing! And when you're down and out, remember what did it. When you're rotting somewhere beside the railroad tracks, remember, and don't you dare blame it on me!
BIFF: I'm not blaming it on you!
WILLY: I won't take the rap for this, you hear?

Happy comes down the stairs and stands on the bottom step, watching.

BIFF: That's just what I'm telling you!
WILLY, *sinking into a chair at the table, with full accusation:* You're trying to put a knife in me—don't think I don't know what you're doing!
BIFF: All right, phony! Then let's lay it on the line. *He whips the rubber tube out of his pocket and puts it on the table.*
HAPPY: You crazy—
LINDA: Biff! *She moves to grab the hose, but Biff holds it down with his hand.*
BIFF: Leave it there! Don't move it!
WILLY, *not looking at it:* What is that?
BIFF: You know goddam well what that is.
WILLY, *caged, wanting to escape:* I never saw that.
BIFF: You saw it. The mice didn't bring it into the cellar! What is this supposed to do, make a hero out of you? This supposed to make me sorry for you?
WILLY: Never heard of it.
BIFF: There'll be no pity for you, you hear it? No pity!
WILLY, *to Linda:* You hear the spite!

BIFF: No, you're going to hear the truth—what you are and what I am!

LINDA: Stop it!

WILLY: Spite!

HAPPY, *coming down toward Biff:* You cut it now!

BIFF, *to Happy:* The man don't know who we are! The man is gonna know! *To Willy:* We never told the truth for ten minutes in this house!

HAPPY: We always told the truth!

BIFF, *turning on him:* You big blow, are you the assistant buyer? You're one of the two assistants to the assistant, aren't you?

HAPPY: Well, I'm practically—

BIFF: You're practically full of it! We all are! And I'm through with it. *To Willy:* Now hear this, Willy, this is me.

WILLY: I know you!

BIFF: You know why I had no address for three months? I stole a suit in Kansas City and I was in jail. *To Linda, who is sobbing:* Stop crying. I'm through with it.

Linda turns away from them, her hands covering her face.

WILLY: I suppose that's my fault!

BIFF: I stole myself out of every good job since high school!

WILLY: And whose fault is that?

BIFF: And I never got anywhere because you blew me so full of hot air I could never stand taking orders from anybody! That's whose fault it is!

WILLY: I hear that!

LINDA: Don't, Biff!

BIFF: It's goddam time you heard that! I had to be boss big shot in two weeks, and I'm through with it!

WILLY: Then hang yourself! For spite, hang yourself!

BIFF: No! Nobody's hanging himself, Willy! I ran down eleven flights with a pen in my hand today. And suddenly I stopped, you hear me? And in the middle of that office building, do you hear this? I stopped in the middle of that building and I saw—the sky. I saw the things that I love in this world. The work and the food and time to sit and smoke. And I looked at the pen and said to myself, what the hell am I grabbing this for? Why am I trying to become what I don't want to be? What am I doing in an office, making a con-

temptuous, begging fool of myself, when all I want is out there, waiting for me the minute I say I know who I am! Why can't I say that, Willy? *He tries to make Willy face him, but Willy pulls away and moves to the left.*

WILLY, *with hatred, threateningly:* The door of your life is wide open!

BIFF: Pop! I'm a dime a dozen, and so are you!

WILLY, *turning on him now in an uncontrolled outburst:* I am not a dime a dozen! I am Willy Loman, and you are Biff Loman!

Biff starts for Willy, but is blocked by Happy. In his fury, Biff seems on the verge of attacking his father.

BIFF: I am not a leader of men, Willy, and neither are you. You were never anything but a hard-working drummer who landed in the ash can like all the rest of them! I'm one dollar an hour, Willy! I tried seven states and couldn't raise it. A buck an hour! Do you gather my meaning? I'm not bringing home any prizes any more, and you're going to stop waiting for me to bring them home!

WILLY, *directly to Biff:* You vengeful, spiteful mut!

Biff breaks from Happy. Willy, in fright, starts up the stairs. Biff grabs him.

BIFF, *at the peak of his fury:* Pop, I'm nothing! I'm nothing, Pop. Can't you understand that? There's no spite in it any more. I'm just what I am, that's all.

Biff's fury has spent itself, and he breaks down, sobbing, holding on to Willy, who dumbly fumbles for Biff's face.

WILLY, *astonished:* What're you doing? What're you doing? *To Linda:* Why is he crying?

BIFF, *crying, broken:* Will you let me go, for Christ's sake? Will you take that phony dream and burn it before something happens? *Struggling to contain himself, he pulls away and moves to the stairs.* I'll go in the morning. Put him—put him to bed. *Exhausted, Biff moves up the stairs to his room.*

WILLY, *after a long pause, astonished, elevated:* Isn't that—isn't that remarkable? Biff—he likes me!

LINDA: He loves you, Willy!

HAPPY, *deeply moved:* Always did, Pop.

WILLY: Oh, Biff! *Staring wildly:* He cried! Cried to me. *He is choking with his love, and now cries out his promise:* That boy—that boy is going to be magnificent!

Ben appears in the light just outside the kitchen.

BEN: Yes, outstanding, with twenty thousand behind him.

LINDA, *sensing the racing of his mind, fearfully, carefully:* Now come to bed, Willy. It's all settled now.

WILLY, *finding it difficult not to rush out of the house:* Yes, we'll sleep. Come on. Go to sleep, Hap.

BEN: And it does take a great kind of a man to crack the jungle.

In accents of dread, Ben's idyllic music starts up.

HAPPY, *his arm around Linda:* I'm getting married, Pop, don't forget it. I'm changing everything. I'm gonna run that department before the year is up. You'll see, Mom. *He kisses her.*

BEN: The jungle is dark but full of diamonds, Willy.

Willy turns, moves, listening to Ben.

LINDA: Be good. You're both good boys, just act that way, that's all.

HAPPY: 'Night, Pop. *He goes upstairs.*

LINDA, *to Willy:* Come, dear.

BEN, *with greater force:* One must go in to fetch a diamond out.

WILLY, *to Linda, as he moves slowly along the edge of the kitchen, toward the door:* I just want to get settled down, Linda. Let me sit alone for a little.

LINDA, *almost uttering her fear:* I want you upstairs.

WILLY, *taking her in his arms:* In a few minutes, Linda. I couldn't sleep right now. Go on, you look awful tired. *He kisses her.*

BEN: Not like an appointment at all. A diamond is rough and hard to the touch.

WILLY: Go on now. I'll be right up.

LINDA: I think this is the only way, Willy.
WILLY: Sure, it's the best thing.
BEN: Best thing!
WILLY: The only way. Everything is gonna be—go on, kid, get to bed. You look so tired.
LINDA: Come right up.
WILLY: Two minutes.

Linda goes into the living-room, then reappears in her bedroom. Willy moves just outside the kitchen door.

WILLY: Loves me. *Wonderingly:* Always loved me. Isn't that a remarkable thing? Ben, he'll worship me for it!
BEN, *with promise:* It's dark there, but full of diamonds.
WILLY: Can you imagine that magnificence with twenty thousand dollars in his pocket?
LINDA, *calling from her room:* Willy! Come up!
WILLY, *calling into the kitchen:* Yes! Yes. Coming! It's very smart, you realize that, don't you, sweetheart? Even Ben sees it. I gotta go, baby. 'By! 'By! *Going over to Ben, almost dancing:* Imagine? When the mail comes he'll be ahead of Bernard again!
BEN: A perfect proposition all around.
WILLY: Did you see how he cried to me? Oh, if I could kiss him, Ben!
BEN: Time, William, time!
WILLY: Oh, Ben, I always knew one way or another we were gonna make it, Biff and I!
BEN, *looking at his watch:* The boat. We'll be late. *He moves slowly off into the darkness.*
WILLY, *elegiacally, turning to the house:* Now when you kick off, boy, I want a seventy-yard boot, and get right down the field under the ball, and when you hit, hit low and hit hard, because it's important, boy. *He swings around and faces the audience.* There's all kinds of important people in the stands, and the first thing you know . . . *Suddenly realizing he is alone:* Ben! Ben, where do I . . . ? *He makes a sudden movement of search.* Ben, how do I . . . ?
LINDA, *calling:* Willy, you coming up?
WILLY, *uttering a gasp of fear, whirling about as if to quiet her:* Sh! *He turns around as if to find his way; sounds, faces, voices,*

seem to be swarming in upon him and he flicks at them, crying, Sh! Sh! *Suddenly music, faint and high, stops him. It rises in intensity, almost to an unbearable scream. He goes up and down on his toes, and rushes off around the house.* Shhh!

LINDA: Willy?

There is no answer. Linda waits. Biff gets up off his bed. He is still in his clothes. Happy sits up. Biff stands listening.

LINDA, *with real fear:* Willy, answer me! Willy!

There is the sound of a car starting and moving away at full speed.

LINDA: No!

BIFF, *rushing down the stairs:* Pop!

As the car speeds off, the music crashes down in a frenzy of sound, which becomes the soft pulsation of a single cello string. Biff slowly returns to his bedroom. He and Happy gravely don their jackets. Linda slowly walks out of her room. The music has developed into a dead march. The leaves of day are appearing over everything. Charley and Bernard, somberly dressed, appear and knock on the kitchen door. Biff and Happy slowly descend the stairs to the kitchen as Charley and Bernard enter. All stop a moment when Linda, in clothes of mourning, bearing a little bunch of roses, comes through the draped doorway into the kitchen. She goes to Charley and takes his arm. Now all move toward the audience, through the wall-line of the kitchen. At the limit of the apron, Linda lays down the flowers, kneels, and sits back on her heels. All stare down at the grave.

REQUIEM

CHARLEY: It's getting dark, Linda.

Linda doesn't react. She stares at the grave.

BIFF: How about it, Mom? Better get some rest, heh? They'll be closing the gate soon.

Linda makes no move. Pause.

HAPPY, *deeply angered:* He had no right to do that. There was no necessity for it. We would've helped him.
CHARLEY, *grunting:* Hmmm.
BIFF: Come along, Mom.
LINDA: Why didn't anybody come?
CHARLEY: It was a very nice funeral.
LINDA: But where are all the people he knew? Maybe they blame him.
CHARLEY: Naa. It's a rough world, Linda. They wouldn't blame him.
LINDA: I can't understand it. At this time especially. First time in thirty-five years we were just about free and clear. He only needed a little salary. He was even finished with the dentist.
CHARLEY: No man only needs a little salary.
LINDA: I can't understand it.
BIFF: There were a lot of nice days. When he'd come home from a trip; or on Sundays, making the stoop; finishing the cellar; putting on the new porch; when he built the extra bathroom; and put up the garage. You know something, Charley, there's more of him in that front stoop than in all the sales he ever made.
CHARLEY: Yeah. He was a happy man with a batch of cement.
LINDA: He was so wonderful with his hands.
BIFF: He had the wrong dreams. All, all, wrong.
HAPPY, *almost ready to fight Biff:* Don't say that!
BIFF: He never knew who he was.
CHARLEY, *stopping Happy's movement and reply. To Biff:* Nobody dast blame this man. You don't understand: Willy was a salesman. And for a salesman, there is no rock bottom to

the life. He don't put a bolt to a nut, he don't tell you the law or give you medicine. He's a man way out there in the blue, riding on a smile and a shoeshine. And when they start not smiling back—that's an earthquake. And then you get yourself a couple of spots on your hat, and you're finished. Nobody dast blame this man. A salesman is got to dream, boy. It comes with the territory.

BIFF: Charley, the man didn't know who he was.

HAPPY, *infuriated:* Don't say that!

BIFF: Why don't you come with me, Happy?

HAPPY: I'm not licked that easily. I'm staying right in this city, and I'm gonna beat this racket! *He looks at Biff, his chin set.* The Loman Brothers!

BIFF: I know who I am, kid.

HAPPY: All right, boy. I'm gonna show you and everybody else that Willy Loman did not die in vain. He had a good dream. It's the only dream you can have—to come out number-one man. He fought it out here, and this is where I'm gonna win it for him.

BIFF, *with a hopeless glance at Happy, bends toward his mother:* Let's go, Mom.

LINDA: I'll be with you in a minute. Go on, Charley. *He hesitates.* I want to, just for a minute. I never had a chance to say good-by.

Charley moves away, followed by Happy. Biff remains a slight distance up and left of Linda. She sits there, summoning herself. The flute begins, not far away, playing behind her speech.

LINDA: Forgive me, dear. I can't cry. I don't know what it is, but I can't cry. I don't understand it. Why did you ever do that? Help me, Willy, I can't cry. It seems to me that you're just on another trip. I keep expecting you. Willy, dear, I can't cry. Why did you do it? I search and search and I search, and I can't understand it, Willy. I made the last payment on the house today. Today, dear. And there'll be nobody home. *A sob rises in her throat.* We're free and clear. *Sobbing more fully, released:* We're free. *Biff comes slowly toward her.* We're free . . . We're free . . .

Biff lifts her to her feet and moves out up right with her in his arms. Linda sobs quietly. Bernard and Charley come together and follow them, followed by Happy. Only the music of the flute is left on the darkening stage as over the house the hard towers of the apartment buildings rise into sharp focus.

CURTAIN

Arthur Miller's
adaptation of

AN ENEMY OF THE PEOPLE

by Henrik Ibsen

Preface

1

AT the outset it ought to be said that the word "adaptation" is very distasteful to me. It seems to mean that one writer has ventured into another's chickencoop, or worse, into the sacred chamber of another's personal creations and rearranged things without permission. Most of the time an adaptation is a playwright's excuse for not writing his own plays, and since I am not yet with my back against that particular wall, I think it wise to set down what I have tried to do with *An Enemy of the People*, and why I did it.

There is one quality in Ibsen that no serious writer can afford to overlook. It lies at the very center of his force, and I found in it—as I hope others will—a profound source of strength. It is his insistence, his utter conviction, that he is going to say what he has to say, and that the audience, by God, is going to listen. It is the very same quality that makes a star actor, a great public speaker, and a lunatic. Every Ibsen play begins with the unwritten words: "Now listen here!" And these words have shown me a path through the wall of "entertainment," a path that leads beyond the formulas and dried-up precepts, the pretense and fraud, of the business of the stage. Whatever else Ibsen has to teach, this is his first and greatest contribution.

In recent years Ibsen has fallen into a kind of respectful obscurity that is not only undeserved but really quite disrespectful of culture—and a disservice to the theater besides. I decided to work on *An Enemy of the People* because I had a private wish to demonstrate that Ibsen is really pertinent today, that he is not "old-fashioned," and, implicitly, that those who condemn him are themselves misleading our theater and our playwrights into a blind alley of senseless sensibility, triviality, and the inevitable waste of our dramatic talents; for it has become the fashion for plays to reduce the "thickness" of life to a fragile facsimile, to avoid portraying the complexities of life, the contradictions of character, the fascinating interplay of cause and effect that have long been part of the novel. And I wished also

to buttress the idea that the dramatic writer has, and must again demonstrate, the right to entertain with his brains as well as his heart. It is necessary that the public understand again that the stage is *the* place for ideas, for philosophies, for the most intense discussion of man's fate. One of the masters of such a discussion is Henrik Ibsen, and I have presumed to point this out once again.

2

I have attempted to make *An Enemy of the People* as alive to Americans as it undoubtedly was to Norwegians, while keeping it intact. I had no interest in exhuming anything, in asking people to sit respectfully before the work of a celebrated but neglected writer. There are museums for such activities; the theater has no truck with them, and ought not to have.

And I believed this play could be alive for us because its central theme is, in my opinion, the central theme of our social life today. Simply, it is the question of whether the democratic guarantees protecting political minorities ought to be set aside in time of crisis. More personally, it is the question of whether one's vision of the truth ought to be a source of guilt at a time when the mass of men condemn it as a dangerous and devilish lie. It is an enduring theme—in fact, possibly the most enduring of all Ibsen's themes—because there never was, nor will there ever be, an organized society able to countenance calmly the individual who insists that he is right while the vast majority is absolutely wrong.

The play is the story of a scientist who discovers an evil and, innocently believing that he has done a service to humanity, expects that he will at least be thanked. However, the town has a vested interest in the perpetuation of that evil, and his "truth," when confronted with that interest, must be made to conform. The scientist cannot change the truth for any reason disconnected with the evil. He clings to the truth and suffers the social consequences. At rock bottom, then, the play is concerned with the inviolability of objective truth. Or, put more dynamically, that those who attempt to warp the truth for ulterior purposes must inevitably become warped and corrupted themselves. This theme is valid today, just as it will always be,

but some of the examples given by Ibsen to prove it may no longer be.

I am told that Ibsen wrote this play as a result of his being practically stoned off the stage for daring to present *Ghosts*. The plot is supposed to have come from a news item which told of an Hungarian scientist who had discovered poisoned water in the town's water supply and had been pilloried for his discovery. If this was the case, my interpretation of the theme is doubly justified, for it then seems beyond doubt that Ibsen meant above and beyond all else to defend his right to stand "at the outpost of society," alone with the truth, and to speak from there to his fellow men.

However, there are a few speeches, and one scene in particular, which have been taken to mean that Ibsen was a fascist. In the original meeting scene in which Dr. Stockmann sets forth his—and Ibsen's—point of view most completely and angrily, Dr. Stockmann makes a speech in which he turns to biology to prove that there are indeed certain individuals "bred" to a superior apprehension of truths and who have the natural right to lead, if not to govern, the mass.

If the entire play is to be understood as the working-out of this speech, then one has no justification for contending that it is other than racist and fascist—certainly it could not be thought of as a defense of any democratic idea. But, structurally speaking, the theme is not wholly contained in the meeting scene alone. In fact, this speech is in some important respects in contradiction to the actual dramatic working-out of the play. But that Ibsen never really believed that idea in the first place is amply proved by a speech he delivered to a workers' club after the production of *An Enemy of the People*. He said then: "Of course I do not mean the aristocracy of birth, or of the purse, or even the aristocracy of the intellect. I mean the aristocracy of character, of will, of mind—that alone can free us."

I have taken as justification for removing those examples which no longer prove the theme—examples I believe Ibsen would have removed were he alive today—the line in the original manuscript that reads: "There is no established truth that can remain true for more than seventeen, eighteen, at most twenty years." In light of genocide, the holocaust that has

swept our world on the wings of the black ideology of racism, it is inconceivable that Ibsen would insist today that certain individuals are by breeding, or race, or "innate" qualities superior to others or possessed of the right to dictate to others. The man who wrote *A Doll's House*, the clarion call for the equality of women, cannot be equated with a fascist. The whole cast of his thinking was such that he could not have lived a day under an authoritarian regime of any kind. He was an individualist sometimes to the point of anarchism, and in such a man there is too explosive a need for self-expression to permit him to conform to any rigid ideology. It is impossible, therefore, to set him beside Hitler.

3

On reading the standard translations of Ibsen's work it quickly became obvious that the false impressions that have been connected with the man would seem to be justified were he to be produced in "translated" form. For one thing, his language in English sounds impossibly pedantic. Combine this with the fact that he wore a beard and half-lenses in his eyeglasses, and that his plays have always been set forth with yards of fringe on every tablecloth and drapery, and it was guaranteed that a new production on the traditional basis would truly bury the man for good.

I set out to transform his language into contemporary English. Working from a pidgin-English, word-for-word rendering of the Norwegian, done by Mr. Lars Nordenson, I was able to gather the meaning of each speech and scene without the obstruction of any kind of English construction.

For instance, Mr. Nordenson, working from the original Norwegian manuscript, set before me speeches such as: "But, dear Thomas, what have you then done to him again?" Or: "The Mayor being your brother, I would not wish to touch it, but you are as convinced as I am that truth goes ahead of all other considerations." Or: "Well, what do you say, Doctor? Don't you think it is high time that we stir a little life into the slackness and sloppiness of halfheartedness and cowardliness?" This last speech now reads: "Well, what do you say to a little hypodermic for these fence-sitting deadheads?"

It was possible to peer into the original play with as clear an eye as one could who knew no Norwegian. There were no English sentences to correct and rewrite, only the bare literalness of the original. This version of the play, then, is really in the nature of a new translation into spoken English.

But it is more too. The original has a tendency to indulge in transitions between scenes that are themselves uninteresting, and although as little as possible of the original construction has been changed and the play is exactly as it was, scene for scene, I have made each act seem of one piece, instead of separate scenes. And my reason for doing this is simply that the tradition of Ibsen's theater allowed the opera-like separation of scenes, while ours demands that the audience never be conscious that a "scene" has taken place at all.

Structurally the largest change is in the third act—Ibsen's fifth. In the original the actual dramatic end comes a little past the middle of the act, but it is followed by a wind-up that keeps winding endlessly to the curtain. I think this overwriting was the result of Ibsen's insistence that his meaning be driven home—and from the front door right through to the back, lest the audience fail to understand him. Generally, in this act, I have brought out the meaning of the play in terms of dramatic action, action which was already there and didn't need to be newly invented, but which was separated by tendentious speeches spoken into the blue.

Throughout the play I have tried to peel away its trappings of the moment, its relatively accidental details which ring the dull green tones of Victorianism, and to show that beneath them there still lives the terrible wrath of Henrik Ibsen, who could make a play as men make watches, precisely, intelligently, and telling not merely the minute and the hour but the age.

CAST

(IN ORDER OF APPEARANCE)

MORTEN KIIL
BILLING
MRS. STOCKMANN
PETER STOCKMANN
HOVSTAD
DR. STOCKMANN
MORTEN
EJLIF
CAPTAIN HORSTER
PETRA
ASLAKSEN
THE DRUNK
TOWNSPEOPLE

SYNOPSIS OF SCENES

THE ACTION TAKES PLACE IN A NORWEGIAN TOWN

ACT ONE

Scene 1: Dr. Stockmann's living room.
Scene 2: The same, the following morning.

ACT TWO

Scene 1: Editorial office of the *People's Daily Messenger.*
Scene 2: A room in Captain Horster's house.

ACT THREE

Scene: Dr. Stockmann's living room the following morning.

Throughout, in the stage directions, right and left mean stage right and stage left.

ACT ONE

SCENE I

It is evening. Dr. Stockmann's living room is simply but cheerfully furnished. A doorway, upstage right, leads into the entrance hall, which extends from the front door to the dining room, running unseen behind the living room. At the left is another door, which leads to the Doctor's study and other rooms. In the upstage left corner is a stove. Toward the left foreground is a sofa with a table behind it. In the right foreground are two chairs, a small table between them, on which stand a lamp and a bowl of apples. At the back, to the left, an open doorway leads to the dining room, part of which is seen. The windows are in the right wall, a bench in front of them.

As the curtain rises, Billing and Morten Kiil are eating in the dining room. Billing is junior editor of the People's Daily Messenger. *Kiil is a slovenly old man who is feeding himself in a great hurry. He gulps his last bite and comes into the living room, where he puts on his coat and ratty fur hat. Billing comes in to help him.*

BILLING: You sure eat fast, Mr. Kiil. *Billing is an enthusiast to the point of foolishness.*

KIIL: Eating don't get you anywhere, boy. Tell my daughter I went home.

Kiil starts across to the front door. Billing returns to his food in the dining room. Kiil halts at the bowl of apples; he takes one, tastes it, likes it, takes another and puts it in his pocket, then continues on toward the door. Again he stops, returns, and takes another apple for his pocket. Then he sees a tobacco can on the table. He covers his action from Billing's possible glance, opens the can, smells it, pours some into his side pocket. He is just closing the can when Catherine Stockmann enters from the dining room.

MRS. STOCKMANN: Father! You're not going, are you?

KIIL: Got business to tend to.

MRS. STOCKMANN: Oh, you're only going back to your room and you know it. Stay! Mr. Billing's here, and Hovstad's coming. It'll be interesting for you.

KIIL: Got all kinds of business. The only reason I came over was the butcher told me you bought roast beef today. Very tasty, dear.

MRS. STOCKMANN: Why don't you wait for Tom? He only went for a little walk.

KIIL, *taking out his pipe:* You think he'd mind if I filled my pipe?

MRS. STOCKMANN: No, go ahead. And here—take some apples. You should always have some fruit in your room.

KIIL: No, no, wouldn't think of it.

The doorbell rings.

MRS. STOCKMANN: That must be Hovstad. *She goes to the door and opens it.*

Peter Stockmann, the Mayor, enters. He is a bachelor, nearing sixty. He has always been one of those men who make it their life work to stand in the center of the ship to keep it from overturning. He probably envies the family life and warmth of this house, but when he comes he never wants to admit he came and often sits with his coat on.

MRS. STOCKMANN: Peter! Well, this is a surprise!

PETER STOCKMANN: I was just passing by . . . *He sees Kiil and smiles, amused.* Mr. Kiil!

KIIL, *sarcastically:* Your Honor! *He bites into his apple and exits.*

MRS. STOCKMANN: You mustn't mind him, Peter, he's getting terribly old. Would you like a bite to eat?

PETER STOCKMANN: No, no thanks. *He sees Billing now, and Billing nods to him from the dining room.*

MRS. STOCKMANN, *embarrassed:* He just happened to drop in.

PETER STOCKMANN: That's all right. I can't take hot food in the evening. Not with my stomach.

MRS. STOCKMANN: Can't I ever get you to eat anything in this house?

PETER STOCKMANN: Bless you, I stick to my tea and toast. Much healthier and more economical.

MRS. STOCKMANN, *smiling:* You sound as though Tom and I throw money out the window.

PETER STOCKMANN: Not you, Catherine. He wouldn't be home, would he?

MRS. STOCKMANN: He went for a little walk with the boys.

PETER STOCKMANN: You don't think that's dangerous, right after dinner? *There is a loud knocking on the front door.* That sounds like my brother.

MRS. STOCKMANN: I doubt it, so soon. Come in, please.

Hovstad enters. He is in his early thirties, a graduate of the peasantry struggling with a terrible conflict. For while he hates authority and wealth, he cannot bring himself to cast off a certain desire to partake of them. Perhaps he is dangerous because he wants more than anything to belong, and in a radical that is a withering wish, not easily to be borne.

MRS. STOCKMANN: Mr. Hovstad—

HOVSTAD: Sorry I'm late. I was held up at the printing shop. *Surprised:* Good evening, Your Honor.

PETER STOCKMANN, *rather stiffly:* Hovstad. On business, no doubt.

HOVSTAD: Partly. It's about an article for the paper—

PETER STOCKMANN, *sarcastically:* Ha! I don't doubt it. I understand my brother has become a prolific contributor to—what do you call it?—the *People's Daily Liberator*?

HOVSTAD, *laughing, but holding his ground:* The *People's Daily Messenger*, sir. The Doctor sometimes honors the *Messenger* when he wants to uncover the real truth of some subject.

PETER STOCKMANN: The truth! Oh, yes, I see.

MRS. STOCKMANN, *nervously to Hovstad:* Would you like to . . . *She points to dining room.*

PETER STOCKMANN: I don't want you to think I blame the Doctor for using your paper. After all, every performer goes for the audience that applauds him most. It's really not your paper I have anything against, Mr. Hovstad.

HOVSTAD: I really didn't think so, Your Honor.

PETER STOCKMANN: As a matter of fact, I happen to admire the spirit of tolerance in our town. It's magnificent. Just don't forget that we have it because we all believe in the same thing; it brings us together.

HOVSTAD: Kirsten Springs, you mean.

PETER STOCKMANN: The springs, Mr. Hovstad, our wonderful new springs. They've changed the soul of this town. Mark my words, Kirsten Springs are going to put us on the map, and there is no question about it.

MRS. STOCKMANN: That's what Tom says too.

PETER STOCKMANN: Everything is shooting ahead—real estate going up, money changing hands every hour, business humming—

HOVSTAD: And no more unemployment.

PETER STOCKMANN: Right. Give us a really good summer, and sick people will be coming here in carloads. The springs will turn into a regular fad, a new Carlsbad. And for once the well-to-do people won't be the only ones paying taxes in this town.

HOVSTAD: I hear reservations are really starting to come in?

PETER STOCKMANN: Coming in every day. Looks very promising, very promising.

HOVSTAD: That's fine. *To Mrs. Stockmann:* Then the Doctor's article will come in handy.

PETER STOCKMANN: He's written something again?

HOVSTAD: No, it's a piece he wrote at the beginning of the winter, recommending the water. But at the time I let the article lie.

PETER STOCKMANN: Why, some hitch in it?

HOVSTAD: Oh, no, I just thought it would have a bigger effect in the spring, when people start planning for the summer.

PETER STOCKMANN: That's smart, Mr. Hovstad, very smart.

MRS. STOCKMANN: Tom is always so full of ideas about the springs; every day he—

PETER STOCKMANN: Well, he ought to be, he gets his salary from the springs, my dear.

HOVSTAD: Oh, I think it's more than that, don't you? After all, Doctor Stockmann *created* Kirsten Springs.

PETER STOCKMANN: You don't say! I've been hearing that lately, but I did think I had a certain modest part—

MRS. STOCKMANN: Oh, Tom always says—

HOVSTAD: I only meant the original idea was—

PETER STOCKMANN: My good brother is never at a loss for ideas. All sorts of ideas. But when it comes to putting them

into action you need another kind of man, and I did think that at least people in this house would—

MRS. STOCKMANN: But Peter, dear—we didn't mean to— Go get yourself a bite, Mr. Hovstad, my husband will be here any minute.

HOVSTAD: Thank you, maybe just a little something. *He goes into the dining room and joins Billing at the table.*

PETER STOCKMANN, *lowering his voice:* Isn't it remarkable? Why is it that people without background can never learn tact?

MRS. STOCKMANN: Why let it bother you? Can't you and Thomas share the honor like good brothers?

PETER STOCKMANN: The trouble is that certain men are never satisfied to share, Catherine.

MRS. STOCKMANN: Nonsense. You've always gotten along beautifully with Tom— That must be him now.

She goes to the front door, opens it. Dr. Stockmann is laughing and talking outside. He is in the prime of his life. He might be called the eternal amateur—a lover of things, of people, of sheer living, a man for whom the days are too short, and the future fabulous with discoverable joys. And for all this most people will not like him—he will not compromise for less than God's own share of the world while they have settled for less than Man's.

DR. STOCKMANN, *in the entrance hall:* Hey, Catherine! Here's another guest for you! Here's a hanger for your coat, Captain. Oh, that's right, you don't wear overcoats! Go on in, boys. You kids must be hungry all over again. Come here, Captain Horster, I want you to get a look at this roast. *He pushes Captain Horster along the hallway to the dining room. Ejlif and Morten also go to the dining room.*

MRS. STOCKMANN: Tom, dear . . . *She motions toward Peter in the living room.*

DR. STOCKMANN, *turns around in the doorway to the living room and sees Peter:* Oh, Peter . . . *He walks across and stretches out his hand.* Say now, this is really nice.

PETER STOCKMANN: I'll have to go in a minute.

DR. STOCKMANN: Oh, nonsense, not with the toddy on the table. You haven't forgotten the toddy, have you, Catherine?

MRS. STOCKMANN: Of course not, I've got the water boiling. *She goes into the dining room.*

PETER STOCKMANN: Toddy too?

DR. STOCKMANN: Sure, just sit down and make yourself at home.

PETER STOCKMANN: No, thanks, I don't go in for drinking parties.

DR. STOCKMANN: But this is no party.

PETER STOCKMANN: What else do you call it? *He looks toward the dining room.* It's extraordinary how you people can consume all this food and live.

DR. STOCKMANN, *rubbing his hands:* Why? What's finer than to watch young people eat? Peter, those are the fellows who are going to stir up the whole future.

PETER STOCKMANN, *a little alarmed:* Is that so! What's there to stir up? *He sits in a chair to the left.*

DR. STOCKMANN, *walking around:* Don't worry, they'll let us know when the time comes. Old idiots like you and me, we'll be left behind like—

PETER STOCKMANN: I've never been called *that* before.

DR. STOCKMANN: Oh, Peter, don't jump on me every minute! You know your trouble, Peter? Your impressions are blunted. You ought to sit up there in that crooked corner of the north for five years, the way I did, and then come back here. It's like watching the first seven days of creation!

PETER STOCKMANN: Here!

DR. STOCKMANN: Things to work and fight for, Peter! Without that you're dead. Catherine, you sure the mailman came today?

MRS. STOCKMANN, *from the dining room:* There wasn't any mail today.

DR. STOCKMANN: And another thing, Peter—a good income; *that's* something you learn to value after you've lived on a starvation diet.

PETER STOCKMANN: When did you starve?

DR. STOCKMANN: Damned near! It was pretty tough going a lot of the time up there. And now, to be able to live like a prince! Tonight, for instance, we had roast beef for dinner, and, by God, there was enough left for supper too. Please have a piece—come here.

PETER STOCKMANN: Oh, no, no—please, certainly not.

DR. STOCKMANN: At least let me show it to you! Come in here—we even have a tablecloth. *He pulls his brother toward the dining room.*

PETER STOCKMANN: I saw it.

DR. STOCKMANN: Live to the hilt! that's my motto. Anyway, Catherine says I'm earning almost as much as we spend.

PETER STOCKMANN, *refusing an apple:* Well, you are improving.

DR. STOCKMANN: Peter, that was a joke! You're supposed to laugh! *He sits in the other chair to the left.*

PETER STOCKMANN: Roast beef twice a day is no joke.

DR. STOCKMANN: Why can't I give myself the pleasure of having people around me? It's a necessity for me to see young, lively, happy people, free people burning with a desire to do something. You'll see. When Hovstad comes in we'll talk and—

PETER STOCKMANN: Oh, yes, Hovstad. That reminds me. He told me he was going to print one of your articles.

DR. STOCKMANN: One of my articles?

PETER STOCKMANN: Yes, about the springs—an article you wrote during the winter?

DR. STOCKMANN: Oh, that one! In the first place, I don't want that one printed right now.

PETER STOCKMANN: No? It sounded to me like it would be very timely.

DR. STOCKMANN: Under normal conditions, maybe so. *He gets up and walks across the floor.*

PETER STOCKMANN, *looking after him:* Well, what is abnormal about the conditions now?

DR. STOCKMANN, *stopping:* I can't say for the moment, Peter—at least not tonight. There could be a great deal abnormal about conditions; then again, there could be nothing at all.

PETER STOCKMANN: Well, you've managed to sound mysterious. Is there anything wrong? Something you're keeping from me? Because I wish once in a while you'd remind yourself that I am chairman of the board for the springs.

DR. STOCKMANN: And I would like *you* to remember that, Peter. Look, let's not get into each other's hair.

PETER STOCKMANN: I don't make a habit of getting into people's hair! But I'd like to underline that everything con-

cerning Kirsten Springs must be treated in a businesslike manner, through the proper channels, and dealt with by the legally constituted authorities. I can't allow anything done behind my back in a roundabout way.

DR. STOCKMANN: When did I ever go behind your back, Peter?

PETER STOCKMANN: You have an ingrained tendency to go your own way, Thomas, and that simply can't go on in a well-organized society. The individual really must subordinate himself to the over-all, or—*groping for words, he points to himself*—to the authorities who are in charge of the general welfare. *He gets up.*

DR. STOCKMANN: Well, that's probably so. But how the hell does that concern me, Peter?

PETER STOCKMANN: My dear Thomas, this is exactly what you will never learn. But you had better watch out because someday you might pay dearly for it. Now I've said it. Good-by.

DR. STOCKMANN: Are you out of your mind? You're absolutely on the wrong track.

PETER STOCKMANN: I am usually not. Anyway, may I be excused? *He nods toward the dining room.* Good-by, Catherine. Good evening, gentlemen. *He leaves.*

MRS. STOCKMANN, *entering the living room:* He left?

DR. STOCKMANN: And burned up!

MRS. STOCKMANN: What did you do to him now?

DR. STOCKMANN: What does he want from me? He can't expect me to give him an accounting of every move I make, every thought I think, until I am ready to do it.

MRS. STOCKMANN: Why? What should you give him an accounting of?

DR. STOCKMANN, *hesitantly:* Just leave that to me, Catherine. Peculiar the mailman didn't come today.

Hovstad, Billing, and Captain Horster have gotten up from the dining-room table and enter the living room. Ejlif and Morten come in a little later. Catherine exits.

BILLING, *stretching out his arms:* After a meal like that, by God, I feel like a new man. This house is so—

HOVSTAD, *cutting him off:* The Mayor certainly wasn't in a glowing mood tonight.

DR. STOCKMANN: It's his stomach. He has a lousy digestion.

HOVSTAD: I think two editors from the *People's Daily Messenger* didn't help either.

DR. STOCKMANN: No, it's just that Peter is a lonely man. Poor fellow, all he knows is official business and duties, and then all that damn weak tea that he pours into himself. Catherine, may we have the toddy?

MRS. STOCKMANN, *calling from the dining room:* I'm just getting it.

DR. STOCKMANN: Sit down here on the couch with me, Captain Horster—a rare guest like you—sit here. Sit down, friends.

HORSTER: This used to be such an ugly house. Suddenly it's beautiful!

Billing and Hovstad sit down at the right. Mrs. Stockmann brings a tray with pot, glasses, bottles, etc. on it, and puts it on the table behind the couch.

BILLING, *to Horster, intimately, indicating Stockmann:* Great man!

MRS. STOCKMANN: Here you are. Help yourselves.

DR. STOCKMANN, *taking a glass:* We sure will. *He mixes the toddy.* And the cigars, Ejlif—you know where the box is. And Morten, get my pipe. *The boys go out to the left.* I have a sneaking suspicion that Ejlif is snitching a cigar now and then, but I don't pay any attention. Catherine, you know where I put it? Oh, he's got it. Good boys! *The boys bring the various things in.* Help yourselves, fellows. I'll stick to the pipe. This one's gone through plenty of blizzards with me up in the north. Skol! *He looks around.* Home! What an invention, heh?

The boys sit down on the bench near the windows.

MRS. STOCKMANN, *who has sat down and is now knitting:* Are you sailing soon, Captain Horster?

HORSTER: I expect to be ready next week.

MRS. STOCKMANN: And then to America, Captain?

HORSTER: Yes, that's the plan.

BILLING: Oh, then you won't be home for the new election?

HORSTER: Is there going to be another election?

BILLING: Didn't you know?

HORSTER: No, I don't get mixed up in those things.
BILLING: But you are interested in public affairs, aren't you?
HORSTER: Frankly, I don't understand a thing about it.

He does, really, although not very much. Captain Horster is one of the longest silent roles in dramatic literature, but he is not to be thought of as characterless therefor. It is not a bad thing to have a courageous, quiet man for a friend, even if it has gone out of fashion.

MRS. STOCKMANN, *sympathetically:* Neither do I, Captain. Maybe that's why I'm always so glad to see you.
BILLING: Just the same, you ought to vote, Captain.
HORSTER: Even if I don't understand anything about it?
BILLING: Understand! What do you mean by that? Society, Captain, is like a ship—every man should do something to help navigate the ship.
HORSTER: That may be all right on shore, but on board a ship it doesn't work out so well.

Petra in hat and coat and with textbooks and notebooks under her arm comes into the entrance hall. She is Ibsen's clear-eyed hope for the future—and probably ours. She is forthright, determined, and knows the meaning of work, which to her is the creation of good on the earth.

PETRA, *from the hall:* Good evening.
DR. STOCKMANN, *warmly:* Good evening, Petra!
BILLING, *to Horster:* Great young woman!

There are mutual greetings. Petra removes her coat and hat and places the books on a chair in the entrance hall.

PETRA, *entering the living room:* And here you are, lying around like lizards while I'm out slaving.
DR. STOCKMANN: Well, you come and be a lizard too. Come here, Petra, sit with me. I look at her and say to myself, "How did I do it?"

Petra goes over to her father and kisses him.

BILLING: Shall I mix a toddy for you?
PETRA, *coming up to the table:* No, thanks, I had better do it

myself—you always mix it too strong. Oh, Father, I forgot—I have a letter for you. *She goes to the chair where her books are.*

DR. STOCKMANN, *alerted:* Who's it from?

PETRA: I met the mailman on the way to school this morning and he gave me your mail too, and I just didn't have time to run back.

DR. STOCKMANN, *getting up and walking toward her:* And you don't give it to me until now!

PETRA: I really didn't have time to run back, Father.

MRS. STOCKMANN: If she didn't have time . . .

DR. STOCKMANN: Let's see it—come on, child! *He takes the letter and looks at the envelope.* Yes, indeed.

MRS. STOCKMANN: Is that the one you've been waiting for?

DR. STOCKMANN: I'll be right back. There wouldn't be a light on in my room, would there?

MRS. STOCKMANN: The lamp is on the desk, burning away.

DR. STOCKMANN: Please excuse me for a moment. *He goes into his study and quickly returns. Mrs. Stockmann hands him his glasses. He goes out again.*

PETRA: What is that, Mother?

MRS. STOCKMANN: I don't know. The last couple of days he's been asking again and again about the mailman.

BILLING: Probably an out-of-town patient of his.

PETRA: Poor Father, he's got much too much to do. *She mixes her drink.* This ought to taste good.

HOVSTAD: By the way, what happened to that English novel you were going to translate for us?

PETRA: I started it, but I've gotten so busy—

HOVSTAD: Oh, teaching evening school again?

PETRA: Two hours a night.

BILLING: Plus the high school every day?

PETRA, *sitting down on the couch:* Yes, five hours, and every night a pile of lessons to correct!

MRS. STOCKMANN: She never stops going.

HOVSTAD: Maybe that's why I always think of you as kind of breathless and—well, breathless.

PETRA: I love it. I get so wonderfully tired.

BILLING, *to Horster:* She looks tired.

MORTEN: You must be a wicked woman, Petra.

PETRA, *laughing:* Wicked?
MORTEN: You work so much. My teacher says that work is a punishment for our sins.
EJLIF: And you believe that?
MRS. STOCKMANN: Ejlif! Of course he believes his teacher!
BILLING, *smiling:* Don't stop him . . .
HOVSTAD: Don't you like to work, Morten?
MORTEN: Work? No.
HOVSTAD: Then what will you ever amount to in this world?
MORTEN: Me? I'm going to be a Viking.
EJLIF: You can't! You'd have to be a heathen!
MORTEN: So I'll be a heathen.
MRS. STOCKMANN: I think it's getting late, boys.
BILLING: I agree with you, Morten. I think—
MRS. STOCKMANN, *making signs to Billing:* You certainly don't, Mr. Billing.
BILLING: Yes, by God, I do. I am a real heathen and proud of it. You'll see, pretty soon we're all going to be heathens!
MORTEN: And then we can do anything we want!
BILLING: Right! You see, Morten—
MRS. STOCKMANN, *interrupting:* Don't you have any homework for tomorrow, boys? Better go in and do it.
EJLIF: Oh, can't we stay in here a while?
MRS. STOCKMANN: No, neither of you. Now run along.

The boys say good night and go off at the left.

HOVSTAD: You really think it hurts them to listen to such talk?
MRS. STOCKMANN: I don't know, but I don't like it.

Dr. Stockmann enters from his study, an open letter in his hand. He is like a sleepwalker, astonished, engrossed. He walks toward the front door.

MRS. STOCKMANN: Tom!

He turns, suddenly aware of them.

DR. STOCKMANN: Boys, there is going to be news in this town!
BILLING: News?
MRS. STOCKMANN: What kind of news?
DR. STOCKMANN: A terrific discovery, Catherine.

HOVSTAD: Really?

MRS. STOCKMANN: That you made?

DR. STOCKMANN: That I made. *He walks back and forth.* Now let the baboons running this town call me a lunatic! Now they'd better watch out. Oh, how the mighty have fallen!

PETRA: What is it, Father?

DR. STOCKMANN: Oh, if Peter were only here! Now you'll see how human beings can walk around and make judgments like blind rats.

HOVSTAD: What in the world's happened, Doctor?

DR. STOCKMANN, *stopping at the table:* It's the general opinion, isn't it, that our town is a sound and healthy spot?

HOVSTAD: Of course.

MRS. STOCKMANN: What happened?

DR. STOCKMANN: Even a rather unusually healthy spot! Oh, God, a place that can be recommended not only to all people but to sick people!

MRS. STOCKMANN: But, Tom, what are you—

DR. STOCKMANN: And we certainly have recommended it. I myself have written and written, in the *People's Messenger*, pamphlets—

HOVSTAD: Yes, yes, but—

DR. STOCKMANN: The miraculous springs that cost such a fortune to build, the whole Health Institute, is a pesthole!

PETRA: Father! The springs?

MRS. STOCKMANN, *simultaneously:* Our springs?

BILLING: That's unbelievable!

DR. STOCKMANN: You know the filth up in Windmill Valley? That stuff that has such a stinking smell? It comes down from the tannery up there, and the same damn poisonous mess comes right out into the blessed, miraculous water we're supposed to *cure* people with!

HORSTER: You mean actually where our beaches are?

DR. STOCKMANN: Exactly.

HOVSTAD: How are you so sure about this, Doctor?

DR. STOCKMANN: I had a suspicion about it a long time ago—last year there were too many sick cases among the visitors, typhoid and gastric disturbances.

MRS. STOCKMANN: That did happen. I remember Mrs. Svensen's niece—

DR. STOCKMANN: Yes, dear. At the time we thought that the visitors brought the bug, but later this winter I got a new idea and I started investigating the water.

MRS. STOCKMANN: So that's what you've been working on!

DR. STOCKMANN: I sent samples of the water to the University for an exact chemical analysis.

HOVSTAD: And that's what you have just received?

DR. STOCKMANN, *waving the letter again:* This is it. It proves the existence of infectious organic matter in the water.

MRS. STOCKMANN: Well, thank God you discovered it in time.

DR. STOCKMANN: I think we can say that, Catherine.

MRS. STOCKMANN: Isn't it wonderful!

HOVSTAD: And what do you intend to do now, Doctor?

DR. STOCKMANN: Put the thing right, of course.

HOVSTAD: Do you think that can be done?

DR. STOCKMANN: Maybe. If not, the whole Institute is useless. But there's nothing to worry about—I am quite clear on what has to be done.

MRS. STOCKMANN: But, Tom, why did you keep it so secret?

DR. STOCKMANN: What did you want me to do? Go out and shoot my mouth off before I really knew? *He walks around, rubbing his hands.* You don't realize what this means, Catherine—the whole water system has got to be changed.

MRS. STOCKMANN: The *whole* water system?

DR. STOCKMANN: The whole water system. The intake is too low, it's got to be raised to a much higher spot. The whole construction's got to be ripped out!

PETRA: Well, Father, at last you can prove they should have listened to you!

DR. STOCKMANN: Ha, she remembers!

MRS. STOCKMANN: That's right, you did warn them—

DR. STOCKMANN: Of course I warned them. When they started the damned thing I told them not to build it down there! But who am I, a mere scientist, to tell politicians where to build a health institute! Well, now they're going to get it, both barrels!

BILLING: This is tremendous! *To Horster:* He's a great man!

DR. STOCKMANN: It's bigger than tremendous. *He starts toward his study.* Wait'll they see this! *He stops.* Petra, my report is on my desk . . . *Petra goes into his study.* An envelope, Catherine!

She goes for it. Gentlemen, this final proof from the University—*Petra comes out with the report, which he takes*—and my report—*he flicks the pages*—five solid, explosive pages . . .

MRS. STOCKMANN, *handing him an envelope:* Is this big enough?

DR. STOCKMANN: Fine. Right to the Board of Directors! *He inserts the report, seals the envelope, and hands it to Catherine.* Will you give this to the maid—what's her name again?

MRS. STOCKMANN: Randine, dear, Randine.

DR. STOCKMANN: Tell our darling Randine to wipe her nose and run over to the Mayor right now.

Mrs. Stockmann just stands there looking at him.

DR. STOCKMANN: What's the matter, dear?

MRS. STOCKMANN: I don't know . . .

PETRA: What's Uncle Peter going to say about this?

MRS. STOCKMANN: That's what I'm wondering.

DR. STOCKMANN: What can he say! He ought to be damn glad that such an important fact is brought out before we start an epidemic! Hurry, dear!

Catherine exits at the left.

HOVSTAD: I would like to put a brief item about this discovery in the *Messenger.*

DR. STOCKMANN: Go ahead. I'd really be grateful for that now.

HOVSTAD: Because the public ought to know soon.

DR. STOCKMANN: Right away.

BILLING: By God, you'll be the leading man in this town, Doctor.

DR. STOCKMANN, *walking around with an air of satisfaction:* Oh, there was nothing to it. Every detective gets a lucky break once in his life. But just the same I—

BILLING: Hovstad, don't you think the town ought to pay Dr. Stockmann some tribute?

DR. STOCKMANN: Oh, no, no . . .

HOVSTAD: Sure, let's all put in a word for—

BILLING: I'll talk to Aslaksen about it!

Catherine enters.

DR. STOCKMANN: No, no, fellows, no fooling around! I won't put up with any commotion. Even if the Board of Directors

wants to give me an increase I won't take it—I just won't take it, Catherine.

MRS. STOCKMANN, *dutifully:* That's right, Tom.

PETRA, *lifting her glass:* Skol, Father!

EVERYBODY: Skol, Doctor!

HORSTER: Doctor, I hope this will bring you great honor and pleasure.

DR. STOCKMANN: Thanks, friends, thanks. There's one blessing above all others. To have earned the respect of one's neighbors is—is— Catherine, I'm going to dance!

He grabs his wife and whirls her around. There are shouts and struggles, general commotion. The boys in nightgowns stick their heads through the doorway at the right, wondering what is going on. Mrs. Stockmann, seeing them, breaks away and chases them upstairs as

The Curtain Falls.

SCENE TWO

Dr. Stockmann's living room the following morning. As the curtain rises, Mrs. Stockmann comes in from the dining room, a sealed letter in her hand. She goes to the study door and peeks in.

MRS. STOCKMANN: Are you there, Tom?

DR. STOCKMANN, *from within:* I just got in. *He enters the living room.* What's up?

MRS. STOCKMANN: From Peter. It just came. *She hands him the envelope.*

DR. STOCKMANN: Oh, let's see. *He opens the letter and reads:* "I am returning herewith the report you submitted . . ." *He continues to read, mumbling to himself.*

MRS. STOCKMANN: Well, what does he say? Don't stand there!

DR. STOCKMANN, *putting the letter in his pocket:* He just says he'll come around this afternoon.

MRS. STOCKMANN: Oh. Well, maybe you ought to try to remember to be home then.

DR. STOCKMANN: Oh, I sure will. I'm through with my morning visits anyway.

MRS. STOCKMANN: I'm dying to see how he's going to take it.

DR. STOCKMANN: Why, is there any doubt? He'll probably make it look like he made the discovery, not I.

MRS. STOCKMANN: But aren't you a little bit afraid of that?

DR. STOCKMANN: Oh, underneath he'll be happy, Catherine. It's just that Peter is so afraid that somebody else is going to do something good for this town.

MRS. STOCKMANN: I wish you'd go out of your way and share the honors with him. Couldn't we say that he put you on the right track or something?

DR. STOCKMANN: Oh, I don't mind—as long as it makes everybody happy.

Morten Kiil sticks his head through the doorway. He looks around searchingly and chuckles. He will continue chuckling until he leaves the house. He is the archetype of the little twinkle-eyed man who sneaks into so much of Ibsen's work. He will chuckle you right over the precipice. He is the dealer, the man with the rat's finely tuned brain. But he is sometimes likable because he is without morals and announces the fact by laughing.

KIIL, *slyly:* Is it really true?

MRS. STOCKMANN, *walking toward him:* Father!

DR. STOCKMANN: Well, good morning!

MRS. STOCKMANN: Come on in.

KIIL: It better be true or I'm going.

DR. STOCKMANN: What had better be true?

KIIL: This crazy story about the water system. Is it true?

MRS. STOCKMANN: Of course it's true! How did you find out about it?

KIIL: Petra came flying by on her way to school this morning.

DR. STOCKMANN: Oh, she did?

KIIL: Ya. I thought she was trying to make a fool out of me—

MRS. STOCKMANN: Now why would she do that?

KIIL: Nothing gives more pleasure to young people than to make fools out of old people. But this is true, eh?

DR. STOCKMANN: Of course it's true. Sit down here. It's pretty lucky for the town, eh?

KIIL, *fighting his laughter:* Lucky for the town!

DR. STOCKMANN: I mean, that I made the discovery before it was too late.

KIIL: Tom, I never thought you had the imagination to pull your own brother's leg like this.

DR. STOCKMANN: Pull his leg?

MRS. STOCKMANN: But, Father, he's not—

KIIL: How does it go now, let me get it straight. There's some kind of—like cockroaches in the waterpipes—

DR. STOCKMANN, *laughing:* No, not cockroaches.

KIIL: Well, some kind of little animals.

MRS. STOCKMANN: Bacteria, Father.

KIIL, *who can barely speak through his laughter:* Ah, but a whole mess of them, eh?

DR. STOCKMANN: Oh, there'd be millions and millions.

KIIL: And nobody can see them but you, is that it?

DR. STOCKMANN: Yes, that's—well, of course anybody with a micro— *He breaks off.* What are you laughing at?

MRS. STOCKMANN, *smiling at Kiil:* You don't understand, Father. Nobody can actually see bacteria, but that doesn't mean they're not there.

KIIL: Good girl, you stick with him! By God, this is the best thing I ever heard in my life!

DR. STOCKMANN, *smiling:* What do you mean?

KIIL: But tell me, you think you are actually going to get your brother to believe this?

DR. STOCKMANN: Well, we'll see soon enough!

KIIL: You really think he's that crazy?

DR. STOCKMANN: I hope the whole town will be that crazy, Morten.

KIIL: Ya, they probably are, and it'll serve them right too—they think they're so much smarter than us old-timers. Your good brother ordered them to bounce me out of the council, so they chased me out like a dog! Make jackasses out of all of them, Stockmann!

DR. STOCKMANN: Yes, but, Morten—

KIIL: Long-eared, short-tailed jackasses! *He gets up.* Stockmann, if you can make the Mayor and his elegant friends grab at this bait, I will give a couple of hundred crowns to charity, and right now, right on the spot.

DR. STOCKMANN: Well, that would be very kind of you, but I'm—

KIIL: I haven't got much to play around with, but if you can pull the rug out from under him with this cockroach business, I'll give at least fifty crowns to some poor people on Christmas Eve. Maybe this'll teach them to put some brains back in Town Hall!

Hovstad enters from the hall.

HOVSTAD: Good morning! Oh, pardon me . . .

KIIL, *enjoying this proof immensely:* Oh, this one is in on it, too?

HOVSTAD: What's that, sir?

DR. STOCKMANN: Of course he's in on it.

KIIL: Couldn't I have guessed that! And it's going to be in the papers, I suppose. You're sure tying down the corners, aren't you? Well, lay it on thick. I've got to go.

DR. STOCKMANN: Oh, no, stay a while, let me explain it to you!

KIIL: Oh, I get it, don't worry! Only you can see them, heh? That's the best idea I've ever—damn it, you shouldn't do this for nothing! *He goes toward the hall.*

MRS. STOCKMANN, *following him out, laughing:* But, Father, you don't understand about bacteria.

DR. STOCKMANN, *laughing:* The old badger doesn't believe a word of it.

HOVSTAD: What does he think you're doing?

DR. STOCKMANN: Making an idiot out of my brother—imagine that?

HOVSTAD: You got a few minutes?

DR. STOCKMANN: Sure, as long as you like.

HOVSTAD: Have you heard from the Mayor?

DR. STOCKMANN: Only that he's coming over later.

HOVSTAD: I've been thinking about this since last night—

DR. STOCKMANN: Don't say?

HOVSTAD: For you as a medical man, a scientist, this is a really rare opportunity. But I've been wondering if you realize that it ties in with a lot of other things.

DR. STOCKMANN: How do you mean? Sit down. *They sit at the right.* What are you driving at?

HOVSTAD: You said last night that the pollution comes from impurities in the ground—

DR. STOCKMANN: It comes from the poisonous dump up in Windmill Valley.

HOVSTAD: Doctor, I think it comes from an entirely different dump.

DR. STOCKMANN: What do you mean?

HOVSTAD, *with growing zeal:* The same dump that is poisoning and polluting our whole social life in this town.

DR. STOCKMANN: For God's sake, Hovstad, what are you babbling about?

HOVSTAD: Everything that matters in this town has fallen into the hands of a few bureaucrats.

DR. STOCKMANN: Well, they're not all bureaucrats—

HOVSTAD: They're all rich, all with old reputable names, and they've got everything in the palm of their hands.

DR. STOCKMANN: Yes, but they happen to have ability and knowledge.

HOVSTAD: Did they show ability and knowledge when they built the water system where they did?

DR. STOCKMANN: No, of course not, but that happened to be a blunder, and we'll clear it up now.

HOVSTAD: You really imagine it's going to be as easy as all that?

DR. STOCKMANN: Easy or not easy, it's got to be done.

HOVSTAD: Doctor, I've made up my mind to give this whole scandal very special treatment.

DR. STOCKMANN: Now wait. You can't call it a scandal yet.

HOVSTAD: Doctor, when I took over the *People's Messenger* I swore I'd blow that smug cabal of old, stubborn, self-satisfied fogies to bits. This is the story that can do it.

DR. STOCKMANN: But I still think we owe them a deep debt of gratitude for building the springs.

HOVSTAD: The Mayor being your brother, I wouldn't ordinarily want to touch it, but I know you'd never let that kind of thing obstruct the truth.

DR. STOCKMANN: Of course not, but . . .

HOVSTAD: I want you to understand me. I don't have to tell you I come from a simple family. I know in my bones what the underdog needs—he's got to have a say in the govern-

ment of society. That's what brings out ability, intelligence, and self-respect in people.

DR. STOCKMANN: I understand that, but . . .

HOVSTAD: I think a newspaperman who turns down any chance to give the underdog a lift is taking on a responsibility that I don't want. I know perfectly well that in fancy circles they call it agitation, and they can call it anything they like if it makes them happy, but I have my own conscience—

DR. STOCKMANN, *interrupting:* I agree with you, Hovstad, but this is just the water supply and— *There is a knock on the door.* Damn it! Come in!

Mr. Aslaksen, the publisher, enters from the hall. He is simply but neatly dressed. He wears gloves and carries a hat and an umbrella in his hand. He is so utterly drawn it is unnecessary to say anything at all about him.

ASLAKSEN: I beg your pardon, Doctor, if I intrude . . .

HOVSTAD, *standing up:* Are you looking for me, Aslaksen?

ASLAKSEN: No, I didn't know you were here. I want to see the Doctor.

DR. STOCKMANN: What can I do for you?

ASLAKSEN: Is it true, Doctor, what I hear from Mr. Billing, that you intend to campaign for a better water system?

DR. STOCKMANN: Yes, for the Institute. But it's not a campaign.

ASLAKSEN: I just wanted to call and tell you that we are behind you a hundred per cent.

HOVSTAD, *to Dr. Stockmann:* There, you see!

DR. STOCKMANN: Mr. Aslaksen, I thank you with all my heart. But you see—

ASLAKSEN: We can be important, Doctor. When the little businessman wants to push something through, he turns out to be the majority, you know, and it's always good to have the majority on your side.

DR. STOCKMANN: That's certainly true, but I don't understand what this is all about. It seems to me it's a simple, straightforward business. The water—

ASLAKSEN: Of course we intend to behave with moderation, Doctor. I always try to be a moderate and careful man.

DR. STOCKMANN: You are known for that, Mr. Aslaksen, but—

ASLAKSEN: The water system is very important to us little businessmen, Doctor. Kirsten Springs are becoming a gold mine for this town, especially for the property owners, and that is why, in my capacity as chairman of the Property Owners Association—

DR. STOCKMANN: Yes.

ASLAKSEN: And furthermore, as a representative of the Temperance Society— You probably know, Doctor, that I am active for prohibition.

DR. STOCKMANN: So I have heard.

ASLAKSEN: As a result, I come into contact with all kinds of people, and since I am known to be a law-abiding and solid citizen, I have a certain influence in this town—you might even call it a little power.

DR. STOCKMANN: I know that very well, Mr. Aslaksen.

ASLAKSEN: That's why you can see that it would be practically nothing for me to arrange a demonstration.

DR. STOCKMANN: Demonstration! What are you going to demonstrate about?

ASLAKSEN: The citizens of the town complimenting you for bringing this important matter to everybody's attention. Obviously it would have to be done with the utmost moderation so as not to hurt the authorities.

HOVSTAD: This could knock the big-bellies right into the garbage can!

ASLAKSEN: No indiscretion or extreme aggressiveness toward the authorities, Mr. Hovstad! I don't want any wild-eyed radicalism on this thing. I've had enough of that in my time, and no good ever comes of it. But for a good solid citizen to express his calm, frank, and free opinion is something nobody can deny.

DR. STOCKMANN, *shaking the publisher's hand:* My dear Aslaksen, I can't tell you how it heartens me to hear this kind of support. I am happy—I really am—I'm happy. Listen! Wouldn't you like a glass of sherry?

ASLAKSEN: I am a member of the Temperance Society. I—

DR. STOCKMANN: Well, how about a glass of beer?

ASLAKSEN, *considers, then:* I don't think I can go quite that far, Doctor. I never take anything. Well, good day, and I want

you to remember that the little man is behind you like a wall.

DR. STOCKMANN: Thank you.

ASLAKSEN: You have the solid majority on your side, because when the little—

DR. STOCKMANN, *trying to stop Aslaksen's talk:* Thanks for that, Mr. Aslaksen, and good day.

ASLAKSEN: Are you going back to the printing shop, Mr. Hovstad?

HOVSTAD: I just have a thing or two to attend to here.

ASLAKSEN: Very well. *He leaves.*

HOVSTAD: Well, what do you say to a little hypodermic for these fence-sitting deadheads?

DR. STOCKMANN, *surprised:* Why? I think Aslaksen is a very sincere man.

HOVSTAD: Isn't it time we pumped some guts into these well-intentioned men of good will? Under all their liberal talk they still idolize authority, and that's got to be rooted out of this town. This blunder of the water system has to be made clear to every voter. Let me print your report.

DR. STOCKMANN: Not until I talk to my brother.

HOVSTAD: I'll write an editorial in the meantime, and if the Mayor won't go along with us—

DR. STOCKMANN: I don't see how you can imagine such a thing!

HOVSTAD: Believe me, Doctor, it's possible, and then—

DR. STOCKMANN: Listen, I promise you: he will go along, and then you can print my report, every word of it.

HOVSTAD: On your word of honor?

DR. STOCKMANN, *giving Hovstad the manuscript:* Here it is. Take it. It can't do any harm for you to read it. Return it to me later.

HOVSTAD: Good day, Doctor.

DR. STOCKMANN: Good day. You'll see, it's going to be easier than you think, Hovstad!

HOVSTAD: I hope so, Doctor. Sincerely. Let me know as soon as you hear from His Honor. *He leaves.*

DR. STOCKMANN, *goes to dining room and looks in:* Catherine! Oh, you're home already, Petra!

PETRA, *coming in:* I just got back from school.

MRS. STOCKMANN, *entering:* Hasn't he been here yet?

DR. STOCKMANN: Peter? No, but I just had a long chat with Hovstad. He's really fascinated with my discovery, and you know, it has more implications than I thought at first. Do you know what I have backing me up?

MRS. STOCKMANN: What in heaven's name have you got backing you up?

DR. STOCKMANN: The solid majority.

MRS. STOCKMANN: Is that good?

DR. STOCKMANN: Good? It's wonderful. You can't imagine the feeling, Catherine, to know that your own town feels like a brother to you. I have never felt so at home in this town since I was a boy. *A noise is heard.*

MRS. STOCKMANN: That must be the front door.

DR. STOCKMANN: Oh, it's Peter then. Come in.

PETER STOCKMANN, *entering from the hall:* Good morning!

DR. STOCKMANN: It's nice to see you, Peter.

MRS. STOCKMANN: Good morning. How are you today?

PETER STOCKMANN: Well, so so. *To Dr. Stockmann:* I received your thesis about the condition of the springs yesterday.

DR. STOCKMANN: I got your note. Did you read it?

PETER STOCKMANN: I read it.

DR. STOCKMANN: Well, what do you have to say?

Peter Stockmann clears his throat and glances at the women.

MRS. STOCKMANN: Come on, Petra. *She and Petra leave the room at the left.*

PETER STOCKMANN, *after a moment:* Thomas, was it really necessary to go into this investigation behind my back?

DR. STOCKMANN: Yes. Until I was convinced myself, there was no point in—

PETER STOCKMANN: And now you are convinced?

DR. STOCKMANN: Well, certainly. Aren't you too, Peter? *Pause.* The University chemists corroborated . . .

PETER STOCKMANN: You intend to present this document to the Board of Directors, officially, as the medical officer of the springs?

DR. STOCKMANN: Of course, something's got to be done, and quick.

PETER STOCKMANN: You always use such strong expressions, Thomas. Among other things, in your report you say that we *guarantee* our guests and visitors a permanent case of poisoning.

DR. STOCKMANN: But, Peter, how can you describe it any other way? Imagine! Poisoned internally and externally!

PETER STOCKMANN: So you merrily conclude that we must build a waste-disposal plant—and reconstruct a brand-new water system from the bottom up!

DR. STOCKMANN: Well, do you know some other way out? I don't.

PETER STOCKMANN: I took a little walk over to the city engineer this morning and in the course of conversation I sort of jokingly mentioned these changes—as something we might consider for the future, you know.

DR. STOCKMANN: The future won't be soon enough, Peter.

PETER STOCKMANN: The engineer kind of smiled at my extravagance and gave me a few facts. I don't suppose you have taken the trouble to consider what your proposed changes would cost?

DR. STOCKMANN: No, I never thought of that.

PETER STOCKMANN: Naturally. Your little project would come to at least three hundred thousand crowns.

DR. STOCKMANN, *astonished:* That expensive!

PETER STOCKMANN: Oh, don't look so upset—it's only money. The worst thing is that it would take some two years.

DR. STOCKMANN: Two years?

PETER STOCKMANN: At the least. And what do you propose we do about the springs in the meantime? Shut them up, no doubt! Because we would have to, you know. As soon as the rumor gets around that the water is dangerous, we won't have a visitor left. So that's the picture, Thomas. You have it in your power literally to ruin your own town.

DR. STOCKMANN: Now look, Peter! I don't want to ruin anything.

PETER STOCKMANN: Kirsten Springs are the blood supply of this town, Thomas—the only future we've got here. Now will you stop and think?

DR. STOCKMANN: Good God! Well, what do you think we ought to do?

PETER STOCKMANN: Your report has not convinced me that the conditions are as dangerous as you try to make them.

DR. STOCKMANN: Now listen; they are even worse than the report makes them out to be. Remember, summer is coming, and the warm weather!

PETER STOCKMANN: I think you're exaggerating. A capable physician ought to know what precautions to take.

DR. STOCKMANN: And what then?

PETER STOCKMANN: The existing water supply for the springs is a fact, Thomas, and has got to be treated as a fact. If you are reasonable and act with discretion, the directors of the Institute will be inclined to take under consideration any means to make possible improvements, reasonably and without financial sacrifices.

DR. STOCKMANN: Peter, do you imagine that I would ever agree to such trickery?

PETER STOCKMANN: Trickery?

DR. STOCKMANN: Yes, a trick, a fraud, a lie! A treachery, a downright crime, against the public and against the whole community!

PETER STOCKMANN: I said before that I am not convinced that there is any actual danger.

DR. STOCKMANN: Oh, you aren't? Anything else is impossible! My report is an absolute fact. The only trouble is that you and your administration were the ones who insisted that the water supply be built where it is, and now you're afraid to admit the blunder you committed. Damn it! Don't you think I can see through it all?

PETER STOCKMANN: All right, let's suppose that's true. Maybe I do care a little about my reputation. I still say I do it for the good of the town—without moral authority there can be no government. And that is why, Thomas, it is my duty to prevent your report from reaching the Board. Some time later I will bring up the matter for discussion. In the meantime, not a single word is to reach the public.

DR. STOCKMANN: Oh, my dear Peter, do you imagine you can prevent that!

PETER STOCKMANN: It will be prevented.

DR. STOCKMANN: It can't be. There are too many people who already know about it.

PETER STOCKMANN, *angered:* Who? It can't possibly be those people from the *Daily Messenger* who—

DR. STOCKMANN: Exactly. The liberal, free, and independent press will stand up and do its duty!

PETER STOCKMANN: You are an unbelievably irresponsible man, Thomas! Can't you imagine what consequences that is going to have for you?

DR. STOCKMANN: For me?

PETER STOCKMANN: Yes, for you and your family.

DR. STOCKMANN: What the hell are you saying now!

PETER STOCKMANN: I believe I have the right to think of myself as a helpful brother, Thomas.

DR. STOCKMANN: You have been, and I thank you deeply for it.

PETER STOCKMANN: Don't mention it. I often couldn't help myself. I had hoped that by improving your finances I would be able to keep you from running completely hog wild.

DR. STOCKMANN: You mean it was only for your own sake?

PETER STOCKMANN: Partly, yes. What do you imagine people think of an official whose closest relatives get themselves into trouble time and time again?

DR. STOCKMANN: And that's what I have done?

PETER STOCKMANN: You do it without knowing it. You're like a man with an automatic brain—as soon as an idea breaks into your head, no matter how idiotic it may be, you get up like a sleepwalker and start writing a pamphlet about it.

DR. STOCKMANN: Peter, don't you think it's a citizen's duty to share a new idea with the public?

PETER STOCKMANN: The public doesn't need new ideas—the public is much better off with old ideas.

DR. STOCKMANN: You're not even embarrassed to say that?

PETER STOCKMANN: Now look, I'm going to lay this out once and for all. You're always barking about authority. If a man gives you an order he's persecuting you. Nothing is important enough to respect once you decide to revolt against your superiors. All right then, I give up. I'm not going to try to change you any more. I told you the stakes you are playing for here, and now I am going to give you an order. And I warn you, you had better obey it if you value your career.

DR. STOCKMANN: What kind of an order?

PETER STOCKMANN: You are going to deny these rumors officially.

DR. STOCKMANN: How?

PETER STOCKMANN: You simply say that you went into the examination of the water more thoroughly and you find that you overestimated the danger.

DR. STOCKMANN: I see.

PETER STOCKMANN: And that you have complete confidence that whatever improvements are needed, the management will certainly take care of them.

DR. STOCKMANN, *after a pause:* My convictions come from the condition of the water. My convictions will change when the water changes, and for no other reason.

PETER STOCKMANN: What are you talking about convictions? You're an official, you keep your convictions to yourself!

DR. STOCKMANN: To myself?

PETER STOCKMANN: As an official, I said. God knows, as a private person that's something else, but as a subordinate employee of the Institute, you have no right to express any convictions or personal opinions about anything connected with policy.

DR. STOCKMANN: Now you listen to me. I am a doctor and a scientist—

PETER STOCKMANN: This has nothing to do with science!

DR. STOCKMANN: Peter, I have the right to express my opinion on anything in the world!

PETER STOCKMANN: Not about the Institute—that I forbid.

DR. STOCKMANN: You forbid!

PETER STOCKMANN: I forbid you as your superior, and when I give orders you obey.

DR. STOCKMANN: Peter, if you weren't my brother—

PETRA, *throwing the door at the left open:* Father! You aren't going to stand for this! *She enters.*

MRS. STOCKMANN, *coming in after her:* Petra, Petra!

PETER STOCKMANN: What have you two been doing, eavesdropping?

MRS. STOCKMANN: You were talking so loud we couldn't help . . .

PETRA: Yes, I was eavesdropping!

PETER STOCKMANN: That makes me very happy.

DR. STOCKMANN, *approaching his brother:* You said something to me about forbidding—

PETER STOCKMANN: You forced me to.

DR. STOCKMANN: So you want me to spit in my own face officially—is that it?

PETER STOCKMANN: Why must you always be so colorful?

DR. STOCKMANN: And if I don't obey?

PETER STOCKMANN: Then we will publish our own statement, to calm the public.

DR. STOCKMANN: Good enough! And I will write against you. I will stick to what I said, and I will prove that I am right and that you are wrong, and what will you do then?

PETER STOCKMANN: Then I simply won't be able to prevent your dismissal.

DR. STOCKMANN: What!

PETRA: Father!

PETER STOCKMANN: Dismissed from the Institute is what I said. If you want to make war on Kirsten Springs, you have no right to be on the Board of Directors.

DR. STOCKMANN, *after a pause:* You'd dare to do that?

PETER STOCKMANN: Oh, no, you're the daring man.

PETRA: Uncle, this is a rotten way to treat a man like Father!

MRS. STOCKMANN: Will you be quiet, Petra!

PETER STOCKMANN: So young and you've got opinions already —but that's natural. *To Mrs. Stockmann:* Catherine dear, you're probably the only sane person in this house. Knock some sense into his head, will you? Make him realize what he's driving his whole family into.

DR. STOCKMANN: My family concerns nobody but myself.

PETER STOCKMANN: His family and his own town.

DR. STOCKMANN: I'm going to show you who loves his town. The people are going to get the full stink of this corruption, Peter, and then we will see who loves his town!

PETER STOCKMANN: You love your town when you blindly, spitefully, stubbornly go ahead trying to cut off our most important industry?

DR. STOCKMANN: That source is poisoned, man. We are getting fat by peddling filth and corruption to innocent people!

PETER STOCKMANN: I think this has gone beyond opinions and convictions, Thomas. A man who can throw that kind of insinuation around is nothing but a traitor to society!

DR. STOCKMANN, *starting toward his brother in a fury:* How dare you to—

MRS. STOCKMANN, *stepping between them:* Tom!

PETRA, *grabbing her father's arm:* Be careful, Father!

PETER STOCKMANN, *with dignity:* I won't expose myself to violence. You have been warned. Consider what you owe yourself and your family! Good day! *He exits.*

DR. STOCKMANN, *walking up and down:* He's insulted. *He's* insulted!

MRS. STOCKMANN: It's shameful, Tom.

PETRA: Oh, I would love to give him a piece of my mind!

DR. STOCKMANN: It was my own fault! I should have shown my teeth right from the beginning. He called me a traitor to society. Me! Damn it all, that's not going to stick!

MRS. STOCKMANN: Please, think! He's got all the power on his side.

DR. STOCKMANN: Yes, but I have the truth on mine.

MRS. STOCKMANN: Without power, what good is the truth?

PETRA: Mother, how can you say such a thing?

DR. STOCKMANN: That's ridiculous, Catherine. I have the liberal press with me, and the majority. If that isn't power, what is?

MRS. STOCKMANN: But, for heaven's sake, Tom, you aren't going to—

DR. STOCKMANN: What am I not going to do?

MRS. STOCKMANN: You aren't going to fight it out in public with your brother!

DR. STOCKMANN: What the hell else do you want me to do?

MRS. STOCKMANN: But it won't do you any earthly good. If they won't do it, they won't. All you'll get out of it is a notice that you're fired.

DR. STOCKMANN: I am going to do my duty, Catherine. Me, the man he calls a traitor to society!

MRS. STOCKMANN: And how about your duty toward your family—the people you're supposed to provide for?

PETRA: Don't always think of us first, Mother.

MRS. STOCKMANN, *to Petra:* You can talk! If worst comes to

worst, you can manage for yourself. But what about the boys, Tom, and you and me?

DR. STOCKMANN: What about you? You want me to be the miserable animal who'd crawl up the boots of that damn gang? Will you be happy if I can't face myself the rest of my life?

MRS. STOCKMANN: Tom, Tom, there's so much injustice in the world! You've simply got to learn to live with it. If you go on this way, God help us, we'll have no money again. Is it so long since the north that you've forgotten what it was to live like we lived? Haven't we had enough of that for one lifetime? *The boys enter.* What will happen to them? We've got nothing if you're fired!

DR. STOCKMANN: Stop it! *He looks at the boys.* Well, boys, did you learn anything in school today?

MORTEN, *looking at them, puzzled:* We learned what an insect is.

DR. STOCKMANN: You don't say!

MORTEN: What happened here? Why is everybody—

DR. STOCKMANN: Nothing, nothing. You know what I'm going to do, boys? From now on I'm going to teach you what a man is. *He looks at Mrs. Stockmann. She cries as*

The Curtain Falls.

ACT TWO

SCENE ONE

The editorial office of the People's Daily Messenger. *At the back of the room, to the left, is a door leading to the printing room. Near it, in the left wall, is another door. At the right of the stage is the entrance door. In the middle of the room there is a large table covered with papers, newspapers, and books. Around it are a few chairs. A writing desk stands against the right wall. The room is dingy and cheerless, the furniture shabby.*

As the curtain rises, Billing is sitting at the desk, reading the manuscript. Hovstad comes in after a moment from the printing room. Billing looks up.

BILLING: The Doctor not come yet?
HOVSTAD: No, not yet. You finish it?

Billing holds up a hand to signal "just a moment." He reads on, the last paragraph of the manuscript. Hovstad comes and stands over him, reading with him. Now Billing closes the manuscript, glances up at Hovstad with some trepidation, then looks off. Hovstad, looking at Billing, walks a few steps away.

HOVSTAD: Well? What do you think of it?
BILLING, *with some hesitation:* It's devastating. The Doctor is a brilliant man. I swear, I myself never really understood how incompetent those fat fellows are, on top. *He picks up the manuscript and waves it a little.* I hear the rumble of revolution in this.
HOVSTAD, *looking toward the door:* Sssh! Aslaksen's inside.
BILLING: Aslaksen's a coward. With all that moderation talk, all he's saying is, he's yellow. You're going to print this, aren't you?
HOVSTAD: Sure, I'm just waiting for the Doctor to give the word. If his brother hasn't given in, we put it on the press anyway.
BILLING: Yes, but if the Mayor's against this it's going to get pretty rough. You know that, don't you?

HOVSTAD: Just let him try to block the reconstruction—the little businessmen and the whole town'll be screaming for his head. Aslaksen'll see to that.

BILLING, *ecstatically:* The stockholders'll have to lay out a fortune of money if this goes through!

HOVSTAD: My boy, I think it's going to bust them. And when the springs go busted, the people are finally going to understand the level of genius that's been running this town. Those five sheets of paper are going to put in a liberal administration once and for all.

BILLING: It's a revolution. You know that? *With hope and fear:* I mean it, we're on the edge of a real revolution!

DR. STOCKMANN, *entering:* Put it on the press!

HOVSTAD, *excited:* Wonderful! What did the Mayor say?

DR. STOCKMANN: The Mayor has declared war, so war is what it's going to be! *He takes the manuscript from Billing.* And this is only the beginning! You know what he tried to do?

BILLING, *calling into the printing room:* Mr. Aslaksen, the Doctor's here!

DR. STOCKMANN, *continuing:* He actually tried to blackmail me! He's got the nerve to tell me that I'm not allowed to speak my mind without his permission! Imagine the shameless effrontery!

HOVSTAD: He actually said it right out?

DR. STOCKMANN: Right to my face! The trouble with me was I kept giving them credit for being our kind of people, but they're dictators! They're people who'll try to hold power even if they have to poison the town to do it.

Toward the last part of Dr. Stockmann's speech Aslaksen enters.

ASLAKSEN: Now take it easy, Doctor, you—you mustn't always be throwing accusations. I'm with you, you understand, but moderation—

DR. STOCKMANN, *cutting him off:* What'd you think of the article, Hovstad?

HOVSTAD: It's a masterpiece. In one blow you've managed to prove beyond any doubt what kind of men are running us.

ASLAKSEN: May we print it now, then?

DR. STOCKMANN: I should say *so*!

HOVSTAD: We'll have it ready for tomorrow's paper.

DR. STOCKMANN: And listen, Mr. Aslaksen, do me a favor, will you? You run a fine paper, but supervise the printing personally, eh? I'd hate to see the weather report stuck into the middle of my article.

ASLAKSEN, *laughing:* Don't worry, that won't happen this time!

DR. STOCKMANN: Make it perfect, eh? Like you were printing money. You can't imagine how I'm dying to see it in print. After all the lies in the papers, the half-lies, the quarter-lies—to finally see the absolute, unvarnished truth about something important. And this is only the beginning. We'll go on to other subjects and blow up every lie we live by! What do you say, Aslaksen?

ASLAKSEN, *nodding in agreement:* But just remember . . .

BILLING *and* HOVSTAD *together with* ASLAKSEN: Moderation!

ASLAKSEN, *to Billing and Hovstad:* I don't know what's so funny about that!

BILLING, *enthralled:* Doctor Stockmann, I feel as though I were standing in some historic painting. Goddammit, this is a historic day! Someday this scene'll be in a museum, entitled, "The Day the Truth Was Born."

DR. STOCKMANN, *suddenly:* Oh! I've got a patient half-bandaged down the street. *He leaves.*

HOVSTAD, *to Aslaksen:* I hope you realize how useful he could be to us.

ASLAKSEN: I don't like that business about "this is only the beginning." Let him stick to the springs.

BILLING: What makes you so scared all the time?

ASLAKSEN: I have to live here. It'd be different if he were attacking the national government or something, but if he thinks I'm going to start going after the whole town administration—

BILLING: What's the difference? Bad is bad!

ASLAKSEN: Yes, but there is a difference. You attack the national government, what's going to happen? Nothing. They go right on. But a town administration—they're liable to be overthrown or something! I represent the small property owners in this town—

BILLING: Ha! It's always the same. Give a man a little property and the truth can go to hell!

ASLAKSEN: Mr. Billing, I'm older than you are. I've seen fire-eaters before. You know who used to work at that desk before you? Councilman Stensford—*councilman!*

BILLING: Just because I work at a renegade's desk, does that mean—

ASLAKSEN: You're a politician. A politician never knows where he's going to end up. And besides you applied for a job as secretary to the Magistrate, didn't you?

HOVSTAD, *surprised, laughs:* Billing!

BILLING, *to Hovstad:* Well, why not? If I get it I'll have a chance to put across some good things. I could put plenty of big boys on the spot with a job like that!

ASLAKSEN: All right, I'm just saying. *He goes to the printing-room door.* People change. Just remember when you call me a coward—I may not have made the hot speeches, but I never went back on my beliefs either. Unlike some of the big radicals around here, I didn't change. Of course, I *am* a little more moderate, but moderation is—

HOVSTAD: Oh, God!

ASLAKSEN: I don't see what's so funny about that! *He glares at Hovstad and goes out.*

BILLING: If we could get rid of him we—

HOVSTAD: Take it easy—he pays the printing bill, he's not that bad. *He picks up the manuscript.* I'll get the printer on this. *He starts out.*

BILLING: Say, Hovstad, how about asking Stockmann to back us? Then we could really put out a paper!

HOVSTAD: What would he do for money?

BILLING: His father-in-law.

HOVSTAD: Kiil? Since when has he got money?

BILLING: I think he's loaded with it.

HOVSTAD: No! Why, as long as I've known him he's worn the same overcoat, the same suit—

BILLING: Yeah, and the same ring on his right hand. You ever get a look at that boulder? *He points to his finger.*

HOVSTAD: No, I never—

BILLING: All year he wears the diamond inside, but on New Year's Eve he turns it around. Figure it out—when a man has no visible means of support, what is he living on? Money, right?

Petra enters, carrying a book.

PETRA: Hello.
HOVSTAD: Well, fancy seeing you here. Sit down. What—
PETRA, *walking slowly up to Hovstad:* I want to ask you a question. *She starts to open the book.*
BILLING: What's that?
PETRA: The English novel you wanted translated.
HOVSTAD: Aren't you going to do it?
PETRA, *with deadly seriousness and curiosity:* I don't get this.
HOVSTAD: You don't get what?
PETRA: This book is absolutely against everything you people believe.
HOVSTAD: Oh, it isn't that bad.
PETRA: But, Mr. Hovstad, it says if you're good there's a supernatural force that'll fix it so you end up happy. And if you're bad you'll be punished. Since when does the world work that way?
HOVSTAD: Yes, Petra, but this is a newspaper, people like to read that kind of thing. They buy the paper for that and then we slip in our political stuff. A newspaper can't buck the public—
PETRA, *astonished, beginning to be angry:* You don't say! *She starts to go.*
HOVSTAD, *hurrying after her:* Now, wait a minute, I don't want you to go feeling that way. *He holds the manuscript out to Billing.* Here, take this to the printer, will you?
BILLING, *taking the manuscript:* Sure. *He goes.*
HOVSTAD: I just want you to understand something: I never even read that book. It was Billing's idea.
PETRA, *trying to penetrate his eyes:* I thought he was a radical.
HOVSTAD: He is. But he's also a—
PETRA, *testily:* A newspaperman.
HOVSTAD: Well, that too, but I was going to say that Billing is trying to get the job as secretary to the Magistrate.
PETRA: What?
HOVSTAD: People are—people, Miss Stockmann.
PETRA: But the Magistrate! He's been fighting everything progressive in this town for thirty years.
HOVSTAD: Let's not argue about it, I just didn't want you to

go out of here with a wrong idea of me. I guess you know that I—I happen to admire women like you. I've never had a chance to tell you, but I—well, I want you to know it. Do you mind? *He smiles.*

PETRA: No, I don't mind, but—reading that book upset me. I really don't understand. Will you tell me why you're supporting my father?

HOVSTAD: What's the mystery? It's a matter of principle.

PETRA: But a paper that'll print a book like this has no principle.

HOVSTAD: Why do you jump to such extremes? You're just like . . .

PETRA: Like what?

HOVSTAD: I simply mean that . . .

PETRA, *moving away from him:* Like my father, you mean. You really have no use for him, do you?

HOVSTAD: Now wait a minute!

PETRA: What's behind this? Are you just trying to hold my hand or something?

HOVSTAD: I happen to agree with your father, and that's why I'm printing his stuff.

PETRA: You're trying to put something over, I think. Why are you in this?

HOVSTAD: Who're you accusing? Billing gave you that book, not me!

PETRA: But you don't mind printing it, do you? What are you trying to do with my father? You have no principles—what are you up to here?

Aslaksen hurriedly enters from the printing shop, Stockmann's manuscript in his hand.

ASLAKSEN: My God! Hovstad! *He sees Petra.* Miss Stockmann.

PETRA, *looking at Hovstad:* I don't think I've been so frightened in my life. *She goes out.*

HOVSTAD, *starting after her:* Please, you mustn't think I—

ASLAKSEN, *stopping him:* Where are you going? The Mayor's out there.

HOVSTAD: The Mayor!

ASLAKSEN: He wants to speak to you. He came in the back door. He doesn't want to be seen.

HOVSTAD: What does he want? *He goes to the printing-room door, opens it, calls out with a certain edge of servility:* Come in, Your Honor!

PETER STOCKMANN, *entering:* Thank you.

Hovstad carefully closes the door.

PETER STOCKMANN, *walking around:* It's clean! I always imagined this place would look dirty. But it's clean. *Commendingly:* Very nice, Mr. Aslaksen. *He puts his hat on the desk.*

ASLAKSEN: Not at all, Your Honor—I mean to say, I always . . .

HOVSTAD: What can I do for you, Your Honor? Sit down?

PETER STOCKMANN, *sits, placing his cane on the table:* I had a very annoying thing happen today, Mr. Hovstad.

HOVSTAD: That so?

PETER STOCKMANN: It seems my brother has written some sort of—memorandum. About the springs.

HOVSTAD: You don't say.

PETER STOCKMANN, *looking at Hovstad now:* He mentioned it . . . to you?

HOVSTAD: Yes. I think he said something about it.

ASLAKSEN, *nervously starts to go out, attempting to hide the manuscript:* Will you excuse me, gentlemen . . .

PETER STOCKMANN, *pointing to the manuscript:* That's it, isn't it?

ASLAKSEN: This? I don't know, I haven't had a chance to look at it, the printer just handed it to me . . .

HOVSTAD: Isn't that the thing the printer wanted the spelling checked?

ASLAKSEN: That's it, it's only a question of spelling. I'll be right back.

PETER STOCKMANN: I'm very good at spelling. *He holds out his hand.* Maybe I can help you.

HOVSTAD: No, Your Honor, there's some Latin in it. You wouldn't know Latin, would you?

PETER STOCKMANN: Oh, yes. I used to help my brother with his Latin all the time. Let me have it.

Aslaksen gives him the manuscript. Peter Stockmann looks at the title on the first page, then glances up sarcastically at Hovstad, who avoids his eyes.

PETER STOCKMANN: You're going to print this?

HOVSTAD: I can't very well refuse a signed article. A signed article is the author's responsibility.

PETER STOCKMANN: Mr. Aslaksen, you're going to allow this?

ASLAKSEN: I'm the publisher, not the editor, Your Honor. My policy is freedom for the editor.

PETER STOCKMANN: You have a point—I can see that.

ASLAKSEN, *reaching for the manuscript:* So if you don't mind . . .

PETER STOCKMANN: Not at all. *But he holds on to the manuscript. After a pause:* This reconstruction of the springs—

ASLAKSEN: I realize, Your Honor—it does mean tremendous sacrifices for the stockholders.

PETER STOCKMANN: Don't upset yourself. The first thing a Mayor learns is that the less wealthy can always be prevailed upon to demand a spirit of sacrifice for the public good.

ASLAKSEN: I'm glad you see that.

PETER STOCKMANN: Oh, yes. Especially when it's the wealthy who are going to do the sacrificing. What you don't seem to understand, Mr. Aslaksen, is that so long as I am Mayor, any changes in those springs are going to be paid for by a municipal loan.

ASLAKSEN: A municipal—you mean you're going to tax the people for this?

PETER STOCKMANN: Exactly.

HOVSTAD: But the springs are a private corporation!

PETER STOCKMANN: The corporation built Kirsten Springs out of its own money. If the people want them changed, the people naturally must pay the bill. The corporation is in no position to put out any more money. It simply can't do it.

ASLAKSEN, *to Hovstad:* That's impossible! People will never stand for a new tax. *To the Mayor:* Is this a fact or your opinion?

PETER STOCKMANN: It happens to be a fact. Plus another fact—you'll forgive me for talking about facts in a newspaper office—but don't forget that the springs will take two years to make over. Two years without income for your small businessmen, Mr. Aslaksen, and a heavy new tax besides. And all because—*his private emotion comes to the surface; he*

throttles the manuscript in his hand—because of this dream, this hallucination, that we live in a pesthole!

HOVSTAD: That's based on science.

PETER STOCKMANN, *raising the manuscript and throwing it down on the table:* This is based on vindictiveness, on his hatred of authority and nothing else. *He pounds on the manuscript.* This is the mad dream of a man who is trying to blow up our way of life! It has nothing to do with reform or science or anything else, but pure and simple destruction! And I intend to see to it that the people understand it exactly so!

ASLAKSEN, *hit by this:* My God! *To Hovstad:* Maybe . . . You sure you want to support this thing, Hovstad?

HOVSTAD, *nervously:* Frankly I'd never thought of it in quite that way. I mean . . . *To the Mayor:* When you think of it psychologically it's completely possible, of course, that the man is simply out to— I don't know what to say, Your Honor. I'd hate to hurt the town in any way. I never imagined we'd have to have a new tax.

PETER STOCKMANN: You should have imagined it because you're going to have to advocate it. Unless, of course, liberal and radical newspaper readers enjoy high taxes. But you'd know that better than I. I happen to have here a brief story of the actual facts. It proves that, with a little care, nobody need be harmed at all by the water. *He takes out a long envelope.* Of course, in time we'd have to make a few minor structural changes and we'd pay for those.

HOVSTAD: May I see that?

PETER STOCKMANN: I want you to *study* it, Mr. Hovstad, and see if you don't agree that—

BILLING, *entering quickly:* Are you expecting the Doctor?

PETER STOCKMANN, *alarmed:* He's here?

BILLING: Just coming across the street.

PETER STOCKMANN: I'd rather not run into him here. How can I . . .

BILLING: Right this way, sir, hurry up!

ASLAKSEN, *at the entrance door, peeking:* Hurry up!

PETER STOCKMANN, *going with Billing through the door at the left:* Get him out of here right away! *They exit.*

HOVSTAD: Do something, do something!

Aslaksen pokes among some papers on the table. Hovstad sits at the desk, starts to "write." Dr. Stockmann enters.

DR. STOCKMANN: Any proofs yet? *He sees they hardly turn to him.* I guess not, eh?

ASLAKSEN, *without turning:* No, you can't expect them for some time.

DR. STOCKMANN: You mind if I wait?

HOVSTAD: No sense in that, Doctor, it'll be quite a while yet.

DR. STOCKMANN, *laughing, places his hand on Hovstad's back:* Bear with me, Hovstad, I just can't wait to see it in print.

HOVSTAD: We're pretty busy, Doctor, so . . .

DR. STOCKMANN, *starting toward the door:* Don't let me hold you up. That's the way to be, busy, busy. We'll make this town shine like a jewel! *He has opened the door, now he comes back.* Just one thing. I—

HOVSTAD: Couldn't we talk some other time? We're very—

DR. STOCKMANN: Two words. Just walking down the street now, I looked at the people, in the stores, driving the wagons, and suddenly I was—well, touched, you know? By their innocence, I mean. What I'm driving at is, when this exposé breaks they're liable to start making a saint out of me or something, and I—Aslaksen, I want you to promise me that you're not going to try to get up any dinner for me or—

ASLAKSEN, *turning toward the Doctor:* Doctor, there's no use concealing—

DR. STOCKMANN: I knew it. Now look, I will simply not attend a dinner in my honor.

HOVSTAD, *getting up:* Doctor, I think it's time we—

Mrs. Stockmann enters.

MRS. STOCKMANN: I thought so. Thomas, I want you home. Now come. I want you to talk to Petra.

DR. STOCKMANN: What happened? What are you doing here?

HOVSTAD: Something wrong, Mrs. Stockmann?

MRS. STOCKMANN, *leveling a look of accusation at Hovstad:* Doctor Stockmann is the father of three children, Mr. Hovstad.

DR. STOCKMANN: Now look, dear, everybody knows that. What's the—

MRS. STOCKMANN, *restraining an outburst at her husband:* Nobody would *believe* it from the way you're dragging us into this disaster!

DR. STOCKMANN: What disaster?

MRS. STOCKMANN, *to Hovstad:* He treated you like a son, now you make a fool of him?

HOVSTAD: *I'm* not making a—

DR. STOCKMANN: Catherine! *He indicates Hovstad.* How can you accuse—

MRS. STOCKMANN, *to Hovstad:* He'll lose his job at the springs, do you realize that? You print the article, and they'll grind him up like a piece of flesh!

DR. STOCKMANN: Catherine, you're embarrassing me! I beg your pardon, gentlemen . . .

MRS. STOCKMANN: Mr. Hovstad, what are you up to?

DR. STOCKMANN: I won't have you jumping at Hovstad, Catherine!

MRS. STOCKMANN: I want you home! This man is not your friend!

DR. STOCKMANN: He is my friend! Any man who shares my risk is my friend! You simply don't understand that as soon as this breaks everybody in this town is going to come out in the streets and drive that gang of— *He picks up the Mayor's cane from the table, notices what it is, and stops. He looks from it to Hovstad and Aslaksen.* What's this? *They don't reply. Now he notices the hat on the desk and picks it up with the tip of the cane. He looks at them again. He is angry, incredulous.* What the hell is he doing here?

ASLAKSEN: All right, Doctor, now let's be calm and—

DR. STOCKMANN, *starting to move:* Where is he? What'd he do, talk you out of it? Hovstad! *Hovstad remains immobile.* He won't get away with it! Where'd you hide him? *He opens the door at the left.*

ASLAKSEN: Be careful, Doctor!

Peter Stockmann enters with Billing through the door Dr. Stockmann opened. Peter Stockmann tries to hide his embarrassment.

DR. STOCKMANN: Well, Peter, poisoning the water was not

enough! You're working on the press now, eh? *He crosses to the entrance door.*

PETER STOCKMANN: My hat, please. And my stick. *Dr. Stockmann puts on the Mayor's hat.* Now what's *this* nonsense! Take that off, that's official insignia!

DR. STOCKMANN: I just wanted you to realize, Peter—*he takes off the hat and looks at it*—that anyone may wear this hat in a democracy, and that a free citizen is not afraid to touch it. *He hands him the hat.* And as for the baton of command, Your Honor, it can pass from hand to hand. *He hands the cane to Peter Stockmann.* So don't gloat yet. The people haven't spoken. *He turns to Hovstad and Aslaksen.* And I have the people because I have the truth, my friends!

ASLAKSEN: Doctor, we're not scientists. We can't judge whether your article is really true.

DR. STOCKMANN: Then print it under my name. Let *me* defend it!

HOVSTAD: I'm not printing it. I'm not going to sacrifice this newspaper. When the whole story gets out the public is not going to stand for any changes in the springs.

ASLAKSEN: His Honor just told us, Doctor—you see, there will have to be a new tax—

DR. STOCKMANN: Ahhhhh! Yes. I see. That's why you're not scientists suddenly and can't decide if I'm telling the truth. Well. So!

HOVSTAD: Don't take that attitude. The point is—

DR. STOCKMANN: The point, the point, oh, the point is going to fly through this town like an arrow, and I am going to fire it! *To Aslaksen:* Will you print this article as a pamphlet? I'll pay for it.

ASLAKSEN: I'm not going to ruin this paper and this town. Doctor, for the sake of your family—

MRS. STOCKMANN: You can leave his family out of this, Mr. Aslaksen. God help me, I think you people are horrible!

DR. STOCKMANN: My article, if you don't mind.

ASLAKSEN, *giving it to him:* Doctor, you won't get it printed in this town.

PETER STOCKMANN: Can't you forget it? *He indicates Hovstad and Aslaksen.* Can't you see now that everybody—

DR. STOCKMANN: Your Honor, I can't forget it, and you will

never forget it as long as you live. I am going to call a mass meeting, and I—

PETER STOCKMANN: And who is going to rent you a hall?

DR. STOCKMANN: Then I will take a drum and go from street to street, proclaiming that the springs are befouled and poison is rotting the body politic! *He starts for the door.*

PETER STOCKMANN: And I believe you really are that mad!

DR. STOCKMANN: Mad? Oh, my brother, you haven't even heard me raise my voice yet. Catherine? *He holds out his hand, she gives him her elbow. They go stiffly out.*

Peter Stockmann looks regretfully toward the exit, then takes out his manuscript and hands it to Hovstad, who in turn gives it to Billing, who hands it to Aslaksen, who takes it and exits. Peter Stockmann puts his hat on and moves toward the door. Blackout.

The Curtain Falls.

SCENE TWO

A room in Captain Horster's house. The room is bare, as though unused for a long time. A large doorway is at the left, two shuttered windows at the back, and another door at the right. Upstage right, packing cases have been set together, forming a platform, on which are a chair and a small table. There are two chairs next to the platform at the right. One chair stands downstage left.

The room is angled, thus making possible the illusion of a large crowd off in the wing to the left. The platform faces the audience at an angle, thus giving the speakers the chance to speak straight out front and creating the illusion of a large crowd by addressing "people" in the audience.

As the curtain rises the room is empty. Captain Horster enters, carrying a pitcher of water, a glass, and a bell. He is putting these on the table when Billing enters. A crowd is heard talking outside in the street.

BILLING: Captain Horster?

HORSTER, *turning:* Oh, come in. I don't have enough chairs for a lot of people so I decided not to have chairs at all.

BILLING: My name is Billing. Don't you remember, at the Doctor's house?

HORSTER, *a little coldly:* Oh, yes, sure. I've been so busy I didn't recognize you. *He goes to a window and looks out.* Why don't those people come inside?

BILLING: I don't know, I guess they're waiting for the Mayor or somebody important so they can be sure it's respectable in here. I wanted to ask you a question before it begins, Captain. Why are you lending your house for this? I never heard of you connected with anything political.

HORSTER, *standing still:* I'll answer that. I travel most of the year and—did you ever travel?

BILLING: Not abroad, no.

HORSTER: Well, I've been in a lot of places where people aren't allowed to say unpopular things. Did you know that?

BILLING: Sure, I've read about it.

HORSTER, *simply:* Well, I don't like it. *He starts to go out.*

BILLING: One more question. What's your opinion about the Doctor's proposition to rebuild the springs?

HORSTER, *turning, thinks, then:* Don't understand a thing about it.

Three citizens enter.

HORSTER: Come in, come in. I don't have enough chairs so you'll just have to stand. *He goes out.*

FIRST CITIZEN: Try the horn.

SECOND CITIZEN: No, let him start to talk first.

THIRD CITIZEN, *a big beef of a man, takes out a horn:* Wait'll they hear this! I could blow your mustache off with this!

Horster returns. He sees the horn and stops abruptly.

HORSTER: I don't want any roughhouse, you hear me?

Mrs. Stockmann and Petra enter.

HORSTER: Come in. I've got chairs just for you.

MRS. STOCKMANN, *nervously:* There's quite a crowd on the sidewalk. Why don't they come in?

HORSTER: I suppose they're waiting for the Mayor.

PETRA: Are all those people on his side?

HORSTER: Who knows? People are bashful, and it's so unusual to come to a meeting like this, I suppose they—

BILLING, *going over to this group:* Good evening, ladies. *They simply look at him.* I don't blame you for not speaking. I just wanted to say I don't think this is going to be a place for ladies tonight.

MRS. STOCKMANN: I don't remember asking your advice, Mr. Billing.

BILLING: I'm not as bad as you think, Mrs. Stockmann.

MRS. STOCKMANN: Then why did you print the Mayor's statement and not a word about my husband's report? Nobody's had a chance to find out what he really stands for. Why, everybody on the street there is against him already!

BILLING: If we printed his report it only would have hurt your husband.

MRS. STOCKMANN: Mr. Billing, I've never said this to anyone in my life, but I think you're a liar.

Suddenly the third citizen lets out a blast on his horn. The women jump, Billing and Horster turn around quickly.

HORSTER: You do that once more and I'll throw you out of here!

Peter Stockmann enters. Behind him comes the crowd. He pretends to be unconnected with them. He goes straight to Mrs. Stockmann, bows.

PETER STOCKMANN: Catherine? Petra?

PETRA: Good evening.

PETER STOCKMANN: Why so coldly? He wanted a meeting and he's got it. *To Horster:* Isn't he here?

HORSTER: The Doctor is going around town to be sure there's a good attendance.

PETER STOCKMANN: Fair enough. By the way, Petra, did you paint that poster? The one somebody stuck on the Town Hall?

PETRA: If you can call it painting, yes.

PETER STOCKMANN: You know I could arrest you? It's against the law to deface the Town Hall.

PETRA: Well, here I am. *She holds out her hands for the handcuffs.*

MRS. STOCKMANN, *taking it seriously:* If you arrest her, Peter, I'll never speak to you!

PETER STOCKMANN, *laughing:* Catherine, you have no sense of humor!

He crosses and sits down at the left. They sit right. A drunk comes out of the crowd.

DRUNK: Say, Billy, who's runnin'? Who's the candidate?

HORSTER: You're drunk, Mister, now get out of here!

DRUNK: There's no law says a man who's drunk can't vote!

HORSTER, *pushing the drunk toward the door as the crowd laughs:* Get out of here! Get out!

DRUNK: I wanna vote! I got a right to vote!

Aslaksen enters hurriedly, sees Peter Stockmann, and rushes to him.

ASLAKSEN: Your Honor . . . *He points to the door.* He's . . .

DR. STOCKMANN, *offstage:* Right this way, gentlemen! In you go, come on, fellows!

Hovstad enters, glances at Peter Stockmann and Aslaksen, then at Dr. Stockmann and another crowd behind him, who enter.

DR. STOCKMANN: Sorry, no chairs, gentlemen, but we couldn't get a hall, y'know, so just relax. It won't take long anyway. *He goes to the platform, sees Peter Stockmann.* Glad you're here, Peter!

PETER STOCKMANN: Wouldn't miss it for the world.

DR. STOCKMANN: How do you feel, Catherine?

MRS. STOCKMANN, *nervously:* Just promise me, don't lose your temper . . .

HORSTER, *seeing the drunk pop in through the door:* Did I tell you to get out of here!

DRUNK: Look, if you ain't votin', what the hell's going on here? *Horster starts after him.* Don't push!

PETER STOCKMANN, *to the drunk:* I order you to get out of here and stay out!

DRUNK: I don't like the tone of your voice! And if you don't watch your step I'm gonna tell the Mayor right now, and

he'll throw yiz all in the jug! *To all:* What're you, a revolution here?

The crowd bursts out laughing; the drunk laughs with them, and they push him out. Dr. Stockmann mounts the platform.

DR. STOCKMANN, *quieting the crowd:* All right, gentlemen, we might as well begin. Quiet down, please. *He clears his throat.* The issue is very simple—

ASLAKSEN: We haven't elected a chairman, Doctor.

DR. STOCKMANN: I'm sorry, Mr. Aslaksen, this isn't a meeting. I advertised a lecture and I—

A CITIZEN: I came to a meeting, Doctor. There's got to be some kind of control here.

DR. STOCKMANN: What do you mean, control? What is there to control?

SECOND CITIZEN: Sure, let him speak, this is no meeting!

THIRD CITIZEN: Your Honor, why don't you take charge of this—

DR. STOCKMANN: Just a minute now!

THIRD CITIZEN: Somebody responsible has got to take charge. There's a big difference of opinion here—

DR. STOCKMANN: What makes you so sure? You don't even know yet what I'm going to say.

THIRD CITIZEN: I've got a pretty good idea what you're going to say, and I don't like it! If a man doesn't like it here, let him go where it suits him better. We don't want any troublemakers here!

There is assent from much of the crowd. Dr. Stockmann looks at them with new surprise.

DR. STOCKMANN: Now look, friend, you don't know anything about me—

FOURTH CITIZEN: We know plenty about you, Stockmann!

DR. STOCKMANN: From what? From the newspapers? How do you know I don't like this town? *He picks up his manuscript.* I'm here to save the life of this town!

PETER STOCKMANN, *quickly:* Now just a minute, Doctor, I think the democratic thing to do is to elect a chairman.

FIFTH CITIZEN: I nominate the Mayor!

Seconds are heard.

PETER STOCKMANN: No, no, no! That wouldn't be fair. We want a neutral person. I suggest Mr. Aslaksen—

SECOND CITIZEN: I came to a lecture, I didn't—

THIRD CITIZEN, *to second citizen:* What're you afraid of, a fair fight? *To the Mayor:* Second Mr. Aslaksen!

The crowd assents.

DR. STOCKMANN: All right, if that's your pleasure. I just want to remind you that the reason I called this meeting was that I have a very important message for you people and I couldn't get it into the press, and nobody would rent me a hall. *To Peter Stockmann:* I just hope I'll be given time to speak here. Mr. Aslaksen?

As Aslaksen mounts the platform and Dr. Stockmann steps down, Kiil enters, looks shrewdly around.

ASLAKSEN: I just have one word before we start. Whatever is said tonight, please remember, the highest civic virtue is moderation. *He can't help turning to Dr. Stockmann, then back to the crowd.* Now if anybody wants to speak—

The drunk enters suddenly.

DRUNK, *pointing at Aslaksen:* I heard that! Since when you allowed to electioneer at the poles? *Citizens push him toward the door amid laughter.* I'm gonna report this to the Mayor, goddammit! *They push him out and close the door.*

ASLAKSEN: Quiet, please, quiet. Does anybody want the floor?

Dr. Stockmann starts to come forward, raising his hand, but Peter Stockmann also has his hand raised.

PETER STOCKMANN: Mr. Chairman!

ASLAKSEN, *quickly recognizing Peter Stockmann:* His Honor the Mayor will address the meeting.

Dr. Stockmann stops, looks at Peter Stockmann, and, suppressing a remark, returns to his place. The Mayor mounts the platform.

PETER STOCKMANN: Gentlemen, there's no reason to take very long to settle this tonight and return to our ordinary, calm,

and peaceful life. Here's the issue: Doctor Stockmann, my brother—and believe me, it is not easy to say this—has decided to destroy Kirsten Springs, our Health Institute—

DR. STOCKMANN: Peter!

ASLAKSEN, *ringing his bell:* Let the Mayor continue, please. There mustn't be any interruptions.

PETER STOCKMANN: He has a long and very involved way of going about it, but that's the brunt of it, believe me.

THIRD CITIZEN: Then what're we wasting time for? Run him out of town!

Others join in the cry.

PETER STOCKMANN: Now wait a minute. I want no violence here. I want you to understand his motives. He is a man, always has been, who is never happy unless he is badgering authority, ridiculing authority, destroying authority. He wants to attack the springs so he can prove that the administration blundered in the construction.

DR. STOCKMANN, *to Aslaksen:* May I speak? I—

ASLAKSEN: The Mayor's not finished.

PETER STOCKMANN: Thank you. Now there are a number of people here who seem to feel that the Doctor has a right to say anything he pleases. After all, we are a democratic country. Now, God knows, in ordinary times I'd agree a hundred per cent with anybody's right to say anything. But these are not ordinary times. Nations have crises, and so do towns. There are ruins of nations, and there are ruins of towns all over the world, and they were wrecked by people who, in the guise of reform, and pleading for justice, and so on, broke down all authority and left only revolution and chaos.

DR. STOCKMANN: What the hell are you talking about!

ASLAKSEN: I'll have to insist, Doctor—

DR. STOCKMANN: I called a lecture! I didn't invite him to attack me. He's got the press and every hall in town to attack me, and I've got nothing but this room tonight!

ASLAKSEN: I don't think you're making a very good impression, Doctor.

Assenting laughter and catcalls. Again Dr. Stockmann is taken aback by this reaction.

ASLAKSEN: Please continue, Your Honor.

PETER STOCKMANN: Now this is our crisis. We know what this town was without our Institute. We could barely afford to keep the streets in condition. It was a dead, third-rate hamlet. Today we're just on the verge of becoming internationally known as a resort. I predict that within five years the income of every man in this room will be immensely greater. I predict that our schools will be bigger and better. And in time this town will be crowded with fine carriages; great homes will be built here; first-class stores will open all along Main Street. I predict that if we are not defamed and maliciously attacked we will someday be one of the richest and most beautiful resort towns in the world. There are your choices. Now all you've got to do is ask yourselves a simple question: Has any one of us the right, the "democratic right," as they like to call it, to pick at minor flaws in the springs, to exaggerate the most picayune faults? *Cries of No, No!* And to attempt to publish these defamations for the whole world to see? We live or die on what the outside world thinks of us. I believe there is a line that must be drawn, and if a man decides to cross that line, we the people must finally take him by the collar and declare, "You cannot say that!"

There is an uproar of assent. Aslaksen rings the bell.

PETER STOCKMANN, *continuing:* All right then. I think we all understand each other. Mr. Aslaksen, I move that Doctor Stockmann be prohibited from reading his report at this meeting! *He goes back to his chair, which meanwhile Kiil has occupied.*

Aslaksen rings the bell to quiet the enthusiasm. Dr. Stockmann is jumping to get up on the platform, the report in his hand.

ASLAKSEN: Quiet, please. Please now. I think we can proceed to the vote.

DR. STOCKMANN: Well, aren't you going to let me speak at all?

ASLAKSEN: Doctor, we are just about to vote on that question.

DR. STOCKMANN: But damn it, man, I've got a right to—

PETRA, *standing up:* Point of order, Father!

DR. STOCKMANN, *picking up the cue:* Yes, point of order!

ASLAKSEN, *turning to him now:* Yes, Doctor.

Dr. Stockmann, at a loss, turns to Petra for further instructions.

PETRA: You want to discuss the motion.

DR. STOCKMANN: That's right, damn it, I want to discuss the motion!

ASLAKSEN: Ah . . . *He glances at Peter Stockmann.* All right, go ahead.

DR. STOCKMANN, *to the crowd:* Now, listen. *He points at Peter Stockmann.* He talks and he talks and he talks, but not a word about the facts! *He holds up the manuscript.*

THIRD CITIZEN: We don't want to hear any more about the water!

FOURTH CITIZEN: You're just trying to blow up everything!

DR. STOCKMANN: Well, judge for yourselves, let me read—

Cries of No, No, No! The man with the horn blows it. Aslaksen rings the bell. Dr. Stockmann is utterly shaken. Astonished, he looks at the maddened faces. He lowers the hand holding the manuscript and steps back, defeated.

ASLAKSEN: Please, please now, quiet. We can't have this uproar! *Quiet returns.* I think, Doctor, that the majority wants to take the vote before you start to speak. If they so will, you can speak. Otherwise, majority rules. You won't deny that.

DR. STOCKMANN, *turns, tosses the manuscript on the floor, turns back to Aslaksen:* Don't bother voting. I understand everything now. Can I have a few minutes—

PETER STOCKMANN: Mr. Chairman!

DR. STOCKMANN, *to his brother:* I won't mention the Institute. I have a new discovery that's a thousand times more important than all the Institutes in the world. *To Aslaksen:* May I have the platform.

ASLAKSEN, *to the crowd:* I don't see how we can deny him that, as long as he confines himself to—

DR. STOCKMANN: The springs are not the subject. *He mounts the platform, looks at the crowd.* Before I go into my subject I want to congratulate the liberals and radicals among us, like Mr. Hovstad—

HOVSTAD: What do you mean, radical! Where's your evidence to call me a radical!

DR. STOCKMANN: You've got me there. There isn't any evidence. I guess there never really was. I just wanted to congratulate you on your self-control tonight—you who have fought in every parlor for the principle of free speech these many years.

HOVSTAD: I believe in democracy. When my readers are overwhelmingly against something, I'm not going to impose my will on the majority.

DR. STOCKMANN: You have begun my remarks, Mr. Hovstad. *He turns to the crowd.* Gentlemen, Mrs. Stockmann, Miss Stockmann. Tonight I was struck by a sudden flash of light, a discovery second to none. But before I tell it to you—a little story. I put in a good many years in the north of our country. Up there the rulers of the world are the great seal and the gigantic squadrons of duck. Man lives on ice, huddled together in little piles of stones. His whole life consists of grubbing for food. Nothing more. He can barely speak his own language. And it came to me one day that it was romantic and sentimental for a man of my education to be tending these people. They had not yet reached the stage where they needed a doctor. If the truth were to be told, a veterinary would be more in order.

BILLING: Is that the way you refer to decent hard-working people!

DR. STOCKMANN: I expected that, my friend, but don't think you can fog up my brain with that magic word—the People! Not any more! Just because there is a mass of organisms with the human shape, they do not automatically become a People. That honor has to be earned! Nor does one automatically become a Man by having human shape, and living in a house, and feeding one's face—and agreeing with one's neighbors. That name *also* has to be earned. Now, when I came to my conclusions about the springs—

PETER STOCKMANN: You have no right to—

DR. STOCKMANN: That's a picayune thing, to catch me on a word, Peter. I am not going into the springs. *To the crowd:* When I became convinced of my theory about the water,

the authorities moved in at once, and I said to myself, I will fight them to the death, because—

THIRD CITIZEN: What're you trying to do, make a revolution here? He's a revolutionist!

DR. STOCKMANN: Let me finish. I thought to myself: The majority, I have the majority! And let me tell you, friends, it was a grand feeling. Because that's the reason I came back to this place of my birth. I wanted to give my education to this town. I loved it so, I spent months without pay or encouragement and dreamed up the whole project of the springs. And why? Not as my brother says, so that fine carriages could crowd our streets, but so that we might cure the sick, so that we might meet people from all over the world and learn from them, and become broader and more civilized. In other words, more like Men, more like A People.

A CITIZEN: You don't like anything about this town, do you?

ANOTHER CITIZEN: Admit it, you're a revolutionist, aren't you? Admit it!

DR. STOCKMANN: I don't admit it! I proclaim it now! I am a revolutionist! I am in revolt against the age-old lie that the majority is always right!

HOVSTAD: He's an aristocrat all of a sudden!

DR. STOCKMANN: And more! I tell you now that the majority is always wrong, and in this way!

PETER STOCKMANN: Have you lost your mind! Stop talking before—

DR. STOCKMANN: Was the majority right when they stood by while Jesus was crucified? *Silence.* Was the majority right when they refused to believe that the earth moved around the sun and let Galileo be driven to his knees like a dog? It takes fifty years for the majority to be right. The majority is never right until it *does* right.

HOVSTAD: I want to state right now, that although I've been this man's friend, and I've eaten at his table many times, I now cut myself off from him absolutely.

DR. STOCKMANN: Answer me this! Please, one more moment! A platoon of soldiers is walking down a road toward the enemy. Every one of them is convinced he is on the right road, the safe road. But two miles ahead stands one lonely man, the outpost. He sees that this road is dangerous, that

his comrades are walking into a trap. He runs back, he finds the platoon. Isn't it clear that this man must have the right to warn the majority, to argue with the majority, to fight with the majority if he believes he has the truth? Before many can know something, *one* must know it! *His passion has silenced the crowd.* It's always the same. Rights are sacred until it hurts for somebody to use them. I beg you now—I realize the cost is great, the inconvenience is great, the risk is great that other towns will get the jump on us while we're rebuilding—

PETER STOCKMANN: Aslaksen, he's not allowed to—

DR. STOCKMANN: Let me prove it to you! The water is poisoned!

THIRD CITIZEN, *steps up on the platform, waves his fist in Dr. Stockmann's face:* One more word about poison and I'm gonna take you outside!

The crowd is roaring; some try to charge the platform. The horn is blowing. Aslaksen rings his bell. Peter Stockmann steps forward, raising his hands. Kiil quietly exits.

PETER STOCKMANN: That's enough. Now stop it! Quiet! There is not going to be any violence here! *There is silence. He turns to Dr. Stockmann.* Doctor, come down and give Mr. Aslaksen the platform.

DR. STOCKMANN, *staring down at the crowd with new eyes:* I'm not through yet.

PETER STOCKMANN: Come down or I will not be responsible for what happens.

MRS. STOCKMANN: I'd like to go home. Come on, Tom.

PETER STOCKMANN: I move the chairman order the speaker to leave the platform.

VOICES: Sit down! Get off that platform!

DR. STOCKMANN: All right. Then I'll take this to out-of-town newspapers until the whole country is warned!

PETER STOCKMANN: You wouldn't dare!

HOVSTAD: You're trying to ruin this town—that's all; trying to ruin it.

DR. STOCKMANN: You're trying to build a town on a morality so rotten that it will infect the country and the world! If the only way you can prosper is this murder of freedom and

truth, then I say with all my heart, "Let it be destroyed! Let the people perish!"

He leaves the platform.

FIRST CITIZEN, *to the Mayor:* Arrest him! Arrest him!
SECOND CITIZEN: He's a traitor!

Cries of "Enemy! Traitor! Revolution!"

ASLAKSEN, *ringing for quiet:* I would like to submit the following resolution: The people assembled here tonight, decent and patriotic citizens, in defense of their town and their country, declare that Doctor Stockmann, medical officer of Kirsten Springs, is an enemy of the people and of his community.

An uproar of assent starts.

MRS. STOCKMANN, *getting up:* That's not true! He loves this town!
DR. STOCKMANN: You damned fools, you fools!

The Doctor and his family are all standing together, at the right, in a close group.

ASLAKSEN, *shouting over the din:* Is there anyone against this motion! Anyone against!
HORSTER, *raising his hand:* I am.
ASLAKSEN: One? *He looks around.*
DRUNK, *who has returned, raising his hand:* Me too! You can't do without a doctor! Anybody'll . . . tell you . . .
ASLAKSEN: Anyone else? With all votes against two, this assembly formally declares Doctor Thomas Stockmann to be the people's enemy. In the future, all dealings with him by decent, patriotic citizens will be on that basis. The meeting is adjourned.

Shouts and applause. People start leaving. Dr. Stockmann goes over to Horster.

DR. STOCKMANN: Captain, do you have room for us on your ship to America?
HORSTER: Any time you say, Doctor.
DR. STOCKMANN: Catherine? Petra?

The three start for the door, but a gantlet has formed, dangerous and silent, except for

THIRD CITIZEN: You'd better get aboard soon, Doctor!
MRS. STOCKMANN: Let's go out the back door.
HORSTER: Right this way.
DR. STOCKMANN: No, no. No back doors. *To the crowd:* I don't want to mislead anybody—the enemy of the people is not finished in this town—not quite yet. And if anybody thinks—

The horn blasts, cutting him off. The crowd starts yelling hysterically: "Enemy! Traitor! Throw him in the river! Come on, throw him in the river! Enemy! Enemy! Enemy!" The Stockmanns, erect, move out through the crowd, with Horster. Some of the crowd follow them out, yelling.

Downstage, watching, are Peter Stockmann, Billing, Aslaksen, and Hovstad. The stage is throbbing with the chant, "Enemy, Enemy, Enemy!" as

The Curtain Falls.

ACT THREE

Dr. Stockmann's living room the following morning. The windows are broken. There is great disorder. As the curtain rises, Dr. Stockmann enters, a robe over shirt and trousers—it's cold in the house. He picks up a stone from the floor, lays it on the table.

DR. STOCKMANN: Catherine! Tell what's-her-name there are still some rocks to pick up in here.

MRS. STOCKMANN, *from inside:* She's not finished sweeping up the glass.

As Dr. Stockmann bends down to get at another stone under a chair a rock comes through one of the last remaining panes. He rushes to the window, looks out. Mrs. Stockmann rushes in.

MRS. STOCKMANN, *frightened:* You all right?

DR. STOCKMANN, *looking out:* A little boy. Look at him run! *He picks up the stone.* How fast the poison spreads—even to the children!

MRS. STOCKMANN, *looking out the window:* It's hard to believe this is the same town.

DR. STOCKMANN, *adding this rock to the pile on the table:* I'm going to keep these like sacred relics. I'll put them in my will. I want the boys to have them in their homes to look at every day. *He shudders.* Cold in here. Why hasn't what's-her-name got the glazier here?

MRS. STOCKMANN: She's getting him . . .

DR. STOCKMANN: She's been getting him for two hours! We'll freeze to death in here.

MRS. STOCKMANN, *unwillingly:* He won't come here, Tom.

DR. STOCKMANN, *stops moving:* No! The glazier's afraid to fix my windows?

MRS. STOCKMANN: You don't realize—people don't like to be pointed out. He's got neighbors, I suppose, and— *She hears something.* Is that someone at the door, Randine?

She goes to front door. He continues picking up stones. She comes back.

MRS. STOCKMANN: Letter for you.

DR. STOCKMANN, *taking and opening it:* What's this now?

MRS. STOCKMANN, *continuing his pick-up for him:* I don't know how we're going to do any shopping with everybody ready to bite my head off and—

DR. STOCKMANN: Well, what do you know? We're evicted.

MRS. STOCKMANN: Oh, no!

DR STOCKMANN: He hates to do it, but with public opinion what it is . . .

MRS. STOCKMANN, *frightened:* Maybe we shouldn't have let the boys go to school today.

DR. STOCKMANN: Now don't get all frazzled again.

MRS. STOCKMANN: But the landlord is such a nice man. If he's got to throw us out, the town must be ready to murder us!

DR. STOCKMANN: Just calm down, will you? We'll go to America, and the whole thing'll be like a dream.

MRS. STOCKMANN: But I don't want to go to America— *She notices his pants.* When did this get torn?

DR. STOCKMANN, *examining the tear:* Must've been last night.

MRS. STOCKMANN: Your best pants!

DR. STOCKMANN: Well, it just shows you, that's all—when a man goes out to fight for the truth he should never wear his best pants. *He calms her.* Stop worrying, will you? You'll sew them up, and in no time at all we'll be three thousand miles away.

MRS. STOCKMANN: But how do you know it'll be any different there?

DR. STOCKMANN: I don't know. It just seems to me, in a big country like that, the spirit must be bigger. Still, I suppose they must have the solid majority there too. I don't know, at least there must be more room to hide there.

MRS. STOCKMANN: Think about it more, will you? I'd hate to go half around the world and find out we're in the same place.

DR. STOCKMANN: You know, Catherine, I don't think I'm ever going to forget the face of that crowd last night.

MRS. STOCKMANN: Don't think about it.

DR. STOCKMANN: Some of them had their teeth bared, like animals in a pack. And who leads them? Men who call

themselves liberals! Radicals! *She starts looking around at the furniture, figuring.* The crowd lets out one roar, and where are they, my liberal friends? I bet if I walked down the street now not one of them would admit he ever met me! Are you listening to me?

MRS. STOCKMANN: I was just wondering what we'll ever do with this furniture if we go to America.

DR. STOCKMANN: Don't you ever listen when I talk, dear?

MRS. STOCKMANN: Why must I listen? I know you're right.

Petra enters.

MRS. STOCKMANN: Petra! Why aren't you in school?

DR. STOCKMANN: What's the matter?

PETRA, *with deep emotion, looks at Dr. Stockmann, goes up and kisses him:* I'm fired.

MRS. STOCKMANN: They wouldn't!

PETRA: As of two weeks from now. But I couldn't bear to stay there.

DR. STOCKMANN, *shocked:* Mrs. Busk fired you?

MRS. STOCKMANN: Who'd ever imagine she could do such a thing!

PETRA: It hurt her. I could see it, because we've always agreed so about things. But she didn't dare do anything else.

DR. STOCKMANN: The glazier doesn't dare fix the windows, the landlord doesn't dare let us stay on—

PETRA: The landlord!

DR. STOCKMANN: Evicted, darling! Oh, God, on the wreckage of all the civilizations in the world there ought to be a big sign: "They Didn't Dare!"

PETRA: I really can't blame her, Father. She showed me three letters she got this morning—

DR. STOCKMANN: From whom?

PETRA: They weren't signed.

DR. STOCKMANN: Oh, naturally. The big patriots with their anonymous indignation, scrawling out the darkness of their minds onto dirty little slips of paper—that's morality, and *I'm* the traitor! What did the letters say?

PETRA: Well, one of them was from somebody who said that he'd heard at the club that somebody who visits this house said that I had radical opinions about certain things.

DR. STOCKMANN: Oh, wonderful! Somebody heard that somebody heard that she heard, that he heard . . . ! Catherine, pack as soon as you can. I feel as though vermin were crawling all over me.

Horster enters.

HORSTER: Good morning.
DR. STOCKMANN: Captain! You're just the man I want to see.
HORSTER: I thought I'd see how you all were.
MRS. STOCKMANN: That's awfully nice of you, Captain, and I want to thank you for seeing us through the crowd last night.
PETRA: Did you get home all right? We hated to leave you alone with that mob.
HORSTER: Oh, nothing to it. In a storm there's just one thing to remember: it will pass.
DR. STOCKMANN: Unless it kills you.
HORSTER: You mustn't let yourself get too bitter.
DR. STOCKMANN: I'm trying, I'm trying. But I don't guarantee how I'll feel when I try to walk down the street with "Traitor" branded on my forehead.
MRS. STOCKMANN: Don't think about it.
HORSTER: Ah, what's a word?
DR. STOCKMANN: A word can be like a needle sticking in your heart, Captain. It can dig and corrode like an acid, until you become what they want you to be—really an enemy of the people.
HORSTER: You mustn't ever let that happen, Doctor.
DR. STOCKMANN: Frankly, I don't give a damn any more. Let summer come, let an epidemic break out, then they'll know whom they drove into exile. When are you sailing?
PETRA: You really decided to go, Father?
DR. STOCKMANN: Absolutely. When do you sail, Captain?
HORSTER: That's really what I came to talk to you about.
DR. STOCKMANN: Why? Something happen to the ship?
MRS. STOCKMANN, *happily, to Dr. Stockmann:* You see! We can't go!
HORSTER: No, the ship will sail. But I won't be aboard.
DR. STOCKMANN: No!
PETRA: You fired too? 'Cause I was this morning.

MRS. STOCKMANN: Oh, Captain, you shouldn't have given us your house.

HORSTER: Oh, I'll get another ship. It's just that the owner, Mr. Vik, happens to belong to the same party as the Mayor, and I suppose when you belong to a party, and the party takes a certain position . . . Because Mr. Vik himself is a very decent man.

DR. STOCKMANN: Oh, they're all decent men!

HORSTER: No, really, he's not like the others.

DR. STOCKMANN: He doesn't have to be. A party is like a sausage grinder: it mashes up clearheads, longheads, fatheads, blockheads—and what comes out? Meatheads!

There is a knock on the hall door. Petra goes to answer.

MRS. STOCKMANN: Maybe that's the glazier!

DR. STOCKMANN: Imagine, Captain! *He points to the window.* Refused to come all morning!

Peter Stockmann enters, his hat in his hand. Silence.

PETER STOCKMANN: If you're busy . . .

DR. STOCKMANN: Just picking up broken glass. Come in, Peter. What can I do for you this fine, brisk morning? *He demonstratively pulls his robe tighter around his throat.*

MRS. STOCKMANN: Come inside, won't you, Captain?

HORSTER: Yes, I'd like to finish our talk, Doctor.

DR. STOCKMANN: Be with you in a minute, Captain.

Horster follows Petra and Catherine out through the dining-room doorway. Peter Stockmann says nothing, looking at the damage.

DR. STOCKMANN: Keep your hat on if you like, it's a little drafty in here today.

PETER STOCKMANN: Thanks, I believe I will. *He puts his hat on.* I think I caught cold last night—that house was freezing.

DR. STOCKMANN: I thought it was kind of warm—suffocating, as a matter of fact. What do you want?

PETER STOCKMANN: May I sit down? *He indicates a chair near the window.*

DR. STOCKMANN: Not there. A piece of the solid majority is liable to open your skull. Here.

They sit on the couch. Peter Stockmann takes out a large envelope.

DR. STOCKMANN: Now don't tell me.

PETER STOCKMANN: Yes. *He hands the Doctor the envelope.*

DR. STOCKMANN: I'm fired.

PETER STOCKMANN: The Board met this morning. There was nothing else to do, considering the state of public opinion.

DR. STOCKMANN, *after a pause:* You look scared, Peter.

PETER STOCKMANN: I—I haven't completely forgotten that you're still my brother.

DR. STOCKMANN: I doubt that.

PETER STOCKMANN: You have no practice left in this town, Thomas.

DR. STOCKMANN: Oh, people always need a doctor.

PETER STOCKMANN: A petition is going from house to house. Everybody is signing it. A pledge not to call you any more. I don't think a single family will dare refuse to sign it.

DR. STOCKMANN: You started that, didn't you?

PETER STOCKMANN: No. As a matter of fact, I think it's all gone a little too far. I never wanted to see you ruined, Thomas. This will ruin you.

DR. STOCKMANN: No, it won't.

PETER STOCKMANN: For once in your life, will you act like a responsible man?

DR. STOCKMANN: Why don't you say it, Peter? You're afraid I'm going out of town to start publishing about the springs, aren't you?

PETER STOCKMANN: I don't deny that. Thomas, if you really have the good of the town at heart, you can accomplish everything without damaging anybody, including yourself.

DR. STOCKMANN: What's this now?

PETER STOCKMANN: Let me have a signed statement saying that in your zeal to help the town you went overboard and exaggerated. Put it any way you like, just so you calm anybody who might feel nervous about the water. If you'll give me that, you've got your job. And I give you my word, you can gradually make all the improvements you feel are necessary. Now, that gives you what you want . . .

DR. STOCKMANN: You're nervous, Peter.

PETER STOCKMANN, *nervously:* I am not nervous!

DR. STOCKMANN: You expect me to remain in charge while people are being poisoned? *He gets up.*

PETER STOCKMANN: In time you can make your changes.

DR. STOCKMANN: When, five years, ten years? You know your trouble, Peter? You just don't grasp—even now—that there are certain men you can't buy.

PETER STOCKMANN: I'm quite capable of understanding that. But you don't happen to be one of those men.

DR. STOCKMANN, *after a slight pause:* What do you mean by that now?

PETER STOCKMANN: You know damned well what I mean by that. Morten Kiil is what I mean by that.

DR. STOCKMANN: Morten Kiil?

PETER STOCKMANN: Your father-in-law, Morten Kiil.

DR. STOCKMANN: I swear, Peter, one of us is out of his mind! What are you talking about?

PETER STOCKMANN: Now don't try to charm me with that professional innocence!

DR. STOCKMANN: What are you talking about?

PETER STOCKMANN: You don't know that your father-in-law has been running around all morning buying up stock in Kirsten Springs?

DR. STOCKMANN, *perplexed:* Buying up stock?

PETER STOCKMANN: Buying up stock, every share he can lay his hands on!

DR. STOCKMANN: Well, I don't understand, Peter. What's that got to do with—

PETER STOCKMANN, *walking around agitatedly:* Oh, come now, come now, come now!

DR. STOCKMANN: I hate you when you do that! Don't just walk around gabbling "Come now, come now!" What the hell are you talking about?

PETER STOCKMANN: Very well, if you insist on being dense. A man wages a relentless campaign to destroy confidence in a corporation. He even goes so far as to call a mass meeting against it. The very next morning, when people are still in a state of shock about it all, his father-in-law runs all over town, picking up shares at half their value.

DR. STOCKMANN, *realizing, turns away:* My God!

PETER STOCKMANN: And you have the nerve to speak to me about principles!

DR. STOCKMANN: You mean you actually believe that I . . . ?

PETER STOCKMANN: I'm not interested in psychology! I believe what I see! And what I see is nothing but a man doing a dirty, filthy job for Morten Kiil. And let me tell you—by tonight every man in this town'll see the same thing!

DR. STOCKMANN: Peter, you, you . . .

PETER STOCKMANN: Now go to your desk and write me a statement denying everything you've been saying, or . . .

DR. STOCKMANN: Peter, you're a low creature!

PETER STOCKMANN: All right then, you'd better get this one straight, Thomas. If you're figuring on opening another attack from out of town, keep this in mind: the morning it's published I'll send out a subpoena for you and begin a prosecution for conspiracy. I've been trying to make you respectable all my life; now if you want to make the big jump there'll be nobody there to hold you back. Now do we understand each other?

DR. STOCKMANN: Oh, we do, Peter! *Peter Stockmann starts for the door.* Get the girl—what the hell is her name—scrub the floors, wash down the walls, a pestilence has been here!

Kiil enters. Peter Stockmann almost runs into him. Peter turns to his brother.

PETER STOCKMANN, *pointing to Kiil:* Ha! *He turns and goes out.*

Kiil, humming quietly, goes to a chair.

DR. STOCKMANN: Morten! What have you done? What's the matter with you? Do you realize what this makes me look like?

Kiil has started taking some papers out of his pocket. Dr. Stockmann breaks off on seeing them. Kiil places them on the table.

DR. STOCKMANN: Is that—them?

KIIL: That's them, yes. Kirsten Springs shares. And very easy to get this morning.

DR. STOCKMANN: Morten, don't play with me—what is this all about?

KIIL: What are you so nervous about? Can't a man buy some stock without . . . ?
DR. STOCKMANN: I want an explanation, Morten.
KIIL, *nodding:* Thomas, they hated you last night—
DR. STOCKMANN: You don't have to tell me that.
KIIL: But they also believed you. They'd love to murder you, but they believe you. *Slight pause.* The way they say it, the pollution is coming down the river from Windmill Valley.
DR. STOCKMANN: That's exactly where it's coming from.
KIIL: Yes. And that's exactly where my tannery is.

Pause. Dr. Stockmann sits down slowly.

DR. STOCKMANN: Well, Morten, I never made a secret to you that the pollution was tannery waste.
KIIL: I'm not blaming you. It's my fault. I didn't take you seriously. But it's very serious now. Thomas, I got that tannery from my father; he got it from his father; and his father got it from my great-grandfather. I do not intend to allow my family's name to stand for the three generations of murdering angels who poisoned this town.
DR. STOCKMANN: I've waited a long time for this talk, Morten. I don't think you can stop that from happening.
KIIL: No, but you can.
DR. STOCKMANN: I?
KIIL, *nudging the shares:* I've bought these shares because—
DR. STOCKMANN: Morten, you've thrown your money away. The springs are doomed.
KIIL: I never throw my money away, Thomas. These were bought with your money.
DR. STOCKMANN: My money? What . . . ?
KIIL: You've probably suspected that I might leave a little something for Catherine and the boys?
DR. STOCKMANN: Well, naturally, I'd hoped you'd . . .
KIIL, *touching the shares:* I decided this morning to invest that money in some stock.
DR. STOCKMANN, *slowly getting up:* You bought that junk with Catherine's money!
KIIL: People call me "badger," and that's an animal that roots out things, but it's also some kind of a pig, I understand.

I've lived a clean man and I'm going to die clean. You're going to clean my name for me.

DR. STOCKMANN: Morten . . .

KIIL: Now I want to see if you really belong in a strait jacket.

DR. STOCKMANN: How could you do such a thing? What's the matter with you!

KIIL: Now don't get excited, it's very simple. If you should make another investigation of the water—

DR. STOCKMANN: I don't *need* another investigation, I—

KIIL: If you think it over and decide that you ought to change your opinion about the water—

DR. STOCKMANN: But the water is poisoned! It is poisoned!

KIIL: If you simply go on insisting the water is poisoned—*he holds up the shares*—with these in your house, then there's only one explanation for you—you're absolutely crazy. *He puts the shares down on the table again.*

DR. STOCKMANN: You're right! I'm mad! I'm insane!

KIIL, *with more force:* You're stripping the skin off your family's back! Only a madman would do a thing like that!

DR. STOCKMANN: Morten, Morten, I'm a penniless man! Why didn't you tell me before you bought this junk?

KIIL: Because you would understand it better if I told you after. *He goes up to Dr. Stockmann, holds him by the lapels. With terrific force, and the twinkle still in his eye:* And, goddammit, I think you do understand it now, don't you? Millions of tons of water come down that river. How do you know the day you made your tests there wasn't something unusual about the water?

DR. STOCKMANN, *not looking at Kiil:* Yes, but I . . .

KIIL: How do you know? Why couldn't those little animals have clotted up only the patch of water you souped out of the river? How do you know the rest of it wasn't pure?

DR. STOCKMANN: It's not probable. People were getting sick last summer . . .

KIIL: They were sick when they came here or they wouldn't have come!

DR. STOCKMANN, *breaking away:* Not intestinal diseases, skin diseases . . .

KIIL, *following him:* The only place anybody gets a bellyache is

here! There are no carbuncles in Norway? Maybe the food was bad. Did you ever think of the food?

DR. STOCKMANN, *with the desire to agree with him:* No, I didn't look into the food . . .

KIIL: Then what makes you so sure it's the water?

DR. STOCKMANN: Because I tested the water and—

KIIL, *taking hold of him again:* Admit it! We're all alone here. You have some doubt.

DR. STOCKMANN: Well, there's always a possible . . .

KIIL: Then part of it's imaginary.

DR. STOCKMANN: Well, nothing is a hundred per cent on this earth, but—

KIIL: Then you have a perfect right to doubt the other way! You have a scientific right! And did you ever think of some disinfectant? I bet you never even thought of that.

DR. STOCKMANN: Not for a mass of water like that, you can't . . .

KIIL: Everything can be killed. That's science! Thomas, I never liked your brother either, you have a perfect right to hate him.

DR. STOCKMANN: I didn't do it because I hate my brother.

KIIL: Part of it, part of it, don't deny it! You admit there's some doubt in your mind about the water, you admit there may be ways to disinfect it, and yet you went after your brother as though these doubts didn't exist; as though the only way to cure the thing was to blow up the whole Institute! There's hatred in that, boy, don't forget it. *He points to the shares.* These can belong to you now, so be sure, be sure! Tear the hatred out of your heart, stand naked in front of yourself—*are you sure?*

DR. STOCKMANN: What right have you to gamble my family's future on the strength of my convictions?

KIIL: Aha! Then the convictions are not really that strong!

DR. STOCKMANN: I am ready to hang for my convictions! But no man has a right to make martyrs of others; my family is innocent. Sell back those shares, give her what belongs to her. I'm a penniless man!

KIIL: Nobody is going to say Morten Kiil wrecked this town. *He gathers up the shares.* You retract your convictions—or these go to my charity.

DR. STOCKMANN: Everything?

KIIL: There'll be a little something for Catherine, but not much. I want my good name. It's exceedingly important to me.

DR. STOCKMANN, *bitterly:* And charity . . .

KIIL: Charity will do it, or you will do it. It's a serious thing to destroy a town.

DR. STOCKMANN: Morten, when I look at you, I swear to God I see the devil!

The door opens, and before we see who is there . . .

DR. STOCKMANN: You!

Aslaksen enters, holding up his hand defensively.

ASLAKSEN: Now don't get excited! Please!

Hovstad enters. He and Aslaksen stop short and smile on seeing Kiil.

KIIL: Too many intellectuals here: I'd better go.

ASLAKSEN, *apologetically:* Doctor, can we have five minutes of—

DR. STOCKMANN: I've got nothing to say to you.

KIIL, *going to the door:* I want an answer right away. You hear? I'm waiting. *He leaves.*

DR. STOCKMANN: All right, say it quick, what do you want?

HOVSTAD: We don't expect you to forgive our attitude at the meeting, but . . .

DR. STOCKMANN, *groping for the word:* Your attitude was prone . . . prostrated . . . prostituted!

HOVSTAD: All right, call it whatever you—

DR. STOCKMANN: I've got a lot on my mind, so get to the point. What do you want?

ASLAKSEN: Doctor, you should have told us what was in back of it all. You could have had the *Messenger* behind you all the way.

HOVSTAD: You'd have had public opinion with you now. Why didn't you tell us?

DR. STOCKMANN: Look, I'm very tired, let's not beat around the bush!

HOVSTAD, *gesturing toward the door where Kiil went out:* He's

been all over town buying up stock in the springs. It's no secret any more.

DR. STOCKMANN, *after a slight pause:* Well, what about it?

HOVSTAD, *in a friendly way:* You don't want me to spell it out, do you?

DR. STOCKMANN: I certainly wish you would. I—

HOVSTAD: All right, let's lay it on the table. Aslaksen, you want to . . . ?

ASLAKSEN: No, no, go ahead.

HOVSTAD: Doctor, in the beginning we supported you. But it quickly became clear that if we kept on supporting you in the face of public hysteria—

DR. STOCKMANN: Your paper created the hysteria.

HOVSTAD: One thing at a time, all right? *Slowly, to drive it into Dr. Stockmann's head:* We couldn't go on supporting you because, in simple language, we didn't have the money to withstand the loss in circulation. You're boycotted now? Well, the paper would have been boycotted too, if we'd stuck with you.

ASLAKSEN: You can see that, Doctor.

DR. STOCKMANN: Oh, yes. But what do you want?

HOVSTAD: *The People's Messenger* can put on such a campaign that in two months you will be hailed as a hero in this town.

ASLAKSEN: We're ready to go.

HOVSTAD: We will prove to the public that you had to buy up the stock because the management would not make the changes required for public health. In other words, you did it for absolutely scientific, public-spirited reasons. Now what do you say, Doctor?

DR. STOCKMANN: You want money from me, is that it?

ASLAKSEN: Well, now, Doctor . . .

HOVSTAD, *to Aslaksen:* No, don't walk around it. *To Dr. Stockmann:* If we started to support you again, Doctor, we'd lose circulation for a while. We'd like you—or Mr. Kiil rather—to make up the deficit. *Quickly:* Now that's open and above-board, and I don't see anything wrong with it. Do you?

Pause. Dr. Stockmann looks at him, then turns and walks to the windows, deep in thought.

ASLAKSEN: Remember, Doctor, you need the paper, you need it desperately.

DR. STOCKMANN, *returning:* No, there's nothing wrong with it at all. I—I'm not at all averse to cleaning up my name—although for myself it never was dirty. But I don't *enjoy* being hated, if you know what I mean.

ASLAKSEN: Exactly.

HOVSTAD: Aslaksen, will you show him the budget . . .

Aslaksen reaches into his pocket.

DR. STOCKMANN: Just a minute. There is one point. I hate to keep repeating the same thing, but the water is poisoned.

HOVSTAD: Now, Doctor . . .

DR. STOCKMANN: Just a minute. The Mayor says that he will levy a tax on everybody to pay for the reconstruction. I assume you are ready to support that tax at the same time you're supporting me.

ASLAKSEN: That tax would be extremely unpopular.

HOVSTAD: Doctor, with you back in charge of the baths, I have absolutely no fear that anything can go wrong.

DR. STOCKMANN: In other words, you will clean up my name—so that I can be in charge of the corruption.

HOVSTAD: But we can't tackle everything at once. A new tax—there'd be an uproar!

ASLAKSEN: It would ruin the paper!

DR. STOCKMANN: Then you don't intend to do anything about the water?

HOVSTAD: We have faith you won't let anyone get sick.

DR. STOCKMANN: In other words, gentlemen, you are looking for someone to blackmail into paying your printing bill.

HOVSTAD, *indignantly:* We are trying to clear your name, Doctor Stockmann! And if you refuse to cooperate, if that's going to be your attitude . . .

DR. STOCKMANN: Yes? Go on. What will you do?

HOVSTAD, *to Aslaksen:* I think we'd better go.

DR. STOCKMANN, *stepping in their way:* What will you do? I would like you to tell me. Me, the man two minutes ago you were going to make into a hero—what will you do now that I won't pay you?

ASLAKSEN: Doctor, the public is almost hysterical.

DR. STOCKMANN: To my face, tell me what you are going to do!

HOVSTAD: The Mayor will prosecute you for conspiracy to destroy a corporation, and without a paper behind you, you will end up in prison.

DR. STOCKMANN: And you'll support him, won't you? I want it from your mouth, Hovstad. This little victory you will not deny me. *Hovstad starts for the door. Dr. Stockmann steps into his way.* Tell the hero, Hovstad. You're going to go on crucifying the hero, are you not? Say it to me! You will not leave here until I get this from your mouth!

HOVSTAD, *looking directly at Dr. Stockmann:* You are a madman. You are insane with egotism. And don't excuse it with humanitarian slogans, because a man who'll drag his family through a lifetime of disgrace is a demon in his heart! *He advances on Dr. Stockmann.* You hear me? A demon who cares more for the purity of a public bath than the lives of his wife and children. Doctor Stockmann, you deserve everything you're going to get!

Dr. Stockmann is struck by Hovstad's ferocious conviction. Aslaksen comes toward him, taking the budget out of his pocket.

ASLAKSEN, *nervously:* Doctor, please consider it. It won't take much money, and in two months' time I promise you your whole life will change and . . .

Offstage Mrs. Stockmann is heard calling in a frightened voice, "What happened? My God, what's the matter?" She runs to the front door. Dr. Stockmann, alarmed, goes quickly to the hallway. Ejlif and Morten enter. Morten's head is bruised. Petra and Captain Horster enter from the left.

MRS. STOCKMANN: Something happened! Look at him!

MORTEN: I'm all right, they just . . .

DR. STOCKMANN, *looking at the bruise:* What happened here?

MORTEN: Nothing, Papa, I swear . . .

DR. STOCKMANN, *to Ejlif:* What happened? Why aren't you in school?

EJLIF: The teacher said we better stay home the rest of the week.

DR. STOCKMANN: The boys hit him?

EJLIF: They started calling you names, so he got sore and began to fight with one kid, and all of a sudden the whole bunch of them . . .

MRS. STOCKMANN, *to Morten:* Why did you answer!

MORTEN, *indignantly:* They called him a traitor! My father is no traitor!

EJLIF: But you didn't have to answer!

MRS. STOCKMANN: You should've known they'd all jump on you! They could have killed you!

MORTEN: I don't care!

DR. STOCKMANN, *to quiet him—and his own heart:* Morten . . .

MORTEN, *pulling away from his father:* I'll kill them! I'll take a rock and the next time I see one of them I'll kill him!

Dr. Stockmann reaches for Morten, who, thinking his father will chastise him, starts to run. Dr. Stockmann catches him and grips him by the arm.

MORTEN: Let me go! Let me . . . !

DR. STOCKMANN: Morten . . . Morten . . .

MORTEN, *crying in his father's arms:* They called you traitor, an enemy . . . *He sobs.*

DR. STOCKMANN: Sssh. That's all. Wash your face.

Mrs. Stockmann takes Morten. Dr. Stockmann stands erect, faces Aslaksen and Hovstad.

DR. STOCKMANN: Good day, gentlemen.

HOVSTAD: Let us know what you decide and we'll—

DR. STOCKMANN: I've decided. I am an enemy of the people.

MRS. STOCKMANN: Tom, what are you . . . ?

DR. STOCKMANN: To such people, who teach their own children to think with their fists—to them I'm an enemy! And my boy . . . my boys . . . my family . . . I think you can count us all enemies.

ASLAKSEN: Doctor, you could have everything you want!

DR. STOCKMANN: Except the truth. I could have everything but that—that the water is poisoned!

HOVSTAD: But you'll be in charge.

DR. STOCKMANN: But the children are poisoned, the people are poisoned! If the only way I can be a friend of the people is to take charge of that corruption, then I am an enemy! The

water is poisoned, poisoned, poisoned! That's the beginning of it and that's the end of it! Now get out of here!

HOVSTAD: You know where you're going to end?

DR. STOCKMANN: I said get out of here! *He grabs Aslaksen's umbrella out of his hand.*

MRS. STOCKMANN: What are you doing?

Aslaksen and Hovstad back toward the door as Dr. Stockmann starts to swing.

ASLAKSEN: You're a fanatic, you're out of your mind!

MRS. STOCKMANN, *grabbing Dr. Stockmann to take the umbrella:* What are you doing?

DR. STOCKMANN: They want me to buy the paper, the public, the pollution of the springs, buy the whole pollution of this town! They'll make a hero out of me for that! *Furiously, to Aslaksen and Hovstad:* But I'm not a hero, I'm the enemy—and now you're first going to find out what kind of enemy I am! I will sharpen my pen like a dagger—you, all you friends of the people, are going to bleed before I'm done! Go, tell them to sign the petitions! Warn them not to call me when they're sick! Beat up my children! And never let her—*he points to Petra*—in the school again or she'll destroy the immaculate purity of the vacuum there! See to all the barricades—the truth is coming! Ring the bells, sound the alarm! The truth, the truth is out, and soon it will be prowling like a lion in the streets!

HOVSTAD: Doctor, you're out of your mind.

He and Aslaksen turn to go. They are in the doorway.

EJLIF, *rushing at them:* Don't you say that to him!

DR. STOCKMANN, *as Mrs. Stockmann cries out, rushes them with the umbrella:* Out of here!

They rush out. Dr. Stockmann throws the umbrella after them, then slams the door. Silence. He has his back pressed against the door, facing his family.

DR. STOCKMANN: I've had all the ambassadors of hell today, but there'll be no more. Now, now listen, Catherine! Children, listen. Now we're besieged. They'll call for blood now,

they'll whip the people like oxen— *A rock comes through a remaining pane. The boys start for the window.* Stay away from there!

MRS. STOCKMANN: The Captain knows where we can get a ship.

DR. STOCKMANN: No ships.

PETRA: We're staying?

MRS. STOCKMANN: But they can't go back to school! I won't let them out of the house!

DR. STOCKMANN: We're staying.

PETRA: Good!

DR. STOCKMANN: We must be careful now. We must live through this. Boys, no more school. I'm going to teach you, and Petra will. Do you know any kids, street louts, hookey-players—

EJLIF: Oh, sure, we—

DR. STOCKMANN: We'll want about twelve of them to start. But I want them good and ignorant, absolutely uncivilized. Can we use your house, Captain?

HORSTER: Sure, I'm never there.

DR. STOCKMANN: Fine. We'll begin, Petra, and we'll turn out not taxpayers and newspaper subscribers, but free and independent people, hungry for the truth. Oh, I forgot! Petra, run to Grandpa and tell him—tell him as follows: NO!

MRS. STOCKMANN, *puzzled:* What do you mean?

DR. STOCKMANN, *going over to Mrs. Stockmann:* It means, my dear, that we are all alone. And there'll be a long night before it's day—

A rock comes through a paneless window. Horster goes to the window. A crowd is heard approaching.

HORSTER: Half the town is out!

MRS. STOCKMANN: What's going to happen? Tom! What's going to happen?

DR. STOCKMANN, *holding his hands up to quiet her, and with a trembling mixture of trepidation and courageous insistence:* I don't know. But remember now, everybody. You are fighting for the truth, and that's why you're alone. And that makes you strong. We're the strongest people in the world . . .

The crowd is heard angrily calling outside. Another rock comes through a window.

DR. STOCKMANN: . . . and the strong must learn to be lonely!

The crowd noise gets louder. He walks upstage toward the windows as a wind rises and the curtains start to billow out toward him.

The Curtain Falls.

THE CRUCIBLE

A Play in Four Acts

A NOTE ON THE HISTORICAL ACCURACY OF THIS PLAY

This play is not history in the sense in which the word is used by the academic historian. Dramatic purposes have sometimes required many characters to be fused into one; the number of girls involved in the "crying-out" has been reduced; Abigail's age has been raised; while there were several judges of almost equal authority, I have symbolized them all in Hathorne and Danforth. However, I believe that the reader will discover here the essential nature of one of the strangest and most awful chapters in human history. The fate of each character is exactly that of his historical model, and there is no one in the drama who did not play a similar—and in some cases exactly the same—role in history.

As for the characters of the persons, little is known about most of them excepting what may be surmised from a few letters, the trial record, certain broadsides written at the time, and references to their conduct in sources of varying reliability. They may therefore be taken as creations of my own, drawn to the best of my ability in conformity with their known behavior, except as indicated in the commentary I have written for this text.

ACT ONE
(AN OVERTURE)

A small upper bedroom in the home of Reverend Samuel Parris, Salem, Massachusetts, in the spring of the year 1692.

There is a narrow window at the left. Through its leaded panes the morning sunlight streams. A candle still burns near the bed, which is at the right. A chest, a chair, and a small table are the other furnishings. At the back a door opens on the landing of the stairway to the ground floor. The room gives off an air of clean spareness. The roof rafters are exposed, and the wood colors are raw and unmellowed.

As the curtain rises, Reverend Parris is discovered kneeling beside the bed, evidently in prayer. His daughter, Betty Parris, aged ten, is lying on the bed, inert.

At the time of these events Parris was in his middle forties. In history he cut a villainous path, and there is very little good to be said for him. He believed he was being persecuted wherever he went, despite his best efforts to win people and God to his side. In meeting, he felt insulted if someone rose to shut the door without first asking his permission. He was a widower with no interest in children, or talent with them. He regarded them as young adults, and until this strange crisis he, like the rest of Salem, never conceived that the children were anything but thankful for being permitted to walk straight, eyes slightly lowered, arms at the sides, and mouths shut until bidden to speak.

His house stood in the "town"—but we today would hardly call it a village. The meeting house was nearby, and from this point outward—toward the bay or inland—there were a few small-windowed, dark houses snuggling against the raw Massachusetts winter. Salem had been established hardly forty years before. To the European world the whole province was a barbaric frontier inhabited by a sect of fanatics who, nevertheless, were shipping out products of slowly increasing quantity and value.

No one can really know what their lives were like. They had no novelists—and would not have permitted anyone to read a novel if one were handy. Their creed forbade anything resembling a theater or "vain enjoyment." They did not celebrate Christmas, and a holiday from work meant only that they must concentrate even more upon prayer.

Which is not to say that nothing broke into this strict and somber way of life. When a new farmhouse was built, friends assembled to "raise the roof," and there would be special foods cooked and probably some potent cider passed around. There was a good supply of ne'er-do-wells in Salem, who dallied at the shovelboard in Bridget Bishop's tavern. Probably more than the creed, hard work kept the morals of the place from spoiling, for the people were forced to fight the land like heroes for every grain of corn, and no man had very much time for fooling around.

That there were some jokers, however, is indicated by the practice of appointing a two-man patrol whose duty was to "walk forth in the time of God's worship to take notice of such as either lye about the meeting house, without attending to the word and ordinances, or that lye at home or in the fields without giving good account thereof, and to take the names of such persons, and to present them to the magistrates, whereby they may be accordingly proceeded against." This predilection for minding other people's business was time-honored among the people of Salem, and it undoubtedly created many of the suspicions which were to feed the coming madness. It was also, in my opinion, one of the things that a John Proctor would rebel against, for the time of the armed camp had almost passed, and since the country was reasonably—although not wholly—safe, the old disciplines were beginning to rankle. But, as in all such matters, the issue was not clear-cut, for danger was still a possibility, and in unity still lay the best promise of safety.

The edge of the wilderness was close by. The American continent stretched endlessly west, and it was full of mystery for them. It stood, dark and threatening, over their shoulders night and day, for out of it Indian tribes marauded from time to time, and Reverend Parris had parishioners who had lost relatives to these heathen.

The parochial snobbery of these people was partly responsible for their failure to convert the Indians. Probably they also preferred to take land from heathens rather than from fellow Christians. At any rate, very few Indians were converted, and the Salem folk believed that the virgin forest was the Devil's last preserve, his home base and the citadel of his final stand. To the best of their knowledge the American forest was the last place on earth that was not paying homage to God.

For these reasons, among others, they carried about an air of innate resistance, even of persecution. Their fathers had, of course, been persecuted in England. So now they and their church found it necessary to deny any other sect its freedom, lest their New Jerusalem be defiled and corrupted by wrong ways and deceitful ideas.

They believed, in short, that they held in their steady hands the candle that would light the world. We have inherited this belief, and it has helped and hurt us. It helped them with the discipline it gave them. They were a dedicated folk, by and large, and they had to be to survive the life they had chosen or been born into in this country.

The proof of their belief's value to them may be taken from the opposite character of the first Jamestown settlement, farther south, in Virginia. The Englishmen who landed there were motivated mainly by a hunt for profit. They had thought to pick off the wealth of the new country and then return rich to England. They were a band of individualists, and a much more ingratiating group than the Massachusetts men. But Virginia destroyed them. Massachusetts tried to kill off the Puritans, but they combined; they set up a communal society which, in the beginning, was little more than an armed camp with an autocratic and very devoted leadership. It was, however, an autocracy by consent, for they were united from top to bottom by a commonly held ideology whose perpetuation was the reason and justification for all their sufferings. So their self-denial, their purposefulness, their suspicion of all vain pursuits, their hard-handed justice, were altogether perfect instruments for the conquest of this space so antagonistic to man.

But the people of Salem in 1692 were not quite the dedicated folk that arrived on the *Mayflower*. A vast differentiation had taken place, and in their own time a revolution had unseated

the royal government and substituted a junta which was at this moment in power. The times, to their eyes, must have been out of joint, and to the common folk must have seemed as insoluble and complicated as do ours today. It is not hard to see how easily many could have been led to believe that the time of confusion had been brought upon them by deep and darkling forces. No hint of such speculation appears on the court record, but social disorder in any age breeds such mystical suspicions, and when, as in Salem, wonders are brought forth from below the social surface, it is too much to expect people to hold back very long from laying on the victims with all the force of their frustrations.

The Salem tragedy, which is about to begin in these pages, developed from a paradox. It is a paradox in whose grip we still live, and there is no prospect yet that we will discover its resolution. Simply, it was this: for good purposes, even high purposes, the people of Salem developed a theocracy, a combine of state and religious power whose function was to keep the community together, and to prevent any kind of disunity that might open it to destruction by material or ideological enemies. It was forged for a necessary purpose and accomplished that purpose. But all organization is and must be grounded on the idea of exclusion and prohibition, just as two objects cannot occupy the same space. Evidently the time came in New England when the repressions of order were heavier than seemed warranted by the dangers against which the order was organized. The witch-hunt was a perverse manifestation of the panic which set in among all classes when the balance began to turn toward greater individual freedom.

When one rises above the individual villainy displayed, one can only pity them all, just as we shall be pitied someday. It is still impossible for man to organize his social life without repressions, and the balance has yet to be struck between order and freedom.

The witch-hunt was not, however, a mere repression. It was also, and as importantly, a long overdue opportunity for everyone so inclined to express publicly his guilt and sins, under the cover of accusations against the victims. It suddenly became possible—and patriotic and holy—for a man to say that Martha Corey had come into his bedroom at night, and that, while his

wife was sleeping at his side, Martha laid herself down on his chest and "nearly suffocated him." Of course it was her spirit only, but his satisfaction at confessing himself was no lighter than if it had been Martha herself. One could not ordinarily speak such things in public.

Long-held hatreds of neighbors could now be openly expressed, and vengeance taken, despite the Bible's charitable injunctions. Land-lust which had been expressed before by constant bickering over boundaries and deeds, could now be elevated to the arena of morality; one could cry witch against one's neighbor and feel perfectly justified in the bargain. Old scores could be settled on a plane of heavenly combat between Lucifer and the Lord; suspicions and the envy of the miserable toward the happy could and did burst out in the general revenge.

Reverend Parris is praying now, and, though we cannot hear his words, a sense of his confusion hangs about him. He mumbles, then seems about to weep; then he weeps, then prays again; but his daughter does not stir on the bed.

The door opens, and his Negro slave enters. Tituba is in her forties. Parris brought her with him from Barbados, where he spent some years as a merchant before entering the ministry. She enters as one does who can no longer bear to be barred from the sight of her beloved, but she is also very frightened because her slave sense has warned her that, as always, trouble in this house eventually lands on her back.

TITUBA, *already taking a step backward:* My Betty be hearty soon?

PARRIS: Out of here!

TITUBA, *backing to the door:* My Betty not goin' die . . .

PARRIS, *scrambling to his feet in a jury:* Out of my sight! *She is gone.* Out of my— *He is overcome with sobs. He clamps his teeth against them and closes the door and leans against it, exhausted.* Oh, my God! God help me! *Quaking with fear, mumbling to himself through his sobs, he goes to the bed and gently takes Betty's hand.* Betty. Child. Dear child. Will you wake, will you open up your eyes! Betty, little one . . .

He is bending to kneel again when his niece, Abigail Williams,

seventeen, enters—a strikingly beautiful girl, an orphan, with an endless capacity for dissembling. Now she is all worry and apprehension and propriety.

ABIGAIL: Uncle? *He looks to her.* Susanna Walcott's here from Doctor Griggs.

PARRIS: Oh? Let her come, let her come.

ABIGAIL, *leaning out the door to call to Susanna, who is down the hall a few steps:* Come in, Susanna.

Susanna Walcott, a little younger than Abigail, a nervous, hurried girl, enters.

PARRIS, *eagerly:* What does the doctor say, child?

SUSANNA, *craning around Parris to get a look at Betty:* He bid me come and tell you, reverend sir, that he cannot discover no medicine for it in his books.

PARRIS: Then he must search on.

SUSANNA: Aye, sir, he have been searchin' his books since he left you, sir. But he bid me tell you, that you might look to unnatural things for the cause of it.

PARRIS, *his eyes going wide:* No—no. There be no unnatural cause here. Tell him I have sent for Reverend Hale of Beverly, and Mr. Hale will surely confirm that. Let him look to medicine and put out all thought of unnatural causes here. There be none.

SUSANNA: Aye, sir. He bid me tell you. *She turns to go.*

ABIGAIL: Speak nothin' of it in the village, Susanna.

PARRIS: Go directly home and speak nothing of unnatural causes.

SUSANNA: Aye, sir. I pray for her. *She goes out.*

ABIGAIL: Uncle, the rumor of witchcraft is all about; I think you'd best go down and deny it yourself. The parlor's packed with people, sir. I'll sit with her.

PARRIS, *pressed, turns on her:* And what shall I say to them? That my daughter and my niece I discovered dancing like heathen in the forest?

ABIGAIL: Uncle, we did dance; let you tell them I confessed it —and I'll be whipped if I must be. But they're speakin' of witchcraft. Betty's not witched.

PARRIS: Abigail, I cannot go before the congregation when I know you have not opened with me. What did you do with her in the forest?

ABIGAIL: We did dance, uncle, and when you leaped out of the bush so suddenly, Betty was frightened and then she fainted. And there's the whole of it.

PARRIS: Child. Sit you down.

ABIGAIL, *quavering, as she sits:* I would never hurt Betty. I love her dearly.

PARRIS: Now look you, child, your punishment will come in its time. But if you trafficked with spirits in the forest I must know it now, for surely my enemies will, and they will ruin me with it.

ABIGAIL: But we never conjured spirits.

PARRIS: Then why can she not move herself since midnight? This child is desperate! *Abigail lowers her eyes.* It must come out—my enemies will bring it out. Let me know what you done there. Abigail, do you understand that I have many enemies?

ABIGAIL: I have heard of it, uncle.

PARRIS: There is a faction that is sworn to drive me from my pulpit. Do you understand that?

ABIGAIL: I think so, sir.

PARRIS: Now then, in the midst of such disruption, my own household is discovered to be the very center of some obscene practice. Abominations are done in the forest—

ABIGAIL: It were sport, uncle!

PARRIS, *pointing at Betty:* You call this sport? *She lowers her eyes. He pleads:* Abigail, if you know something that may help the doctor, for God's sake tell it to me. *She is silent.* I saw Tituba waving her arms over the fire when I came on you. Why was she doing that? And I heard a screeching and gibberish coming from her mouth. She were swaying like a dumb beast over that fire!

ABIGAIL: She always sings her Barbados songs, and we dance.

PARRIS: I cannot blink what I saw, Abigail, for my enemies will not blink it. I saw a dress lying on the grass.

ABIGAIL, *innocently:* A dress?

PARRIS—*it is very hard to say:* Aye, a dress. And I thought I saw—someone naked running through the trees!

ABIGAIL, *in terror:* No one was naked! You mistake yourself, uncle!

PARRIS, *with anger:* I saw it! *He moves from her. Then, resolved:* Now tell me true, Abigail. And I pray you feel the weight of truth upon you, for now my ministry's at stake, my ministry and perhaps your cousin's life. Whatever abomination you have done, give me all of it now, for I dare not be taken unaware when I go before them down there.

ABIGAIL: There is nothin' more. I swear it, uncle.

PARRIS, *studies her, then nods, half convinced:* Abigail, I have fought here three long years to bend these stiff-necked people to me, and now, just now when some good respect is rising for me in the parish, you compromise my very character. I have given you a home, child, I have put clothes upon your back—now give me upright answer. Your name in the town—it is entirely white, is it not?

ABIGAIL, *with an edge of resentment:* Why, I am sure it is, sir. There be no blush about my name.

PARRIS, *to the point:* Abigail, is there any other cause than you have told me, for your being discharged from Goody Proctor's service? I have heard it said, and I tell you as I heard it, that she comes so rarely to the church this year for she will not sit so close to something soiled. What signified that remark?

ABIGAIL: She hates me, uncle, she must, for I would not be her slave. It's a bitter woman, a lying, cold, sniveling woman, and I will not work for such a woman!

PARRIS: She may be. And yet it has troubled me that you are now seven month out of their house, and in all this time no other family has ever called for your service.

ABIGAIL: They want slaves, not such as I. Let them send to Barbados for that. I will not black my face for any of them! *With ill-concealed resentment at him:* Do you begrudge my bed, uncle?

PARRIS: No—no.

ABIGAIL, *in a temper:* My name is good in the village! I will not have it said my name is soiled! Goody Proctor is a gossiping liar!

Enter Mrs. Ann Putnam. She is a twisted soul of forty-five, a death-ridden woman, haunted by dreams.

PARRIS, *as soon as the door begins to open:* No—no, I cannot have anyone. *He sees her, and a certain deference springs into him, although his worry remains.* Why, Goody Putnam, come in.

MRS. PUTNAM, *full of breath, shiny-eyed:* It is a marvel. It is surely a stroke of hell upon you.

PARRIS: No, Goody Putnam, it is—

MRS. PUTNAM, *glancing at Betty:* How high did she fly, how high?

PARRIS: No, no, she never flew—

MRS. PUTNAM, *very pleased with it:* Why, it's sure she did. Mr. Collins saw her goin' over Ingersoll's barn, and come down light as bird, he says!

PARRIS: Now, look you, Goody Putnam, she never— *Enter Thomas Putnam, a well-to-do hard-handed landowner, near fifty.* Oh, good morning, Mr. Putnam.

PUTNAM: It is a providence the thing is out now! It is a providence. *He goes directly to the bed.*

PARRIS: What's out, sir, what's—?

Mrs. Putnam goes to the bed.

PUTNAM, *looking down at Betty:* Why, *her* eyes is closed! Look you, Ann.

MRS. PUTNAM: Why, that's strange. *To Parris:* Ours is open.

PARRIS, *shocked:* Your Ruth is sick?

MRS. PUTNAM, *with vicious certainty:* I'd not call it sick; the Devil's touch is heavier than sick. It's death, y'know, it's death drivin' into them, forked and hoofed.

PARRIS: Oh, pray not! Why, how does Ruth ail?

MRS. PUTNAM: She ails as she must—she never waked this morning, but her eyes open and she walks, and hears naught, sees naught, and cannot eat. Her soul is taken, surely.

Parris is struck.

PUTNAM, *as though for further details:* They say you've sent for Reverend Hale of Beverly?

PARRIS, *with dwindling conviction now:* A precaution only. He has much experience in all demonic arts, and I—

MRS. PUTNAM: He has indeed; and found a witch in Beverly last year, and let you remember that.

PARRIS: Now, Goody Ann, they only thought that were a witch, and I am certain there be no element of witchcraft here.

PUTNAM: No witchcraft! Now look you, Mr. Parris—

PARRIS: Thomas, Thomas, I pray you, leap not to witchcraft. I know that you—you least of all, Thomas, would ever wish so disastrous a charge laid upon me. We cannot leap to witchcraft. They will howl me out of Salem for such corruption in my house.

A word about Thomas Putnam. He was a man with many grievances, at least one of which appears justified. Some time before, his wife's brother-in-law, James Bayley, had been turned down as minister of Salem. Bayley had all the qualifications, and a two-thirds vote into the bargain, but a faction stopped his acceptance, for reasons that are not clear.

Thomas Putnam was the eldest son of the richest man in the village. He had fought the Indians at Narragansett, and was deeply interested in parish affairs. He undoubtedly felt it poor payment that the village should so blatantly disregard his candidate for one of its more important offices, especially since he regarded himself as the intellectual superior of most of the people around him.

His vindictive nature was demonstrated long before the witchcraft began. Another former Salem minister, George Burroughs, had had to borrow money to pay for his wife's funeral, and, since the parish was remiss in his salary, he was soon bankrupt. Thomas and his brother John had Burroughs jailed for debts the man did not owe. The incident is important only in that Burroughs succeeded in becoming minister where Bayley, Thomas Putnam's brother-in-law, had been rejected; the motif of resentment is clear here. Thomas Putnam felt that his own name and the honor of his family had been smirched by the village, and he meant to right matters however he could.

Another reason to believe him a deeply embittered man was his attempt to break his father's will, which left a disproportionate amount to a stepbrother. As with every other public cause in which he tried to force his way, he failed in this.

So it is not surprising to find that so many accusations against people are in the handwriting of Thomas Putnam, or that his name is so often found as a witness corroborating the super-

natural testimony, or that his daughter led the crying-out at the most opportune junctures of the trials, especially when— But we'll speak of that when we come to it.

PUTNAM—*at the moment he is intent upon getting Parris, for whom he has only contempt, to move toward the abyss:* Mr. Parris, I have taken your part in all contention here, and I would continue; but I cannot if you hold back in this. There are hurtful, vengeful spirits layin' hands on these children.

PARRIS: But, Thomas, you cannot—

PUTNAM: Ann! Tell Mr. Parris what you have done.

MRS. PUTNAM: Reverend Parris, I have laid seven babies unbaptized in the earth. Believe me, sir, you never saw more hearty babies born. And yet, each would wither in my arms the very night of their birth. I have spoke nothin', but my heart has clamored intimations. And now, this year, my Ruth, my only—I see her turning strange. A secret child she has become this year, and shrivels like a sucking mouth were pullin' on her life too. And so I thought to send her to your Tituba—

PARRIS: To Tituba! What may Tituba—?

MRS. PUTNAM: Tituba knows how to speak to the dead, Mr. Parris.

PARRIS: Goody Ann, it is a formidable sin to conjure up the dead!

MRS. PUTNAM: I take it on my soul, but who else may surely tell us what person murdered my babies?

PARRIS, *horrified:* Woman!

MRS. PUTNAM: They were murdered, Mr. Parris! And mark this proof! Mark it! Last night my Ruth were ever so close to their little spirits; I know it, sir. For how else is she struck dumb now except some power of darkness would stop her mouth? It is a marvelous sign, Mr. Parris!

PUTNAM: Don't you understand it, sir? There is a murdering witch among us, bound to keep herself in the dark. *Parris turns to Betty, a frantic terror rising in him.* Let your enemies make of it what they will, you cannot blink it more.

PARRIS, *to Abigail:* Then you were conjuring spirits last night.

ABIGAIL, *whispering:* Not I, sir—Tituba and Ruth.

PARRIS *turns now, with new fear, and goes to Betty, looks down*

at her, and then, gazing off: Oh, Abigail, what proper payment for my charity! Now I am undone.

PUTNAM: You are not undone! Let you take hold here. Wait for no one to charge you—declare it yourself. You have discovered witchcraft—

PARRIS: In my house? In my house, Thomas? They will topple me with this! They will make of it a—

Enter Mercy Lewis, the Putnams' servant, a fat, sly, merciless girl of eighteen.

MERCY: Your pardons. I only thought to see how Betty is.

PUTNAM: Why aren't you home? Who's with Ruth?

MERCY: Her grandma come. She's improved a little, I think—she give a powerful sneeze before.

MRS. PUTNAM: Ah, there's a sign of life!

MERCY: I'd fear no more, Goody Putnam. It were a grand sneeze; another like it will shake her wits together, I'm sure. *She goes to the bed to look.*

PARRIS: Will you leave me now, Thomas? I would pray a while alone.

ABIGAIL: Uncle, you've prayed since midnight. Why do you not go down and—

PARRIS: No—no. *To Putnam:* I have no answer for that crowd. I'll wait till Mr. Hale arrives. *To get Mrs. Putnam to leave:* If you will, Goody Ann . . .

PUTNAM: Now look you, sir. Let you strike out against the Devil, and the village will bless you for it! Come down, speak to them—pray with them. They're thirsting for your word, Mister! Surely you'll pray with them.

PARRIS, *swayed:* I'll lead them in a psalm, but let you say nothing of witchcraft yet. I will not discuss it. The cause is yet unknown. I have had enough contention since I came; I want no more.

MRS. PUTNAM: Mercy, you go home to Ruth, dy'y'hear?

MERCY: Aye, mum.

Mrs. Putnam goes out.

PARRIS, *to Abigail:* If she starts for the window, cry for me at once.

ABIGAIL: I will, uncle.

PARRIS, *to Putnam:* There is a terrible power in her arms today. *He goes out with Putnam.*

ABIGAIL, *with hushed trepidation:* How is Ruth sick?

MERCY: It's weirdish, I know not—she seems to walk like a dead one since last night.

ABIGAIL, *turns at once and goes to Betty, and now, with fear in her voice:* Betty? *Betty doesn't move. She shakes her.* Now stop this! Betty! Sit up now!

Betty doesn't stir. Mercy comes over.

MERCY: Have you tried beatin' her? I gave Ruth a good one and it waked her for a minute. Here, let me have her.

ABIGAIL, *holding Mercy back:* No, he'll be comin' up. Listen, now; if they be questioning us, tell them we danced—I told him as much already.

MERCY: Aye. And what more?

ABIGAIL: He knows Tituba conjured Ruth's sisters to come out of the grave.

MERCY: And what more?

ABIGAIL: He saw you naked.

MERCY, *clapping her hands together with a frightened laugh:* Oh, Jesus!

Enter Mary Warren, breathless. She is seventeen, a subservient, naive, lonely girl.

MARY WARREN: What'll we do? The village is out! I just come from the farm; the whole country's talkin' witchcraft! They'll be callin' us witches, Abby!

MERCY, *pointing and looking at Mary Warren:* She means to tell, I know it.

MARY WARREN: Abby, we've got to tell. Witchery's a hangin' error, a hangin' like they done in Boston two year ago! We must tell the truth, Abby! You'll only be whipped for dancin', and the other things!

ABIGAIL: Oh, *we'll* be whipped!

MARY WARREN: I never done none of it, Abby. I only looked!

MERCY, *moving menacingly toward Mary:* Oh, you're a great one for lookin', aren't you, Mary Warren? What a grand peeping courage you have!

Betty, on the bed, whimpers. Abigail turns to her at once.

ABIGAIL: Betty? *She goes to Betty.* Now, Betty, dear, wake up now. It's Abigail. *She sits Betty up and furiously shakes her.* I'll beat you, Betty! *Betty whimpers.* My, you seem improving. I talked to your papa and I told him everything. So there's nothing to—

BETTY, *darts off the bed, frightened of Abigail, and flattens herself against the wall:* I want my mama!

ABIGAIL, *with alarm, as she cautiously approaches Betty:* What ails you, Betty? Your mama's dead and buried.

BETTY: I'll fly to Mama. Let me fly! *She raises her arms as though to fly, and streaks for the window, gets one leg out.*

ABIGAIL, *pulling her away from the window:* I told him everything; he knows now, he knows everything we—

BETTY: You drank blood, Abby! You didn't tell him that!

ABIGAIL: Betty, you never say that again! You will never—

BETTY: You did, you did! You drank a charm to kill John Proctor's wife! You drank a charm to kill Goody Proctor!

ABIGAIL, *smashes her across the face:* Shut it! Now shut it!

BETTY, *collapsing on the bed:* Mama, Mama! *She dissolves into sobs.*

ABIGAIL: Now look you. All of you. We danced. And Tituba conjured Ruth Putnam's dead sisters. And that is all. And mark this. Let either of you breathe a word, or the edge of a word, about the other things, and I will come to you in the black of some terrible night and I will bring a pointy reckoning that will shudder you. And you know I can do it; I saw Indians smash my dear parents' heads on the pillow next to mine, and I have seen some reddish work done at night, and I can make you wish you had never seen the sun go down! *She goes to Betty and roughly sits her up.* Now, you—sit up and stop this!

But Betty collapses in her hands and lies inert on the bed.

MARY WARREN, *with hysterical fright:* What's got her? *Abigail stares in fright at Betty.* Abby, she's going to die! It's a sin to conjure, and we—

ABIGAIL, *starting for Mary:* I say shut it, Mary Warren!

Enter John Proctor. On seeing him, Mary Warren leaps in fright.

Proctor was a farmer in his middle thirties. He need not have been a partisan of any faction in the town, but there is evidence to suggest that he had a sharp and biting way with hypocrites. He was the kind of man—powerful of body, even-tempered, and not easily led—who cannot refuse support to partisans without drawing their deepest resentment. In Proctor's presence a fool felt his foolishness instantly—and a Proctor is always marked for calumny therefore.

But as we shall see, the steady manner he displays does not spring from an untroubled soul. He is a sinner, a sinner not only against the moral fashion of the time, but against his own vision of decent conduct. These people had no ritual for the washing away of sins. It is another trait we inherited from them, and it has helped to discipline us as well as to breed hypocrisy among us. Proctor, respected and even feared in Salem, has come to regard himself as a kind of fraud. But no hint of this has yet appeared on the surface, and as he enters from the crowded parlor below it is a man in his prime we see, with a quiet confidence and an unexpressed, hidden force. Mary Warren, his servant, can barely speak for embarrassment and fear.

MARY WARREN: Oh! I'm just going home, Mr. Proctor.

PROCTOR: Be you foolish, Mary Warren? Be you deaf? I forbid you leave the house, did I not? Why shall I pay you? I am looking for you more often than my cows!

MARY WARREN: I only come to see the great doings in the world.

PROCTOR: I'll show you a great doin' on your arse one of these days. Now get you home; my wife is waitin' with your work!

Trying to retain a shred of dignity, she goes slowly out.

MERCY LEWIS, *both afraid of him and strangely titillated:* I'd best be off. I have my Ruth to watch. Good morning, Mr. Proctor.

Mercy sidles out. Since Proctor's entrance, Abigail has stood as though on tiptoe, absorbing his presence, wide-eyed. He glances at her, then goes to Betty on the bed.

ABIGAIL: Gah! I'd almost forgot how strong you are, John Proctor!

PROCTOR, *looking at Abigail now, the faintest suggestion of a knowing smile on his face:* What's this mischief here?

ABIGAIL, *with a nervous laugh:* Oh, she's only gone silly somehow.

PROCTOR: The road past my house is a pilgrimage to Salem all morning. The town's mumbling witchcraft.

ABIGAIL: Oh, posh! *Winningly she comes a little closer, with a confidential, wicked air.* We were dancin' in the woods last night, and my uncle leaped in on us. She took fright, is all.

PROCTOR, *his smile widening:* Ah, you're wicked yet, aren't y'! *A trill of expectant laughter escapes her, and she dares come closer, feverishly looking into his eyes.* You'll be clapped in the stocks before you're twenty.

He takes a step to go, and she springs into his path.

ABIGAIL: Give me a word, John. A soft word. *Her concentrated desire destroys his smile.*

PROCTOR: No, no, Abby. That's done with.

ABIGAIL, *tauntingly:* You come five mile to see a silly girl fly? I know you better.

PROCTOR, *setting her firmly out of his path:* I come to see what mischief your uncle's brewin' now. *With final emphasis:* Put it out of mind, Abby.

ABIGAIL, *grasping his hand before he can release her:* John—I am waitin' for you every night.

PROCTOR: Abby, I never give you hope to wait for me.

ABIGAIL, *now beginning to anger—she can't believe it:* I have something better than hope, I think!

PROCTOR: Abby, you'll put it out of mind. I'll not be comin' for you more.

ABIGAIL: You're surely sportin' with me.

PROCTOR: You know me better.

ABIGAIL: I know how you clutched my back behind your house and sweated like a stallion whenever I come near! Or did I dream that? It's she put me out, you cannot pretend it were you. I saw your face when she put me out, and you loved me then and you do now!

PROCTOR: Abby, that's a wild thing to say—

ABIGAIL: A wild thing may say wild things. But not so wild, I

think. I have seen you since she put me out; I have seen you nights.

PROCTOR: I have hardly stepped off my farm this sevenmonth.

ABIGAIL: I have a sense for heat, John, and yours has drawn me to my window, and I have seen you looking up, burning in your loneliness. Do you tell me you've never looked up at my window?

PROCTOR: I may have looked up.

ABIGAIL, *now softening:* And you must. You are no wintry man. I know you, John. I *know* you. *She is weeping.* I cannot sleep for dreamin'; I cannot dream but I wake and walk about the house as though I'd find you comin' through some door. *She clutches him desperately.*

PROCTOR, *gently pressing her from him, with great sympathy but firmly:* Child—

ABIGAIL, *with a flash of anger:* How do you call me child!

PROCTOR: Abby, I may think of you softly from time to time. But I will cut off my hand before I'll ever reach for you again. Wipe it out of mind. We never touched, Abby.

ABIGAIL: Aye, but we did.

PROCTOR: Aye, but we did not.

ABIGAIL, *with a bitter anger:* Oh, I marvel how such a strong man may let such a sickly wife be—

PROCTOR, *angered—at himself as well:* You'll speak nothin' of Elizabeth!

ABIGAIL: She is blackening my name in the village! She is telling lies about me! She is a cold, sniveling woman, and you bend to her! Let her turn you like a—

PROCTOR, *shaking her:* Do you look for whippin'?

A psalm is heard being sung below.

ABIGAIL, *in tears:* I look for John Proctor that took me from my sleep and put knowledge in my heart! I never knew what pretense Salem was, I never knew the lying lessons I was taught by all these Christian women and their covenanted men! And now you bid me tear the light out of my eyes? I will not, I cannot! You loved me, John Proctor, and whatever sin it is, you love me yet! *He turns abruptly to go out. She rushes to him.* John, pity me, pity me!

The words "going up to Jesus" are heard in the psalm, and Betty claps her ears suddenly and whines loudly.

ABIGAIL: Betty? *She hurries to Betty, who is now sitting up and screaming. Proctor goes to Betty as Abigail is trying to pull her hands down, calling "Betty!"*

PROCTOR, *growing unnerved:* What's she doing? Girl, what ails you? Stop that wailing!

The singing has stopped in the midst of this, and now Parris rushes in.

PARRIS: What happened? What are you doing to her? Betty! *He rushes to the bed, crying, "Betty, Betty!" Mrs. Putnam enters, feverish with curiosity, and with her Thomas Putnam and Mercy Lewis. Parris, at the bed, keeps lightly slapping Betty's face, while she moans and tries to get up.*

ABIGAIL: She heard you singin' and suddenly she's up and screamin'.

MRS. PUTNAM: The psalm! The psalm! She cannot bear to hear the Lord's name!

PARRIS: No, God forbid. Mercy, run to the doctor! Tell him what's happened here! *Mercy Lewis rushes out.*

MRS. PUTNAM: Mark it for a sign, mark it!

Rebecca Nurse, seventy-two, enters. She is white-haired, leaning upon her walking-stick.

PUTNAM, *pointing at the whimpering Betty:* That is a notorious sign of witchcraft afoot, Goody Nurse, a prodigious sign!

MRS. PUTNAM: My mother told me that! When they cannot bear to hear the name of—

PARRIS, *trembling:* Rebecca, Rebecca, go to her, we're lost. She suddenly cannot bear to hear the Lord's—

Giles Corey, eighty-three, enters. He is knotted with muscle, canny, inquisitive, and still powerful.

REBECCA: There is hard sickness here, Giles Corey, so please to keep the quiet.

GILES: I've not said a word. No one here can testify I've said a word. Is she going to fly again? I hear she flies.

PUTNAM: Man, be quiet now!

Everything is quiet. Rebecca walks across the room to the bed. Gentleness exudes from her. Betty is quietly whimpering, eyes shut. Rebecca simply stands over the child, who gradually quiets.

And while they are so absorbed, we may put a word in for Rebecca. Rebecca was the wife of Francis Nurse, who, from all accounts, was one of those men for whom both sides of the argument had to have respect. He was called upon to arbitrate disputes as though he were an unofficial judge, and Rebecca also enjoyed the high opinion most people had for him. By the time of the delusion, they had three hundred acres, and their children were settled in separate homesteads within the same estate. However, Francis had originally rented the land, and one theory has it that, as he gradually paid for it and raised his social status, there were those who resented his rise.

Another suggestion to explain the systematic campaign against Rebecca, and inferentially against Francis, is the land war he fought with his neighbors, one of whom was a Putnam. This squabble grew to the proportions of a battle in the woods between partisans of both sides, and it is said to have lasted for two days. As for Rebecca herself, the general opinion of her character was so high that to explain how anyone dared cry her out for a witch—and more, how adults could bring themselves to lay hands on her—we must look to the fields and boundaries of that time.

As we have seen, Thomas Putnam's man for the Salem ministry was Bayley. The Nurse clan had been in the faction that prevented Bayley's taking office. In addition, certain families allied to the Nurses by blood or friendship, and whose farms were contiguous with the Nurse farm or close to it, combined to break away from the Salem town authority and set up Topsfield, a new and independent entity whose existence was resented by old Salemites.

That the guiding hand behind the outcry was Putnam's is indicated by the fact that, as soon as it began, this Topsfield-Nurse faction absented themselves from church in protest and disbelief. It was Edward and Jonathan Putnam who signed the first complaint against Rebecca; and Thomas Putnam's little daughter was the one who fell into a fit at the hearing and pointed to Rebecca as her attacker. To top it all, Mrs.

Putnam—who is now staring at the bewitched child on the bed—soon accused Rebecca's spirit of "tempting her to iniquity," a charge that had more truth in it than Mrs. Putnam could know.

MRS. PUTNAM, *astonished:* What have you done?

Rebecca, in thought, now leaves the bedside and sits.

PARRIS, *wondrous and relieved:* What do you make of it, Rebecca?

PUTNAM, *eagerly:* Goody Nurse, will you go to my Ruth and see if you can wake her?

REBECCA, *sitting:* I think she'll wake in time. Pray calm yourselves. I have eleven children, and I am twenty-six times a grandma, and I have seen them all through their silly seasons, and when it come on them they will run the Devil bowlegged keeping up with their mischief. I think she'll wake when she tires of it. A child's spirit is like a child, you can never catch it by running after it; you must stand still, and, for love, it will soon itself come back.

PROCTOR: Aye, that's the truth of it, Rebecca.

MRS. PUTNAM: This is no silly season, Rebecca. My Ruth is bewildered, Rebecca; she cannot eat.

REBECCA: Perhaps she is not hungered yet. *To Parris:* I hope you are not decided to go in search of loose spirits, Mr. Parris. I've heard promise of that outside.

PARRIS: A wide opinion's running in the parish that the Devil may be among us, and I would satisfy them that they are wrong.

PROCTOR: Then let you come out and call them wrong. Did you consult the wardens before you called this minister to look for devils?

PARRIS: He is not coming to look for devils!

PROCTOR: Then what's he coming for?

PUTNAM: There be children dyin' in the village, Mister!

PROCTOR: I seen none dyin'. This society will not be a bag to swing around your head, Mr. Putnam. *To Parris:* Did you call a meeting before you—?

PUTNAM: I am sick of meetings; cannot the man turn his head without he have a meeting?

PROCTOR: He may turn his head, but not to Hell!

REBECCA: Pray, John, be calm. *Pause. He defers to her.* Mr. Parris, I think you'd best send Reverend Hale back as soon as he come. This will set us all to arguin' again in the society, and we thought to have peace this year. I think we ought rely on the doctor now, and good prayer.

MRS. PUTNAM: Rebecca, the doctor's baffled!

REBECCA: If so he is, then let us go to God for the cause of it. There is prodigious danger in the seeking of loose spirits. I fear it, I fear it. Let us rather blame ourselves and—

PUTNAM: How may we blame ourselves? I am one of nine sons; the Putnam seed have peopled this province. And yet I have but one child left of eight—and now she shrivels!

REBECCA: I cannot fathom that.

MRS. PUTNAM, *with a growing edge of sarcasm:* But I must! You think it God's work you should never lose a child, nor grandchild either, and I bury all but one? There are wheels within wheels in this village, and fires within fires!

PUTNAM, *to Parris:* When Reverend Hale comes, you will proceed to look for signs of witchcraft here.

PROCTOR, *to Putnam:* You cannot command Mr. Parris. We vote by name in this society, not by acreage.

PUTNAM: I never heard you worried so on this society, Mr. Proctor. I do not think I saw you at Sabbath meeting since snow flew.

PROCTOR: I have trouble enough without I come five mile to hear him preach only hellfire and bloody damnation. Take it to heart, Mr. Parris. There are many others who stay away from church these days because you hardly ever mention God any more.

PARRIS, *now aroused:* Why, that's a drastic charge!

REBECCA: It's somewhat true; there are many that quail to bring their children—

PARRIS: I do not preach for children, Rebecca. It is not the children who are unmindful of their obligations toward this ministry.

REBECCA: Are there really those unmindful?

PARRIS: I should say the better half of Salem village—

PUTNAM: And more than that!

PARRIS: Where is my wood? My contract provides I be supplied

with all my firewood. I am waiting since November for a stick, and even in November I had to show my frostbitten hands like some London beggar!

GILES: You are allowed six pound a year to buy your wood, Mr. Parris.

PARRIS: I regard that six pound as part of my salary. I am paid little enough without I spend six pound on firewood.

PROCTOR: Sixty, plus six for firewood—

PARRIS: The salary is sixty-six pound, Mr. Proctor! I am not some preaching farmer with a book under my arm; I am a graduate of Harvard College.

GILES: Aye, and well instructed in arithmetic!

PARRIS: Mr. Corey, you will look far for a man of my kind at sixty pound a year! I am not used to this poverty; I left a thrifty business in the Barbados to serve the Lord. I do not fathom it, why am I persecuted here? I cannot offer one proposition but there be a howling riot of argument. I have often wondered if the Devil be in it somewhere; I cannot understand you people otherwise.

PROCTOR: Mr. Parris, you are the first minister ever did demand the deed to this house—

PARRIS: Man! Don't a minister deserve a house to live in?

PROCTOR: To live in, yes. But to ask ownership is like you shall own the meeting house itself; the last meeting I were at you spoke so long on deeds and mortgages I thought it were an auction.

PARRIS: I want a mark of confidence, is all! I am your third preacher in seven years. I do not wish to be put out like the cat whenever some majority feels the whim. You people seem not to comprehend that a minister is the Lord's man in the parish; a minister is not to be so lightly crossed and contradicted—

PUTNAM: Aye!

PARRIS: There is either obedience or the church will burn like Hell is burning!

PROCTOR: Can you speak one minute without we land in Hell again? I am sick of Hell!

PARRIS: It is not for you to say what is good for you to hear!

PROCTOR: I may speak my heart, I think!

PARRIS, *in a fury:* What, are we Quakers? We are not Quakers here yet, Mr. Proctor. And you may tell that to your followers!

PROCTOR: My followers!

PARRIS—*now he's out with it:* There is a party in this church. I am not blind; there is a faction and a party.

PROCTOR: Against you?

PUTNAM: Against him and all authority!

PROCTOR: Why, then I must find it and join it.

There is shock among the others.

REBECCA: He does not mean that.

PUTNAM: He confessed it now!

PROCTOR: I mean it solemnly, Rebecca; I like not the smell of this "authority."

REBECCA: No, you cannot break charity with your minister. You are another kind, John. Clasp his hand, make your peace.

PROCTOR: I have a crop to sow and lumber to drag home. *He goes angrily to the door and turns to Corey with a smile.* What say you, Giles, let's find the party. He says there's a party.

GILES: I've changed my opinion of this man, John. Mr. Parris, I beg your pardon. I never thought you had so much iron in you.

PARRIS, *surprised:* Why, thank you, Giles!

GILES: It suggests to the mind what the trouble be among us all these years. *To all:* Think on it. Wherefore is everybody suing everybody else? Think on it now, it's a deep thing, and dark as a pit. I have been six time in court this year—

PROCTOR, *familiarly, with warmth, although he knows he is approaching the edge of Giles' tolerance with this:* Is it the Devil's fault that a man cannot say you good morning without you clap him for defamation? You're old, Giles, and you're not hearin' so well as you did.

GILES—*he cannot be crossed:* John Proctor, I have only last month collected four pound damages for you publicly sayin' I burned the roof off your house, and I—

PROCTOR, *laughing:* I never said no such thing, but I've paid you for it, so I hope I can call you deaf without charge. Now come along, Giles, and help me drag my lumber home.

PUTNAM: A moment, Mr. Proctor. What lumber is that you're draggin', if I may ask you?

PROCTOR: My lumber. From out my forest by the riverside.

PUTNAM: Why, we are surely gone wild this year. What anarchy is this? That tract is in my bounds, it's in my bounds, Mr. Proctor.

PROCTOR: In your bounds! *Indicating Rebecca:* I bought that tract from Goody Nurse's husband five months ago.

PUTNAM: He had no right to sell it. It stands clear in my grandfather's will that all the land between the river and—

PROCTOR: Your grandfather had a habit of willing land that never belonged to him, if I may say it plain.

GILES: That's God's truth; he nearly willed away my north pasture but he knew I'd break his fingers before he'd set his name to it. Let's get your lumber home, John. I feel a sudden will to work coming on.

PUTNAM: You load one oak of mine and you'll fight to drag it home!

GILES: Aye, and we'll win too, Putnam—this fool and I. Come on! *He turns to Proctor and starts out.*

PUTNAM: I'll have my men on you, Corey! I'll clap a writ on you!

Enter Reverend John Hale of Beverly.

Mr. Hale is nearing forty, a tight-skinned, eager-eyed intellectual. This is a beloved errand for him; on being called here to ascertain witchcraft he felt the pride of the specialist whose unique knowledge has at last been publicly called for. Like almost all men of learning, he spent a good deal of his time pondering the invisible world, especially since he had himself encountered a witch in his parish not long before. That woman, however, turned into a mere pest under his searching scrutiny, and the child she had allegedly been afflicting recovered her normal behavior after Hale had given her his kindness and a few days of rest in his own house. However, that experience never raised a doubt in his mind as to the reality of the underworld or the existence of Lucifer's many-faced lieutenants. And his belief is not to his discredit. Better minds than Hale's were—and still are—convinced that there is a society of spirits

beyond our ken. One cannot help noting that one of his lines has never yet raised a laugh in any audience that has seen this play; it is his assurance that "We cannot look to superstition in this. The Devil is precise." Evidently we are not quite certain even now whether diabolism is holy and not to be scoffed at. And it is no accident that we should be so bemused.

Like Reverend Hale and the others on this stage, we conceive the Devil as a necessary part of a respectable view of cosmology. Ours is a divided empire in which certain ideas and emotions and actions are of God, and their opposites are of Lucifer. It is as impossible for most men to conceive of a morality without sin as of an earth without "sky." Since 1692 a great but superficial change has wiped out God's beard and the Devil's horns, but the world is still gripped between two diametrically opposed absolutes. The concept of unity, in which positive and negative are attributes of the same force, in which good and evil are relative, ever-changing, and always joined to the same phenomenon—such a concept is still reserved to the physical sciences and to the few who have grasped the history of ideas. When it is recalled that until the Christian era the underworld was never regarded as a hostile area, that all gods were useful and essentially friendly to man despite occasional lapses; when we see the steady and methodical inculcation into humanity of the idea of man's worthlessness—until redeemed —the necessity of the Devil may become evident as a weapon, a weapon designed and used time and time again in every age to whip men into a surrender to a particular church or church-state.

Our difficulty in believing the—for want of a better word—political inspiration of the Devil is due in great part to the fact that he is called up and damned not only by our social antagonists but by our own side, whatever it may be. The Catholic Church, through its Inquisition, is famous for cultivating Lucifer as the arch-fiend, but the Church's enemies relied no less upon the Old Boy to keep the human mind enthralled. Luther was himself accused of alliance with Hell, and he in turn accused his enemies. To complicate matters further, he believed that he had had contact with the Devil and had argued theology with him. I am not surprised at this, for at my own university a professor of history—a Lutheran, by the way—used to

assemble his graduate students, draw the shades, and commune in the classroom with Erasmus. He was never, to my knowledge, officially scoffed at for this, the reason being that the university officials, like most of us, are the children of a history which still sucks at the Devil's teats. At this writing, only England has held back before the temptations of contemporary diabolism. In the countries of the Communist ideology, all resistance of any import is linked to the totally malign capitalist succubi, and in America any man who is not reactionary in his views is open to the charge of alliance with the Red hell. Political opposition, thereby, is given an inhumane overlay which then justifies the abrogation of all normally applied customs of civilized intercourse. A political policy is equated with moral right, and opposition to it with diabolical malevolence. Once such an equation is effectively made, society becomes a congerie of plots and counterplots, and the main role of government changes from that of the arbiter to that of the scourge of God.

The results of this process are no different now from what they ever were, except sometimes in the degree of cruelty inflicted, and not always even in that department. Normally the actions and deeds of a man were all that society felt comfortable in judging. The secret intent of an action was left to the ministers, priests, and rabbis to deal with. When diabolism rises, however, actions are the least important manifests of the true nature of a man. The Devil, as Reverend Hale said, is a wily one, and, until an hour before he fell, even God thought him beautiful in Heaven.

The analogy, however, seems to falter when one considers that, while there were no witches then, there are Communists and capitalists now, and in each camp there is certain proof that spies of each side are at work undermining the other. But this is a snobbish objection and not at all warranted by the facts. I have no doubt that people *were* communing with, and even worshiping, the Devil in Salem, and if the whole truth could be known in this case, as it is in others, we should discover a regular and conventionalized propitiation of the dark spirit. One certain evidence of this is the confession of Tituba, the slave of Reverend Parris, and another is the behavior of the

children who were known to have indulged in sorceries with her.

There are accounts of similar *klatches* in Europe, where the daughters of the towns would assemble at night and, sometimes with fetishes, sometimes with a selected young man, give themselves to love, with some bastardly results. The Church, sharp-eyed as it must be when gods long dead are brought to life, condemned these orgies as witchcraft and interpreted them, rightly, as a resurgence of the Dionysiac forces it had crushed long before. Sex, sin, and the Devil were early linked, and so they continued to be in Salem, and are today. From all accounts there are no more puritanical mores in the world than those enforced by the Communists in Russia, where women's fashions, for instance, are as prudent and all-covering as any American Baptist would desire. The divorce laws lay a tremendous responsibility on the father for the care of his children. Even the laxity of divorce regulations in the early years of the revolution was undoubtedly a revulsion from the nineteenth-century Victorian immobility of marriage and the consequent hypocrisy that developed from it. If for no other reasons, a state so powerful, so jealous of the uniformity of its citizens, cannot long tolerate the atomization of the family. And yet, in American eyes at least, there remains the conviction that the Russian attitude toward women is lascivious. It is the Devil working again, just as he is working within the Slav who is shocked at the very idea of a woman's disrobing herself in a burlesque show. Our opposites are always robed in sexual sin, and it is from this unconscious conviction that demonology gains both its attractive sensuality and its capacity to infuriate and frighten.

Coming into Salem now, Reverend Hale conceives of himself much as a young doctor on his first call. His painfully acquired armory of symptoms, catchwords, and diagnostic procedures are now to be put to use at last. The road from Beverly is unusually busy this morning, and he has passed a hundred rumors that make him smile at the ignorance of the yeomanry in this most precise science. He feels himself allied with the best minds of Europe—kings, philosophers, scientists, and ecclesiasts of all churches. His goal is light, goodness and its preservation, and he knows the exaltation of the blessed

whose intelligence, sharpened by minute examinations of enormous tracts, is finally called upon to face what may be a bloody fight with the Fiend himself.

He appears loaded down with half a dozen heavy books.

HALE: Pray you, someone take these!

PARRIS, *delighted:* Mr. Hale! Oh! it's good to see you again! *Taking some books:* My, they're heavy!

HALE, *setting down his books:* They must be; they are weighted with authority.

PARRIS, *a little scared:* Well, you do come prepared!

HALE: We shall need hard study if it comes to tracking down the Old Boy. *Noticing Rebecca:* You cannot be Rebecca Nurse?

REBECCA: I am, sir. Do you know me?

HALE: It's strange how I knew you, but I suppose you look as such a good soul should. We have all heard of your great charities in Beverly.

PARRIS: Do you know this gentleman? Mr. Thomas Putnam. And his good wife Ann.

HALE: Putnam! I had not expected such distinguished company, sir.

PUTNAM, *pleased:* It does not seem to help us today, Mr. Hale. We look to you to come to our house and save our child.

HALE: Your child ails too?

MRS. PUTNAM: Her soul, her soul seems flown away. She sleeps and yet she walks . . .

PUTNAM: She cannot eat.

HALE: Cannot eat! *Thinks on it. Then, to Proctor and Giles Corey:* Do you men have afflicted children?

PARRIS: No, no, these are farmers. John Proctor—

GILES COREY: He don't believe in witches.

PROCTOR, *to Hale:* I never spoke on witches one way or the other. Will you come, Giles?

GILES: No—no, John, I think not. I have some few queer questions of my own to ask this fellow.

PROCTOR: I've heard you to be a sensible man, Mr. Hale. I hope you'll leave some of it in Salem.

Proctor goes. Hale stands embarrassed for an instant.

PARRIS, *quickly:* Will you look at my daughter, sir? *Leads Hale to the bed.* She has tried to leap out the window; we discovered her this morning on the highroad, waving her arms as though she'd fly.

HALE, *narrowing his eyes:* Tries to fly.

PUTNAM: She cannot bear to hear the Lord's name, Mr. Hale; that's a sure sign of witchcraft afloat.

HALE, *holding up his hands:* No, no. Now let me instruct you. We cannot look to superstition in this. The Devil is precise; the marks of his presence are definite as stone, and I must tell you all that I shall not proceed unless you are prepared to believe me if I should find no bruise of hell upon her.

PARRIS: It is agreed, sir—it is agreed—we will abide by your judgment.

HALE: Good then. *He goes to the bed, looks down at Betty. To Parris:* Now, sir, what were your first warning of this strangeness?

PARRIS: Why, sir—I discovered her—*indicating Abigail*—and my niece and ten or twelve of the other girls, dancing in the forest last night.

HALE, *surprised:* You permit dancing?

PARRIS: No, no, it were secret—

MRS. PUTNAM, *unable to wait:* Mr. Parris's slave has knowledge of conjurin', sir.

PARRIS, *to Mrs. Putnam:* We cannot be sure of that, Goody Ann—

MRS. PUTNAM, *frightened, very softly:* I know it, sir. I sent my child—she should learn from Tituba who murdered her sisters.

REBECCA, *horrified:* Goody Ann! You sent a child to conjure up the dead?

MRS. PUTNAM: Let God blame me, not you, not you, Rebecca! I'll not have you judging me any more! *To Hale:* Is it a natural work to lose seven children before they live a day?

PARRIS: Sssh!

Rebecca, with great pain, turns her face away. There is a pause.

HALE: Seven dead in childbirth.

MRS. PUTNAM, *softly:* Aye. *Her voice breaks; she looks up at him. Silence. Hale is impressed. Parris looks to him. He goes to his books, opens one, turns pages, then reads. All wait, avidly.*

PARRIS, *hushed:* What book is that?

MRS. PUTNAM: What's there, sir?

HALE, *with a tasty love of intellectual pursuit:* Here is all the invisible world, caught, defined, and calculated. In these books the Devil stands stripped of all his brute disguises. Here are all your familiar spirits—your incubi and succubi; your witches that go by land, by air, and by sea; your wizards of the night and of the day. Have no fear now—we shall find him out if he has come among us, and I mean to crush him utterly if he has shown his face! *He starts for the bed.*

REBECCA: Will it hurt the child, sir?

HALE: I cannot tell. If she is truly in the Devil's grip we may have to rip and tear to get her free.

REBECCA: I think I'll go, then. I am too old for this. *She rises.*

PARRIS, *striving for conviction:* Why, Rebecca, we may open up the boil of all our troubles today!

REBECCA: Let us hope for that. I go to God for you, sir.

PARRIS, *with trepidation—and resentment:* I hope you do not mean we go to Satan here! *Slight pause.*

REBECCA: I wish I knew. *She goes out; they feel resentful of her note of moral superiority.*

PUTNAM, *abruptly:* Come, Mr. Hale, let's get on. Sit you here.

GILES: Mr. Hale, I have always wanted to ask a learned man—what signifies the readin' of strange books?

HALE: What books?

GILES: I cannot tell; she hides them.

HALE: Who does this?

GILES: Martha, my wife. I have waked at night many a time and found her in a corner, readin' of a book. Now what do you make of that?

HALE: Why, that's not necessarily—

GILES: It discomfits me! Last night—mark this—I tried and tried and could not say my prayers. And then she close her book and walks out of the house, and suddenly—mark this—I could pray again!

Old Giles must be spoken for, if only because his fate was to be so remarkable and so different from that of all the others. He was in his early eighties at this time, and was the most comical hero in the history. No man has ever been blamed for so much. If a cow was missed, the first thought was to look for her around Corey's house; a fire blazing up at night brought suspicion of arson to his door. He didn't give a hoot for public opinion, and only in his last years—after he had married Martha—did he bother much with the church. That she stopped his prayer is very probable, but he forgot to say that he'd only recently learned any prayers and it didn't take much to make him stumble over them. He was a crank and a nuisance, but withal a deeply innocent and brave man. In court, once, he was asked if it were true that he had been frightened by the strange behavior of a hog and had then said he knew it to be the Devil in an animal's shape. "What frighted you?" he was asked. He forgot everything but the word "frighted," and instantly replied, "I do not know that I ever spoke that word in my life."

HALE: Ah! The stoppage of prayer—that is strange. I'll speak further on that with you.

GILES: I'm not sayin' she's touched the Devil, now, but I'd admire to know what books she reads and why she hides them. She'll not answer me, y' see.

HALE: Aye, we'll discuss it. *To all:* Now mark me, if the Devil is in her you will witness some frightful wonders in this room, so please to keep your wits about you. Mr. Putnam, stand close in case she flies. Now, Betty, dear, will you sit up? *Putnam comes in closer, ready-handed. Hale sits Betty up, but she hangs limp in his hands.* Hmmm. *He observes her carefully. The others watch breathlessly.* Can you hear me? I am John Hale, minister of Beverly. I have come to help you, dear. Do you remember my two little girls in Beverly? *She does not stir in his hands.*

PARRIS, *in fright:* How can it be the Devil? Why would he choose my house to strike? We have all manner of licentious people in the village!

HALE: What victory would the Devil have to win a soul already bad? It is the best the Devil wants, and who is better than the minister?

GILES: That's deep, Mr. Parris, deep, deep!

PARRIS, *with resolution now:* Betty! Answer Mr. Hale! Betty!

HALE: Does someone afflict you, child? It need not be a woman, mind you, or a man. Perhaps some bird invisible to others comes to you—perhaps a pig, a mouse, or any beast at all. Is there some figure bids you fly? *The child remains limp in his hands. In silence he lays her back on the pillow. Now, holding out his hands toward her, he intones:* In nomine Domini Sabaoth sui filiique ite ad infernos. *She does not stir. He turns to Abigail, his eyes narrowing.* Abigail, what sort of dancing were you doing with her in the forest?

ABIGAIL: Why—common dancing is all.

PARRIS: I think I ought to say that I—I saw a kettle in the grass where they were dancing.

ABIGAIL: That were only soup.

HALE: What sort of soup were in this kettle, Abigail?

ABIGAIL: Why, it were beans—and lentils, I think, and—

HALE: Mr. Parris, you did not notice, did you, any living thing in the kettle? A mouse, perhaps, a spider, a frog—?

PARRIS, *fearfully:* I—do believe there were some movement—in the soup.

ABIGAIL: That jumped in, we never put it in!

HALE, *quickly:* What jumped in?

ABIGAIL: Why, a very little frog jumped—

PARRIS: A frog, Abby!

HALE, *grasping Abigail:* Abigail, it may be your cousin is dying. Did you call the Devil last night?

ABIGAIL: I never called him! Tituba, Tituba . . .

PARRIS, *blanched:* She called the Devil?

HALE: I should like to speak with Tituba.

PARRIS: Goody Ann, will you bring her up? *Mrs. Putnam exits.*

HALE: How did she call him?

ABIGAIL: I know not—she spoke Barbados.

HALE: Did you feel any strangeness when she called him? A sudden cold wind, perhaps? A trembling below the ground?

ABIGAIL: I didn't see no Devil! *Shaking Betty:* Betty, wake up. Betty! Betty!

HALE: You cannot evade me, Abigail. Did your cousin drink any of the brew in that kettle?

ABIGAIL: She never drank it!

HALE: Did you drink it?

ABIGAIL: No, sir!

HALE: Did Tituba ask you to drink it?

ABIGAIL: She tried, but I refused.

HALE: Why are you concealing? Have you sold yourself to Lucifer?

ABIGAIL: I never sold myself! I'm a good girl! I'm a proper girl!

Mrs. Putnam enters with Tituba, and instantly Abigail points at Tituba.

ABIGAIL: She made me do it! She made Betty do it!

TITUBA, *shocked and angry:* Abby!

ABIGAIL: She makes me drink blood!

PARRIS: Blood!!

MRS. PUTNAM: My baby's blood?

TITUBA: No, no, chicken blood. I give she chicken blood!

HALE: Woman, have you enlisted these children for the Devil?

TITUBA: No, no, sir, I don't truck with no Devil!

HALE: Why can she not wake? Are you silencing this child?

TITUBA: I love me Betty!

HALE: You have sent your spirit out upon this child, have you not? Are you gathering souls for the Devil?

ABIGAIL: She sends her spirit on me in church; she makes me laugh at prayer!

PARRIS: She have often laughed at prayer!

ABIGAIL: She comes to me every night to go and drink blood!

TITUBA: You beg *me* to conjure! She beg *me* make charm—

ABIGAIL: Don't lie! *To Hale:* She comes to me while I sleep; she's always making me dream corruptions!

TITUBA: Why you say that, Abby?

ABIGAIL: Sometimes I wake and find myself standing in the open doorway and not a stitch on my body! I always hear her laughing in my sleep. I hear her singing her Barbados songs and tempting me with—

TITUBA: Mister Reverend, I never—

HALE, *resolved now:* Tituba, I want you to wake this child.

TITUBA: I have no power on this child, sir.

HALE: You most certainly do, and you will free her from it now! When did you compact with the Devil?

TITUBA: I don't compact with no Devil!

PARRIS: You will confess yourself or I will take you out and whip you to your death, Tituba!

PUTNAM: This woman must be hanged! She must be taken and hanged!

TITUBA, *terrified, falls to her knees:* No, no, don't hang Tituba! I tell him I don't desire to work for him, sir.

PARRIS: The Devil?

HALE: Then you saw him! *Tituba weeps.* Now Tituba, I know that when we bind ourselves to Hell it is very hard to break with it. We are going to help you tear yourself free—

TITUBA, *frightened by the coming process:* Mister Reverend, I do believe somebody else be witchin' these children.

HALE: Who?

TITUBA: I don't know, sir, but the Devil got him numerous witches.

HALE: Does he! *It is a clue.* Tituba, look into my eyes. Come, look into me. *She raises her eyes to his fearfully.* You would be a good Christian woman, would you not, Tituba?

TITUBA: Aye, sir, a good Christian woman.

HALE: And you love these little children?

TITUBA: Oh, yes, sir, I don't desire to hurt little children.

HALE: And you love God, Tituba?

TITUBA: I love God with all my bein'.

HALE: Now, in God's holy name—

TITUBA: Bless Him. Bless Him. *She is rocking on her knees, sobbing in terror.*

HALE: And to His glory—

TITUBA: Eternal glory. Bless Him—bless God . . .

HALE: Open yourself, Tituba—open yourself and let God's holy light shine on you.

TITUBA: Oh, bless the Lord.

HALE: When the Devil comes to you does he ever come—with another person? *She stares up into his face.* Perhaps another person in the village? Someone you know.

PARRIS: Who came with him?

PUTNAM: Sarah Good? Did you ever see Sarah Good with him? Or Osburn?

PARRIS: Was it man or woman came with him?

TITUBA: Man or woman. Was—was woman.

PARRIS: What woman? A woman, you said. What woman?
TITUBA: It was black dark, and I—
PARRIS: You could see him, why could you not see her?
TITUBA: Well, they was always talking; they was always runnin' round and carryin' on—
PARRIS: You mean out of Salem? Salem witches?
TITUBA: I believe so, yes, sir.

Now Hale takes her hand. She is surprised.

HALE: Tituba. You must have no fear to tell us who they are, do you understand? We will protect you. The Devil can never overcome a minister. You know that, do you not?
TITUBA, *kisses Hale's hand:* Aye, sir, oh, I do.
HALE: You have confessed yourself to witchcraft, and that speaks a wish to come to Heaven's side. And we will bless you, Tituba.
TITUBA, *deeply relieved:* Oh, God bless you, Mr. Hale!
HALE, *with rising exaltation:* You are God's instrument put in our hands to discover the Devil's agents among us. You are selected, Tituba, you are chosen to help us cleanse our village. So speak utterly, Tituba, turn your back on him and face God—face God, Tituba, and God will protect you.
TITUBA, *joining with him:* Oh, God, protect Tituba!
HALE, *kindly:* Who came to you with the Devil? Two? Three? Four? How many?

Tituba pants, and begins rocking back and forth again, staring ahead.

TITUBA: There was four. There was four.
PARRIS, *pressing in on her:* Who? Who? Their names, their names!
TITUBA, *suddenly bursting out:* Oh, how many times he bid me kill you, Mr. Parris!
PARRIS: Kill me!
TITUBA, *in a fury:* He say Mr. Parris must be kill! Mr. Parris no goodly man, Mr. Parris mean man and no gentle man, and he bid me rise out of my bed and cut your throat! *They gasp.* But I tell him "No! I don't hate that man. I don't want kill that man." But he say, "You work for me, Tituba, and I make you free! I give you pretty dress to wear, and put you way

high up in the air, and you gone fly back to Barbados!" And I say, "You lie, Devil, you lie!" And then he come one stormy night to me, and he say, "Look! I have *white* people belong to me." And I look—and there was Goody Good.

PARRIS: Sarah Good!

TITUBA, *rocking and weeping:* Aye, Sir, and Goody Osburn.

MRS. PUTNAM: I knew it! Goody Osburn were midwife to me three times. I begged you, Thomas, did I not? I begged him not to call Osburn because I feared her. My babies always shriveled in her hands!

HALE: Take courage, you must give us all their names. How can you bear to see this child suffering? Look at her, Tituba. *He is indicating Betty on the bed.* Look at her God-given innocence; her soul is so tender; we must protect her, Tituba; the Devil is out and preying on her like a beast upon the flesh of the pure lamb. God will bless you for your help.

Abigail rises, staring as though inspired, and cries out.

ABIGAIL: I want to open myself! *They turn to her, startled. She is enraptured, as though in a pearly light.* I want the light of God, I want the sweet love of Jesus! I danced for the Devil; I saw him; I wrote in his book; I go back to Jesus; I kiss His hand. I saw Sarah Good with the Devil! I saw Goody Osburn with the Devil! I saw Bridget Bishop with the Devil!

As she is speaking, Betty is rising from the bed, a fever in her eyes, and picks up the chant.

BETTY, *staring too:* I saw George Jacobs with the Devil! I saw Goody Howe with the Devil!

PARRIS: She speaks! *He rushes to embrace Betty.* She speaks!

HALE: Glory to God! It is broken, they are free!

BETTY, *calling out hysterically and with great relief:* I saw Martha Bellows with the Devil!

ABIGAIL: I saw Goody Sibber with the Devil! *It is rising to a great glee.*

PUTNAM: The marshal, I'll call the marshal!

Parris is shouting a prayer of thanksgiving.

BETTY: I saw Alice Barrow with the Devil!

The curtain begins to fall.

HALE, *as Putnam goes out:* Let the marshal bring irons!
ABIGAIL: I saw Goody Hawkins with the Devil!
BETTY: I saw Goody Bibber with the Devil!
ABIGAIL: I saw Goody Booth with the Devil!

On their ecstatic cries—

CURTAIN

ACT TWO

The common room of Proctor's house, eight days later.

At the right is a door opening on the fields outside. A fireplace is at the left, and behind it a stairway leading upstairs. It is the low, dark, and rather long living room of the time. As the curtain rises, the room is empty. From above, Elizabeth is heard softly singing to the children. Presently the door opens and John Proctor enters, carrying his gun. He glances about the room as he comes toward the fireplace, then halts for an instant as he hears her singing. He continues on to the fireplace, leans the gun against the wall as he swings a pot out of the fire and smells it. Then he lifts out the ladle and tastes. He is not quite pleased. He reaches to a cupboard, takes a pinch of salt, and drops it into the pot. As he is tasting again, her footsteps are heard on the stair. He swings the pot into the fireplace and goes to a basin and washes his hands and face. Elizabeth enters.

ELIZABETH: What keeps you so late? It's almost dark.

PROCTOR: I were planting far out to the forest edge.

ELIZABETH: Oh, you're done then.

PROCTOR: Aye, the farm is seeded. The boys asleep?

ELIZABETH: They will be soon. *And she goes to the fireplace, proceeds to ladle up stew in a dish.*

PROCTOR: Pray now for a fair summer.

ELIZABETH: Aye.

PROCTOR: Are you well today?

ELIZABETH: I am. *She brings the plate to the table, and, indicating the food:* It is a rabbit.

PROCTOR, *going to the table:* Oh, is it! In Jonathan's trap?

ELIZABETH: No, she walked into the house this afternoon; I found her sittin' in the corner like she come to visit.

PROCTOR: Oh, that's a good sign walkin' in.

ELIZABETH: Pray God. It hurt my heart to strip her, poor rabbit. *She sits and watches him taste it.*

PROCTOR: It's well seasoned.

ELIZABETH, *blushing with pleasure:* I took great care. She's tender?

PROCTOR: Aye. *He eats. She watches him.* I think we'll see green fields soon. It's warm as blood beneath the clods.
ELIZABETH: That's well.

Proctor eats, then looks up.

PROCTOR: If the crop is good I'll buy George Jacob's heifer. How would that please you?
ELIZABETH: Aye, it would.
PROCTOR, *with a grin:* I mean to please you, Elizabeth.
ELIZABETH—*it is hard to say:* I know it, John.

He gets up, goes to her, kisses her. She receives it. With a certain disappointment, he returns to the table.

PROCTOR, *as gently as he can:* Cider?
ELIZABETH, *with a sense of reprimanding herself for having forgot:* Aye! *She gets up and goes and pours a glass for him. He now arches his back.*
PROCTOR: This farm's a continent when you go foot by foot droppin' seeds in it.
ELIZABETH, *coming with the cider:* It must be.
PROCTOR, *drinks a long draught, then, putting the glass down:* You ought to bring some flowers in the house.
ELIZABETH: Oh! I forgot! I will tomorrow.
PROCTOR: It's winter in here yet. On Sunday let you come with me, and we'll walk the farm together; I never see such a load of flowers on the earth. *With good feeling he goes and looks up at the sky through the open doorway.* Lilacs have a purple smell. Lilac is the smell of nightfall, I think. Massachusetts is a beauty in the spring!
ELIZABETH: Aye, it is.

There is a pause. She is watching him from the table as he stands there absorbing the night. It is as though she would speak but cannot. Instead, now, she takes up his plate and glass and fork and goes with them to the basin. Her back is turned to him. He turns to her and watches her. A sense of their separation rises.

PROCTOR: I think you're sad again. Are you?
ELIZABETH—*she doesn't want friction, and yet she must:* You come so late I thought you'd gone to Salem this afternoon.

PROCTOR: Why? I have no business in Salem.

ELIZABETH: You did speak of going, earlier this week.

PROCTOR—*he knows what she means:* I thought better of it since.

ELIZABETH: Mary Warren's there today.

PROCTOR: Why'd you let her? You heard me forbid her go to Salem any more!

ELIZABETH: I couldn't stop her.

PROCTOR, *holding back a full condemnation of her:* It is a fault, it is a fault, Elizabeth—you're the mistress here, not Mary Warren.

ELIZABETH: She frightened all my strength away.

PROCTOR: How may that mouse frighten you, Elizabeth? You—

ELIZABETH: It is a mouse no more. I forbid her go, and she raises up her chin like the daughter of a prince and says to me, "I must go to Salem, Goody Proctor; I am an official of the court!"

PROCTOR: Court! What court?

ELIZABETH: Aye, it is a proper court they have now. They've sent four judges out of Boston, she says, weighty magistrates of the General Court, and at the head sits the Deputy Governor of the Province.

PROCTOR, *astonished:* Why, she's mad.

ELIZABETH: I would to God she were. There be fourteen people in the jail now, she says. *Proctor simply looks at her, unable to grasp it.* And they'll be tried, and the court have power to hang them too, she says.

PROCTOR, *scoffing, but without conviction:* Ah, they'd never hang—

ELIZABETH: The Deputy Governor promise hangin' if they'll not confess, John. The town's gone wild, I think. She speak of Abigail, and I thought she were a saint, to hear her. Abigail brings the other girls into the court, and where she walks the crowd will part like the sea for Israel. And folks are brought before them, and if they scream and howl and fall to the floor—the person's clapped in the jail for bewitchin' them.

PROCTOR, *wide-eyed:* Oh, it is a black mischief.

ELIZABETH: I think you must go to Salem, John. *He turns to her.* I think so. You must tell them it is a fraud.

PROCTOR, *thinking beyond this:* Aye, it is, it is surely.

ELIZABETH: Let you go to Ezekiel Cheever—he knows you well. And tell him what she said to you last week in her uncle's house. She said it had naught to do with witchcraft, did she not?

PROCTOR, *in thought:* Aye, she did, she did. *Now, a pause.*

ELIZABETH, *quietly, fearing to anger him by prodding:* God forbid you keep that from the court, John. I think they must be told.

PROCTOR, *quietly, struggling with his thought:* Aye, they must, they must. It is a wonder they do believe her.

ELIZABETH: I would go to Salem now, John—let you go tonight.

PROCTOR: I'll think on it.

ELIZABETH, *with her courage now:* You cannot keep it, John.

PROCTOR, *angering:* I know I cannot keep it. I say I will think on it!

ELIZABETH, *hurt, and very coldly:* Good, then, let you think on it. *She stands and starts to walk out of the room.*

PROCTOR: I am only wondering how I may prove what she told me, Elizabeth. If the girl's a saint now, I think it is not easy to prove she's fraud, and the town gone so silly. She told it to me in a room alone—I have no proof for it.

ELIZABETH: You were alone with her?

PROCTOR, *stubbornly:* For a moment alone, aye.

ELIZABETH: Why, then, it is not as you told me.

PROCTOR, *his anger rising:* For a moment, I say. The others come in soon after.

ELIZABETH, *quietly—she has suddenly lost all faith in him:* Do as you wish, then. *She starts to turn.*

PROCTOR: Woman. *She turns to him.* I'll not have your suspicion any more.

ELIZABETH, *a little loftily: I* have no—

PROCTOR: I'll not have it!

ELIZABETH: Then let you not earn it.

PROCTOR, *with a violent undertone:* You doubt me yet?

ELIZABETH, *with a smile, to keep her dignity:* John, if it were not Abigail that you must go to hurt, would you falter now? I think not.

PROCTOR: Now look you—

ELIZABETH: I see what I see, John.

PROCTOR, *with solemn warning:* You will not judge me more, Elizabeth. I have good reason to think before I charge fraud on Abigail, and I will think on it. Let you look to your own improvement before you go to judge your husband any more. I have forgot Abigail, and—

ELIZABETH: And I.

PROCTOR: Spare me! You forget nothin' and forgive nothin'. Learn charity, woman. I have gone tiptoe in this house all seven month since she is gone. I have not moved from there to there without I think to please you, and still an everlasting funeral marches round your heart. I cannot speak but I am doubted, every moment judged for lies, as though I come into a court when I come into this house!

ELIZABETH: John, you are not open with me. You saw her with a crowd, you said. Now you—

PROCTOR: I'll plead my honesty no more, Elizabeth.

ELIZABETH—*now she would justify herself:* John, I am only—

PROCTOR: No more! I should have roared you down when first you told me your suspicion. But I wilted, and, like a Christian, I confessed. Confessed! Some dream I had must have mistaken you for God that day. But you're not, you're not, and let you remember it! Let you look sometimes for the goodness in me, and judge me not.

ELIZABETH: I do not judge you. The magistrate sits in your heart that judges you. I never thought you but a good man, John—*with a smile*—only somewhat bewildered.

PROCTOR, *laughing bitterly:* Oh, Elizabeth, your justice would freeze beer! *He turns suddenly toward a sound outside. He starts for the door as Mary Warren enters. As soon as he sees her, he goes directly to her and grabs her by her cloak, furious.* How do you go to Salem when I forbid it? Do you mock me? *Shaking her.* I'll whip you if you dare leave this house again!

Strangely, she doesn't resist him, but hangs limply by his grip.

MARY WARREN: I am sick, I am sick, Mr. Proctor. Pray, pray, hurt me not. *Her strangeness throws him off, and her evident pallor and weakness. He frees her.* My insides are all shuddery; I am in the proceedings all day, sir.

PROCTOR, *with draining anger—his curiosity is draining it:* And what of these proceedings here? When will you proceed to keep this house, as you are paid nine pound a year to do—and my wife not wholly well?

As though to compensate, Mary Warren goes to Elizabeth with a small rag doll.

MARY WARREN: I made a gift for you today, Goody Proctor. I had to sit long hours in a chair, and passed the time with sewing.

ELIZABETH, *perplexed, looking at the doll:* Why, thank you, it's a fair poppet.

MARY WARREN, *with a trembling, decayed voice:* We must all love each other now, Goody Proctor.

ELIZABETH, *amazed at her strangeness:* Aye, indeed we must.

MARY WARREN, *glancing at the room:* I'll get up early in the morning and clean the house. I must sleep now. *She turns and starts off.*

PROCTOR: Mary. *She halts.* Is it true? There be fourteen women arrested?

MARY WARREN: No, sir. There be thirty-nine now— *She suddenly breaks off and sobs and sits down, exhausted.*

ELIZABETH: Why, she's weepin'! What ails you, child?

MARY WARREN: Goody Osburn—will hang!

There is a shocked pause, while she sobs.

PROCTOR: Hang! *He calls into her face.* Hang, y'say?

MARY WARREN, *through her weeping:* Aye.

PROCTOR: The Deputy Governor will permit it?

MARY WARREN: He sentenced her. He must. *To ameliorate it:* But not Sarah Good. For Sarah Good confessed, y'see.

PROCTOR: Confessed! To what?

MARY WARREN: That she—*in horror at the memory*—she sometimes made a compact with Lucifer, and wrote her name in his black book—with her blood—and bound herself to torment Christians till God's thrown down—and we all must worship Hell forevermore.

Pause.

PROCTOR: But—surely you know what a jabberer she is. Did you tell them that?

MARY WARREN: Mr. Proctor, in open court she near to choked us all to death.

PROCTOR: How, choked you?

MARY WARREN: She sent her spirit out.

ELIZABETH: Oh, Mary, Mary, surely you—

MARY WARREN, *with an indignant edge:* She tried to kill me many times, Goody Proctor!

ELIZABETH: Why, I never heard you mention that before.

MARY WARREN: I never knew it before. I never knew anything before. When she come into the court I say to myself, I must not accuse this woman, for she sleep in ditches, and so very old and poor. But then—then she sit there, denying and denying, and I feel a misty coldness climbin' up my back, and the skin on my skull begin to creep, and I feel a clamp around my neck and I cannot breathe air; and then—*entranced*—I hear a voice, a screamin' voice, and it were my voice—and all at once I remembered everything she done to me!

PROCTOR: Why? What did she do to you?

MARY WARREN, *like one awakened to a marvelous secret insight:* So many time, Mr. Proctor, she come to this very door, beggin' bread and a cup of cider—and mark this: whenever I turned her away empty, she mumbled.

ELIZABETH: Mumbled! She may mumble if she's hungry.

MARY WARREN: But *what* does she mumble? You must remember, Goody Proctor. Last month—a Monday, I think—she walked away, and I thought my guts would burst for two days after. Do you remember it?

ELIZABETH: Why—I do, I think, but—

MARY WARREN: And so I told that to Judge Hathorne, and he asks her so. "Goody Osburn," says he, "what curse do you mumble that this girl must fall sick after turning you away?" And then she replies—*mimicking an old crone*—"Why, your excellence, no curse at all. I only say my commandments; I hope I may say my commandments," says she!

ELIZABETH: And that's an upright answer.

MARY WARREN: Aye, but then Judge Hathorne say, "Recite for

us your commandments!"—*leaning avidly toward them*—and of all the ten she could not say a single one. She never knew no commandments, and they had her in a flat lie!

PROCTOR: And so condemned her?

MARY WARREN, *now a little strained, seeing his stubborn doubt:* Why, they must when she condemned herself.

PROCTOR: But the proof, the proof!

MARY WARREN, *with greater impatience with him:* I told you the proof. It's hard proof, hard as rock, the judges said.

PROCTOR, *pauses an instant, then:* You will not go to court again, Mary Warren.

MARY WARREN: I must tell you, sir, I will be gone every day now. I am amazed you do not see what weighty work we do.

PROCTOR: What work you do! It's strange work for a Christian girl to hang old women!

MARY WARREN: But, Mr. Proctor, they will not hang them if they confess. Sarah Good will only sit in jail some time—*recalling*—and here's a wonder for you; think on this. Goody Good is pregnant!

ELIZABETH: Pregnant! Are they mad? The woman's near to sixty!

MARY WARREN: They had Doctor Griggs examine her, and she's full to the brim. And smokin' a pipe all these years, and no husband either! But she's safe, thank God, for they'll not hurt the innocent child. But be that not a marvel? You must see it, sir, it's God's work we do. So I'll be gone every day for some time. I'm—I am an official of the court, they say, and I— *She has been edging toward offstage.*

PROCTOR: I'll official you! *He strides to the mantel, takes down the whip hanging there.*

MARY WARREN, *terrified, but coming erect, striving for her authority:* I'll not stand whipping any more!

ELIZABETH, *hurriedly, as Proctor approaches:* Mary, promise now you'll stay at home—

MARY WARREN, *backing from him, but keeping her erect posture, striving, striving for her way:* The Devil's loose in Salem, Mr. Proctor; we must discover where he's hiding!

PROCTOR: I'll whip the Devil out of you! *With whip raised he reaches out for her, and she streaks away and yells.*

MARY WARREN, *pointing at Elizabeth:* I saved her life today!

Silence. His whip comes down.

ELIZABETH, *softly:* I am accused?
MARY WARREN, *quaking:* Somewhat mentioned. But I said I never see no sign you ever sent your spirit out to hurt no one, and seeing I do live so closely with you, they dismissed it.
ELIZABETH: Who accused me?
MARY WARREN: I am bound by law, I cannot tell it. *To Proctor:* I only hope you'll not be so sarcastical no more. Four judges and the King's deputy sat to dinner with us but an hour ago. I—I would have you speak civilly to me, from this out.
PROCTOR, *in horror, muttering in disgust at her:* Go to bed.
MARY WARREN, *with a stamp of her foot:* I'll not be ordered to bed no more, Mr. Proctor! I am eighteen and a woman, however single!
PROCTOR: Do you wish to sit up? Then sit up.
MARY WARREN: I wish to go to bed!
PROCTOR, *in anger:* Good night, then!
MARY WARREN: Good night. *Dissatisfied, uncertain of herself, she goes out. Wide-eyed, both, Proctor and Elizabeth stand staring.*
ELIZABETH, *quietly:* Oh, the noose, the noose is up!
PROCTOR: There'll be no noose.
ELIZABETH: She wants me dead. I knew all week it would come to this!
PROCTOR, *without conviction:* They dismissed it. You heard her say—
ELIZABETH: And what of tomorrow? She will cry me out until they take me!
PROCTOR: Sit you down.
ELIZABETH: She wants me dead, John, you know it!
PROCTOR: I say sit down! *She sits, trembling. He speaks quietly, trying to keep his wits.* Now we must be wise, Elizabeth.
ELIZABETH, *with sarcasm, and a sense of being lost:* Oh, indeed, indeed!
PROCTOR: Fear nothing. I'll find Ezekiel Cheever. I'll tell him she said it were all sport.
ELIZABETH: John, with so many in the jail, more than Cheever's

help is needed now, I think. Would you favor me with this? Go to Abigail.

PROCTOR, *his soul hardening as he senses . . . :* What have I to say to Abigail?

ELIZABETH, *delicately:* John—grant me this. You have a faulty understanding of young girls. There is a promise made in any bed—

PROCTOR, *striving against his anger:* What promise!

ELIZABETH: Spoke or silent, a promise is surely made. And she may dote on it now—I am sure she does—and thinks to kill me, then to take my place.

Proctor's anger is rising; he cannot speak.

ELIZABETH: It is her dearest hope, John, I know it. There be a thousand names; why does she call mine? There be a certain danger in calling such a name—I am no Goody Good that sleeps in ditches, nor Osburn, drunk and half-witted. She'd dare not call out such a farmer's wife but there be monstrous profit in it. She thinks to take my place, John.

PROCTOR: She cannot think it! *He knows it is true.*

ELIZABETH, *"reasonably":* John, have you ever shown her somewhat of contempt? She cannot pass you in the church but you will blush—

PROCTOR: I may blush for my sin.

ELIZABETH: I think she sees another meaning in that blush.

PROCTOR: And what see you? What see you, Elizabeth?

ELIZABETH, *"conceding":* I think you be somewhat ashamed, for I am there, and she so close.

PROCTOR: When will you know me, woman? Were I stone I would have cracked for shame this seven month!

ELIZABETH: Then go and tell her she's a whore. Whatever promise she may sense—break it, John, break it.

PROCTOR, *between his teeth:* Good, then. I'll go. *He starts for his rifle.*

ELIZABETH, *trembling, fearfully:* Oh, how unwillingly!

PROCTOR, *turning on her, rifle in hand:* I will curse her hotter than the oldest cinder in hell. But pray, begrudge me not my anger!

ELIZABETH: Your anger! I only ask you—

PROCTOR: Woman, am I so base? Do you truly think me base?

ELIZABETH: I never called you base.

PROCTOR: Then how do you charge me with such a promise? The promise that a stallion gives a mare I gave that girl!

ELIZABETH: Then why do you anger with me when I bid you break it?

PROCTOR: Because it speaks deceit, and I am honest! But I'll plead no more! I see now your spirit twists around the single error of my life, and I will never tear it free!

ELIZABETH, *crying out:* You'll tear it free—when you come to know that I will be your only wife, or no wife at all! She has an arrow in you yet, John Proctor, and you know it well!

Quite suddenly, as though from the air, a figure appears in the doorway. They start slightly. It is Mr. Hale. He is different now—drawn a little, and there is a quality of deference, even of guilt, about his manner now.

HALE: Good evening.

PROCTOR, *still in his shock:* Why, Mr. Hale! Good evening to you, sir. Come in, come in.

HALE, *to Elizabeth:* I hope I do not startle you.

ELIZABETH: No, no, it's only that I heard no horse—

HALE: You are Goodwife Proctor.

PROCTOR: Aye; Elizabeth.

HALE, *nods, then:* I hope you're not off to bed yet.

PROCTOR, *setting down his gun:* No, no. *Hale comes further into the room. And Proctor, to explain his nervousness:* We are not used to visitors after dark, but you're welcome here. Will you sit you down, sir?

HALE: I will. *He sits.* Let you sit, Goodwife Proctor.

She does, never letting him out of her sight. There is a pause as Hale looks about the room.

PROCTOR, *to break the silence:* Will you drink cider, Mr. Hale?

HALE: No, it rebels my stomach; I have some further traveling yet tonight. Sit you down, sir. *Proctor sits.* I will not keep you long, but I have some business with you.

PROCTOR: Business of the court?

HALE: No—no, I come of my own, without the court's authority. Hear me. *He wets his lips.* I know not if you are aware, but your wife's name is—mentioned in the court.

PROCTOR: We know it, sir. Our Mary Warren told us. We are entirely amazed.

HALE: I am a stranger here, as you know. And in my ignorance I find it hard to draw a clear opinion of them that come accused before the court. And so this afternoon, and now tonight, I go from house to house—I come now from Rebecca Nurse's house and—

ELIZABETH, *shocked:* Rebecca's charged!

HALE: God forbid such a one be charged. She is, however—mentioned somewhat.

ELIZABETH, *with an attempt at a laugh:* You will never believe, I hope, that Rebecca trafficked with the Devil.

HALE: Woman, it is possible.

PROCTOR, *taken aback:* Surely you cannot think so.

HALE: This is a strange time, Mister. No man may longer doubt the powers of the dark are gathered in monstrous attack upon this village. There is too much evidence now to deny it. You will agree, sir?

PROCTOR, *evading:* I—have no knowledge in that line. But it's hard to think so pious a woman be secretly a Devil's bitch after seventy year of such good prayer.

HALE: Aye. But the Devil is a wily one, you cannot deny it. However, she is far from accused, and I know she will not be. *Pause.* I thought, sir, to put some questions as to the Christian character of this house, if you'll permit me.

PROCTOR, *coldly, resentful:* Why, we—have no fear of questions, sir.

HALE: Good, then. *He makes himself more comfortable.* In the book of record that Mr. Parris keeps, I note that you are rarely in the church on Sabbath Day.

PROCTOR: No, sir, you are mistaken.

HALE: Twenty-six time in seventeen month, sir. I must call that rare. Will you tell me why you are so absent?

PROCTOR: Mr. Hale, I never knew I must account to that man for I come to church or stay at home. My wife were sick this winter.

HALE: So I am told. But you, Mister, why could you not come alone?

PROCTOR: I surely did come when I could, and when I could not I prayed in this house.

HALE: Mr. Proctor, your house is not a church; your theology must tell you that.

PROCTOR: It does, sir, it does; and it tells me that a minister may pray to God without he have golden candlesticks upon the altar.

HALE: What golden candlesticks?

PROCTOR: Since we built the church there were pewter candlesticks upon the altar; Francis Nurse made them, y'know, and a sweeter hand never touched the metal. But Parris came, and for twenty week he preach nothin' but golden candlesticks until he had them. I labor the earth from dawn of day to blink of night, and I tell you true, when I look to heaven and see my money glaring at his elbows—it hurt my prayer, sir, it hurt my prayer. I think, sometimes, the man dreams cathedrals, not clapboard meetin' houses.

HALE, *thinks, then:* And yet, Mister, a Christian on Sabbath Day must be in church. *Pause.* Tell me—you have three children?

PROCTOR: Aye. Boys.

HALE: How comes it that only two are baptized?

PROCTOR, *starts to speak, then stops, then, as though unable to restrain this:* I like it not that Mr. Parris should lay his hand upon my baby. I see no light of God in that man. I'll not conceal it.

HALE: I must say it, Mr. Proctor; that is not for you to decide. The man's ordained, therefore the light of God is in him.

PROCTOR, *flushed with resentment but trying to smile:* What's your suspicion, Mr. Hale?

HALE: No, no, I have no—

PROCTOR: I nailed the roof upon the church, I hung the door—

HALE: Oh, did you! That's a good sign, then.

PROCTOR: It may be I have been too quick to bring the man to book, but you cannot think we ever desired the destruction of religion. I think that's in your mind, is it not?

HALE, *not altogether giving way:* I—have—there is a softness in your record, sir, a softness.

ELIZABETH: I think, maybe, we have been too hard with Mr. Parris. I think so. But sure we never loved the Devil here.

HALE, *nods, deliberating this. Then, with the voice of one ad-*

ministering a secret test: Do you know your Commandments, Elizabeth?

ELIZABETH, *without hesitation, even eagerly:* I surely do. There be no mark of blame upon my life, Mr. Hale. I am a convenanted Christian woman.

HALE: And you, Mister?

PROCTOR, *a trifle unsteadily:* I—am sure I do, sir.

HALE, *glances at her open face, then at John, then:* Let you repeat them, if you will.

PROCTOR: The Commandments.

HALE: Aye.

PROCTOR, *looking off, beginning to sweat:* Thou shalt not kill.

HALE: Aye.

PROCTOR, *counting on his fingers:* Thou shalt not steal. Thou shalt not covet thy neighbor's goods, nor make unto thee any graven image. Thou shalt not take the name of the Lord in vain; thou shalt have no other gods before me. *With some hesitation:* Thou shalt remember the Sabbath Day and keep it holy. *Pause. Then:* Thou shalt honor thy father and mother. Thou shalt not bear false witness. *He is stuck. He counts back on his fingers, knowing one is missing.* Thou shalt not make unto thee any graven image.

HALE: You have said that twice, sir.

PROCTOR, *lost:* Aye. *He is flailing for it.*

ELIZABETH, *delicately: Adultery*, John.

PROCTOR, *as though a secret arrow had pained his heart:* Aye. *Trying to grin it away—to Hale:* You see, sir, between the two of us we do know them all. *Hale only looks at Proctor, deep in his attempt to define this man. Proctor grows more uneasy.* I think it be a small fault.

HALE: Theology, sir, is a fortress; no crack in a fortress may be accounted small. *He rises; he seems worried now. He paces little, in deep thought.*

PROCTOR: There be no love for Satan in this house, Mister,

HALE: I pray it, I pray it dearly. *He looks to both of them, an attempt at a smile on his face, but his misgivings are clear.* Well, then—I'll bid you good night.

ELIZABETH, *unable to restrain herself:* Mr. Hale. *He turns.* I do think you are suspecting me somewhat? Are you not?

HALE, *obviously disturbed—and evasive:* Goody Proctor, I do not judge you. My duty is to add what I may to the godly wisdom of the court. I pray you both good health and good fortune. *To John:* Good night, sir. *He starts out.*

ELIZABETH, *with a note of desperation:* I think you must tell him, John.

HALE: What's that?

ELIZABETH, *restraining a call:* Will you tell him?

Slight pause. Hale looks questioningly at John.

PROCTOR, *with difficulty:* I—I have no witness and cannot prove it, except my word be taken. But I know the children's sickness had naught to do with witchcraft.

HALE, *stopped, struck:* Naught to do—?

PROCTOR: Mr. Parris discovered them sportin' in the woods. They were startled and took sick.

Pause.

HALE: Who told you this?

PROCTOR, *hesitates, then:* Abigail Williams.

HALE: Abigail!

PROCTOR: Aye.

HALE, *his eyes wide:* Abigail Williams told you it had naught to do with witchcraft!

PROCTOR: She told me the day you came, sir.

HALE, *suspiciously:* Why—why did you keep this?

PROCTOR: I never knew until tonight that the world is gone daft with this nonsense.

HALE: Nonsense! Mister, I have myself examined Tituba, Sarah Good, and numerous others that have confessed to dealing with the Devil. They have *confessed* it.

PROCTOR: And why not, if they must hang for denyin' it? There are them that will swear to anything before they'll hang; have you never thought of that?

HALE: I have. I—I have indeed. *It is his own suspicion, but he resists it. He glances at Elizabeth, then at John.* And you—would you testify to this in court?

PROCTOR: I—had not reckoned with goin' into court. But if I must I will.

HALE: Do you falter here?

PROCTOR: I falter nothing, but I may wonder if my story will be credited in such a court. I do wonder on it, when such a steady-minded minister as you will suspicion such a woman that never lied, and cannot, and the world knows she cannot! I may falter somewhat, Mister; I am no fool.

HALE, *quietly—it has impressed him:* Proctor, let you open with me now, for I have a rumor that troubles me. It's said you hold no belief that there may even be witches in the world. Is that true, sir?

PROCTOR—*he knows this is critical, and is striving against his disgust with Hale and with himself for even answering:* I know not what I have said, I may have said it. I have wondered if there be witches in the world—although I cannot believe they come among us now.

HALE: Then you do not believe—

PROCTOR: I have no knowledge of it; the Bible speaks of witches, and I will not deny them.

HALE: And you, woman?

ELIZABETH: I—I cannot believe it.

HALE, *shocked:* You cannot!

PROCTOR: Elizabeth, you bewilder him!

ELIZABETH, *to Hale:* I cannot think the Devil may own a woman's soul, Mr. Hale, when she keeps an upright way, as I have. I am a good woman, I know it; and if you believe I may do only good work in the world, and yet be secretly bound to Satan, then I must tell you, sir, I do not believe it.

HALE: But, woman, you do believe there are witches in—

ELIZABETH: If you think that I am one, then I say there are none.

HALE: You surely do not fly against the Gospel, the Gospel—

PROCTOR: She believe in the Gospel, every word!

ELIZABETH: Question Abigail Williams about the Gospel, not myself!

Hale stares at her.

PROCTOR: She do not mean to doubt the Gospel, sir, you cannot think it. This be a Christian house, sir, a Christian house.

HALE: God keep you both; let the third child be quickly baptized, and go you without fail each Sunday in to Sabbath prayer; and keep a solemn, quiet way among you. I think—

Giles Corey appears in doorway.

GILES: John!
PROCTOR: Giles! What's the matter?
GILES: They take my wife.

Francis Nurse enters.

GILES: And his Rebecca!
PROCTOR, *to Francis:* Rebecca's in the *jail!*
FRANCIS: Aye, Cheever come and take her in his wagon. We've only now come from the jail, and they'll not even let us in to see them.
ELIZABETH: They've surely gone wild now, Mr. Hale!
FRANCIS, *going to Hale:* Reverend Hale! Can you not speak to the Deputy Governor? I'm sure he mistakes these people—
HALE: Pray calm yourself, Mr. Nurse.
FRANCIS: My wife is the very brick and mortar of the church, Mr. Hale—*indicating Giles*—and Martha Corey, there cannot be a woman closer yet to God than Martha.
HALE: How is Rebecca charged, Mr. Nurse?
FRANCIS, *with a mocking, half-hearted laugh:* For murder, she's charged! *Mockingly quoting the warrant:* "For the marvelous and supernatural murder of Goody Putnam's babies." What am I to do, Mr. Hale?
HALE, *turns from Francis, deeply troubled, then:* Believe me, Mr. Nurse, if Rebecca Nurse be tainted, then nothing's left to stop the whole green world from burning. Let you rest upon the justice of the court; the court will send her home, I know it.
FRANCIS: You cannot mean she will be tried in court!
HALE, *pleading:* Nurse, though our hearts break, we cannot flinch; these are new times, sir. There is a misty plot afoot so subtle we should be criminal to cling to old respects and ancient friendships. I have seen too many frightful proofs in court—the Devil is alive in Salem, and we dare not quail to follow wherever the accusing finger points!
PROCTOR, *angered:* How may such a woman murder children?
HALE, *in great pain:* Man, remember, until an hour before the Devil fell, God thought him beautiful in Heaven.

GILES: I never said my wife were a witch, Mr. Hale; I only said she were reading books!

HALE: Mr. Corey, exactly what complaint were made on your wife?

GILES: That bloody mongrel Walcott charge her. Y'see, he buy a pig of my wife four or five year ago, and the pig died soon after. So he come dancin' in for his money back. So my Martha, she says to him, "Walcott, if you haven't the wit to feed a pig properly, you'll not live to own many," she says. Now he goes to court and claims that from that day to this he cannot keep a pig alive for more than four weeks because my Martha bewitch them with her books!

Enter Ezekiel Cheever. A shocked silence.

CHEEVER: Good evening to you, Proctor.

PROCTOR: Why, Mr. Cheever. Good evening.

CHEEVER: Good evening, all. Good evening, Mr. Hale.

PROCTOR: I hope you come not on business of the court.

CHEEVER: I do, Proctor, aye. I am clerk of the court now, y'know.

Enter Marshal Herrick, a man in his early thirties, who is somewhat shamefaced at the moment.

GILES: It's a pity, Ezekiel, that an honest tailor might have gone to Heaven must burn in Hell. You'll burn for this, do you know it?

CHEEVER: You know yourself I must do as I'm told. You surely know that, Giles. And I'd as lief you'd not be sending me to Hell. I like not the sound of it, I tell you; I like not the sound of it. *He fears Proctor, but starts to reach inside his coat.* Now believe me, Proctor, how heavy be the law, all its tonnage I do carry on my back tonight. *He takes out a warrant.* I have a warrant for your wife.

PROCTOR, *to Hale:* You said she were not charged!

HALE: I know nothin' of it. *To Cheever:* When were she charged?

CHEEVER: I am given sixteen warrant tonight, sir, and she is one.

PROCTOR: Who charged her?

CHEEVER: Why, Abigail Williams charge her.

PROCTOR: On what proof, what proof?

CHEEVER, *looking about the room:* Mr. Proctor, I have little time. The court bid me search your house, but I like not to search a house. So will you hand me any poppets that your wife may keep here?

PROCTOR: Poppets?

ELIZABETH: I never kept no poppets, not since I were a girl.

CHEEVER, *embarrassed, glancing toward the mantel where sits Mary Warren's poppet:* I spy a poppet, Goody Proctor.

ELIZABETH: Oh! *Going for it:* Why, this is Mary's.

CHEEVER, *shyly:* Would you please to give it to me?

ELIZABETH, *handing it to him, asks Hale:* Has the court discovered a text in poppets now?

CHEEVER, *carefully holding the poppet:* Do you keep any others in this house?

PROCTOR: No, nor this one either till tonight. What signifies a poppet?

CHEEVER: Why, a poppet—*he gingerly turns the poppet over*—a poppet may signify— Now, woman, will you please to come with me?

PROCTOR: She will not! *To Elizabeth:* Fetch Mary here.

CHEEVER, *ineptly reaching toward Elizabeth:* No, no, I am forbid to leave her from my sight.

PROCTOR, *pushing his arm away:* You'll leave her out of sight and out of mind, Mister. Fetch Mary, Elizabeth. *Elizabeth goes upstairs.*

HALE: What signifies a poppet, Mr. Cheever?

CHEEVER, *turning the poppet over in his hands:* Why, they say it may signify that she— *He has lifted the poppet's skirt, and his eyes widen in astonished fear.* Why, this, this—

PROCTOR, *reaching for the poppet:* What's there?

CHEEVER: Why— *He draws out a long needle from the poppet*— it is a needle! Herrick, Herrick, it is a needle!

Herrick comes toward him.

PROCTOR, *angrily, bewildered:* And what signifies a needle!

CHEEVER, *his hands shaking:* Why, this go hard with her, Proctor, this— I had my doubts, Proctor, I had my doubts, but here's calamity. *To Hale, showing the needle:* You see it, sir, it is a needle!

HALE: Why? What meanin' has it?

CHEEVER, *wide-eyed, trembling:* The girl, the Williams girl, Abigail Williams, sir. She sat to dinner in Reverend Parris's house tonight, and without word nor warnin' she falls to the floor. Like a struck beast, he says, and screamed a scream that a bull would weep to hear. And he goes to save her, and, stuck two inches in the flesh of her belly, he draw a needle out. And demandin' of her how she come to be so stabbed, she—*to Proctor now*—testify it were your wife's familiar spirit pushed it in.

PROCTOR: Why, she done it herself! *To Hale:* I hope you're not takin this for proof, Mister!

Hale, struck by the proof, is silent.

CHEEVER: 'Tis hard proof! *To Hale:* I find here a poppet Goody Proctor keeps. I have found it, sir. And in the belly of the poppet a needle's stuck. I tell you true, Proctor, I never warranted to see such proof of Hell, and I bid you obstruct me not, for I—

Enter Elizabeth with Mary Warren. Proctor, seeing Mary Warren, draws her by the arm to Hale.

PROCTOR: Here now! Mary, how did this poppet come into my house?

MARY WARREN, *frightened for herself, her voice very small:* What poppet's that, sir?

PROCTOR, *impatiently, pointing at the doll in Cheever's hand:* This poppet, this poppet.

MARY WARREN, *evasively, looking at it:* Why, I—I think it is mine.

PROCTOR: It is your poppet, is it not?

MARY WARREN, *not understanding the direction of this:* It—is, sir.

PROCTOR: And how did it come into this house?

MARY WARREN, *glancing about at the avid faces:* Why—I made it in the court, sir, and—give it to Goody Proctor tonight.

PROCTOR, *to Hale:* Now, sir—do you have it?

HALE: Mary Warren, a needle have been found inside this poppet.

MARY WARREN, *bewildered:* Why, I meant no harm by it, sir.

PROCTOR, *quickly:* You stuck that needle in yourself?

MARY WARREN: I—I believe I did, sir, I—

PROCTOR, *to Hale:* What say you now?

HALE, *watching Mary Warren closely:* Child, you are certain this be your natural memory? May it be, perhaps, that someone conjures you even now to say this?

MARY WARREN: Conjures me? Why, no, sir, I am entirely myself, I think. Let you ask Susanna Walcott—she saw me sewin' it in court. *Or better still:* Ask Abby, Abby sat beside me when I made it.

PROCTOR, *to Hale, of Cheever:* Bid him begone. Your mind is surely settled now. Bid him out, Mr. Hale.

ELIZABETH: What signifies a needle?

HALE: Mary—you charge a cold and cruel murder on Abigail.

MARY WARREN: Murder! I charge no—

HALE: Abigail were stabbed tonight; a needle were found stuck into her belly—

ELIZABETH: And she charges me?

HALE: Aye.

ELIZABETH, *her breath knocked out:* Why—! The girl is murder! She must be ripped out of the world!

CHEEVER, *pointing at Elizabeth:* You've heard that, sir! Ripped out of the world! Herrick, you heard it!

PROCTOR, *suddenly snatching the warrant out of Cheever's hands:* Out with you.

CHEEVER: Proctor, you dare not touch the warrant.

PROCTOR, *ripping the warrant:* Out with you!

CHEEVER: You've ripped the Deputy Governor's warrant, man!

PROCTOR: Damn the Deputy Governor! Out of my house!

HALE: Now, Proctor, Proctor!

PROCTOR: Get y'gone with them! You are a broken minister.

HALE: Proctor, if she is innocent, the court—

PROCTOR: If *she* is innocent! Why do you never wonder if Parris be innocent, or Abigail? Is the accuser always holy now? Were they born this morning as clean as God's fingers? I'll tell you what's walking Salem—vengeance is walking Salem. We are what we always were in Salem, but now the little crazy children are jangling the keys of the kingdom, and common vengeance writes the law! This warrant's vengeance! I'll not give my wife to vengeance!

ELIZABETH: I'll go, John—

PROCTOR: You will not go!

HERRICK: I have nine men outside. You cannot keep her. The law binds me, John, I cannot budge.

PROCTOR, *to Hale, ready to break him:* Will you see her taken?

HALE: Proctor, the court is just—

PROCTOR: Pontius Pilate! God will not let you wash your hands of this!

ELIZABETH: John—I think I must go with them. *He cannot bear to look at her.* Mary, there is bread enough for the morning; you will bake, in the afternoon. Help Mr. Proctor as you were his daughter—you owe me that, and much more. *She is fighting her weeping. To Proctor:* When the children wake, speak nothing of witchcraft—it will frighten them. *She cannot go on.*

PROCTOR: I will bring you home. I will bring you soon.

ELIZABETH: Oh, John, bring me soon!

PROCTOR: I will fall like an ocean on that court! Fear nothing, Elizabeth.

ELIZABETH, *with great fear:* I will fear nothing. *She looks about the room, as though to fix it in her mind.* Tell the children I have gone to visit someone sick.

She walks out the door, Herrick and Cheever behind her. For a moment, Proctor watches from the doorway. The clank of chain is heard.

PROCTOR: Herrick! Herrick, don't chain her! *He rushes out the door. From outside:* Damn you, man, you will not chain her! Off with them! I'll not have it! I will not have her chained!

There are other men's voices against his. Hale, in a fever of guilt and uncertainty, turns from the door to avoid the sight; Mary Warren bursts into tears and sits weeping. Giles Corey calls to Hale.

GILES: And yet silent, minister? It is fraud, you know it is fraud! What keeps you, man?

Proctor is half braced, half pushed into the room by two deputies and Herrick.

PROCTOR: I'll pay you, Herrick, I will surely pay you!

HERRICK, *panting:* In God's name, John, I cannot help myself. I must chain them all. Now let you keep inside this house till I am gone! *He goes out with his deputies.*

Proctor stands there, gulping air. Horses and a wagon creaking are heard.

HALE, *in great uncertainty:* Mr. Proctor—
PROCTOR: Out of my sight!
HALE: Charity, Proctor, charity. What I have heard in her favor, I will not fear to testify in court. God help me, I cannot judge her guilty or innocent—I know not. Only this consider: the world goes mad, and it profit nothing you should lay the cause to the vengeance of a little girl.
PROCTOR: You are a coward! Though you be ordained in God's own tears, you are a coward now!
HALE: Proctor, I cannot think God be provoked so grandly by such a petty cause. The jails are packed—our greatest judges sit in Salem now—and hangin's promised. Man, we must look to cause proportionate. Were there murder done, perhaps, and never brought to light? Abomination? Some secret blasphemy that stinks to Heaven? Think on cause, man, and let you help me to discover it. For there's your way, believe it, there is your only way, when such confusion strikes upon the world. *He goes to Giles and Francis.* Let you counsel among yourselves; think on your village and what may have drawn from heaven such thundering wrath upon you all. I shall pray God open up our eyes.

Hale goes out.

FRANCIS, *struck by Hale's mood:* I never heard no murder done in Salem.
PROCTOR—*he has been reached by Hale's words:* Leave me, Francis, leave me.
GILES, *shaken:* John—tell me, are we lost?
PROCTOR: Go home now, Giles. We'll speak on it tomorrow.
GILES: Let you think on it. We'll come early, eh?
PROCTOR: Aye. Go now, Giles.
GILES: Good night, then.

Giles Corey goes out. After a moment:

MARY WARREN, *in a fearful squeak of a voice:* Mr. Proctor, very likely they'll let her come home once they're given proper evidence.

PROCTOR: You're coming to the court with me, Mary. You will tell it in the court.

MARY WARREN: I cannot charge murder on Abigail.

PROCTOR, *moving menacingly toward her:* You will tell the court how that poppet come here and who stuck the needle in.

MARY WARREN: She'll kill me for sayin' that! *Proctor continues toward her.* Abby'll charge lechery on you, Mr. Proctor!

PROCTOR, *halting:* She's told you!

MARY WARREN: I have known it, sir. She'll ruin you with it, I know she will.

PROCTOR, *hesitating, and with deep hatred of himself:* Good. Then her saintliness is done with. *Mary backs from him.* We will slide together into our pit; you will tell the court what you know.

MARY WARREN, *in terror:* I cannot, they'll turn on me—

Proctor strides and catches her, and she is repeating, "I cannot, I cannot!"

PROCTOR: My wife will never die for me! I will bring your guts into your mouth but that goodness will not die for me!

MARY WARREN, *struggling to escape him:* I cannot do it, I cannot!

PROCTOR, *grasping her by the throat as though he would strangle her:* Make your peace with it! Now Hell and Heaven grapple on our backs, and all our old pretense is ripped away—make your peace! *He throws her to the floor, where she sobs, "I cannot, I cannot . . . " And now, half to himself, staring, and turning to the open door:* Peace. It is a providence, and no great change; we are only what we always were, but naked now. *He walks as though toward a great horror, facing the open sky.* Aye, naked! And the wind, God's icy wind, will blow!

And she is over and over again sobbing, "I cannot, I cannot, I cannot."

CURTAIN

ACT THREE

The vestry room of the Salem meeting house, now serving as the anteroom of the General Court.

As the curtain rises, the room is empty, but for sunlight pouring through two high windows in the back wall. The room is solemn, even forbidding. Heavy beams jut out, boards of random widths make up the walls. At the right are two doors leading into the meeting house proper, where the court is being held. At the left another door leads outside.

There is a plain bench at the left, and another at the right. In the center a rather long meeting table, with stools and a considerable armchair snugged up to it.

Through the partitioning wall at the right we hear a prosecutor's voice, Judge Hathorne's, asking a question; then a woman's voice, Martha Corey's, replying.

HATHORNE'S VOICE: Now, Martha Corey, there is abundant evidence in our hands to show that you have given yourself to the reading of fortunes. Do you deny it?

MARTHA COREY'S VOICE: I am innocent to a witch. I know not what a witch is.

HATHORNE'S VOICE: How do you know, then, that you are not a witch?

MARTHA COREY'S VOICE: If I were, I would know it.

HATHORNE'S VOICE: Why do you hurt these children?

MARTHA COREY'S VOICE: I do not hurt them. I scorn it!

GILES' VOICE, *roaring:* I have evidence for the court!

Voices of townspeople rise in excitement.

DANFORTH'S VOICE: You will keep your seat!

GILES' VOICE: Thomas Putnam is reaching out for land!

DANFORTH'S VOICE: Remove that man, Marshal!

GILES' VOICE: You're hearing lies, lies!

A roaring goes up from the people.

HATHORNE'S VOICE: Arrest him, excellency!

GILES' VOICE: I have evidence. Why will you not hear my evidence?

The door opens and Giles is half carried into the vestry room by Herrick.

GILES: Hands off, damn you, let me go!
HERRICK: Giles, Giles!
GILES: Out of my way, Herrick! I bring evidence—
HERRICK: You cannot go in there, Giles; it's a court!

Enter Hale from the court.

HALE: Pray be calm a moment.
GILES: You, Mr. Hale, go in there and demand I speak.
HALE: A moment, sir, a moment.
GILES. They'll be hangin' my wife!

Judge Hathorne enters. He is in his sixties, a bitter, remorseless Salem judge.

HATHORNE: How do you dare come roarin' into this court! Are you gone daft, Corey?
GILES: You're not a Boston judge yet, Hathorne. You'll not call me daft!

Enter Deputy Governor Danforth and, behind him, Ezekiel Cheever and Parris. On his appearance, silence falls. Danforth is a grave man in his sixties, of some humor and sophistication that does not, however, interfere with an exact loyalty to his position and his cause. He comes down to Giles, who awaits his wrath.

DANFORTH, *looking directly at Giles:* Who is this man?
PARRIS: Giles Corey, sir, and a more contentious—
GILES, *to Parris:* I am asked the question, and I am old enough to answer it! *To Danforth, who impresses him and to whom he smiles through his strain:* My name is Corey, sir, Giles Corey. I have six hundred acres, and timber in addition. It is my wife you be condemning now. *He indicates the courtroom.*
DANFORTH: And how do you imagine to help her cause with such contemptuous riot? Now be gone. Your old age alone keeps you out of jail for this.

GILES, *beginning to plead:* They be tellin' lies about my wife, sir, I—

DANFORTH: Do you take it upon yourself to determine what this court shall believe and what it shall set aside?

GILES: Your Excellency, we mean no disrespect for—

DANFORTH: Disrespect indeed! It is disruption, Mister. This is the highest court of the supreme government of this province, do you know it?

GILES, *beginning to weep:* Your Excellency, I only said she were readin' books, sir, and they come and take her out of my house for—

DANFORTH, *mystified:* Books! What books?

GILES, *through helpless sobs:* It is my third wife, sir; I never had no wife that be so taken with books, and I thought to find the cause of it, d'y'see, but it were no witch I blamed her for. *He is openly weeping.* I have broke charity with the woman, I have broke charity with her. *He covers his face, ashamed. Danforth is respectfully silent.*

HALE: Excellency, he claims hard evidence for his wife's defense. I think that in all justice you must—

DANFORTH: Then let him submit his evidence in proper affidavit. You are certainly aware of our procedure here, Mr. Hale. *To Herrick:* Clear this room.

HERRICK: Come now, Giles. *He gently pushes Corey out.*

FRANCIS: We are desperate, sir; we come here three days now and cannot be heard.

DANFORTH: Who is this man?

FRANCIS: Francis Nurse, Your Excellency.

HALE: His wife's Rebecca that were condemned this morning.

DANFORTH: Indeed! I am amazed to find you in such uproar. I have only good report of your character, Mr. Nurse.

HATHORNE: I think they must both be arrested in contempt, sir.

DANFORTH, *to Francis:* Let you write your plea, and in due time I will—

FRANCIS: Excellency, we have proof for your eyes; God forbid you shut them to it. The girls, sir, the girls are frauds.

DANFORTH: What's that?

FRANCIS: We have proof of it, sir. They are all deceiving you.

Danforth is shocked, but studying Francis.

HATHORNE: This is contempt, sir, contempt!

DANFORTH: Peace, Judge Hathorne. Do you know who I am, Mr. Nurse?

FRANCIS: I surely do, sir, and I think you must be a wise judge to be what you are.

DANFORTH: And do you know that near to four hundred are in the jails from Marblehead to Lynn, and upon my signature?

FRANCIS: I—

DANFORTH: And seventy-two condemned to hang by that signature?

FRANCIS: Excellency, I never thought to say it to such a weighty judge, but you are deceived.

Enter Giles Corey from left. All turn to see as he beckons in Mary Warren with Proctor. Mary is keeping her eyes to the ground; Proctor has her elbow as though she were near collapse.

PARRIS, *on seeing her, in shock:* Mary Warren! *He goes directly to bend close to her face.* What are you about here?

PROCTOR, *pressing Parris away from her with a gentle but firm motion of protectiveness:* She would speak with the Deputy Governor.

DANFORTH, *shocked by this, turns to Herrick:* Did you not tell me Mary Warren were sick in bed?

HERRICK: She were, Your Honor. When I go to fetch her to the court last week, she said she were sick.

GILES: She has been strivin' with her soul all week, Your Honor; she comes now to tell the truth of this to you.

DANFORTH: Who is this?

PROCTOR: John Proctor, sir. Elizabeth Proctor is my wife.

PARRIS: Beware this man, Your Excellency, this man is mischief.

HALE, *excitedly:* I think you must hear the girl, sir, she—

DANFORTH, *who has become very interested in Mary Warren and only raises a hand toward Hale:* Peace. What would you tell us, Mary Warren?

Proctor looks at her, but she cannot speak.

PROCTOR: She never saw no spirits, sir.

DANFORTH, *with great alarm and surprise, to Mary:* Never saw no spirits!

GILES, *eagerly:* Never.

PROCTOR, *reaching into his jacket:* She has signed a deposition, sir—

DANFORTH, *instantly:* No, no, I accept no depositions. *He is rapidly calculating this; he turns from her to Proctor.* Tell me, Mr. Proctor, have you given out this story in the village?

PROCTOR: We have not.

PARRIS: They've come to overthrow the court, sir! This man is—

DANFORTH: I pray you, Mr. Parris. Do you know, Mr. Proctor, that the entire contention of the state in these trials is that the voice of Heaven is speaking through the children?

PROCTOR: I know that, sir.

DANFORTH, *thinks, staring at Proctor, then turns to Mary Warren:* And you, Mary Warren, how came you to cry out people for sending their spirits against you?

MARY WARREN: It were pretense, sir.

DANFORTH: I cannot hear you.

PROCTOR: It were pretense, she says.

DANFORTH: Ah? And the other girls? Susanna Walcott, and—the others? They are also pretending?

MARY WARREN: Aye, sir.

DANFORTH, *wide-eyed:* Indeed. *Pause. He is baffled by this. He turns to study Proctor's face.*

PARRIS, *in a sweat:* Excellency, you surely cannot think to let so vile a lie be spread in open court!

DANFORTH: Indeed not, but it strike hard upon me that she will dare come here with such a tale. Now, Mr. Proctor, before I decide whether I shall hear you or not, it is my duty to tell you this. We burn a hot fire here; it melts down all concealment.

PROCTOR: I know that, sir.

DANFORTH: Let me continue. I understand well, a husband's tenderness may drive him to extravagance in defense of a wife. Are you certain in your conscience, Mister, that your evidence is the truth?

PROCTOR: It is. And you will surely know it.

DANFORTH: And you thought to declare this revelation in the open court before the public?

PROCTOR: I thought I would, aye—with your permission.

DANFORTH, *his eyes narrowing:* Now, sir, what is your purpose in so doing?

PROCTOR: Why, I—I would free my wife, sir.

DANFORTH: There lurks nowhere in your heart, nor hidden in your spirit, any desire to undermine this court?

PROCTOR, *with the faintest faltering:* Why, no, sir.

CHEEVER, *clears his throat, awakening:* I— Your Excellency.

DANFORTH: Mr. Cheever.

CHEEVER: I think it be my duty, sir— *Kindly, to Proctor:* You'll not deny it, John. *To Danforth:* When we come to take his wife, he damned the court and ripped your warrant.

PARRIS: Now you have it!

DANFORTH: He did that, Mr. Hale?

HALE, *takes a breath:* Aye, he did.

PROCTOR: It were a temper, sir. I knew not what I did.

DANFORTH, *studying him:* Mr. Proctor.

PROCTOR: Aye, sir.

DANFORTH, *straight into his eyes:* Have you ever seen the Devil?

PROCTOR: No, sir.

DANFORTH: You are in all respects a Gospel Christian?

PROCTOR: I am, sir.

PARRIS: Such a Christian that will not come to church but once in a month!

DANFORTH, *restrained—he is curious:* Not come to church?

PROCTOR: I—I have no love for Mr. Parris. It is no secret. But God I surely love.

CHEEVER: He plow on Sunday, sir.

DANFORTH: Plow on Sunday!

CHEEVER, *apologetically:* I think it be evidence, John. I am an official of the court, I cannot keep it.

PROCTOR: I—I have once or twice plowed on Sunday. I have three children, sir, and until last year my land give little.

GILES: You'll find other Christians that do plow on Sunday if the truth be known.

HALE: Your Honor, I cannot think you may judge the man on such evidence.

DANFORTH: I judge nothing. *Pause. He keeps watching Proctor, who tries to meet his gaze.* I tell you straight, Mister—I have seen marvels in this court. I have seen people choked before my eyes by spirits; I have seen them stuck by pins and slashed by daggers. I have until this moment not the slightest reason to suspect that the children may be deceiving me. Do you understand my meaning?

PROCTOR: Excellency, does it not strike upon you that so many of these women have lived so long with such upright reputation, and—

PARRIS: Do you read the Gospel, Mr. Proctor?

PROCTOR: I read the Gospel.

PARRIS: I think not, or you should surely know that Cain were an upright man, and yet he did kill Abel.

PROCTOR: Aye, God tells us that. *To Danforth:* But who tells us Rebecca Nurse murdered seven babies by sending out her spirit on them? It is the children only, and this one will swear she lied to you.

Danforth considers, then beckons Hathorne to him. Hathorne leans in, and he speaks in his ear. Hathorne nods.

HATHORNE: Aye, she's the one.

DANFORTH: Mr. Proctor, this morning, your wife sent me a claim in which she states that she is pregnant now.

PROCTOR: My wife pregnant!

DANFORTH: There be no sign of it—we have examined her body.

PROCTOR: But if she say she is pregnant, then she must be! That woman will never lie, Mr. Danforth.

DANFORTH: She will not?

PROCTOR: Never, sir, never.

DANFORTH: We have thought it too convenient to be credited. However, if I should tell you now that I will let her be kept another month; and if she begin to show her natural signs, you shall have her living yet another year until she is delivered—what say you to that? *John Proctor is struck silent.* Come now. You say your only purpose is to save your wife. Good, then, she is saved at least this year, and a year is long. What say you, sir? It is done now. *In conflict, Proctor glances at Francis and Giles.* Will you drop this charge?

PROCTOR: I—I think I cannot.

DANFORTH, *now an almost imperceptible hardness in his voice:* Then your purpose is somewhat larger.

PARRIS: He's come to overthrow this court, Your Honor!

PROCTOR: These are my friends. Their wives are also accused—

DANFORTH, *with a sudden briskness of manner:* I judge you not, sir. I am ready to hear your evidence.

PROCTOR: I come not to hurt the court; I only—

DANFORTH, *cutting him off:* Marshal, go into the court and bid Judge Stoughton and Judge Sewall declare recess for one hour. And let them go to the tavern, if they will. All witnesses and prisoners are to be kept in the building.

HERRICK: Aye, sir. *Very deferentially:* If I may say it, sir, I know this man all my life. It is a good man, sir.

DANFORTH—*it is the reflection on himself he resents:* I am sure of it, Marshal. *Herrick nods, then goes out.* Now, what deposition do you have for us, Mr. Proctor? And I beg you be clear, open as the sky, and honest.

PROCTOR, *as he takes out several papers:* I am no lawyer, so I'll—

DANFORTH: The pure in heart need no lawyers. Proceed as you will.

PROCTOR, *handing Danforth a paper:* Will you read this first, sir? It's a sort of testament. The people signing it declare their good opinion of Rebecca, and my wife, and Martha Corey. Danforth looks down at the paper.

PARRIS, *to enlist Danforth's sarcasm:* Their good opinion! *But Danforth goes on reading, and Proctor is heartened.*

PROCTOR: These are all landholding farmers, members of the church. *Delicately, trying to point out a paragraph:* If you'll notice, sir—they've known the women many years and never saw no sign they had dealings with the Devil.

Parris nervously moves over and reads over Danforth's shoulder.

DANFORTH, *glancing down a long list:* How many names are here?

FRANCIS: Ninety-one, Your Excellency.

PARRIS, *sweating:* These people should be summoned. *Danforth looks up at him questioningly.* For questioning.

FRANCIS, *trembling with anger:* Mr. Danforth, I gave them all my word no harm would come to them for signing this.

PARRIS: This is a clear attack upon the court!

HALE, *to Parris, trying to contain himself:* Is every defense an attack upon the court? Can no one—?

PARRIS: All innocent and Christian people are happy for the courts in Salem! These people are gloomy for it. *To Danforth directly:* And I think you will want to know, from each and every one of them, what discontents them with you!

HATHORNE: I think they ought to be examined, sir.

DANFORTH: It is not necessarily an attack, I think. Yet—

FRANCIS: These are all covenanted Christians, sir.

DANFORTH: Then I am sure they may have nothing to fear. *Hands Cheever the paper.* Mr. Cheever, have warrants drawn for all of these—arrest for examination. *To Proctor:* Now, Mister, what other information do you have for us? *Francis is still standing, horrified.* You may sit, Mr. Nurse.

FRANCIS: I have brought trouble on these people; I have—

DANFORTH: No, old man, you have not hurt these people if they are of good conscience. But you must understand, sir, that a person is either with this court or he must be counted against it, there be no road between. This is a sharp time, now, a precise time—we live no longer in the dusky afternoon when evil mixed itself with good and befuddled the world. Now, by God's grace, the shining sun is up, and them that fear not light will surely praise it. I hope you will be one of those. *Mary Warren suddenly sobs.* She's not hearty, I see.

PROCTOR: No, she's not, sir. *To Mary, bending to her, holding her hand, quietly:* Now remember what the angel Raphael said to the boy Tobias. Remember it.

MARY WARREN, *hardly audible:* Aye.

PROCTOR: "Do that which is good, and no harm shall come to thee."

MARY WARREN: Aye.

DANFORTH: Come, man, we wait you.

Marshal Herrick returns, and takes his post at the door.

GILES: John, my deposition, give him mine.

PROCTOR: Aye. *He hands Danforth another paper.* This is Mr. Corey's deposition.

DANFORTH: Oh? *He looks down at it. Now Hathorne comes behind him and reads with him.*

HATHORNE, *suspiciously:* What lawyer drew this, Corey?

GILES: You know I never hired a lawyer in my life, Hathorne.

DANFORTH, *finishing the reading:* It is very well phrased. My compliments. Mr. Parris, if Mr. Putnam is in the court, will you bring him in? *Hathorne takes the deposition, and walks to the window with it. Parris goes into the court.* You have no legal training, Mr. Corey?

GILES, *very pleased:* I have the best, sir—I am thirty-three time in court in my life. And always plaintiff, too.

DANFORTH: Oh, then you're much put-upon.

GILES: I am never put-upon; I know my rights, sir, and I will have them. You know, your father tried a case of mine—might be thirty-five year ago, I think.

DANFORTH: Indeed.

GILES: He never spoke to you of it?

DANFORTH: No, I cannot recall it.

GILES: That's strange, he give me nine pound damages. He were a fair judge, your father. Y'see, I had a white mare that time, and this fellow come to borrow the mare— *Enter Parris with Thomas Putnam. When he sees Putnam, Giles' ease goes; he is hard.* Aye, there he is.

DANFORTH: Mr. Putnam, I have here an accusation by Mr. Corey against you. He states that you coldly prompted your daughter to cry witchery upon George Jacobs that is now in jail.

PUTNAM: It is a lie.

DANFORTH, *turning to Giles:* Mr. Putnam states your charge is a lie. What say you to that?

GILES, *furious, his fists clenched:* A fart on Thomas Putnam, that is what I say to that!

DANFORTH: What proof do you submit for your charge, sir?

GILES: My proof is there! *Pointing to the paper.* If Jacobs hangs for a witch he forfeit up his property—that's law! And there is none but Putnam with the coin to buy so great a piece. This man is killing his neighbors for their land!

DANFORTH: But proof, sir, proof.

GILES, *pointing at his deposition:* The proof is there! I have it from an honest man who heard Putnam say it! The day his daughter cried out on Jacobs, he said she'd given him a fair gift of land.

HATHORNE: And the name of this man?

GILES, *taken aback:* What name?

HATHORNE: The man that give you this information.

GILES, *hesitates, then:* Why, I—I cannot give you his name.

HATHORNE: And why not?

GILES, *hesitates, then bursts out:* You know well why not! He'll lay in jail if I give his name!

HATHORNE: This is contempt of the court, Mr. Danforth!

DANFORTH, *to avoid that:* You will surely tell us the name.

GILES: I will not give you no name. I mentioned my wife's name once and I'll burn in hell long enough for that. I stand mute.

DANFORTH: In that case, I have no choice but to arrest you for contempt of this court, do you know that?

GILES: This is a hearing; you cannot clap me for contempt of a hearing.

DANFORTH: Oh, it is a proper lawyer! Do you wish me to declare the court in full session here? Or will you give me good reply?

GILES, *faltering:* I cannot give you no name, sir, I cannot.

DANFORTH: You are a foolish old man. Mr. Cheever, begin the record. The court is now in session. I ask you, Mr. Corey—

PROCTOR, *breaking in:* Your Honor—he has the story in confidence, sir, and he—

PARRIS: The Devil lives on such confidences! *To Danforth:* Without confidences there could be no conspiracy, Your Honor!

HATHORNE: I think it must be broken, sir.

DANFORTH, *to Giles:* Old man, if your informant tells the truth let him come here openly like a decent man. But if he hide in anonymity I must know why. Now sir, the government and central church demand of you the name of him who reported Mr. Thomas Putnam a common murderer.

HALE: Excellency—

DANFORTH: Mr. Hale.

HALE: We cannot blink it more. There is a prodigious fear of this court in the country—

DANFORTH: Then there is a prodigious guilt in the country. Are you afraid to be questioned here?

HALE: I may only fear the Lord, sir, but there is fear in the country nevertheless.

DANFORTH, *angered now:* Reproach me not with the fear in the country; there is fear in the country because there is a moving plot to topple Christ in the country!

HALE: But it does not follow that everyone accused is part of it.

DANFORTH: No uncorrupted man may fear this court, Mr. Hale! None! *To Giles:* You are under arrest in contempt of this court. Now sit you down and take counsel with yourself, or you will be set in the jail until you decide to answer all questions.

Giles Corey makes a rush for Putnam. Proctor lunges and holds him.

PROCTOR: No, Giles!

GILES, *over Proctor's shoulder at Putnam:* I'll cut your throat, Putnam, I'll kill you yet!

PROCTOR, *forcing him into a chair:* Peace, Giles, peace. *Releasing him.* We'll prove ourselves. Now we will. *He starts to turn to Danforth.*

GILES: Say nothin' more, John. *Pointing at Danforth:* He's only playin' you! You means to hang us all!

Mary Warren bursts into sobs.

DANFORTH: This is a court of law, Mister. I'll have no effrontery here!

PROCTOR: Forgive him, sir, for his old age. Peace, Giles, we'll prove it all now. *He lifts up Mary's chin.* You cannot weep, Mary. Remember the angel, what he say to the boy. Hold to it, now; there is your rock. *Mary quiets. He takes out a paper, and turns to Danforth.* This is Mary Warren's deposition. I—I would ask you remember, sir, while you read it, that until two week ago she were no different than the other children are today. *He is speaking reasonably, restraining all his fears, his anger, his anxiety.* You saw her scream, she howled, she swore familiar spirits choked her; she even testified that Satan, in the form of women now in jail, tried to win her soul away, and then when she refused—

DANFORTH: We know all this.

PROCTOR: Aye, sir. She swears now that she never saw Satan; nor any spirit, vague or clear, that Satan may have sent to hurt her. And she declares her friends are lying now.

Proctor starts to hand Danforth the deposition, and Hale comes up to Danforth in a trembling state.

HALE: Excellency, a moment. I think this goes to the heart of the matter.

DANFORTH, *with deep misgivings:* It surely does.

HALE: I cannot say he is an honest man; I know him little. But in all justice, sir, a claim so weighty cannot be argued by a farmer. In God's name, sir, stop here; send him home and let him come again with a lawyer—

DANFORTH, *patiently:* Now look you, Mr. Hale—

HALE: Excellency, I have signed, seventy-two death warrants; I am a minister of the Lord, and I dare not take a life without there be a proof so immaculate no slightest qualm of conscience may doubt it.

DANFORTH: Mr. Hale, you surely do not doubt my justice.

HALE: I have this morning signed away the soul of Rebecca Nurse, Your Honor. I'll not conceal it, my hand shakes yet as with a wound! I pray you, sir, *this* argument let lawyers present to you.

DANFORTH: Mr. Hale, believe me; for a man of such terrible learning you are most bewildered—I hope you will forgive me. I have been thirty-two year at the bar, sir, and I should be confounded were I called upon to defend these people. Let you consider, now— *To Proctor and the others:* And I bid you all do likewise. In an ordinary crime, how does one defend the accused? One calls up witnesses to prove his innocence. But witchcraft is *ipso facto*, on its face and by its nature, an invisible crime, is it not? Therefore, who may possibly be witness to it? The witch and the victim. None other. Now we cannot hope the witch will accuse herself; granted? Therefore, we must rely upon her victims—and they do testify, the children certainly do testify. As for the witches, none will deny that we are most eager for all their confessions. Therefore, what is left for a lawyer to bring out? I think I have made my point. Have I not?

HALE: But this child claims the girls are not truthful, and if they are not—

DANFORTH: That is precisely what I am about to consider, sir.

What more may you ask of me? Unless you doubt my probity?

HALE, *defeated:* I surely do not, sir. Let you consider it, then.

DANFORTH: And let you put your heart to rest. Her deposition, Mr. Proctor.

Proctor hands it to him. Hathorne rises, goes beside Danforth, and starts reading. Parris comes to his other side. Danforth looks at John Proctor, then proceeds to read. Hale gets up, finds position near the judge, reads too. Proctor glances at Giles. Francis prays silently, hands pressed together. Cheever waits placidly, the sublime official, dutiful. Mary Warren sobs once. John Proctor touches her head reassuringly. Presently Danforth lifts his eyes, stands up, takes out a kerchief and blows his nose. The others stand aside as he moves in thought toward the window.

PARRIS, *hardly able to contain his anger and fear:* I should like to question—

DANFORTH—*his first real outburst, in which his contempt for Parris is clear:* Mr. Parris, I bid you be silent! *He stands in silence, looking out the window. Now, having established that he will set the gait:* Mr. Cheever, will you go into the court and bring the children here? *Cheever gets up and goes out upstage. Danforth now turns to Mary.* Mary Warren, how came you to this turnabout? Has Mr. Proctor threatened you for this deposition?

MARY WARREN: No, sir.

DANFORTH: Has he ever threatened you?

MARY WARREN, *weaker:* No, sir.

DANFORTH, *sensing a weakening:* Has he threatened you?

MARY WARREN: No, sir.

DANFORTH: Then you tell me that you sat in my court, callously lying, when you knew that people would hang by your evidence? *She does not answer.* Answer me!

MARY WARREN, *almost inaudibly:* I did, sir.

DANFORTH: How were you instructed in your life? Do you not know that God damns all liars? *She cannot speak.* Or is it now that you lie?

MARY WARREN: No, sir—I am with God now.

DANFORTH: You are with God now.

MARY WARREN: Aye, sir.

DANFORTH, *containing himself:* I will tell you this—you are either lying now, or you were lying in the court, and in either case you have committed perjury and you will go to jail for it. You cannot lightly say you lied, Mary. Do you know that?

MARY WARREN: I cannot lie no more. I am with God, I am with God.

But she breaks into sobs at the thought of it, and the right door opens, and enter Susanna Walcott, Mercy Lewis, Betty Parris, and finally Abigail. Cheever comes to Danforth.

CHEEVER: Ruth Putnam's not in the court, sir, nor the other children.

DANFORTH: These will be sufficient. Sit you down, children. *Silently they sit.* Your friend, Mary Warren, has given us a deposition. In which she swears that she never saw familiar spirits, apparitions, nor any manifest of the Devil. She claims as well that none of you have seen these things either. *Slight pause.* Now, children, this is a court of law. The law, based upon the Bible, and the Bible, writ by Almighty God, forbid the practice of witchcraft, and describe death as the penalty thereof. But likewise, children, the law and Bible damn all bearers of false witness. *Slight pause.* Now then. It does not escape me that this deposition may be devised to blind us; it may well be that Mary Warren has been conquered by Satan, who sends her here to distract our sacred purpose. If so, her neck will break for it. But if she speak true, I bid you now drop your guile and confess your pretense, for a quick confession will go easier with you. *Pause.* Abigail Williams, rise. *Abigail slowly rises.* Is there any truth in this?

ABIGAIL: No, sir.

DANFORTH, *thinks, glances at Mary, then back to Abigail:* Children, a very augur bit will now be turned into your souls until your honesty is proved. Will either of you change your positions now, or do you force me to hard questioning?

ABIGAIL: I have naught to change, sir. She lies.

DANFORTH, *to Mary:* You would still go on with this?

MARY WARREN, *faintly:* Aye, Sir.

DANFORTH, *turning to Abigail:* A poppet were discovered in

Mr. Proctor's house, stabbed by a needle. Mary Warren claims that you sat beside her in the court when she made it, and that you saw her make it and witnessed how she herself stuck her needle into it for safe-keeping. What say you to that?

ABIGAIL, *with a slight note of indignation:* It is a lie, sir.

DANFORTH, *after a slight pause:* While you worked for Mr. Proctor, did you see poppets in that house?

ABIGAIL: Goody Proctor always kept poppets.

PROCTOR: Your honor, my wife never kept no poppets. Mary Warren confesses it was her poppet.

CHEEVER: Your Excellency.

DANFORTH: Mr. Cheever.

CHEEVER: When I spoke with Goody Proctor in that house, she said she never kept no poppets. But she said she did keep poppets when she were a girl.

PROCTOR: She has not been a girl these fifteen years, Your Honor.

HATHORNE: But a poppet will keep fifteen years, will it not?

PROCTOR: It will keep if it is kept, but Mary Warren swears she never saw no poppets in my house, nor anyone else.

PARRIS: Why could there not have been poppets hid where no one ever saw them?

PROCTOR, *furious:* There might also be a dragon with five legs in my house, but no one has ever seen it.

PARRIS: We are here, Your Honor, precisely to discover what no one has ever seen.

PROCTOR: Mr. Danforth, what profit this girl to turn herself about? What may Mary Warren gain but hard questioning and worse?

DANFORTH: You are charging Abigail Williams with a marvelous cool plot to murder, do you understand that?

PROCTOR: I do, sir. I believe she means to murder.

DANFORTH, *pointing at Abigail, incredulously:* This child would murder your wife?

PROCTOR: It is not a child. Now hear me, sir. In the sight of the congregation she were twice this year put out of this meetin' house for laughter during prayer.

DANFORTH, *shocked, turning to Abigail:* What's this? Laughter during—!

PARRIS: Excellency, she were under Tituba's power at that time, but she is solemn now.

GILES: Aye, now she is solemn and goes to hang people!

DANFORTH: Quiet, man.

HATHORNE: Surely it have no bearing on the question, sir. He charges contemplation of murder.

DANFORTH: Aye. *He studies Abigail for a moment, then:* Continue, Mr. Proctor.

PROCTOR: Mary. Now tell the Governor how you danced in the woods.

PARRIS, *instantly:* Excellency, since I come to Salem this man is blackening my name. He—

DANFORTH: In a moment, sir. *To Mary Warren, sternly, and surprised:* What is this dancing?

MARY WARREN: I— *She glances at Abigail, who is staring down at her remorselessly. Then, appealing to Proctor:* Mr. Proctor—

PROCTOR, *taking it right up:* Abigail leads the girls to the woods, Your Honor, and they have danced there naked—

PARRIS: Your Honor, this—

PROCTOR, *at once:* Mr. Parris discovered them himself in the dead of night! There's the "child" she is!

DANFORTH—*it is growing into a nightmare, and he turns, astonished, to Parris:* Mr. Parris—

PARRIS: I can only say, sir, that I never found any of them naked, and this man is—

DANFORTH: But you discovered them dancing in the woods? *Eyes on Parris, he points at Abigail.* Abigail?

HALE: Excellency, when I first arrived from Beverly, Mr. Parris told me that.

DANFORTH: Do you deny it, Mr. Parris?

PARRIS: I do not, sir, but I never saw any of them naked.

DANFORTH: But she have *danced*?

PARRIS, *unwillingly:* Aye, sir.

Danforth, as though with new eyes, looks at Abigail.

HATHORNE: Excellency, will you permit me? *He points at Mary Warren.*

DANFORTH, *with great worry:* Pray, proceed.

HATHORNE: You say you never saw no spirits, Mary, were

never threatened or afflicted by any manifest of the Devil or the Devil's agents.

MARY WARREN, *very faintly:* No, Sir.

HATHORNE, *with a gleam of victory:* And yet, when people accused of witchery confronted you in court, you would faint, saying their spirits came out of their bodies and choked you—

MARY WARREN: That were pretense, sir.

DANFORTH: I cannot hear you.

MARY WARREN: Pretense, sir.

PARRIS: But you did turn cold, did you not? I myself picked you up many times, and your skin were icy. Mr. Danforth, you—

DANFORTH: I saw that many times.

PROCTOR: She only pretended to faint, Your Excellency. They're all marvelous pretenders.

HATHORNE: Then can she pretend to faint now?

PROCTOR: Now?

PARRIS: Why not? Now there are no spirits attacking her, for none in this room is accused of witchcraft. So let her turn herself cold now, let her pretend she is attacked now, let her faint. *He turns to Mary Warren.* Faint!

MARY WARREN: Faint?

PARRIS: Aye, faint. Prove to us how you pretended in the court so many times.

MARY WARREN, *looking to Proctor:* I—cannot faint now, sir.

PROCTOR, *alarmed, quietly:* Can you not pretend it?

MARY WARREN: I— *She looks about as though searching for the passion to faint.* I—have no *sense* of it now, I—

DANFORTH: Why? What is lacking now?

MARY WARREN: I—cannot tell, sir, I—

DANFORTH: Might it be that here we have no afflicting spirit loose, but in the court there were some?

MARY WARREN: I never saw no spirits.

PARRIS: Then see no spirits now, and prove to us that you can faint by your own will, as you claim.

MARY WARREN, *stares, searching for the emotion of it, and then shakes her head:* I—cannot do it.

PARRIS: Then you will confess, will you not? It were attacking spirits made you faint!

MARY WARREN: No, sir, I—

PARRIS: Your Excellency, this is a trick to blind the court!

MARY WARREN: It's not a trick! *She stands.* I—I used to faint because I—I thought I saw spirits.

DANFORTH: *Thought* you saw them!

MARY WARREN: But I did not, Your Honor.

HATHORNE: How could you think you saw them unless you saw them?

MARY WARREN: I—I cannot tell how, but I did. I—I heard the other girls screaming, and you, Your Honor, you seemed to believe them, and I— It were only sport in the beginning, sir, but then the whole world cried spirits, spirits, and I—I promise you, Mr. Danforth, I only thought I saw them but I did not.

Danforth peers at her.

PARRIS, *smiling, but nervous because Danforth seems to be struck by Mary Warren's story:* Surely Your Excellency is not taken by this simple lie.

DANFORTH, *turning worriedly to Abigail:* Abigail. I bid you now search your heart and tell me this—and beware of it, child, to God every soul is precious and His vengeance is terrible on them that take life without cause. Is it possible, child, that the spirits you have seen are illusion only, some deception that may cross your mind when—

ABIGAIL: Why, this—this—is a base question, sir.

DANFORTH: Child, I would have you consider it—

ABIGAIL: I have been hurt, Mr. Danforth; I have seen my blood runnin' out! I have been near to murdered every day because I done my duty pointing out the Devil's people—and this is my reward? To be mistrusted, denied, questioned like a—

DANFORTH, *weakening:* Child, I do not mistrust you—

ABIGAIL, *in an open threat:* Let *you* beware, Mr. Danforth. Think you to be so mighty that the rower of Hell may not turn your wits? Beware of it! There is— *Suddenly, from an accusatory attitude, her face turns, looking into the air above —it is truly frightened.*

DANFORTH, *apprehensively:* What is it, child?

ABIGAIL, *looking about in the air, clasping her arms about her as though cold:* I—I know not. A wind, a cold wind, has come. *Her eyes fall on Mary Warren.*

MARY WARREN, *terrified, pleading:* Abby!

MERCY LEWIS, *shivering:* Your Honor, I freeze!

PROCTOR: They're pretending!

HATHORNE, *touching Abigail's hand:* She is cold, Your Honor, touch her!

MERCY LEWIS, *through chattering teeth:* Mary, do you send this shadow on me?

MARY WARREN: Lord, save me!

SUSANNA WALCOTT: I freeze, I freeze!

ABIGAIL, *shivering visibly:* It is a wind, a wind!

MARY WARREN: Abby, don't do that!

DANFORTH, *himself engaged and entered by Abigail:* Mary Warren, do you witch her? I say to you, do you send your spirit out?

With a hysterical cry Mary Warren starts to run. Proctor catches her.

MARY WARREN, *almost collapsing:* Let me go, Mr. Proctor, I cannot, I cannot—

ABIGAIL, *crying to Heaven:* Oh, Heavenly Father, take away this shadow!

Without warning or hesitation, Proctor leaps at Abigail and, grabbing her by the hair, pulls her to her feet. She screams in pain. Danforth, astonished, cries, "What are you about?" and Hathorne and Parris call, "Take your hands off her!" and out of all comes Proctor's roaring voice.

PROCTOR: How do you call Heaven! Whore! Whore!

Herrick breaks Proctor from her.

HERRICK: John!

DANFORTH: Man! Man, what do you—

PROCTOR, *breathless and in agony:* It is a whore!

DANFORTH, *dumfounded:* You charge—?

ABIGAIL: Mr. Danforth, he is lying!—

PROCTOR: Mark her! Now she'll suck a scream to stab me with but—

DANFORTH: You will prove this! This will not pass!

PROCTOR, *trembling, his life collapsing about him:* I have known her, sir. I have known her.

DANFORTH: You—you are a lecher?

FRANCIS, *horrified:* John, you cannot say such a—

PROCTOR: Oh, Francis, I wish you had some evil in you that you might know me! *To Danforth:* A man will not cast away his good name. You surely know that.

DANFORTH, *dumfounded:* In—in what time? In what place?

PROCTOR, *his voice about to break, and his shame great:* In the proper place—where my beasts are bedded. On the last night of my joy, some eight months past. She used to serve me in my house, sir. *He has to clamp his jaw to keep from weeping.* A man may think God sleeps, but God sees everything, I know it now. I beg you, sir, I beg you—see her what she is. My wife, my dear, good wife, took this girl soon after, sir, and put her out on the highroad. And being what she is, a lump of vanity, sir— *He is being overcome.* Excellency, forgive me, forgive me. *Angrily against himself, he turns away from the Governor for a moment. Then, as though to cry out is his only means of speech left:* She thinks to dance with me on my wife's grave! And well she might, for I thought of her softly. God help me, I lusted, and there *is* a promise in such sweat. But it is a whore's vengeance, and you must see it; I set myself entirely in your hands. I know you must see it now.

DANFORTH, *blanched, in horror, turning to Abigail:* You deny every scrap and tittle of this?

ABIGAIL: If I must answer that, I will leave and I will not come back again!

Danforth seems unsteady.

PROCTOR: I have made a bell of my honor! I have rung the doom of my good name—you will believe me, Mr. Danforth! My wife is innocent, except she knew a whore when she saw one!

ABIGAIL, *stepping up to Danforth:* What look do you give me?

Danforth cannot speak. I'll not have such looks! *She turns and starts for the door.*

DANFORTH: You will remain where you are! *Herrick steps into her path. She comes up short, fire in her eyes.* Mr. Parris, go into the court and bring Goodwife Proctor out.

PARRIS, *objecting:* Your Honor, this is all a—

DANFORTH, *sharply to Parris:* Bring her out! And tell her not one word of what's been spoken here. And let you knock before you enter. *Parris goes out.* Now we shall touch the bottom of this swamp. *To Proctor:* Your wife, you say, is an honest woman.

PROCTOR: In her life, sir, she have never lied. There are them that cannot sing, and them that cannot weep—my wife cannot lie. I have paid much to learn it, sir.

DANFORTH: And when she put this girl out of your house, she put her out for a harlot?

PROCTOR: Aye, sir.

DANFORTH: And knew her for a harlot?

PROCTOR: Aye, sir, she knew her for a harlot.

DANFORTH: Good then. *To Abigail:* And if she tell me, child, it were for harlotry, may God spread His mercy on you! *There is a knock. He calls to the door.* Hold! *To Abigail:* Turn your back. Turn your back. *To Proctor:* Do likewise. *Both turn their backs—Abigail with indignant slowness.* Now let neither of you turn to face Goody Proctor. No one in this room is to speak one word, or raise a gesture aye or nay. *He turns toward the door, calls:* Enter! *The door opens. Elizabeth enters with Parris. Parris leaves her. She stands alone, her eyes looking for Proctor.* Mr. Cheever, report this testimony in all exactness. Are you ready?

CHEEVER: Ready, sir.

DANFORTH: Come here, woman. *Elizabeth comes to him, glancing at Proctor's back.* Look at me only, not at your husband. In my eyes only.

ELIZABETH, *faintly:* Good, sir.

DANFORTH: We are given to understand that at one time you dismissed your servant, Abigail Williams.

ELIZABETH: That is true, sir.

DANFORTH: For what cause did you dismiss her? *Slight pause.*

Then Elizabeth tries to glance at Proctor. You will look in my eyes only and not at your husband. The answer is in your memory and you need no help to give it to me. Why did you dismiss Abigail Williams?

ELIZABETH, *not knowing what to say, sensing a situation, wetting her lips to stall for time:* She—dissatisfied me. *Pause.* And my husband.

DANFORTH: In what way dissatisfied you?

ELIZABETH: She were— *She glances at Proctor for a cue.*

DANFORTH: Woman, look at me! *Elizabeth does.* Were she slovenly? Lazy? What disturbance did she cause?

ELIZABETH: Your Honor, I—in that time I were sick. And I— My husband is a good and righteous man. He is never drunk as some are, nor wastin' his time at the shovelboard, but always at his work. But in my sickness—you see, sir, I were a long time sick after my last baby, and I thought I saw my husband somewhat turning from me. And this girl— *She turns to Abigail.*

DANFORTH: Look at me.

ELIZABETH: Aye, sir. Abigail Williams— *She breaks off.*

DANFORTH: What of Abigail Williams?

ELIZABETH: I came to think he fancied her. And so one night I lost my wits, I think, and put her out on the highroad.

DANFORTH: Your husband—did he indeed turn from you?

ELIZABETH, *in agony:* My husband—is a goodly man, sir.

DANFORTH: Then he did not turn from you.

ELIZABETH, *starting to glance at Proctor:* He—

DANFORTH, *reaches out and holds her face, then:* Look at me! To your own knowledge, has John Proctor ever committed the crime of lechery? *In a crisis of indecision she cannot speak.* Answer my question! Is your husband a lecher!

ELIZABETH, *faintly:* No, sir.

DANFORTH: Remove her, Marshal.

PROCTOR: Elizabeth, tell the truth!

DANFORTH: She has spoken. Remove her!

PROCTOR, *crying out:* Elizabeth, I have confessed it!

ELIZABETH: Oh, God! *The door closes behind her.*

PROCTOR: She only thought to save my name!

HALE: Excellency, it is a natural lie to tell; I beg you, stop now before another is condemned! I may shut my conscience to

it no more—private vengeance is working through this testimony! From the beginning this man has struck me true. By my oath to Heaven, I believe him now, and I pray you call back his wife before we—

DANFORTH: She spoke nothing of lechery, and this man has lied!

HALE: I believe him! *Pointing at Abigail:* This girl has always struck me false! She has—

Abigail, with a weird, wild, chilling cry, screams up to the ceiling.

ABIGAIL: You will not! Begone! Begone, I say!

DANFORTH: What is it, child? *But Abigail, pointing with fear, is now raising up her frightened eyes, her awed face, toward the ceiling—the girls are doing the same—and now Hathorne, Hale, Putnam, Cheever, Herrick, and Danforth do the same.* What's there? *He lowers his eyes from the ceiling, and now he is frightened; there is real tension in his voice.* Child! *She is transfixed—with all the girls, she is whimpering open-mouthed, agape at the ceiling.* Girls! Why do you—?

MERCY LEWIS, *pointing:* It's on the beam! Behind the rafter!

DANFORTH, *looking up:* Where!

ABIGAIL: Why—? *She gulps.* Why do you come, yellow bird?

PROCTOR: Where's a bird? I see no bird!

ABIGAIL, *to the ceiling:* My face? My face?

PROCTOR: Mr. Hale—

DANFORTH: Be quiet!

PROCTOR, *to Hale:* Do you see a bird?

DANFORTH: Be quiet!!

ABIGAIL, *to the ceiling, in a genuine conversation with the "bird," as though trying to talk it out of attacking her:* But God made my face; you cannot want to tear my face. Envy is a deadly sin, Mary.

MARY WARREN, *on her feet with a spring, and horrified, pleading:* Abby!

ABIGAIL, *unperturbed, continuing to the "bird":* Oh, Mary, this is a black art to change your shape. No, I cannot, I cannot stop my mouth; it's God's work I do.

MARY WARREN: Abby, I'm *here*!

PROCTOR, *frantically:* They're pretending, Mr. Danforth!

ABIGAIL—*now she takes a backward step, as though in fear the bird will swoop down momentarily:* Oh, please, Mary! Don't come down.

SUSANNA WALCOTT: Her claws, she's stretching her claws!

PROCTOR: Lies, lies.

ABIGAIL, *backing further, eyes still fixed above:* Mary, please don't hurt me!

MARY WARREN, *to Danforth:* I'm not hurting her!

DANFORTH, *to Mary Warren:* Why does she see this vision?

MARY WARREN: She sees nothin'!

ABIGAIL, *now staring full front as though hypnotized, and mimicking the exact tone of Mary Warren's cry:* She sees nothin'!

MARY WARREN, *pleading:* Abby, you mustn't!

ABIGAIL AND ALL THE GIRLS, *all transfixed:* Abby, you mustn't!

MARY WARREN, *to all the girls:* I'm here, I'm here!

GIRLS: I'm here, I'm here!

DANFORTH, *horrified:* Mary Warren! Draw back your spirit out of them!

MARY WARREN: Mr. Danforth!

GIRLS, *cutting her off:* Mr. Danforth!

DANFORTH: Have you compacted with the Devil? Have you?

MARY WARREN: Never, never!

GIRLS: Never, never!

DANFORTH, *growing hysterical:* Why can they only repeat you?

PROCTOR: Give me a whip—I'll stop it!

MARY WARREN: They're sporting. They—!

GIRLS: They're sporting!

MARY WARREN, *turning on them all hysterically and stamping her feet:* Abby, stop it!

GIRLS, *stamping their feet:* Abby, stop it!

MARY WARREN: Stop it!

GIRLS: Stop it!

MARY WARREN, *screaming it out at the top of her lungs, and raising her fists:* Stop it!!

GIRLS, *raising their fists:* Stop it!!

Mary Warren, utterly confounded, and becoming overwhelmed by Abigail's—and the girls'—utter conviction, starts to whimper, hands half raised, powerless, and all the girls begin whimpering exactly as she does.

DANFORTH: A little while ago you were afflicted. Now it seems you afflict others; where did you find this power?

MARY WARREN, *staring at Abigail:* I—have no power.

GIRLS: I have no power.

PROCTOR: They're gulling you, Mister!

DANFORTH: Why did you turn about this past two weeks? You have seen the Devil, have you not?

HALE, *indicating Abigail and the girls:* You cannot believe them!

MARY WARREN: I—

PROCTOR, *sensing her weakening:* Mary, God damns all liars!

DANFORTH, *pounding it into her:* You have seen the Devil, you have made compact with Lucifer, have you not?

PROCTOR: God damns liars, Mary!

Mary utters something unintelligible, staring at Abigail, who keeps watching the "bird" above.

DANFORTH: I cannot hear you. What do you say? *Mary utters again unintelligibly.* You will confess yourself or you will hang! *He turns her roughly to face him.* Do you know who I am? I say you will hang if you do not open with me!

PROCTOR: Mary, remember the angel Raphael—do that which is good and—

ABIGAIL, *pointing upward:* The wings! Her wings are spreading! Mary, please, don't, don't—!

HALE: I see nothing, Your Honor!

DANFORTH: Do you confess this power! *He is an inch from her face.* Speak!

ABIGAIL: She's going to come down! She's walking the beam!

DANFORTH: Will you speak!

MARY WARREN, *staring in horror:* I cannot!

GIRLS: I cannot!

PARRIS: Cast the Devil out! Look him in the face! Trample him! We'll save you, Mary, only stand fast against him and—

ABIGAIL, *looking up:* Look out! She's coming down!

She and all the girls run to one wall, shielding their eyes. And now, as though cornered, they let out a gigantic scream, and Mary, as though infected, opens her mouth and screams with them. Gradually Abigail and the girls leave off, until only

Mary is left there, staring up at the "bird," screaming madly. All watch her, horrified by this evident fit. Proctor strides to her.

PROCTOR: Mary, tell the Governor what they— *He has hardly got a word out, when, seeing him coming for her, she rushes out of his reach, screaming in horror.*

MARY WARREN: Don't touch me—don't touch me! *At which the girls halt at the door.*

PROCTOR, *astonished:* Mary!

MARY WARREN, *pointing at Proctor:* You're the Devil's man!

He is stopped in his tracks.

PARRIS: Praise God!

GIRLS: Praise God!

PROCTOR, *numbed:* Mary, how—?

MARY WARREN: I'll not hang with you! I love God, I love God.

DANFORTH, *to Mary:* He bid you do the Devil's work?

MARY WARREN, *hysterically, indicating Proctor:* He come at me by night and every day to sign, to sign, to—

DANFORTH: Sign what?

PARRIS: The Devil's book? He come with a book?

MARY WARREN, *hysterically, pointing at Proctor, fearful of him:* My name, he want my name. "I'll murder you," he says, "if my wife hangs! We must go and overthrow the court," he says!

Danforth's head jerks toward Proctor, shock and horror in his face.

PROCTOR, *turning, appealing to Hale:* Mr. Hale!

MARY WARREN, *her sobs beginning:* He wake me every night, his eyes were like coals and his fingers claw my neck, and I sign, I sign . . .

HALE: Excellency, this child's gone wild!

PROCTOR, *as Danforth's wide eyes pour on him:* Mary, Mary!

MARY WARREN, *screaming at him:* No, I love God; I go your way no more. I love God, I bless God. *Sobbing, she rushes to Abigail.* Abby, Abby, I'll never hurt you more! *They all watch, as Abigail, out of her infinite charity, reaches out and draws the sobbing Mary to her, and then looks up to Danforth.*

DANFORTH, *to Proctor:* What are you? *Proctor is beyond speech*

in his anger. You are combined with anti-Christ, are you not? I have seen your power; you will not deny it! What say you, Mister?

HALE: Excellency—

DANFORTH: I will have nothing from you, Mr. Hale! *To Proctor:* Will you confess yourself befouled with Hell, or do you keep that black allegiance yet? What say you?

PROCTOR, *his mind wild, breathless:* I say—I say—God is dead!

PARRIS: Hear it, hear it!

PROCTOR, *laughs insanely, then:* A fire, a fire is burning! I hear the boot of Lucifer, I see his filthy face! And it is my face, and yours, Danforth! For them that quail to bring men out of ignorance, as I have quailed, and as you quail now when you know in all your black hearts that this be fraud—God damns our kind especially, and we will burn, we will burn together!

DANFORTH: Marshal! Take him and Corey with him to the jail!

HALE, *starting across to the door:* I denounce these proceedings!

PROCTOR: You are pulling Heaven down and raising up a whore!

HALE: I denounce these proceedings, I quit this court! *He slams the door to the outside behind him.*

DANFORTH, *calling to him in a fury:* Mr. Hale! Mr. Hale!

CURTAIN

ACT FOUR

A cell in Salem jail, that fall.

At the back is a high barred window; near it, a great, heavy door. Along the walls are two benches.

The place is in darkness but for the moonlight seeping through the bars. It appears empty. Presently footsteps are heard coming down a corridor beyond the wall, keys rattle, and the door swings open. Marshal Herrick enters with a lantern.

He is nearly drunk, and heavy-footed. He goes to a bench and nudges a bundle of rags lying on it.

HERRICK: Sarah, wake up! Sarah Good! *He then crosses to the other bench.*

SARAH GOOD, *rising in her rags:* Oh, Majesty! Comin', comin'! Tituba, he's here, His Majesty's come!

HERRICK: Go to the north cell; this place is wanted now. *He hangs his lantern on the wall. Tituba sits up.*

TITUBA: That don't look to me like His Majesty; look to me like the marshal.

HERRICK, *taking out a flask:* Get along with you now, clear this place. *He drinks, and Sarah Good comes and peers up into his face.*

SARAH GOOD: Oh, is it you, Marshal! I thought sure you be the Devil comin' for us. Could I have a sip of cider for me goin'-away?

HERRICK, *handing her the flask:* And where are you off to, Sarah?

TITUBA, *as Sarah drinks:* We goin' to Barbados, soon the Devil, gits here with the feathers and the wings.

HERRICK: Oh? A happy voyage to you.

SARAH GOOD: A pair of bluebirds wingin' southerly, the two of us! Oh, it be a grand transformation, Marshal! *She raises the flask to drink again.*

HERRICK, *taking the flask from her lips:* You'd best give me that or you'll never rise off the ground. Come along now.

TITUBA: I'll speak to him for you, if you desires to come along, Marshal.

HERRICK: I'd not refuse it, Tituba; it's the proper morning to fly into Hell.

TITUBA: Oh, it be no Hell in Barbados. Devil, him be pleasure-man in Barbados, him be singin' and dancin' in Barbados. It's you folks—you riles him up 'round here; it be too cold 'round here for that Old Boy. He freeze his soul in Massachusetts, but in Barbados he just as sweet and— *A bellowing cow is heard, and Tituba leaps up and calls to the window:* Aye, sir! That's him, Sarah!

SARAH GOOD: I'm here, Majesty! *They hurriedly pick up their rags as Hopkins, a guard, enters.*

HOPKINS: The Deputy Governor's arrived.

HERRICK, *grabbing Tituba:* Come along, come along.

TITUBA, *resisting him:* No, he comin' for me. I goin' home!

HERRICK, *pulling her to the door:* That's not Satan, just a poor old cow with a hatful of milk. Come along now, out with you!

TITUBA, *calling to the window:* Take me home, Devil! Take me home!

SARAH GOOD, *following the shouting Tituba out:* Tell him I'm goin', Tituba! Now you tell him Sarah Good is goin' too!

In the corridor outside Tituba calls on—"Take me home, Devil; Devil take me home!" and Hopkins' voice orders her to move on. Herrick returns and begins to push old rags and straw into a corner. Hearing footsteps, he turns, and enter Danforth and Judge Hathorne. They are in greatcoats and wear hats against the bitter cold. They are followed in by Cheever, who carries a dispatch case and a flat wooden box containing his writing materials.

HERRICK: Good morning, Excellency.

DANFORTH: Where is Mr. Parris?

HERRICK: I'll fetch him. *He starts for the door.*

DANFORTH: Marshal. *Herrick stops.* When did Reverend Hale arrive?

HERRICK: It were toward midnight, I think.

DANFORTH, *suspiciously:* What is he about here?

HERRICK: He goes among them that will hang, sir. And he prays with them. He sits with Goody Nurse now. And Mr. Parris with him.

DANFORTH: Indeed. That man have no authority to enter here, Marshal. Why have you let him in?

HERRICK: Why, Mr. Parris command me, sir. I cannot deny him.

DANFORTH: Are you drunk, Marshal?

HERRICK: No, sir; it is a bitter night, and I have no fire here.

DANFORTH, *containing his anger:* Fetch Mr. Parris.

HERRICK: Aye, sir.

DANFORTH: There is a prodigious stench in this place.

HERRICK: I have only now cleared the people out for you.

DANFORTH: Beware hard drink, Marshal.

HERRICK: Aye, sir. *He waits an instant for further orders. But Danforth, in dissatisfaction, turns his back on him, and Herrick goes out. There is a pause. Danforth stands in thought.*

HATHORNE: Let you question Hale, Excellency; I should not be surprised he have been preaching in Andover lately.

DANFORTH: We'll come to that; speak nothing of Andover. Parris prays with him. That's strange. *He blows on his hands, moves toward the window, and looks out.*

HATHORNE: Excellency, I wonder if it be wise to let Mr. Parris so continuously with the prisoners. *Danforth turns to him, interested.* I think, sometimes, the man has a mad look these days.

DANFORTH: Mad?

HATHORNE: I met him yesterday coming out of his house, and I bid him good morning—and he wept and went his way. I think it is not well the village sees him so unsteady.

DANFORTH: Perhaps he have some sorrow.

CHEEVER, *stamping his feet against the cold:* I think it be the cows, sir.

DANFORTH: Cows?

CHEEVER: There be so many cows wanderin' the highroads, now their masters are in the jails, and much disagreement who they will belong to now. I know Mr. Parris be arguin' with farmers all yesterday—there is great contention, sir, about the cows. Contention make him weep, sir; it were always a man that weep for contention. *He turns, as do Hathorne and Danforth, hearing someone coming up the corridor. Danforth raises his head as Parris enters. He is gaunt, frightened, and sweating in his greatcoat.*

PARRIS, *to Danforth, instantly:* Oh, good morning, sir, thank

A wakin' you so early. Good

you for coming, I be... ve no right to enter this—

morning, Judge H...ent. *He hurries back and shuts the*

DANFORTH: Rever...

PARRIS: Excellen... leave him alone with the prisoners?

door.

HATHORNE: ...s his business here?

DANFORTH ...*fully holding up his hands:* Excellency, hear me.

PARRIS, ...vidence. Reverend Hale has returned to bring Re-

It is ... Nurse to God.

bec...

DA...ORTH, *surprised:* He bids her confess?

PARRIS, *sitting:* Hear me. Rebecca have not given me a word this three month since she came. Now she sits with him, and her sister and Martha Corey and two or three others, and he pleads with them, confess their crimes and save their lives.

DANFORTH: Why—this is indeed a providence. And they soften, they soften?

PARRIS: Not yet, not yet. But I thought to summon you, sir, that we might think on whether it be not wise, to— *He dares not say it.* I had thought to put a question, sir, and I hope you will not—

DANFORTH: Mr. Parris, be plain, what troubles you?

PARRIS: There is news, sir, that the court—the court must reckon with. My niece, sir, my niece—I believe she has vanished.

DANFORTH: Vanished!

PARRIS: I had thought to advise you of it earlier in the week, but—

DANFORTH: Why? How long is she gone?

PARRIS: This be the third night. You see, sir, she told me she would stay a night with Mercy Lewis. And next day, when she does not return, I send to Mr. Lewis to inquire. Mercy told him she would sleep in *my* house for a night.

DANFORTH: They are both gone?!

PARRIS, *in fear of him:* They are, sir.

DANFORTH, *alarmed:* I will send a party for them. Where may they be?

PARRIS: Excellency, I think they be aboard a ship. *Danforth stands agape.* My daughter tells me how she heard them speaking of ships last week, and tonight I discover my—my

strongbox is broke into. *He pr ers against his eyes to keep back tears.*

HATHORNE, *astonished:* She have rob

PARRIS: Thirty-one pound is gone. I am p *He covers his face and sobs.*

DANFORTH: Mr. Parris, you are a brainless m *e walks in thought, deeply worried.*

PARRIS: Excellency, it profit nothing you should b e me. I cannot think they would run off except they fear to keep in Salem any more. *He is pleading.* Mark it, sir, Abigail had close knowledge of the town, and since the news of Ando r has broken here—

DANFORTH: Andover is remedied. The court returns there on Friday, and will resume examinations.

PARRIS: I am sure of it, sir. But the rumor here speaks rebellion in Andover, and it—

DANFORTH: There is no rebellion in Andover!

PARRIS: I tell you what is said here, sir. Andover have thrown out the court, they say, and will have no part of witchcraft. There be a faction here, feeding on that news, and I tell you true, sir, I fear there will be riot here.

HATHORNE: Riot! Why at every execution I have seen naught but high satisfaction in the town.

PARRIS: Judge Hathorne—it were another sort that hanged till now. Rebecca Nurse is no Bridget that lived three year with Bishop before she married him. John Proctor is not Isaac Ward that drank his family to ruin. *To Danforth:* I would to God it were not so, Excellency, but these people have great weight yet in the town. Let Rebecca stand upon the gibbet and send up some righteous prayer, and I fear she'll wake a vengeance on you.

HATHORNE: Excellency, she is condemend a witch. The court have—

DANFORTH, *in deep concern, raising a hand to Hathorne:* Pray you. *To Parris:* How do you propose, then?

PARRIS: Excellency, I would postpone these hangin's for a time.

DANFORTH: There will be no postponement.

PARRIS: Now Mr. Hale's returned, there is hope, I think—for if he bring even one of these to God, that confession surely

damns the others in the public eye, and none may doubt more that they are all linked to Hell. This way, unconfessed and claiming innocence, doubts are multiplied, many honest people will weep for them, and our good purpose is lost in their tears.

DANFORTH, *after thinking a moment, then going to Cheever:* Give me the list.

Cheever opens the dispatch case, searches.

PARRIS: It cannot be forgot, sir, that when I summoned the congregation for John Proctor's excommunication there were hardly thirty people come to hear it. That speak a discontent, I think, and—

DANFORTH, *studying the list:* There will be no postponement.

PARRIS: Excellency—

DANFORTH: Now, sir—which of these in your opinion may be brought to God? I will myself strive with him till dawn. *He hands the list to Parris, who merely glances at it.*

PARRIS: There is not sufficient time till dawn.

DANFORTH: I shall do my utmost. Which of them do you have hope for?

PARRIS, *not even glancing at the list now, and in a quavering voice, quietly:* Excellency—a dagger— He chokes up.

DANFORTH: What do you say?

PARRIS: Tonight, when I open my door to leave my house—a dagger clattered to the ground. *Silence. Danforth absorbs this. Now Parris cries out:* You cannot hang this sort. There is danger for me. I dare not step outside at night!

Reverend Hale enters. They look at him for an instant in silence. He is steeped in sorrow, exhausted, and more direct than he ever was.

DANFORTH: Accept my congratulations, Reverend Hale; we are gladdened to see you returned to your good work.

HALE, *coming to Danforth now:* You must pardon them. They will not budge.

Herrick enters, waits.

DANFORTH, *conciliatory:* You misunderstand, sir; I cannot

pardon these when twelve are already hanged for the same crime. It is not just.

PARRIS, *with failing heart:* Rebecca will not confess?

HALE: The sun will rise in a few minutes. Excellency, I must have more time.

DANFORTH: Now hear me, and beguile yourselves no more. I will not receive a single plea for pardon or postponement. Them that will not confess will hang. Twelve are already executed; the names of these seven are given out, and the village expects to see them die this morning. Postponement now speaks a floundering on my part; reprieve or pardon must cast doubt upon the guilt of them that died till now. While I speak God's law, I will not crack its voice with whimpering. If retaliation is your fear, know this—I should hang ten thousand that dared to rise against the law, and an ocean of salt tears could not melt the resolution of the statutes. Now draw yourselves up like men and help me, as you are bound by Heaven to do. Have you spoken with them all, Mr. Hale?

HALE: All but Proctor. He is in the dungeon.

DANFORTH, *to Herrick:* What's Proctor's way now?

HERRICK: He sits like some great bird; you'd not know he lived except he will take food from time to time.

DANFORTH, *after thinking a moment:* His wife—his wife must be well on with child now.

HERRICK: She is, sir.

DANFORTH: What think you, Mr. Parris? You have closer knowledge of this man; might her presence soften him?

PARRIS: It is possible, sir. He have not laid eyes on her these three months. I should summon her.

DANFORTH, *to Herrick:* Is he yet adamant? Has he struck at you again?

HERRICK: He cannot, sir, he is chained to the wall now.

DANFORTH, *after thinking on it:* Fetch Goody Proctor to me. Then let you bring him up.

HERRICK: Aye, sir. *Herrick goes. There is silence.*

HALE: Excellency, if you postpone a week and publish to the town that you are striving for their confessions, that speak mercy on your part, not faltering.

DANFORTH: Mr. Hale, as God have not empowered me like Joshua to stop this sun from rising, so I cannot withhold from them the perfection of their punishment.

HALE, *harder now:* If you think God wills you to raise rebellion, Mr. Danforth, you are mistaken!

DANFORTH, *instantly:* You have heard rebellion spoken in the town?

HALE: Excellency, there are orphans wandering from house to house; abandoned cattle bellow on the highroads, the stink of rotting crops hangs everywhere, and no man knows when the harlots' cry will end his life—and you wonder yet if rebellion's spoke? Better you should marvel how they do not burn your province!

DANFORTH: Mr. Hale, have you preached in Andover this month?

HALE: Thank God they have no need of me in Andover.

DANFORTH: You baffle me, sir. Why have you returned here?

HALE: Why, it is all simple. I come to do the Devil's work. I come to counsel Christians they should belie themselves. *His sarcasm collapses.* There is blood on my head! Can you not see the blood on my head!!

PARRIS: Hush! *For he has heard footsteps. They all face the door. Herrick enters with Elizabeth. Her wrists are linked by heavy chain, which Herrick now removes. Her clothes are dirty; her face is pale and gaunt. Herrick goes out.*

DANFORTH, *very politely:* Goody Proctor. *She is silent.* I hope you are hearty?

ELIZABETH, *as a warning reminder:* I am yet six month before my time.

DANFORTH: Pray be at your ease, we come not for your life. We—*uncertain how to plead, for he is not accustomed to it.* Mr. Hale, will you speak with the woman?

HALE: Goody Proctor, your husband is marked to hang this morning.

Pause.

ELIZABETH, *quietly:* I have heard it.

HALE: You know, do you not, that I have no connection with the court? *She seems to doubt it.* I come of my own, Goody

Proctor. I would save your husband's life, for if he is taken I count myself his murderer. Do you understand me?

ELIZABETH: What do you want of me?

HALE: Goody Proctor, I have gone this three month like our Lord into the wilderness. I have sought a Christian way, for damnation's doubled on a minister who counsels men to lie.

HATHORNE: It is no lie, you cannot speak of lies.

HALE: It is a lie! They are innocent!

DANFORTH: I'll hear no more of that!

HALE, *continuing to Elizabeth:* Let you not mistake your duty as I mistook my own. I came into this village like a bridegroom to his beloved, bearing gifts of high religion; the very crowns of holy law I brought, and what I touched with my bright confidence, it died; and where I turned the eye of my great faith, blood flowed up. Beware, Goody Proctor—cleave to no faith when faith brings blood. It is mistaken law that leads you to sacrifice. Life, woman, life is God's most precious gift; no principle, however glorious, may justify the taking of it. I beg you, woman, prevail upon your husband to confess. Let him give his lie. Quail not before God's judgment in this, for it may well be God damns a liar less than he that throws his life away for pride. Will you plead with him? I cannot think he will listen to another.

ELIZABETH, *quietly:* I think that be the Devil's argument.

HALE, *with a climactic desperation:* Woman, before the laws of God we are as swine! We cannot read His will!

ELIZABETH: I cannot dispute with you, sir; I lack learning for it.

DANFORTH, *going to her:* Goody Proctor, you are not summoned here for disputation. Be there no wifely tenderness within you? He will die with the sunrise. Your husband. Do you understand it? *She only looks at him.* What say you? Will you contend with him? *She is silent.* Are you stone? I tell you true, woman, had I no other proof of your unnatural life, your dry eyes now would be sufficient evidence that you delivered up your soul to Hell! A very ape would weep at such calamity! Have the devil dried up any tear of pity in you? *She is silent.* Take her out. It profit nothing she should speak to him!

ELIZABETH, *quietly:* Let me speak with him, Excellency.

PARRIS, *with hope:* You'll strive with him? *She hesitates.*
DANFORTH: Will you plead for his confession or will you not?
ELIZABETH: I promise nothing. Let me speak with him.

A sound—the sibilance of dragging feet on stone. They turn. A pause. Herrick enters with John Proctor. His wrists are chained. He is another man, bearded, filthy, his eyes misty as though webs had overgrown them. He halts inside the doorway, his eye caught by the sight of Elizabeth. The emotion flowing between them prevents anyone from speaking for an instant. Now Hale, visibly affected, goes to Danforth and speaks quietly.

HALE: Pray, leave them, Excellency.
DANFORTH, *pressing Hale impatiently aside:* Mr. Proctor, you have been notified, have you not? *Proctor is silent, staring at Elizabeth.* I see light in the sky, Mister; let you counsel with your wife, and may God help you turn your back on Hell. *Proctor is silent, staring at Elizabeth.*
HALE, *quietly:* Excellency, let—

Danforth brushes past Hale and walks out. Hale follows. Cheever stands and follows, Hathorne behind. Herrick goes. Parris from a safe distance, offers:

PARRIS: If you desire a cup of cider, Mr. Proctor, I am sure I— *Proctor turns an icy stare at him, and he breaks off. Parris raises his palms toward Proctor.* God lead you now. *Parris goes out.*

Alone. Proctor walks to her, halts. It is as though they stood in a spinning world. It is beyond sorrow, above it. He reaches out his hand as though toward an embodiment not quite real, and as he touches her, a strange soft sound, half laughter, half amazement, comes from his throat. He pats her hand. She covers his hand with hers. And then, weak, he sits. Then she sits, facing him.

PROCTOR: The child?
ELIZABETH: It grows.
PROCTOR: There is no word of the boys?
ELIZABETH: They're well. Rebecca's Samuel keeps them.
PROCTOR: You have not seen them?

ELIZABETH: I have not. *She catches a weakening in herself and downs it.*

PROCTOR: You are a—marvel, Elizabeth.

ELIZABETH: You—have been tortured?

PROCTOR: Aye. *Pause. She will not let herself be drowned in the sea that threatens her.* They come for my life now.

ELIZABETH: I know it.

Pause.

PROCTOR: None—have yet confessed?

ELIZABETH: There be many confessed.

PROCTOR: Who are they?

ELIZABETH: There be a hundred or more, they say. Goody Ballard is one; Isaiah Goodkind is one. There be many.

PROCTOR: Rebecca?

ELIZABETH: Not Rebecca. She is one foot in Heaven now; naught may hurt her more.

PROCTOR: And Giles?

ELIZABETH: You have not heard of it?

PROCTOR: I hear nothin', where I am kept.

ELIZABETH: Giles is dead.

He looks at her incredulously.

PROCTOR: When were he hanged?

ELIZABETH, *quietly, factually:* He were not hanged. He would not answer aye or nay to his indictment; for if he denied the charge they'd hang him surely, and auction out his property. So he stand mute, and died Christian under the law. And so his sons will have his farm. It is the law, for he could not be condemned a wizard without he answer the indictment, aye or nay.

PROCTOR: Then how does he die?

ELIZABETH, *gently:* They press him, John.

PROCTOR: Press?

ELIZABETH: Great stones they lay upon his chest until he plead aye or nay. *With a tender smile for the old man:* They say he give them but two words. "More weight," he says. And died.

PROCTOR, *numbed—a thread to weave into his agony:* "More weight."

ELIZABETH: Aye. It were a fearsome man, Giles Corey.

Pause.

PROCTOR, *with great force of will, but not quite looking at her:* I have been thinking I would confess to them, Elizabeth. *She shows nothing.* What say you? If I give them that?

ELIZABETH: I cannot judge you, John.

Pause.

PROCTOR, *simply—a pure question:* What would you have me do?

ELIZABETH: As you will, I would have it. *Slight pause:* I want you living, John. That's sure.

PROCTOR, *pauses, then with a flailing of hope:* Giles' wife? Have she confessed?

ELIZABETH: She will not.

Pause.

PROCTOR: It is a pretense, Elizabeth.

ELIZABETH: What is?

PROCTOR: I cannot mount the gibbet like a saint. It is a fraud. I am not that man. *She is silent.* My honesty is broke, Elizabeth; I am no good man. Nothing's spoiled by giving them this lie that were not rotten long before.

ELIZABETH: And yet you've not confessed till now. That speak goodness in you.

PROCTOR: Spite only keeps me silent. It is hard to give a lie to dogs. *Pause, for the first time he turns directly to her.* I would have your forgiveness, Elizabeth.

ELIZABETH: It is not for me to give, John, I am—

PROCTOR: I'd have you see some honesty in it. Let them that never lied die now to keep their souls. It is pretense for me, a vanity that will not blind God nor keep my children out of the wind. *Pause.* What say you?

ELIZABETH, *upon a heaving sob that always threatens:* John, it come to naught that I should forgive you, if you'll not forgive yourself. *Now he turns away a little, in great agony.* It is not my soul, John, it is yours. *He stands, as though in physical pain, slowly rising to his feet with a great immortal longing to find his answer. It is difficult to say, and she is on the verge of tears.* Only be sure of this, for I know it now:

Whatever you will do, it is a good man does it. *He turns his doubting, searching gaze upon her.* I have read my heart this three month, John. *Pause.* I have sins of my own to count. It needs a cold wife to prompt lechery.

PROCTOR, *in great pain:* Enough, enough—

ELIZABETH, *now pouring out her heart:* Better you should know me!

PROCTOR: I will not hear it! I know you!

ELIZABETH: You take my sins upon you, John—

PROCTOR, *in agony:* No, I take my own, my own!

ELIZABETH: John, I counted myself so plain, so poorly made, no honest love could come to me! Suspicion kissed you when I did; I never knew how I should say my love. It were a cold house I kept! *In fright, she swerves, as Hathorne enters.*

HATHORNE: What say you, Proctor? The sun is soon up.

Proctor, his chest heaving, stares, turns to Elizabeth. She comes to him as though to plead, her voice quaking.

ELIZABETH: Do what you will. But let none be your judge. There be no higher judge under Heaven than Proctor is! Forgive me, forgive me, John—I never knew such goodness in the world! *She covers her face, weeping.*

Proctor turns from her to Hathorne; he is off the earth, his voice hollow.

PROCTOR: I want my life.

HATHORNE, *electrified, surprised:* You'll confess yourself?

PROCTOR: I will have my life.

HATHORNE, *with a mystical tone:* God be praised! It is a providence! *He rushes out the door, and his voice is heard calling down the corridor:* He will confess! Proctor will confess!

PROCTOR, *with a cry, as he strides to the door:* Why do you cry it? *In great pain he turns back to her.* It is evil, is it not? It is evil.

ELIZABETH, *in terror, weeping:* I cannot judge you, John, I cannot!

PROCTOR: Then who will judge me? *Suddenly clasping his hands:* God in Heaven, what is John Proctor, what is John Proctor? *He moves as an animal, and a fury is riding in him, a tantalized search.* I think it is honest, I think so; I am no

saint. *As though she had denied this he calls angrily at her:* Let Rebecca go like a saint; for me it is fraud!

Voices are heard in the hall, speaking together in suppressed excitement.

ELIZABETH: I am not your judge, I cannot be. *As though giving him release:* Do as you will, do as you will!

PROCTOR: Would you give them such a lie? Say it. Would you ever give them this? *She cannot answer.* You would not, if tongs of fire were singeing you you would not! It is evil. Good, then—it is evil, and I do it!

Hathorne enters with Danforth, and, with them, Cheever, Parris, and Hale. It is a businesslike, rapid entrance, as though the ice had been broken.

DANFORTH, *with great relief and gratitude:* Praise to God, man, praise to God; you shall be blessed in Heaven for this. *Cheever has hurried to the bench with pen, ink, and paper. Proctor watches him.* Now then, let us have it. Are you ready, Mr. Cheever?

PROCTOR, *with a cold, cold horror at their efficiency:* Why must it be written?

DANFORTH: Why, for the good instruction of the village, Mister; this we shall post upon the church door! *To Parris, urgently:* Where is the marshal?

PARRIS, *runs to the door and calls down the corridor:* Marshal! Hurry!

DANFORTH: Now, then, Mister, will you speak slowly, and directly to the point, for Mr. Cheever's sake. *He is on record now, and is really dictating to Cheever, who writes.* Mr. Proctor, have you seen the Devil in your life? *Proctor's jaws lock.* Come, man, there is light in the sky; the town waits at the scaffold; I would give out this news. Did you see the Devil?

PROCTOR: I did.

PARRIS: Praise God!

DANFORTH: And when he come to you, what were his demand? *Proctor is silent. Danforth helps.* Did he bid you to do his work upon the earth?

PROCTOR: He did.

DANFORTH: And you bound yourself to his service? *Danforth turns, as Rebecca Nurse enters, with Herrick helping to support her. She is barely able to walk.* Come in, come in, woman!

REBECCA, *brightening as she sees Proctor:* Ah, John! You are well, then, eh?

Proctor turns his face to the wall.

DANFORTH: Courage, man, courage—let her witness your good example that she may come to God herself. Now hear it, Goody Nurse! Say on, Mr. Proctor. Did you bind yourself to the Devil's Service?

REBECCA, *astonished:* Why, John!

PROCTOR, *through his teeth, his face turned from Rebecca:* I did.

DANFORTH: Now, woman, you surely see it profit nothin' to keep this conspiracy any further. Will you confess yourself with him?

REBECCA: Oh, John—God send his mercy on you!

DANFORTH: I say, will you confess yourself, Goody Nurse?

REBECCA: Why, it is a lie, it is a lie; how may I damn myself? I cannot, I cannot.

DANFORTH: Mr. Proctor. When the Devil came to you did you see Rebecca Nurse in his company? *Proctor is silent.* Come, man, take courage—did you ever see her with the Devil?

PROCTOR, *almost inaudibly:* No.

Danforth, now sensing trouble, glances at John and goes to the table, and picks up a sheet—the list of condemned.

DANFORTH: Did you ever see her sister, Mary Easty, with the Devil?

PROCTOR: No, I did not.

DANFORTH, *his eyes narrow on Proctor:* Did you ever see Martha Corey with the Devil?

PROCTOR: I did not.

DANFORTH, *realizing, slowly putting the sheet down:* Did you ever see anyone with the Devil?

PROCTOR: I did not.

DANFORTH: Proctor, you mistake me. I am not empowered to trade your life for a lie. You have most certainly seen some person with the Devil. *Proctor is silent.* Mr. Proctor, a score

of people have already testified they saw this woman with the Devil.

PROCTOR: Then it is proved. Why must I say it?

DANFORTH: Why "must" you say it! Why, you should rejoice to say it if your soul is truly purged of any love for Hell!

PROCTOR: They think to go like saints. I like not to spoil their names.

DANFORTH, *inquiring, incredulous:* Mr. Proctor, do you think they go like saints?

PROCTOR, *evading:* This woman never thought she done the Devil's work.

DANFORTH: Look you, sir. I think you mistake your duty here. It matters nothing what she thought—she is convicted of the unnatural murder of children, and you for sending your spirit out upon Mary Warren. Your soul alone is the issue here, Mister, and you will prove its whiteness or you cannot live in a Christian country. Will you tell me now what persons conspired with you in the Devil's company? *Proctor is silent.* To your knowledge was Rebecca Nurse ever—

PROCTOR: I speak my own sins; I cannot judge another. *Crying out, with hatred:* I have no tongue for it.

HALE, *quickly to Danforth:* Excellency, it is enough he confess himself. Let him sign it, let him sign it.

PARRIS, *feverishly:* It is a great service, sir. It is a weighty name; it will strike the village that Proctor confess. I beg you, let him sign it. The sun is up, Excellency!

DANFORTH, *considers; then with dissatisfaction:* Come, then, sign your testimony. *To Cheever:* Give it to him. *Cheever goes to Proctor, the confession and a pen in hand. Proctor does not look at it.* Come, man, sign it.

PROCTOR, *after glancing at the confession:* You have all witnessed it—it is enough.

DANFORTH: You will not sign it?

PROCTOR: You have all witnessed it; what more is needed?

DANFORTH: Do you sport with me? You will sign your name or it is no confession, Mister! *His breast heaving with agonized breathing, Proctor now lays the paper down and signs his name.*

PARRIS: Praise be to the Lord!

Proctor has just finished signing when Danforth reaches for the paper. But Proctor snatches it up, and now a wild terror is rising in him, and a boundless anger.

DANFORTH, *perplexed; but politely extending his hand:* If you please, sir.

PROCTOR: No.

DANFORTH, *as though Proctor did not understand:* Mr. Proctor, I must have—

PROCTOR: No, no. I have signed it. You have seen me. It is done! You have no need for this.

PARRIS: Proctor, the village must have proof that—

PROCTOR: Damn the village! I confess to God, and God has seen my name on this! It is enough!

DANFORTH: No, sir, it is—

PROCTOR: You came to save my soul, did you not? Here! I have confessed myself; it is enough!

DANFORTH: You have not con—

PROCTOR: I have confessed myself! Is there no good penitence but it be public? God does not need my name nailed upon the church! God sees my name; God knows how black my sins are! It is enough!

DANFORTH: Mr. Proctor—

PROCTOR: You will not use me! I am no Sarah Good or Tituba, I am John Proctor! You will not use me! It is no part of salvation that you should use me!

DANFORTH: I do not wish to—

PROCTOR: I have three children—how may I teach them to walk like men in the world, and I sold my friends?

DANFORTH: You have not sold your friends—

PROCTOR: Beguile me not! I blacken all of them when this is nailed to the church the very day they hang for silence!

DANFORTH: Mr. Proctor, I must have good and legal proof that you—

PROCTOR: You are the high court, your word is good enough! Tell them I confessed myself; say Proctor broke his knees and wept like a woman; say what you will, but my name cannot—

DANFORTH, *with suspicion:* It is the same, is it not? If I report it or you sign to it?

PROCTOR—*he knows it is insane:* No, it is not the same! What others say and what I sign to is not the same!

DANFORTH: Why? Do you mean to deny this confession when you are free?

PROCTOR: I mean to deny nothing!

DANFORTH: Then explain to me, Mr. Proctor, why you will not let—

PROCTOR, *with a cry of his whole soul:* Because it is my name! Because I cannot have another in my life! Because I lie and sign myself to lies! Because I am not worth the dust on the feet of them that hang! How may I live without my name? I have given you my soul; leave me my name!

DANFORTH, *pointing at the confession in Proctor's hand:* Is that document a lie? If it is a lie I will not accept it! What say you? I will not deal in lies, Mister! *Proctor is motionless.* You will give me your honest confession in my hand, or I cannot keep you from the rope. *Proctor does not reply.* Which way do you go, Mister?

His breast heaving, his eyes staring, Proctor tears the paper and crumples it, and he is weeping in fury, but erect.

DANFORTH: Marshal!

PARRIS, *hysterically, as though the tearing paper were his life:* Proctor, Proctor!

HALE: Man, you will hang! You cannot!

PROCTOR, *his eyes full of tears:* I can. And there's your first marvel, that I can. You have made your magic now, for now I do think I see some shred of goodness in John Proctor. Not enough to weave a banner with, but white enough to keep it from such dogs. *Elizabeth, in a burst of terror, rushes to him and weeps against his hand.* Give them no tear! Tears pleasure them! Show honor now, show a stony heart and sink them with it! *He has lifted her, and kisses her now with great passion.*

REBECCA: Let you fear nothing! Another judgment waits us all!

DANFORTH: Hang them high over the town! Who weeps for these, weeps for corruption! *He sweeps out past them. Herrick starts to lead Rebecca, who almost collapses, but Proctor catches her, and she glances up at him apologetically.*

REBECCA: I've had no breakfast.

HERRICK: Come, man.

Herrick escorts them out, Hathorne and Cheever behind them. Elizabeth stands staring at the empty doorway.

PARRIS, *in deadly fear, to Elizabeth:* Go to him, Goody Proctor! There is yet time!

From outside a drumroll strikes the air. Parris is startled. Elizabeth jerks about toward the window.

PARRIS: Go to him! *He rushes out the door, as though to hold back his fate.* Proctor! Proctor!

Again, a short burst of drums.

HALE: Woman, plead with him! *He starts to rush out the door, and then goes back to her.* Woman! It is pride, it is vanity. *She avoids his eyes, and moves to the window. He drops to his knees.* Be his helper!—What profit him to bleed? Shall the dust praise him? Shall the worms declare his truth? Go to him, take his shame away!

ELIZABETH, *supporting herself against collapse, grips the bars of the window, and with a cry:* He have his goodness now. God forbid I take it from him!

The final drumroll crashes, then heightens violently. Hale weeps in frantic prayer, and the new sun is pouring in upon her face, and the drums rattle like bones in the morning air.

CURTAIN

ECHOES DOWN THE CORRIDOR

Not long after the fever died, Parris was voted from office, walked out on the highroad, and was never heard of again.

The legend has it that Abigail turned up later as a prostitute in Boston.

Twenty years after the last execution, the government awarded compensation to the victims still living, and to the families of the dead. However, it is evident that some people still were unwilling to admit their total guilt, and also that the factionalism was still alive, for some beneficiaries were actually not victims at all, but informers.

Elizabeth Proctor married again, four years after Proctor's death.

In solemn meeting, the congregation rescinded the excommunications—this in March 1712. But they did so upon orders of the government. The jury, however, wrote a statement praying forgiveness of all who had suffered.

Certain farms which had belonged to the victims were left to ruin, and for more than a century no one would buy them or live on them.

To all intents and purposes, the power of theocracy in Massachusetts was broken.

A MEMORY OF TWO MONDAYS

A Play in One Act

THE CHARACTERS

BERT
RAYMOND
AGNES
PATRICIA
GUS
JIM
KENNETH
LARRY
FRANK
JERRY
WILLIAM
TOM
MECHANIC
MR. EAGLE

A MEMORY OF TWO MONDAYS

The shipping room of a large auto-parts warehouse. This is but the back of a large loft in an industrial section of New York. The front of the loft, where we cannot see, is filled with office machinery, records, the telephone switchboard, and the counter where customers may come who do not order by letter or phone.

The two basic structures are the long packing table which curves upstage at the left, and the factory-type windows which reach from floor to ceiling and are encrusted with the hard dirt of years. These windows are the background and seem to surround the entire stage.

At the back, near the center, is a door to the toilet; on it are hooks for clothing. The back wall is bare but for a large spindle on which orders are impaled every morning and taken off and filled by the workers all day long. At center there is an ancient desk and chair. Downstage right is a small bench. Boxes, a roll of packing paper on the table, and general untidiness. This place is rarely swept.

The right and left walls are composed of corridor openings, a louverlike effect, leading out into the alleys which are lined with bins reaching to the ceiling. Downstage center there is a large cast-iron floor scale with weights and balance exposed.

The nature of the work is simple. The men take orders off the hook, go out into the bin-lined alleys, fill the orders, bring the merchandise back to the table, where Kenneth packs and addresses everything. The desk is used by Gus and/or Tom Kelly to figure postage or express rates on, to eat on, to lean on, or to hide things in. It is just home base, generally.

A warning: The place must seem dirty and unmanageably chaotic, but since it is seen in this play with two separate visions it is also romantic. It is a little world, a home to which, unbelievably perhaps, these people like to come every Monday morning, despite what they say.

It is a hot Monday morning in summer, just before nine.

The stage is empty for a moment; then Bert enters. He is eighteen. His trousers are worn at the knees but not unrespectable; he has rolled-up sleeves and is tieless. He carries a thick book, a large

lunch in a brown paper bag, and a New York Times. *He stores the lunch behind the packing table, clears a place on the table, sits and opens the paper, reads.*

Enter Raymond Ryan, the manager. He wears a tie, white shirt, pressed pants, carries a clean towel, a tabloid, and in the other hand a sheaf of orders.

Raymond is forty, weighed down by responsibilities, afraid to be kind, quite able to be tough. He walks with the suggestion of a stoop.

He goes directly to a large hook set in the back wall and impales the orders. Bert sees him but, getting no greeting, returns to his paper. Preoccupied, Raymond walks past Bert toward the toilet, then halts in thought, turns back to Bert.

RAYMOND: Tommy Kelly get in yet?

BERT: I haven't seen him, but I just got here myself. *Raymond nods slightly, worried.* He'll probably make it all right.

RAYMOND: What are you doing in so early?

BERT: I wanted to get a seat on the subway for once. Boy, it's nice to walk around in the streets before the crowds get out . . .

RAYMOND—*he has never paid much attention to Bert, is now curious, has time for it:* How do you get time to read that paper?

BERT: Well, I've got an hour and ten minutes on the subway. I don't read it all, though. Just reading about Hitler.

RAYMOND: Who's that?

BERT: He took over the German government last week.

RAYMOND, *nodding, uninterested:* Listen, I want you to sweep up that excelsior laying around the freight elevator.

BERT: Okay. I had a lot of orders on Saturday, so I didn't get to it.

RAYMOND, *self-consciously; thus almost in mockery:* I hear you're going to go to college. Is that true?

BERT, *embarrassed:* Oh, I don't know, Mr. Ryan. They may not even let me in, I got such bad marks in high school.

RAYMOND: *You* did?

BERT: Oh, yeah. I just played ball and fooled around, that's all. I think I wasn't listening, y'know?

RAYMOND: How much it going to cost you?

BERT: I guess about four, five hundred for the first year. So I'll be here a long time—if I ever do go. You ever go to college?

RAYMOND, *shaking his head negatively:* My kid brother went to pharmacy though. What are you going to take up?

BERT: I really don't know. You look through that catalogue—boy, you feel like taking it all, you know?

RAYMOND: This the same book you been reading?

BERT: Well, it's pretty long, and I fall asleep right after supper.

RAYMOND, *turning the book up:* "War and Peace"?

BERT: Yeah, he's supposed to be a great writer.

RAYMOND: How long it take you to read a book like this?

BERT: Oh, probably about three, four months, I guess. It's hard on the subway, with all those Russian names.

RAYMOND, *putting the book down:* What do you get out of a book like that?

BERT: Well, it's—it's literature.

RAYMOND, *nodding, mystified:* Be sure to open those three crates of axles that came in Saturday, will you? *He starts to go toward the toilet.*

BERT: I'll get to it this morning.

RAYMOND: And let me know when you decide to leave. I'll have to get somebody—

BERT: Oh, that'll be another year. Don't worry about it. I've got to save it all up first. I'm probably just dreaming anyway.

RAYMOND: How much do you save?

BERT: About eleven or twelve a week.

RAYMOND: Out of fifteen?

BERT: Well, I don't buy much. And my mother gives me my lunch.

RAYMOND: Well, sweep up around the elevator, will you?

Raymond starts for the toilet as Agnes enters. She is a spinster in her late forties, always on the verge of laughter.

AGNES: Morning, Ray!

RAYMOND: Morning, Agnes. *He exits into the toilet.*

AGNES, *to Bert:* Bet you wish you could go swimming, heh?

BERT: Boy, I wouldn't mind. It's starting to boil already.

AGNES: You ought to meet my nephew sometime, Bert. He's a wonderful swimmer. Really, you'd like him. He's very serious.

BERT: How old is he now?

AGNES: He's only thirteen, but he reads the *New York Times* too.

BERT: Yeah?

AGNES, *noticing the book:* You still reading that book?

BERT, *embarrassed:* Well, I only get time on the subway, Agnes—

AGNES: Don't let any of them kid you, Bert. You go ahead. You read the *New York Times* and all that. What happened today?

BERT: Hitler took over the German government.

AGNES: Oh, yes; my nephew knows about him. He loves civics. Last week one night he made a regular speech to all of us in the living room, and I realized that everything Roosevelt has done is absolutely illegal. Did you know that? Even my brother-in-law had to admit it, and he's a Democrat.

Enter Patricia on her way to the toilet. She is twenty-three, blankly pretty, dressed just a little too tightly. She is not quite sure who she is yet.

PATRICIA: Morning!

AGNES: Morning, Patricia! Where did you get that pin?

PATRICIA: It was given. *She glances at Bert, who blushes.*

AGNES: Oh, Patricia! Which one is he?

PATRICIA: Oh, somebody. *She starts past for the toilet; Bert utters a warning "Ugh," and she remains.*

AGNES—*she tends to laugh constantly, softly:* Did you go to the dance Saturday night?

PATRICIA, *fixing her clothing:* Well, they're always ending up with six guys in the hospital at that dance, and like that, so we went bowling.

AGNES: Did he give you that pin?

PATRICIA: No, I had a date after him.

AGNES, *laughing, titillated:* Pat!

PATRICIA: Well, I forgot all about him. So when I got home he was still sitting in front of the house in his car. I thought he was going to murder me. But isn't it an unusual pin? *To Bert, who has moved off:* What are you always running away for?

BERT, *embarrassed:* I was just getting ready to work, that's all.

Enter Gus. He is sixty-eight, a barrel-bellied man, totally bald, with a long, fierce, gray mustache that droops on the right side. He wears a bowler, and his pants are a little too short. He has a ready-made clip-on tie. He wears winter underwear all summer long, changes once a week. There is something neat and dusty about him—a rolling gait, bandy legs, a belly hard as a rock and full of beer. He speaks with a gruff Slavic accent.

PATRICIA: Oh, God, here's King Kong. *She goes out up one of the corridors.*

GUS, *calling after her halfheartedly—he is not completely sober, not bright yet:* You let me get my hands on you I give you King Kong!

AGNES, *laughing:* Oh, Gus, don't say those things!

GUS, *going for her:* Aggie, you make me crazy for you!

AGNES, *laughing and running from him toward the toilet door:* Gus!

GUS: Agnes, let's go Atlantic City!

Agnes starts to open the toilet door. Raymond emerges from it.

AGNES, *surprised by Raymond:* Oh!

RAYMOND, *with plaintive anger:* Gus! Why don't you cut it out, heh?

GUS: Oh, I'm sick and tired, Raymond.

Agnes goes into the toilet.

RAYMOND: How about getting all the orders shipped out by tonight, heh, Gus—for once?

GUS: What I did? I did something?

RAYMOND: Where's Jim?

GUS: How do I know where's Jim? Jim is my brother?

Jim enters, stiff. He is in his mid-seventies, wears bent eyeglasses; has a full head of hair; pads about with careful tread.

JIM, *dimly:* Morning, Raymond. *He walks as though he will fall forward. All watch as Jim aims his jacket for a hook, then, with a sudden motion, makes it. But he never really sways.*

GUS: Attaboy, Jim! *To Raymond:* What you criticize Jim? Look at that!

JIM, *turning to Raymond with an apologetic smile:* Morning,

Raymond. Hot day today. *He goes to the spike and takes orders off it.*

RAYMOND: Now look, Gus, Mr. Eagle is probably going to come today, so let's have everything going good, huh?

GUS: You can take Mr. Eagle and you shove him!

Agnes enters from the toilet.

RAYMOND: What's the matter with you? I don't want that language around here any more. I'm not kidding, either. It's getting worse and worse, and we've got orders left over every night. Let's get straightened out here, will you? It's the same circus every Monday morning. *He goes out.*

AGNES: How's Lilly? Feeling better?

GUS: She's all the time sick, Agnes. I think she gonna die.

AGNES: Oh, don't say that. Pray to God, Gus.

GUS, *routinely:* Aggie, come with me Atlantic City. *He starts taking off his shirt.*

AGNES, *going from him:* Oh, how you smell!

GUS, *loudly:* I stink, Aggie!

AGNES, *closing her ears, laughing:* Oh, Gus, you're so terrible! *She rushes out.*

Gus *laughs loudly, tauntingly, and turns to Bert:* What are you doin'? It's nine o'clock.

BERT: Oh. *He gets off the bench.* I've got five to. Is your wife really sick? *He gets an order from the hook.*

GUS: You don't see Jim wait till nine o'clock! *He goes to Jim, who is looking through the orders, and puts an arm around him.* Goddam Raymond. You hear what he says to me?

JIM: Ssh, Gus, it's all right. Maybe better call Lilly.

GUS, *grasping Jim's arm:* Wanna beer?

JIM, *trying to disengage himself:* No, Gus, let's behave ourselves. Come on.

GUS, *looking around:* Oh, boy. Oh, goddam boy. Monday morning. Ach.

JIM, *to Bert, as he starts out:* Did you unpack those axles yet?

GUS, *taking the order out of Jim's hand:* What are you doing with axles? Man your age! *He gives Bert Jim's order.* Bert! Here! You let him pick up heavy stuff I show you something! Go!

BERT: I always take Jim's heavy orders, Gus. *He goes out with the orders.*

GUS: Nice girls, heh, Jim?

JIM: Oh, darn nice. Darn nice girls, Gus.

GUS: I keep my promise, hah, Jim?

JIM: You did, Gus. I enjoyed myself. But maybe you ought to call up your wife. She might be wonderin' about you. You been missin' since Saturday, Gus.

GUS, *asking for a reminder:* Where we was yesterday?

JIM: That's when we went to Staten Island, I think. On the ferry? Remember? With the girls? I think we was on a ferry. So it must've been to Staten Island. You better call her.

GUS: Ach— She don't hear nothing, Jim.

JIM: But if the phone rings, Gus, she'll know you're all right.

GUS: All right, I ring the phone. *He goes and dials. Jim leaves with his orders.*

Patricia enters.

PATRICIA: Morning, Kong!

GUS: Shatap. *She goes into the toilet as Gus listens on the phone. Then he roars:* Hallo! *Hallo!* Lilly! Gus! *Gus!* How you feel? *Gus!* Working! Ya! Ya! *Gus!* Oh, shatap! *He hangs up the phone angrily, confused.*

Jim enters with a few small boxes, which he sets in a pile on the table.

JIM: You call her?

GUS: Oh, Jim, she don't hear nothing. *He goes idly to the toilet, opens the door. Patricia screams within, and Gus stands there in the open doorway, screaming with her in parody, then lets the door shut.*

Jim starts out, examining his order, a pencil in his hand, as Kenneth enters, lunch in hand. Kenneth is twenty-six, a strapping, fair-skinned man, with thinning hair, delicately shy, very strong. He has only recently come to the country.

JIM: Morning, Kenneth.

KENNETH: And how are you this fine exemplary morning, James?

JIM: Oh, comin' along. Goin' to be hot today. *He goes out.*

Kenneth hangs up his jacket and stores his lunch. Gus is standing in thought, picking his ear with a pencil.

KENNETH: Havin' yourself a thought this morning, Gus? *Gus just looks at him, then goes back to his thought and his excavation.* Gus, don't you think something could be done about the dust constantly fallin' through the air of this place? Don't you imagine a thing or two could be done about that?

GUS: Because it's dusty, that's why. *He goes to the desk, sits.*

KENNETH: That's what I was sayin'—it's dusty. Tommy Kelly get in?

GUS: No.

KENNETH: Oh, poor Tommy Kelly. *Bert enters.* Good morning to you, Bert. Have you finished your book yet?

BERT, *setting two heavy axles on the bench:* Not yet, Kenneth.

KENNETH, *his jacket in his hand:* Well, don't lose heart. *He orates:*

"Courage, brother! do not stumble
Though thy path be dark as night;
There's a star to guide the humble;
Trust in God, and do the Right."

By Norman Macleod.

BERT, *with wonder, respect:* How'd you learn all that poetry?

KENNETH, *hanging up his jacket:* Why, in Ireland, Bert; there's all kinds of useless occupations in Ireland. "When lilacs last in the dooryard bloomed . . ."

GUS, *from the desk:* What the hell you doin'? *Bert goes to order hook.*

KENNETH: Why, it's the poetry hour, Gus, don't you know that? This is the hour all men rise to thank God for the blue of the sky, the roundness of the everlasting globe, and the cheerful cleanliness of the subway system. And here we have some axles. Oh, Bert, I never thought I would end me life wrappin' brown paper around strange axles. *He wraps.* And what's the latest in the *New York Times* this morning?

BERT, *looking through orders on the hook:* Hitler took over the German government.

KENNETH: Oh, did he! Strange, isn't it, about the Germans?

A great people they are for mustaches. You take Bismarck, now, or you take Frederick the Great, or even take Gus over here—

GUS: I'm no Heinie.

KENNETH: Why, I always thought you were, Gus. What are you, then?

GUS: American.

KENNETH: I know that, but what *are* you?

GUS: I fought in submarine.

KENNETH: Did you, now? An American submarine?

GUS: What the hell kind of submarine I fight in, Hungarian? *He turns back to his desk.*

KENNETH: Well, don't take offense, Gus. There's all kinds of submarines, y'know. *Bert starts out, examining his order.* How's this to be wrapped, Bert? Express?

BERT: I think that goes parcel post. It's for Skaneateles.

GUS, *erupting at his desk:* Axles parcel post? You crazy? You know how much gonna cost axles parcel post?

BERT: That's right. I guess it goes express.

GUS: And you gonna go college? Barber college you gonna go!

BERT: Well, I forgot it was axles, Gus.

GUS, *muttering over his desk:* Stupid.

KENNETH: I've never been to Skaneateles. Where would that be?

BERT: It's a little town upstate. It's supposed to be pretty there.

KENNETH: That a sweet thought? Sendin' these two grimy axles out into the green countryside? I spent yesterday in the park. What did you do, Bert? Go swimmin' again, I suppose?

GUS, *turning:* You gonna talk all day?

BERT: We're working. *He goes out. Kenneth wraps.*

KENNETH: You're rubbin' that poor kid pretty hard, Gus; he's got other things on his mind than parcel post and—

GUS: What the hell I care what he got on his mind? Axles he gonna send parcel post! *He returns to his work on the desk.*

KENNETH *wraps, then:* Can you feel the heat rising in this building! If only some of it could be saved for the winter. *Pause. He is wrapping.* The fiery furnace. Nebuchadnezzar was the architect. *Pause.* What do you suppose would happen, Gus, if a man took it into his head to wash these

windows? They'd snatch him off to the nuthouse, heh? *Pause.* I wonder if he's only kiddin'—Bert. About goin' to college someday.

GUS, *not turning from his desk:* Barber College he gonna go.

KENNETH—*he works, thinking:* He must have a wealthy family. Still and all, he don't spend much. I suppose he's just got some strong idea in his mind. That's the thing, y'know. I often conceive them myself, but I'm all the time losin' them, though. It's the holdin' on—that's what does it. You can almost see it in him, y'know? He's holdin' on to somethin'. *He shakes his head in wonder, then sings:*

Oh, the heat of the summer,
The cool of the fall.
The lady went swimming
With nothing at all.

Ah, that's a filthy song, isn't it! *Pause. He wraps.* Gus, you suppose Mr. Roosevelt'll be makin' it any better than it is? *He sings:*

The minstrel boy to the war has gone,
In the ranks of death . . .

Patricia enters from the toilet.

PATRICIA: Was that an Irish song?

KENNETH, *shyly:* All Irish here and none of yiz knows an Irish song.

PATRICIA: You have a terrific voice, Kenneth.

GUS, *to Patricia:* Why don't you make date with him?

KENNETH, *stamping his foot:* Oh, that's a nasty thing to say in front of a girl, Gus!

Gus rises.

PATRICIA, *backing away from Gus:* Now don't start with me, kid, because—

Gus lunges for her. She turns to run, and he squeezes her buttocks mercilessly as she runs out and almost collides with Larry, who is entering. Larry is thirty-nine, a troubled but phlegmatic man, good-looking. He is carrying a container of coffee and a lighted cigarette. On the collision he spills a little coffee.

LARRY, *with a slight humor:* Hey! Take it easy.

PATRICIA, *quite suddenly all concerned for Larry, to Gus:* Look what you did, you big horse!

Larry sets the coffee on the table.

LARRY: Jesus, Gus.

GUS: Tell her stop makin' all the men crazy! *He returns to his desk.*

PATRICIA: I'm sorry, Larry. *She is alone, in effect, with Larry. Both of them wipe the spot on his shirt.* Did you buy it?

LARRY, *embarrassed but courageous, as though inwardly flaunting his own fears:* Yeah, I got it yesterday.

PATRICIA: Gee, I'd love to see it. You ever going to bring it to work?

LARRY—*now he meets her eyes:* I might. On a Saturday, maybe.

PATRICIA: 'Cause I love those Auburns, y'know?

LARRY: Yeah, they got nice valves. Maybe I'll drive you home some night. For the ride.

PATRICIA—*the news stuns her:* Oh, boy! Well—I'll see ya. *She goes.*

GUS: You crazy? Buy Auburn?

LARRY, *with depth—a profound conclusion:* I like the valves, Gus.

GUS: Yeah, but when you gonna go sell it who gonna buy an Auburn?

LARRY: Didn't you ever get to where you don't care about that? I *always* liked those valves, and I decided, that's all.

GUS: Yeah, but when you gonna go sell it—

LARRY: I don't care.

GUS: You don't care!

LARRY: I'm sick of dreaming about things. They've got the most beautifully laid-out valves in the country on that car, and I want it, that's all.

Kenneth is weighing a package on the scales.

GUS: Yeah, but when you gonna go sell it—

LARRY: I just don't care, Gus. Can't you understand that? *He stares away, inhaling his cigarette.*

KENNETH, *stooped over, sliding the scale weights:* There's a remarkable circumstance, Larry. Raymond's got twins, and now you with the triplets. And both in the same corporation.

We ought to send that to the *Daily News* or something. I think they give you a dollar for an item like that.

Bert enters, puts goods on the table.

BERT: Gee, I'm getting hungry. Want a sandwich, Kenneth? *He reaches behind the packing table for his lunch bag.*
KENNETH: Thank you, Bert. I might take one later.
GUS, *turning from the desk to Bert:* Lunch you gonna eat nine o'clock?
BERT: I got up too early this morning. You want some?
KENNETH: He's only a growing boy, Gus—and by the way, if you care to bend down, Gus—*indicating under the scale platform*—there's more mice than ever under here.
GUS, *without turning:* Leave them mice alone.
KENNETH: Well, you're always complainin' the number of crayons I'm using, and I'm only tellin' you they're the ones is eatin' them up. *He turns to Larry.* It's a feast of crayons goin' on here every night, Larry.

Enter Jim with goods, padding along.

JIM: Goin' to be hot today, Gus.
GUS: Take easy, what you running for? *Jim stops to light his cigar butt.*
KENNETH, *reading off the scale weights:* Eighty-one pounds, Gus. For Skaneateles, in the green countryside of upper New York State.
GUS: What? What you want?
KENNETH: I want the express order—eighty-one pounds to Skaneateles, New York.
GUS: Then why don't you say that, goddam Irishman? You talk so much. When you gonna stop talkin'? *He proceeds to make out the slip.*
KENNETH: Oh, when I'm rich, Gus, I'll have very little more to say. *Gus is busy making out the slip; Kenneth turns to Larry.* No sign yet of Tommy Kelly in the place, Larry.
LARRY: What'd you, cut a hole in your shoe?
KENNETH: A breath of air for me little toe. I only paid a quarter for them, y'know; feller was sellin' them in Bryant Park. Slightly used, but they're a fine pair of shoes, you can see that.
LARRY: They look small for you.

KENNETH: They are at that. But you can't complain for a quarter, I guess.
GUS: Here.

Gus hands Kenneth an express slip, which Kenneth now proceeds to attach to the package on the table. Meanwhile Jim has been leafing through the orders on the hook and is now leaving with two in his hand.

KENNETH: How do you keep up your strength, Jim? I'm always exhausted. You never stop movin', do ya? *Jim just shakes his head with a "Heh, heh."* I bet it's because you never got married, eh?
JIM: No, I guess I done everything there is but that.
LARRY: How come you never did get married, Jim?
JIM: Well, I was out West so long, you know, Larry. Out West. *He starts to go again.*
KENNETH: Oh, don't they get married much out there?
JIM: Well, the cavalry was amongst the Indians most of the time.
BERT: How old are you now, Jim? No kidding.
KENNETH: I'll bet he's a hundred.
JIM: Me? No. I ain't no hunderd. I ain't near a hunderd. You don't have to be a hunderd to've fought the Indians. They was more Indians was fought than they tells in the schoolbooks, y'know. They was a hell of a lot of fightin' up to McKinley and all in there. I ain't no hunderd. *He starts out.*
KENNETH: Well, how old would you say you are, Jim?
JIM: Oh, I'm seventy-four, seventy-five, seventy-six—around in there. But I ain't no hunderd. *He exits, and Kenneth sneezes.*
BERT—*he has put his lunch bag away and is about to leave:* Boy, I was hungry!
KENNETH, *irritated:* Larry, don't you suppose a word might be passed to Mr. Eagle about the dust? It's rainin' dust from the ceiling!

Bert goes out.

GUS: What the hell Mr. Eagle gonna do about the dust?
KENNETH: Why, he's supposed to be a brilliant man, isn't he? Dartmouth College graduate and all? I've been five and a half

months in this country, and I never sneezed so much in my entire life before. My nose is all—

Enter Frank, the truckdriver, an impassive, burly man in his thirties.

FRANK: Anything for the West Bronx?
KENNETH: Nothin' yet, Frank. I've only started, though.

Jim enters with little boxes, which he adds to the pile on the bench.

FRANK: You got anything for West Bronx, Jim? I've got the truck on the elevator.
GUS: What's the hurry?
FRANK: I got the truck on the elevator.
GUS: Well, take it off the elevator! You got one little box of bearings for the West Bronx. You can't go West Bronx with one little box.
FRANK: Well, I gotta go.
GUS: You got a little pussy in the West Bronx.
FRANK: Yeah, I gotta make it before lunch.
JIM, *riffling through his orders:* I think I got something for the East Bronx.
FRANK: No, West Bronx.
JIM, *removing one order from his batch:* How about Brooklyn?
FRANK: What part? *He takes Jim's order, reads the address, looks up, thinking.*
JIM: Didn't you have a girl around Williamsburg?
FRANK: I'll have to make a call. I'll be right back.
GUS: You gonna deliver only where you got a woman?
FRANK: No, Gus, I go any place you tell me. But as long as I'm goin' someplace I might as well—you know. *He starts out.*
GUS: You some truckdriver.
FRANK: You said it, Gus. *He goes out.*
GUS: Why don't you go with him sometime, Kenneth? Get yourself nice piece ding-a-ling—
KENNETH: Oh, don't be nasty now, Gus. You're only tryin' to be nasty to taunt me.

Raymond enters.

RAYMOND: Didn't Tommy Kelly get here?
GUS: Don't worry for Tommy. Tommy going to be all right.
LARRY: Can I see you a minute, Ray? *He moves with Raymond over to the left.*
RAYMOND: Eagle's coming today, and if he sees him drunk again I don't know what I'm going to do.
LARRY: Ray, I'd like you to ask Eagle something for me.
RAYMOND: What?
LARRY: I've got to have more money.
RAYMOND: You and me both, boy.
LARRY: No, I can't make it any more, Ray. I mean it. The car put me a hundred and thirty bucks in the hole. If one of the kids gets sick I'll be strapped.
RAYMOND: Well, what'd you buy the car for?
LARRY: I'm almost forty, Ray. What am I going to be careful for?
RAYMOND: See, the problem is, Larry, if you go up, I'm only making thirty-eight myself, and I'm the manager, so it's two raises—
LARRY: Ray, I hate to make it tough for you, but my wife is driving me nuts. Now—

Enter Jerry Maxwell and Willy Hogan, both twenty-three. Jerry has a black eye; both are slick dressers.

JERRY AND WILLY: Morning. Morning, Gus.
RAYMOND: Aren't you late, fellas?
JERRY, *glancing at his gold wristwatch:* I've got one minute to nine, Mr. Ryan.
WILLY: That's Hudson Tubes time, Mr. Ryan.
GUS: The stopwatch twins.
RAYMOND, *to Jerry:* You got a black eye?
JERRY: Yeah, we went to a dance in Jersey City last night.
WILLY: Ran into a wise guy in Jersey City, Mr. Ryan.
JERRY, *with his taunting grin; he is very happy with himself:* Tried to take his girl away from us.
RAYMOND: Well, get on the ball. Mr. Eagle's—

Enter Tom Kelly. Gus rises from the desk. Bert enters, stands still. Raymond and Larry stand watching. Kenneth stops

wrapping. Tom is stiff; he moves in a dream to the chair Gus has left and sits rigidly. He is a slight, graying clerk in his late forties.

GUS, *to Raymond:* Go 'way, go 'head.

Raymond comes up and around the desk to face Tom, who sits there, staring ahead, immobile, his hands in his lap.

RAYMOND: Tommy.

Jerry and Willy titter.

GUS, *to them:* Shatap, goddam bums!
JERRY: Hey, don't call me—
GUS: Shatap, goddamit I break you goddam head! *He has an axle in his hand, and Raymond and Larry are pulling his arm down. Jim enters and goes directly to him. All are crying, "Gus! Cut it out! Put it down!"*
JERRY: What'd we do? What'd I say?
GUS: Watch out! Just watch out you make fun of this man! I break you head, both of you! *Silence. He goes to Tom, who has not moved since arriving.* Tommy. Tommy, you hear Gus? Tommy? *Tom is transfixed.*
RAYMOND: Mr. Eagle is coming today, Tommy.
GUS, *to all:* Go 'head, go to work, go to work! *They all move; Jerry and Willy go out.*
RAYMOND: Can you hear me, Tom? Mr. Eagle is coming to look things over today, Tom.
JIM: Little shot of whisky might bring him to.
GUS: Bert! *He reaches into his pocket.* Here, go downstairs bring a shot. Tell him for Tommy. *He sees what is in his hand.* I only got ten cents.
RAYMOND: Here. *He reaches into his pocket as Jim, Kenneth, and Larry all reach into their own pockets.*
BERT, *taking a coin from Raymond:* Okay, I'll be right up. *He hurries out.*
RAYMOND: Well, this is it, Gus. I gave him his final warning.
GUS—*he is worried:* All right, go 'way, go 'way.

Agnes enters.

AGNES: Is he—?

RAYMOND: You heard me, Agnes. I told him on Saturday, didn't I? *He starts past her.*

AGNES: But Ray, look how nice and clean he came in today. His hair is all combed, and he's much neater.

RAYMOND: I did my best, Agnes. *He goes out.*

GUS, *staring into Tommy's dead eyes:* Ach. He don't see nothin', Agnes.

AGNES, *looking into Tommy's face:* And he's supposed to be saving for his daughter's confirmation dress! Oh, Tommy. I'd better cool his face. *She goes into the toilet.*

KENNETH, *to Larry:* Ah, you can't blame the poor feller; sixteen years of his life in this place.

LARRY: You said it.

KENNETH: There's a good deal of monotony connected with the life, isn't it?

LARRY: You ain't kiddin'.

KENNETH: Oh, there must be a terrible lot of Monday mornings in sixteen years. And no philosophical idea at all, y'know, to pass the time?

GUS, *to Kenneth:* When you gonna shut up?

Agnes comes from the toilet with a wet cloth. They watch as she washes Tom's face.

KENNETH: Larry, you suppose we could get these windows washed sometime? I've often thought if we could see a bit of the sky now and again it would help matters now and again.

LARRY: They've never been washed since I've been here.

KENNETH: I'd do it myself if I thought they wouldn't all be laughin' at me for a greenhorn. *He looks out through the open window, which only opens out a few inches.* With all this glass we might observe the clouds and the various signs of approaching storms. And there might even be a bird now and again.

AGNES: Look at that—he doesn't even move. And he's been trying so hard! Nobody gives him credit, but he does try hard. *To Larry:* See how nice and clean he comes in now?

Jim enters, carrying parts.

JIM: Did you try blowing in his ear?

GUS: Blow in his ear?

JIM: Yeah, the Indians used to do that. Here, wait a minute. *He comes over, takes a deep breath, and blows into Tom's ear. A faint smile begins to appear on Tom's face, but, as Jim runs out of breath, it fades.*

KENNETH: Well, I guess he's not an Indian.

JIM: That's the truth, y'know. Out West, whenever there'd be a drunken Indian, they used to blow in his ear.

Enter Bert, carefully carrying a shotglass of whisky.

GUS: Here, gimme that. *He takes it.*

BERT, *licking his fingers:* Boy, that stuff is strong.

GUS: Tommy? *He holds the glass in front of Tom's nose.* Whisky. *Tom doesn't move.* Mr. Eagle is coming today, Tommy.

JIM: Leave it on the desk. He might wake up to it.

BERT: How's he manage to make it here, I wonder.

AGNES: Oh, he's awake. Somewhere inside, y'know. He just can't show it, somehow. It's not really like being drunk, even.

KENNETH: Well, it's pretty close, though, Agnes.

Agnes resumes wetting Tom's brow.

LARRY: Is that a fact, Jim, about blowing in a guy's ear?

JIM: Oh, sure. Indians always done that. *He goes to the order hook, leafs through.*

KENNETH: What did yiz all have against the Indians?

JIM: The Indians? Oh, we didn't have nothin' against the Indians. Just law and order, that's all. Talk about heat, though. It was so hot out there we—

Jim exits with an order as Frank enters.

FRANK: All right, I'll go to Brooklyn.

GUS: Where you running? I got nothing packed yet.

Enter Jerry, who puts goods on the table.

FRANK: Well, you beefed that I want to go Bronx, so I'm tellin' you now I'll go to Brooklyn.

GUS: You all fixed up in Brooklyn?

FRANK: Yeah, I just made a call.

AGNES, *laughing:* Oh, you're all so terrible! *She goes out.*

JERRY: How you doin', Kenny? You gittin' any?

KENNETH: Is that all two fine young fellas like you is got on your minds?
JERRY: Yeah, that's all. What's on your mind?

Frank is loading himself with packages.

GUS, *of Tommy:* What am I gonna do with him, Larry? The old man's comin'.
LARRY: Tell you the truth, Gus, I'm sick and tired of worrying about him, y'know? Let him take care of himself.

Gus goes to Larry, concerned, and they speak quietly.

GUS: What's the matter with you these days?
LARRY: Two years I'm asking for a lousy five-dollar raise. Meantime my brother's into me for fifty bucks for his wife's special shoes; my sister's got me for sixty-five to have her kid's teeth fixed. So I buy a car, and they're all on my back—how'd I dare buy a car! Whose money is it? Y'know, Gus? I mean—
GUS: Yeah, but an Auburn, Larry—
LARRY, *getting hot:* I happen to like the valves! What's so unusual about that?

Enter Willy and Jerry with goods.

WILLY, *to Jerry:* Here! Ask Frank. *To Frank:* Who played shortstop for Pittsburgh in nineteen-twenty-four?
FRANK: Pittsburgh? Honus Wagner, wasn't it?
WILLY, *to Jerry:* What I tell ya?
JERRY: How could it be Honus Wagner? Honus Wagner—

Raymond enters with a mechanic, and Willy and Jerry exit, arguing. Frank goes out with his packages. Gus returns to his desk.

RAYMOND: Larry, you want to help this man? He's got a part here.

Larry simply turns, silent, with a hurt and angry look. The mechanic goes to him, holds out the part; but Larry does not take it, merely inspects it, for it is greasy, as is the man.

RAYMOND, *going to the desk, where Gus is now seated at work beside Tom Kelly:* Did he move at all, Gus?

GUS: He's feeling much better, I can see. Go, go 'way, Raymond.

Raymond worriedly stands there.

LARRY, *to mechanic:* Where you from?

MECHANIC: I'm mechanic over General Truck.

LARRY: What's that off?

MECHANIC, *as Bert stops to watch, and Kenneth stops packing to observe:* That's the thing—I don't know. It's a very old coal truck, see, and I thought it was a Mack, because it says Mack on the radiator, see? But I went over to Mack, and they says there's no part like that on any Mack in their whole history, see?

LARRY: Is there any name on the engine?

MECHANIC: I'm tellin' you; on the engine it says American-LaFrance—must be a replacement engine.

LARRY: That's not off a LaFrance.

MECHANIC: I know! I went over to American-LaFrance, but they says they never seen nothin' like that in their whole life since the year one.

Raymond joins them.

LARRY: What is it, off the manifold?

MECHANIC: Well, it ain't exactly off the manifold. It like sticks out, see, except it don't stick out, it's like stuck in there—I mean it's like in a little hole there on top of the head, except it ain't exactly a hole, it's a thing that comes up in like a bump, see, and then it goes down. Two days I'm walkin' the streets with this, my boss is goin' crazy.

LARRY: Well, go and find out what it is, and if we got it we'll sell it to you.

RAYMOND: Don't you have any idea, Larry?

LARRY: I might, Ray, but I'm not getting paid for being an encyclopedia. There's ten thousand obsolete parts upstairs—it was never my job to keep all that in my head. If the old man wants that service, let him pay somebody to do it.

RAYMOND: Ah, Larry, the guy's here with the part.

LARRY: The guy is always here with the part, Ray. Let him hire somebody to take an inventory up there and see what it costs him.

RAYMOND, *taking the part off the table:* Well, I'll see what I can find up there.

LARRY: You won't find it, Ray. Put it down. *Raymond does, and Larry, blinking with hurt, turns to the mechanic.* What is that truck, about nineteen-twenty-two?

MECHANIC: That truck? *He shifts onto his right foot in thought.*

LARRY: Nineteen-twenty?

MECHANIC, *in a higher voice, shifting to the left foot:* That truck?

LARRY: Well, it's at least nineteen-twenty, isn't it?

MECHANIC: Oh, it's at least. I brung over a couple a friend of mines, and one of them is an old man and he says when he was a boy already that truck was an old truck, and he's an old, old man, that guy. *Larry takes the part now and sets it on the packing bench. Now even Gus gets up to watch as he stares at the part. There is a hush. Raymond goes out. Larry turns the part a little and stares at it again. Now he sips his coffee.* I understand this company's got a lot of old parts from the olden days, heh?

LARRY: We may have one left, if it's what I think it is, but you'll have to pay for it.

MECHANIC: Oh, I know; that's why my boss says try all the other places first, because he says youse guys charge. But looks to me like we're stuck.

LARRY: Bert. *He stares in thought.* Get the key to the third floor from Miss Molloy. Go up there, and when you open the door you'll see those Model-T mufflers stacked up.

BERT: Okay.

LARRY: You ever been up there?

BERT: No, but I always wanted to go.

LARRY: Well, go past the mufflers and you'll see a lot of bins going up to the ceiling. They're full of Marmon valves and ignition stuff.

BERT: Yeah?

LARRY: Go past them, and you'll come to a little corridor, see?

BERT: Yeah?

LARRY: At the end of the corridor is a pile of crates—I think there's some Maxwell differentials in there.

BERT: Yeah?

LARRY: Climb over the crates, but don't keep goin', see. Stand on top of the crates and turn right. Then bend down, and

there's a bin— No, I tell you, get off the crates, and you can reach behind them, but to the right, and reach into that bin. There's a lot of Locomobile headnuts in there, but way back—you gotta stick your hand way in, see, and you'll find one of these.

BERT: Geez, Larry, how do you remember all that?

Agnes rushes in.

AGNES: Eagle's here! Eagle's here!

LARRY, *to the mechanic:* Go out front and wait at the counter, will ya? *The mechanic nods and leaves. Larry indicates the glass on the desk.* Better put that whisky away, Gus.

GUS, *alarmed now:* What should we do with him?

Larry goes to Tom, peeved, and speaks in his ear.

LARRY: Tommy. Tommy!

AGNES: Larry, why don't you put him up on the third floor? He got a dozen warnings already. Eagle's disgusted—

GUS: Maybe he's sick. I never seen him like this.

Jim enters with goods.

JIM: Eagle's here.

LARRY: Let's try to walk him around. Come on.

Gus looks for a place to hide the whisky, then drinks it.

GUS: All right, Tommy, come on, get up. *They hoist him up to his feet, then let him go. He starts to sag; they catch him.* I don't think he feel so good.

LARRY: Come on, walk him. *To Agnes:* Watch out for Eagle. *She stands looking off and praying silently.* Let's go, Tom. *They try to walk Tom, but he doesn't lift his feet.*

AGNES, *trembling, watching Tommy:* He's so kindhearted, y'see? That's his whole trouble—he's too kindhearted.

LARRY, *angering, but restrained, shaking Tom:* For God's sake, Tom, come on! Eagle's here! *He shakes Tom more violently.* Come on! What the hell is the matter with you, you want to lose your job? Goddamit, you a baby or something?

AGNES: Sssh!

They all turn to the left. In the distance is heard the clacking of heel taps on a concrete floor.

GUS: Put him down. Larry! *They seat Tom before the desk. Agnes swipes back his mussed hair. Gus sets his right hand on top of an invoice on the desk.* Here, put him like he's writing. Where's my pencil? Who's got pencil? *Larry, Kenneth, Agnes search themselves for a pencil.*

KENNETH: Here's a crayon.

GUS: Goddam, who take my pencil! Bert! Where's that Bert! He always take my pencil!

Bert enters, carrying a heavy axle.

BERT: Hey, Eagle's here!

GUS: Goddam you, why you take my pencil?

BERT: I haven't got your pencil. This is mine.

Gus grabs the pencil out of Bert's shirt pocket and sticks it upright into Tom's hand. They have set him up to look as if he is writing. They step away. Tom starts sagging toward one side.

AGNES, *in a loud whisper:* Here he comes!

She goes to the order spike and pretends she is examining it. Larry meanwhile rushes to Tom, sets him upright, then walks away, pretending to busy himself. But Tom starts falling off the chair again, and Bert rushes and props him up.

The sound of the heel taps is on us now, and Bert starts talking to Tom, meantime supporting him with one hand on his shoulder.

BERT, *overloudly:* Tommy, the reason I ask, see, is because on Friday I filled an order for the same amount of coils for Scranton, see, and it just seems they wouldn't be ordering the same exact amount again.

During his speech Eagle has entered—a good-looking man in his late forties, wearing palm beach trousers, a shirt and tie, sleeves neatly folded up, a new towel over one arm. He walks across the shipping room, not exactly looking at anyone, but clearly observing everything. He goes into the toilet, past Agnes, who turns.

AGNES: Good morning, Mr. Eagle.
EAGLE, *nodding:* Morning. *He goes into the toilet.*
KENNETH, *indicating the toilet:* Keep it up, keep it up now!
BERT, *loudly:* Ah—another thing that's bothering me, Tommy, is those rear-end gears for Riverhead. I can't find any invoice for Riverhead. I can't find any invoice for gears to Riverhead. *He is getting desperate, looks to the others, but they only urge him on.* So what happened to the invoice? That's the thing we're all wondering about, Tommy. What happened to that invoice? You see, Tom? That invoice—it was blue, I remember, blue with a little red around the edges—
KENNETH, *loudly:* That's right there, Bert, it was a blue invoice—and it had numbers on it—

Suddenly Tom stands, swaying a little, blinking. There is a moment's silence.

TOM: No, no, Glen Wright was shortstop for Pittsburgh, not Honus Wagner.

Eagle emerges from the toilet. Bert goes to the order spike.

LARRY: Morning, sir. *He goes out.*
TOM, *half bewildered, shifting from foot to foot:* Who was talking about Pittsburgh? *He turns about and almost collides with Eagle.* Morning, Mr. Eagle.
EAGLE—*as he passes Tom he lets his look linger on his face:* Morning, Kelly.

Eagle crosses the shipping room and goes out. Agnes, Kenneth, and Gus wait an instant. Jim enters, sees Tom is up.

JIM: Attaboy, Tommy, knew you'd make it.
TOM: Glen Wright was shortstop. Who asked about that?
GUS, *nodding sternly his approbation to Bert:* Very good, Bert, you done good.
BERT, *wiping his forehead:* Boy!
TOM: Who was talking about Pittsburgh? *Agnes is heard weeping. They turn.* Agnes? *He goes to her.* What's the matter, Ag?
AGNES: Oh, Tommy, why do you do that?

PATRICIA, *calling from offstage left:* Aggie? Your switchboard's ringing.

AGNES: Oh, Tommy! *Weeping, she hurries out.*

TOM, *to the others:* What happened? What is she cryin' for?

GUS, *indicating the desk:* Why don't you go to work, Tommy? You got lotta parcel post this morning.

Tom always has a defensive smile. He shifts from foot to foot as he talks, as though he were always standing on a hot stove. He turns to the desk, sees Kenneth. He wants to normalize everything.

TOM: Kenny! I didn't even see ya!

KENNETH: Morning, Tommy. Good to see you up and about.

TOM, *with a put-on brogue:* Jasus, me bye, y'r hair is fallin' like the dew of the evenin'.

KENNETH, *self-consciously wiping his hair:* Oh, Tommy, now—

TOM: Kenny, bye, y'r gittin' an awful long face to wash!

KENNETH, *gently cuffing him:* Oh, now, stop that talk!

TOM, *backing toward his desk:* Why, ya donkey, ya. I bet they had to back you off the boat!

KENNETH, *with mock anger:* Oh, don't you be callin' me a donkey now!

Enter Raymond.

RAYMOND: Tom? *He is very earnest, even deadly.*

TOM, *instantly perceiving his own guilt:* Oh, mornin', Ray, how's the twins? *He gasps little chuckles as he sits at his desk, feeling about for a pencil.*

Raymond goes up close to the desk and leans over, as the others watch—pretending not to.

RAYMOND, *quietly:* Eagle wants to see you.

TOM, *with foreboding, looking up into Raymond's face:* Eagle? I got a lot of parcel post this morning, Ray. *He automatically presses down his hair.*

RAYMOND: He's in his office waiting for you now, Tom.

TOM: Oh, sure. It's just that there's a lot of parcel post on Monday. . . . *He feels for his tie as he rises, and walks out. Raymond starts out after him, but Gus, intercedes.*

GUS, *going up to Raymond:* What Eagle wants?

RAYMOND: I warned him, Gus, I warned him a dozen times.

GUS: He's no gonna fire him.
RAYMOND: Look, it's all over, Gus, so there's nothing—
GUS: He gonna fire Tommy?
RAYMOND: Now don't raise your voice.
GUS: Sixteen year Tommy work here! He got daughter gonna be in church confirmation!
RAYMOND: Now listen, I been nursing him along for—
GUS: Then you fire me! You fire Tommy, you fire me!
RAYMOND: Gus!

With a stride Gus goes to the hook, takes his shirt down, thrusts himself into it.

GUS: Goddam son-of-a-bitch.
RAYMOND: Now don't be crazy, Gus.
GUS: I show who crazy! Tommy Kelly he gonna fire! *He grabs his bowler off the hook. Enter Agnes, agitated.*
AGNES: Gus! Go to the phone!
GUS, *not noticing her, and with bowler on, to Raymond:* Come on, he gonna fire me now, son-of-a-bitch! *He starts out, shirt-tails flying, and Agnes stops him.*
AGNES, *indicating the phone:* Gus, your neighbor's—
GUS, *trying to disengage himself:* No, he gonna fire me now. He fire Tommy Kelly, he fire me!
AGNES: Lilly, Gus! Your neighbor wants to talk to you. Go, go to the phone.

Gus halts, looks at Agnes.

GUS: What, Lilly?
AGNES: Something's happened. Go, go to the phone.
GUS: Lilly? *Perplexed, he goes to the phone.* Hallo. Yeah, Gus. Ha? *He listens, stunned. His hand, of itself, goes to his hatbrim as though to doff the hat, but it stays there. Jim enters, comes to a halt, sensing the attention, and watches Gus.* When? When it happen? *He listens, and then mumbles:* Ya. Thank you. I come home right away. *He hangs up. Jim comes forward to him questioningly. To Jim, perplexed:* My Lilly. Die.
JIM: Oh? Hm!

Larry enters. Gus dumbly turns to him.

GUS, *to Larry:* Die. My Lilly.

LARRY: Oh, that's tough, Gus.
RAYMOND: You better go home. *Pause.* Go ahead, Gus. Go home.

Gus stands blinking. Raymond takes his jacket from the hook and helps him on with it. Agnes starts to push his shirttails into his pants.

GUS: We shouldn't've go to Staten Island, Jim. Maybe she don't feel good yesterday. Ts, I was in Staten Island, maybe she was sick. *Tommy Kelly enters, goes directly to his desk, sits, his back to the others. Pause. To Tom:* He fire you, Tommy?
TOM, *holding tears back:* No, Gus, I'm all right.
GUS, *going up next to him:* Give you another chance?
TOM—*he is speaking with his head lowered:* Yeah. It's all right, Gus, I'm goin' to be all right from now on.
GUS: Sure. Be a man, Tommy. Don't be no drunken bum. Be a man. You hear? Don't let nobody walk on top you. Be man.
TOM: I'm gonna be all right, Gus.
GUS, *nodding:* One more time you come in drunk I gonna show you something. *Agnes sobs. He turns to her.* What for you cry all the time? *He goes past her and out. Agnes then goes. A silence.*
RAYMOND, *breaking the silence:* What do you say, fellas, let's get going, heh? *He claps his hands and walks out as all move about their work. Soon all are gone but Tommy Kelly, slumped at his desk; Kenneth, wrapping; and Bert, picking an order from the hook. Now Kenneth faces Bert suddenly.*
KENNETH—*he has taken his feeling from the departing Gus, and turns now to Bert:* Bert? How would you feel about washing these windows—you and I—once and for all? Let a little of God's light in the place?
BERT, *excitedly, happily:* Would you?
KENNETH: Well, I would if you would.
BERT: Okay, come on! Let's do a little every day; couple of months it'll all be clean! Gee! Look at the sun!
KENNETH: Hey, look down there!
See the old man sitting in a chair?
And roses all over the fence!
Oh, that's a lovely back yard!

A rag in hand, Bert mounts the table; they make one slow swipe of the window before them and instantly all the windows

around the stage burst into the yellow light of summer that floods into the room.

BERT: Boy, they've got a tree!
And all those cats!
KENNETH: It'll be nice to watch the seasons pass.
That pretty up there now, a real summer sky
And a little white cloud goin' over?
I can just see autumn comin' in
And the leaves falling on the gray days.
You've got to have a sky to look at!

Gradually, as they speak, all light hardens to that of winter, finally.

BERT, *turning to Kenneth:* Kenny, were you ever fired from a job?
KENNETH: Oh, sure; two-three times.
BERT: Did you feel bad?
KENNETH: The first time, maybe. But you have to get used to that, Bert. I'll bet you never went hungry in your life, did you?
BERT: No, I never did. Did you?
KENNETH: Oh, many and many a time. You get used to that too, though.
BERT, *turning and looking out:* That tree is turning red.
KENNETH: It must be spectacular out in the country now.
BERT: How does the cold get through these walls?
Feel it, it's almost a wind!
KENNETH: Don't cats walk dainty in the snow!
BERT: Gee, you'd never know it was the same place—
How clean it is when it's white!
Gus doesn't say much any more, y'know?
KENNETH: Well, he's showin' his age. Gus is old.
When do you buy your ticket for the train?
BERT: I did. I've got it.
KENNETH: Oh, then you're off soon!
You'll confound all the professors, I'll bet!

He sings softly.

"The minstrel boy to the war has gone . . ."

Bert moves a few feet away; thus he is alone. Kenneth remains at the window, looking out, polishing, and singing softly.

BERT: There's something so terrible here!
There always was, and I don't know what.
Gus, and Agnes, and Tommy and Larry, Jim and Patricia—
Why does it make me so sad to see them every morning?
It's like the subway;
Every day I see the same people getting on
And the same people getting off,
And all that happens is that they get older. God!
Sometimes it scares me; like all of us in the world
Were riding back and forth across a great big room,
From wall to wall and back again,
And no end ever! Just no end!

He turns to Kenneth, but not quite looking at him, and with a deeper anxiety.

Didn't you ever want to be anything, Kenneth?

KENNETH: I've never been able to keep my mind on it, Bert. . . .
I shouldn't've cut a hole in me shoe.
Now the snow's slushin' in, and me feet's all wet.

BERT: If you studied, Kenneth, if you put your mind to something great, I know you'd be able to learn anything, because you're clever, you're much smarter than I am!

KENNETH: You've got something steady in your mind, Bert;
Something far away and steady.
I never could hold my mind on a far-away thing . . .

His tone changes as though he were addressing a group of men; his manner is rougher, angrier, less careful of proprieties.

She's not giving me the heat I'm entitled to.
Eleven dollars a week room and board,
And all she puts in the bag is a lousy pork sandwich,
The same every day and no surprises.
Is that right? Is that right now?
How's a man to live,
Freezing all day in this palace of dust
And night comes with one window and a bed
And the streets full of strangers

And not one of them's read a book through,
Or seen a poem from beginning to end
Or knows a song worth singing.
Oh, this is an ice-cold city, Mother,
And Roosevelt's not makin' it warmer, somehow.

He sits on the table, holding his head.

And here's another grand Monday!

They are gradually appearing in natural light now, but it is a cold wintry light which has gradually supplanted the hot light of summer. Bert goes to the hook for a sweater.

Jesus, me head'll murder me. I never had the headache till this year.

BERT, *delicately:* You're not taking up drinking, are you?

KENNETH—*he doesn't reply. Suddenly, as though to retrieve something slipping by, he gets to his feet, and roars out:*

"The Ship of State," by Walt Whitman!
"O Captain! my Captain! our fearful trip is done!
The ship has weathered every wrack,
The prize we sought is won . . ."

Now what in the world comes after that?

BERT: I don't know that poem.

KENNETH: Dammit all! I don't remember the bloody poems any more the way I did! It's the drinkin' does it, I think. I've got to stop the drinkin'!

BERT: Well, why do you drink, Kenny, if it makes you feel—

KENNETH: Good God, Bert, you can't always be doin' what you're better off to do! There's all kinds of unexpected turns, y'know, and things not workin' out the way they ought! What in hell *is* the next stanza of that poem? "The prize we sought is won . . ." God, I'd never believe I could forget that poem! I'm thinkin', Bert, y'know—maybe I ought to go onto the Civil Service. The only trouble is there's no jobs open except for the guard in the insane asylum. And that'd be a nervous place to work, I think.

BERT: It might be interesting, though.

KENNETH: I suppose it might. They tell me it's only the more intelligent people goes mad, y'know. But it's sixteen hundred a year, Bert, and I've a feelin' I'd never dare leave it,

y'know? And I'm not ready for me last job yet, I think. I don't want nothin' to be the last, yet. Still and all . . .

Raymond enters, going to toilet. He wears a blue button-up sweater.

RAYMOND: Morning, boys. *He impales a batch of orders on the desk.*

KENNETH, *in a routine way:* Morning, Mr. Ryan. Have a nice New Year's, did you?

RAYMOND: Good enough. *To Bert, seeing the book on the table.* Still reading that book?

BERT: Oh, I'm almost finished now. *Raymond nods, continues on. Bert jumps off the table.* Mr. Ryan? Can I see you a minute? *He goes to Raymond.* I wondered if you hired anybody yet, to take my place.

RAYMOND, *pleasantly surprised:* Why? Don't you have enough money to go?

BERT: No, I'm going. I just thought maybe I could help you break in the new boy. I won't be leaving till after lunch tomorrow.

RAYMOND, *with resentment, even an edge of sarcasm:* We'll break him in all right. Why don't you just get on to your own work? There's a lot of excelsior laying around the freight elevator.

Raymond turns and goes into the toilet. For an instant Bert is left staring after him. Then he turns to Kenneth, perplexed.

BERT: Is he sore at me?

KENNETH, *deprecatingly:* Ah, why would he be sore at you? *He starts busying himself at the table, avoiding Bert's eyes. Bert moves toward him, halts.*

BERT: I hope you're not, are you?

KENNETH, *with an evasive air:* Me? Ha! Why, Bert, you've got the heartfelt good wishes of everybody in the place for your goin'-away! *But he turns away to busy himself at the table—and on his line Larry has entered with a container of coffee and a cigarette.*

BERT: Morning, Larry. *He goes to the hook, takes an order.*

LARRY, *leaning against the table:* Jesus, it'd be just about per-

fect in here for penguins. *Bert passes him.* You actually leaving tomorrow?

BERT, *eagerly:* I guess so, yeah.

LARRY, *with a certain embarrassed envy:* Got all the dough, heh?

BERT: Well, for the first year anyway. *He grins in embarrassment.* You mind if I thank you?

LARRY: What for?

BERT: I don't know—just for teaching me everything. I'd have been fired the first month without you, Larry.

LARRY, *with some wonder, respect:* Got all your dough, heh?

BERT: Well, that's all I've been doing is saving.

Enter Tom Kelly. He is bright, clean, sober.

TOM: Morning!

KENNETH, *with an empty kind of heartiness:* Why, here comes Tommy Kelly!

TOM, *passing to hang up his coat and hat:* Ah, y're gettin' an awful long face to wash, Kenny, me bye.

KENNETH: Oh, cut it out with me face, Tommy. I'm as sick of it as you are.

TOM: Go on, ya donkey ya, they backed you off the boat.

KENNETH: Why, I'll tear you limb from limb, Tom Kelly! *He mocks a fury, and Tom laughs as he is swung about. And then, with a quick hug and a laugh:* Oh, Tommy, you're the first man I ever heard of done it. How'd you do it, Tom?

TOM: Will power, Kenny. *He walks to his desk, sits.* Just made up my mind, that's all.

KENNETH: Y'know the whole world is talking about you, Tom—the way you mixed all the drinks at the Christmas party and never weakened? Y'know, when I heard it was you going to mix the drinks I was prepared to light a candle for you.

TOM: I just wanted to see if I could do it, that's all. When I done that—mixin' the drinks for three hours, and givin' them away—I realized I made it. You don't look so hot to me, you know that?

KENNETH, *with a sigh:* Oh, I'm all right. It's the sight of Monday, that's all, is got me down.

TOM: You better get yourself a little will power, Kenny. I think you're gettin' a fine taste for the hard stuff.

KENNETH: Ah, no, I'll never be a drunk, Tommy.

TOM: You're a drunk now.

KENNETH: Oh, don't say that, please!

TOM: I'm tellin' you, I can see it comin' on you.

KENNETH, *deeply disturbed:* You can't either. Don't say that, Tommy!

Agnes enters.

AGNES: Morning! *She wears sheets of brown paper for leggins.*

KENNETH: Winter's surely here when Agnes is wearin' her leggins.

AGNES, *with her laughter:* Don't they look awful? But that draft under the switchboard is enough to kill ya.

LARRY: This place is just right for penguins.

AGNES: Haven't you got a heavier sweater, Bert? I'm surprised at your mother.

BERT: Oh, it's warm; she knitted it.

KENNETH: Bert's got the idea. Get yourself an education.

TOM: College guys are sellin' ties all over Macy's. Accountancy, Bert, that's my advice to you. You don't even have to go to college for it either.

BERT: Yeah, but I don't want to be an accountant.

TOM, *with a superior grin:* You don't want to be an accountant?

LARRY: What's so hot about an accountant?

TOM: Well, try runnin' a business without one. That's what you should've done, Larry. If you'd a took accountancy, you'd a—

LARRY: You know, Tommy, I'm beginning to like you better drunk? *Tommy laughs, beyond criticism.* I mean it. Before, we only had to pick you up all the time; now you got opinions about everything.

TOM: Well, if I happen to know something, why shouldn't I say—

Enter Raymond from the toilet.

RAYMOND: What do you say we get on the ball early today, fellas? Eagle's coming today. Bert, how about gettin' those carburetor crates open, will ya?

BERT: I was just going to do that.

Bert and Raymond are starting out, and Agnes is moving to

go, when Gus and Jim enter. Both of them are on the verge of staggering. Gus has a bright new suit and checked overcoat, a new bowler, and new shoes. He is carrying upright a pair of Ford fenders, still in their brown paper wrappings—they stand about seven feet in height. Jim aids him in carefully resting the fenders against the wall.

Kenneth, Agnes, and Larry watch in silence.

Patricia enters and watches. She is wearing leggins.

Willy and Jerry enter in overcoats, all jazzed up.

WILLY: Morning!
JERRY: Morn— *Both break off and slowly remove their coats as they note the scene and the mood. Gus, now that the fenders are safely stacked, turns.*
GUS, *dimly:* Who's got a hanger?
KENNETH: Hanger? You mean a coat-hanger, Gus?
GUS: Coat-hanger.
JERRY: Here! Here's mine! *He gives a wire hanger to Gus. Gus is aided by Jim in removing his overcoat, and they both hang it on the hanger, then on a hook. Both give it a brush or two, and Gus goes to his chair, sits. He raises his eyes to them all.*
GUS: So what everybody is looking at?

Bert, Willy, Jerry go to work, gradually going out with orders. Jim also takes orders off the hook, and the pattern of going-and-coming emerges. Patricia goes to the toilet. Tom Kelly works at the desk.

LARRY, *half-kidding, but in a careful tone:* What are you all dressed up about?

Gus simply glowers in his fumes and thoughts. Raymond goes over to Jim.

RAYMOND: What's he all dressed up for?
JIM: Oh, don't talk to me about him, Ray, I'm sick and tired of him. Spent all Saturday buyin' new clothes to go to the cemetery; then all the way the hell over to Long Island City to get these damned fenders for that old wreck of a Ford he's got. Never got to the cemetery, never got the fenders

on—and we been walkin' around all weekend carryin' them damn things.

RAYMOND: Eagle'll be here this morning. See if you can get him upstairs. I don't want him to see him crocked again.

JIM: I'd just let him sit there, Ray, if I was you. I ain't goin' to touch him. You know what he went and done? Took all his insurance money outa the bank Saturday. Walkin' around with all that cash in his pocket—I tell ya, I ain't been to sleep since Friday night. 'Cause you can't let him loose with all that money and so low in his mind, y'know . . .

GUS: Irishman! *All turn to him. He takes a wad out of his pocket, peels one bill off.* Here. Buy new pair shoes.

KENNETH: Ah, thank you, no, Gus, I couldn't take that.

RAYMOND: Gus, Eagle's coming this morning; why don't you—

GUS, *stuffing a bill into Kenneth's pocket:* Go buy pair shoes.

RAYMOND: Gus, he's going to be here right away; why don't you—

GUS: I don't give one goddam for Eagle! Why he don't make one more toilet?

RAYMOND: What?

Bert enters with goods.

GUS: Toilet! That's right? Have one toilet for so many people? That's very bad, Raymond. That's no nice. *Offering Bert a bill:* Here, boy, go—buy book, buy candy.

Larry goes to Gus before he gives the bill, puts an arm around him, and walks away from the group.

LARRY: Come on, Gussy, let me take you upstairs.

GUS: I don't care Eagle sees me, I got my money now, goddam. Oh, Larry, Larry, twenty-two year I workin' here.

LARRY: Why don't you give me the money, Gus? I'll put in the bank for you.

GUS: What for I put in bank? I'm sixty-eight years old, Larry. I got no children, nothing. What for I put in bank? *Suddenly, reminded, he turns back to Raymond, pointing at the floor scale.* Why them goddam mice nobody does nothing?

RAYMOND, *alarmed by Gus's incipient anger:* Gus, I want you to go upstairs!

Patricia enters from toilet.

GUS, *at the scale:* Twenty-two years them goddam mice! That's very bad, Raymond, so much mice! *He starts rocking the scale.* Look at them goddam mice! *Patricia screams as mice come running out from under the scale. A mêlée of shouts begins, everyone dodging mice or swinging brooms and boxes at them. Raymond is pulling Gus away from the scale, yelling at him to stop it. Agnes rushes in and, seeing the mice, screams and rushes out. Jerry and Willy rush in and join in chasing the mice, laughing. Patricia, wearing leggins, is helped onto the packing table by Larry, and Gus shouts up at her.* Come with me Atlantic City, Patricia! *He pulls out the wad.* Five thousand dollars I got for my wife!

PATRICIA: You rotten thing, you! You dirty rotten thing, Gus!

GUS: I make you happy, Patricia! I make you— *Suddenly his hand goes to his head; he is dizzy. Larry goes to him, takes one look.*

LARRY: Come, come on. *He walks Gus into the toilet.*

PATRICIA, *out of the momentary silence:* Oh, that louse! Did you see what he did, that louse? *She gets down off the table, and, glancing angrily toward the toilet, she goes out.*

RAYMOND: All right, fellas, what do you say, heh? Let's get going.

Work proceeds—the going and coming.

TOM, *as Raymond passes him:* I tried talking to him a couple of times, Ray, but he's got no will power! There's nothing you can do if there's no will power, y'know?

RAYMOND: Brother! It's a circus around here. Every Monday morning! I never saw anything like . . .

He is gone. Kenneth is packing. Tom works at his desk. Jim comes and, leaving goods on the packing table, goes to the toilet, peeks in, then goes out, studying an order. Bert enters with goods.

KENNETH: There's one thing you have to say for the Civil Service; it seals the fate and locks the door. A man needn't wonder what he'll do with his life any more.

Jerry enters with goods.

BERT, *glancing at the toilet door:* Gee, I never would've thought Gus liked his wife, would you?

Tom, studying a letter, goes out.

JERRY, *looking up and out the window:* Jesus!
BERT, *not attending to Jerry:* I thought he always hated his wife—
JERRY: Jesus, boy!
KENNETH, *to Jerry:* What're you doin'? What's—?
JERRY: Look at the girls up in there. One, two, three, four windows—full a girls, look at them! Them two is naked!

Willy enters with goods.

KENNETH: Oh, my God!
WILLY, *rushing to the windows:* Where? Where?
KENNETH: Well, what're you gawkin' at them for!

Gus and Larry enter from the toilet.

JERRY: There's another one down there! Look at her on the bed! What a beast!
WILLY, *overjoyed:* It's a cathouse! Gus! A whole cathouse moved in!

Willy and Jerry embrace and dance around wildly; Gus stands with Larry, staring out, as does Bert.

KENNETH: Aren't you ashamed of yourself!!

Tom enters with his letter.

TOM: Hey, fellas, Eagle's here.
JERRY, *pointing out:* There's a new cathouse, Tommy! *Tom goes and looks out the windows.*
KENNETH: Oh, that's a terrible thing to be lookin' at, Tommy! *Agnes enters; Kenneth instantly goes to her to get her out.* Oh, Agnes, you'd best not be comin' back here any more now—
AGNES: What? What's the matter?

Jerry has opened a window, and he and Willy whistle sharply through their fingers. Agnes looks out.

KENNETH: Don't, Agnes, don't look at that!

AGNES: Well, for heaven's sake! What are all those women doing there?

GUS: That's whorehouse, Aggie.

KENNETH: Gus, for God's sake! *He walks away in pain.*

AGNES: What are they sitting on the beds like that for?

TOM: The sun is pretty warm this morning—probably trying to get a little tan.

AGNES: Oh, my heavens. Oh, Bert, it's good you're leaving! *She turns to them.* You're not all going, are you? *Gus starts to laugh, then Tom, then Jerry and Willy, then Larry, and she is unstrung and laughing herself, but shocked.* Oh, my heavens! *She is gone, as Jim enters with goods.*

KENNETH: All right, now, clear off, all of you. I can't be workin' with a lot of sex maniacs blockin' off me table!

GUS: Look, Jim! *Jim looks out.*

JIM: Oh, nice.

JERRY: How about it, fellas? Let's all go lunchtime! What do you say, Kenny? I'll pay for you!

Gus goes to the desk, drags the chair over to the window.

KENNETH: I'd sooner roll meself around in the horse manure of the gutter!

JERRY: I betcha you wouldn't even know what to do!

KENNETH, *bristling, fists shut:* I'll show you what I do! I'll show you right now!

Enter Raymond, furious.

RAYMOND: What the hell is this? What's going on here?

GUS, *sitting in his chair, facing the windows:* Whorehouse. *Raymond looks out the windows.*

KENNETH: You'd better pass a word to Mr. Eagle about this, Raymond, or the corporation's done for. Poor Agnes, she's all mortified, y'know.

RAYMOND: Oh, my God! *To all:* All right, break it up, come on, break it up, Eagle's here. *Willy, Jerry, Bert, and Jim disperse, leaving with orders. Tommy returns to the desk.* What're you going to do, Gus? You going to sit there? *Gus doesn't answer; sits staring out thoughtfully.* What's going on with you? Gus! Eagle's here! All right, cook in your own juice. Sit

there. *He glances out the windows.* Brother, I needed this now! *He goes out angrily.*

LARRY: Give me the money, Gus, come on. I'll hold it for you.

GUS—*an enormous sadness is on him:* Go way.

Enter Patricia. She glances at Larry and Gus, then looks out the windows.

KENNETH, *wrapping:* Ah, Patricia, don't look out there. It's disgraceful.

TOM: It's only a lot of naked women.

KENNETH: Oh, Tommy, now! In front of a girl!

PATRICIA, *to Kenneth:* What's the matter? Didn't you ever see that before? *She sees Gus sitting there.* Look at Kong, will ya? *She laughs.* Rememberin' the old days, heh, Kong?

Larry is walking toward an exit at left.

GUS: Oh, shatap!

PATRICIA, *catching up with Larry at the edge of the stage, quietly:* What's Ray sayin' about you sellin' the Auburn?

LARRY: Yeah, I'm kinda fed up with it. It's out of my class anyway.

PATRICIA: That's too bad. I was just gettin' to enjoy it.

LARRY, *very doubtfully:* Yeah?

PATRICIA: What're you mad at me for?

LARRY: Why should I be mad?

PATRICIA: You're married, what're you—?

LARRY: Let me worry about that, will you?

PATRICIA: Well, I gotta worry about it too, don't I?

LARRY: Since when do you worry about anything, Pat?

PATRICIA: Well, what did you expect me to do? How did I know you were serious?

Gus goes to his coat, searches in a pocket.

LARRY: What did you think I was telling you all the time?

PATRICIA: Yeah, but Larry, anybody could say those kinda things.

LARRY: I know, Pat. But I never did. *With a cool, hurt smile:* You know, kid, you better start believing people when they tell you something. Or else you're liable to end up in there. *He points out the windows.*

PATRICIA, *with quiet fury:* You take that back! *He walks away; she goes after him.* You're going to take that back, Larry!

Eagle enters, nods to Larry and Patricia.

EAGLE: Morning.
PATRICIA, *with a mercurial change to sunny charm:* Good morning, Mr. Eagle!

Larry is gone, and she exits. Eagle crosses, noticing Gus, who is standing beside his coat, drinking out of a pint whisky bottle.

EAGLE: Morning, Gus.
GUS, *lowering the bottle:* Good morning. *Eagle exits into the toilet.*
TOM, *to Gus:* You gone nuts?

Gus returns, holding the bottle, to his chair, where he sits, looking out the window. He is growing sodden and mean. Bert enters with goods.

KENNETH, *sotto voce:* Eagle's in there, and look at him. He'll get the back of it now for sure.
TOM, *going to Gus:* Gimme the bottle, Gus!
GUS: I goin' go someplace, Tommy. I goin' go cemetery. I wasn't one time in cemetery. I go see my Lilly. My Lilly die, I was in Staten Island. All alone she was in the house. Ts! *Jerry enters with goods, sees him, and laughs.*
BERT: Gus, why don't you give Tommy the bottle?
GUS: Twenty-two years I work here.
KENNETH, *to Jerry, who is staring out the window:* Will you quit hangin' around me table, please?
JERRY: Can't I look out the window?

Willy enters with goods.

WILLY: How's all the little pussies?
KENNETH: Now cut that out! *They laugh at him.*
TOM, *sotto voce:* Eagle's in there!
KENNETH: Is that all yiz know of the world—filthy women and dirty jokes and the ignorance drippin' off your faces? *Eagle enters from the toilet.* There's got to be somethin' done about this, Mr. Eagle. It's an awful humiliation for the women here. *He points, and Eagle looks.* I mean to say, it's a

terrible disorganizing sight starin' a man in the face eight hours a day, sir.

EAGLE: Shouldn't have washed the windows, I guess. *He glances down at Gus and his bottle and walks out.*

KENNETH: Shouldn't have washed the windows, he says! *They are laughing; Gus is tipping the bottle up. Jim enters with goods.*

JERRY: What a donkey that guy is!

Kenneth lunges for Jerry and grabs him by the tie, one fist ready.

KENNETH: I'll donkey you! *Jerry starts a swing at him, and Bert and Tom rush to separate them as Raymond enters.*

RAYMOND: Hey! Hey!

JERRY, *as they part:* All right, donkey, I'll see you later.

KENNETH: You'll see me later, all right—with one eye closed!

RAYMOND: Cut it out! *Kenneth, muttering, returns to work at his table. Jerry rips an order off the hook and goes out. Willy takes an order. Bert goes out with an order. Raymond has been looking down at Gus, who is sitting with the bottle.* You going to work, Gus? Or you going to do that? *Gus gets up and goes to his coat, takes it off the hanger.* What're you doing?

GUS: Come on, Jim, we go someplace. Here—put on you coat.

RAYMOND: Where you going? It's half-past nine in the morning.

Enter Agnes.

AGNES: What's all the noise here? *She breaks off, seeing Gus dressing.*

GUS: That's when I wanna go—half-past nine. *He hands Jim his coat.* Here. Put on. Cold outside.

JIM, *quietly:* Maybe I better go with him, Ray. He's got all his money in—

Bert enters with goods.

RAYMOND, *reasonably, deeply concerned:* Gus, now look; where you gonna go now? Why don't you lie down upstairs?

GUS, *swaying, to Bert:* Twenty-two years I was here.

BERT: I know, Gus.

Larry enters, watches.

GUS: I was here before you was born I was here.

BERT: I know.

GUS: Them mice was here before you was born. *Bert nods uncomfortably, full of sadness.* When Mr. Eagle was in high school I was already here. When there was Winton Six I was here. When was Minerva car I was here. When was Stanley Steamer I was here, and Stearns Knight, and Marmon was good car; I was here all them times. I was here first day Raymond come; he was young boy; work hard be manager. When Agnes still think she was gonna get married I was here. When was Locomobile, and Model K Ford and Model N Ford—all them different Fords, and Franklin was good car, Jordan car, Reo car, Pierce Arrow, Cleveland car—all them was good cars. All them times I was here.

BERT: I know.

GUS: You don't know nothing. Come on, Jim. *He goes and gets a fender. Jim gets the other.* Button up you coat, cold outside. Tommy? Take care everything good.

He walks out with Jim behind him, each carrying a fender upright. Raymond turns and goes out, then Larry. Agnes goes into the toilet. The lights lower as this movement takes place, until Bert is alone in light, still staring at the point where Gus left.

BERT: I don't understand;
I don't know anything:
How is it me that gets out?
I don't know half the poems Kenneth does,
Or a quarter of what Larry knows about an engine.

I don't understand how they come every morning,
Every morning and every morning,
And no end in sight.
That's the thing—there's no end!
Oh, there ought to be a statue in the park—
"To All the Ones That Stay."
One to Larry, to Agnes, Tom Kelly, Gus . . .

Gee, it's peculiar to leave a place—forever!
Still, I always hated coming here;
The same dried-up jokes, the dust;
Especially in spring, walking in from the sunshine,

Or any Monday morning in the hot days.

In the darkness men appear and gather around the packing table, eating lunch out of bags; we see them as ghostly figures, silent.

God, it's so peculiar to leave a place!
I know I'll remember them as long as I live,
As long as I live they'll never die,
And still I know that in a month or two
They'll forget my name, and mix me up
With another boy who worked here once,
And went. Gee, it's a mystery!

As full light rises Bert moves into the group, begins eating from a bag.

JERRY, *looking out the window:* You know what's a funny thing? It's a funny thing how you get used to that.

WILLY: Tommy, what would you say Cobb's average was for lifetime?

TOM: Cobb? Lifetime? *He thinks. Pause. Kenneth sings.*

KENNETH: "The minstrel boy to the war has gone—

Patricia enters, crossing to toilet—

In the ranks of death you will find him."

PATRICIA: Is that an Irish song?

KENNETH: All Irish here, and none of yiz knows an Irish song!

She laughs, exits into the toilet.

TOM: I'd say three-eighty lifetime for Ty Cobb. *To Larry:* You're foolish sellin' that car with all the work you put in it.

LARRY: Well, it was one of those crazy ideas. Funny how you get an idea, and then suddenly you wake up and you look at it and it's like—dead or something. I can't afford a car.

Agnes enters, going toward the toilet.

AGNES: I think it's even colder today than yesterday.

Raymond enters.

RAYMOND: It's five after one, fellas; what do you say?

They begin to get up as Jim enters in his overcoat and hat.

KENNETH: Well! The old soldier returns!
RAYMOND: Where's Gus, Jim?

Agnes has opened the toilet door as Patricia emerges.

AGNES: Oh! You scared me. I didn't know you were in there!
JIM, *removing his coat:* He died, Ray.
RAYMOND: What?

The news halts everyone—but one by one—in midair, as it were.

LARRY: He what?
AGNES: What'd you say?
JIM: Gus died.
KENNETH: Gus died!
BERT: Gus?
AGNES, *going to Jim:* Oh, good heavens. When? What happened?
LARRY: What'd you have an accident?
JIM: No, we—we went home and got the fenders on all right, and he wanted to go over and start at the bottom, and go right up Third Avenue and hit the bars on both sides. And we got up to about Fourteenth Street, in around there, and we kinda lost track of the car someplace. I have to go back there tonight, see if I can find—
AGNES: Well, what happened?
Jim: Well, these girls got in the cab, y'know, and we seen a lot of places and all that—we was to some real high-class places, forty cents for a cup of coffee and all that; and then he put me in another cab, and we rode around a while; and then he got another cab to follow us. Case one of our cabs got a flat, see? He just didn't want to be held up for a minute, Gus didn't.
LARRY: Where were you going?
JIM: Oh, just all over. And we stopped for a light, y'know, and I thought I'd go up and see how he was gettin' along, y'know, and I open his cab door, and—the girl was fast asleep, see—and he—was dead. Right there in the seat. It was just gettin' to be morning.
AGNES: Oh, poor Gus!

JIM: I tell ya, Agnes, he didn't look too good to me since she died, the old lady. I never knowed it. He—liked that woman.

RAYMOND: Where's his money?

JIM: Oh—*with a wasting wave of the hand*—it's gone, Ray. We was stoppin' off every couple minutes so he call long distance. I didn't even know it, he had a brother someplace in California. Called him half a dozen times. And there was somebody he was talkin' to in Texas someplace, somebody that was in the Navy with him. He was tryin' to call all the guys that was in the submarine with him, and he was callin' all over hell and gone—and givin' big tips, and he bought a new suit, and give the cab driver a wristwatch and all like that. I think he got himself too sweated. Y'know it got pretty cold last night, and he was all sweated up. I kept tellin' him, I says, "Gus," I says, "you're gettin' yourself all sweated, y'know, and it's a cold night," I says; and all he kept sayin' to me all night he says, "Jim," he says, "I'm gonna do it right, Jim." That's all he says practically all night. "I'm gonna do it right," he says. "I'm gonna do it right." *Pause. Jim shakes his head.* Oh, when I open that cab door I knowed it right away. I takes one look at him and I knowed it. *There is a moment of silence, and Agnes turns and goes into the toilet.* Oh, poor Agnes, I bet she's gonna cry now.

Jim goes to the order hook, takes an order off, and, putting a cigar into his mouth, he goes out, studying the order. Raymond crosses and goes out; then Patricia goes. Willy and Jerry exit in different directions with orders in their hands; Kenneth begins wrapping. Tom goes to his desk and sits, clasps his hands, and for a moment he prays.

Bert goes and gets his jacket. He slowly puts it on.

Enter Frank, the truckdriver.

FRANK: Anything for West Bronx, Tommy?

TOM: There's some stuff for Sullivan's there.

FRANK: Okay. *He pokes through the packages, picks some.*

KENNETH: Gus died.

FRANK: No kiddin'!

KENNETH: Ya, last night.

FRANK: What do you know. Hm. *He goes on picking packages out.* Is this all for West Bronx, Tom?

TOM: I guess so for now.

FRANK, *to Kenneth:* Died.

KENNETH: Yes, Jim was with him. Last night.

FRANK: Jesus. *Pause. He stares, shakes his head.* I'll take Brooklyn when I get back, Tommy. *He goes out, loaded with packages. Bert is buttoning his overcoat. Agnes comes out of the toilet.*

BERT: Agnes?

AGNES, *seeing the coat on, the book in his hand:* Oh, you're leaving, Bert!

BERT: Yeah.

AGNES: Well. You're leaving.

BERT, *expectantly:* Yeah.

Patricia enters.

PATRICIA: Agnes? Your switchboard's ringing.

Jerry enters with goods.

AGNES: Okay! *Patricia goes out.* Well, good luck. I hope you pass everything.

BERT: Thanks, Aggie. *She walks across and out, wiping a hair across her forehead. Willy enters with goods as Jerry goes out. Jim enters with goods. Bert seems about to say good-by to each of them, but they are engrossed and he doesn't quite want to start a scene with them; but now Jim is putting his goods on the table, so Bert goes over to him.* I'm leaving, Jim, so—uh—

JIM: Oh, leavin'? Heh! Well, that's—

TOM, *from his place at the desk, offering an order to Jim:* Jim? See if these transmissions came in yet, will ya? This guy's been ordering them all month.

JIM: Sure, Tom.

Jim goes out past Bert, studying his order. Bert glances at Kenneth, who is busy wrapping. He goes to Tom, who is working at the desk.

BERT: Well, so long, Tommy.

TOM, *turning:* Oh, you goin', heh?
BERT: Yeah, I'm leavin' right now.
TOM: Well, keep up the will power, y'know. That's what does it.
BERT: Yeah. I—uh—I wanted to—

Raymond enters.

RAYMOND, *handing Tom an order:* Tommy, make this a special, will you? The guy's truck broke down in Peekskill. Send it out special today.
TOM: Right.

Raymond turns to go out, sees Bert, who seems to expect some moment from him.

RAYMOND: Oh! 'By, Bert.
BERT: So long, Raymond, I— *Raymond is already on his way, and he is gone. Jim enters with goods. Bert goes over to Kenneth and touches his back. Kenneth turns to him. Jim goes out as Willy enters with goods—Jerry too, and this work goes on without halt.* Well, good-by, Kenny.
KENNETH—*he is embarrassed as he turns to Bert:* Well, it's our last look, I suppose, isn't it?
BERT: No, I'll come back sometime. I'll visit you.
KENNETH: Oh, not likely; it'll all be out of mind as soon as you turn the corner. I'll probably not be here anyway.
BERT: You made up your mind for Civil Service?
KENNETH: Well, you've got to keep movin', and—I'll move there, I guess. I done a shockin' thing last night, Bert; I knocked over a bar.
BERT: Knocked it over?
KENNETH: It's disgraceful, what I done. I'm standin' there, havin' a decent conversation, that's all, and before I know it I start rockin' the damned thing, and it toppled over and broke every glass in the place, and the beer spoutin' out of the pipes all over the floor. They took all me money; I'll be six weeks payin' them back. I'm for the Civil Service, I think; I'll get back to regular there, I think.
BERT: Well—good luck, Kenny. *Blushing:* I hope you'll remember the poems again.
KENNETH, *as though they were unimportant:* No, they're gone,

Bert. There's too much to do in this country for that kinda stuff.

Willy enters with goods.

TOM: Hey, Willy, get this right away; it's a special for Peekskill.
WILLY: Okay.

Willy takes the order and goes, and when Bert turns back to Kenneth he is wrapping again. So Bert moves away from the table. Jerry enters, leaves; and Jim enters, drops goods on the table, and leaves. Larry enters with a container of coffee, goes to the order hook, and checks through the orders. Bert goes to him.

BERT: I'm goin', Larry.
LARRY, *over his shoulder:* Take it easy, kid.

Patricia enters and crosses past Bert, looking out through the windows. Tom gets up and bumbles through a pile of goods on the table, checking against an order in his hand. It is as though Bert wished it could stop for a moment, and as each person enters he looks expectantly, but nothing much happens. And so he gradually moves—almost is *moved—toward an exit, and with his book in his hand he leaves.*

Now Kenneth turns and looks about, sees Bert is gone. He resumes his work and softly sings.

KENNETH: "The minstrel boy to the war has gone!" Tommy, I'll be needin' more crayon before the day is out.
TOM, *without turning from the desk:* I'll get some for you.
KENNETH, *looking at a crayon, peeling it down to a nub:* Oh, the damn mice. But they've got to live too, I suppose. *He marks a package and softly sings:*

"... in the ranks of death you will find him.
His father's sword he has girded on,
And his wild harp slung behind him."

CURTAIN

A VIEW FROM THE BRIDGE

A Play in One Act

CAST

LOUIS
MIKE
ALFIERI
EDDIE
CATHERINE
BEATRICE
MARCO
TONY
RODOLPHO
FIRST IMMIGRATION OFFICER
SECOND IMMIGRATION OFFICER
MR. LIPARI
MRS. LIPARI
TWO "SUBMARINES"

A VIEW FROM THE BRIDGE

A tenement house and the street before it.

Like the play, the set is stripped of everything but its essential elements. The main acting area is Eddie Carbone's living-dining room, furnished with a round table, a few chairs, a rocker, and a phonograph.

This room is slightly elevated from the stage floor and is shaped in a free form designed to contain the acting space required, and that is all. At its back is an opaque wall-like shape, around whose right and left sides respectively entrances are made to an unseen kitchen and bedrooms.

Downstage, still in this room, and to the left, are two columnar shapes ending in air, and indicating the house front and entrance. Suspended over the entire front is an architectural element indicating a pediment over the columns, as well as the facing of a tenement building. Through this entrance a stairway is seen, beginning at floor level of the living-dining room, then curving upstage and around the back to the second-floor landing overhead.

Downstage center is the street. At the right, against the proscenium are a desk and chair belonging to Mr. Alfieri, whose office this is, and a coat hook or rack. Near the office, but separated from it, is a low iron railing such as might form a barrier on a street to guard a basement stair. Later in the play a coin telephone will appear against the proscenium at the left.

The intention is to make concrete the ancient element of this tale through the unmitigated forms of the commonest life of the big-city present, the one playing against the other to form a new world on the stage.

As the curtain rises, Louis and Mike, longshoremen, are pitching coins against the building at left.

A distant foghorn blows.

Enter Alfieri, a lawyer in his fifties, turning gray, portly, good-humored, and thoughtful. The two pitchers nod to him as he passes; he crosses the stage to his desk and removes his hat and coat, hangs them, then turns to the audience.

ALFIERI: I am smiling because they nod so uneasily to me.
That's because I am a lawyer, and in this neighborhood a lawyer's like a priest—
They only think of us when disaster comes. So we're unlucky.

Good evening. Welcome to the theater.

My name is Alfieri. I'll come directly to the point, even though I am a lawyer. I am getting on. And I share the weakness of so many of my profession—I believe I have had some amazingly interesting cases.

When one is still young the more improbable vagaries of life only make one impatient. One looks for logic.

But when one is old, facts become precious; in facts I find all the poetry, all the wonder, all the amazement of spring. And spring is especially beautiful after fifty-five. I love what happened, instead of what might or ought to have happened.

My wife has warned me, so have my friends: they tell me the people in this neighborhood lack elegance, glamour. After all, who have I dealt with in my life? Longshoremen and their wives and fathers and grandfathers—compensation cases, evictions, family squabbles—the petty troubles of the poor—and yet . . .

When the tide is right,
And the wind blows the sea air against these houses,
I sit here in my office,
Thinking it is all so timeless here.
I think of Sicily, from where these people came,
The Roman rocks of Calabria,
Siracusa on the cliff, where Carthaginian and Greek
Fought such bloody fights. I think of Hannibal,
Who slew the fathers of these people; Caesar,
Whipping them on in Latin.

Which is all, of course, ridiculous.
Al Capone learned his trade on these pavements,
And Frankie Yale was cut in half
On the corner of Union Street and President,

Where so many were so justly shot,
By unjust men.

It's different now, of course.
I no longer keep a pistol in my filing cabinet;
We are quite American, quite civilized—
Now we settle for half. And I like it better.

And yet, when the tide is right,
And the green smell of the sea
Floats through my window,
I must look up at the circling pigeons of the poor,
And I see falcons there,
The hunting eagles of the olden time,
Fierce above Italian forests. . . .

This is Red Hook, a slum that faces the bay,
Seaward from Brooklyn Bridge.

Enter Eddie along the street. He joins the penny-pitchers.

Once in every few years there is a case,
And as the parties tell me what the trouble is,
I see cobwebs tearing, Adriatic ruins rebuilding themselves;
Calabria;
The eyes of the plaintiff seem suddenly carved,
His voice booming toward me over many fallen stones.

This one's name was Eddie Carbone,
A longshoreman working the docks
From Brooklyn Bridge to the breakwater. . . .

Eddie picks up pennies.

EDDIE: Well, I'll see ya, fellas.
LOUIS: You workin' tomorrow?
EDDIE: Yeah, there's another day yet on that ship. See ya, Louis. *Eddie goes into the house, climbs the stairs, as light rises in the apartment. Eddie is forty, a husky, slightly overweight longshoreman.*

Catherine, his niece, is discovered standing at the window of the apartment, waving down at Louis, who now sees her and

waves back up. She is seventeen and is now holding dishes in her hand, preparatory to laying out the dinner on the table.

Eddie enters, and she immediately proceeds to lay the table.

The lights go out on Alfieri and the street.

CATHERINE—*she has a suppressed excitement on her:* Hi, Eddie.
EDDIE, *with a trace of wryness:* What's the shoes for?
CATHERINE: I didn't go outside with them.
EDDIE, *removing his zipper jacket and hat:* Do me a favor, heh?
CATHERINE: Why can't I wear them in the house?
EDDIE: Take them off, will you please?
You're beautiful enough without the shoes.
CATHERINE: I'm only trying them out.
EDDIE: When I'm home I'm not in the movies,
I don't wanna see young girls
Walking around in spike-heel shoes.
CATHERINE: Oh, brother.

Enter Beatrice, Eddie's wife; she is his age.

BEATRICE: You find out anything?
EDDIE, *sitting in a rocker:* The ship came in. They probably get off anytime now.
BEATRICE, *softly clapping her hands together, half in prayer, half in joy:* Oh, boy. You find Tony?
EDDIE, *preoccupied:* Yeah, I talked to him. They're gonna let the crew off tonight. So they'll be here any time, he says.
CATHERINE: Boy, they must be shakin'.
EDDIE: Naa, they'll get off all right. They got regular seamen papers; they walk off with the crew. *To Beatrice:* I just hope they know where they're going to sleep, heh?
BEATRICE: I told them in the letter we got no room.
CATHERINE: You didn't meet them, though, heh? You didn't see them?
EDDIE: They're still on board. I only met Tony on the pier. What are you all hopped up about?
CATHERINE: I'm not hopped up.
BEATRICE, *in an ameliorative tone:* It's something new in the house, she's excited.

EDDIE, *to Catherine:* 'Cause they ain't comin' here for parties, they're only comin' here to work.

CATHERINE, *blushing, even enjoying his ribbing:* Who's lookin' for parties?

EDDIE: Why don't you wear them nice shoes you got? *He indicates her shoes.* Those are for an actress. Go ahead.

CATHERINE: Don't tell nothin' till I come back. *She hurries out, kicking off her shoes.*

EDDIE, *as Beatrice comes toward him:* Why do you let her wear stuff like that? That ain't her type. *Beatrice bends and kisses his cheek.* What's that for?

BEATRICE: For bein' so nice about it.

EDDIE: As long as they know we got nothin', B.; that's all I'm worried about.

BEATRICE: They're gonna pay for everything; I told them in the letter.

EDDIE: Because this ain't gonna end up with you on the floor, like when your mother's house burned down.

BEATRICE: Eddie, I told them in the letter we got no room.

CATHERINE *enters in low-heeled shoes.*

EDDIE: Because as soon as you see a relative I turn around you're on the floor.

BEATRICE, *half amused, half serious:* All right, stop it already. You want a beer? The sauce is gotta cook a little more.

EDDIE, *to Beatrice:* No, it's too cold. *To Catherine:* You do your lessons today, Garbo?

CATHERINE: Yeah; I'm way ahead anyway. I just gotta practice from now on.

BEATRICE: She could take it down almost as fast as you could talk already. She's terrific. Read something to her later, you'll be surprised.

EDDIE: That's the way, Katie. You're gonna be all right, kid, you'll see.

CATHERINE, *proudly:* I could get a job right now, Eddie. I'm not even afraid.

EDDIE: You got time. Wait'll you're eighteen. We'll look up the ads—find a nice company, or maybe a lawyer's office or somethin' like that.

CATHERINE: Oh, boy! I could go to work now, my teacher said.

EDDIE: Be eighteen first. I want you to have a little more head on your shoulders. You're still dizzy yet. *To Beatrice:* Where's the kids? They still outside?

BEATRICE: I put them with my mother for tonight. They'd never go to sleep otherwise. So what kinda cargo you have today?

EDDIE: Coffee. It was nice.

BEATRICE: I thought all day I smelled coffee here!

EDDIE: Yeah, Brazil. That's one time, boy, to be a longshoreman is a pleasure. The whole ship smelled from coffee. It was like flowers. We'll bust a bag tomorrow; I'll bring you some. Well, let's eat, heh?

BEATRICE: Two minutes. I want the sauce to cook a little more.

Eddie goes to a bowl of grapes.

CATHERINE: How come he's not married, Beatrice, if he's so old? The younger one.

BEATRICE, *to Eddie:* Twenty-five is old!

EDDIE, *to Catherine:* Is that all you got on your mind?

CATHERINE, *wryly:* What else should I have on my mind?

EDDIE: There's plenty a things.

CATHERINE: Like what?

EDDIE: What the hell are you askin' me? I shoulda been struck by lightning when I promised your mother I would take care of you.

CATHERINE: You and me both.

EDDIE, *laughing:* Boy, God bless you, you got a tongue in your mouth like the Devil's wife. You oughta be on the television.

CATHERINE: Oh, I wish!

EDDIE: You wish! You'd be scared to death.

CATHERINE: Yeah? Try me.

EDDIE: Listen, by the way, Garbo, what'd I tell you about wavin' from the window?

CATHERINE: I was wavin' to Louis!

EDDIE: Listen, I could tell you things about Louis which you wouldn't wave to him no more.

CATHERINE, *to Beatrice, who is grinning:* Boy, I wish I could find one guy that he couldn't tell me things about!

EDDIE, *going to her, cupping her cheek:* Now look, Catherine, don't joke with me.
I'm responsible for you, kid.
I promised your mother on her deathbed.
So don't joke with me. I mean it.
I don't like the sound of them high heels on the sidewalk,
I don't like that clack, clack, clack,
I don't like the looks they're givin' you.

BEATRICE: How can she help it if they look at her?

EDDIE: She don't walk right. *To Catherine:* Don't walk so wavy like that.

Beatrice goes out into the kitchen.

CATHERINE: Who's walkin' wavy?

EDDIE: Now don't aggravate me, Katie, you are walkin' wavy!

CATHERINE: Those guys look at all the girls, you know that.

EDDIE: They got mothers and fathers. You gotta be more careful.

Beatrice enters with a tureen.

CATHERINE: Oh, Jesus! *She goes out into the kitchen.*

EDDIE, *calling after her:* Hey, lay off the language, heh?

BEATRICE, *alone with him, loading the plates—she is riding lightly over a slightly sore issue:* What do you want from her all the time?

EDDIE: Boy, she grew up! Your sister should see her now. I'm tellin' you, it's like a miracle—one day she's a baby; you turn around and she's— *Enter Catherine with knives and forks.* Y'know? When she sets a table she looks like a Madonna. *Beatrice wipes a strand of hair off Catherine's face. To Catherine:* You're the Madonna type. That's why you shouldn't be flashy, Kate. For you it ain't beautiful. You're more the Madonna type. And anyway, it ain't nice in an office. They don't go for that in an office. *He sits at the table.*

BEATRICE, *sitting to eat:* Sit down, Katie-baby. *Catherine sits. They eat.*

EDDIE: Geez, how quiet it is here without the kids!

CATHERINE: What happens? How they gonna find the house here?

EDDIE: Tony'll take them from the ship and bring them here.

BEATRICE: That Tony must be makin' a nice dollar off this.

EDDIE: Naa, the syndicate's takin' the heavy cream.

CATHERINE: What happens when the ship pulls out and they ain't on it, though?

EDDIE: Don't worry; captain's pieced-off.

CATHERINE: Even the captain?

EDDIE: Why, the captain don't have to live? Captain gets a piece, maybe one of the mates, a piece for the guy in Italy who fixed the papers for them— *To Beatrice:* They're gonna have to work six months for that syndicate before they keep a dime for theirselfs; they know that, I hope.

BEATRICE: Yeah, but Tony'll fix jobs for them, won't he?

EDDIE: Sure, as long as they owe him money he'll fix jobs; it's after the pay-off—they're gonna have to scramble like the rest of us. I just hope they know that.

BEATRICE: Oh, they must know. Boy, they must've been starvin' there. To go through all this just to make a couple a dollars. I'm tellin' ya, it could make you cry.

EDDIE: By the way, what are you going to tell the people in the house? If somebody asks what they're doin' here?

BEATRICE: Well, I'll tell 'em— Well, who's gonna ask? They probably know anyway.

EDDIE: What do you mean, they know? Listen, Beatrice, the Immigration Bureau's got stool pigeons all over the neighborhood.

BEATRICE: Yeah, but not in this house—?

EDDIE: How do you know, not in this house? Listen, both a yiz. If anybody asks you, they're your cousins visitin' here from Philadelphia.

CATHERINE: Yeah, but what would they know about Philadelphia? I mean if somebody asks them—

EDDIE: Well—they don't talk much, that's all. But don't get confidential with nobody, you hear me? Because there's a lotta guys do anything for a couple a dollars, and the Immigration pays good for that kinda news.

CATHERINE: I could teach them about Philadelphia.

EDDIE: Do me a favor, baby, will ya? Don't teach them, and don't mix in with them. Because with that blabbermouth the less you know the better off we're all gonna be. They're gonna work, and they're gonna come home here and go to

sleep, and I don't want you payin' no attention to them. This is a serious business; this is the United States Government. So you don't know they're alive. I mean don't get dizzy with your friends about it. It's nobody's business. *Slight pause.* Where's the salt?

Pause.

CATHERINE: It's gettin' dark.
EDDIE: Yeah, gonna snow tomorrow, I think.

Pause.

BEATRICE—*she is frightened:* Geez, remember that Vinny Bolzano years ago? Remember him?
EDDIE: That funny? I was just thinkin' about him before.
CATHERINE: Who's he?
BEATRICE: You were a baby then. But there was a kid, Vinny, about sixteen. Lived over there on Sackett Street. And he snitched on somebody to the Immigration. He had five brothers, and the old man. And they grabbed him in the kitchen, and they pulled him down three flights, his head was bouncin' like a coconut—we lived in the next house. And they spit on him in the street, his own father and his brothers. It was so terrible.
CATHERINE: So what happened to him?
BEATRICE: He went away, I think. *To Eddie:* Did you ever see him again?
EDDIE: Him? Naa, you'll never see him no more. A guy do a thing like that—how could he show his face again? There's too much salt in here.
BEATRICE: So what'd you put salt for?

Eddie lays the spoon down, leaves the table.

EDDIE: Geez, I'm gettin' nervous, y'know?
BEATRICE: What's the difference; they'll only sleep here; you won't hardly see them. Go ahead, eat. *He looks at her, disturbed.* What could I do? They're my cousins. *He returns to her and clasps her face admiringly as the lights fade on them and rise on Alfieri.*
ALFIERI: I only know that they had two children;
He was as good a man as he had to be

In a life that was hard and even.
He worked on the piers when there was work,
He brought home his pay, and he lived.
And toward ten o'clock of that night,
After they had eaten, the cousins came.

While he is speaking Eddie goes to the window and looks out. Catherine and Beatrice clear the dishes. Eddie sits down and reads the paper.

Enter Tony, escorting Marco and Rodolpho, each with a valise. Tony halts, indicates the house. They stand for a moment, looking at it.

MARCO—*he is a square-built peasant of thirty-two, suspicious and quiet-voiced:* Thank you.
TONY: You're on your own now. Just be careful, that's all. Ground floor.
MARCO: Thank you.
TONY: I'll see you on the pier tomorrow. You'll go to work.

Marco nods. Tony continues on, walking down the street.

Rodolpho is in his early twenties, an eager boy, one moment a gamin, the next a brooding adult. His hair is startlingly blond.

RODOLPHO: This will be the first house I ever walked into in America!
MARCO: Sssh! Come. *They mount the stoop.*
RODOLPHO: Imagine! She said they were poor!
MARCO: Ssh!

They pass between the columns. Light rises inside the apartment. Eddie, Catherine, Beatrice hear and raise their heads toward the door. Marco knocks. Beatrice and Catherine look to Eddie, who rises and goes and opens the door. Enter Marco and Rodolpho, removing their caps.

EDDIE: You Marco?

Marco nods, looks to the women, and fixes on Beatrice.

MARCO: Are you my cousin?
BEATRICE, *touching her chest with her hand:* Beatrice. This is

my husband, Eddie. *All nod.* Catherine, my sister Nancy's daughter. *The brothers nod.*

MARCO, *indicating Rodolpho:* My brother. Rodolpho. *Rodolpho nods. Marco comes with a certain formal stiffness to Eddie.* I want to tell you now, Eddie—when you say go, we will go.

EDDIE: Oh, no—

MARCO: I see it's a small house, but soon, maybe, we can have our own house.

EDDIE: You're welcome, Marco, we got plenty of room here. Katie, give them supper, heh?

CATHERINE: Come here, sit down. I'll get you some soup.

They go to the table.

MARCO: We ate on the ship. Thank you. *To Eddie:* Thank you.

BEATRICE: Get some coffee. We'll all have coffee. Come sit down.

CATHERINE: How come he's so dark and you're so light, Rodolpho?

RODOLPHO: I don't know. A thousand years ago, they say, the Danes invaded Sicily. *He laughs.*

CATHERINE, *to Beatrice:* He's practically blond!

EDDIE: How's the coffee doin'?

CATHERINE, *brought up short:* I'm gettin' it. *She hurries out.*

EDDIE: Yiz have a nice trip?

MARCO: The ocean is always rough in the winter. But we are good sailors.

EDDIE: No trouble gettin' here?

MARCO: No. The man brought us. Very nice man.

RODOLPHO: He says we start to work tomorrow. Is he honest?

EDDIE: No. But as long as you owe them money they'll get you plenty of work. *To Marco:* Yiz ever work on the piers in Italy?

MARCO: Piers? Ts! No.

RODOLPHO, *smiling at the smallness of his town:* In our town there are no piers,
Only the beach, and little fishing boats.

BEATRICE: So what kinda work did yiz do?

MARCO: *shrugging shyly, even embarrassed:* Whatever there is, anything.

RODOLPHO: Sometimes they build a house,

Or if they fix the bridge—
Marco is a mason,
And I bring him the cement.

He laughs.

In harvest time we work in the fields—
If there is work. Anything.
EDDIE: Still bad there, heh?
MARCO: Bad, yes.
RODOLPHO: It's terrible.
We stand around all day in the piazza,
Listening to the fountain like birds.

He laughs.

Everybody waits only for the train.
BEATRICE: What's on the train?
RODOLPHO: Nothing. But if there are many passengers
And you're lucky you make a few lire
To push the taxi up the hill.

Enter Catherine, who sits, listens.

BEATRICE: You gotta push a taxi?
RODOLPHO, *with a laugh:* Oh, sure! It's a feature in our town.
The horses in our town are skinnier than goats.
So if there are too many passengers
We help to push the carriages up to the hotel.

He laughs again.

In our town the horses are only for the show.
CATHERINE: Why don't they have automobile taxis?
RODOLPHO: There is one—we push that too.

They laugh.

Everything in our town, you gotta push.
BEATRICE, *to Eddie, sorrowfully:* How do you like that—
EDDIE, *to Marco:* So what're you wanna do, you gonna stay here in this country or you wanna go back?
MARCO, *surprised:* Go back?
EDDIE: Well, you're married, ain't you?
MARCO: Yes. I have three children.

BEATRICE: Three! I thought only one.

MARCO: Oh, no. I have three now.
Four years, five years, six years.

BEATRICE: Ah, I bet they're cryin' for you already, heh?

MARCO: What can I do?
The older one is sick in his chest;
My wife—she feeds them from her own mouth.
I tell you the truth,
If I stay there they will never grow up.
They eat the sunshine.

BEATRICE: My God. So how long you want to stay?

MARCO: With your permission, we will stay maybe a—

EDDIE: She don't mean in this house, she means in the country.

MARCO: Oh. Maybe four, five, six years, I think.

RODOLPHO, *smiling:* He trusts his wife.

BEATRICE: Yeah, but maybe you'll get enough,
You'll be able to go back quicker.

MARCO: I hope. I don't know. *To Eddie:* I understand it's not so good here either.

EDDIE: Oh, you guys'll be all right—till you pay them off, anyway. After that, you'll have to scramble, that's all. But you'll make better here than you could there.

RODOLPHO: How much? We hear all kinds of figures.
How much can a man make? We work hard,
We'll work all day, all night . . .

EDDIE—*he is coming more and more to address Marco only:* On the average a whole year? Maybe—well, it's hard to say, see. Sometimes we lay off, there's no ships three-four weeks.

MARCO: Three, four weeks! Ts!

EDDIE: But I think you could probably— Thirty, forty a week over the whole twelve months of the year.

MARCO: Dollars.

EDDIE: Sure dollars.

MARCO, *looking happily at Rodolpho:* If we can stay here a few months, Beatrice—

BEATRICE: Listen, you're welcome, Marco—

MARCO: Because I could send them a little more if I stay here—

BEATRICE: As long as you want; we got plenty a room—

MARCO, *his eyes showing tears:* My wife—my wife . . .
I want to send right away maybe twenty dollars.
EDDIE: You could send them something next week already.
MARCO, *near tears:* Eduardo—
EDDIE: Don't thank me. Listen, what the hell, it's no skin off me. *To Catherine:* What happened to the coffee?
CATHERINE: I got it on. *To Rodolpho:* You married too? No.
RODOLPHO: Oh, no.
BEATRICE: I told you he—
CATHERINE, *to her:* I know, I just thought maybe he got married recently.
RODOLPHO: I have no money to get married.
I have a nice face, but no money. *He laughs.*
CATHERINE, *to Beatrice:* He's a real blond!
BEATRICE, *to Rodolpho:* You want to stay here too, heh? For good?
RODOLPHO: Me? Yes, forever! Me,
I want to be an American.
And then I want to go back to Italy
When I am rich. And I will buy a motorcycle. *He smiles.*
CATHERINE: A motorcycle!
RODOLPHO: With a motorcycle in Italy you will never starve any more.
BEATRICE: I'll get you coffee. *She exits.*
EDDIE: What're you do with a motorcycle?
MARCO: He dreams, he dreams.
RODOLPHO: Why? Messages! The rich people in the hotel
Always need someone who will carry a message.
But quickly, and with a great noise.
With a blue motorcycle I would station myself
In the courtyard of the hotel,
And in a little while I would have messages.
MARCO: When you have no wife you have dreams.
EDDIE: Why can't you just walk, or take a trolley or sump'm?

Enter Beatrice with coffee.

RODOLPHO: Oh, no, the machine, the machine is necessary.
A man comes into a great hotel and says,
"I am a messenger." Who is this man?
He disappears walking, there is no noise, nothing—

Maybe he will never come back,
Maybe he will never deliver the message.
But a man who rides up on a great machine,
This man is responsible, this man exists.
He will be given messages.
I am also a singer, though.

EDDIE: You mean a regular—?

RODOLPHO: Oh, yes. One night last year
Andreola got sick. Baritone.
And I took his place in the garden of the hotel.
Three arias I sang without a mistake;
Thousand-lire notes they threw from the tables,
Money was falling like a storm in the treasury;
It was magnificent.
We lived six months on that night, eh, Marco?

Marco nods doubtfully.

MARCO: Two months.

BEATRICE: Can't you get a job in that place?

RODOLPHO: Andreola got better.
He's a baritone, very strong; otherwise I—

MARCO, *to Beatrice:* He sang too loud.

RODOLPHO: Why too loud!

MARCO: Too loud. The guests in that hotel are all Englishmen. They don't like too loud.

RODOLPHO: Then why did they throw so much money?

MARCO: They pay for your courage. *To Eddie:* The English like courage, but once is enough.

RODOLPHO, *to all but Marco:* I never heard anybody say it was too loud.

CATHERINE: Did you ever hear of jazz?

RODOLPHO: Oh, sure! I sing jazz.

CATHERINE: You could sing jazz?

RODOLPHO: Oh, I sing Napolidan, jazz, bel canto—
I sing "Paper Doll"; you like "Paper Doll"?

CATHERINE: Oh, sure, I'm crazy for "Paper Doll." Go ahead, sing it.

RODOLPHO—*he takes his stance, and with a high tenor voice:*
"I'll tell you boys it's tough to be alone,
And it's tough to love a doll that's not your own.

I'm through with all of them,
I'll never fall again,
Hey, boy, what you gonna do—

I'm goin' to buy a paper doll that I can call my own,
A doll that other fellows cannot steal,
And then the flirty, flirty guys
With their flirty, flirty eyes
Will have to flirt with dollies that are real.
When I come home at night she will be waiting.
She'll be the truest doll in all this world—"

EDDIE—*he has been slowly moving in agitation:* Hey, kid—hey, wait a minute—

CATHERINE, *enthralled:* Leave him finish. It's beautiful! *To Beatrice:* He's terrific! It's terrific, Rodolpho!

EDDIE: Look, kid; you don't want to be picked up, do ya?

MARCO: No-no!

EDDIE, *indicating the rest of the building:* Because we never had no singers here—and all of a sudden there's a singer in the house, y'know what I mean?

MARCO: Yes, yes. You will be quiet, Rodolpho.

EDDIE, *flushed:* They got guys all over the place, Marco. I mean.

MARCO: Yes. He will be quiet. *To Rodolpho:* Quiet.

EDDIE, *with iron control, even a smile:* You got the shoes again, Garbo?

CATHERINE: I figured for tonight—

EDDIE: Do me a favor, will you? *He indicates the bedroom.* Go ahead.

Embarrassed now, angered, Catherine goes out into the bedroom. Beatrice watches her go and gets up, and, in passing, gives Eddie a cold look, restrained only by the strangers, and goes to the table to pour coffee.

EDDIE, *to Marco, but directed as much to Beatrice:* All actresses they want to be around here. *He goes to draw a shade down.*

RODOLPHO, *happy about it:* In Italy too! All the girls.

EDDIE, *sizing up Rodolpho—there is a concealed suspicion:* Yeah, heh?

RODOLPHO: Yes! *He laughs, indicating Catherine with his head—her bedroom.* Especially when they are so beautiful!

Catherine emerges from the bedroom in low-heeled shoes, comes to the table. Rodolpho is lifting a cup.

CATHERINE: You like sugar?
RODOLPHO: Sugar? Yes! I like sugar very much!

Eddie is downstage, watching, as she pours a spoonful of sugar into Rodolpho's cup. Eddie turns and draws a shade, his face puffed with trouble, and the room dies. Light rises on Alfieri.

ALFIERI: Who can ever know what will be discovered?

Sunlight rises on the street and house.

Eddie Carbone had never expected to have a destiny.

Eddie comes slowly, ambling, down the stairs into the street.

A man works, raises his family, goes bowling,
Eats, gets old, and then he dies.
Now, as the weeks passed, there was a future,
There was a trouble that would not go away.

Beatrice appears with a shopping bag. Seeing her, Eddie meets her at the stoop.

EDDIE: It's after four.
BEATRICE: Well, it's a long show at the Paramount.
EDDIE: They must've seen every picture in Brooklyn by now. He's supposed to stay in the house when he ain't workin'. He ain't supposed to go advertising himself.
BEATRICE: So what am I gonna do?
EDDIE: Last night they went to the park. You know that? Louis seen them in the park.
BEATRICE: She's goin' on eighteen, what's so terrible?
EDDIE: I'm responsible for her.
BEATRICE: I just wish once in a while you'd be responsible for me, you know that?
EDDIE: What're you beefin'?
BEATRICE: You don't know why I'm beefin'? *He turns away, making as though to scan the street, his jaws clamped.* What's eatin' you? You're gonna bust your teeth, you grind them so much in bed, you know that? It's like a factory all night. *He doesn't answer, looks peeved.* What's the matter, Eddie?
EDDIE: It's all right with you? You don't mind this?

BEATRICE: Well what you want, keep her in the house a little baby all her life? What do you want, Eddie?

EDDIE: That's what I brung her up for? For that character?

BEATRICE: Why? He's a nice fella. Hard-workin', he's a good-lookin' fella—

EDDIE: That's good-lookin'?

BEATRICE: He's handsome, for God's sake.

EDDIE: He gives me the heeby-jeebies. I don't like his whole way.

BEATRICE, *smiling:* You're jealous, that's all.

EDDIE: Of *him*? Boy, you don't think much of me.

BEATRICE, *going to him:* What are you worried about? She knows how to take care of herself.

EDDIE: She don't know nothin'. He's got her rollin'; you see the way she looks at him? The house could burn down she wouldn't know.

BEATRICE: Well, she's got a boy-friend finally, so she's excited. So?

EDDIE: He sings on the ships, didja know that?

BEATRICE, *mystified:* What do you mean, he sings?

EDDIE: He sings. Right on the deck, all of a sudden—a whole song. They're callin' him Paper Doll, now. Canary. He's like a weird. Soon as he comes onto the pier it's a regular free show.

BEATRICE: Well, he's a kid; he don't know how to behave himself yet.

EDDIE: And with that wacky hair; he's like a chorus girl or sump'm.

BEATRICE: So he's blond, so—

EDDIE, *not looking at her:* I just hope that's his regular hair, that's all I hope.

BEATRICE, *alarmed:* You crazy or sump'm?

EDDIE, *only glancing at her:* What's so crazy? You know what I heard them call him on Friday? I was on line for my check, somebody calls out, "Blondie!" I turn around, they're callin' *him!* Blondie now!

BEATRICE: You never seen a blond guy in your life? What about Whitey Balso?

EDDIE: Sure, but Whitey don't sing; he don't do like that on the ships—

BEATRICE: Well, maybe that's the way they do in Italy.

EDDIE: Then why don't his brother sing? Marco goes around like a man; nobody kids Marco. *He shifts, with a glance at her.* I don't like him, B. And I'm tellin' you now, I'm not gonna stand for it. For that character I didn't bring her up.

BEATRICE: All right—well, go tell her, then.

EDDIE: How am I gonna tell her? She won't listen to me, she can't even see me. I come home, she's in a dream. Look how thin she got, she could walk through a wall—

BEATRICE: All right, listen—

EDDIE: It's eatin' me out, B. I can't stand to look at his face. And what happened to the stenography? She don't practice no more, does she?

BEATRICE: All right, listen. I want you to lay off, you hear me? Don't work yourself up. You hear? This is her business.

EDDIE: B., he's takin' her for a ride!

BEATRICE: All right, that's her ride. It's time already; let her be somebody else's Madonna now. Come on, come in the house, you got your own to worry about. *She glances around.* She ain't gonna come any quicker if you stand on the street, Eddie. It ain't nice.

EDDIE: I'll be up right away. I want to take a walk. *He walks away.*

BEATRICE: Come on, look at the kids for once.

EDDIE: I'll be up right away. Go ahead.

BEATRICE, *with a shielded tone:* Don't stand around, please. It ain't nice. I mean it.

She goes into the house. He reaches the upstage right extremity, stares at nothing for a moment; then, seeing someone coming, he goes to the railing downstage and sits, as Louis and Mike enter and join him.

LOUIS: Wanna go bowlin' tonight?

EDDIE: I'm too tired. Goin' to sleep.

LOUIS: How's your two submarines?

EDDIE: They're okay.

LOUIS: I see they're gettin' work allatime.

EDDIE: Oh yeah, they're doin' all right.

MIKE: That's what we oughta do. We oughta leave the country and come in under the water. Then we get work.

EDDIE: You ain't kiddin'.

LOUIS: Well, what the hell. Y'know?

EDDIE: Sure.

LOUIS: Believe me, Eddie, you got a lotta credit comin' to you.

EDDIE: Aah, they don't bother me, don't cost me nutt'n.

MIKE: That older one, boy, he's a regular bull. I seen him the other day liftin' coffee bags over the Matson Line. They leave him alone he woulda load the whole ship by himself.

EDDIE: Yeah, he's a strong guy, that guy. My Frankie takes after him, I think. Their father was a regular giant, supposed to be.

LOUIS: Yeah, you could see. He's a regular slave.

MIKE: That blond one, though—*Eddie looks at him.* He's got a sense a humor.

EDDIE, *searchingly:* Yeah. He's funny—

MIKE, *laughing through his speech:* Well, he ain't ezackly funny, but he's always like makin' remarks, like, y'know? He comes around, everybody's laughin'.

EDDIE, *uncomfortably:* Yeah, well—he's got a sense a humor.

MIKE: Yeah, I mean, he's always makin' like remarks, like, y'know? *Louis is quietly laughing with him.*

EDDIE: Yeah, I know. But he's a kid yet, y'know? He—he's just a kid, that's all.

MIKE: I know. You take one look at him—everybody's happy. I worked one day with him last week over the Moore-MacCormack, I'm tellin' you they was all hysterical.

EDDIE: Why? What'd he do?

MIKE: I don't know—he was just humorous. You never can remember what he says, y'know? But it's the way he says it. I mean he gives you a look sometimes and you start laughin'!

EDDIE: Yeah. *Troubled:* He's got a sense a humor.

MIKE, *laughing:* Yeah.

LOUIS: Well, well see ya, Eddie.

EDDIE: Take it easy.

LOUIS: Yeah. See ya.

MIKE: If you wanna come bowlin' later we're goin' Flatbush Avenue.

They go. Eddie, in troubled thought, stares after them; they arrive at the left extremity, and their laughter, untroubled and

friendly, rises as they see Rodolpho, who is entering with Catherine on his arm. The longshoremen exit. Rodolpho waves a greeting to them.

CATHERINE: Hey, Eddie, what a picture we saw! Did we laugh!
EDDIE—*he can't help smiling at sight of her:* Where'd you go?
CATHERINE: Paramount. It was with those two guys, y'know? That—
EDDIE: Brooklyn Paramount?
CATHERINE, *with an edge of anger, embarrassed before Rodolpho:* Sure the Brooklyn Paramount. I told you we wasn't goin' to New York.
EDDIE, *retreating before the threat of her anger:* All right, I only asked you. *To Rodolpho:* I just don't want her hangin' around Times Square, see; it's full of tramps over there.
RODOLPHO: I would like to go to Broadway once, Eddie.
I would like to walk with her once
Where the theaters are, and the opera;
Since I was a boy I see pictures of those lights—
EDDIE, *his little patience waning:* I want to talk to her a minute, Rodolpho; go upstairs, will you?
RODOLPHO: Eddie, we only walk together in the streets,
She teaches me—
CATHERINE: You know what he can't get over?
That there's no fountains in Brooklyn!
EDDIE, *smiling unwillingly, to Rodolpho:* Fountains?

Rodolpho smiles at his own naïveté.

CATHERINE: In Italy, he says, every town's got fountains,
And they meet there. And you know what?
They got oranges on the trees where he comes from,
And lemons. Imagine? On the trees?
I mean it's interesting. But he's crazy for New York!
RODOLPHO, *attempting familiarity:* Eddie, why can't we go once to Broadway?
EDDIE: Look, I gotta tell her something—

Rodolpho nods, goes to the stoop.

RODOLPHO: Maybe you can come too.
I want to see all those lights . . .

He sees no response in Eddie's face. He glances at Catherine and goes into the house.

CATHERINE: Why don't you talk to him, Eddie? He blesses you, and you don't talk to him hardly.

EDDIE, *enveloping her with his eyes:* I bless you, and you don't talk to me. *He tries to smile.*

CATHERINE: *I* don't talk to you? *She hits his arm.* What do you mean!

EDDIE: I don't see you no more. I come home you're runnin' around someplace—

Catherine takes his arm, and they walk a little.

CATHERINE: Well, he wants to see everything, that's all, so we go. You mad at me?

EDDIE: No. *He is smiling sadly, almost moony.* It's just I used to come home, you was always there. Now, I turn around, you're a big girl. I don't know how to talk to you.

CATHERINE: Why!

EDDIE: I don't know, you're runnin', you're runnin', Katie. I don't think you listening any more to me.

CATHERINE: Ah, Eddie, sure I am. What's the matter? You don't like him?

Slight pause.

EDDIE: *You* like him, Katie?

CATHERINE, *with a blush, but holding her ground:* Yeah. I like him.

EDDIE—*his smile goes:* You like him.

CATHERINE, *looking down:* Yeah. *Now she looks at him for the consequences, smiling but tense. He looks at her like a lost boy.* What're you got against him? I don't understand. He only blesses you.

EDDIE: He don't bless me, Katie.

CATHERINE: He does! You're like a father to him!

EDDIE: Katie.

CATHERINE: What, Eddie?

EDDIE: You gonna marry him?

CATHERINE: I don't know. We just been—goin' around, that's all.

EDDIE: He don't respect you, Katie.

CATHERINE: Why!

EDDIE: Katie, if you wasn't an orphan, wouldn't he ask your father permission before he run around with you like this?

CATHERINE: Oh, well, he didn't think you'd mind.

EDDIE: He knows I mind, but it don't bother him if I mind, don't you see that?

CATHERINE: No, Eddie, he's got all kinds of respect for me. And you too! We walk across the street, he takes my arm—he almost bows to me! You got him all wrong, Eddie; I mean it, you—

EDDIE: Katie, he's only bowin' to his passport.

CATHERINE: His passport!

EDDIE: That's right. He marries you he's got the right to be an American citizen. That's what's goin' on here. *She is puzzled and surprised.* You understand what I'm tellin' you? The guy is lookin' for his break, that's all he's lookin' for.

CATHERINE, *pained:* Oh, no, Eddie, I don't think so.

EDDIE: You don't think so! Katie, you're gonna make me cry here. Is that a workin' man? What does he do with his first money? A snappy new jacket he buys, records, a pointy pair new shoes, and his brother's kids are starvin' with tuberculosis over there? That's a hit-and-run guy, baby; he's got bright lights in his head, Broadway—them guys don't think of nobody but theirself! You marry him and the next time you see him it'll be for the divorce!

CATHERINE: Eddie, he never said a word about his papers or—

EDDIE: You mean he's supposed to tell you that?

CATHERINE: I don't think he's even thinking about it.

EDDIE: What's better for him to think about? He could be picked up any day here and he's back pushin' taxis up the hill!

CATHERINE: No, I don't believe it.

EDDIE, *grabbing her hand:* Katie, don't break my heart, listen to me—

CATHERINE: I don't want to hear it. Lemme go.

EDDIE, *holding her:* Katie, listen—

CATHERINE: He loves me!

EDDIE, *with deep alarm:* Don't say that, for God's sake! This is the oldest racket in the country.

CATHERINE, *desperately, as though he had made his imprint:* I don't believe it!

EDDIE: They been pullin' this since the immigration law was put in! They grab a green kid that don't know nothin' and they—

CATHERINE: I don't believe it and I wish to hell you'd stop it!

She rushes, sobbing, into the house.

EDDIE: Katie!

He starts in after her, but halts as though realizing he has no force over her. From within, music is heard now, radio jazz. He glances up and down the street, then moves off, his chest beginning to rise and fall in anger.

Light rises on Alfieri, seated behind his desk.

ALFIERI: It was at this time that he first came to me.
I had represented his father in an accident case some years before,
And I was acquainted with the family in a casual way.
I remember him now as he walked through my doorway—
His eyes were like tunnels;
My first thought was that he had committed a crime,

Eddie enters, sits beside the desk, cap in hand, looking out.

But soon I saw it was only a passion
That had moved into his body, like a stranger.

Alfieri pauses, looks down at his desk, then to Eddie, as though he were continuing a conversation with him.

I don't quite understand what I can do for you. Is there a question of law somewhere?

EDDIE: That's what I want to ask you.

ALFIERI: Because there's nothing illegal about a girl falling in love with an immigrant.

EDDIE: Yeah, but what about if the only reason for it is to get his papers?

ALFIERI: First of all, you don't know that—

EDDIE: I see it in his eyes; he's laughin' at her and he's laughin' at me.

ALFIERI: Eddie, I'm a lawyer; I can only deal in what's provable. You understand that, don't you? Can you prove that?

EDDIE: I know what's in his mind, Mr. Alfieri!

ALFIERI: Eddie, even if you could prove that—

EDDIE: Listen—Will you listen to me a minute? My father always said you was a smart man. I want you to listen to me.

ALFIERI: I'm only a lawyer, Eddie—

EDDIE: Will you listen a minute? I'm talkin' about the law. Lemme just bring out what I mean. A man, which he comes into the country illegal, don't it stand to reason he's gonna take every penny and put it in the sock? Because they don't know from one day to the nother, right?

ALFIERI: All right.

EDDIE: He's spendin'. Records he buys now. Shoes. Jackets. Y'understand me? This guy ain't worried. This guy is *here*. So it must be that he's got it all laid out in his mind already —he's stayin'. Right?

ALFIERI: Well? What about it?

EDDIE: All right. *He glances over his shoulder as though for intruders, then back to Alfieri, then down to the floor.* I'm talkin' to you confidential, ain't I?

ALFIERI: Certainly.

EDDIE: I mean it don't go no place but here. Because I don't like to say this about anybody. Even to my wife I didn't exactly say this.

ALFIERI: What is it?

EDDIE—*he takes a breath:* The guy ain't right, Mr. Alfieri.

ALFIERI: What do you mean?

EDDIE, *glancing over his shoulder again:* I mean he ain't right.

ALFIERI: I don't get you.

EDDIE—*he shifts to another position in the chair:* Dja ever get a look at him?

ALFIERI: Not that I know of, no.

EDDIE: He's a blond guy. Like—platinum. You know what I mean?

ALFIERI: No.

EDDIE: I mean if you close the paper fast—you could blow him over.

ALFIERI: Well, that doesn't mean—

EDDIE: Wait a minute, I'm tellin' you sump'm. He sings, see. Which is—I mean it's all right, but sometimes he hits a note, see. I turn around. I mean—high. You know what I mean?

ALFIERI: Well, that's a tenor.

EDDIE: I know a tenor, Mr. Alfieri. This ain't no tenor. I mean if you came in the house and you didn't know who was singin', you wouldn't be lookin' for him, you'd be lookin' for her.

ALFIERI: Yes, but that's not—

EDDIE: I'm tellin' you sump'm, wait a minute; please, Mr. Alfieri. I'm tryin' to bring out my thoughts here. Couple a nights ago my niece brings out a dress, which it's too small for her, because she shot up like a light this last year. He takes the dress, lays it on the table, he cuts it up; one-two-three, he makes a new dress. I mean he looked so sweet there, like an angel—you could kiss him he was so sweet.

ALFIERI: Now look, Eddie—

EDDIE: Mr. Alfieri, they're laughin' at him on the piers. I'm ashamed. Paper Doll, they call him. Blondie now. His brother thinks it's because he's got a sense a humor, see—which he's got—but that ain't what they're laughin'. Which they're not goin' to come out with it because they know he's my relative, which they have to see me if they make a crack, y'know? But I know what they're laughin' at, and when I think of that guy layin' his hands on her I could—I mean it's eatin' me out, Mr. Alfieri, because I struggled for that girl. And now he comes in my house—

ALFIERI: Eddie, look. I have my own children, I understand you. But the law is very specific. The law does not—

EDDIE, *with a fuller flow of indignation:* You mean to tell me that there's no law that a guy which he ain't right can go to work and marry a girl and—?

ALFIERI: You have no recourse in the law, Eddie.

EDDIE: Yeah, but if he ain't right, Mr. Alfieri, you mean to tell me—

ALFIERI: There is nothing you can do, Eddie, believe me.

EDDIE: Nothin'.

ALFIERI: Nothing at all. There's only one legal question here.

EDDIE: What?

ALFIERI: The manner in which they entered the country. But I don't think you want to do anything about that, do you?

EDDIE: You mean—?

ALFIERI: Well, they entered illegally.

EDDIE: Oh, Jesus, no, I wouldn't do nothin' about that. I mean—

ALFIERI: All right, then, let me talk now, eh?

EDDIE: Mr. Alfieri, I can't believe what you tell me. I mean there must be some kinda law which—

ALFIERI: Eddie, I want you to listen to me.

Pause.

You know, sometimes God mixes up the people.
We all love somebody, the wife, the kids—
Every man's got somebody that he loves, heh?
But sometimes—there's too much. You know?
There's too much, and it goes where it mustn't.
A man works hard, he brings up a child,
Sometimes it's a niece, sometimes even a daughter,
And he never realizes it, but through the years—
There is too much love for the daughter,
There is too much love for the niece.
Do you understand what I'm saying to you?

EDDIE, *sardonically:* What do you mean, I shouldn't look out for her good?

ALFIERI: Yes, but these things have to end, Eddie, that's all.
The child has to grow up and go away,
And the man has to learn how to forget.
Because after all, Eddie—
What other way can it end?

Pause.

Let her go. That's my advice. You did your job,
Now it's her life; wish her luck,
And let her go.

Pause.

Will you do that? Because there's no law, Eddie;
Make up your mind to it; the law is not interested in this.

EDDIE: You mean to tell me, even if he's a punk? If he's—

ALFIERI: There's nothing you can do.

Eddie sits almost grinding his jaws. He stands, wipes one eye.

EDDIE: Well, all right, thanks. Thanks very much.

ALFIERI: What are you going to do?

EDDIE, *with a helpless but ironic gesture:* What can I do? I'm a patsy, what can a patsy do? I worked like a dog twenty years so a punk could have her, so that's what I done. I mean, in the worst times, in the worst, when there wasn't a ship comin' in the harbor, I didn't stand around lookin' for relief—I hustled. When there was empty piers in Brooklyn I went to Hoboken, Staten Island, the West Side, Jersey, all over—because I made a promise. I took out of my own kids' mouths to give to her. I took out of my own mouth. I walked hungry plenty days in this city! *It begins to break through.* And now I gotta sit in my own house and look at a son-of-a-bitch punk like that!—which he came out of nowhere! I give him my house to sleep! I take the blankets off my bed for him, and he takes and puts his dirty filthy hands on her like a goddam thief!

ALFIERI: But Eddie, she's a woman now—

EDDIE: He's stealin' from me!

ALFIERI: She wants to get married, Eddie. She can't marry you, can she?

EDDIE, *furiously:* What're you talkin' about, marry me! I don't know what the hell you're talkin' about!

Pause.

ALFIERI: I gave you my advice, Eddie. That's it.

Eddie gathers himself. A pause.

EDDIE: Well, thanks. Thanks very much. It just—it's breakin' my heart, y'know. I—

ALFIERI: I understand. Put it out of your mind. Can you do that?

EDDIE: I'm—*He feels the threat of sobs, and with a helpless wave:* I'll see you around. *He goes out.*

ALFIERI: There are times when you want to spread an alarm,
But nothing has happened. I knew, I knew then and there—
I could have finished the whole story that afternoon.
It wasn't as though there were a mystery to unravel.
I could see every step coming, step after step,
Like a dark figure walking down a hall toward a certain door.
I knew where he was heading for;

I knew where he was going to end.
And I sat here many afternoons,
Asking myself why, being an intelligent man,
I was so powerless to stop it.
I even went to a certain old lady in the neighborhood,
A very wise old woman, and I told her,
And she only nodded, and said,
"Pray for him."
And so I—*he sits*—waited here.

As the light goes out on Alfieri it rises in the apartment, where all are finishing dinner. There is silence, but for the clink of a dish. Now Catherine looks up.

CATHERINE: You know where they went?

BEATRICE: Where?

CATHERINE: They went to Africa once. On a fishing boat. *Eddie glances at her.* It's true, Eddie.

EDDIE: I didn't say nothin'. *He finishes his coffee and leaves the table.*

CATHERINE: And I was never even in Staten Island.

EDDIE, *sitting with a paper in his rocker:* You didn't miss nothin'. *Pause. Catherine takes dishes out; Beatrice and Rodolpho stack the others.* How long that take you, Marco—to get to Africa?

MARCO: Oh—two days. We go all over.

RODOLPHO: Once we went to Yugoslavia.

EDDIE, *to Marco:* They pay all right on them boats?

MARCO: If they catch fish they pay all right.

RODOLPHO: They're family boats, though. And nobody in our family owned one. So we only worked when one of the families was sick.

Catherine re-enters.

BEATRICE: Y'know, Marco, what I don't understand—there's an ocean full of fish and yiz are all starvin'.

EDDIE: They gotta have boats, nets, you need money.

BEATRICE: Yeah, but couldn't they like fish from the beach? You see them down Coney Island—

MARCO: Sardines.

EDDIE: Sure. How you gonna catch sardines on a hook?

BEATRICE: Oh, I didn't know they're sardines. *To Catherine:* They're sardines!

CATHERINE: Yeah, they follow them all over the ocean—Africa, Greece, Yugoslavia . . .

BEATRICE, *to Eddie:* It's funny, y'know? You never think of it, that sardines are swimming in the ocean!

CATHERINE: I know. It's like oranges and lemons on a tree. *To Eddie:* I mean you ever think of oranges and lemons on a tree?

EDDIE: Yeah, I know. It's funny. *To Marco:* I heard that they paint the oranges to make them look orange.

MARCO: Paint?

EDDIE: Yeah, I heard that they grow like green—

MARCO: No, in Italy the oranges are orange.

RODOLPHO: Lemons are green.

EDDIE, *resenting his instruction:* I know lemons are green, for Christ's sake, you see them in the store they're green sometimes. I said oranges they paint, I didn't say nothin' about lemons.

BEATRICE, *diverting their attention:* Your wife is gettin' the money all right, Marco?

MARCO: Oh, yes. She bought medicine for my boy.

BEATRICE: That's wonderful. You feel better, heh?

MARCO: Oh, yes! But I'm lonesome.

BEATRICE: I just hope you ain't gonna do like some of them around here. They're here twenty-five years, some men, and they didn't get enough together to go back twice.

MARCO: Oh, I know. We have many families in our town, the children never saw the father. But I will go home. Three, four years, I think.

BEATRICE: Maybe you should keep more here, no? Because maybe she thinks it comes so easy you'll never get ahead of yourself.

MARCO: Oh, no, she saves. I send everything. My wife is very lonesome. *He smiles shyly.*

BEATRICE: She must be nice. She pretty? I bet, heh?

MARCO, *blushing:* No, but she understands everything.

RODOLPHO: Oh, he's got a clever wife!

EDDIE: I betcha there's plenty surprises sometimes when those guys get back there, heh?

MARCO: Surprises?

EDDIE: I mean, you know—they count the kids and there's a couple extra than when they left?

MARCO: No—no. The women wait, Eddie. Most. Most. Very few surprises.

RODOLPHO: It's more strict in our town. *Eddie looks at him now.* It's not so free.

EDDIE: It ain't so free here either, Rodolpho, like you think. I seen greenhorns sometimes get in trouble that way—they think just because a girl don't go around with a shawl over her head that she ain't strict, y'know? Girl don't have to wear black dress to be strict. Know what I mean?

RODOLPHO: Well, I always have respect—

EDDIE: I know, but in your town you wouldn't just drag off some girl without permission, I mean. *He turns.* You know what I mean, Marco? It ain't that much different here.

MARCO, *cautiously:* Yes.

EDDIE, *to Rodolpho:* I mean I seen some a yiz get the wrong idea sometimes. I mean it might be a little more free here but it's just as strict.

RODOLPHO: I have respect for her, Eddie. I do anything wrong?

EDDIE: Look, kid, I ain't her father, I'm only her uncle—

MARCO: No, Eddie, if he does wrong you must tell him. What does he do wrong?

EDDIE: Well, Marco, till he came here she was never out on the street twelve o'clock at night.

MARCO, *to Rodolpho:* You come home early now.

CATHERINE: Well, the movie ended late.

EDDIE: I'm just sayin'—he thinks you always stayed out like that. I mean he don't understand, honey, see?

MARCO: You come home early now, Rodolpho.

RODOLPHO, *embarrassed:* All right, sure.

EDDIE: It's not only for her, Marco. *To Catherine:* I mean it, kid, he's gettin' careless. The more he runs around like that the more chance he's takin'. *To Rodolpho:* I mean suppose you get hit by a car or sump'm, where's your papers, who are you? Know what I mean?

RODOLPHO: But I can't stay in the house all the time, I—

BEATRICE: Listen, he's gotta go out sometime—

EDDIE: Well, listen, it depends, Beatrice. If he's here to work, then he should work; if he's here for a good time, then he

could fool around! *To Marco:* But I understood, Marco, that you was both comin' to make a livin' for your family. You understand me, don't you, Marco?

MARCO—*he sees it nearly in the open now, and with reserve:* I beg your pardon, Eddie.

EDDIE: I mean that's what I understood in the first place, see?

MARCO: Yes. That's why we came.

EDDIE: Well, that's all I'm askin'.

There is a pause, an awkwardness. Now Catherine gets up and puts a record on the phonograph. Music.

CATHERINE, *flushed with revolt:* You wanna dance, Rodolpho?

RODOLPHO, *in deference to Eddie:* No, I—I'm tired.

CATHERINE: Ah, come on. He plays a beautiful piano, that guy. Come. *She has taken his hand, and he stiffly rises, feeling Eddie's eyes on his back, and they dance.*

EDDIE, *to Catherine:* What's that, a new record?

CATHERINE: It's the same one. We bought it the other day.

BEATRICE, *to Eddie:* They only bought three records. *She watches them dance; Eddie turns his head away. Marco just sits there, waiting. Now Beatrice turns to Eddie.* Must be nice to go all over in one of them fishin' boats. I would like that myself. See all them other countries?

EDDIE: Yeah.

BEATRICE, *to Marco:* But the women don't go along, I bet.

MARCO: No, not on the boats. Hard work.

BEATRICE: What're you got, a regular kitchen and everything?

MARCO: Yes, we eat very good on the boats—especially when Rodolpho comes along; everybody gets fat.

BEATRICE: Oh, he cooks?

MARCO: Sure, very good cook. Rice, pasta, fish, everything.

EDDIE: He's a cook too! *He looks at Rodolpho.* He sings, he cooks . . .

Rodolpho smiles thankfully.

BEATRICE: Well, it's good; he could always make a living.

EDDIE: It's wonderful. He sings, he cooks, he could make dresses . . .

CATHERINE: They get some high pay, them guys. The head chefs in all the big hotels are men. You read about them.

EDDIE: That's what I'm sayin'.

Catherine and Rodolpho continue dancing.

CATHERINE: Yeah, well, I mean.

EDDIE, *to Beatrice:* He's lucky, believe me. *A slight pause; he looks away, then back to Beatrice.* That's why the waterfront is no place for him. I mean, like me—I can't cook, I can't sing, I can't make dresses, so I'm on the waterfront. But if I could cook, if I could sing, if I could makes dresses, I wouldn't be on the waterfront. *They are all regarding him now; he senses he is exposing the issue, but he is driven on.* I would be someplace else. I would be like in a dress store. *He suddenly gets up and pulls his pants up over his belly.* What do you say, Marco, we go to the bouts next Saturday night? You never seen a fight, did you?

MARCO, *uneasily:* Only in the moving pictures.

EDDIE: I'll treat yiz. What do you say, Danish? You wanna come along? I'll buy the tickets.

RODOLPHO: Sure. I like to go.

CATHERINE, *nervously happy now:* I'll make some coffee, all right?

EDDIE: Go ahead, make some! *He draws her near him.* Make it nice and strong. *Mystified, she smiles and goes out. He is weirdly elated; he is rubbing his fists into his palms.* You wait, Marco, you see some real fights here. You ever do any boxing?

MARCO: No, I never.

EDDIE, *to Rodolpho:* Betcha you done some, heh?

RODOLPHO: No.

EDDIE: Well, get up, come on, I'll teach you.

BEATRICE: What's he got to learn that for?

EDDIE: Ya can't tell, one a these days somebody's liable to step on his foot, or sump'm. Come on, Rodolpho, I show you a couple a passes.

BEATRICE, *unwillingly, carefully:* Go ahead, Rodolpho. He's a good boxer; he could teach you.

RODOLPHO, *embarrassed:* Well, I don't know how to—

EDDIE: Just put your hands up. Like this, see? That's right. That's very good, keep your left up, because you lead with the left, see, like this. *He gently moves his left into Rodolpho's*

face. See? Now what you gotta do is you gotta block me, so when I come in like that you— *Rodolpho parries his left.* Hey, that's very good! *Rodolpho laughs.* All right, now come into me. Come on.

RODOLPHO: I don't want to hit you, Eddie.

EDDIE: Don't pity me, come on. Throw it; I'll show you how to block it. *Rodolpho jabs at him, laughing.* 'At's it. Come on, again. For the jaw, right here. *Rodolpho jabs with more assurance.* Very good!

BEATRICE, *to Marco:* He's very good!

EDDIE: Sure, he's great! Come on, kid, put sump'm behind it; you can't hurt me. *Rodolpho, more seriously, jabs at Eddie's jaw and grazes it.* Attaboy. Now I'm gonna hit you, so block me, see?

Catherine comes from the kitchen, watches.

CATHERINE, *with beginning alarm:* What are they doin'?

They are lightly boxing now.

BEATRICE—*she senses only the comradeship in it now:* He's teachin' him; he's very good!

EDDIE: Sure, he's terrific! Look at him go! *Rodolpho lands a blow.* 'At's it! Now watch out, here I come, Danish! *He feints with his left hand and lands with his right. It mildly staggers Rodolpho.*

CATHERINE, *rushing to Rodolpho:* Eddie!

EDDIE: Why? I didn't hurt him. *Going to help the dizzy Rodolpho:* Did I hurt you, kid?

RODOLPHO: No, no, he didn't hurt me. *To Eddie, with a certain gleam and a smile:* I was only surprised.

BEATRICE: That's enough, Eddie; he did pretty good, though.

EDDIE: Yeah. *He rubs his fists together.* He could be very good, Marco. I'll teach him again.

Marco nods at him dubiously.

RODOLPHO, *as a new song comes on the radio, his voice betraying a new note of command:* Dance, Catherine. Come.

Rodolpho takes her in his arms. They dance. Eddie, in thought, sits in his chair, and Marco rises and comes downstage to a chair and looks down at it. Beatrice and Eddie watch him.

MARCO: Can you lift this chair?

EDDIE: What do you mean?

MARCO: From here. *He gets on one knee with one hand behind his back, and grasps the bottom of one of the chair legs but does not raise it.*

EDDIE: Sure, why not? *He comes to the chair, kneels, grasps the leg, raises the chair one inch, but it leans over to the floor.* Gee, that's hard, I never knew that. *He tries again, and again fails.* It's on an angle, that's why, heh?

MARCO: Here. *He kneels, grasps, and with strain slowly raises the chair higher and higher, getting to his feet now.*

And Rodolpho and Catherine have stopped dancing as Marco raises the chair over his head.

He is face to face with Eddie, a strained tension gripping his eyes and jaw, his neck stiff, the chair raised like a weapon—and he transforms what might appear like a glare of warning into a smile of triumph, and Eddie's grin vanishes as he absorbs the look; as the lights go down.

The stage remains dark for a moment. Ships' horns are heard. Light rises on Alfieri at his desk. He is discovered in dejection, his face bent to the desk, on which his arms rest. Now he looks up and front.

ALFIERI: On the twenty-third of that December
A case of Scotch whisky slipped from a net
While being unloaded—as a case of Scotch whisky
Is inclined to do on the twenty-third of December
On Pier Forty-one. There was no snow, but it was cold.
His wife was out shopping.
Marco was still at work.
The boy had not been hired that day;
Catherine told me later that this was the first time
They had been alone together in the house.

Light is rising on Catherine, who is ironing in the apartment. Music is playing. Rodolpho is in Eddie's rocker, his head leaning back. A piano jazz cadenza begins. Luxuriously he turns his head to her and smiles, and she smiles at him, then continues ironing. He comes to the table and sits beside her.

CATHERINE: You hungry?

RODOLPHO: Not for anything to eat. *He leans his chin on the back of his hand on the table, watching her iron.* I have nearly three hundred dollars. *He looks up at her.* Catherine?

CATHERINE: I heard you.

Rodolpho reaches out and takes her hand and kisses it, then lets it go. She resumes ironing. He rests his head again on the back of his hand.

RODOLPHO: You don't like to talk about it any more?

CATHERINE: Sure, I don't mind talkin' about it.

RODOLPHO: What worries you, Catherine?

Catherine continues ironing. He now reaches out and takes her hand off the iron, and she sits back in her chair, not looking directly at him.

CATHERINE: I been wantin' to ask you about something. Could I?

RODOLPHO: All the answers are in my eyes, Catherine. But you don't look in my eyes lately. You're full of secrets. *She looks at him. He presses her hand against his cheek. She seems withdrawn.* What is the question?

CATHERINE: Suppose I wanted to live in Italy.

RODOLPHO, *smiling at the incongruity:* You going to marry somebody rich?

CATHERINE: No, I mean live there—you and me.

RODOLPHO—*his smile is vanishing:* When?

CATHERINE: Well—when we get married.

RODOLPHO, *astonished:* You want to be an Italian?

CATHERINE: No, but I could live there without being Italian. Americans live there.

RODOLPHO: Forever?

CATHERINE: Yeah.

RODOLPHO: You're fooling.

CATHERINE: No, I mean it.

RODOLPHO: Where do you get such an idea?

CATHERINE: Well, you're always saying it's so beautiful there, with the mountains and the ocean and all the—

RODOLPHO: You're fooling me.

CATHERINE: I mean it.

RODOLPHO: Catherine, if I ever brought you home
With no money, no business, nothing,
They would call the priest and the doctor
And they would say Rodolpho is crazy.
CATHERINE: I know, but I think we would be happier there.
RODOLPHO: Happier! What would you eat? You can't cook the view!
CATHERINE: Maybe you could be a singer, like in Rome or—
RODOLPHO: Rome! Rome is full of singers.
CATHERINE: Well, I could work then.
RODOLPHO: Where?
CATHERINE: God, there must be jobs somewhere!
RODOLPHO: There's nothing! Nothing, nothing,
Nothing. Now tell me what you're talking about.
How can I bring you from a rich country
To suffer in a poor country?
What are you talking about?

She searches for words.

I would be a criminal stealing your face;
In two years you would have an old, hungry face.
When my brothers' babies cry they give them water,
Water that boiled a bone.
Don't you believe that?
CATHERINE, *quietly:* I'm afraid of Eddie here.

A slight pause.

RODOLPHO: We wouldn't live here.
Once I am a citizen I could work anywhere,
And I would find better jobs,
And we would have a house, Catherine.
If I were not afraid to be arrested
I would start to be something wonderful here!
CATHERINE, *steeling herself:* Tell me something. I mean just tell me, Rodolpho. Would you still want to do it if it turned out we had to go live in Italy? I mean just if it turned out that way.
RODOLPHO: This is your question or his question?
CATHERINE: I would like to know, Rodolpho. I mean it.
RODOLPHO: To go there with nothing?

CATHERINE: Yeah.
RODOLPHO: No. *She looks at him wide-eyed.* No.
CATHERINE: You wouldn't?
RODOLPHO: No; I will not marry you to live in Italy.
I want you to be my wife
And I want to be a citizen.
Tell him that, or I will. Yes.

He moves about angrily.

And tell him also, and tell yourself, please,
That I am not a beggar,
And you are not a horse, a gift,
A favor for a poor immigrant.
CATHERINE: Well, don't get mad!
RODOLPHO: I am furious!
Do you think I am so desperate?
My brother is desperate, not me.
You think I would carry on my back
The rest of my life a woman I didn't love
Just to be an American? It's so wonderful?
You think we have no tall buildings in Italy?
Electric lights? No wide streets? No flags?
No automobiles? Only work we don't have.
I want to be an American so I can work,
That is the only wonder here—work!
How can you insult me, Catherine?
CATHERINE: I didn't mean that—
RODOLPHO: My heart dies to look at you.
Why are you so afraid of him?
CATHERINE, *near tears:* I don't know!

Rodolpho turns her to him.

RODOLPHO: Do you trust me, Catherine? You?
CATHERINE: It's only that I—
He was good to me, Rodolpho.
You don't know him; he was always the sweetest guy to me.
Good. He razzes me all the time,
But he don't mean it. I know.
I would—just feel ashamed if I made him sad.
'Cause I always dreamt that when I got married

He would be happy at the wedding, and laughin'.
And now he's—mad all the time, and nasty.

She is weeping.

Tell him you'd live in Italy—just tell him,
And maybe he would start to trust you a little, see?
Because I want him to be happy; I mean—
I like him, Rodolpho—and I can't stand it!

She weeps, and he holds her.

RODOLPHO: Catherine—oh, little girl—
CATHERINE: I love you, Rodolpho, I love you.
RODOLPHO: I think that's what you have to tell him, eh?
Can't you tell him?
CATHERINE: I'm ascared, I'm so scared.
RODOLPHO: Ssssh. Listen, now. Tonight when he comes home
We will both sit down after supper
And we will tell him—you and I.

He sees her fear rising.

But you must believe me yourself, Catherine.
It's true—you have very much to give me;
A whole country! Sure, I hold America when I hold you.
But if you were not my love,
If every day I did not smile so many times
When I think of you,
I could never kiss you, not for a hundred Americas.
Tonight I'll tell him,
And you will not be frightened any more, eh?
And then in two, three months I'll have enough,
We will go to the church, and we'll come back to our own—

He breaks off, seeing the conquered longing in her eyes, her smile.

Catherine—
CATHERINE: Now. There's nobody here.
RODOLPHO: Oh, my little girl. Oh God!
CATHERINE, *kissing his face:* Now!

He turns her upstage. They walk embraced, her head on his shoulder, and he sings to her softly. They go into a bedroom.

A pause. Ships' horns sound in the distance. Eddie enters on the street. He is unsteady, drunk. He mounts the stairs. The sounds continue. He enters the apartment, looks around, takes out a bottle from one pocket, puts it on the table; then another bottle from another pocket; and a third from an inside pocket. He sees the iron, goes over to it and touches it, pulls his hand quickly back, turns toward upstage.

EDDIE: Beatrice? *He goes to the open kitchen door and looks in. He turns to a bedroom door.* Beatrice? *He starts for this door; it opens, and Catherine is standing there; under his gaze she adjusts her dress.*

CATHERINE: You got home early.

EDDIE, *trying to unravel what he senses:* Knocked off for Christmas early. *She goes past him to the ironing board. Indicating the iron:* You start a fire that way.

CATHERINE: I only left it for a minute.

Rodolpho appears in the bedroom doorway. Eddie sees him, and his arm jerks slightly in shock. Rodolpho nods to him testingly. Eddie looks to Catherine, who is looking down at the ironing as she works.

RODOLPHO: Beatrice went to buy shoes for the children.

EDDIE: Pack it up. Go ahead. Get your stuff and get outa here. *Catherine puts down the iron and walks toward the bedroom, and Eddie grabs her arm.* Where you goin'?

CATHERINE: Don't bother me, Eddie. I'm goin' with him.

EDDIE: You goin' with him. You goin' with him, heh? *He grabs her face in the vise of his two hands.* You goin' with him!

He kisses her on the mouth as she pulls at his arms; he will not let go, keeps his face pressed against hers. Rodolpho comes to them now.

RODOLPHO, *tentatively at first:* Eddie! No, Eddie! *He now pulls full force on Eddie's arms to break his grip.* Don't! No!

Catherine breaks free, and Eddie is spun around by Rodolpho's force, to face him.

EDDIE: You want something?

RODOLPHO: She'll be my wife.

EDDIE: But what're you gonna be? That's what I wanna know! What're you gonna be!

RODOLPHO, *with tears of rage:* Don't say that to me!

Rodolpho flies at him in attack. Eddie pins his arms, laughing, and suddenly kisses him.

CATHERINE: Eddie! Let go, ya hear me! I'll kill you! Leggo of him!

She tears at Eddie's face, and Eddie releases Rodolpho and stands there, tears rolling down his face as he laughs mockingly at Rodolpho. She is staring at him in horror, her breasts heaving. Rodolpho is rigid; they are like animals that have torn at each other and broken up without a decision, each waiting for the other's mood.

EDDIE: I give you till tomorrow, kid. Get outa here. Alone. You hear me? Alone.

CATHERINE: I'm goin' with him, Eddie.

EDDIE, *indicating Rodolpho with his head:* Not with that. *He sits, still panting for breath, and they watch him helplessly as he leans his head back on the chair and, striving to catch his breath, closes his eyes.* Don't make me do nuttin', Catherine.

The lights go down on Eddie's apartment and rise on Alfieri.

ALFIERI: On December twenty-seventh I saw him next.
I normally go home well before six,
But that day I sat around,
Looking out my window at the bay,
And when I saw him walking through my doorway
I knew why I had waited.
And if I seem to tell this like a dream,
It was that way. Several moments arrived
In the course of the two talks we had
When it occurred to me how—almost transfixed
I had come to feel. I had lost my strength somewhere.

Eddie enters, removing his cap, sits in the chair, looks thoughtfully out.

I looked in his eyes more than I listened—
In fact, I can hardly remember the conversation.

But I will never forget how dark the room became
When he looked at me; his eyes were like tunnels.
I kept wanting to call the police,
But nothing had happened.
Nothing at all had really happened.

He breaks off and looks down at the desk. Then he turns to Eddie.

So in other words, he won't leave?

EDDIE: My wife is talkin' about renting a room upstairs for them. An old lady on the top floor is got an empty room.

ALFIERI: What does Marco say?

EDDIE: He just sits there. Marco don't say much.

ALFIERI: I guess they didn't tell him, heh? What happened?

EDDIE: I don't know; Marco don't say much.

ALFIERI: What does your wife say?

EDDIE, *unwilling to pursue this:* Nobody's talkin' much in the house. So what about that?

ALFIERI: But you didn't prove anything about him.

EDDIE: Mr. Alfieri, I'm tellin' you—

ALFIERI: You're not telling me anything, Eddie;
It sounds like he just wasn't strong enough to break your grip.

EDDIE: I'm tellin' you I know—he ain't right.
Somebody that don't want it can break it.
Even a mouse, if you catch a teeny mouse
And you hold it in your hand, that mouse
Can give you the right kind of fight,
And he didn't give me the right kind of fight.
I know it, Mr. Alfieri, the guy ain't right.

ALFIERI: What did you do that for, Eddie?

EDDIE: To show her what he is! So she would see, once and for all! Her mother'll turn over in the grave! *He gathers himself almost peremptorily.* So what do I gotta do now? Tell me what to do.

ALFIERI: She actually said she's marrying him?

EDDIE: She told me, yeah. So what do I do?

A slight pause.

ALFIERI: This is my last word, Eddie,

Take it or not, that's your business.
Morally and legally you have no rights;
You cannot stop it; she is a free agent.

EDDIE, *angering:* Didn't you hear what I told you?

ALFIERI, *with a tougher tone:* I heard what you told me,
And I'm telling you what the answer is.
I'm not only telling you now, I'm warning you—
The law is nature.
The law is only a word for what has a right to happen.
When the law is wrong it's because it's unnatural,
But in this case it is natural,
And a river will drown you
If you buck it now.
Let her go. And bless her.

As he speaks, a phone begins to glow on the opposite side of the stage, a faint, lonely blue. Eddie stands up, jaws clenched.

Somebody had to come for her, Eddie, sooner or later.

Eddie starts to turn to go, and Alfieri rises with new anxiety.

You won't have a friend in the world, Eddie!
Even those who understand will turn against you,
Even the ones who feel the same will despise you!

Eddie moves off quickly.

Put it out of your mind! Eddie!

The light goes out on Alfieri. Eddie has at the same time appeared beside the phone, and he lifts it.

EDDIE: I want to report something. Illegal immigrants. Two of them. That's right. Four-forty-one Saxon Street, Brooklyn, yeah. Ground floor. Heh? *With greater difficulty:* I'm just around the neighborhood, that's all. Heh?

Evidently he is being questioned further, and he slowly hangs up. He comes out of the booth just as Louis and Mike come down the street. They are privately laughing at some private joke.

LOUIS: Go bowlin', Eddie?

EDDIE: No, I'm due home.

LOUIS: Well, take it easy.

EDDIE: I'll see yiz.

They leave him, and he watches them go. They resume their evidently amusing conversation. He glances about, then goes up into the house, and, as he enters, the lights go on in the apartment. Beatrice is seated, sewing a pair of child's pants.

BEATRICE: Where you been so late?

EDDIE: I took a walk, I told you. *He gets out of his zipper jacket, picks up a paper that is lying in a chair, prepares to sit.* Kids sleepin'?

BEATRICE: Yeah, they're all sleepin'.

Pause. Eddie looks out the window.

EDDIE: Where's Marco?

BEATRICE: They decided to move upstairs with Mrs. Dondero.

EDDIE, *turning to her:* They're up there now?

BEATRICE: They moved all their stuff. Catherine decided. It's better, Eddie, they'll be outa your way. They're happy and we'll be happy.

EDDIE: Catherine's up there too?

BEATRICE: She just went up to bring pillow cases. She'll be down right away.

EDDIE, *nodding:* Well, they're better off up there; the whole house knows they were here anyway, so there's nothin' to hide no more.

BEATRICE: That's what I figured. And besides, with the other ones up there maybe it'll look like they're just boarders too, or sump'm. You want eat?

EDDIE: What other ones?

BEATRICE: The two guys she rented the other room to. She's rentin' two rooms. She bought beds and everything: I told you.

EDDIE: When'd you tell me?

BEATRICE: I don't know; I think we were talkin' about it last week, even. She's startin' like a little boarding house up there. Only she's got no pillow cases yet.

EDDIE: I didn't hear nothin' about no boarding house.

BEATRICE: Sure, I loaned her my big fryin' pan beginning of the week. I told you. *She smiles and goes to him.* You gotta come to yourself, kid; you're in another world all the time.

He is silent, peering; she touches his head. I wanna tell you, Eddie; it was my fault, and I'm sorry. No kiddin'. I shoulda put them up there in the first place.

EDDIE: Dja ever see these guys?

BEATRICE: I see them on the stairs every couple a days. They're kinda young guys. You look terrible, y'know?

EDDIE: They longshoremen?

BEATRICE: I don't know; they never said only hello, and she don't say nothin', so I don't ask, but they look like nice guys. *Eddie, silent, stares.* What's the matter? I thought you would like it.

EDDIE: I'm just wonderin'—where they come from? She's got no sign outside; she don't know nobody. How's she find boarders all of a sudden?

BEATRICE: What's the difference? She—

EDDIE: The difference is they could be cops, that's all.

BEATRICE: Oh, no, I don't think so.

EDDIE: It's all right with me, I don't care. Except for this kinda work they don't wear badges, y'know. I mean you gotta face it, they could be cops. And Rodolpho'll start to shoot his mouth off up there, and they got him.

BEATRICE: I don't think so. You want some coffee?

EDDIE: No. I don't want nothin'.

BEATRICE: You gettin' sick or sump'm?

EDDIE: Me—no, I'm all right. *Mystified:* When did you tell me she had boarders?

BEATRICE: Couple a times.

EDDIE: Geez, I don't even remember. I thought she had the one room. *He touches his forehead, alarmed.*

BEATRICE: Sure, we was all talkin' about it last week. I loaned her my big fryin' pan. I told you.

EDDIE: I must be dizzy or sump'm.

BEATRICE: I think you'll come to yourself now, Eddie. I mean it, we shoulda put them up there in the first place. You can never bring strangers in a house. *Pause. They are seated.* You know what?

EDDIE: What?

BEATRICE: Why don't you go to her and tell her it's all right—Katie? Give her a break. A wedding should be happy.

EDDIE: I don't care. Let her do what she wants to do.

BEATRICE: Why don't you tell her you'll go to the wedding? It's terrible, there wouldn't be no father there. She's broken-hearted.

EDDIE: They made up the date already?

BEATRICE: She wants him to have like six, seven hundred. I told her, I says, "If you start off with a little bit you never gonna get ahead of yourself," I says. So they're gonna wait yet. I think maybe the end of the summer. But if you would tell them you'll be at the wedding—I mean, it would be nice, they would both be happy. I mean live and let live, Eddie, I mean?

EDDIE, *as though he doesn't care:* All right, I'll go to the wedding. *Catherine is descending the stairs from above.*

BEATRICE, *darting a glance toward the sound:* You want me to tell her?

EDDIE—*he thinks, then turns to her with a certain deliberativeness:* If you want, go ahead.

Catherine enters, sees him, and starts for the bedroom door.

BEATRICE: Come here, Katie. *Catherine looks doubtfully at her.* Come here, honey. *Catherine comes to her, and Beatrice puts an arm around her. Eddie looks off.* He's gonna come to the wedding.

CATHERINE: What do I care if he comes? *She starts upstage, but Beatrice holds her.*

BEATRICE: Ah, Katie, don't be that way. I want you to make up with him; come on over here. You're his baby! *She tries to draw Catherine near Eddie.*

CATHERINE: I got nothin' to make up with him, he's got somethin' to make up with me.

EDDIE: Leave her alone, Beatrice, she knows what she wants to do. *Now, however, he turns for a second to Catherine.* But if I was you I would watch out for those boarders up there.

BEATRICE: He's worried maybe they're cops.

CATHERINE: Oh, no, they ain't cops. Mr. Lipari from the butcher store—they're his nephews; they just come over last week.

EDDIE, *coming alive:* They're submarines?

CATHERINE: Yeah, they come from around Bari. They ain't cops.

She walks to her bedroom. Eddie tries to keep silent, and when he speaks it has an unwilling sharpness of anxiety.

EDDIE: Catherine. *She turns to him. He is getting to his feet in a high but subdued terror.* You think that's a good idea?

CATHERINE: What?

EDDIE: How do you know what enemies Lipari's got? Which they would love to stab him in the back? I mean you never do that, Catherine, put in two strange pairs like that together. They track one, they'll catch 'em all. I ain't tryin' to advise you, kid, but that ain't smart. Anybody tell you that. I mean you just takin' a double chance, y'understand?

CATHERINE: Well, what'll I do with them?

EDDIE: What do you mean? The neighborhood's full of rooms. Can't you stand to live a couple a blocks away from him? He's got a big family, Lipari—these guys get picked up he's liable to blame you or me, and we got his whole family on our head. That's no joke, kid. They got a temper, that family.

CATHERINE: Well, maybe tomorrow I'll find some other place—

EDDIE: Kid, I'm not tellin' you nothin' no more because I'm just an ignorant jerk. I know that; but if I was you I would get them outa this house tonight, see?

CATHERINE: How'm I gonna find a place tonight?

EDDIE, *his temper rising:* Catherine, don't mix yourself with somebody else's family, Catherine.

Two men in overcoats and felt hats appear on the street, start into the house.

EDDIE: You want to do yourself a favor? Go up and get them out of the house, kid.

CATHERINE: Yeah, but they been in the house so long already—

EDDIE: You think I'm always tryin' to fool you or sump'm? What's the matter with you? Don't you believe I could think of your good? *He is breaking into tears.* Didn't I work like a horse keepin' you? You think I got no feelin's? I never told you nothin' in my life that wasn't for your good. Nothin'! And look at the way you talk to me! Like I was an enemy! Like I— *There is a knock on the door. His head swerves. They all stand motionless. Another knock. Eddie firmly draws*

Catherine to him. And, in a whisper, pointing upstage: Go out the back up the fire escape; get them out over the back fence.

FIRST OFFICER, *in the hall:* Open up in there! Immigration!

EDDIE: Go, go. Hurry up! *He suddenly pushes her upstage, and she stands a moment, staring at him in a realized horror.* Well what're you lookin' at?

FIRST OFFICER: Open up!

EDDIE: Who's that there?

FIRST OFFICER: Immigration. Open up.

With a sob of fury and that glance, Catherine streaks into a bedroom. Eddie looks at Beatrice, who sinks into a chair, turning her face from him.

EDDIE: All right, take it easy, take it easy. *He goes and opens the door. The officers step inside.* What's all this?

FIRST OFFICER: Where are they?

EDDIE: Where's who?

FIRST OFFICER: Come on, come on, where are they?

EDDIE: Who? We got nobody here. *The first officer opens the door and exits into a bedroom. Second officer goes and opens the other bedroom door and exits through it. Beatrice now turns her head to look at Eddie. He goes to her, reaches for her, and involuntarily she withdraws herself. Then, pugnaciously, furious:* What's the matter with *you*?

The first officer enters from the bedroom, calls quietly into the other bedroom.

FIRST OFFICER: Dominick?

Enter second officer from bedroom.

SECOND OFFICER: Maybe it's a different apartment.

FIRST OFFICER: There's only two more floors up there. I'll take the front, you go up the fire escape. I'll let you in. Watch your step up there.

SECOND OFFICER: Okay, right, Charley. *He re-enters the bedroom. The first officer goes to the apartment door, turns to Eddie.*

FIRST OFFICER: This is Four-forty-one, isn't it?

EDDIE: That's right.

The officer goes out into the hall, closing the door, and climbs up out of sight. Beatrice slowly sits at the table. Eddie goes to the closed door and listens. Knocking is heard from above, voices. Eddie turns to Beatrice. She looks at him now and sees his terror, and, weakened with fear, she leans her head on the table.

BEATRICE: Oh, Jesus, Eddie.

EDDIE: What's the matter with *you? He starts toward her, but she swiftly rises, pressing her palms against her face, and walks away from him.*

BEATRICE: Oh, my God, my God.

EDDIE: What're you, accusin' me?

BEATRICE—*her final thrust is to turn toward him instead of running from him:* My God, what did you do!

Many steps on the outer stair draw his attention. We see the first officer descending with Marco, behind him Rodolpho, and Catherine and two strange men, followed by second officer. Beatrice hurries and opens the door.

CATHERINE, *as they appear on the stairs:* What do yiz want from them? They work, that's all. They're boarders upstairs, they work on the piers.

BEATRICE, *now appearing in the hall, to first officer:* Ah, mister, what do you want from them? Who do they hurt?

CATHERINE, *pointing to Rodolpho:* They ain't no submarines; he was born in Philadelphia.

FIRST OFFICER: Step aside, lady.

CATHERINE: What do you mean? You can't just come in a house and—

FIRST OFFICER: All right, take it easy. *To Rodolpho:* What street were you born in Philadelphia?

CATHERINE: What do you mean, what street? Could you tell me what street you were born?

FIRST OFFICER: Sure. Four blocks away, One-eleven Union Street. Let's go, fellas.

CATHERINE, *fending him off Rodolpho:* No, you can't! Now, get outa here!

FIRST OFFICER, *moving her into the apartment:* Look, girlie, if they're all right they'll be back tomorrow. If they're illegal they go back where they came from. If you want, get yourself

a lawyer, although I'm tellin' you now you're wasting your money. *He goes back to the group in the hall.* Let's get them in the car, Dom. *To the men:* Andiamo, andiamo, let's go.

The men start out toward the street—but Marco hangs back, letting them pass.

BEATRICE: Who're they hurtin', for God's sake? What do you want from them? They're starvin' over there, what do you want!

Marco suddenly breaks from the group and dashes into the room and faces Eddie, and Beatrice and the first officer rush in as Marco spits into Eddie's face. Catherine has arrived at the door and sees it. Eddie, with an enraged cry, lunges for Marco.

EDDIE: Oh, you mother's—!

The first officer quickly intercedes and pushes Eddie from Marco, who stands there accusingly.

FIRST OFFICER, *pushing Eddie from Marco:* Cut it out!

EDDIE, *over the first officer's shoulder to Marco:* I'll kill you for that, you son of a bitch!

FIRST OFFICER: Hey! *He shakes Eddie.* Stay in here now, don't come down, don't bother him. You hear me? Don't come down, fella.

For an instant there is silence. Then the first officer turns and takes Marco's arm and then gives a last, informative look at Eddie; and as he and Marco are going out into the hall Eddie erupts.

EDDIE: I don't forget that, Marco! You hear what I'm sayin'?

Out in the hall, the first officer and Marco go down the stairs. Catherine rushes out of the room and past them toward Rodolpho, who, with the second officer and the two strange men, is emerging into the street. Now, in the street, Louis, Mike, and several neighbors, including the butcher, Lipari, a stout, intense, middle-aged man are gathering around the stoop.

Eddie follows Catherine and calls down after Marco. Beatrice watches him from within the room, her hands clasped together in fear and prayer.

EDDIE: That's the thanks I get? Which I took the blanket off my bed for yiz? *He hurries down the stairs, shouting. Beatrice descends behind him, ineffectually trying to hold him back.* You gonna apologize to me, Marco! *Marco!*

Eddie appears on the stoop and sees the little crowd looking up at him, and falls silent, expectant. Lipari, the butcher, walks over to the two strange men, and he kisses them. His wife, keening, goes and kisses their hands.

FIRST OFFICER: All right, lady, let them go. Get in the car, fellas, it's right over there.

The second officer begins moving off with the two strange men and Rodolpho. Catherine rushes to the first officer, who is drawing Marco off now.

CATHERINE: He was born in Philadelphia! What do you want from him?

FIRST OFFICER: Step aside, lady, come on now—

MARCO: *suddenly, taking advantage of the first officer's being occupied with Catherine, freeing himself and pointing up at Eddie:* That one! I accuse that one!

FIRST OFFICER, *grabbing him and moving him quickly off:* Come on!

MARCO, *as he is taken off, pointing back and up the stoop at Eddie:* That one! He killed my children! That one stole the food from my children!

Marco is gone. The crowd has turned to Eddie.

EDDIE: He's crazy. I give them the blankets off my bed. Six months I kept them like my own brothers! *Lipari, the butcher, turns and starts off with his wife behind him.* Lipari! *Eddie comes down and reaches Lipari and turns him about.* For Christ's sake, I kept them, I give them the blankets off my bed! *Lipari turns away in disgust and anger and walks off with his keening wife. The crowd is now moving away. Eddie calls:* Louis! *Louis barely turns, then walks away with Mike.* LOUIS! *Only Beatrice is left on the stoop—and Catherine now returns, blank-eyed, from offstage and the car. Eddie turns to Catherine.* He's gonna take that back. He's gonna take that back or I'll kill him! *He faces all the buildings, the*

street down which the crowd has vanished. You hear me? I'll kill him!

Blackout

There is a pause in darkness before the lights rise. On the left—opposite where the desk stands—is a backless wooden bench. Seated on it are Rodolpho and Marco. There are two wooden chairs. It is a room in the jail. Catherine and Alfieri are seated on the chairs.

ALFIERI: I'm waiting, Marco. What do you say? *Marco glances at him, then shrugs.* That's not enough; I want an answer from you.

RODOLPHO: Marco never hurt anybody.

ALFIERI: I can bail you out until your hearing comes up.
But I'm not going to do it—you understand me?—
Unless I have your promise. You're an honorable man,
I will believe your promise. Now what do you say?

MARCO: In my country he would be dead now.
He would not live this long.

ALFIERI: All right, Rodolpho, you come with me now. *He rises.*

RODOLPHO: No! Please, mister. Marco—
Promise the man. Please, I want you to watch the wedding.
How can I be married and you're in here?
Please, you're not going to do anything; you know you're not—

Marco is silent.

CATHERINE: Marco, don't you understand? He can't bail you out if you're gonna do something bad. To hell with Eddie. Nobody is gonna talk to him again if he lives to a hundred. Everybody knows you spit in his face, that's enough, isn't it? Give me the satisfaction—I want you at the wedding. You got a wife and kids, Marco—you could be workin' till the hearing comes up, instead of layin' around here. You're just giving him satisfaction layin' here.

MARCO, *after a slight pause, to Alfieri:* How long you say before the hearing?

ALFIERI: I'll try to stretch it out, but it wouldn't be more than five or six weeks.

CATHERINE: So you could make a couple of dollars in the meantime, y'see?

MARCO, *to Alfieri:* I have no chance?

ALFIERI: No, Marco. You're going back. The hearing is a formality, that's all.

MARCO: But him? There is a chance, eh?

ALFIERI: When she marries him he can start to become an American. They permit that, if the wife is born here.

MARCO, *looking at Rodolpho:* Well—we did something. *He lays a palm on Rodolpho's cheek, then lowers his hand.*

RODOLPHO: Marco, tell the man.

MARCO: What will I tell him? *He looks at Alfieri.* He knows such a promise is dishonorable.

ALFIERI: To promise not to kill is not dishonorable.

MARCO: No?

ALFIERI: No.

MARCO, *gesturing with his head— this is a new idea.* Then what is done with such a man?

ALFIERI: Nothing. If he obeys the law, he lives. That's all.

MARCO: The law? All the law is not in a book.

ALFIERI: Yes. In a book. There is no other law.

MARCO, *his anger rising:* He degraded my brother—my blood. He robbed my children, he mocks my work. I work to come here, mister!

ALFIERI: I know, Marco—

MARCO: There is no law for that? Where is the law for that?

ALFIERI: There is none.

MARCO, *shaking his head:* I don't understand this country. *Pause. He stands staring in fury.*

ALFIERI: Well? What is your answer? You have five or six weeks you could work. Or else you sit here. What do you say to me?

Marco lowers his eyes. It almost seems he is ashamed.

MARCO: All right.

ALFIERI: You won't touch him. This is your promise.

Slight pause.

MARCO: Maybe he wants to apologize to me.

ALFIERI, *taking one of his hands:* This is not God, Marco. You hear? Only God makes justice.

Marco withdraws his hand and covers it with the other.

MARCO: All right.

ALFIERI: Is your uncle going to the wedding?

CATHERINE: No. But he wouldn't do nothin' anyway. He just keeps talkin' so people will think he's in the right, that's all. He talks. I'll take them to the church, and they could wait for me there.

ALFIERI: Why, where are you going?

CATHERINE: Well, I gotta get Beatrice.

ALFIERI: I'd rather you didn't go home.

CATHERINE: Oh, no, for my wedding I gotta get Beatrice. Don't worry, he just talks big, he ain't gonna do nothin', Mr. Alfieri. I could go home.

ALFIERI, *nodding, not with assurance:* All right, then—let's go. *Marco rises. Rodolpho suddenly embraces him. Marco pats him on the back, his mind engrossed. Rodolpho goes to Catherine, kisses her hand. She pulls his head to her shoulder, and they go out. Marco faces Alfieri.* Only God, Marco.

Marco turns and walks out. Alfieri, with a certain processional tread, leaves the stage. The lights dim out.

Light rises in the apartment. Eddie is alone in the rocker, rocking back and forth in little surges. Pause. Now Beatrice emerges from a bedroom, then Catherine. Both are in their best clothes, wearing hats.

BEATRICE, *with fear:* I'll be back in about an hour, Eddie. All right?

EDDIE: What, have I been talkin' to myself?

BEATRICE: Eddie, for God's sake, it's her wedding.

EDDIE: Didn't you hear what I told you? You walk out that door to that wedding you ain't comin' back here, Beatrice.

BEATRICE: Why? What do you want?

EDDIE: I want my respect. Didn't you ever hear of that? From my wife?

CATHERINE: It's after three; we're supposed to be there already, Beatrice. The priest won't wait.

BEATRICE: Eddie. It's her wedding. There'll be nobody there from her family. For my sister let me go. I'm goin' for my sister.

EDDIE: Look, I been arguin' with you all day already, Beatrice, and I said what I'm gonna say. He's gonna come here and apologize to me or nobody from this house is goin' into that church today. Now if that's more to you than I am, then go. But don't come back. You be on my side or on their side, that's all.

CATHERINE, *suddenly:* Who the hell do you think you are?

BEATRICE: Sssh!

CATHERINE: You got no more right to tell nobody nothin'! Nobody! The rest of your life, nobody!

BEATRICE: Shut up, Katie!

CATHERINE, *pulling Beatrice by the arm:* You're gonna come with me!

BEATRICE: I can't, Katie, I can't—

CATHERINE: How can you listen to him? This rat!

Eddie gets up.

BEATRICE, *to Catherine, in terror at sight of his face:* Go, go—I'm not goin'—

CATHERINE: What're you scared of? He's a rat! He belongs in the sewer! In the garbage he belongs! *She is addressing him.* He's a rat from under the piers! He bites people when they sleep! He comes when nobody's lookin' and he poisons decent people!

Eddie rushes at her with his hand raised, and Beatrice struggles with him. Rodolpho appears, hurrying along the street, and runs up the stairs.

BEATRICE, *screaming:* Get out of here, Katie! *To Eddie:* Please, Eddie, Eddie, please!

EDDIE, *trying to free himself of Beatrice:* Don't bother me!

Rodolpho enters the apartment. A pause.

EDDIE: Get outa here.

RODOLPHO: Marco is coming, Eddie. *Pause. Beatrice raises her hands.* He's praying in the church. You understand?

Pause.

BEATRICE, *in terror:* Eddie. Eddie, get out.

EDDIE: What do you mean, get out?

BEATRICE: Eddie, you got kids, go 'way, go 'way from here! Get outa the house!

EDDIE: Me get outa the house? *Me* get outa the house?
What did I do that I gotta get outa the house?
That I wanted a girl not to turn into a tramp?
That I made a promise and I kept my promise
She should be sump'm in her life?

Catherine goes trembling to him.

CATHERINE: Eddie—

EDDIE: What do *you* want?

CATHERINE: Please, Eddie, go away. He's comin' for you.

EDDIE: What do you care? What do you care he's comin' for me?

CATHERINE—*weeping, she embraces him:* I never meant to do nothin' bad to you in my life, Eddie!

EDDIE, *with tears in his eyes:* Then who meant somethin' bad? How'd it get bad?

CATHERINE: I don't know, I don't know!

EDDIE, *pointing to Rodolpho with the new confidence of the embrace:* They made it bad! This one and his brother made it bad which they came like thieves to rob, to rob!

He grabs her arm and swings her behind him so that he is between her and Rodolpho, who is alone at the door.

You go tell him to come and come quick.
You go tell him I'm waitin' here for him to apologize
For what he said to me in front of the neighborhood!
Now get goin'!

RODOLPHO, *starting around Eddie toward Catherine:* Come, Catherine, we—

EDDIE, *nearly throwing Rodolpho out the door:* Get away from her!

RODOLPHO, *starting back in:* Catherine!

EDDIE, *turning on Catherine:* Tell him to get out! *She stands paralyzed before him.* Katie! I'll do somethin' if he don't get outa here!

BEATRICE, *rushing to him, her open hands pressed together before him as though in prayer:* Eddie, it's her husband, it's her husband! Let her go, it's her husband!

Catherine, moaning, breaks for the door, and she and Rodolpho start down the stairs; Eddie lunges and catches her; he holds her, and she weeps up into his face. And he kisses her on the lips.

EDDIE, *like a lover, out of his madness:* It's me, ain't it?
BEATRICE, *hitting his body:* Eddie! God, Eddie!
EDDIE: Katie, it's me, ain't it? You know it's me!
CATHERINE: Please, please, Eddie, lemme go. Heh? Please?

She moves to go. Marco appears on the street.

EDDIE, *to Rodolpho:* Punk! Tell her what you are! You know what you are, you punk!
CATHERINE, *pulling Rodolpho out the doorway:* Come on!

Eddie rushes after them to the doorway.

EDDIE: Make him tell you what he is! Tell her, punk! *He is on the stairway, calling down.* Why don't he answer me! Punk, answer me! *He rushes down the stairs, Beatrice after him.*
BEATRICE: Eddie, come back!

Outside, Rodolpho sees Marco and cries out, "No, Marco. Marco, go away, go away!" But Marco nears the stoop, looking up at the descending Eddie.

EDDIE, *emerging from the house:* Punk, what are you gonna do with a girl! I'm waitin' for your answer, punk. Where's your —answer!

He sees Marco. Two other neighbors appear on the street, stand and watch. Beatrice now comes in front of him.

BEATRICE: Go in the house, Eddie!
EDDIE, *pushing her aside, coming out challengingly on the stoop, and glaring down at Marco:* What do you mean, go in the house? Maybe he came to apologize to me.

To the people:

Which I took the blankets off my bed for them;
Which I brought up a girl, she wasn't even my daughter,
And I took from my own kids to give to her—
And they took her like you take from a stable,
Like you go in and rob from your own family!

And never a word to me!
And now accusations in the bargain?
Makin' my name like a dirty rag?

He faces Marco now, and moves toward him.

You gonna take that back?
BEATRICE: Eddie! Eddie!
EDDIE: I want my good name, Marco! You took my name!

Beatrice rushes past him to Marco and tries to push him away.

BEATRICE: Go, go!
MARCO: Animal! You go on your knees to me!

He strikes Eddie powerfully on the side of the head. Eddie falls back and draws a knife. Marco springs to a position of defense, both men circling each other. Eddie lunges, and Mike, Louis, and all the neighbors move in to stop them, and they fight up the steps of the stoop, and there is a wild scream—Beatrice's—and they all spread out, some of them running off.

Marco is standing over Eddie, who is on his knees, a bleeding knife in his hands. Eddie falls forward on his hands and knees, and he crawls a yard to Catherine. She raises her face away—but she does not move as he reaches over and grasps her leg, and, looking up at her, he seems puzzled, questioning, betrayed.

EDDIE: Catherine—why—?

He falls forward and dies. Catherine covers her face and weeps. She sinks down beside the weeping Beatrice. The lights fade, and Alfieri is illuminated in his office.

ALFIERI: Most of the time now we settle for half,
And I like it better.
And yet, when the tide is right
And the green smell of the sea
Floats in through my window,
The waves of this bay
Are the waves against Siracusa,
And I see a face that suddenly seems carved;
The eyes look like tunnels

Leading back toward some ancestral beach
Where all of us once lived.

And I wonder at those times
How much of all of us
Really lives there yet,
And when we will truly have moved on,
On and away from that dark place,
That world that has fallen to stones?

This is the end of the story. Good night.

THE CURTAIN FALLS

A VIEW FROM THE BRIDGE

A Play in Two Acts

THE CHARACTERS

LOUIS
MIKE
ALFIERI
EDDIE
CATHERINE
BEATRICE
MARCO
TONY
RODOLPHO
FIRST IMMIGRATION OFFICER
SECOND IMMIGRATION OFFICER
MR. LIPARI
MRS. LIPARI
TWO "SUBMARINES"
NEIGHBORS

ACT ONE

The street and house front of a tenement building. The front is skeletal entirely. The main acting area is the living room–dining room of Eddie's apartment. It is a worker's flat, clean, sparse, homely. There is a rocker down front; a round dining table at center, with chairs; and a portable phonograph.

At back are a bedroom door and an opening to the kitchen; none of these interiors are seen.

At the right, forestage, a desk. This is Mr. Alfieri's law office.

There is also a telephone booth. This is not used until the last scenes, so it may be covered or left in view.

A stairway leads up to the apartment, and then farther up to the next story, which is not seen.

Ramps, representing the street, run upstage and off to right and left.

As the curtain rises, Louis and Mike, longshoremen, are pitching coins against the building at left.

A distant foghorn blows.

Enter Alfieri, a lawyer in his fifties turning gray; he is portly, good-humored, and thoughtful. The two pitchers nod to him as he passes. He crosses the stage to his desk, removes his hat, runs his fingers through his hair, and grinning, speaks to the audience.

ALFIERI: You wouldn't have known it, but something amusing has just happened. You see how uneasily they nod to me? That's because I am a lawyer. In this neighborhood to meet a lawyer or a priest on the street is unlucky. We're only thought of in connection with disasters, and they'd rather not get too close.

I often think that behind that suspicious little nod of theirs lie three thousand years of distrust. A lawyer means the law, and in Sicily, from where their fathers came, the law has not been a friendly idea since the Greeks were beaten.

I am inclined to notice the ruins in things, perhaps because I was born in Italy. . . . I only came here when I was twenty-five. In those days, Al Capone, the greatest Carthaginian of all, was learning his trade on these pavements, and Frankie

Yale himself was cut precisely in half by a machine gun on the corner of Union Street, two blocks away. Oh, there were many here who were justly shot by unjust men. Justice is very important here.

But this is Red Hook, not Sicily. This is the slum that faces the bay on the seaward side of Brooklyn Bridge. This is the gullet of New York swallowing the tonnage of the world. And now we are quite civilized, quite American. Now we settle for half, and I like it better. I no longer keep a pistol in my filing cabinet.

And my practice is entirely unromantic.

My wife has warned me, so have my friends; they tell me the people in this neighborhood lack elegance, glamour. After all, who have I dealt with in my life? Longshoremen and their wives, and fathers and grandfathers, compensation cases, evictions, family squabbles—the petty troubles of the poor—and yet . . . every few years there is still a case, and as the parties tell me what the trouble is, the flat air in my office suddenly washes in with the green scent of the sea, the dust in this air is blown away and the thought comes that in some Caesar's year, in Calabria perhaps or on the cliff at Syracuse, another lawyer, quite differently dressed, heard the same complaint and sat there as powerless as I, and watched it run its bloody course.

Eddie has appeared and has been pitching coins with the men and is highlighted among them. He is forty—a husky, slightly overweight longshoreman.

This one's name was Eddie Carbone, a longshoreman working the docks from Brooklyn Bridge to the breakwater where the open sea begins.

Alfieri walks into darkness.

EDDIE, *moving up steps into doorway:* Well, I'll see ya, fellas.

Catherine enters from kitchen, crosses down to window, looks out.

LOUIS: You workin' tomorrow?
EDDIE: Yeah, there's another day yet on that ship. See ya, Louis.

Eddie goes into the house, as light rises in the apartment.

Catherine is waving to Louis from the window and turns to him.

CATHERINE: Hi, Eddie!

Eddie is pleased and therefore shy about it; he hangs up his cap and jacket.

EDDIE: Where you goin' all dressed up?
CATHERINE, *running her hands over her skirt:* I just got it. You like it?
EDDIE: Yeah, it's nice. And what happened to your hair?
CATHERINE: You like it? I fixed it different. *Calling to kitchen:* He's here, B.!
EDDIE: Beautiful. Turn around, lemme see in the back. *She turns for him.* Oh, if your mother was alive to see you now! She wouldn't believe it.
CATHERINE: You like it, huh?
EDDIE: You look like one of them girls that went to college. Where you goin'?
CATHERINE, *taking his arm:* Wait'll B. comes in, I'll tell you something. Here, sit down. *She is walking him to the arm-chair. Calling offstage:* Hurry up, will you, B.?
EDDIE, *sitting:* What's goin' on?
CATHERINE: I'll get you a beer, all right?
EDDIE: Well, tell me what happened. Come over here, talk to me.
CATHERINE: I want to wait till B. comes in. *She sits on her heels beside him.* Guess how much we paid for the skirt.
EDDIE: I think it's too short, ain't it?
CATHERINE, *standing:* No! not when I stand up.
EDDIE: Yeah, but you gotta sit down sometimes.
CATHERINE: Eddie, it's the style now. *She walks to show him.* I mean, if you see me walkin' down the street—
EDDIE: Listen, you been givin' me the willies the way you walk down the street, I mean it.
CATHERINE: Why?
EDDIE: Catherine, I don't want to be a pest, but I'm tellin' you you're walkin' wavy.

CATHERINE: I'm walkin' wavy?

EDDIE: Now don't aggravate me, Katie, you are walkin' wavy! I don't like the looks they're givin' you in the candy store. And with them new high heels on the sidewalk—clack, clack, clack. The heads are turnin' like windmills.

CATHERINE: But those guys look at all the girls, you know that.

EDDIE: You ain't "all the girls."

CATHERINE, *almost in tears because he disapproves:* What do you want me to do? You want me to—

EDDIE: Now don't get mad, kid.

CATHERINE: Well, I don't know what you want from me.

EDDIE: Katie, I promised your mother on her deathbed. I'm responsible for you. You're a baby, you don't understand these things. I mean like when you stand here by the window, wavin' outside.

CATHERINE: I was wavin' to Louis!

EDDIE: Listen, I could tell you things about Louis which you wouldn't wave to him no more.

CATHERINE, *trying to joke him out of his warning:* Eddie, I wish there was one guy you couldn't tell me things about!

EDDIE: Catherine, do me a favor, will you? You're gettin' to be a big girl now, you gotta keep yourself more, you can't be so friendly, kid. *Calls:* Hey, B., what're you doin' in there? *To Catherine:* Get her in here, will you? I got news for her.

CATHERINE, *starting out:* What?

EDDIE: Her cousins landed.

CATHERINE, *clapping her hands together:* No! *She turns instantly and starts for the kitchen.* B.! Your cousins!

Beatrice enters, wiping her hands with a towel.

BEATRICE, *in the face of Catherine's shout:* What?

CATHERINE: Your cousins got in!

BEATRICE, *astounded, turns to Eddie:* What are you talkin' about? Where?

EDDIE: I was just knockin' off work before and Tony Bereli come over to me; he says the ship is in the North River.

BEATRICE—*her hands are clasped at her breast; she seems half in fear, half in unutterable joy:* They're all right?

EDDIE: He didn't see them yet, they're still on board. But as

soon as they get off he'll meet them. He figures about ten o'clock they'll be here.

BEATRICE *sits, almost weak from tension:* And they'll let them off the ship all right? That's fixed, heh?

EDDIE: Sure, they give them regular seamen papers and they walk off with the crew. Don't worry about it, B., there's nothin' to it. Couple of hours they'll be here.

BEATRICE: What happened? They wasn't supposed to be till next Thursday.

EDDIE: I don't know; they put them on any ship they can get them out on. Maybe the other ship they was supposed to take there was some danger— What you cryin' about?

BEATRICE, *astounded and afraid:* I'm— I just—I can't believe it! I didn't even buy a new table cloth; I was gonna wash the walls—

EDDIE: Listen, they'll think it's a millionaire's house compared to the way they live. Don't worry about the walls. They'll be thankful. *To Catherine:* Whyn't you run down buy a table cloth. Go ahead, here. *He is reaching into his pocket.*

CATHERINE: There's no stores open now.

EDDIE, *to Beatrice:* You was gonna put a new cover on the chair.

BEATRICE: I know—well, I thought it was gonna be next week! I was gonna clean the walls, I was gonna wax the floors. *She stands disturbed.*

CATHERINE, *pointing upward:* Maybe Mrs. Dondero upstairs—

BEATRICE, *of the table cloth:* No, hers is worse than this one. *Suddenly:* My God, I don't even have nothin' to eat for them! *She starts for the kitchen.*

EDDIE, *reaching out and grabbing her arm:* Hey, hey! Take it easy.

BEATRICE: No, I'm just nervous, that's all. *To Catherine:* I'll make the fish.

EDDIE: You're savin' their lives, what're you worryin' about the table cloth? They probably didn't see a table cloth in their whole life where they come from.

BEATRICE, *looking into his eyes:* I'm just worried about you, that's all I'm worried.

EDDIE: Listen, as long as they know where they're gonna sleep.

BEATRICE: I told them in the letters. They're sleepin' on the floor.

EDDIE: Beatrice, all I'm worried about is you got such a heart that I'll end up on the floor with you, and they'll be in our bed.

BEATRICE: All right, stop it.

EDDIE: Because as soon as you see a tired relative, I end up on the floor.

BEATRICE: When did you end up on the floor?

EDDIE: When your father's house burned down I didn't end up on the floor?

BEATRICE: Well, their house burned down!

EDDIE: Yeah, but it didn't keep burnin' for two weeks!

BEATRICE: All right, look, I'll tell them to go someplace else. *She starts into the kitchen.*

EDDIE: Now wait a minute. Beatrice! *She halts. He goes to her.* I just don't want you bein' pushed around, that's all. You got too big a heart. *He touches her hand.* What're you so touchy?

BEATRICE: I'm just afraid if it don't turn out good you'll be mad at me.

EDDIE: Listen, if everybody keeps his mouth shut, nothin' can happen. They'll pay for their board.

BEATRICE: Oh, I told them.

EDDIE: Then what the hell. *Pause. He moves.* It's an honor, B. I mean it. I was just thinkin' before, comin' home, suppose my father didn't come to this country, and I was starvin' like them over there . . . and I had people in America could keep me a couple of months? The man would be honored to lend me a place to sleep.

BEATRICE—*there are tears in her eyes. She turns to Catherine:* You see what he is? *She turns and grabs Eddie's face in her hands.* Mmm! You're an angel! God'll bless you. *He is gratefully smiling.* You'll see, you'll get a blessing for this!

EDDIE, *laughing:* I'll settle for my own bed.

BEATRICE: Go, Baby, set the table.

CATHERINE: We didn't tell him about me yet.

BEATRICE: Let him eat first, then we'll tell him. Bring everything in. *She hurries Catherine out.*

EDDIE, *sitting at the table:* What's all that about? Where's she goin'?

BEATRICE: Noplace. It's very good news, Eddie. I want you to be happy.

EDDIE: What's goin' on?

Catherine enters with plates, forks.

BEATRICE: She's got a job.

Pause. Eddie looks at Catherine, then back to Beatrice.

EDDIE: What job? She's gonna finish school.
CATHERINE: Eddie, you won't believe it—
EDDIE: No—no, you gonna finish school. What kinda job, what do you mean? All of a sudden you—
CATHERINE: Listen a minute, it's wonderful.
EDDIE: It's not wonderful. You'll never get nowheres unless you finish school. You can't take no job. Why didn't you ask me before you take a job?
BEATRICE: She's askin' you now, she didn't take nothin' yet.
CATHERINE: Listen a minute! I came to school this morning and the principal called me out of the class, see? To go to his office.
EDDIE: Yeah?
CATHERINE: So I went in and he says to me he's got my records, y'know? And there's a company wants a girl right away. It ain't exactly a secretary, it's a stenographer first, but pretty soon you get to be secretary. And he says to me that I'm the best student in the whole class—
BEATRICE: You hear that?
EDDIE: Well why not? Sure she's the best.
CATHERINE: I'm the best student, he says, and if I want, I should take the job and the end of the year he'll let me take the examination and he'll give me the certificate. So I'll save practically a year!
EDDIE, *strangely nervous:* Where's the job? What company?
CATHERINE: It's a big plumbing company over Nostrand Avenue.
EDDIE: Nostrand Avenue and where?
CATHERINE: It's someplace by the Navy Yard.
BEATRICE: Fifty dollars a week, Eddie.
EDDIE, *to Catherine, surprised:* Fifty?
CATHERINE: I swear.

Pause.

EDDIE: What about all the stuff you wouldn't learn this year, though?

CATHERINE: There's nothin' more to learn, Eddie, I just gotta practice from now on. I know all the symbols and I know the keyboard. I'll just get faster, that's all. And when I'm workin' I'll keep gettin' better and better, you see?

BEATRICE: Work is the best practice anyway.

EDDIE: That ain't what I wanted, though.

CATHERINE: Why! It's a great big company—

EDDIE: I don't like that neighborhood over there.

CATHERINE: It's a block and half from the subway, he says.

EDDIE: Near the Navy Yard plenty can happen in a block and a half. And a plumbin' company! That's one step over the water front. They're practically longshoremen.

BEATRICE: Yeah, but she'll be in the office, Eddie.

EDDIE: I know she'll be in the office, but that ain't what I had in mind.

BEATRICE: Listen, she's gotta go to work sometime.

EDDIE: Listen, B., she'll be with a lotta plumbers? And sailors up and down the street? So what did she go to school for?

CATHERINE: But it's fifty a week, Eddie.

EDDIE: Look, did I ask you for money? I supported you this long I support you a little more. Please, do me a favor, will ya? I want you to be with different kind of people. I want you to be in a nice office. Maybe a lawyer's office someplace in New York in one of them nice buildings. I mean if you're gonna get outa here then get out; don't go practically in the same kind of neighborhood.

Pause. Catherine lowers her eyes.

BEATRICE: Go, Baby, bring in the supper. *Catherine goes out.* Think about it a little bit, Eddie. Please. She's crazy to start work. It's not a little shop, it's a big company. Some day she could be a secretary. They picked her out of the whole class. *He is silent, staring down at the tablecloth, fingering the pattern.* What are you worried about? She could take care of herself. She'll get out of the subway and be in the office in two minutes.

EDDIE, *somehow sickened:* I know that neighborhood, B., I don't like it.

BEATRICE: Listen, if nothin' happened to her in this neighborhood it ain't gonna happen noplace else. *She turns his face to her.* Look, you gotta get used to it, she's no baby no more. Tell her to take it. *He turns his head away.* You hear me? *She is angering.* I don't understand you; she's seventeen years old, you gonna keep her in the house all her life?

EDDIE, *insulted:* What kinda remark is that?

BEATRICE, *with sympathy but insistent force:* Well, I don't understand when it ends. First it was gonna be when she graduated high school, so she graduated high school. Then it was gonna be when she learned stenographer, so she learned stenographer. So what're we gonna wait for now? I mean it, Eddie, sometimes I don't understand you; they picked her out of the whole class, it's an honor for her.

Catherine enters with food, which she silently sets on the table. After a moment of watching her face, Eddie breaks into a smile, but it almost seems that tears will form in his eyes.

EDDIE: With your hair that way you look like a madonna, you know that? You're the madonna type. *She doesn't look at him, but continues ladling out food onto the plates.* You wanna go to work, heh, Madonna?

CATHERINE, *softly:* Yeah.

EDDIE, *with a sense of her childhood, her babyhood, and the years:* All right, go to work. *She looks at him, then rushes and hugs him.* Hey, hey! Take it easy! *He holds her face away from him to look at her.* What're you cryin' about? *He is affected by her, but smiles his emotion away.*

CATHERINE, *sitting at her place:* I just— *Bursting out:* I'm gonna buy all new dishes with my first pay! *They laugh warmly.* I mean it. I'll fix up the whole house! I'll buy a rug!

EDDIE: And then you'll move away.

CATHERINE: No, Eddie!

EDDIE, *grinning:* Why not? That's life. And you'll come visit on Sundays, then once a month, then Christmas and New Year's, finally.

CATHERINE, *grasping his arm to reassure him and to erase the accusation:* No, please!

EDDIE, *smiling but hurt:* I only ask you one thing—don't trust

nobody. You got a good aunt but she's got too big a heart, you learned bad from her. Believe me.

BEATRICE: Be the way you are, Katie, don't listen to him.

EDDIE, *to Beatrice—strangely and quickly resentful:* You lived in a house all your life, what do you know about it? You never worked in your life.

BEATRICE: She likes people. What's wrong with that?

EDDIE: Because most people ain't people. She's goin' to work; plumbers; they'll chew her to pieces if she don't watch out. *To Catherine:* Believe me, Katie, the less you trust, the less you be sorry.

Eddie crosses himself and the women do the same, and they eat.

CATHERINE: First thing I'll buy is a rug, heh, B.?

BEATRICE: I don't mind. *To Eddie:* I smelled coffee all day today. You unloadin' coffee today?

EDDIE: Yeah, a Brazil ship.

CATHERINE: I smelled it too. It smelled all over the neighborhood.

EDDIE: That's one time, boy, to be a longshoreman is a pleasure. I could work coffee ships twenty hours a day. You go down in the hold, y'know? It's like flowers, that smell. We'll bust a bag tomorrow, I'll bring you some.

BEATRICE: Just be sure there's no spiders in it, will ya? I mean it. *She directs this to Catherine, rolling her eyes upward.* I still remember that spider coming out of that bag he brung home. I nearly died.

EDDIE: You call that a spider? You oughta see what comes outa the bananas sometimes.

BEATRICE: Don't talk about it!

EDDIE: I seen spiders could stop a Buick.

BEATRICE, *clapping her hands over her ears:* All right, shut up!

EDDIE, *laughing and taking a watch out of his pocket:* Well, who started with spiders?

BEATRICE: All right, I'm sorry, I didn't mean it. Just don't bring none home again. What time is it?

EDDIE: Quarter nine. *Puts watch back in his pocket.*

They continue eating in silence.

CATHERINE: He's bringin' them ten o'clock, Tony?

EDDIE: Around, yeah. *He eats.*

CATHERINE: Eddie, suppose somebody asks if they're livin' here. *He looks at her as though already she had divulged something publicly. Defensively:* I mean if they ask.

EDDIE: Now look, Baby, I can see we're gettin' mixed up again here.

CATHERINE: No, I just mean . . . people'll see them goin' in and out.

EDDIE: I don't care who sees them goin' in and out as long as you don't see them goin' in and out. And this goes for you too, B. You don't see nothin' and you don't know nothin'.

BEATRICE: What do you mean? I understand.

EDDIE: You don't understand; you still think you can talk about this to somebody just a little bit. Now lemme say it once and for all, because you're makin' me nervous again, both of you. I don't care if somebody comes in the house and sees them sleepin' on the floor, it never comes out of your mouth who they are or what they're doin' here.

BEATRICE: Yeah, but my mother'll know—

EDDIE: Sure she'll know, but just don't you be the one who told her, that's all. This is the United States government you're playin' with now, this is the Immigration Bureau. If you said it you knew it, if you didn't say it you didn't know it.

CATHERINE: Yeah, but Eddie, suppose somebody—

EDDIE: I don't care what question it is. You—don't—know—nothin'. They got stool pigeons all over this neighborhood they're payin' them every week for information, and you don't know who they are. It could be your best friend. You hear? *To Beatrice:* Like Vinny Bolzano, remember Vinny?

BEATRICE: Oh, yeah. God forbid.

EDDIE: Tell her about Vinny. *To Catherine:* You think I'm blowin' steam here? *To Beatrice:* Go ahead, tell her. *To Catherine:* You was a baby then. There was a family lived next door to her mother, he was about sixteen—

BEATRICE: No, he was no more than fourteen, cause I was to his confirmation in Saint Agnes. But the family had an uncle that they were hidin' in the house, and he snitched to the Immigration.

CATHERINE: The kid snitched?

EDDIE: On his own uncle!

CATHERINE: What, was he crazy?

EDDIE: He was crazy after, I tell you that, boy.

BEATRICE: Oh, it was terrible. He had five brothers and the old father. And they grabbed him in the kitchen and pulled him down the stairs—three flights his head was bouncin' like a coconut. And they spit on him in the street, his own father and his brothers. The whole neighborhood was cryin'.

CATHERINE: Ts! So what happened to him?

BEATRICE: I think he went away. *To Eddie:* I never seen him again, did you?

EDDIE *rises during this, taking out his watch:* Him? You'll never see him no more, a guy do a thing like that? How's he gonna show his face? *To Catherine, as he gets up uneasily:* Just remember, kid, you can quicker get back a million dollars that was stole than a word that you gave away. *He is standing now, stretching his back.*

CATHERINE: Okay, I won't say a word to nobody, I swear.

EDDIE: Gonna rain tomorrow. We'll be slidin' all over the decks. Maybe you oughta put something on for them, they be here soon.

BEATRICE: I only got fish, I hate to spoil it if they ate already. I'll wait, it only takes a few minutes; I could broil it.

CATHERINE: What happens, Eddie, when that ship pulls out and they ain't on it, though? Don't the captain say nothin'?

EDDIE, *slicing an apple with his pocket knife:* Captain's pieced off, what do you mean?

CATHERINE: Even the captain?

EDDIE: What's the matter, the captain don't have to live? Captain gets a piece, maybe one of the mates, piece for the guy in Italy who fixed the papers for them, Tony here'll get a little bite. . . .

BEATRICE: I just hope they get work here, that's all I hope.

EDDIE: Oh, the syndicate'll fix jobs for them; till they pay 'em off they'll get them work every day. It's after the pay-off, then they'll have to scramble like the rest of us.

BEATRICE: Well, it be better than they got there.

EDDIE: Oh sure, well, listen. So you gonna start Monday, heh, Madonna?

CATHERINE, *embarrassed:* I'm supposed to, yeah.

Eddie is standing facing the two seated women. First Beatrice smiles, then Catherine, for a powerful emotion is on him, a childish one and a knowing fear, and the tears show in his eyes —and they are shy before the avowal.

EDDIE, *sadly smiling, yet somehow proud of her:* Well . . . I hope you have good luck. I wish you the best. You know that, kid.

CATHERINE, *rising, trying to laugh:* You sound like I'm goin' a million miles!

EDDIE: I know. I guess I just never figured on one thing.

CATHERINE, *smiling:* What?

EDDIE: That you would ever grow up. *He utters a soundless laugh at himself, feeling his breast pocket of his shirt.* I left a cigar in my other coat, I think. *He starts for the bedroom.*

CATHERINE: Stay there! I'll get it for you.

She hurries out. There is a slight pause, and Eddie turns to Beatrice, who has been avoiding his gaze.

EDDIE: What are you mad at me lately?

BEATRICE: Who's mad? *She gets up, clearing the dishes.* I'm not mad. *She picks up the dishes and turns to him.* You're the one is mad. *She turns and goes into the kitchen as Catherine enters from the bedroom with a cigar and a pack of matches.*

CATHERINE: Here! I'll light it for you! *She strikes a match and holds it to his cigar. He puffs. Quietly:* Don't worry about me, Eddie, heh?

EDDIE: Don't burn yourself. *Just in time she blows out the match.* You better go in help her with the dishes.

CATHERINE *turns quickly to the table, and, seeing the table cleared, she says, almost guiltily:* Oh! *She hurries into the kitchen, and as she exits there:* I'll do the dishes, B.!

Alone, Eddie stands looking toward the kitchen for a moment. Then he takes out his watch, glances at it, replaces it in his pocket, sits in the armchair, and stares at the smoke flowing out of his mouth.

The lights go down, then come up on Alfieri, who has moved onto the forestage.

ALFIERI: He was as good a man as he had to be in a life that

was hard and even. He worked on the piers when there was work, he brought home his pay, and he lived. And toward ten o'clock of that night, after they had eaten, the cousins came.

The lights fade on Alfieri and rise on the street.

Enter Tony, escorting Marco and Rodolpho, each with a valise. Tony halts, indicates the house. They stand for a moment looking at it.

MARCO—*he is a square-built peasant of thirty-two, suspicious, tender, and quiet-voiced:* Thank you.
TONY: You're on your own now. Just be careful, that's all. Ground floor.
MARCO: Thank you.
TONY, *indicating the house:* I'll see you on the pier tomorrow. You'll go to work.

Marco nods. Tony continues on walking down the street.

RODOLPHO: This will be the first house I ever walked into in America! Imagine! She said they were poor!
MARCO: Ssh! Come. *They go to door.*

Marco knocks. The lights rise in the room. Eddie goes and opens the door. Enter Marco and Rodolpho, removing their caps. Beatrice and Catherine enter from the kitchen. The lights fade in the street.

EDDIE: You Marco?
MARCO: Marco.
EDDIE: Come on in! *He shakes Marco's hand.*
BEATRICE: Here, take the bags!
MARCO *nods, looks to the women and fixes on Beatrice. Crosses to Beatrice.* Are you my cousin?

She nods. He kisses her hand.

BEATRICE, *above the table, touching her chest with her hand:* Beatrice. This is my husband, Eddie. *All nod.* Catherine, my sister Nancy's daughter. *The Brothers nod.*
MARCO, *indicating Rodolpho:* My brother. Rodolpho. *Rodol-*

pho nods. Marco comes with a certain formal stiffness to Eddie. I want to tell you now Eddie—when you say go, we will go.

EDDIE: Oh, no . . . *Takes Marco's bag.*

MARCO: I see it's a small house, but soon, maybe, we can have our own house.

EDDIE: You're welcome, Marco, we got plenty of room here. Katie, give them supper, heh? *Exits into bedroom with their bags.*

CATHERINE: Come here, sit down. I'll get you some soup.

MARCO, *as they go to the table:* We ate on the ship. Thank you. *To Eddie, calling off to bedroom:* Thank you.

BEATRICE: Get some coffee. We'll all have coffee. Come sit down.

Rodolpho and Marco sit, at the table.

CATHERINE, *wondrously:* How come he's so dark and you're so light, Rodolpho?

RODOLPHO, *ready to laugh:* I don't know. A thousand years ago, they say, the Danes invaded Sicily.

Beatrice kisses Rodolpho. They laugh as Eddie enters.

CATHERINE, *to Beatrice:* He's practically blond!

EDDIE: How's the coffee doin'?

CATHERINE, *brought up:* I'm gettin' it. *She hurries out to kitchen.*

EDDIE *sits on his rocker:* Yiz have a nice trip?

MARCO: The ocean is always rough. But we are good sailors.

EDDIE: No trouble gettin' here?

MARCO: No. The man brought us. Very nice man.

RODOLPHO, *to Eddie:* He says we start to work tomorrow. Is he honest?

EDDIE, *laughing:* No. But as long as you owe them money, they'll get you plenty of work. *To Marco:* Yiz ever work on the piers in Italy?

MARCO: Piers? Ts!—no.

RODOLPHO, *smiling at the smallness of his town:* In our town there are no piers, only the beach, and little fishing boats.

BEATRICE: So what kinda work did yiz do?

MARCO, *shrugging shyly, even embarrassed:* Whatever there is, anything.

RODOLPHO: Sometimes they build a house, or if they fix the

bridge—Marco is a mason and I bring him the cement. *He laughs.* In harvest time we work in the fields . . . if there is work. Anything.

EDDIE: Still bad there, heh?

MARCO: Bad, yes.

RODOLPHO, *laughing:* It's terrible! We stand around all day in the piazza listening to the fountain like birds. Everybody waits only for the train.

BEATRICE: What's on the train?

RODOLPHO: Nothing. But if there are many passengers and you're lucky you make a few lire to push the taxi up the hill.

Enter Catherine; she listens.

BEATRICE: You gotta push a taxi?

RODOLPHO, *laughing:* Oh, sure! It's a feature in our town. The horses in our town are skinnier than goats. So if there are too many passengers we help to push the carriages up to the hotel. *He laughs.* In our town the horses are only for show.

CATHERINE: Why don't they have automobile taxis?

RODOLPHO: There is one. We push that too. *They laugh.* Everything in our town, you gotta push!

BEATRICE, *to Eddie:* How do you like that!

EDDIE, *to Marco:* So what're you wanna do, you gonna stay here in this country or you wanna go back?

MARCO, *surprised:* Go back?

EDDIE: Well, you're married, ain't you?

MARCO: Yes. I have three children.

BEATRICE: Three! I thought only one.

MARCO: Oh, no. I have three now. Four years, five years, six years.

BEATRICE: Ah . . . I bet they're cryin' for you already, heh?

MARCO: What can I do? The older one is sick in his chest. My wife—she feeds them from her own mouth. I tell you the truth, if I stay there they will never grow up. They eat the sunshine.

BEATRICE: My God. So how long you want to stay?

MARCO: With your permission, we will stay maybe a—

EDDIE: She don't mean in this house, she means in the country.

MARCO: Oh. Maybe four, five, six years, I think.

RODOLPHO, *smiling:* He trusts his wife.

BEATRICE: Yeah, but maybe you'll get enough, you'll be able to go back quicker.

MARCO: I hope. I don't know. *To Eddie:* I understand it's not so good here either.

EDDIE: Oh, you guys'll be all right—till you pay them off, anyway. After that, you'll have to scramble, that's all. But you'll make better here than you could there.

RODOLPHO: How much? We hear all kinds of figures. How much can a man make? We work hard, we'll work all day, all night—

Marco raises a hand to hush him.

EDDIE—*he is coming more and more to address Marco only:* On the average a whole year? Maybe—well, it's hard to say, see. Sometimes we lay off, there's no ships three four weeks.

MARCO: Three, four weeks!—Ts!

EDDIE: But I think you could probably—thirty, forty a week, over the whole twelve months of the year.

MARCO, *rises, crosses to Eddie:* Dollars.

EDDIE: Sure dollars.

Marco puts an arm round Rodolpho and they laugh.

MARCO: If we can stay here a few months, Beatrice—

BEATRICE: Listen, you're welcome, Marco—

MARCO: Because I could send them a little more if I stay here.

BEATRICE: As long as you want, we got plenty a room.

MARCO, *his eyes are showing tears:* My wife— *To Eddie:* My wife —I want to send right away maybe twenty dollars—

EDDIE: You could send them something next week already.

MARCO—*he is near tears:* Eduardo . . . *He goes to Eddie, offering his hand.*

EDDIE: Don't thank me. Listen, what the hell, it's no skin off me. *To Catherine:* What happened to the coffee?

CATHERINE: I got it on. *To Rodolpho:* You married too? No.

RODOLPHO *rises:* Oh, no . . .

BEATRICE, *to Catherine:* I told you he—

CATHERINE: I know, I just thought maybe he got married recently.

RODOLPHO: I have no money to get married. I have a nice face, but no money. *He laughs.*

CATHERINE, *to Beatrice:* He's a real blond!

BEATRICE, *to Rodolpho:* You want to stay here too, heh? For good?

RODOLPHO: Me? Yes, forever! Me, I want to be an American. And then I want to go back to Italy when I am rich, and I will buy a motorcycle. *He smiles. Marco shakes him affectionately.*

CATHERINE: A motorcycle!

RODOLPHO: With a motorcycle in Italy you will never starve any more.

BEATRICE: I'll get you coffee. *She exits to the kitchen.*

EDDIE: What you do with a motorcycle?

MARCO: He dreams, he dreams.

RODOLPHO, *to Marco:* Why? *To Eddie:* Messages! The rich people in the hotel always need someone who will carry a message. But quickly, and with a great noise. With a blue motorcycle I would station myself in the courtyard of the hotel, and in a little while I would have messages.

MARCO: When you have no wife you have dreams.

EDDIE: Why can't you just walk, or take a trolley or sump'm?

Enter Beatrice with coffee.

RODOLPHO: Oh, no, the machine, the machine is necessary. A man comes into a great hotel and says, I am a messenger. Who is this man? He disappears walking, there is no noise, nothing. Maybe he will never come back, maybe he will never deliver the message. But a man who rides up on a great machine, this man is responsible, this man exists. He will be given messages. *He helps Beatrice set out the coffee things.* I am also a singer, though.

EDDIE: You mean a regular—?

RODOLPHO: Oh, yes. One night last year Andreola got sick. Baritone. And I took his place in the garden of the hotel. Three arias I sang without a mistake! Thousand-lire notes they threw from the tables, money was falling like a storm in the treasury. It was magnificent. We lived six months on that night, eh, Marco?

Marco nods doubtfully.

MARCO: Two months.

Eddie laughs.

BEATRICE: Can't you get a job in that place?
RODOLPHO: Andreola got better. He's a baritone, very strong.

Beatrice laughs.

MARCO, *regretfully, to Beatrice:* He sang too loud.
RODOLPHO: Why too loud?
MARCO: Too loud. The guests in that hotel are all Englishmen. They don't like too loud.
RODOLPHO, *to Catherine:* Nobody ever said it was too loud!
MARCO: I say. It was too loud. *To Beatrice:* I knew it as soon as he started to sing. Too loud.
RODOLPHO: Then why did they throw so much money?
MARCO: They paid for your courage. The English like courage. But once is enough.
RODOLPHO, *to all but Marco:* I never heard anybody say it was too loud.
CATHERINE: Did you ever hear of jazz?
RODOLPHO: Oh, sure! I *sing* jazz.
CATHERINE *rises:* You could sing jazz?
RODOLPHO: Oh, I sing Napolidan, jazz, bel canto— I sing "Paper Doll," you like "Paper Doll"?
CATHERINE: Oh, sure, I'm crazy for "Paper Doll." Go ahead, sing it.
RODOLPHO *takes his stance after getting a nod of permission from Marco, and with a high tenor voice begins singing:*

"I'll tell you boys it's tough to be alone,
And it's tough to love a doll that's not your own.
I'm through with all of them,
I'll never fall again,
Hey, boy, what you gonna do?
I'm gonna buy a paper doll that I can call my own,
A doll that other fellows cannot steal.

Eddie rises and moves upstage.

And then those flirty, flirty guys
With their flirty, flirty eyes
Will have to flirt with dollies that are real—

EDDIE: Hey, kid—hey, wait a minute—

CATHERINE, *enthralled:* Leave him finish, it's beautiful! *To Beatrice:* He's terrific! It's terrific, Rodolpho.

EDDIE: Look, kid; you don't want to be picked up, do ya?

MARCO: No—no! *He rises.*

EDDIE, *indicating the rest of the building:* Because we never had no singers here . . . and all of a sudden there's a singer in the house, y'know what I mean?

MARCO: Yes, yes. You'll be quiet, Rodolpho.

EDDIE—*he is flushed:* They got guys all over the place, Marco. I mean.

MARCO: Yes. He'll be quiet. *To Rodolpho:* You'll be quiet.

Rodolpho nods.

Eddie has risen, with iron control, even a smile. He moves to Catherine.

EDDIE: What's the high heels for, Garbo?

CATHERINE: I figured for tonight—

EDDIE: Do me a favor, will you? Go ahead.

Embarrassed now, angered, Catherine goes out into the bedroom. Beatrice watches her go and gets up; in passing, she gives Eddie a cold look, restrained only by the strangers, and goes to the table to pour coffee.

EDDIE, *striving to laugh, and to Marco, but directed as much to Beatrice:* All actresses they want to be around here.

RODOLPHO, *happy about it:* In Italy too! All the girls.

Catherine emerges from the bedroom in low-heel shoes, comes to the table. Rodolpho is lifting a cup.

EDDIE—*he is sizing up Rodolpho, and there is a concealed suspicion:* Yeah, heh?

RODOLPHO: Yes! *Laughs, indicating Catherine:* Especially when they are so beautiful!

CATHERINE: You like sugar?

RODOLPHO: Sugar? Yes! I like sugar very much!

Eddie is downstage, watching as she pours a spoonful of sugar into his cup, his face puffed with trouble, and the room dies.

Lights rise on Alfieri.

ALFIERI: Who can ever know what will be discovered? Eddie Carbone had never expected to have a destiny. A man works, raises his family, goes bowling, eats, gets old, and then he dies. Now, as the weeks passed, there was a future, there was a trouble that would not go away.

The lights fade on Alfieri, then rise on Eddie standing at the doorway of the house. Beatrice enters on the street. She sees Eddie, smiles at him. He looks away.

She starts to enter the house when Eddie speaks.

EDDIE: It's after eight.
BEATRICE: Well, it's a long show at the Paramount.
EDDIE: They must've seen every picture in Brooklyn by now. He's supposed to stay in the house when he ain't working. He ain't supposed to go advertising himself.
BEATRICE: Well that's his trouble, what do you care? If they pick him up they pick him up, that's all. Come in the house.
EDDIE: What happened to the stenography? I don't see her practice no more.
BEATRICE: She'll get back to it. She's excited, Eddie.
EDDIE: She tell you anything?
BEATRICE *comes to him, now the subject is opened:* What's the matter with you? He's a nice kid, what do you want from him?
EDDIE: That's a nice kid? He gives me the heeby-jeebies.
BEATRICE, *smiling:* Ah, go on, you're just jealous.
EDDIE: Of *him*? Boy, you don't think much of me.
BEATRICE: I don't understand you. What's so terrible about him?
EDDIE: You mean it's all right with you? That's gonna be her husband?
BEATRICE: Why? He's a nice fella, hard workin', he's a good-lookin' fella.
EDDIE: He sings on the ships, didja know that?
BEATRICE: What do you mean, he sings?
EDDIE: Just what I said, he sings. Right on the deck, all of a sudden, a whole song comes out of his mouth—with motions. You know what they're callin' him now? Paper Doll

they're callin' him, Canary. He's like a weird. He comes out on the pier, one-two-three, it's a regular free show.

BEATRICE: Well, he's a kid; he don't know how to behave himself yet.

EDDIE: And with that wacky hair; he's like a chorus girl or sump'm.

BEATRICE: So he's blond, so—

EDDIE: I just hope that's his regular hair, that's all I hope.

BEATRICE: You crazy or sump'm? *She tries to turn him to her.*

EDDIE—*he keeps his head turned away:* What's so crazy? I don't like his whole way.

BEATRICE: Listen, you never seen a blond guy in your life? What about Whitey Balso?

EDDIE, *turning to her victoriously:* Sure, but Whitey don't sing; he don't do like that on the ships.

BEATRICE: Well, maybe that's the way they do in Italy.

EDDIE: Then why don't his brother sing? Marco goes around like a man; nobody kids Marco. *He moves from her, halts. She realizes there is a campaign solidified in him.* I tell you the truth I'm surprised I have to tell you all this. I mean I'm surprised, B.

BEATRICE—*she goes to him with purpose now:* Listen, you ain't gonna start nothin' here.

EDDIE: I ain't startin' nothin', but I ain't gonna stand around lookin' at that. For that character I didn't bring her up. I swear, B., I'm surprised at you; I sit there waitin' for you to wake up but everything is great with you.

BEATRICE: No, everything ain't great with me.

EDDIE: No?

BEATRICE: No. But I got other worries.

EDDIE: Yeah. *He is already weakening.*

BEATRICE: Yeah, you want me to tell you?

EDDIE, *in retreat:* Why? What worries you got?

BEATRICE: When am I gonna be a wife again, Eddie?

EDDIE: I ain't been feelin' good. They bother me since they came.

BEATRICE: It's almost three months you don't feel good; they're only here a couple of weeks. It's three months, Eddie.

EDDIE: I don't know, B. I don't want to talk about it.
BEATRICE: What's the matter, Eddie, you don't like me, heh?
EDDIE: What do you mean, I don't like you? I said I don't feel good, that's all.
BEATRICE: Well, tell me, am I doing something wrong? Talk to me.
EDDIE—*Pause. He can't speak, then:* I can't. I can't talk about it.
BEATRICE: Well tell me what—
EDDIE: I got nothin' to say about it!

She stands for a moment; he is looking off; she turns to go into the house.

EDDIE: I'll be all right, B.; just lay off me, will ya? I'm worried about her.
BEATRICE: The girl is gonna be eighteen years old, it's time already.
EDDIE: B., he's taking her for a ride!
BEATRICE: All right, that's her ride. What're you gonna stand over her till she's forty? Eddie, I want you to cut it out now, you hear me? I don't like it! Now come in the house.
EDDIE: I want to take a walk, I'll be in right away.
BEATRICE: They ain't goin' to come any quicker if you stand in the street. It ain't nice, Eddie.
EDDIE: I'll be in right away. Go ahead. *He walks off.*

She goes into the house. Eddie glances up the street, sees Louis and Mike coming, and sits on an iron railing. Louis and Mike enter.

LOUIS: Wanna go bowlin' tonight?
EDDIE: I'm too tired. Goin' to sleep.
LOUIS: How's your two submarines?
EDDIE: They're okay.
LOUIS: I see they're gettin' work allatime.
EDDIE: Oh yeah, they're doin' all right.
MIKE: That's what we oughta do. We oughta leave the country and come in under the water. Then we get work.
EDDIE: You ain't kiddin'.

LOUIS: Well, what the hell. Y'know?

EDDIE: Sure.

LOUIS—*sits on railing beside Eddie:* Believe me, Eddie, you got a lotta credit comin' to you.

EDDIE: Aah, they don't bother me, don't cost me nutt'n.

MIKE: That older one, boy, he's a regular bull. I seen him the other day liftin' coffee bags over the Matson Line. They leave him alone he woulda load the whole ship by himself.

EDDIE: Yeah, he's a strong guy, that guy. Their father was a regular giant, supposed to be.

LOUIS: Yeah, you could see. He's a regular slave.

MIKE, *grinning:* That blond one, though— *Eddie looks at him.* He's got a sense of humor. *Louis snickers.*

EDDIE, *searchingly:* Yeah. He's funny—

MIKE, *starting to laugh:* Well he ain't exackly funny, but he's always like makin' remarks like, y'know? He comes around, everybody's laughin'. *Louis laughs.*

EDDIE, *uncomfortably, grinning:* Yeah, well . . . he's got a sense of humor.

MIKE, *laughing:* Yeah, I mean, he's always makin' like remarks, like, y'know?

EDDIE: Yeah, I know. But he's a kid yet, y'know? He—he's just a kid, that's all.

MIKE, *getting hysterical with Louis:* I know. You take one look at him—everybody's happy. *Louis laughs.* I worked one day with him last week over the Moore-MacCormack Line, I'm tellin' you they was all hysterical. *Louis and he explode in laughter.*

EDDIE: Why? What'd he do?

MIKE: I don't know . . . he was just humorous. You never can remember what he says, y'know? But it's the way he says it. I mean he gives you a look sometimes and you start laughin'!

EDDIE: Yeah. *Troubled:* He's got a sense of humor.

MIKE, *gasping:* Yeah.

LOUIS, *rising:* Well, we see ya, Eddie.

EDDIE: Take it easy.

LOUIS: Yeah. See ya.

MIKE: If you wanna come bowlin' later we're goin' Flatbush Avenue.

Laughing, they move to exit, meeting Rodolpho and Catherine entering on the street. Their laughter rises as they see Rodolpho, who does not understand but joins in. Eddie moves to enter the house as Louis and Mike exit. Catherine stops him at the door.

CATHERINE: Hey, Eddie—what a picture we saw! Did we laugh!

EDDIE—*he can't help smiling at sight of her:* Where'd you go?

CATHERINE: Paramount. It was with those two guys, y'know? That—

EDDIE: Brooklyn Paramount?

CATHERINE, *with an edge of anger, embarrassed before Rodolpho:* Sure, the Brooklyn Paramount. I told you we wasn't goin' to New York.

EDDIE, *retreating before the threat of her anger:* All right, I only asked you. *To Rodolpho:* I just don't want her hangin' around Times Square, see? It's full of tramps over there.

RODOLPHO: I would like to go to Broadway once, Eddie. I would like to walk with her once where the theaters are and the opera. Since I was a boy I see pictures of those lights.

EDDIE, *his little patience waning:* I want to talk to her a minute, Rodolpho. Go inside, will you?

RODOLPHO: Eddie, we only walk together in the streets. She teaches me.

CATHERINE: You know what he can't get over? That there's no fountains in Brooklyn!

EDDIE, *smiling unwillingly:* Fountains? *Rodolpho smiles at his own naïveté.*

CATHERINE: In Italy he says, every town's got fountains, and they meet there. And you know what? They got oranges on the trees where he comes from, and lemons. Imagine —on the trees? I mean it's interesting. But he's crazy for New York.

RODOLPHO, *attempting familiarity:* Eddie, why can't we go once to Broadway—?

EDDIE: Look, I gotta tell her something—

RODOLPHO: Maybe you can come too. I want to see all those lights. *He sees no response in Eddie's face. He glances at Catherine.* I'll walk by the river before I go to sleep. *He walks off down the street.*

CATHERINE: Why don't you talk to him, Eddie? He blesses you, and you don't talk to him hardly.

EDDIE, *enveloping her with his eyes:* I bless you and you don't talk to me. *He tries to smile.*

CATHERINE: *I* don't talk to you? *She hits his arm.* What do you mean?

EDDIE: I don't see you no more. I come home you're runnin' around someplace—

CATHERINE: Well, he wants to see everything, that's all, so we go. . . . You mad at me?

EDDIE: No. *He moves from her, smiling sadly.* It's just I used to come home, you was always there. Now, I turn around, you're a big girl. I don't know how to talk to you.

CATHERINE: Why?

EDDIE: I don't know, you're runnin', you're runnin', Katie. I don't think you listening any more to me.

CATHERINE, *going to him:* Ah, Eddie, sure I am. What's the matter? You don't like him?

Slight pause.

EDDIE, *turns to her: You* like him, Katie?

CATHERINE, *with a blush but holding her ground:* Yeah. I like him.

EDDIE—*his smile goes:* You like him.

CATHERINE, *looking down:* Yeah. *Now she looks at him for the consequences, smiling but tense. He looks at her like a lost boy.* What're you got against him? I don't understand. He only blesses you.

EDDIE *turns away:* He don't bless me, Katie.

CATHERINE: He does! You're like a father to him!

EDDIE *turns to her:* Katie.

CATHERINE: What, Eddie?

EDDIE: You gonna marry him?

CATHERINE: I don't know. We just been . . . goin' around, that's all. *Turns to him:* What're you got against him, Eddie? Please, tell me. What?

EDDIE: He don't respect you.

CATHERINE: Why?

EDDIE: Katie . . . if you wasn't an orphan, wouldn't he ask

your father's permission before he run around with you like this?

CATHERINE: Oh, well, he didn't think you'd mind.

EDDIE: He knows I mind, but it don't bother him if I mind, don't you see that?

CATHERINE: No, Eddie, he's got all kinds of respect for me. And you too! We walk across the street he takes my arm—he almost bows to me! You got him all wrong, Eddie; I mean it, you—

EDDIE: Katie, he's only bowin' to his passport.

CATHERINE: His passport!

EDDIE: That's right. He marries you he's got the right to be an American citizen. That's what's goin' on here. *She is puzzled and surprised.* You understand what I'm tellin' you? The guy is lookin' for his break, that's all he's lookin' for.

CATHERINE, *pained:* Oh, no, Eddie, I don't think so.

EDDIE: You don't think so! Katie, you're gonna make me cry here. Is that a workin' man? What does he do with his first money? A snappy new jacket he buys, records, a pointy pair new shoes and his brother's kids are starvin' over there with tuberculosis? That's a hit-and-run guy, baby; he's got bright lights in his head, Broadway. Them guys don't think of nobody but theirself! You marry him and the next time you see him it'll be for divorce!

CATHERINE *steps toward him:* Eddie, he never said a word about his papers or—

EDDIE: You mean he's supposed to tell you that?

CATHERINE: I don't think he's even thinking about it.

EDDIE: What's better for him to think about! He could be picked up any day here and he's back pushin' taxis up the hill!

CATHERINE: No, I don't believe it.

EDDIE: Katie, don't break my heart, listen to me.

CATHERINE: I don't want to hear it.

EDDIE: Katie, listen . . .

CATHERINE: He loves me!

EDDIE, *with deep alarm:* Don't say that, for God's sake! This is the oldest racket in the country—

CATHERINE, *desperately, as though he had made his imprint:* I don't believe it! *She rushes to the house.*

EDDIE, *following her:* They been pullin' this since the Immigration Law was put in! They grab a green kid that don't know nothin' and they—

CATHERINE, *sobbing:* I don't believe it and I wish to hell you'd stop it!

EDDIE: Katie!

They enter the apartment. The lights in the living room have risen and Beatrice is there. She looks past the sobbing Catherine at Eddie, who in the presence of his wife, makes an awkward gesture of eroded command, indicating Catherine.

EDDIE: Why don't you straighten her out?

BEATRICE, *inwardly angered at his flowing emotion, which in itself alarms her:* When are you going to leave her alone?

EDDIE: B., the guy is no good!

BEATRICE, *suddenly, with open fright and fury:* You going to leave her alone? Or you gonna drive me crazy? *He turns, striving to retain his dignity, but nevertheless in guilt walks out of the house, into the street and away. Catherine starts into a bedroom.* Listen, Catherine. *Catherine halts, turns to her sheepishly.* What are you going to do with yourself?

CATHERINE: I don't know.

BEATRICE: Don't tell me you don't know; you're not a baby any more, what are you going to do with yourself?

CATHERINE: He won't listen to me.

BEATRICE: I don't understand this. He's not your father, Catherine. I don't understand what's going on here.

CATHERINE, *as one who herself is trying to rationalize a buried impulse:* What am I going to do, just kick him in the face with it?

BEATRICE: Look, honey, you wanna get married, or don't you wanna get married? What are you worried about, Katie?

CATHERINE, *quietly, trembling:* I don't know B. It just seems wrong if he's against it so much.

BEATRICE, *never losing her aroused alarm:* Sit down, honey, I want to tell you something. Here, sit down. Was there ever any fella he liked for you? There wasn't, was there?

CATHERINE: But he says Rodolpho's just after his papers.

BEATRICE: Look, he'll say anything. What does he care what

he says? If it was a prince came here for you it would be no different. You know that, don't you?

CATHERINE: Yeah, I guess.

BEATRICE: So what does that mean?

CATHERINE *slowly turns her head to Beatrice:* What?

BEATRICE: It means you gotta be your own self more. You still think you're a little girl, honey. But nobody else can make up your mind for you any more, you understand? You gotta give him to understand that he can't give you orders no more.

CATHERINE: Yeah, but how am I going to do that? He thinks I'm a baby.

BEATRICE: Because *you* think you're a baby. I told you fifty times already, you can't act the way you act. You still walk around in front of him in your slip—

CATHERINE: Well I forgot.

BEATRICE: Well you can't do it. Or like you sit on the edge of the bathtub talkin' to him when he's shavin' in his underwear.

CATHERINE: When'd I do that?

BEATRICE: I seen you in there this morning.

CATHERINE: Oh . . . well, I wanted to tell him something and I—

BEATRICE: I know, honey. But if you act like a baby and he be treatin' you like a baby. Like when he comes home sometimes you throw yourself at him like when you was twelve years old.

CATHERINE: Well I like to see him and I'm happy so I—

BEATRICE: Look, I'm not tellin' you what to do honey, but—

CATHERINE: No, you could tell me, B.! Gee, I'm all mixed up. See, I— He looks so sad now and it hurts me.

BEATRICE: Well look Katie, if it's goin' to hurt you so much you're gonna end up an old maid here.

CATHERINE: No!

BEATRICE: I'm tellin' you, I'm not makin' a joke. I tried to tell you a couple of times in the last year or so. That's why I was so happy you were going to go out and get work, you wouldn't be here so much, you'd be a little more independent. I mean it. It's wonderful for a whole family to love each

other, but you're a grown woman and you're in the same house with a grown man. So you'll act different now, heh?

CATHERINE: Yeah, I will. I'll remember.

BEATRICE: Because it ain't only up to him, Katie, you understand? I told him the same thing already.

CATHERINE, *quickly:* What?

BEATRICE: That he should let you go. But, you see, if only I tell him, he thinks I'm just bawlin' him out, or maybe I'm jealous or somethin', you know?

CATHERINE, *astonished:* He said you was jealous?

BEATRICE: No, I'm just sayin' maybe that's what he thinks. *She reaches over to Catherine's hand; with a strained smile:* You think I'm jealous of you, honey?

CATHERINE: No! It's the first I thought of it.

BEATRICE, *with a quiet sad laugh:* Well you should have thought of it before . . . but I'm not. We'll be all right. Just give him to understand; you don't have to fight, you're just—You're a woman, that's all, and you got a nice boy, and now the time came when you said good-by. All right?

CATHERINE, *strangely moved at the prospect:* All right. . . . If I can.

BEATRICE: Honey . . . you gotta.

Catherine, sensing now an imperious demand, turns with some fear, with a discovery, to Beatrice. She is at the edge of tears, as though a familiar world had shattered.

CATHERINE: Okay.

Lights out on them and up on Alfieri, seated behind his desk.

ALFIERI: It was at this time that he first came to me. I had represented his father in an accident case some years before, and I was acquainted with the family in a casual way. I remember him now as he walked through my doorway—

Enter Eddie down right ramp.

His eyes were like tunnels; my first thought was that he had committed a crime,

Eddie sits beside the desk, cap in hand, looking out.

but soon I saw it was only a passion that had moved into his body, like a stranger. *Alfieri pauses, looks down at his desk, then to Eddie as though he were continuing a conversation with him.* I don't quite understand what I can do for you. Is there a question of law somewhere?

EDDIE: That's what I want to ask you.

ALFIERI: Because there's nothing illegal about a girl falling in love with an immigrant.

EDDIE: Yeah, but what about it if the only reason for it is to get his papers?

ALFIERI: First of all you don't know that.

EDDIE: I see it in his eyes; he's laughin' at her and he's laughin' at me.

ALFIERI: Eddie, I'm a lawyer. I can only deal in what's provable. You understand that, don't you? Can you prove that?

EDDIE: *I know what's in his mind, Mr. Alfieri!*

ALFIERI: Eddie, even if you could prove that—

EDDIE: Listen . . . will you listen to me a minute? My father always said you was a smart man. I want you to listen to me.

ALFIERI: I'm only a lawyer, Eddie.

EDDIE: Will you listen a minute? I'm talkin' about the law. Lemme just bring out what I mean. A man, which he comes into the country illegal, don't it stand to reason he's gonna take every penny and put it in the sock? Because they don't know from one day to another, right?

ALFIERI: All right.

EDDIE: He's spendin'. Records he buys now. Shoes. Jackets. Y'understand me? This guy ain't worried. This guy is *here*. So it must be that he's got it all laid out in his mind already—he's stayin'. Right?

ALFIERI: Well? What about it?

EDDIE: All right. *He glances at Alfieri, then down to the floor.* I'm talking to you confidential, ain't I?

ALFIERI: Certainly.

EDDIE: I mean it don't go no place but here. Because I don't like to say this about anybody. Even my wife I didn't exactly say this.

ALFIERI: What is it?

EDDIE *takes a breath and glances briefly over each shoulder:* The guy ain't right, Mr. Alfieri.

ALFIERI: What do you mean?

EDDIE: I mean he ain't right.

ALFIERI: I don't get you.

EDDIE, *shifts to another position in the chair:* Dja ever get a look at him?

ALFIERI: Not that I know of, no.

EDDIE: He's a blond guy. Like . . . platinum. You know what I mean?

ALFIERI: No.

EDDIE: I mean if you close the paper fast—you could blow him over.

ALFIERI: Well that doesn't mean—

EDDIE: Wait a minute, I'm tellin' you sump'm. He sings, see. Which is— I mean it's all right, but sometimes he hits a note, see. I turn around. I mean—high. You know what I mean?

ALFIERI: Well, that's a tenor.

EDDIE: I know a tenor, Mr. Alfieri. This ain't no tenor. I mean if you came in the house and you didn't know who was singin', you wouldn't be lookin' for him you be lookin' for her.

ALFIERI: Yes, but that's not—

EDDIE: I'm tellin' you sump'm, wait a minute. Please, Mr. Alfieri. I'm tryin' to bring out my thoughts here. Couple of nights ago my niece brings out a dress which it's too small for her, because she shot up like a light this last year. He takes the dress, lays it on the table, he cuts it up; one-two-three, he makes a new dress. I mean he looked so sweet there, like an angel—you could kiss him he was so sweet.

ALFIERI: Now look, Eddie—

EDDIE: Mr. Alfieri, they're laughin' at him on the piers. I'm ashamed. Paper Doll they call him. Blondie now. His brother thinks it's because he's got a sense of humor, see—which he's got—but that ain't what they're laughin'. Which they're not goin' to come out with it because they know he's my relative, which they have to see me if they make a crack, y'know? But I know what they're laughin' at, and when I think of that guy layin' his hands on her I could—I mean it's eatin' me out, Mr. Alfieri, because I struggled for that girl. And now he comes in my house and—

ALFIERI: Eddie, look—I have my own children. I understand you. But the law is very specific. The law does not . . .

EDDIE, *with a fuller flow of indignation:* You mean to tell me that there's no law that a guy which he ain't right can go to work and marry a girl and—?

ALFIERI: You have no recourse in the law, Eddie.

EDDIE: Yeah, but if he ain't right, Mr. Alfieri, you mean to tell me—

ALFIERI: There is nothing you can do, Eddie, believe me.

EDDIE: Nothin'.

ALFIERI: Nothing at all. There's only one legal question here.

EDDIE: What?

ALFIERI: The manner in which they entered the country. But I don't think you want to do anything about that, do you?

EDDIE: You mean—?

ALFIERI: Well, they entered illegally.

EDDIE: Oh, Jesus, no, I wouldn't do nothin' about that, I mean—

ALFIERI: All right, then, let me talk now, eh?

EDDIE: Mr. Alfieri, I can't believe what you tell me. I mean there must be some kinda law which—

ALFIERI: Eddie, I want you to listen to me. *Pause.* You know, sometimes God mixes up the people. We all love somebody, the wife, the kids—every man's got somebody that he loves, heh? But sometimes . . . there's too much. You know? There's too much, and it goes where it mustn't. A man works hard, he brings up a child, sometimes it's a niece, sometimes even a daughter, and he never realizes it, but through the years—there is too much love for the daughter, there is too much love for the niece. Do you understand what I'm saying to you?

EDDIE, *sardonically:* What do you mean, I shouldn't look out for her good?

ALFIERI: Yes, but these things have to end, Eddie, that's all. The child has to grow up and go away, and the man has to learn to forget. Because after all, Eddie—what other way can it end? *Pause.* Let her go. That's my advice. You did your job, now it's her life; wish her luck, and let her go. *Pause.* Will you do that? Because there's no law, Eddie; make up your mind to it; the law is not interested in this.

EDDIE: You mean to tell me, even if he's a punk? If he's—

ALFIERI: There's nothing you can do.

Eddie stands.

EDDIE: Well, all right, thanks. Thanks very much.

ALFIERI: What are you going to do?

EDDIE, *with a helpless but ironic gesture:* What can I do? I'm a patsy, what can a patsy do? I worked like a dog twenty years so a punk could have her, so that's what I done. I mean, in the worst times, in the worst, when there wasn't a ship comin' in the harbor, I didn't stand around lookin' for relief —I hustled. When there was empty piers in Brooklyn I went to Hoboken, Staten Island, the West Side, Jersey, all over— because I made a promise. I took out of my own mouth to give to her. I took out of my wife's mouth. I walked hungry plenty days in this city! *It begins to break through.* And now I gotta sit in my own house and look at a son-of-a-bitch punk like that—which he came out of nowhere! I give him my house to sleep! I take the blankets off my bed for him, and he takes and puts his dirty filthy hands on her like a goddam thief!

ALFIERI, *rising:* But, Eddie, she's a woman now.

EDDIE: He's stealing from me!

ALFIERI: She wants to get married, Eddie. She can't marry you, can she?

EDDIE, *furiously:* What're you talkin' about, marry me! I don't know what the hell you're talkin' about!

Pause.

ALFIERI: I gave you my advice, Eddie. That's it.

Eddie gathers himself. A pause.

EDDIE: Well, thanks. Thanks very much. It just—it's breakin' my heart, y'know. I—

ALFIERI: I understand. Put it out of your mind. Can you do that?

EDDIE: I'm— *He feels the threat of sobs, and with a helpless wave.* I'll see you around. *He goes out up the right ramp.*

ALFIERI *sits on desk:* There are times when you want to spread an alarm, but nothing has happened. I knew, I knew then and there—I could have finished the whole story that afternoon. It wasn't as though there was a mystery to unravel. I could

see every step coming, step after step, like a dark figure walking down a hall toward a certain door. I knew where he was heading for, I knew where he was going to end. And I sat here many afternoons asking myself why, being an intelligent man, I was so powerless to stop it. I even went to a certain old lady in the neighborhood, a very wise old woman, and I told her, and she only nodded, and said, "Pray for him . . . " And so I—waited here.

As lights go out on Alfieri, they rise in the apartment where all are finishing dinner. Beatrice and Catherine are clearing the table.

CATHERINE: You know where they went?

BEATRICE: Where?

CATHERINE: They went to Africa once. On a fishing boat. *Eddie glances at her.* It's true, Eddie.

Beatrice exits into the kitchen with dishes.

EDDIE: I didn't say nothin'. *He goes to his rocker, picks up a newspaper.*

CATHERINE: And I was never even in Staten Island.

EDDIE, *sitting with the paper:* You didn't miss nothin'. *Pause. Catherine takes dishes out.* How long that take you, Marco—to get to Africa?

MARCO, *rising:* Oh . . . two days. We go all over.

RODOLPHO, *rising:* Once we went to Yugoslavia.

EDDIE, *to Marco:* They pay all right on them boats?

Beatrice enters. She and Rodolpho stack the remaining dishes.

MARCO: If they catch fish they pay all right. *Sits on a stool.*

RODOLPHO: They're family boats, though. And nobody in our family owned one. So we only worked when one of the families was sick.

BEATRICE: Y'know, Marco, what I don't understand—there's an ocean full of fish and yiz are all starvin'.

EDDIE: They gotta have boats, nets, you need money.

Catherine enters.

BEATRICE: Yeah, but couldn't they like fish from the beach? You see them down Coney Island—

MARCO: Sardines.
EDDIE: Sure. *Laughing:* How you gonna catch sardines on a hook?
BEATRICE: Oh, I didn't know they're sardines. *To Catherine:* They're sardines!
CATHERINE: Yeah, they follow them all over the ocean, Africa, Yugoslavia . . . *She sits and begins to look through a movie magazine. Rodolpho joins her.*
BEATRICE, *to Eddie:* It's funny, y'know. You never think of it, that sardines are swimming in the ocean! *She exits to kitchen with dishes.*
CATHERINE: I know. It's like oranges and lemons on a tree. *To Eddie:* I mean you ever think of oranges and lemons on a tree?
EDDIE: Yeah, I know. It's funny. *To Marco:* I heard that they paint the oranges to make them look orange.

Beatrice enters.

MARCO—*He has been reading a letter:* Paint?
EDDIE: Yeah, I heard that they grow like green.
MARCO: No, in Italy the oranges are orange.
RODOLPHO: Lemons are green.
EDDIE, *resenting his instruction:* I know lemons are green, for Christ's sake, you see them in the store they're green sometimes. I said oranges they paint, I didn't say nothin' about lemons.
BEATRICE, *sitting; diverting their attention:* Your wife is gettin' the money all right, Marco?
MARCO: Oh, yes. She bought medicine for my boy.
BEATRICE: That's wonderful. You feel better, heh?
MARCO: Oh, yes! But I'm lonesome.
BEATRICE: I just hope you ain't gonna do like some of them around here. They're here twenty-five years, some men, and they didn't get enough together to go back twice.
MARCO: Oh, I know. We have many families in our town, the children never saw the father. But I will go home. Three, four years, I think.
BEATRICE: Maybe you should keep more here. Because maybe she thinks it comes so easy you'll never get ahead of yourself.

MARCO: Oh, no, she saves. I send everything. My wife is very lonesome. *He smiles shyly.*

BEATRICE: She must be nice. She pretty? I bet, heh?

MARCO, *blushing:* No, but she understand everything.

RODOLPHO: Oh, he's got a clever wife!

EDDIE: I betcha there's plenty surprises sometimes when those guys get back there, heh?

MARCO: Surprises?

EDDIE, *laughing:* I mean, you know—they count the kids and there's a couple extra than when they left?

MARCO: No—no . . . The women wait, Eddie. Most. Most. Very few surprises.

RODOLPHO: It's more strict in our town. *Eddie looks at him now.* It's not so free.

EDDIE *rises, paces up and down:* It ain't so free here either, Rodolpho, like you think. I seen greenhorns sometimes get in trouble that way—they think just because a girl don't go around with a shawl over her head that she ain't strict, y'know? Girl don't have to wear black dress to be strict. Know what I mean?

RODOLPHO: Well, I always have respect—

EDDIE: I know, but in your town you wouldn't just drag off some girl without permission, I mean. *He turns.* You know what I mean, Marco? It ain't that much different here.

MARCO, *cautiously:* Yes.

BEATRICE: Well, he didn't exactly drag her off though, Eddie.

EDDIE: I know, but I seen some of them get the wrong idea sometimes. *To Rodolpho:* I mean it might be a little more free here but it's just as strict.

RODOLPHO: I have respect for her, Eddie. I do anything wrong?

EDDIE: Look, kid, I ain't her father, I'm only her uncle—

BEATRICE: Well then, be an uncle then. *Eddie looks at her, aware of her criticizing force.* I *mean.*

MARCO: No, Beatrice, if he does wrong you must tell him. *To Eddie:* What does he do wrong?

EDDIE: Well, Marco, till he came here she was never out on the street twelve o'clock at night.

MARCO, *to Rodolpho:* You come home early now.

BEATRICE, *to Catherine:* Well, you said the movie ended late, didn't you?

CATHERINE: Yeah.

BEATRICE: Well, tell him, honey. *To Eddie:* The movie ended late.

EDDIE: Look, B., I'm just sayin'—he thinks she always stayed out like that.

MARCO: You come home early now, Rodolpho.

RODOLPHO, *embarrassed:* All right, sure. But I can't stay in the house all the time, Eddie.

EDDIE: Look, kid, I'm not only talkin' about her. The more you run around like that the more chance you're takin'. *To Beatrice:* I mean suppose he gets hit by a car or something. *To Marco:* Where's his papers, who is he? Know what I mean?

BEATRICE: Yeah, but who is he in the daytime, though? It's the same chance in the daytime.

EDDIE, *holding back a voice full of anger:* Yeah, but he don't have to go lookin' for it, Beatrice. If he's here to work, then he should work; if he's here for a good time then he could fool around! *To Marco:* But I understood, Marco, that you was both comin' to make a livin' for your family. You understand me, don't you, Marco? *He goes to his rocker.*

MARCO: I beg your pardon, Eddie.

EDDIE: I mean, that's what I understood in the first place, see.

MARCO: Yes. That's why we came.

EDDIE *sits on his rocker:* Well, that's all I'm askin'.

Eddie reads his paper. There is a pause, an awkwardness. Now Catherine gets up and puts a record on the phonograph—"Paper Doll."

CATHERINE, *flushed with revolt:* You wanna dance, Rodolpho?

Eddie freezes.

RODOLPHO, *in deference to Eddie:* No, I—I'm tired.

BEATRICE: Go ahead, dance, Rodolpho.

CATHERINE: Ah, come on. They got a beautiful quartet, these guys. Come.

She has taken his hand and he stiffly rises, feeling Eddie's eyes on his back, and they dance.

EDDIE, *to Catherine:* What's that, a new record?

CATHERINE: It's the same one. We bought it the other day.

BEATRICE, *to Eddie:* They only bought three records. *She watches them dance; Eddie turns his head away. Marco just sits there, waiting. Now Beatrice turns to Eddie.* Must be nice to go all over in one of them fishin' boats. I would like that myself. See all them other countries?

EDDIE: Yeah.

BEATRICE, *to Marco:* But the women don't go along, I bet.

MARCO: No, not on the boats. Hard work.

BEATRICE: What're you got, a regular kitchen and everything?

MARCO: Yes, we eat very good on the boats—especially when Rodolpho comes along; everybody gets fat.

BEATRICE: Oh, he cooks?

MARCO: Sure, very good cook. Rice, pasta, fish, everything.

Eddie lowers his paper.

EDDIE: He's a cook, too! *Looking at Rodolpho:* He sings, he cooks . . .

Rodolpho smiles thankfully.

BEATRICE: Well it's good, he could always make a living.

EDDIE: It's wonderful. He sings, he cooks, he could make dresses . . .

CATHERINE: They get some high pay, them guys. The head chefs in all the big hotels are men. You read about them.

EDDIE: That's what I'm sayin'.

Catherine and Rodolpho continue dancing.

CATHERINE: Yeah, well, I mean.

EDDIE, *to Beatrice:* He's lucky, believe me. *Slight pause. He looks away, then back to Beatrice.* That's why the water front is no place for him. *They stop dancing. Rodolpho turns off phonograph.* I mean like me—I can't cook, I can't sing, I can't make dresses, so I'm on the water front. But if I could cook, if I could sing, if I could make dresses, I wouldn't be on the water front. *He has been unconsciously twisting the newspaper into a tight roll. They are all regarding him now; he senses he is exposing the issue and he is driven on.* I would be someplace else. I would be like in a dress store. *He has bent the rolled paper and it suddenly tears in two. He suddenly gets up and pulls his pants up over his belly and goes to Marco.* What do

you say, Marco, we go to the bouts next Saturday night. You never seen a fight, did you?

MARCO, *uneasily:* Only in the moving pictures.

EDDIE, *going to Rodolpho:* I'll treat yiz. What do you say, Danish? You wanna come along? I'll buy the tickets.

RODOLPHO: Sure. I like to go.

CATHERINE *goes to Eddie; nervously happy now:* I'll make some coffee, all right?

EDDIE: Go ahead, make some! Make it nice and strong. *Mystified, she smiles and exits to kitchen. He is weirdly elated, rubbing his fists into his palms. He strides to Marco.* You wait, Marco, you see some real fights here. You ever do any boxing?

MARCO: No, I never.

EDDIE, *to Rodolpho:* Betcha you have done some, heh?

RODOLPHO: No.

EDDIE: Well, come on, I'll teach you.

BEATRICE: What's he got to learn that for?

EDDIE: Ya can't tell, one a these days somebody's liable to step on his foot or sump'm. Come on, Rodolpho, I show you a couple a passes. *He stands below table.*

BEATRICE: Go ahead, Rodolpho. He's a good boxer, he could teach you.

RODOLPHO, *embarrassed:* Well, I don't know how to— *He moves down to Eddie.*

EDDIE: Just put your hands up. Like this, see? That's right. That's very good, keep your left up, because you lead with the left, see, like this. *He gently moves his left into Rodolpho's face.* See? Now what you gotta do is you gotta block me, so when I come in like that you—*Rodolpho parries his left.* Hey, that's very good! *Rodolpho laughs.* All right, now come into me. Come on.

RODOLPHO: I don't want to hit you, Eddie.

EDDIE: Don't pity me, come on. Throw it, I'll show you how to block it. *Rodolpho jabs at him, laughing. The others join.* 'At's it. Come on again. For the jaw right here. *Rodolpho jabs with more assurance.* Very good!

BEATRICE, *to Marco:* He's very good!

Eddie crosses directly upstage of Rodolpho.

EDDIE: Sure, he's great! Come on, kid, put sump'm behind it, you can't hurt me. *Rodolpho, more seriously, jabs at Eddie's jaw and grazes it.* Attaboy.

Catherine comes from the kitchen, watches.

Now I'm gonna hit you, so block me, see?

CATHERINE, *with beginning alarm:* What are they doin'?

They are lightly boxing now.

BEATRICE—*she senses only the comradeship in it now:* He's teachin' him; he's very good!

EDDIE: Sure, he's terrific! Look at him go! *Rodolpho lands a blow.* 'At's it! Now, watch out, here I come, Danish! *He feints with his left hand and lands with his right. It mildly staggers Rodolpho. Marco rises.*

CATHERINE, *rushing to Rodolpho:* Eddie!

EDDIE: Why? I didn't hurt him. Did I hurt you, kid? *He rubs the back of his hand across his mouth.*

RODOLPHO: No, no, he didn't hurt me. *To Eddie with a certain gleam and a smile:* I was only surprised.

BEATRICE, *pulling Eddie down into the rocker:* That's enough, Eddie; he did pretty good, though.

EDDIE: Yeah. *Rubbing his fists together:* He could be very good, Marco. I'll teach him again.

Marco nods at him dubiously.

RODOLPHO: Dance, Catherine. Come. *He takes her hand; they go to phonograph and start it. It plays "Paper Doll."*

Rodolpho takes her in his arms. They dance. Eddie in thought sits in his chair, and Marco takes a chair, places it in front of Eddie, and looks down at it. Beatrice and Eddie watch him.

MARCO: Can you lift this chair?

EDDIE: What do you mean?

MARCO: From here. *He gets on one knee with one hand behind his back, and grasps the bottom of one of the chair legs but does not raise it.*

EDDIE: Sure, why not? *He comes to the chair, kneels, grasps the leg, raises the chair one inch, but it leans over to the floor.* Gee,

that's hard, I never knew that. *He tries again, and again fails.* It's on an angle, that's why, heh?

MARCO: Here. *He kneels, grasps, and with strain slowly raises the chair higher and higher, getting to his feet now. Rodolpho and Catherine have stopped dancing as Marco raises the chair over his head.*

Marco is face to face with Eddie, a strained tension gripping his eyes and jaw, his neck stiff, the chair raised like a weapon over Eddie's head—and he transforms what might appear like a glare of warning into a smile of triumph, and Eddie's grin vanishes as he absorbs his look.

CURTAIN

ACT TWO

Light rises on Alfieri at his desk.

ALFIERI: On the twenty-third of that December a case of Scotch whisky slipped from a net while being unloaded—as a case of Scotch whisky is inclined to do on the twenty-third of December on Pier Forty-one. There was no snow, but it was cold, his wife was out shopping. Marco was still at work. The boy had not been hired that day; Catherine told me later that this was the first time they had been alone together in the house.

Light is rising on Catherine in the apartment. Rodolpho is watching as she arranges a paper pattern on cloth spread on the table.

CATHERINE: You hungry?
RODOLPHO: Not for anything to eat. *Pause.* I have nearly three hundred dollars. Catherine?
CATHERINE: I heard you.
RODOLPHO: You don't like to talk about it any more?
CATHERINE: Sure, I don't mind talkin' about it.
RODOLPHO: What worries you, Catherine?
CATHERINE: I been wantin' to ask you about something. Could I?
RODOLPHO: All the answers are in my eyes, Catherine. But you don't look in my eyes lately. You're full of secrets. *She looks at him. She seems withdrawn.* What is the question?
CATHERINE: Suppose I wanted to live in Italy.
RODOLPHO, *smiling at the incongruity:* You going to marry somebody rich?
CATHERINE: No, I mean live there—you and me.
RODOLPHO, *his smile vanishing:* When?
CATHERINE: Well . . . when we get married.
RODOLPHO, *astonished:* You want to be an Italian?
CATHERINE: No, but I could live there without being Italian. Americans live there.
RODOLPHO: Forever?

CATHERINE: Yeah.

RODOLPHO *crosses to rocker:* You're fooling.

CATHERINE: No, I mean it.

RODOLPHO: Where do you get such an idea?

CATHERINE: Well, you're always saying it's so beautiful there, with the mountains and the ocean and all the—

RODOLPHO: You're fooling me.

CATHERINE: I mean it.

RODOLPHO *goes to her slowly:* Catherine, if I ever brought you home with no money, no business, nothing, they would call the priest and the doctor and they would say Rodolpho is crazy.

CATHERINE: I know, but I think we would be happier there.

RODOLPHO: Happier! What would you eat? You can't cook the view!

CATHERINE: Maybe you could be a singer, like in Rome or—

RODOLPHO: Rome! Rome is full of singers.

CATHERINE: Well, I could work then.

RODOLPHO: Where?

CATHERINE: God, there must be jobs somewhere!

RODOLPHO: There's nothing! Nothing, nothing, nothing. Now tell me what you're talking about. How can I bring you from a rich country to suffer in a poor country? What are you talking about? *She searches for words.* I would be a criminal stealing your face. In two years you would have an old, hungry face. When my brother's babies cry they give them water, water that boiled a bone. Don't you believe that?

CATHERINE, *quietly:* I'm afraid of Eddie here.

Slight pause.

RODOLPHO *steps closer to her:* We wouldn't live here. Once I am a citizen I could work anywhere and I would find better jobs and we would have a house, Catherine. If I were not afraid to be arrested I would start to be something wonderful here!

CATHERINE, *steeling herself:* Tell me something. I mean just tell me, Rodolpho—would you still want to do it if it turned out we had to go live in Italy? I mean just if it turned out that way.

RODOLPHO: This is your question or his question?
CATHERINE: I would like to know, Rodolpho. I mean it.
RODOLPHO: To go there with nothing.
CATHERINE: Yeah.
RODOLPHO: No. *She looks at him wide-eyed.* No.
CATHERINE: You wouldn't?
RODOLPHO: No; I will not marry you to live in Italy. I want you to be my wife, and I want to be a citizen. Tell him that, or I will. Yes. *He moves about angrily.* And tell him also, and tell yourself, please, that I am not a beggar, and you are not a horse, a gift, a favor for a poor immigrant.
CATHERINE: Well, don't get mad!
RODOLPHO: I am furious! *Goes to her.* Do you think I am so desperate? My brother is desperate, not me. You think I would carry on my back the rest of my life a woman I didn't love just to be an American? It's so wonderful? You think we have no tall buildings in Italy? Electric lights? No wide streets? No flags? No automobiles? Only work we don't have. I want to be an American so I can work, that is the only wonder here—work! How can you insult me, Catherine?
CATHERINE: I didn't mean that—
RODOLPHO: My heart dies to look at you. Why are you so afraid of him?
CATHERINE, *near tears:* I don't know!
RODOLPHO: Do you trust me, Catherine? You?
CATHERINE: It's only that I— He was good to me, Rodolpho. You don't know him; he was always the sweetest guy to me. Good. He razzes me all the time but he don't mean it. I know. I would—just feel ashamed if I made him sad. 'Cause I always dreamt that when I got married he would be happy at the wedding, and laughin'—and now he's—mad all the time and nasty— *She is weeping.* Tell him you'd live in Italy—just tell him, and maybe he would start to trust you a little, see? Because I want him to be happy; I mean—I like him, Rodolpho—and I can't stand it!
RODOLPHO: Oh, Catherine—oh, little girl.
CATHERINE: I love you, Rodolpho, I love you.
RODOLPHO: Then why are you afraid? That he'll spank you?
CATHERINE: Don't, don't laugh at me! I've been here all my

life. . . . Every day I saw him when he left in the morning and when he came home at night. You think it's so easy to turn around and say to a man he's nothin' to you no more?

RODOLPHO: I know, but—

CATHERINE: You don't know; nobody knows! I'm not a baby, I know a lot more than people think I know. Beatrice says to be a woman, but—

RODOLPHO: Yes.

CATHERINE: Then why don't she be a woman? If I was a wife I would make a man happy instead of goin' at him all the time. I can tell a block away when he's blue in his mind and just wants to talk to somebody quiet and nice. . . . I can tell when he's hungry or wants a beer before he even says anything. I know when his feet hurt him, I mean I *know* him and now I'm supposed to turn around and make a stranger out of him? I don't know why I have to do that, I mean.

RODOLPHO: Catherine. If I take in my hands a little bird. And she grows and wishes to fly. But I will not let her out of my hands because I love her so much, is that right for me to do? I don't say you must hate him; but anyway you must go, mustn't you? Catherine?

CATHERINE, *softly:* Hold me.

RODOLPHO, *clasping her to him:* Oh, my little girl.

CATHERINE: Teach me. *She is weeping.* I don't know anything, teach me, Rodolpho, hold me.

RODOLPHO: There's nobody here now. Come inside. Come. *He is leading her toward the bedrooms.* And don't cry any more.

Light rises on the street. In a moment Eddie appears. He is unsteady, drunk. He mounts the stairs. He enters the apartment, looks around, takes out a bottle from one pocket, puts it on the table. Then another bottle from another pocket, and a third from an inside pocket. He sees the pattern and cloth, goes over to it and touches it, and turns toward upstage.

EDDIE: Beatrice? *He goes to the open kitchen door and looks in.* Beatrice? Beatrice?

Catherine enters from bedroom; under his gaze she adjusts her dress.

CATHERINE: You got home early.

EDDIE: Knocked off for Christmas early. *Indicating the pattern:* Rodolpho makin' you a dress?

CATHERINE: No. I'm makin' a blouse.

Rodolpho appears in the bedroom doorway. Eddie sees him and his arm jerks slightly in shock. Rodolpho nods to him testingly.

RODOLPHO: Beatrice went to buy presents for her mother.

Pause.

EDDIE: Pack it up. Go ahead. Get your stuff and get outa here. *Catherine instantly turns and walks toward the bedroom, and Eddie grabs her arm.* Where you goin'?

CATHERINE, *trembling with fright:* I think I have to get out of here, Eddie.

EDDIE: No, you ain't goin' nowheres, he's the one.

CATHERINE: I think I can't stay here no more. *She frees her arm, steps back toward the bedroom.* I'm sorry, Eddie. *She sees the tears in his eyes.* Well, don't cry. I'll be around the neighborhood; I'll see you. I just can't stay here no more. You know I can't. *Her sobs of pity and love for him break her composure.* Don't you know I can't? You know that, don't you? *She goes to him.* Wish me luck. *She clasps her hands prayerfully.* Oh, Eddie, don't be like that!

EDDIE: You ain't goin' nowheres.

CATHERINE: Eddie, I'm not gonna be a baby any more! You—

He reaches out suddenly, draws her to him, and as she strives to free herself he kisses her on the mouth.

RODOLPHO: Don't! *He pulls on Eddie's arm.* Stop that! Have respect for her!

EDDIE, *spun round by Rodolpho:* You want something?

RODOLPHO: Yes! She'll be my wife. That is what I want. My wife!

EDDIE: But what're you gonna be?

RODOLPHO: I show you what I be!

CATHERINE: Wait outside; don't argue with him!

EDDIE: Come on, show me! What're you gonna be? Show me!

RODOLPHO, *with tears of rage:* Don't say that to me!

Rodolpho flies at him in attack. Eddie pins his arms, laughing, and suddenly kisses him.

CATHERINE: Eddie! Let go, ya hear me! I'll kill you! Leggo of him!

She tears at Eddie's face and Eddie releases Rodolpho. Eddie stands there with tears rolling down his face as he laughs mockingly at Rodolpho. She is staring at him in horror. Rodolpho is rigid. They are like animals that have torn at one another and broken up without a decision, each waiting for the other's mood.

EDDIE, *to Catherine:* You see? *To Rodolpho:* I give you till tomorrow, kid. Get outa here. Alone. You hear me? Alone.

CATHERINE: I'm going with him, Eddie. *She starts toward Rodolpho.*

EDDIE, *indicating Rodolpho with his head:* Not with that. *She halts, frightened. He sits, still panting for breath, and they watch him helplessly as he leans toward them over the table.* Don't make me do nuttin', Catherine. Watch your step, submarine. By rights they oughta throw you back in the water. But I got pity for you. *He moves unsteadily toward the door, always facing Rodolpho.* Just get outa here and don't lay another hand on her unless you wanna go out feet first. *He goes out of the apartment.*

The lights go down, as they rise on Alfieri.

ALFIERI: On December twenty-seventh I saw him next. I normally go home well before six, but that day I sat around looking out my window at the bay, and when I saw him walking through my doorway, I knew why I had waited. And if I seem to tell this like a dream, it was that way. Several moments arrived in the course of the two talks we had when it occurred to me how—almost transfixed I had come to feel. I had lost my strength somewhere. *Eddie enters, removing his cap, sits in the chair, looks thoughtfully out.* I looked in his eyes more than I listened—in fact, I can hardly remember the conversation. But I will never forget how dark the room became when he looked at me; his eyes were like tunnels. I kept wanting to call the police, but nothing had happened. Nothing at all had really happened. *He breaks off and looks*

down at the desk. Then he turns to Eddie. So in other words, he won't leave?

EDDIE: My wife is talkin' about renting a room upstairs for them. An old lady on the top floor is got an empty room.

ALFIERI: What does Marco say?

EDDIE: He just sits there. Marco don't say much.

ALFIERI: I guess they didn't tell him, heh? What happened?

EDDIE: I don't know; Marco don't say much.

ALFIERI: What does your wife say?

EDDIE, *unwilling to pursue this:* Nobody's talkin' much in the house. So what about that?

ALFIERI: But you didn't prove anything about him. It sounds like he just wasn't strong enough to break your grip.

EDDIE: I'm tellin' you I know—he ain't right. Somebody that don't want it can break it. Even a mouse, if you catch a teeny mouse and you hold it in your hand, that mouse can give you the right kind of fight. He didn't give me the right kind of fight, I know it, Mr. Alfieri, the guy ain't right.

ALFIERI: What did you do that for, Eddie?

EDDIE: To show her what he is! So she would see, once and for all! Her mother'll turn over in the grave! *He gathers himself almost peremptorily.* So what do I gotta do now? Tell me what to do.

ALFIERI: She actually said she's marrying him?

EDDIE: She told me, yeah. So what do I do?

Slight pause.

ALFIERI: This is my last word, Eddie, take it or not, that's your business. Morally and legally you have no rights, you cannot stop it; she is a free agent.

EDDIE, *angering:* Didn't you hear what I told you?

ALFIERI, *with a tougher tone:* I heard what you told me, and I'm telling you what the answer is. I'm not only telling you now, I'm warning you—the law is nature. The law is only a word for what has a right to happen. When the law is wrong it's because it's unnatural, but in this case it is natural and a river will drown you if you buck it now. Let her go. And bless her. *A phone booth begins to glow on the opposite side of the stage; a faint, lonely blue. Eddie stands up, jaws clenched.* Somebody had to come for her, Eddie, sooner or later. *Eddie*

starts turning to go and Alfieri rises with new anxiety. You won't have a friend in the world, Eddie! Even those who understand will turn against you, even the ones who feel the same will despise you! *Eddie moves off.* Put it out of your mind! Eddie! *He follows into the darkness, calling desperately.*

Eddie is gone. The phone is glowing in light now. Light is out on Alfieri. Eddie has at the same time appeared beside the phone.

EDDIE: Give me the number of the Immigration Bureau. Thanks. *He dials.* I want to report something. Illegal immigrants. Two of them. That's right. Four-forty-one Saxon Street, Brooklyn, yeah. Ground floor. Heh? *With greater difficulty:* I'm just around the neighborhood, that's all. Heh?

Evidently he is being questioned further, and he slowly hangs up. He leaves the phone just as Louis and Mike come down the street.

LOUIS: Go bowlin', Eddie?
EDDIE: No, I'm due home.
LOUIS: Well, take it easy.
EDDIE: I'll see yiz.

They leave him, exiting right, and he watches them go. He glances about, then goes up into the house. The lights go on in the apartment. Beatrice is taking down Christmas decorations and packing them in a box.

EDDIE: Where is everybody? *Beatrice does not answer.* I says where is everybody?
BEATRICE, *looking up at him, wearied with it, and concealing a fear of him:* I decided to move them upstairs with Mrs. Dondero.
EDDIE: Oh, they're all moved up there already?
BEATRICE: Yeah.
EDDIE: Where's Catherine? She up there?
BEATRICE: Only to bring pillow cases.
EDDIE: She ain't movin' in with them.
BEATRICE: Look, I'm sick and tired of it. I'm sick and tired of it!
EDDIE: All right, all right, take it easy.

BEATRICE: I don't wanna hear no more about it, you understand? Nothin'!

EDDIE: What're you blowin' off about? Who brought them in here?

BEATRICE: All right, I'm sorry; I wish I'd a drop dead before I told them to come. In the ground I wish I was.

EDDIE: Don't drop dead, just keep in mind who brought them in here, that's all. *He moves about restlessly.* I mean I got a couple of rights here. *He moves, wanting to beat down her evident disapproval of him.* This is my house here not their house.

BEATRICE: What do you want from me? They're moved out; what do you want now?

EDDIE: I want my respect!

BEATRICE: So I moved them out, what more do you want? You got your house now, you got your respect.

EDDIE—*he moves about biting his lip:* I don't like the way you talk to me, Beatrice.

BEATRICE: I'm just tellin' you I done what you want!

EDDIE: I don't like it! The way you talk to me and the way you look at me. This is my house. And she is my niece and I'm responsible for her.

BEATRICE: So that's why you done that to him?

EDDIE: I done what to him?

BEATRICE: What you done to him in front of her; you know what I'm talkin' about. She goes around shakin' all the time, she can't go to sleep! That's what you call responsible for her?

EDDIE, *quietly:* The guy ain't right, Beatrice. *She is silent.* Did you hear what I said?

BEATRICE: Look, I'm finished with it. That's all. *She resumes her work.*

EDDIE, *helping her to pack the tinsel:* I'm gonna have it out with you one of these days, Beatrice.

BEATRICE: Nothin' to have out with me, it's all settled. Now we gonna be like it never happened, that's all.

EDDIE: I want my respect, Beatrice, and you know what I'm talkin' about.

BEATRICE: What?

Pause.

EDDIE—*finally his resolution hardens:* What I feel like doin' in the bed and what I don't feel like doin'. I don't want no—

BEATRICE: When'd I say anything about that?

EDDIE: You said, you said, I ain't deaf. I don't want no more conversations about that, Beatrice. I do what I feel like doin' or what I don't feel like doin'.

BEATRICE: Okay.

Pause.

EDDIE: You used to be different, Beatrice. You had a whole different way.

BEATRICE: *I'm* no different.

EDDIE: You didn't used to jump me all the time about everything. The last year or two I come in the house I don't know what's gonna hit me. It's a shootin' gallery in here and I'm the pigeon.

BEATRICE: Okay, okay.

EDDIE: Don't tell me okay, okay, I'm tellin' you the truth. A wife is supposed to believe the husband. If I tell you that guy ain't right don't tell me he is right.

BEATRICE: But how do you know?

EDDIE: Because I know. I don't go around makin' accusations. He give me the heeby-jeebies the first minute I seen him. And I don't like you sayin' I don't want her marryin' anybody. I broke my back payin' her stenography lessons so she could go out and meet a better class of people. Would I do that if I didn't want her to get married? Sometimes you talk like I was a crazy man or sump'm.

BEATRICE: But she likes him.

EDDIE: Beatrice, she's a baby, how is she gonna know what she likes?

BEATRICE: Well, you kept her a baby, you wouldn't let her go out. I told you a hundred times.

Pause.

EDDIE: All right. Let her go out, then.

BEATRICE: She don't wanna go out now. It's too late, Eddie.

Pause.

EDDIE: Suppose I told her to go out. Suppose I—

BEATRICE: They're going to get married next week, Eddie.

EDDIE—*his head jerks around to her:* She said that?

BEATRICE: Eddie, if you want my advice, go to her and tell her good luck. I think maybe now that you had it out you learned better.

EDDIE: What's the hurry next week?

BEATRICE: Well, she's been worried about him bein' picked up; this way he could start to be a citizen. She loves him, Eddie. *He gets up, moves about uneasily, restlessly.* Why don't you give her a good word? Because I still think she would like you to be a friend, y'know? *He is standing, looking at the floor.* I mean like if you told her you'd go to the wedding.

EDDIE: She asked you that?

BEATRICE: I know she would like it. I'd like to make a party here for her. I mean there oughta be some kinda send-off. Heh? I mean she'll have trouble enough in her life, let's start it off happy. What do you say? Cause in her heart she still loves you, Eddie. I know it. *He presses his fingers against his eyes.* What're you, cryin'? *She goes to him, holds his face.* Go . . . whyn't you go tell her you're sorry? *Catherine is seen on the upper landing of the stairway, and they hear her descending.* There . . . she's comin' down. Come on, shake hands with her.

EDDIE, *moving with suppressed suddenness:* No, I can't, I can't talk to her.

BEATRICE: Eddie, give her a break; a wedding should be happy!

EDDIE: I'm goin', I'm goin' for a walk.

He goes upstage for his jacket. Catherine enters and starts for the bedroom door.

BEATRICE: Katie? . . . Eddie, don't go, wait a minute. *She embraces Eddie's arm with warmth.* Ask him, Katie. Come on, honey.

EDDIE: It's all right, I'm—*He starts to go and she holds him.*

BEATRICE: No, she wants to ask you. Come on, Katie, ask him. We'll have a party! What're we gonna do, hate each other? Come on!

CATHERINE: I'm gonna get married, Eddie. So if you wanna come, the wedding be on Saturday.

Pause.

EDDIE: Okay. I only wanted the best for you, Katie. I hope you know that.

CATHERINE: Okay. *She starts out again.*

EDDIE: Catherine? *She turns to him.* I was just tellin' Beatrice . . . if you wanna go out, like . . . I mean I realize maybe I kept you home too much. Because he's the first guy you ever knew, y'know? I mean now that you got a job, you might meet some fellas, and you get a different idea, y'-know? I mean you could always come back to him, you're still only kids, the both of yiz. What's the hurry? Maybe you'll get around a little bit, you grow up a little more, maybe you'll see different in a couple of months. I mean you be surprised, it don't have to be him.

CATHERINE: No, we made it up already.

EDDIE, *with increasing anxiety:* Katie, wait a minute.

CATHERINE: No, I made up my mind.

EDDIE: But you never knew no other fella, Katie! How could you make up your mind?

CATHERINE: Cause I did. I don't want nobody else.

EDDIE: But, Katie, suppose he gets picked up.

CATHERINE: That's why we gonna do it right away. Soon as we finish the wedding he's goin' right over and start to be a citizen. I made up my mind, Eddie. I'm sorry. *To Beatrice:* Could I take two more pillow cases for the other guys?

BEATRICE: Sure, go ahead. Only don't let her forget where they came from.

Catherine goes into a bedroom.

EDDIE: She's got other boarders up there?

BEATRICE: Yeah, there's two guys that just came over.

EDDIE: What do you mean, came over?

BEATRICE: From Italy. Lipari the butcher—his nephew. They come from Bari, they just got here yesterday. I didn't even know till Marco and Rodolpho moved up there before. *Catherine enters, going toward exit with two pillow cases.* It'll be nice, they could all talk together.

EDDIE: Catherine! *She halts near the exit door. He takes in Bea-*

trice too. What're you, got no brains? You put them up there with two other submarines?

CATHERINE: Why?

EDDIE, *in a driving fright and anger:* Why! How do you know they're not trackin' these guys? They'll come up for them and find Marco and Rodolpho! Get them out of the house!

BEATRICE: But they been here so long already—

EDDIE: How do you know what enemies Lipari's got? Which they'd love to stab him in the back?

CATHERINE: Well what'll I do with them?

EDDIE: The neighborhood is full of rooms. Can't you stand to live a couple of blocks away from him? Get them out of the house!

CATHERINE: Well maybe tomorrow night I'll—

EDDIE: Not tomorrow, do it now. Catherine, you never mix yourself with somebody else's family! These guys get picked up, Lipari's liable to blame you or me and we got his whole family on our head. They got a temper, that family.

Two men in overcoats appear outside, start into the house.

CATHERINE: How'm I gonna find a place tonight?

EDDIE: Will you stop arguin' with me and get them out! You think I'm always tryin' to fool you or sump'm? What's the matter with you, don't you believe I could think of your good? Did I ever ask sump'm for myself? You think I got no feelin's? I never told you nothin' in my life that wasn't for your good. Nothin'! And look at the way you talk to me! Like I was an enemy! Like I— *A knock on the door. His head swerves. They all stand motionless. Another knock. Eddie, in a whisper, pointing upstage.* Go up the fire escape, get them out over the back fence.

Catherine stands motionless, uncomprehending.

FIRST OFFICER, *in the hall:* Immigration! Open up in there!

EDDIE: Go, go. Hurry up! *She stands a moment staring at him in a realized horror.* Well, what're you lookin' at!

FIRST OFFICER: Open up!

EDDIE, *calling toward door:* Who's that there?

FIRST OFFICER: Immigration, open up.

Eddie turns, looks at Beatrice. She sits. Then he looks at Catherine. With a sob of fury Catherine streaks into a bedroom.

Knock is repeated.

EDDIE: All right, take it easy, take it easy. *He goes and opens the door. The Officer steps inside.* What's all this?
FIRST OFFICER: Where are they?

Second Officer sweeps past and, glancing about, goes into the kitchen.

EDDIE: Where's who?
FIRST OFFICER: Come on, come on, where are they? *He hurries into the bedrooms.*
EDDIE: Who? We got nobody here. *He looks at Beatrice, who turns her head away. Pugnaciously, furious, he steps toward Beatrice.* What's the matter with *you*?

First Officer enters from the bedroom, calls to the kitchen.

FIRST OFFICER: Dominick?

Enter Second Officer from kitchen.

SECOND OFFICER: Maybe it's a different apartment.
FIRST OFFICER: There's only two more floors up there. I'll take the front, you go up the fire escape. I'll let you in. Watch your step up there.
SECOND OFFICER: Okay, right, Charley. *First Officer goes out apartment door and runs up the stairs.* This is Four-forty-one, isn't it?
EDDIE: That's right.

Second Officer goes out into the kitchen.

Eddie turns to Beatrice. She looks at him now and sees his terror.

BEATRICE, *weakened with fear:* Oh, Jesus, Eddie.
EDDIE: What's the matter with *you*?
BEATRICE, *pressing her palms against her face:* Oh, my God, my God.
EDDIE: What're you, accusin' me?

BEATRICE—*her final thrust is to turn toward him instead of running from him:* My God, what did you do?

Many steps on the outer stair draw his attention. We see the First Officer descending, with Marco, behind him Rodolpho, and Catherine and the two strange immigrants, followed by Second Officer. Beatrice hurries to door.

CATHERINE, *backing down stairs, fighting with First Officer; as they appear on the stairs:* What do yiz want from them? They work, that's all. They're boarders upstairs, they work on the piers.

BEATRICE, *to First Officer:* Ah, Mister, what do you want from them, who do they hurt?

CATHERINE, *pointing to Rodolpho:* They ain't no submarines, he was born in Philadelphia.

FIRST OFFICER: Step aside, lady.

CATHERINE: What do you mean? You can't just come in a house and—

FIRST OFFICER: All right, take it easy. *To Rodolpho:* What street were you born in Philadelphia?

CATHERINE: What do you mean, what street? Could you tell me what street you were born?

FIRST OFFICER: Sure. Four blocks away, One-eleven Union Street. Let's go fellas.

CATHERINE, *fending him off Rodolpho:* No, you can't! Now, get outa here!

FIRST OFFICER: Look, girlie, if they're all right they'll be out tomorrow. If they're illegal they go back where they came from. If you want, get yourself a lawyer, although I'm tellin' you now you're wasting your money. Let's get them in the car, Dom. *To the men:* Andiamo, Andiamo, let's go.

The men start, but Marco hangs back.

BEATRICE, *from doorway:* Who're they hurtin', for God's sake, what do you want from them? They're starvin' over there, what do you want! Marco!

Marco suddenly breaks from the group and dashes into the room and faces Eddie; Beatrice and First Officer rush in as Marco spits into Eddie's face.

Catherine runs into hallway and throws herself into Rodolpho's arms. Eddie, with an enraged cry, lunges for Marco.

EDDIE: Oh, you mother's—!

First Officer quickly intercedes and pushes Eddie from Marco, who stands there accusingly.

FIRST OFFICER, *between them, pushing Eddie from Marco:* Cut it out!

EDDIE, *over the First Officer's shoulder, to Marco:* I'll kill you for that, you son of a bitch!

FIRST OFFICER: Hey! *Shakes him.* Stay in here now, don't come out, don't bother him. You hear me? Don't come out, fella.

For an instant there is silence. Then First Officer turns and takes Marco's arm and then gives a last, informative look at Eddie. As he and Marco are going out into the hall, Eddie erupts.

EDDIE: I don't forget that, Marco! You hear what I'm sayin'?

Out in the hall, First Officer and Marco go down the stairs. Now, in the street, Louis, Mike, and several neighbors including the butcher, Lipari—a stout, intense, middle-aged man—are gathering around the stoop.

Lipari, the butcher, walks over to the two strange men and kisses them. His wife, keening, goes and kisses their hands. Eddie is emerging from the house shouting after Marco. Beatrice is trying to restrain him.

EDDIE: That's the thanks I get? Which I took the blankets off my bed for yiz? You gonna apologize to me, Marco! *Marco!*

FIRST OFFICER, *in the doorway with Marco:* All right, lady, let them go. Get in the car, fellas, it's right over there.

Rodolpho is almost carrying the sobbing Catherine off up the street, left.

CATHERINE: He was born in Philadelphia! What do you want from him?

FIRST OFFICER: Step aside, lady, come on now . . .

The Second Officer has moved off with the two strange men. Marco, taking advantage of the First Officer's being occupied with Catherine, suddenly frees himself and points back at Eddie.

MARCO: That one! I accuse that one!

Eddie brushes Beatrice aside and rushes out to the stoop.

FIRST OFFICER, *grabbing him and moving him quickly off up the left street:* Come on!

MARCO, *as he is taken off, pointing back at Eddie:* That one! He killed my children! That one stole the food from my children!

Marco is gone. The crowd has turned to Eddie.

EDDIE, *to Lipari and wife:* He's crazy! I give them the blankets off my bed. Six months I kept them like my own brothers!

Lipari, the butcher, turns and starts up left with his arm around his wife.

EDDIE: Lipari! *He follows Lipari up left.* For Christ's sake, I kept them, I give them the blankets off my bed!

Lipari and wife exit. Eddie turns and starts crossing down right to Louis and Mike.

EDDIE: Louis! *Louis!*

Louis barely turns, then walks off and exits down right with Mike. Only Beatrice is left on the stoop. Catherine now returns, blank-eyed, from offstage and the car. Eddie calls after Louis and Mike.

EDDIE: He's gonna take that back. He's gonna take that back or I'll kill him! You hear me? I'll kill him! I'll kill him! *He exits up street calling.*

There is a pause of darkness before the lights rise, on the reception room of a prison. Marco is seated; Alfieri, Catherine, and Rodolpho standing.

ALFIERI: I'm waiting, Marco, what do you say?

RODOLPHO: Marco never hurt anybody.

ALFIERI: I can bail you out until your hearing comes up. But I'm not going to do it, you understand me? Unless I have your promise. You're an honorable man, I will believe your promise. Now what do you say?

MARCO: In my country he would be dead now. He would not live this long.

ALFIERI: All right, Rodolpho—you come with me now.

RODOLPHO: No! Please, Mister. Marco—promise the man. Please, I want you to watch the wedding. How can I be married and you're in here? Please, you're not going to do anything; you know you're not.

Marco is silent.

CATHERINE, *kneeling left of Marco:* Marco, don't you understand? He can't bail you out if you're gonna do something bad. To hell with Eddie. Nobody is gonna talk to him again if he lives to a hundred. Everybody knows you spit in his face, that's enough, isn't it? Give me the satisfaction—I want you at the wedding. You got a wife and kids, Marco. You could be workin' till the hearing comes up, instead of layin' around here.

MARCO, *to Alfieri:* I have no chance?

ALFIERI *crosses to behind Marco:* No, Marco. You're going back. The hearing is a formality, that's all.

MARCO: But him? There is a chance, eh?

ALFIERI: When she marries him he can start to become an American. They permit that, if the wife is born here.

MARCO, *looking at Rodolpho:* Well—we did something. *He lays a palm on Rodolpho's arm and Rodolpho covers it.*

RODOLPHO: Marco, tell the man.

MARCO, *pulling his hand away:* What will I tell him? He knows such a promise is dishonorable.

ALFIERI: To promise not to kill is not dishonorable.

MARCO, *looking at Alfieri:* No?

ALFIERI: No.

MARCO, *gesturing with his head—this is a new idea:* Then what is done with such a man?

ALFIERI: Nothing. If he obeys the law, he lives. That's all.

MARCO, *rises, turns to Alfieri:* The law? All the law is not in a book.

ALFIERI: Yes. In a book. There is no other law.

MARCO, *his anger rising:* He degraded my brother. My blood. He robbed my children, he mocks my work. I work to come here, mister!

ALFIERI: I know, Marco—

MARCO: There is no law for that? Where is the law for that?

ALFIERI: There is none.

MARCO, *shaking his head, sitting:* I don't understand this country.

ALFIERI: Well? What is your answer? You have five or six weeks you could work. Or else you sit here. What do you say to me?

MARCO *lowers his eyes. It almost seems he is ashamed.* All right.

ALFIERI: You won't touch him. This is your promise.

Slight pause.

MARCO: Maybe he wants to apologize to me.

Marco is staring away. Alfieri takes one of his hands.

ALFIERI: This is not God, Marco. You hear? Only God makes justice.

MARCO: All right.

ALFIERI, *nodding, not with assurance:* Good! Catherine, Rodolpho, Marco, let us go.

Catherine kisses Rodolpho and Marco, then kisses Alfieri's hand.

CATHERINE: I'll get Beatrice and meet you at the church. *She leaves quickly.*

Marco rises. Rodolpho suddenly embraces him. Marco pats him on the back and Rodolpho exits after Catherine. Marco faces Alfieri.

ALFIERI: Only God, Marco.

Marco turns and walks out. Alfieri with a certain processional tread leaves the stage. The lights dim out.

The lights rise in the apartment. Eddie is alone in the rocker, rocking back and forth in little surges. Pause. Now Beatrice emerges from a bedroom. She is in her best clothes, wearing a hat.

BEATRICE, *with fear, going to Eddie:* I'll be back in about an hour, Eddie. All right?

EDDIE, *quietly, almost inaudibly, as though drained:* What, have I been talkin' to myself?

BEATRICE: Eddie, for God's sake, it's her wedding.

EDDIE: Didn't you hear what I told you? You walk out that door to that wedding you ain't comin' back here, Beatrice.

BEATRICE: Why! What do you want?

EDDIE: I want my respect. Didn't you ever hear of that? From my wife?

Catherine enters from bedroom.

CATHERINE: It's after three; we're supposed to be there already, Beatrice. The priest won't wait.

BEATRICE: Eddie. It's her wedding. There'll be nobody there from her family. For my sister let me go. I'm goin' for my sister.

EDDIE, *as though hurt:* Look, I been arguin' with you all day already, Beatrice, and I said what I'm gonna say. He's gonna come here and apologize to me or nobody from this house is goin' into that church today. Now if that's more to you than I am, then go. But don't come back. You be on my side or on their side, that's all.

CATHERINE, *suddenly:* Who the hell do you think you are?

BEATRICE: Sssh!

CATHERINE: You got no more right to tell nobody nothin'! Nobody! The rest of your life, nobody!

BEATRICE: Shut up, Katie! *She turns Catherine around.*

CATHERINE: You're gonna come with me!

BEATRICE: I can't Katie, I can't . . .

CATHERINE: How can you listen to him? This rat!

BEATRICE, *shaking Catherine:* Don't you call him that!

CATHERINE, *clearing from Beatrice:* What're you scared of? He's a rat! He belongs in the sewer!

BEATRICE: Stop it!

CATHERINE, *weeping:* He bites people when they sleep! He comes when nobody's lookin' and poisons decent people. In the garbage he belongs!

Eddie seems about to pick up the table and fling it at her.

BEATRICE: No, Eddie! Eddie! *To Catherine:* Then we all belong in the garbage. You, and me too. Don't say that. Whatever happened we all done it, and don't you ever forget it, Catherine. *She goes to Catherine.* Now go, go to your wedding, Katie, I'll stay home. Go. God bless you, God bless your children.

Enter Rodolpho.

RODOLPHO: Eddie?

EDDIE: Who said you could come in here? Get outa here!

RODOLPHO: Marco is coming, Eddie. *Pause. Beatrice raises her hands in terror.* He's praying in the church. You understand? *Pause. Rodolpho advances into the room.* Catherine, I think it is better we go. Come with me.

CATHERINE: Eddie go away please.

BEATRICE, *quietly:* Eddie. Let's go someplace. Come. You and me. *He has not moved.* I don't want you to be here when he comes. I'll get your coat.

EDDIE: Where? Where am I goin'? This is my house.

BEATRICE, *crying out:* What's the use of it! He's crazy now, you know the way they get, what good is it! You got nothin' against Marco, you always liked Marco!

EDDIE: I got nothin' against Marco? Which he called me a rat in front of the whole neighborhood? Which he said I killed his children! Where you been?

RODOLPHO, *quite suddenly, stepping up to Eddie:* It is my fault, Eddie. Everything. I wish to apologize. It was wrong that I do not ask your permission. I kiss your hand. *He reaches for Eddie's hand, but Eddie snaps it away from him.*

BEATRICE: Eddie, he's apologizing!

RODOLPHO: I have made all our troubles. But you have insult me too. Maybe God understand why you did that to me. Maybe you did not mean to insult me at all—

BEATRICE: Listen to him! Eddie, listen what he's tellin' you!

RODOLPHO: I think, maybe when Marco comes, if we can tell him we are comrades now, and we have no more argument between us. Then maybe Marco will not—

EDDIE: Now, listen—

CATHERINE: Eddie, give him a chance!

BEATRICE: What do you want! Eddie, what do you want!

EDDIE: I want my name! He didn't take my name; he's only a punk. Marco's got my name—*to Rodolpho:* and you can run tell him, kid, that he's gonna give it back to me in front of this neighborhood, or we have it out. *Hoisting up his pants:* Come on, where is he? Take me to him.

BEATRICE: Eddie, listen—

EDDIE: I heard enough! Come on, let's go!

BEATRICE: Only blood is good? He kissed your hand!

EDDIE: What he does don't mean nothin' to nobody! *To Rodolpho:* Come on!

BEATRICE, *barring his way to the stairs:* What's gonna mean somethin'? Eddie, listen to me. Who could give you your name? Listen to me, I love you, I'm talkin' to you, I love you; if Marco'll kiss your hand outside, if he goes on his knees, what is he got to give you? That's not what you want.

EDDIE: Don't bother me!

BEATRICE: You want somethin' else, Eddie, and you can never have her!

CATHERINE, *in horror:* B.!

EDDIE, *shocked, horrified, his fists clenching:* Beatrice!

Marco appears outside, walking toward the door from a distant point.

BEATRICE, *crying out, weeping:* The truth is not as bad as blood, Eddie! I'm tellin' you the truth—tell her good-by forever!

EDDIE, *crying out in agony:* That's what you think of me—that I would have such a thoughts? *His fists clench his head as though it will burst.*

MARCO, *calling near the door outside:* Eddie Carbone!

Eddie swerves about; all stand transfixed for an instant. People appear outside.

EDDIE, *as though flinging his challenge:* Yeah, Marco! Eddie Carbone. Eddie Carbone. Eddie Carbone. *He goes up the stairs and emerges from the apartment. Rodolpho streaks up and out past him and runs to Marco.*

RODOLPHO: No, Marco, please! Eddie, please, he has children! You will kill a family!

BEATRICE: Go in the house! Eddie, go in the house!

EDDIE—*he gradually comes to address the people:* Maybe he come to apologize to me. Heh, Marco? For what you said about me in front of the neighborhood? *He is incensing himself and little bits of laughter even escape him as his eyes are murderous and he cracks his knuckles in his hands with a strange sort of relaxation.* He knows that ain't right. To do like that? To a man? Which I put my roof over their head and my food in their mouth? Like in the Bible? Strangers I never seen in my whole life? To come out of the water and grab a girl for a passport? To go and take from your own family like from the stable—and never a word to me? And now accusations in the bargain! *Directly to Marco:* Wipin' the neighborhood with my name like a dirty rag! I want my name, Marco. *He is moving now, carefully, toward Marco.* Now gimme my name and we go together to the wedding.

BEATRICE *and* CATHERINE, *keening:* Eddie! Eddie, don't! Eddie!

EDDIE: No, Marco knows what's right from wrong. Tell the people, Marco, tell them what a liar you are! *He has his arms spread and Marco is spreading his.* Come on, liar, you know what you done! *He lunges for Marco as a great hushed shout goes up from the people.*

Marco strikes Eddie beside the neck.

MARCO: Animal! You go on your knees to me!

Eddie goes down with the blow and Marco starts to raise a foot to stomp him when Eddie springs a knife into his hand and Marco steps back. Louis rushes in toward Eddie.

LOUIS: Eddie, for Christ's sake!

Eddie raises the knife and Louis halts and steps back.

EDDIE: You lied about me, Marco. Now say it. Come on now, say it!

MARCO: Anima-a-a-l!

Eddie lunges with the knife. Marco grabs his arm, turning the blade inward and pressing it home as the women and Louis and Mike rush in and separate them, and Eddie, the knife still

in his hand, falls to his knees before Marco. The two women support him for a moment, calling his name again and again.

CATHERINE: Eddie I never meant to do nothing bad to you.
EDDIE: Then why— Oh, B.!
BEATRICE: Yes, yes!
EDDIE: My B.!

He dies in her arms, and Beatrice covers him with her body. Alfieri, who is in the crowd, turns out to the audience. The lights have gone down, leaving him in a glow, while behind him the dull prayers of the people and the keening of the women continue.

ALFIERI: Most of the time now we settle for half and I like it better. But the truth is holy, and even as I know how wrong he was, and his death useless, I tremble, for I confess that something perversely pure calls to me from his memory—not purely good, but himself purely, for he allowed himself to be wholly known and for that I think I will love him more than all my sensible clients. And yet, it is better to settle for half, it must be! And so I mourn him—I admit it—with a certain . . . alarm.

CURTAIN

THE MISFITS

AUTHOR'S NOTE

A glance at *The Misfits* will show that it is written in an unfamiliar form, neither novel, play, nor screenplay. A word of explanation is perhaps in order.

It is a story conceived as a film, and every word is there for the purpose of telling the camera what to see and the actors what they are to say. However, it is the kind of tale which the telegraphic, diagrammatic manner of screenplay writing cannot alone convey because its sense depends as much on the nuances of character and place as on the plot. It therefore became necessary to do more than merely indicate what happens and to create through words the emotions which the finished film should possess. It was as though a picture were already in being, and the writer were recreating its full effects through language, so that as a result of a purely functional attempt to make a vision of a film clear to others, a film which existed as yet only in the writer's mind, there was gradually suggested a form of fiction itself, a mixed form if you will, but one which it seems to me has vigorous possibilities for reflecting contemporary existence. Movies, the most widespread form of art on earth, have willy-nilly created a particular way of seeing life, and their swift transitions, their sudden bringing together of disparate images, their effect of documentation inevitable in photography, their economy of storytelling, and their concentration on mute action have infiltrated the novel and play writing—especially the latter—without being confessed to or, at times, being consciously realized at all. *The Misfits* avowedly uses the perspectives of the film in order to create a fiction which might have the peculiar immediacy of image and the reflective possibilities of the written word.

ONE

THERE is a permanent steel arch across Main Street bearing a neon sign which reads, WELCOME TO RENO THE BIGGEST LITTLE CITY IN THE WORLD.

It is a quiet little town. We can see through our windshield almost to the end of Main Street, a dozen blocks away. Everything is sharp to the eye at this altitude, the sky is immaculate, and the morning jazz coming from the dashboard is perky. It is a clean town. The great gambling palaces are modernistic, battleship gray, and all their neon signs are lit in the sunshine. The traffic light changes and our vehicle moves cautiously ahead. But a block on we are halted by a policeman who steps off the sidewalk, stops a truck coming the other way, and escorts an old lady slowly across the street. She goes into the sedate bank and trust company next to which is an elegant women's clothing store and next to that a store with "Craps" in gold letters on its windows. Some stores feature "Horse Betting," others "Casino," and others "Wedding Rings." In this momentary halt a loud buzzing draws our attention. A gambling emporium on the left, glistening inside, is broadcasting the buzzing noise into the street and flashing a sign over the sidewalk which says "Jackpot," indicating that somewhere within a customer has struck the full count.

The policeman, who wears gold-framed eyeglasses, waves us on, but a woman steps up to the side window of our vehicle. She is carrying a three-month-old baby on her arm, and a suitcase.

The woman: "Am I headed right for the courthouse, mister?"

Driver's voice: "Straight on one block and then two left."

The woman: "Thank you kindly. It's awfully confusin' here."

Driver's voice: "It sure is, ma'am."

She steps back to the sidewalk. There is a rural pathos in her eyes, an uprooted quality in the intense mistrust with which she walks. She is thin, and her polka-dot dress is too large. She is clutching the baby and the suitcase as though she were continuously counting them.

Our vehicle moves again, keeping pace with her for a

moment. The morning jazz from the dashboard remains bright and untroubled. The neon signs flash in the sunlight. The few people on the sidewalks are almost all women, and women who are alone. Many of them are strolling with the preoccupied air of the disconnected, the tourist, the divorcée who has not yet memorized the town. The jazz number ends and a hillbilly disc jockey greets his listeners. As he drawls we continue on down Main Street. Through the window of a supermarket we see a woman holding a large bag of groceries on one arm while with the other she is pulling down the arm of a slot machine; not even looking at the revolving drums, she walks away and out the door, hoping to be stopped by the crash of money which does not come. Farther on, a couple-in-love stares at bridal gowns in a store window. There is a door next to the store and a sign on it, reading "Divorce Actions One Flight Up." It is a prospering town with one brand-new hotel facing the Truckee River, a gray facade covered with cantilevered balconies. Beyond it rise the dry brown mountains capped with snow. One can see immense distances here, even boulders sticking out of the mountains' face. The disc jockey, in a baritone drawl, says, "Weel, folks . . ." and for a moment there is only the sound of rustling paper coming through the radio as he evidently searches for the commercial. Two Indian young men in dungarees stand on a corner watching us pass by; their faces are like the faces of the blind, which one cannot look at too long.

The commentator chuckles. "Folks? Here's somethin' to think about while you're a-waitin' for your vacuum-packed Rizdale Coffee to come to a boil. For the third month a-runnin', we've beat out Las Vegas. Four hundred and eleven divorces have been granted as of yesterday compared to three hundred and ninety-one for Vegas. No doubt about it, pardners, we are the Divorce Capital of the World. And speakin' of divorce, would you like to cut loose of a bad habit? How about rootin' yourself out of that chair and gettin' over to Haber's Drug Store and treat yourself to a good night's sleep with good old Dream-E-Z?"

We are going down a tree-lined street, almost suburban, the houses very small, some of them frayed and nearly poor. Here

is a peaceful, almost somnolent quality of a hot Nevada day. As we turn . . .

"Now naturally we don't claim to provide you with any special type of dream, friends. Dream-E-Z's only one of them names they made up back East in New York. But it does work. I can rightly swear your sleepless nights are over; you get the dream ready, and we'll give you the sleep. Dream-E-Z's a real little bottle of rest, folks, and relaxation, and peace. Put that burden down, Mother. Daddy? Let yourself go. Dream-E-Z. Come on, folks, let's get together here. . . . Say it with me now like we always do . . . all together . . ." A school of violins soars into a music of wafting sleep. "Dream-Eeeeee-Zeeeeee."

The vehicle comes to a halt at the curb and the engine is shut off and the radio with it.

Guido hops out of what we now see is a tow truck and comes around and lifts a battery out of the back. He walks up the driveway with it. The legend on the back of his jumper reads, "Jack's Reno Garage."

He goes behind the house, where a new Cadillac convertible stands with its hood open. The car is banged up all around, its fenders dented. He is resting the battery on the fender to get a new grip on it before lowering it into place when he hears a plane overhead. He looks up.

A great jet liner roars over, flying quite low. Guido watches it until it disappears toward the mountains, a certain longing and expert appraisal in his eyes. Then he lowers the battery into its rack and works at connecting it. He is about forty—it is hard to tell precisely because he is tanned and healthy, with close-cropped hair, strong arms, and a wrestler's way of moving his neck; from the rear he seems the athlete, even to the pigeon-toed walk and the voice that is a little too high. But face to face, talking with him, he seems to have a university-bred sophistication. Perhaps he is a football-playing poet. Then, quite suddenly, his black eyes seem to thicken into stupidity and he is a local, a naive spender of time underneath broken cars, a man in the usual industrial daze munching his sandwich at lunchtime and watching the girls go by.

Now, as he works at the battery, which is a simple job

requiring only automatic fingers, his gaze spreads, and he seems to see or be longing to see something soft or something vast. The skin around his eyes and over the bridge of his nose is whiter than the rest—the mark of aviator's goggles—so that when he blinks a parrotlike look appears, the look of some heavily blinking tropical bird.

The voice of a woman turns him around.

"Young man? You have the time?"

Holding the screen door open, Isabelle shades her eyes against the morning sun. Her left arm is in a sling but she holds an alarm clock in her hand. She is a sixty-year-old tomboy with hair bobbed high in the manner of the twenties, a Buster Brown cut which somehow marks her as a woman who is impatient of details, for it rarely needs combing. She is in an old wrapper, which she holds together with her elbows. Her nose and cheeks are faintly purpled, her voice cracks and pipes, and she looks on the world with an amused untidiness that approaches an air of wreckage and a misspent intelligence. But with her first words—which cause her to cough and clear her throat—a suggestion of great kindness emerges from her. There is a cut to her speech which banishes the sentimental. She seems never to expect anything in return; she would be kind even to her executioner, perhaps apologizing for getting him up so early in the morning. For people in general she has little but despair, yet she has never met an individual she couldn't forgive. A flavor of the South sweetens her words. Seeing her, Guido feels like smiling, as most people do. She is standing there shading her eyes like an Indian as she waits to hear the time of day. He looks at his watch. As though arraigning the entire clock industry, she adds: "I've got six or eight clocks in this house, and none of them work."

"It's twenty after nine."

"*After!*" Isabelle comes farther out on the porch and calls up to a second-floor window: "Dear girl? It's twenty after!" No answer comes from the window. "Darling?"

Roslyn appears behind the screen; we can barely make out her features. Her voice is excited as she calls down: "Five minutes! What about you?"

"I'm all set. I just ironed my sling. The lawyer said nine-thirty sharp, darling."

"Okay!"

Isabelle turns on hearing the car's engine start. Guido emerges from behind the wheel and stands over the engine, listening. Isabelle comes over to him, still carrying the clock which she has forgotten to set or wind.

"I hope you're not the kind to be miserly. It's brand new, you know. She ought to get a good price."

"Is that the right mileage? Twenty-three miles?"

"We only took two rides in it. It's the damn men in this town—they kept runnin' into her just to start a conversation." With a proud smile: "She's a stunner, y'know."

Roslyn's voice: "Will you come up here, Iz?"

"Coming, dear girl!" Then back to Guido, who is facing the upstairs window for a glimpse: "Now you be your most generous self. You mustn't go by appearances—it's brand new, a divorce present from her husband, don't y'know."

"They giving presents for divorces now?"

"Why not? On the anniversary of *our* divorce my husband has never failed to send me a potted yellow rose. And it'll be nineteen years July." She is already his friend, and laughs, squeezing his arm and leaning in toward his face. "Of course he never paid me the alimony, but I wouldn't want to put a man out anyway—if his heart's not in it, y'know." She starts toward the porch.

"You break your arm in the car?"

"Oh, no. My last roomer before this girl—we celebrated her divorce and I . . . misbehaved. I'm just so sick and tired of myself!"

She is suddenly almost in tears and vanishes into the house. His interest piqued, Guido glances up at the window, then, taking out a pad and pencil, starts circling the car, noting down the damage.

Isabelle hurries through the house and up the stairs and goes into a room. Chaos: bureau drawers hang open; the bed is covered with letters, toilet articles, magazines, hair curlers.

From the closet, Roslyn calls: "Could we do my answers again, Iz?"

"Oh, sure, dear." Isabelle goes to a mirror and takes a slip of paper which is stuck in the frame. She sits on the bed, holding a pair of bent glasses to her nose. "Let's see. 'Did your husband,

Mr. Raymond Taber, act toward you with cruelty?'" There is no answer from the closet. "Darling?"

After a moment: "Well . . . yes."

Isabelle: "Just say yes, dear."

A golden girl comes bursting out of the closet, zipping up her dress, and goes to the bureau, where with her free hand she searches for something in the disorder of jars, papers, and odds and ends, while glancing at her hair in the mirror. Each detail of her appearance is in perfectly good order but the total effect is windy; she can be obsessed with how she looks now, and entirely oblivious as she turns her head too quickly for her hairdo to stay in place and in a freshly pressed dress gets on her hands and knees to look under the bed for something. But, quick as she is, a certain stilled inwardness lies coiled in her gaze. She glances at Isabelle.

"Yes."

She adjusts her dress in the mirror, absorbed at the same time in the effort of answering. As with so many things she does, so many objects she examines, so many events she passes through, a part of her is totally alone, like a little child in a new school, mystified as to how it got here and passionately looking for a friendly face.

Isabelle reads on: " 'In what ways did his cruelty manifest itself?' "

"He . . . How's it go again?"

"'He persistently and cruelly ignored my personal rights and wishes, and resorted on several occasions to physical violence against me.'" The older woman looks up from the slip of paper.

"He persistently . . ." She breaks off, troubled. "Must I say that? Why can't I just say he wasn't *there*? I mean, you could touch him but he wasn't there."

"Darling child, if that was grounds for divorce there'd be about eleven marriages left in the United States. Now just repeat—"

A car horn blows. Isabelle hurries to the window. Below, Guido, putting his notepad away, speaks up to her: "They'll call in their estimate from the office."

Roslyn comes beside Isabelle and calls down: "Those dents weren't my fault, you know!"

Guido now sees Roslyn for the first time, still behind the window screen, but more or less clearly. He is strangely embarrassed and ashamed of his own shyness.

"I'll recommend the best price I can, miss. You can drive her now. I put a battery in."

"Oh, I'll never drive *that* car again. We'll call a cab."

"I'll give you a lift in my truck if you're leavin' right away."

"Swell! Two minutes! Get dressed, Iz! You got to be my witness!"

Isabelle grasps Roslyn's hand with a quick surge of feeling. "This'll be my seventy-seventh time I've witnessed for a divorce. Two sevens is lucky, darlin'."

"Oh, Iz, I hope!"

Roslyn smiles, but fear and a puzzled consternation remain in her eyes. The old lady hurries out of the room, opening the sash of her wrapper with her good hand.

TWO

THERE is a small park across the street from the Reno courthouse. The crosswalks are lined with benches and there is a greenish statue of a man, wife, and child facing the direction of the court—a pioneer family group to remind the litigants of the great treks that passed through here on the way West. It is a pleasant place to sit on a hot day, the shade of the tree being a rare luxury in this territory. Derelicts and old men lounge here to watch the strangers go by—sometimes young people examining proofs of their wedding pictures from the photo shops across the avenue, sometimes land claimants spreading out their maps. Anything that happens sooner or later ends up in court, and this park is where the parties can sit and stare at the issues while the traffic flows past on four sides.

Guido's tow truck pulls up. Quickly he jumps out, comes around to open the door on the other side, and helps Isabelle down.

"Easy does it, now."

"Aren't you a dear!" Isabelle pats his shoulder.

Roslyn is almost out of the truck already, but he reaches and takes her hand, anyway. She is still clutching the slip of paper, and starts past him.

Roslyn: "Thanks a lot. We got to run now."

Guido gently blocks her way. "If you're not going back East right away I'd be glad to take you out and show you the country. Some beautiful country around here, you know."

Roslyn, distracted by her mission, thanks him with her eyes. "I'd love to see it, but I don't know what I'm going to do yet. All I could think about here was when my six weeks would be up."

Guido: "Can I call you?"

"I don't know where I'll be, but okay." Rosyln starts to move, waving back. "Thanks again!"

Isabelle taps his arm. "*My* name is Isabelle Steers."

Guido laughs at her jibe. "Okay, Isabelle. You could come along if you like."

"That's a sweet afterthought! Oh, you Reno men!" She laughs and trots after Roslyn.

Guido, somehow moved, quickened, remains staring as they walk across the paved paths that section the grass in front of the courthouse. Men on park benches look up at Roslyn as she passes; newspapers lower as she goes by.

The young polka-dot woman carrying her baby is shaking hands with a lawyer on the courthouse steps. They part. Gaunt-eyed, the woman passes Roslyn. Roslyn and Isabelle approach the steps of the court; Roslyn is rapidly going over her lines from her prompting paper. Her anxiety is hardened now.

"I can't memorize this; it's not the way it was."

Isabelle laughs. "You take everything so seriously, dear! Just say it; it doesn't have to be true. It's not a quiz show, it's only a court."

They start up the courthouse steps, and as Roslyn looks up after putting her paper away she is stopped by what she sees. A man is descending the steps toward her. He is well built, tall, about thirty-eight, wearing a soft straw hat and a tie with a big design. His mind is constantly trying to tune in on the world, but the message is never clear. He feels self-conscious now, having to plead; he was successful early in life and this pleading threatens his dignity. He expects that the simple fact of his

having come here will somehow convince his wife how guilty she is. But he will forgive her and she will idolize him again. He is Raymond Taber, her husband. He manages a hurt, embarrassed grin, as though confessing to a minor error he made.

"Just got off the plane. I'm not too late, am I?"

Roslyn looks at him; a rising fear for herself holds her silent. He comes down the steps to her.

"Don't, Raymond. Please, I don't want to hear anything."

His resentment floods his face. "Give me five minutes, will you? After two years, five minutes isn't—"

"You can't have me, so now you want me, that's all. Please . . . I'm not blaming you. I never saw it any different. I just don't believe in the whole thing any more." She starts around him and he takes her arm.

"Kid, I understand what—"

"You don't understand it, because nobody understands it!" With her finger she presses his chest. "You aren't *there*, Raymond!" She steps back. "If I'm going to be alone, I want to be alone by myself. Go back, Raymond—you're not going to make me sorry for you any more."

She leaves him standing there in an impotent fury and beckons to Isabelle, who puts her arm around her. Roslyn is inwardly quaking with sobs, but she will not cry as they hurry up the steps together and into the courthouse.

Guido watches from his truck window until the two women disappear. He has seen the argument but could not hear it. Now he drives down Main Street, bemused. A train is parked across Main Street. At the crossing gate he stops, switches off the engine, and settles back in his seat to wait. His eyes show a certain fixed daze of introspection. He happens to turn and comes alert and calls out: "Gay!"

Gay Langland is standing at the foot of the train steps with a woman. His dog is at his heels. He turns toward the truck and waves, calling: "Wait up! I was just going over to see you!"

A conductor stands with a watch in hand a few yards off. The woman, about forty-two, is expensively dressed. She is afraid she has been a fool and is trying to find out by searching Gay's eyes; she wears a joyless smile that is full of fear and unhappiness.

Gay is just turning back from his look at Guido. "Good luck now, Susan. I won't forget you, you can be sure of that."

She glances down at his proffered handclasp, and she clearly feels the formality and rejection in the gesture; she starts to shake his hand, trying to maintain composure, but suddenly she throws her arms around him and tears flood her eyes.

Gay: "Now, now, honey, you be a good sport."

Conductor: "Board!"

Woman: "I don't even know where to write you!"

Gay, reassuring her as he moves her toward the steps: "General Delivery. I'll get it." He gets her onto the step and she turns to him.

"Will you think about it, Gay? It's the second largest laundry in St. Louis."

"I wouldn't want to kid you, Susan. I ain't cut out for business."

The train starts to move. The conductor hops aboard and grasps her arm to help her up. Gay walks along with the train. She has lost all her composure and is weeping.

"Will you think of me? Gay!"

"You know I will, honey! 'Bye!"

She manages a masculine, brave salute as she moves away. Even after the woman is out of sight Gay stands with his arm raised, a compassionate farewell that is full of his relief. Now he walks along the platform, the dog at his heels. Guido has pulled the truck over to the curb; Gay comes and rests his arms on the sill of the window, and he seems weary into his voice.

"How you doin', boy? You ready to cut out of this town? 'Cause I sure am."

"I been thinkin' about it." Guido gestures toward the departed train; there is a certain onlooker's excitement around his eyes, a suggestive yet shy thirst for detail. "Which one was that?"

Gay smiles at his friend's heavy curiosity, but there is a refusal to join Guido in cynicism toward her. "Susan. Damn good sport, that woman."

He opens the door and lets himself down on the edge of the seat. The traffic goes by quietly. Gay is forty-nine years old, a big-knuckled cowboy, a wondrous listener. He takes off his hat

and wipes his sweat band. His mind is elsewhere but not in any particular place—simply not here and not now. It is the middle of a weekday morning with a stateful of sand and mountains around him. Now he seems either contented or exhausted; it is not clear which. Toward Guido he has a business friendliness, but there is no business. Maybe he has many such friends. One senses that he does not expect very much, but that he sets the rhythm for whoever he walks with because he cannot follow. And he has no desire to lead. It is always a question of arranging for the next few days, maybe two weeks; beyond that there is only the state, and he knows people all over it. Homeless, he is always home inside his shoes and jeans and shirt, and interested. When he listens, he seems to feel that life is a pageant that is sometimes loud, sometimes soft, sometimes a headshaking absurdity, and sometimes dangerous. It is a pageant with no head and no tail. He listens, he is interested, and like a woodchuck he can go suddenly into the ground and come up later in another place. He needs no guile because he has never required himself to promise anything, so his betrayals are minor and do not cling. "If you have to you will," he seems to believe. The moral world is full of women and he has, with their gratitude, eased many of them out of it, modestly. His refusal to mock the departed woman encourages Guido to confess his own feeling now.

Guido: "I just met a girl sweet enough to eat, Gay. Hell of a lookin' woman."

Gay, looking at him with pleased surprise: "She sure must be, for you to get worked up. Look, whyn't we take out to the mountains?"

"I wanted to pile up about five hundred this time. I ought to get a new engine."

"Hell, that engine'll fly you anywhere. You been more than two months on this job, fella—that's enough wages for one year. You gonna get the habit. I tell you, I'm just dyin' for some fresh air and no damned people, male or female. Maybe we can even do a little mustangin' up there."

Guido looks off, indecisively. "I'll meet you over the bar later. Let's talk about it."

"That's the way!" Getting out, Gay slams the door shut. "Hope I get a look at that girl!"

"Only trouble is, when I think of all the useless talkin' you gotta do I get discouraged."

"Hell, there's nothin' more useful than talkin' to a good-looking woman. You been moody lately—might perk you up. See you later, now!"

Gay steps back, they wave to each other, and the truck takes off. Gay starts walking, a mildly revived spirit showing in his eyes.

At a certain point Main Street becomes a bridge crossing the narrow Truckee River, which flows between buildings. Roslyn and Isabelle are walking along, but Isabelle stops her at the railing. The heat of noon seems to have wilted them.

Isabelle: "If you throw your ring in you'll never have a divorce again."

Puzzled, Roslyn touches her ring protectively.

Isabelle: "Go ahead, honey, everybody does it. There's more gold in that river than the Klondike."

Roslyn, with a certain revulsion: "Did you do it?"

Isabelle: "Me? Oh, I lost my ring on my honeymoon!"

Roslyn: "Let's get a drink."

Isabelle: "That's my girl!"

A few doors down is a casino. Open to the street, a seeming half-acre of big-chested slot machines reflect rose and blue neon light. Most of the aisles are empty now, but a few early risers are pulling at the levers, blinking in this sea of chrome, staring at glints like fish in a dim underworld. Sound is hushed here. The two women sit at a table near the bar and watch the scattered players.

A waiter comes and Roslyn orders: "Scotch, I guess. On ice."

Isabelle: "Rye and water."

The sound of well-oiled levers is peaceful in the neon gloom. The two women sit in silence for a moment, looking around. An old man nearby makes the sign of the cross over a machine and pulls the lever.

Isabelle touches her friend's arm: "Cheer up, dear!"

"I will, I just hate to fight with anybody. Even if I win I lose. In my heart, you know?"

"Darling, you're free! Maybe the trouble is you're not used to it yet."

"No, the trouble is I'm always back where I started. I never had anybody much, and here I—"

"Well, you had your mother, though, didn't you?"

Roslyn quells a strange feeling of shame. "How do you have somebody who disappears all the time? Both of them weren't . . . *there.* She'd go off with a patient for three months. You know how long three months is to a kid? And he came around when his ship happened to need repairs. . . ."

The waiter comes and sets down their drinks and goes. Isabelle raises her glass. "Well, here's to the whole damned thing, darling!"

Roslyn, suddenly grasping Isabelle's arm: "You're a fine woman, Iz. You're practically the only woman who was ever my friend."

"Listen! Don't leave; settle down here. There's a school here; you could teach dancing. . . . 'Cause there's one thing about this town—it's always full of interesting strangers." Tears show in Roslyn's eyes and Isabelle is surprised. "Oh, my dear girl, I'm sorry; what'd I—"

"I suddenly miss my mother. Isn't that the stupidest thing?" She determinedly raises her drink, smiling. "To . . . to life! Whatever that is."

They laugh and drink. Roslyn sees Gay's dog sitting patiently at the foot of the bar.

Roslyn: "Oh, look at that dear dog! How sweet it sits there!"

Isabelle: "Yeah, dogs are nice."

She and Isabelle see Gay placing a glass of water before the dog, Margaret. Margaret drinks. Gay glances at the two women, nods just for hello, and as he straightens up to turn back to the bar Guido enters, dressed in a clean shirt and dress trousers. Guido sees Roslyn and comes over as Gay starts to greet him.

Guido: "Oh, hello! How'd you make out?"

Roslyn, shyly: "Okay. It's all over."

He nods, uncertain how to proceed, and beckons Gay over, partly as a relief for his tension.

"Like you to meet a friend of mine. This is Gay Langland. Mrs. Taber . . .

Gay, realizing she is the one: "Oh! How-de-do."

Guido, of Isabelle: "And this is . . ."

"Isabelle Steers." To Roslyn: "One thing about Reno men, they do remember the name."

They laugh. Isabelle is blooming. She loves new people. "Why don't you boys sit down?"

Gay: "Well, thank you. Sit down, Guido. Waiter? What're you girls drinkin'?"

Isabelle: "Whiskey. We're celebrating the jail burned down."

The waitress comes to the table.

Gay: "Get four doubles." To Roslyn: "You sure made a big impression on my friend here, and" —to Guido—"I can see why."

Roslyn glances at Guido, but his intensity turns her to Gay and she speaks to him: "You a mechanic too?"

Isabelle: "Him? He's a cowboy."

Gay, grinning: "How'd you know?"

Isabelle: "I can smell, can't I?"

Gay: "You can't smell cows on me."

Isabelle: "I can smell the look in your face, cowboy." She reaches across and laughs. "But I love every miserable one of you! I had a cowboy friend. . . ." She quickly sips. "He had one arm gone, but he was more with one arm than any man with two. I mean like cooking—" They all laugh. "I'm serious! He could throw a whole frying pan full of chops in the air and they'd all come down on the other side. Of course, you're all good-for-nothin', as you know."

Gay: "That may be, but it's better than wages."

The waitress arrives with the drinks.

Guido: "I suppose you're headin' back East now, huh?"

Roslyn: "I can't make up my mind; I don't know what to do."

Gay: "You mean you don't have a business to run, or school to teach, or—"

"Me? I didn't even finish high school."

"Well, that's real *good* news."

"Why? Don't you like educated women?"

"Oh, they're all right. Always wantin' to know what you're *thinkin'*, that's all. There sure must be a load of thinkin' goin' around back East."

"Well, maybe they're trying to get to know you better." Roslyn smiles wryly. "You don't mind that, do you?"

"I don't at all. But did you ever get to know a man by askin' him questions?"

"You mean, he's going to lie."

"Well, he might not—but then again, he just might!"

Isabelle guffaws and the question-and-answer period gives way.

Gay: "Let's get another drink!"

Roslyn: "Sure, let's have some more!" His openness relaxes her; he is avowedly engaging her and it awakens her pleasurably.

Gay, calling to the waiter: "Fella? See if you can get us four more, will ya?" He turns to Guido, relaxed and happy, trying to open the way. "How about it, Pilot? We takin' out of this town today?"

Spurred, awkward, Guido falters into his campaign: "You been out of Reno at all, Mrs. Taber?"

Roslyn: "I walked to the edge of town once, but—it looks like nothing's out there."

Guido: "Oh."

Gay: "That might just be where everything is."

Roslyn: "Like what?"

"The country."

"What do you do there?"

"Just live."

Drawn in, Roslyn searches Gay's eyes, asking: "How can you . . . just live?"

"Well . . . you start by going to sleep. Then, you get up when you feel like it. Then you scratch yourself"—they chuckle—"fry yourself some eggs, see what kind of day it is, throw a stone, ride a horse, visit, whistle . . ."

Roslyn's eyes meet his. "I know what you mean."

Isabelle: "Might be nice, dear, whyn't you go out for a ride?"

Guido: "If it hit you right, I've got an empty house out in the country just beyond Hawleyville. It's yours if you want a little peace and quiet before you go back."

Roslyn, grinning: "Oh, is the last woman gone now?"

"No! No kidding." With a sudden self-exposure that is difficult for Guido: "I never offered it before."

"Well, thanks. I wouldn't stay there, but I *was* thinking of renting a car and seeing what the country—"

"Gay's got a truck, or I could get my car."

"No. Then you'll have to drive me back."

"Oh, I don't mind!"

"It's all right—I always . . ." She is a little flustered at having to stand against him; she touches his hand. ". . . like to feel I'm on my own, y'know? I'll rent a car. Where can I?"

Gay: "Right now?"

Roslyn: "Why not?"

Gay stands up. "Okay! You sure don't waste your time, do you?"

Guido: "I just got to stop over at the garage and tell the boss I quit."

Gay: "Now, that's the boy!"

They go down an aisle of slot machines toward the street. All at once there is a goal, a path through the shapeless day.

THREE

ROSLYN'S rented station wagon is speeding along a straight, endless highway a quarter of a mile behind Gay's ten-year-old pickup truck. Except for the two vehicles the highway is deserted. On both sides the bare Nevada hills are spread out, range beyond range. An occasional dirt trail winding into them raises the surprising thought that one could follow it and arrive at a human place in the interior. No house shows; only an occasional line of fence indicates that cattle range here sometimes. The hills front the highway like great giants' chests; to the eye speeding past, their undulating crests rise and fall as though the earth were silently breathing. The noon sun is lighting up red woundlike stains on their surfaces, a sudden blush of purple on one, the next faintly pink, another buff. Despite the hum of the engines the land seems undisturbed in its silence, a silence that grows in the mind until it becomes a wordless voice.

Roslyn, driving with Isabelle beside her, constantly turns from the road to stare at the great round hills. Her look is inward, her eyes widened by an air of respect.

Roslyn: "What's behind them?"

Isabelle: "More hills."

"What's that beautiful smell? It's like some kind of green perfume."

"Sage, darling."

"Oh, sure! I never smelled it except in a bottle!" Laughing: "Oh, Isabelle, it's beautiful here, isn't it?"

Isabelle, sensing Roslyn's excitement: "I better tell you something about cowboys, dear."

Roslyn laughs warmly: "You really worry about me, don't you!"

"You're too believing, dear. Cowboys are the last real men in the world, but they're as reliable as jackrabbits."

"But what if that's all there is? Really and truly, I mean."

"I guess a person just doesn't want to believe that."

"You think I'm reliable?"

"I guess you would be if you had somebody to be reliable *to*."

"I don't know any more. Maybe you're not supposed to believe anything people say. Maybe it's not even fair to them."

"Well . . . don't ask me, dear. This world and I have always been strangers—down deep, I mean."

They fall silent. The hills and their colors float across Roslyn's eyes.

Up ahead, Guido is at the wheel of the truck. Beside him, Gay dozes with his hat over his eyes.

Guido: "I couldn't hear what he said to her but"—he glances at Gay for corroboration—"it looked like *she* left *him*. The husband." He waits, but Gay is silent. "She's kind of hard to figure out, y'know? One minute she looks dumb and brand new. Like a kid. But maybe he caught her knockin' around, huh?" Gay is silent. "She sure *moves*, doesn't she?"

Gay: "Yeah. She's real prime."

Guido starts to speak again, but, glancing at Gay, decides to let him sleep. They ride in silence. They pass two Indians on brown-and-white paints riding slowly behind a small herd of cattle off to the right. Now Guido slows down and, sticking his head out the window, waves back at Roslyn. He turns off the highway onto a dirt trail, glancing into his mirror.

Roslyn follows in his dust across the sage flat toward the hills. In a moment they are climbing the belly of a hill. Now they are winding around behind it, rising all the time, the road

becoming stony and the curves abrupt. Smashed and splintered outcroppings of rock force the trail to meander. They drive down a gap and then up a steep gorge whose flanks almost blot out the sky. Quite suddenly a house appears at the head of the gorge; Roslyn pulls up behind the truck and the motors are shut off.

She and Isabelle emerge, looking at the house. The men join them. A small cloud of buff dust slowly floats away. For a moment the sudden appearance of this vacant building enforces its silence on them.

An odd, almost otherworldly air emerges from the rather modern, ranch-style house. Its windows look out on the swiftly falling land toward the unseen highway far below and the next swell of hills rising beyond. In this vastness it seems as terribly alone as a stranded boat.

It has never been completed. Black composition sheathing panels show where the clapboards were never put on, and the boards lie in a graying, weathered pile on the ground nearby, morning glories winding through them. The gabled roof is partly shingled, but a large area is still bare to the black tarpaper underneath. Sawhorses stand in weeds and sage. An unfinished wing of bare studs and joists sticks out of one side, little sage bushes starting up through the foundation. There is an abortive look to the place, a sense of its having been immobilized by sudden catastrophe or whimsically left incomplete by people who suddenly ran away to another idea. It is not a farm or a ranch; its only visible reason for being here is that it stands at the focal point of a vast view. Yet someone rich enough to build for that reason would hardly have thought of so conventional and small a house. Its very pointlessness is somehow poetic to Roslyn, like an unrealized longing nailed together.

Roslyn: "Why isn't it finished?"

Guido, cryptically: "It's weather-tight. Come on in."

Guido leads them in through the side door. He stops before they are well inside the doorway and turns to Roslyn, patting the black insulation batting between the open studs of a partition. "Insulated." She nods, not quite sure what he is referring to, and he leads on into the living room. With a wide sweep of his arm he says: "Living room," and she nods, looking around at the complete assortment of furniture, from the Morris chair to

the studio couch, the drapeless dirty windows, the sections of wall lined with knotty-pine boards and the sections which still show bare studs, the dusty Indian blankets on the Grand Rapids couch. The place is not damp but it seems so. Light is grayed by the dust on the windows.

Guido opens a door and presses himself against the jamb, inviting her to look out. "This was going to be a new bedroom."

Roslyn sticks her head into the stud skeleton of a wing built onto the house. The sun is bright in her face, and lights the ground underneath the uncovered floor joists. "It's even nice now!"

Encouraged, Guido rushes to a series of three windows at the front of the room. "Picture windows."

"Oh!"

But when he arrives at the windows and looks out, the view is gray glass, and he hurries to open the front door. "Look at that."

With Gay and Isabelle behind her she stands in the threshold, looking out and down at the oceanic roll of mountains falling away below. "God, it goes forever."

"See the bathroom." Guido touches her elbow and she follows him across the living room. Passing the fireplace, he touches it, glancing up to where it goes through the ceiling. "Fireplace."

She nods. "Brick."

"Kitchen."

She follows into the kitchen area, noting the spider in the sink and the damp-wrinkled box of soap flakes on the stove.

"Gas refrigerator." He opens the freezer door and she looks in. His pride is riding him and she is drawn toward him. He closes the door and hurries through a doorway—quickly, as though he might lose her interest.

"Ceramic tile."

In the bathroom she inspects the tile. He crosses the bathroom and opens another door and she comes up to his side.

"And here's our—" He breaks off at the sight of an ornately framed wedding photograph hanging over the bed. Two rosaries are suspended from the frame. "My wife. She died here."

"Oh. I'm sorry." Roslyn glances at the barren room. A double bed, a dresser, a window, an unpainted composition-board wall. His face, and his wife's in the photograph, are curiously unmarked, new. A sadness presses in on Roslyn, and she looks at Guido's face beside her, seeing for the first time the twisting private agony behind his eyes.

Guido: "She was due to have a baby. I was setting the capstone on the chimney, and . . . she screamed, and that was that."

Roslyn: "Couldn't you call the doctor?"

"She didn't seem to be that sick. Then I got a flat and didn't have a spare. Everything just happened wrong. It'll do that sometimes."

"Oh, I know. Couldn't you live here any more?"

Guido is surprised by her flow of sympathy, and he is swept into cultivating it now. Yet one senses a fear in him of mockery, and his manner with her is tentative and delicate. "We knew each other since we were seven years old, see."

"You should find another girl."

Guido, with a certain trace of vague condescension toward the idea: "I don't know. Being with anybody else, it just seems . . . impossible, you know? She wasn't *like* other women. Stood behind me hundred per cent, uncomplaining as a tree."

Roslyn senses an invidious comparison; she laughs lightly. "But maybe that's what killed her." Quickly, as she sees he feels a slur: "I mean, a little complaining helps sometimes." But he does not understand, and, striving for gaiety—and pardon—she takes his arm, starting him out of the room. "Come! Show me the rest of it! It's beautiful!"

They emerge into the living-room area. Gay is sprawled on the couch; Isabelle is holding up an Indian blanket to examine it.

Roslyn: "Isn't it beautiful here, Iz?"

Isabelle: "It'd be perfect if somebody'd go out in the car and get the bottle of whiskey I bought with my own money."

Guido: "Hey, that's right!" Glad for the reprieve, he jumps to the ground from the front-door threshold—there being no step.

Roslyn wanders about the room, touching things.

Gay: "Glasses are in the kitchen, Isabelle. I'm real tired."

Isabelle: "No, darling, you're just a cowboy. You fella
get up unless it's rainin' down your neck." 't

Gay laughs as the old woman goes into the kitchen area.
turns and watches Roslyn, who has halted at a dirty window t
look out. He runs his eyes over her back, her legs.

"Too rough for you, Roslyn?"

A certain abstracted suspense emanates from her. "Oh, I don't mind that."

"Should've seen his wife. She helped pour the cement, knocked in nails. She was a real good sport."

She looks around at the room as though trying to summon the walls' memories. "And now she's dead. . . . Because he didn't have a spare tire."

"Well, that's the way it goes."

Their eyes meet; hers resent his contradiction of her mood's truth.

"Goes the other way too, though; don't forget that." His immovable resolution keeps her staring at him for a moment, and despite herself a vague gratitude softens her face.

Guido jumps up into the room with a small bag of groceries and a bottle. He looks at them and at Isabelle drying glasses on her sling and calls out: "Boy, it's nice to see people in here! Come on, folks, let's get a drink." Going to Isabelle in the kitchen area: "I'll start the refrigerator. It makes ice quick."

"Ice!" Isabelle calls through the open studs to Roslyn: "We stayin' that long?"

"I don't know. . . ."

She unwittingly looks to Gay for the decision, and he speaks to her uncertainty.

"Sure! come on, there's no better place to be! And you couldn't find better company, either!"

"All right!" Roslyn laughs.

"That's it, sport!" Gay calls to the kitchen: "Turn on that ice, Guido boy!"

Isabelle comes in, balancing a tray and glasses, which Gay leaps up to take—along with the bottle from her sling. Gay pours.

Gay: "Let's get this stuff a-flowin' and make the desert bloom."

Isabelle: "Flow it slow. We only got the one bottle."

asps Roslyn's wrist and puts the glass into her hand.
C you are, now! Put that in your thoughts and see how "ome out."
She smiles at him, warmed by his persistence.
Guido enters and takes a glass. "Come on, sit down, everybody! Let's get comfortable."
Roslyn sits on the couch, Isabelle beside her. The two men take chairs.
Guido addresses Roslyn, his hope flying: "Say, I'm really glad you like this place."
Isabelle: "Well, here's to Nevada, the leave-it state."
Roslyn: "The what state?"
They are already starting to chuckle.
"The leave-it state. You want to gamble your money, leave it here. A wife to get rid of? Get rid of her here. Extra atom bomb you don't need? Just blow it up here and nobody will mind in the slightest. The slogan of Nevada is, 'Anything goes, but don't complain if it went!'"
Gay: "God, that's no lie!"
Guido: "How come you never went back home, Isabelle? You came out here for your divorce, didn't you? Originally?"
Isabelle drinks, glances diffidently at Roslyn. "Tell you the truth, I wasn't beautiful enough to go home."
Roslyn: "Oh, Isabelle!"
"It's true, darling. Beauty helps anywhere, but in Virginia it's a necessity. You practically need it for a driver's license. I love Nevada. Why, they don't even have mealtimes here. I never met so many people didn't own a watch. Might have two wives at the same time, but no watch. Bless 'em all!"
Roslyn, relaxing, is leaning her head back on the couch as they drink. Their rhythm has slowed. Their laughter slides away now.
Roslyn: "How quiet it is here!"
Sprawled out, Gay speaks with avowed seriousness. "Sweetest sound there is."
They sip their drinks. There is a skylike silence in the room.
Guido: "There's an Indian store about five miles"—Roslyn looks at him quizzically—"if you wanted to shop. Groceries, everything. If you decided to stay a while."

Gay, plainly, without any insinuation: "Be glad to come by and do your chores. If you liked."

Roslyn drinks again and gets up. They watch as, in a closed world of her own, she wanders to a half-empty bookcase. Unable to bear the silence she turns to the men. "Could we have a fire?"

Guido: "Sure! It's a good fireplace." He springs up and piles wood into the fireplace. He looks up at her, dares to smile, thankful for her command.

She smiles back abstractedly and, turning from Guido, sees that Gay has been watching the silent exchange. She smiles at Gay and he replies with a frankly intensified gaze at her. She says to Isabelle: "Maybe they know your friend." To the men: "You ever know a fellow named Andy?"

Gay: "Andy who?"

Isabelle: "Stop it, darling! You can't go lookin' for a man."

Gay: "What'd he, take off?"

"Not exactly. He just didn't come back." Isabelle laughs at herself. "Andy Powell? You ever—"

"Sure! Fella with one arm. Call him Andy Gump sometimes?"

Isabelle, a little excited in spite of herself, laughing: "That's him!"

Roslyn, hopefully for Isabelle, asks Gay: "Where is he?"

"Saw him at the rodeo only last month."

Roslyn: "Could you find him if you—"

Isabelle: "Dear girl, you got to stop thinkin' you can change things."

A mystifying flood of protest reddens Roslyn's face. "But if there's something you could do . . . *I* don't know what to *do*, but if I knew, I'd do it!"

She suddenly finds the three of them looking at her in silence, looking at her as though she had challenged them in some secret way. Gay's interest is heightened; Isabelle feels a little ashamed and ineffectual; Guido is vaguely frightened by this burst of feeling and drawn to her. Because there is no one here to receive her meaning as she intends it, she says, almost laughing: "Is there a phonograph or a radio? Let's get some music."

Guido: "There's no electricity."

Roslyn: "How about the car radio?"

Gay: "Now who'd've thought of that? Turn it on, Guido!"

Guido: "You always got an idea, don't you." Excitedly he rushes out, hopping down to the ground.

Gay: "How about another drink, Roslyn? It'll keep the first one warm."

Roslyn: "I'd love it."

The car engine is heard starting outside. With strangely youthful energy Isabelle gets up and heads for the kitchen. "Think I'll make a sandwich. How about you people?"

Roslyn: "Okay."

Isabelle goes into the kitchen area. Gay, close to Roslyn, pours a drink into her glass and says in a private tone: "I hope you're going to stay on here. Any chance?"

Her face fills with a sadness that approaches a strange self-abandonment. "Why? What difference would it make?"

"Might make all the difference in the world as time goes by."

She looks at him with the unconcealed intensity of a searcher, and he does not evade it. Jazz is heard from the car radio outside. The engine is shut off. Gay touches her arm. "Like to dance?"

"Okay."

He draws her to him. He is a fair dancer. Guido enters, and is rather caught in midair by this progress.

Roslyn calls over Gay's shoulder to Guido: "Thanks! Iz, give him another drink. It's a very nice house, Guido."

Isabelle comes out of the kitchen area. Guido goes around them and forces an interest in stoking up the fire. In his face, seen in the firelight, there is rapid, planning thought.

Isabelle, making sandwiches with one hand: "That's pretty good dancing, cowboy!"

Gay: "Hey, what're you makin' my feet do?"

Roslyn is getting quite high; her body is moving more freely. "Relax. Join your partner, don't fight her."

"*I* ain't fightin' her."

She breaks and tries to move him into a lindy. He does it awkwardly, but amazed at himself.

Guido: "What *are* you doin'?"

Guido and Isabelle are watching with intrigued smiles.

Guido drinks deeply now, a competitive tension rising in him. Isabelle speaks with quiet pride to Guido: "She taught dancing, y'know, before she was married."

"No kiddin'! In a dance hall?"

"Something like that, I guess."

The information tends to place Roslyn for Guido. Suddenly he breaks in between her and Gay. "How about the landlord?" Lightly, to Gay: "Move over, boy, huh?"

"Just watch out for those pretty little feet there!"

Guido looks directly at Roslyn, his eyes firing, an almost ludicrous familiarity in his grin. "Oh, she knows how to get out of the way. Let's go!"

With a clap of his hands, he astounds them all by breaking into a boogie lindy. Roslyn immediately, and happily, accepts the challenge. They come together, part, dance back to back, and he puts her to her mettle.

Gay: "Where in hell you learn that, Pilot?" To Isabelle: "I never knew him to dance at all!" Calling: "Look at Pilot comin' out from under the bushel!"

The number ends, and on the last beat Guido has her pressed close, and in the silence she deftly, but definitely—smiling, however—breaks his grip on her body, her expression striving to deny the easy victory in his eyes.

Gay: "You two oughta put on a show! That's some goin', Roslyn!"

Roslyn: "Whew!" Panting, getting high, she staggers to the door. Another number starts from the radio. Guido goes to her, clasps her waist, and turns her around to him familiarly. "Come on, honey, this is a good one. I haven't danced in years." They dance with quicker knowledge of each other now. After a moment she asks: "Didn't your wife dance?"

"Not like you. She had no . . . gracefulness."

Roslyn stays close to him and looks up into his face: "Whyn't you *teach* her to be graceful?"

"You can't learn that."

"How do you know? I mean, how do you *know*?"

Guido is stumped by her veering thought. Resentment mars his face.

Roslyn: "You see? She died, and she never knew how you could dance! It's nobody's fault, but to a certain extent"—she

holds thumb and index finger a half inch apart— "I mean just to a certain extent maybe you were strangers."

Guido, injured, his tone on the verge of contempt: "I don't feel like discussing my wife." He stops dancing.

Roslyn takes his arm. The jazz is going, she is high now, and a depth of sadness comes over her face. "Oh, don't be mad! I just meant that if you loved her you could have taught her anything. Because we have to die, we're really dying right now, aren't we? All the husbands and all the wives are dying every minute, and they are not teaching one another what they really know." She sees he is at a loss and genuinely tries to plead with him. "You're such a nice man, Guido." She wipes her hair out of her eyes to blot out the sight of his resentful face, and suddenly: "I want air!"

Turning quickly to the front door she starts to step out. Gay rushes from the couch and catches her before she goes down where the step is missing. Isabelle rushes right behind him.

Gay: "You better lie down, girl."

Isabelle: "Come on, let's get back home. Heist her down, cowboy."

Roslyn: "No, I'm all right, I'm all—"

She starts once again to walk out the door. Guido leaps down to the ground and she falls into his arms, standing up. She is looking into his face, laughing in surprise at her sudden drop, when he thrusts his lips against hers, squeezing her body to him. She pushes him away.

Above them on the threshold Isabelle calls with fear in her voice: "Help me down! Get in the car, Roslyn!"

Roslyn sends Guido falling a step back and staggers away. Momentarily alone, she looks around her. The radio jazz is still playing. She flies into a warm, longing solo dance among the weeds, and coming to a great tree she halts and then embraces it, pressing her face against its trunk.

Guido, Isabelle, and Gay are watching now in a group at the doorway of the house, mystification on their faces. Guido, still resentful, takes a step toward her, but Gay touches him and he stops. Gay goes through the weeds to the tree and gently tries to turn Roslyn's shoulder, for her face is hidden under her arm. As soon as he touches her she turns and faces him and, as-

tonishingly, her face is bright and laughing. Gay starts to smile, but he is bewildered.

Roslyn: "You were worried about me! That's so sweet!"

Gay: "Just want to keep you in one pretty piece."

He puts his arm around her and she lets herself be led to her station wagon, which is parked beside Gay's beat-up pickup truck. At the car's open door, Gay turns to Guido and begins to speak, but Guido cuts him off: "Go ahead, you drive her, I'll take your truck."

Gay moves Roslyn into the car, and she says: "No, don't leave Guido all alone. Go ahead, Iz. . . . Ride with poor Guido." In apology she reaches toward Guido: "It's a beautiful house, Guido!"

Gay gets in beside her.

Both vehicles descend the rocky trail to the highway below, the truck ahead. Inside the station wagon, Roslyn is sitting beside Gay, one leg tucked under, her foot almost touching Gay's hip. She is in the momentary calm after a quick storm, blurred eyes staring out at the passing hills that rise from the roadside. She turns to look at Gay's profile; a calm seems to exude from him, an absence of uncertainty which has the quality of kindness, a serious concern for which she is grateful. She speaks: "I didn't mean to hurt his feelings. Did I hurt his feelings?"

Gay, grinning: "You sure brought out the little devil in him—surprised me." He laughs. "He did look comical doin' that dance!" He guffaws.

They have arrived at the foot of the trail. The truck has entered the highway, turned, and moved off. Now Gay stops the car, he looks left and right for traffic, and his eyes fall on Roslyn; she is looking at him searchingly, a residual smile lingering on her face.

"You're a real beautiful woman. It's . . . almost kind of an honor sittin' next to you. You just shine in my eyes." She laughs softly, surprised. "That's my true feeling, Roslyn." He pulls up the brake, shifts around to face her. "What makes you so sad? I think you're the saddest girl I ever met."

"You're the first man ever said that. I'm usually told how happy I am."

"You make a man *feel* happy, that's why."

He tries to embrace her; she gently stops him. "I don't feel that way about you, Gay."

Gay, pleased, somehow, holds up her chin. "Well, don't get discouraged, girl—you might! Look, whyn't you try it out here a while? You know, sometimes if a person don't know what to do, the best thing is to just stand still . . . and I guarantee you'd have something out here you wouldn't find on every corner."

She asks him with her eyes.

"I may not amount to much some ways, but I am a good friend."

Roslyn, touching his hand: "Thanks."

Gay, encouraged, quickly puts the car in gear: "Let me take you back, and you get your things. . . ." He drives onto the highway with heightened urgency. "Try it for a week, see what happens." They drive for a moment. "You ever hear the story of the city man out in the country? And he sees this farmer sittin' on his porch, and he says, 'Mister, do you know how I can get back to town?' And the fella says, 'Nope.' And the city man says, 'Well can you tell me how to get to the post office?' And the fella says, 'Nope.' 'Well, do you know how to get to the railroad station?' 'Nope.' 'Mister,' he says, 'you sure don't know much, do you?' And the farmer on the porch says, 'Nope. But I ain't lost.'

They laugh together. A certain reserve dissolves in her, as she senses a delicacy in his feeling, an unwavering attention on her. Even when he turns away she feels herself in the center of his gaze.

She asks: "Don't you have a home?"

"Sure. Never was a better one, either."

"Where is it?"

"Right here."

With a gesture of his head he indicates the open country. She looks out the window for a house on the moonlit land, but seeing only the deserted hills she again faces his profile, drawn by his self-containment. She turns back to the night outside, trying to touch a point of rest in the vastness there.

FOUR

THE end of night. Stars recede and go out, the sun's rim appears above the sea of hills, and the sky swiftly catches fire, sucking the vision of the eye toward the circular horizon and an earth in peace. Bird songs as clear as the air whistle the sun back into the sky. The eye tires of distances and seeks detail, and rapacity emerges; a rabbit hops from under a sage bush and a shadow passes over it. A hawk, serene, floats in narrowing circles above. The bird songs become jagged and strident. Swallows from nowhere dive at the soaring hunter to drive him off. A butterfly lights on a stone and a chameleon's tongue flicks out and takes it.

The sunlight moves into the bedroom of Guido's house, where Roslyn is asleep. The screaming of the birds seems to be penetrating her dreams; her face tenses and one fist begins to close. The empty pillow beside her head is dented.

The door to the living room opens and Gay stands there looking down at her, his gaze fingering the outlines of her body under the sheet. The picture of Guido and his wife is gone from over the bed, only the hook remaining. There is desire in Gay's face and the scent of her body still clings to his, but his eyes are searching as though through a mist emanating from her. Some wonder has taken place and is still unfolding itself within him, an unforetold consequence of pleasure. Unconsciously he smooths his hair back and in the gesture is a worry that he is not quite young any more.

She stirs under his stare and now opens her eyes, and he comes and knee-bends beside the bed. As her eyes open he leans in and kisses her. She seems for a moment not to know where she is. Then she smiles, and her eyes look around the room and she stretches. "Boy, I'm hungry!"

"Come on out, I got a surprise."

He walks out of the room. She sits up, her face showing a pleasurable anticipation, and she starts out of bed.

Gay goes to the stove and turns over some eggs in a pan. Near him is a kitchen table set for two. He turns and sees Roslyn in a terry-cloth robe emerging from the bedroom doorway.

She looks about in surprise. "You been *cleaning*?"

She moves, sees the table set, the breakfast sizzling on the stove, and in a vase a few wild flowers. Something outside the door catches her eyes. She looks and sees a mop standing in an empty pail among the weeds. Now she turns to him. She is moved by this effort. She hurries toward him at the stove. "Here, let me cook."

"Just sit down, it's all done."

He dishes out eggs for both of them and sits opposite her. She stares at him. He starts eating.

"You always do this?"

"Uh-uh. First time for me."

"Really and truly?"

Gay nods; his having gone out of himself is enough.

She starts eating. "Oooo! It's delicious!"

She eats ravenously. He watches with enjoyment. "You really go all out, don't you? Even the way you eat. I like that. Women generally pick."

In reply she smiles and returns to eating, and it joins them for a moment. Now she looks up at him and says with a full mouth: "The air makes you hungry, doesn't it?"

He laughs softly. Now he is sipping his coffee. He lights a cigarette, always trying to sound her.

She eats like one who has starved. Now she stops for a breath. "I love to eat!" Happily she looks around the room. "I'd never know it was the same house. It even smells different."

Suddenly she goes around the table and kisses his cheek. "You like me, huh?"

He draws her down to his lap, kisses her on the mouth, holds her with his head buried in her. She pats his neck, an uneasiness rising into her face mixed with her happiness. He relaxes his hold. She gets up, walks to the doorway, looks out at the endless hills, the horizon, the empty sky.

"Birds must be brave to live out here. Especially at night." She turns to him, explaining. "Whereas they're so small, you know?"

"M-m."

Roslyn, almost laughing: "You think I'm crazy?"

"Uh-uh. I just look that way 'cause I can't make you out."

"Why?"

"I don't know. . . . You got children?"

She shakes her head. Some embarrassment seems to have risen in her at the question; she turns out again, and seeing a butterfly lighting on the threshold, does a knee-bend and holds out her finger toward it but it flies off. She spreads out on her stomach with her head in the doorway. Now she glances back at him and decides to answer him.

"I didn't want children. Not with him."

"He did, though, huh?"

"Children supposedly bring you together. But what if they don't, you know? Because I've known couples, so-called happily married, and one time"—she turns to him, rolling onto her side—"the wife was actually in the hospital to have the baby and he was calling me up. I mean *calling me up*. And they're still supposed to be happily married."

"I guess you believe in true love, don't you?"

"I don't know, but somebody ought to invent where you can't have kids unless you love each other. Because kids know the difference. I always knew." Suddenly, even cheerfully: "If you want to go anywhere I don't mind being alone."

Gay comes over to her and knee-bends beside her, runs his fingers through her hair. "I look like I want to leave?"

"I just want you to do what you feel like."

"I never saw anything like it."

"What?"

"You ain't kiddin'. Even when you're kiddin', you ain't kiddin'."

She laughs. "Most people don't like it."

"Makes me feel peaceful." He sits on the floor. For a moment they are silent. "You know, they come out here from New York, Chicago, St. Louis—and find them a cowboy. Cowboy's supposed to be dumb, y'know, so they'll tell him everything. And they'll do everything, everything they couldn't do back home. And it's pitiful."

"Why is it pitiful?"

"Cowboy's laughin' at them and they don't know it. Sure is nice to meet somebody who's got respect for a man."

"You ever think of getting married again?"

"Oh, I've thought of it lots of times, but never in daylight." She laughs easily, recognizing his nature, and he grins in admission of it.

He comes to a complete stillness, and whatever strategic quality structured their questions and answers falls away. His direct, unwavering gaze awakens a wisp of fear in her. "I'll tell you this, though. I wouldn't know how to say good-bye to you, Roslyn. It surprises me."

The silence suddenly seems like an onrushing wave that will smother her. She reaches thankfully for his hand, but her eyes are growing distant, protecting her.

He looks around at the room. "There'd be a lot to do around this place if you were going to stay awhile."

She is on her feet, drawing him up by the hand. "Let's go in the sun!"

They drop down to the ground from the threshold and walk through the weeds reflectively, hand in hand.

"You got respect for a man. I can't stand these women all the time sayin' what they would do and what they wouldn't do."

She laughs.

"And they go and do it anyway."

They sit on the lumber pile. She looks up at the blue, cloudless sky. "I really make you peaceful?"

He nods. "I sure wish I knew whether you were stayin' or goin'."

She bends to a pebble and cleans the dirt off it. "When I know myself I'll tell you. Okay? Let's just live—like you said in the bar?" Apologetically, with almost a laugh: "I don't know where I am yet—you know?"

She gets off the lumber and her eye happens to fall on a cement block in the weeds. Grateful for even this small escape, she almost dances over to it. "Look! Couldn't we use this for a step?"

He walks over and picks up the block. "Just might at that." He goes the few yards to the front door and sets the block under it. "There now!"

"Let me try it." She hurries and runs up the step into the house, then turns and hops down again. "It's perfect! I can come in and I can go out." Again she jumps up into the house and out again, and her pure enthusiasm moves him, and he laughs with the surprise of a youth. She senses his naive, genuine feeling, and with sudden gratitude and hope cries out:

"Oh, you're a dear man, Gay!" He kisses her speaking mouth as she once more comes dancing out of the doorway.

FIVE

THERE were weeds around the house, hunks of dried cement, and scabs of bare ground. Now Gay is hoeing in a new vegetable garden nearby and flowers have been planted around the rocks, a fallen fence has been repaired, and a hose is spouting water over new grass. Sweat is dripping from his chin as he works the hoe around young vegetable plants. A deep hum in the sky raises his head. The sound grows. He turns in a circle.

Roslyn appears in the doorway, then comes down toward him, carrying a pitcher of lemonade and a glass. The roar is descending on them, and as she reaches him a small biplane zooms over the ridge of the house, waggling its wings. Gay yells: "Guido!" and waves. The plane swings around in a curve over the falling valley and she waves with him. It disappears.

Roslyn: "Where's he going?"

Gay: "Sssh!" He listens. She is puzzled. "He might be gonna land back there. There's a place." They listen. Silence. "I guess not. Probably just sayin' hello."

"Here, have some lemonade."

"Thanks." He takes it and drinks and she sits on a stone.

"What does he do, just fly around?"

He hands back the glass and picks a splinter out of his palm. "He might be goin' for eagles. Now and again the ranchers hire Guido to shoot eagles."

"Why?"

"They kill a lot of lambs. He gets fifty bucks a bird. It's nice work."

"Why doesn't he ever come around? I hope he's not mad at me."

"Oh, no. Women don't mean too much to Guido. He's probably been layin' around readin' his comic books, that's all."

He works the ground again. Squatting on the stone, she seems to join the sun and the earth in staring at him, watching his hoe awakening the soil around the plants. He senses an importance for her in his expertness, and he winks down at her.

She smiles and breaks her stare. "I like you, Gay."

"That's good news."

"You like me?"

"Well, it's close to ninety degrees out here, and I'm hoein' a garden for the first time since I was ten years old, so I guess I must like you pretty good."

She reaches out and touches a plant. "I never really saw anything grow before. How tiny those seeds were—and still they know they're supposed to be lettuces!"

"You say the damnedest things, you know that?"

They laugh quietly. He works the ground. She looks off now at the distant hills. She is almost content; she knows she might well be content but something gnaws at her, and she listens to it.

"In Chicago everybody's busy."

He glances at her; he doesn't quite understand what she means, but the feeling is a welcoming one, so he lets it go.

"You ever get lonesome for your children?"

For a moment he works in silence; it might be reticence or a bad recollection. She starts to change the subject but he speaks.

"I see them couple of times a year. They come whenever I'm in a rodeo. I'm a roper." He works for a moment, bends, and tosses a rock out of the garden. "I do get lonesome. Sure."

"They must like you."

"I guess they do. My daughter's almost your size now. You size twelve?"

"Uh-huh."

"So's she. I bought her a dress for Christmas. Size twelve."

Effortlessly she jumps up and goes to him; her movement is imperative and surprises him. She embraces him and kisses him passionately. Her face is very serious, nearly in pain. He lets the hoe drop from his hand. Roslyn sees he is puzzled. "Go ahead. Work." She returns to the stone and sits. He resumes hoeing. "What happened; you just stop loving your wife?"

He speaks out of vivid memory and it is discomfiting to go into. "Well . . . I come home one night and find her wrapped

up in a car with a fella. Turned out to be one of my real old friends, too. Cousin of mine, matter of fact."

"Huh! And you didn't have any idea, before?"

The intensity of a blush tightens his eyes.

"God, no! In those days I thought you got married, and that was it. But nothin's it. Not forever."

"That's what I could never get used to—everything's always changing, isn't it?"

Gay rests on the hoe, looking down at her. "You been fooled an awful lot, haven't you?"

With a certain shame that is without self-pity, she whispers: "Yes."

"Well, let's just see if it turns out different this time. You're not going anywhere?"

"I'm here."

"Well, let's leave it that way for now. Okay?"

"How dear you are! You didn't get mad at me."

She kisses him again quickly, then, filled with an unspeakable relief, a sense of somehow having been pardoned and accepted, she clasps her hands together with her face toward the sky, her whole body on tiptoe. "I love this whole state!"

She laughs at herself and he grins in surprise. She picks up his hoe and hands it to him as though to keep the present image of him from vanishing. "Here. I love to see a man working around his house."

But his eye has caught something on the ground. He bends to a plant. "Now what have we here?"

He unfolds the leaves of a nibbled lettuce. Now he turns about and sees several more damaged plants farther up the row. He scans the brushy borders of the garden.

"It's plain old rabbit, and I'm gonna get him!" He drops his hoe and starts toward his truck beside the house, calling, "Margaret! Come here now!"

The dog appears around a corner, alert and eager. Gay goes to his truck and takes a shotgun out from behind the seat, then a handful of shells. He is loading the gun when Roslyn comes to him, still carrying the lemonade pitcher. She is trying to appear smiling, but her anxiety is clear.

"Maybe they won't eat any more."

Gay, busy with his gun, eager for the kill, speaks rapidly of

what he knows: "No, ma'am. Once they zeroed in on that garden it's them or us. There won't be a thing left by the end of the week."

He starts past her with his gun. She touches his arm. She is trying to suppress her anxiety and it thins her voice. "Couldn't we wait another day and see? I can't stand to kill anything, Gay."

"Honey, it's only a rabbit."

"But it's alive, and . . . it doesn't know any better, does it?"

"Now you just go in the house and let me—"

She grasps his arm and her adamance astounds him. "Please, Gay! I know how hard you worked—"

"Damn right I worked hard!" He points angrily at the garden and tries to laugh. "I never done that in my life for anybody! And I didn't do it for some bug-eyed rabbit!"

He takes off toward the garden, the eager dog at his heel. She tries to turn back to the house, but is driven to follow him. A little breathless now, with the ice-filled lemonade pitcher still clinking in her hand: "Gay, please listen."

Gay turns on her now, smiling, but his eyes full of anger. "You go in the house now and stop bein' silly!"

"I am not silly!"

He starts off again, she calls: "You have no respect for me!"

Gay turns, suddenly furious, red-faced.

She pleads now: "Gay, I don't care about the lettuce!"

"Well, *I* care about it! How about some respect for me?"

A sound from behind the house turns them both. Gay walks a few steps toward one corner when, from a trail that climbs the hill behind the house, Guido appears, helping Isabelle along. She is no longer wearing a sling, but her arm is still bandaged.

Roslyn runs toward her with high relief and joy. "Isabelle, Guido, how are you?"

Isabelle: "Dear girl!"

The women embrace. Gay comes and shakes Guido's hands, happy at this visit. "How you been, fella? We never heard you land."

Isabelle holds Roslyn before her. "My, you look thrivin'!"

Guido has been glancing at the place, and now walks to get

a better vantage. "Am I in the right place?" His voice cracks into a giggle.

Roslyn is extraordinarily sympathetic toward him, and Guido, despite the conventionality of his remarks, is moved by what he sees.

"Did you see the vegetable garden?" Roslyn turns to draw in Gay and even to give him preeminence. "Gay did it. Took him a whole week just to get the soil turned over."

Gay walks up beside her, and now that her feeling for him has returned he puts an arm around her waist. With wry pride: "Mowed the grass and put in them flowers, too. Even got your windows unstuck, and your fireplace don't smoke any more."

Guido turns from Gay to Roslyn. There is a subtle resentment toward both of them, but at the same time his eyes seem charged with a vision beyond them. "Roslyn, you must be a magician. The only thing this boy ever did for a woman was to get out the ice cubes."

They all laugh, trying to obliterate his evident uneasiness.

Roslyn, pointing to the outdoor furniture and taking Guido's arm: "We got chairs! Come, sit down!"

Gay intercepts them. "Let's show him the inside. Wait'll you see this, Guido! I've moved the furniture around so many times I'm gettin' long ears."

He and Guido move together toward the doorway. Roslyn and Isabelle follow behind. The men go into the house.

Isabelle: "Darling, you look so lovely! You found yourself, haven't you?"

Roslyn tries to dispel her own hesitation and ends by hugging Isabelle. "I'm so glad you came! Look, we have a step now."

She helps Isabelle into the house, Isabelle giving a marveling look at the flower bed beside the step as she mounts up.

"Watch your arm—how is it?"

"It's still weak as a bird's wing, but—" Entering the living room, she breaks off. "Well, I never in my life . . ."

Guido and Isabelle look at each detail in the room. Indian blankets cover the formerly bare studs; wild flowers brighten the tables and window sills; the furniture is rearranged, cleaned; the newly curtained windows are no longer smeared with dust

and cobwebs; and the fireplace is all white. There is a feeling here of a shelter.

Tears flow into Isabelle's eyes. "Well! Huh! My—it's magical!" She looks at Roslyn, then she addresses Gay, almost rebuking him. "I just hope you know that you have finally come in contact with a real woman." She suddenly throws her arms around Roslyn. "Oh, my darling girl!"

"Come, see the bedroom. Come, Guido." Roslyn pulls them both to the bedroom. "I hope you don't mind we changed things around. . . ."

Gay, with an excitement previously unknown to him, opens the refrigerator and takes out cubes. Roslyn, Guido, and Isabelle enter the bedroom; it too is transformed, repainted, brightly curtained, with a carpet on the floor, a few botanical pictures on the walls, a dressing table, a bright spread on the bed. Guido looks about and his eyes fall on the place above the bed where the picture of himself and his dead wife had been. A print of a Western landscape hangs there now.

Roslyn sees the direction of his gaze. "Oh! I put your picture in the living room!"

"Uh-huh. Put a closet in?"

"Gay did it."

She swings the door of the closet open to show him. Inside the door half a dozen photos of her are tacked up. They are girlie photos for the doorway of a second-class nightclub, herself in net tights, on her back, in bizarre costumes. She realizes only now, partly by the flush on his face as he sees the photos, that she has shown them to him.

"Oh, they're stupid, don't look at them!" She closes the door. He looks embarrassed for her, perplexed. "Gay put them up for a joke. Come. Let's have a lot of drinks!"

She shepherds them into the living room and goes on to the kitchen to spread crackers around a piece of cheese on a platter. Gay is coming to them with drinks.

Guido's face is flushed as he strives against his envy. "Man, you sure got it made this time."

Roslyn calls from the kitchen area with high joy: "Sit down, everybody. I got wonderful cheese. It's so nice to have company!" They are dispersing to the couch and chairs, but she rushes to Guido, who is about to sit on the couch. "No! Sit in

the big chair." Leading him—he is embarrassed—to the most imposing chair in the room: "This must have been your chair, wasn't it?"

"Matter of fact it was. I did all my studying in this chair. When I was still ambitious." He sits stiffly, like one who feels vaguely threatened at being served.

She rushes back to the kitchen area. "Maybe you'll get ambitious again, you can't tell. I'll get you some cheese." She gets the cheese tray from the kitchen counter and, returning to Guido, points with it toward his wedding photograph on a table. "I put your picture there—is that all right?"

"Oh, you don't have to keep it out, Roslyn."

"Why? It's part of the house, Guido. Y'know?" She sets the tray down and sits beside Gay on the couch, taking a drink from the table where he set it for her. Now they are settled. "I mean, it's still your house. Here, Isabelle, rest your arm on this." She leaps up with a cushion from the couch and sets it under Isabelle's bandaged arm.

"Oh, don't bother with me, dear."

"Why? Might as well be comfortable."

Roslyn goes back to the couch and sits beside Gay, as Guido speaks. His voice is suddenly portentous. "I'm going to tell you something, Roslyn." With a strained, self-deprecating grin that lowers a driving pressure onto his words: "I hope you don't mind, Gay, because I love this girl, and you might as well know it."

Putting a proprietary arm loosely around Roslyn's shoulders, Gay grins. "Well, you'd be out of your head if you didn't."

Guido faces Roslyn. A formality sets in that is faintly self-pitiful and oddly dangerous. "I spent four years in the war: two tours. Fifty missions. And every time I came back to base I started to design this house. But somehow I could never get it to look like my idea of it. And now it almost does. You just walk in, a stranger out of nowhere, and for the first time it all lights up. And I'm sure you know why, too."

Roslyn, her voice faint in the face of his curiously intense feeling: "Why?"

"Because you have the gift of life, Roslyn. You really want to live, don't you?"

His remorseless sincerity silences the room.

Roslyn: "Doesn't everybody?"

Guido glances at the picture. "No, I think most of us . . . are just looking for a place to hide and watch it all go by."

Isabelle: "Amen!"

Guido, raising his glass, persisting in his formality: "Here's to your life, Roslyn—I hope it goes on forever."

She quickly reaches over and clicks her glass with his. "And yours. And yours, Isabelle." And with the faintest air of an afterthought: "And yours, Gay."

We notice the slightest flicker in Gay, an awareness that he has been placed slightly to one side. They drink.

Roslyn moves closer to Gay. "Gay did all the work, you know."

"Yeah, and the rabbits are really enjoyin' it, too." He grins, and only now puts his arm around her.

Guido sees the reconciliation of a conflict in them and he feigns ignorance, but there is condescension in his question: "You think you could break away from paradise long enough to do some mustangin'?"

"Mustangin'!" Gay's look sharpens. "Now you're sayin' something. You been up to the mountains?"

"I took a quick look up there this morning. Spotted fifteen horses."

"That's not bad. I'd sure like to lay my hand on a rope again. What do you say?"

Isabelle turns to Roslyn, shaking her head. "I will never understand cowboys. All crazy about animals, but the minute they got nothin' to do they go runnin' up the mountains to bother those poor wild horses." Passionlessly, to the men: "Shame on you!"

Roslyn: "Horses?"

Gay: "Sure, honey. Nevada mustang. Used to ship them all over the United States once upon a time. Mostly gone now, though." He turns back to Guido: "We'll have to pick up another man."

"Dayton Rodeo's on today. We could probably find a fella down there."

"Hey, that's an idea! Roslyn, you never saw a rodeo."

Isabelle: "Oh, you gotta see a rodeo."

Roslyn: "I'd love to. If you come with us, Iz."

"I'm all set."

Roslyn springs up. "I'll get dressed up!" She quickly looks at Gay. "Let's have some fun today!"

Gay: "Now that's a girl! Get goin' right now." He gets up and shoos her toward the bedroom, and as she starts away he grabs her hand and she turns back to him, her face warmed by the return of his connection with her. "Honey, when you smile it's like the sun comin' up."

He lets her go and she flies toward the bedroom.

SIX

THE four are silent in the station wagon as they drive into the sun on the empty highway. Gay drives with one hand resting on Roslyn's bright silken dress where it flows off her thigh.

Behind them Guido blinks at time passing by. "I'd like to have stopped home and got cleaned up a little." He feels his stubble, glancing ahead at Roslyn's brushed hair.

She turns back to him. "Why? You look nice, Guido. Doesn't he, Iz?"

"Better than a lot I've known."

Guido smiles moodily. "You're just one mass of compliments, Isabelle. Hey! Hold it!" He grabs Gay's shoulder, at the same time spinning around in his seat to look at something they have passed. "Stop!"

Gay brakes the car, and Guido points back toward a bar and gas station. "The guy next to that phone booth. I think it's that kid from California. Back up!"

Gay turns and cranes out the window. "What kid?"

"That what's-his-name—the rodeo rider was working the Stinson Rodeo with you last year."

"Perce Howland?" Gay shouts and backs the car along the highway, fast.

Perce Howland is sitting on his saddle, his back against a glass-enclosed phone booth beside the highway. He is resting his chin on his hands, his eyes staring at the bare ground. Noticing the reversing car, he looks toward it with sleepy eyes.

He is in his late twenties, a bucking-horse rider—which is to say a resident of nowhere, who sleeps most often in his clothes, rich and broke in the same afternoon, celebrated in the lobbies of small hotels where a month earlier he might have been thrown out for loitering. He does not yet have the cauliflower ear, the missing front teeth, or the dazed eye of his tribe, but his face has been sewn and his bones broken.

Glancing up at the approaching car on the deserted highway, his eyes already show their expectant, seeking quality. There is a naiveté in his strangely soft, gentle movements, a boyishness which is itself a force.

A great glad smile opens on his face as he sees through the side window of the car coming to a halt before him. He gets up and goes to the car. "Gay Langland! Why, you old buzzard, you!"

Gay grabs his arm. "What are you sittin' out here for?"

"I hitched a ride to the Dayton Rodeo but the fella changed his mind and left me here. Hey, Pilot, how you doin'? Boy, it's sure good to see you two scoundrels!"

Gay draws Roslyn closer to his window. "Like you to meet this fella, Roslyn. This is Perce Howland."

She nods.

Perce removes his hat. "Well, old Gay is sure comin' up in the world. How do, ma'am." He shakes her hand; there is a certain embarrassed shyness on him. He regards her as one of Gay's passing divorcées.

Guido starts to introduce him to Isabelle when the bell rings inside the phone booth. Hurrying toward it, he carefully puts his hat on as though he were to face someone in there. "'Scuse me, I been tryin' to call home but they keep puttin' me into Wyoming!"

He steps into the booth and closes the door. "Hello, Ma? Perce, Ma."

The four in the car sit in silence, listening to his muffled voice. Perce's emotion quickly reaches them, holding them still.

"Hello? You there? It's Perce, Ma. I'm okay. No, I'm in Nevada now. I *was* in Colorado. Won another bull-ridin', Ma. Hundred dollars. Yeah, real good rodeo. I was goin' to buy you a birthday present with it but I was comin' out of my boots. . . . No, Ma, I haven't been in a hospital since I told

you. I just bought some boots, that's all, Ma." Astounded: "What in the world would I want to get married for? *I only bought some—*" He breaks off. "Whyn't you try believin' me once in a while, make everybody feel better, huh?" She is obviously berating him. "Okay, okay, I'm sorry." Trying to bring brightness back: "They give me a silver buckle on top of the prize money!" Holding the buckle of his belt toward the phone: "Got a buckin' horse on it and my entire name wrote out underneath. Ain't you proud?" His smile goes; he touches his cheeks. "No, no, my face is all healed up, good as new. You will too recognize me! Okay, operator! Ma? say hello to Frieda and Victoria, will ya?" A silence. He is being severely instructed and his patience is waning. He opens the door for air. Sweat is burning his eyes. "Okay, say hello to him, too. No, Ma, it just slipped my mind, that's all. . . . *Okay*, I'm sayin' it now." Near an outburst: "Well, you married him, I didn't! Tell him hello for me. Maybe I'll call you Christmas. . . . Hello? Hello!" He is cut off, but with a deeply troubled mumble he adds: "God bless you, too."

His somber look is disappearing as he comes out on the sidewalk. He is a little embarrassed at having shown so much emotion before these others, and he tries to laugh, shaking his head and mopping his face. "You wouldn't be goin' down to the Dayton Rodeo, would you?"

Guido: "Why? You entered?"

Perce: "I aim to if I can get a ride out there. . . . And if I can raise ten bucks for the entrance fee. . . . And if I can get a loan of a buckin' horse when I get down there." He laughs. "I'm real equipped!"

Gay: "How'd you like to do some mustangin' with us? We need a third man."

Perce: "Boy, you still flyin' that five-dollar airplane?"

Guido: "Lot safer than a buckin' horse."

Perce: "Lot higher, too, comin' down."

Roslyn: "Your plane that bad?"

Gay: "Now don't start worryin' about him, honey."

Roslyn, laughing: "Well, I just asked."

Gay, to Perce and Guido: "'Cause if she starts worrying, she can *worry*."

Perce is surprised and drawn toward her intensity. "You got

a right to if you ever seen that DC-six-and-seven-eighths he flies. I didn't know they still had mustangs around here."

Guido: "I spotted fifteen this morning."

Gay, quickly: "Well, there might be more, though."

Perce: "What're you gonna get outa fifteen?" He laughs, not knowing why. "Like if there was a thousand or somethin' it'd make some sense. But just to go up there and take fifteen horses . . . I mean the *idea* of it, y'know? Just kinda hits me sideways."

His sensitivity seems to move over into Roslyn's face. She seems grateful he is there.

Gay: "It's better than wages, ain't it?"

Perce: "Hell, anything's better than wages."

Gay: "Tell you what. We'll drive you down to the rodeo, put up ten for the entrance fee, and I'll get a loan of some good stock for you down there. You come along with us tomorrow morning and help us run some mustang."

Perce thinks for a moment, then says: "And you buy a bottle of good whiskey right in there so I'm primed up for the rodeo."

Gay: "Just wait right there." He starts into the bar, putting his hand in his pocket.

Perce turns to Roslyn, intense curiosity and excitement in his face. He cannot place her. "You an . . . old friend of Gay's?"

"Pretty old."

He nods slightly, and awkwardly turns, as though escaping the insoluble, and goes to get his saddle to put it into the car.

SEVEN

THEY are driving through a new kind of territory. There is not even sage here, but only a sterile white alkali waste. It is midday.

Gay is at the wheel, Roslyn beside him, Guido and Perce in the rear seat. Guido has a whiskey bottle tilted to his lips. They are all a little high. Guido passes the bottle to Roslyn over her shoulder; she silently drinks, then hands it over to Gay, who takes a short one and hands it back. Guido never takes his brooding eyes from Roslyn. She makes a half-turn in her seat

and gives the bottle to Perce, who drinks and then holds the bottle on his knee, staring out at the white waste going by.

Their eyes are narrowed against the harsh light. They have been driving a long time. Now Gay overtakes a horse-van trailer hitched to a new car, and as they pass it Perce leans out his window and waves at the Stetson-hatted cowboy driver. Then he speaks to Roslyn, resuming a conversation that had died out.

Perce: "I've broke this arm twice in the same place. You don't do that fakin' a fall, y'know. I don't fake anything. Some of these riders'll drop off and lay there like they're stone dead. Just putting on a show, y'know. I don't fake it, do I, Gay?"

Gay: "That's right. You're just a natural-born damn fool."

Roslyn: "Why! That's wonderful . . . to be that way?" To Perce: "I know what you mean. I used to dance in places . . . and everybody said I was crazy. I mean I really tried, you know? Whereas people don't know the difference."

Guido, who has been looking at her feverishly, as though his several concepts of her were constantly falling to pieces: "What kind of dancing you do?"

Roslyn, with embarrassment: "Oh . . . just what they call interpretive dancing. Nightclubs. You know."

Perce sticks his head in between her and Gay. "I went to a nightclub once—in Kansas City. Name of it was 'The Naked Truth.' And they wasn't kiddin', either!"

He laughs, but an uneasiness on her face dampens him.

Gay calls out, "Here we come!"

Their attention is drawn to the first glimpse of the town. A long, gradual curve of highway lies directly ahead, an arc of concrete raised above the valley bottom of white gypsum. At the distant end of the road is a row of wooden buildings and beyond them the mountains piled up like dumps of slag the color of soot. From this distance the desolation is almost supernatural, the mind struggling with the question of why men would ever have settled here. There is no tree, no bush, no pool of water. To right and left the blank white flatland stretches away, dampened here and there by acid stains of moisture left from the spring rains. Gradually a perverse beauty grows out of the place. It is so absolute, its ugliness is so direct and blatant as to take on honesty and the force of something perfectly defined, itself without remorse or excuse, a town set

up beside a railroad track for the purpose of loading gypsum board from the nearby plant.

Gay and Guido have been here many times for the yearly rodeo, Perce and Roslyn never. As the road straightens and they can see into the town's interior, the silence which has held them is broken by Gay explaining, with a grin, that this is the last wide-open town in the West. There is no police force and practically no law. Except for this one day there are never strangers here, and most of the natives are related closely enough to settle disputes among themselves. He is grinning but he is not making light of his instruction to her to stay close to him. There is no help here; there will not necessarily be trouble, but there has been, and they still carry sidearms in this place, and use them. "Like in the movies," Roslyn says, her eyes wide with incipient laughter, but they do not laugh—not entirely because of fear but from a sense of absurdity, the kind of absurdity so senseless as to rise to a logic, a law, a principle of destruction, as when one is knocked down by a bicycle and killed on the way to a wedding. Without warning, they realize that the town is packed with people, perhaps two thousand, a mob boiling around on the highway between the row of buildings and the railroad tracks. Its uproar strikes at them through the car windows, a clash and rumble of humanity enslaved by its own will a hundred miles out in this sun-stricken powderland.

Gay slows the car to avoid the first humans, men standing in the middle of the highway, talking, looking into the windows as they pass. Now there are cars parked along the roadside, jalopies mostly, and some recent models caked with talc. The door of one of them swings open; a girl of twelve runs out with a little boy, and they dash toward the dense mob as though they knew where they were going. An old man stands peeing in the sun and chewing a wad of tobacco as he turns with the car passing him by. Gay can barely move ahead now as the car is engorged by the crowd.

Perce suddenly sticks his head out of the window. "There's old Rube! Hey, Rube! Whatcha say!" Rube waves back. "Hey, there's old Bernie! Whatcha say, Bernie!" Bernie waves back. Perce draws his head into the car and leans in between Gay and

Roslyn. "Hey, they got some real riders here today! Hope I draw me a good horse!"

Gay: "Just come out in one piece, now, 'cause you gotta go mustangin' tomorrow."

Roslyn is looking at Perce's face, a few inches from her eyes; she sees the pure lust for glory in him. A new emotion flows from her toward him—a kind of pity, a personal involvement in his coming trial.

He jerks away to call out the window again: "There's Franklin! Hey, Franklin boy!"

The car moves into the heart of the crowd.

There are cowboys in working clothes, and many in the tight shirts and jeans they saw in movies. There are many kids, dressed like their elders. There are farmers in overalls, women in Sunday best. A cowboy is trying to back a horse out of a little trailer van right into the stream of traffic; three girls not yet sixteen walk in front of a gang of cowboys who are trying to make them; a mother holds onto her teenage daughter's wrist as she pushes through the crowd. Two overweight deputies, with .45s hanging from their hips, bounce a Cadillac up and down to unhook its bumper from a battered pickup truck behind it. In the pickup is a gang of kids with a farmer driving. In the Cadillac, its convertible top down, are three betting types and a show girl, all bouncing up and down and striving to retain their dignity and their sunglasses.

Above the people and the cars, mixed with their roar, is a cacophony of jazz; each bar's jukebox is pouring its music into the street, one number changing to another as the car passes the screen doorways. An enormously loud voice from a nearby public-address system announces something indistinguishable; then there is the sound of a crowd roaring as in a stadium—the rodeo arena is in action at the far end of the street.

Roslyn suddenly turns to watch an Indian standing perfectly still while the crowd pours around him. He is staring off at something—or at nothing—with a bundle of clothes under his arm.

Gay nudges his car to the left, even letting the fenders press people out of the way, and pulls up facing one of the bars. He takes Roslyn's hand and draws her out of the car past the

steering wheel; the four, with their arms raised against the crush of people, squeeze into the saloon. The dog sits up in the front seat, looking around calmly, seeing everything, turning her head from one familiar face to another. An old man comes out the screen door, sees the dog, and goes to the window to look in at her. She looks at him. He is bleary. His shirtfront is streaked with tobacco juice. Deep blackheads swarm around his nose. He reaches into his pocket and takes out coins from which powdery talc sifts down. He tosses a quarter to the dog and she sniffs it on the seat and looks back at him in puzzlement. He winks at her and disappears into the crowd with his secret.

The sound of money clinking turns people around; a sweet little old lady is hurrying through the crowd, violently shaking a well-filled collection can. She wears a toque hat askew on her gray head and a brocade dress down to her shins. Something like "Oyez, oyez," is coming out of her voice box, and she is smiling wittily under incensed, climactic eyes. She pulls the screen door open and pushes into the saloon.

This bar is fifty feet long. The customers are ranked back to the opposite wall and order drinks from a distance the width of a handball court. There is a spidery atmosphere of a hundred hands raised to pass drinks back and empties returning to the bar. Two jukeboxes are playing different records and a television set on high is speaking, its eye rolling in its head. Five bartenders face the mob, serving and collecting, grimly glancing right and left along the mahogany to ward off any attack upon the vertical platoon of bottles behind them. Overhead, reflected in the yardage of the mirror on the wall, a morose elkhead stares through the smoke. A printed sign hanging from a piece of twine around its neck reads, "Don't shoot this elk again," and the careful eye can see the bullet holes that drew sawdust instead of blood.

The old lady pushes up to a cowboy and his girl at the bar and shakes the can under their surprised faces.

Old lady: "Church Ladies' Auxiliary, Tom."

"Sure." He drops a coin in the collection can.

The old lady turns to his girl. "How about you, sinner?"

"Oh, Ma! I got no money yet!"

The old lady shakes the can at another prospect nearby. "Come on, Frank. Church Ladies' Auxiliary."

"You just got me in the bar next door."

"That'll larn you to stay put. Come on!"

He groans and puts in money.

Roslyn, Gay, Perce, Isabelle, and Guido, with drinks in hand which they can barely raise to their lips, are pressed together at the bar, standing in the paralyzing noise like people in a subway. A grizzled old man with startling silver hair forces his way through and hoists a seven-year-old boy onto the bar. Holding the boy's knees, he explains to Gay, "I gotta hold onto him tight or first thing y'know he run off to school."

Gay nods understandingly, and the old man smiles through his haze, "Hya, Coz, not many of us left."

"Well, things are tough all over, Pop."

The old man yells at the bartender: "Draft of pop for my grandson Lester!" He is full of holiday cheer and, taking a paddleball from the boy, he says to Gay: "Ever try one of these? Damnedest thing I ever saw. Stand clear, now!"

With which he swats away at the elusive ball, while people around him shield their faces from his unpredictable blows. The bartenders come alert.

Roslyn has found room to get her glass to her lips and drinks fast, calling: "Hey, I can do that! Can I try?"

The old man, sensing action, offers her the paddle at once. "Betcha two dollars you can't do ten!"

Perce: "I'll take that! Go ahead, Roz!"

Roslyn, untwisting the rubber band: "Oh, I can do more than ten! I *think*!"

Pushing his back against the crowd, the old man spreads his arms. "Clear away, clear away, we got a bet goin'!"

News of a bet miraculously squeezes the crowd back, and a space opens around Roslyn. She starts to hit the ball and does it obviously well. She has a drink still in one hand. Perce counts each stroke, two dollars in his hand. By the time she gets to six, a cowboy yells at Perce: "Five bucks she don't do fifteen!"

Perce, nodding and still counting: "Nine, ten, eleven . . ."

Perce reaches toward the surprised old man, who hands him the two dollars.

Second cowboy: "Ten she don't make twenty!"

Perce: "Thirteen, fourteen, fifteen, sixteen, seventeen, eighteen, nineteen, twenty, twenty-one, two, three, four, five,

six . . ." Perce collects from both cowboys, counting on. From all over the saloon voices call new bets and money passes in all directions.

"Ten here too!"

"Five here!"

"I'll take five!"

"Fifteen here!"

Roslyn is now working the ball with great earnestness, sipping her drink at the same time, an alcoholic distance spreading in her eyes. Isabelle, counting aloud with Perce, picks up her drink and takes a gulp and looks at it with disgust. She sees a bottle of whiskey and pours some into her glass, drinks, and sets it down. The little boy sitting on the bar beside her, his eyes fascinated at Roslyn's attack on the ball, lifts his pop glass—which Isabelle has just inadvertently spiked—drinks, and studies the new effect upon him, and tastes some more.

The crowd is roaring out Roslyn's count now. The little old lady, trying to push through the circle of men who have formed around Roslyn and Perce, manages to peep through the bodies, and her eyes fasten on the growing wad of money in Perce's upraised hand. With a new spurt of greedy determination she pushes through to Perce, who calls: "Thirty-six, thirty-seven, thirty-eight, thirty-nine, forty! Forty-one, forty-two . . ."

Suddenly she starts hitting the ball at the floor and receiving it back on the bounce. A roar of excited appreciation goes up at this new risk she is taking. Even the bartenders are on tiptoe, stretching to see over the crowd.

"Ten bucks she don't do seventy!"

Perce nods, takes the money without losing his count: "Fifty-four, fifty-five . . ."

A second cowboy suddenly steps out and pats Roslyn low on the back. Guido, standing beside Gay, looks and sees Gay's mild irritation. Gay now scans the faces in the crowd. The eyes around him are coursing Roslyn's body. Guido bursts out laughing: "She'll do anything!" and Gay sees in Guido's expression the same near-lewdness of some of the crowd. A new shout goes up.

Now she is hitting the ball on the bounce, and backhand,

taking a drink at the same time. Perce is continuing his count at her side, absorbed, young, somehow at one with Roslyn as he urges her on with his counting. The old lady steps up close to Roslyn, calling into her ear as she shakes the collection can. "Play for the Lord! Steady, sinner!"

Roslyn, unnerved: "Please!"

Old lady to Perce, demanding the money in his hand: "Help the good work, boy, do it while the spirit's in ya."

Perce: "Seventy-one, seventy-two, *shut up*, four, *seventy-five . . .*"

A shout goes up at this new victory. Roslyn is now a foot from the second cowboy with her back to him, and he grabs her from behind and starts to kiss her. Gay is on him and is about to hit him when he is pulled away by others. Two bartenders leap the bar. Guido appears next to Gay and draws on his arm, grabbing Roslyn with his other hand; he pulls both of them toward the door.

The old man turns to his grandson on the bar, and is about to take the boy down when he notices the bemused look in his face. He takes the half-full glass out of his little hand, sniffs it, then tastes it. First surprise penetrates his fog, and then with a genuinely avaricious wheedling tone, "Lester!" he asks, bending down into the boy's somnolent face, "where'd you get the money?"

On the street outside, Gay draws Roslyn out of the mob into a space between two parked cars. Just behind them, Perce, Guido, and Isabelle are counting the money in Perce's hat. Moved by his protective passion, Roslyn clasps his face. "I'm sorry, Gay, I didn't mean to do it that long! But thanks for helping me! I embarrass you?"

The threat of losing her in the moments earlier, the lust of others for her, has wiped out his reserve. "I'd marry you."

Roslyn, with a sad and joyous mixture: "Oh, no, Gay, you don't have to! But thanks for saying that."

Perce bursts in, Guido behind him. "Hundred and forty-five dollars! Ain't she great, Gay? She is the greatest yet!"

With which Perce throws an arm around her as he puts the money in her hand. Instantly the old lady appears under Perce's arm, shaking the can.

Isabelle: "Don't shake that at me! I'm still payin' off this broken arm!" Suddenly Isabelle, seeing someone in the crowd, shouts, "Charles!" and runs into the passing mob.

The old lady, shaking the can under Roslyn's face, fixes her with her missionary stare. "Sinner! I can tell you want to make a big donation. You got it in the middle of your pretty eyes. You're lookin' for the light, sinner, I know you and I love you for your life of pain and sin. Give it to the one that understands, the only one that loves you in your lonely desert!"

At first amused, then drawn and repelled, then half-frightened, and yet somehow reached by this woman's mad desire to bless her, she starts to hand the old lady the whole wad of money.

But Gay intercepts. "She ain't sinned that much." He hands the old lady one bill. "Here's ten . . ." He gives her another. "And here's ten more to settle for the twenty."

Old lady: "Lord be praised! We're gonna buy a fence around the graveyard, keep these cowboys from pasturing their horses on the graves. Sweetheart, you've gone and helped our dead to rest in peace! Go reborn!"

Isabelle rushes up to Roslyn out of the crowd. "Guess who's here! Dear girl, guess who is here!"

"Who?"

"My husband! I couldn't believe it. They're on vacation."

"Oh. His wife too?"

"Sure! Clara. You remember my talkin' about Clara, she was my best friend? And she's sweeter than ever!"

Gay: "Sure must be, to make you so glad to see her."

"Oh, Charles could never've stayed married to me. I even lost the vacuum cleaner once." The men burst out laughing, and she joins them, and waves her arm toward her former husband, who is evidently somewhere deep in the crowd. "They still haven't found it! Come, you'll meet them."

Gay stops them. "Let's meet you later, Isabelle. We still got to get this boy a horse to ride."

"Okay, we'll be around someplace. But I won't be mustangin' with you—they're gonna stay at my house for a week." She reaches for Perce's hand and squeezes it. "Good luck, young fella!" Patting Roslyn's hand, she backs into the moving crowd, waving happily. "See you, dear girl!"

Pressed together by the surrounding crowd, the four move toward the end of the street and the rodeo arena. Perce puts his head between Gay and Roslyn. "Can I kiss her for luck?"

"Once."

Perce kisses her as they move.

Gay draws him away from her. "You don't need all that luck. Come on, let's get you registered." He starts off ahead with Perce, laughing over his shoulder to Roslyn. She waves to him as he vanishes into the crowd.

The rodeo arena is a homemade corral surrounded by a collapsing post-and-rail fence, with splintered bleachers three tiers high along one side. A chute of planks is at one end and near it a low tower for the judge. A sea of parked cars surrounds the area. From the stands the only visible building is a small church leaning in the direction of the distant mountains, its cross of boards twisting under the weight of weather into the form of an X.

The stands are packed and the mob has surrounded the fence. There is always a certain threading movement of people looking for one another—fathers for their daughters, wives for husbands, fellows for girls, and loners from the hills who want only to move through the only crowd of strangers they will touch until the same time next year.

A rider on a bucking horse charges out of the chute. The timing judge in the tower, his stopwatch in his hand at the end of a heavy gold chain, drinks from a pint bottle, his eyes flicking from watch to rider. The contestant is staying on the black horse. It charges directly toward the fence and the crowd there clambers backward, and for a moment the Indian is left in the clear, watching impassively. The horse swerves away, the crowd surges back, and the Indian is lost among the people again.

Roslyn and Guido are in the stands. Guido looks on, half-interested. She is watching avidly. He turns and stares at her beside him, his eyes absorbing the molding of her face, her neck, her body.

The crowd roars suddenly, and people around them half-stand in their seats. Alarm shows in her face as she stands. The rider scoots from the horse's flying hooves.

"Gee, I didn't know it was so dangerous!"

Guido, deliberatively, as though declaring his determination toward her: "Same as everything else worth doing."

She looks at him with surprise. Whiskey and sun have dissolved his strategy, and he simply stares longingly into her eyes. She turns to see the outrider coming alongside the bucking horse and undoing its bucking strap.

"What'd he just take off?"

"Oh, that's the bucking strap. Grabs them where they don't like it. Makes them buck."

"Well, that's not fair!"

He starts to laugh, but her intensity stops him. "You couldn't have a rodeo otherwise."

"Well, then you shouldn't have a rodeo!"

The crowd suddenly roars and stands, and she and Guido rise, but he is staring at her with deep puzzlement as she turns toward the arena where the bucking horse has chased the rider over the fence. A few yards away Gay and Perce sit straddling the closed chute, their legs slung over the top. Now Gay looks at the people in the stands.

"I hope you're sober."

Perce, following Gay's eyes: "Hell, I've won prizes where I couldn't remember the name of the town." He sees Roslyn in the stands and waves. "There she is!"

Gay waves to her now and she stands up, waving her furred sweater. Guido raises his arm.

Perce, seeing her passionate encouragement, turns to Gay. "I wouldn't try to move in on you, Gay—unless you wouldn't mind."

Gay nearly blushes. "Boy—I'd mind."

They both laugh at this unwitting avowal of their conflict and Gay slaps Perce on the back with warmth as a horse is led into the chute at their feet.

"Well, here I go!"

Perce descends from the fence onto the restive horse with Gay lending a hand, and he looks up at Gay.

"My address is Black River—"

He is cut off by the public-address system.

Public-address system: "On a bucking horse, Perce Howland out of Black River, Wyoming!"

"California, not Wyoming!" he yells over his shoulder.

A cowboy pulls the bucking belt tight. The horse kicks the chute planks.

Gay: "You ready, boy?"

Perce: "Go! Go!"

Gay: "Open up!"

An attendant opens the gate; the horse charges out. The crowd roars. Perce is holding on. The horse bucks under him, high and wild.

In the stands Guido has come alive. "Go it, boy!"

Roslyn is looking on, torn between hope of Perce's victory and terror; she holds her hands to her ears as she watches.

The timing judge drinks, his stopwatch in his hand.

From the chute fence, Gay glances at Roslyn in the stands. She is watching with tears in her eyes. The horse leaps in close to where she is sitting, and for an instant she can see Perce's teeth bared with the tension of his fight as he is flung up and down, the sky over his head.

The horse is twisting Perce, wracking his body as it comes down on the packed earth. Now she shouts as though to rescue Perce, calling his name. She turns to Guido for help. He strikes the air with his fist, a look of near-rage on his face, a flow of animal joy that disconcerts her, and, more alone now than before with her terror, she turns back to the field.

A sudden roar goes up from the crowd, and Gay rises up on the fence with a look of what almost seems like joy on his face, but his rising movement is to help. Perce is being thrown. He lands on his face and lies still.

Gay jumps down from the fence and runs toward Perce. Guido is pushing his way down the bleacher rows to the field; Roslyn remains standing on her bench behind him, stretching to see over the crowd, staring and weeping, her face as blank as if she had been struck. Now she starts down the bleachers toward the field.

Gay reaches Perce and starts to lift him to his feet. Guido arrives and they half-carry Perce toward a gate in the fence, Guido clapping his hat onto his head.

Roslyn catches up with them as they emerge into an area of parked cars. An ambulance is standing in front of the church.

Roslyn: "Where's the doctor?"

Perce: "Where's my hat, Pa?"

Gay: "You got it on, Perce."

Perce suddenly pulls away and yells at Roslyn, who has grasped his arm.

Perce: "Lemme go, Frieda!"

Gay comes up to him, holding out his hand to calm him, "Take it easy, boy, she ain't your sister." Perce is staring, perplexed, at Roslyn. She is cold with fright. But they move him along again. They arrive at the ambulance. An attendant is waiting, an affable grin on his face. "Well now, you've been messin' around with the wrong end of a horse, haven't you?" He holds Perce's face, pressing his cheekbones in his hair-covered hands.

Roslyn: "Let him sit down."

She sits him on the edge of the ambulance floor. The attendant's movements do not quicken. She looks distrustfully at him.

Roslyn: "Are you a doctor?"

Perce starts to rise. "I don't want a doctor."

Attendant: "Hold it, boy. I'm no doctor. I'll just clean you up a little." He presses Perce down, wipes his hands on his trousers, and reaches into the ambulance for something.

Roslyn, with a growing feeling of helplessness: "Well, isn't there a doctor?"

The attendant reappears with a bottle of alcohol and a swab.

Gay: "Not for sixty miles."

Gay bends and looks closely at Perce's face as the attendant swabs it; then he straightens up. "He ain't bad hurt."

"How do you know? Let's take him!" She reaches down to lift Perce. "Come with me, I'll take you in my car."

Gay, forcefully, not too covertly taking her from Perce: "Now don't start runnin' things, Roslyn."

"He's your friend, isn't he? I don't understand anything!"

A loud yelp of pain from Perce turns her about; the attendant is pressing adhesive tape across the bridge of his nose. Perce delicately touches his nose as Gay bends down to him where he sits on the edge of the ambulance floor. "You all right, ain't you, Perce?" Perce exhales a breath of pain, then feels his nose.

"Perce, you all right?"

Perce blinks, looks up at Gay, still dazed. "Did I make the whistle?"

"Almost, boy. You done good, though."

"That was a rank horse. Wasn't it?"

"Oh, that was a killer. You done good."

Perce tries to stand, but falls forward onto his hands and knees. Roslyn quickly bends to lift him up.

Gay: "Leave him alone, Roz, he'll get up." He separates her from Perce, who remains for a moment on all fours, catching his breath.

In horror, in a sea of helpless nonunderstanding, she looks down at him. Now he raises himself with great difficulty to his feet. Guido hands him his hat, which has again fallen off. The public-address system erupts, incomprehensibly.

Perce: "Oh! That me?"

Gay: "Not yet. You still got a coupla minutes."

Roslyn: "What for?"

"He's got a bull to ride. Come on, Perce, walk yourself around a little bit."

Gay, putting Perce's arm over his shoulder, walks down an aisle of parked cars with him. Perce is not surefooted yet, but is getting steadier. They walk slowly, in the sea of steel.

Roslyn: "Guido, he's not going in there again!"

Guido, with an uncertain celebration of life's facts: "I guess he wants to ride that bull."

"But . . ." Frustrated, she runs to Gay and Perce and moves with them.

"Just let him walk it off, Roz, come on now." Gay presses her aside.

She has to squeeze in beside them, sometimes forced behind them by an obstructing fender. "What are you doing it for, Perce? Here, why don't you take what we won in the bar." Struggling with her purse to get money out, she tries to keep up with them. "You helped me win it, Perce, come on, take it. Look, it's over a hundred dollars. You don't have to go back in there!" He halts. She presses up to him. He is staring at her. She feels encouraged now. She gently touches his cheek, smiling pleadingly.

Perce: "I like ya to watch me now. I'm pretty good ridin' bulls."

"But why're you doing it?"

"Why, I put in for it, Roslyn. I'm entered."

The public-address system again erupts incomprehensibly.

Perce: "Get me up there, Gay, I'm just warmin' up!"

They start for the arena. She hurries along with them. Guido is following, still smiling at her concern. He is progressively drunker.

Roslyn: "Gay, please!"

But Perce and Gay continue moving toward the chutes.

Perce turns to her over his shoulder. "I like ya to watch me, Roslyn! Don't you be scared, now!"

Roslyn turns to Guido, who is standing beside her, as though for help. Beneath his troubled look she sees he is blandly accepting the situation. Reasonably, he says, "They don't mind getting busted up!" She turns quickly, scanning the world for help. No human being is in sight—only row after row of cars, mute, iron. The roar of the crowd mixes with the babble of the public-address system.

The bloody-eyed face of an immense white Brahma bull appears under Perce and Gay where they sit on the chute wall. Its handlers are respectfully hogging it into position. Now a handler loops the bucking belt around the bull's hind quarters, letting it hang loose for the moment. Perce is wide-eyed with fear and calculation. He is blinking hard to clear his head and softly working a wad of tobacco in his cheek. Gay turns to him from the bull, which is now directly under them. In Gay's eyes is a look of brutal pride in Perce. "You okay, boy? You want it?"

Perce hesitates, looking down at the bull; he has the excitement of one already injured. Then: "Hell, yes." He leans out over the bull to straddle it.

"Perce!"

He looks up and Gay does. Gay smiles pridefully, almost tauntingly, toward Roslyn, who has climbed the bottom rung of the fence a few yards away and is calling: "Gay, don't let him! Perce, here's your prize! Why . . ." She holds out the money toward him. Guido, no longer smiling, is beside her.

She is cut off by the public-address system: "Now folks, who do you think is back with us? We still got some real men in the West! On a Brahma bull, again, out of Black Hills, Colorado, *Perce Howland!*" The crowd roars.

Roslyn is struck dumb by the inexorable march of it all. She looks down, calling defeatedly: "Gay!"

Gay helps as Perce descends and straddles the bull. Mounted, he turns up to Roslyn. "You watch me now, sport!"

A handler yanks the bucking belt up tight. The bull shoots its head up, the gate opens, and Perce goes charging out into the arena.

Standing so close to the chute, Roslyn can feel the earth shake as the bull pounds out across the arena, and once having felt the thunder of its weight she nearly goes blind, seeing only tattered impressions that filter through her fear: the bull's corded neck, its oddly deadened eyes fixed on some motionless vision of vengeance, the pounding on the earth that seems to call up resounding answers from deep below the ground. The beast humps into the air and shifts direction, coming down, and Perce's body twists and doubles over, straightening only to be wracked again, flung and compressed as though he were tied to the end of a whip. A grimace of teeth-clenching anguish spreads over his face, and when he comes down from a leap his head is thrown back against the darkening sky like that of a supplicant. The crowd is roaring, but she does not hear it; customers are fighting the air with their fists and tearing with bared teeth at a hundred imagined demons, dogs are barking, pop bottles smash, strangers are squeezing one another's arms, a portable radio in the stands is loudly advertising an airline's cuisine, and the sun itself is setting behind the blind mountains; she is in a void, a silence of incomprehension, glimpsing only the bull's steady, remorseless stare and Perce's head snapping back like a doll's, the manly determination of his mouth belied by the helpless desolation in his eyes.

Guido has stopped cheering. Out of his half-drunken lethargy a new inner attention has straightened him, and he turns to her as though to comfort her, but she runs into the crowd behind her. A coarse call, a roar, an "Ohhh" from the crowd turns her around to the arena.

Perce is lying in the dirt, his shoulder twisted over half his face. The silence of the mountains spreads over the arena and the stands. The barebacked bull is lunging and blindly kicking near Perce's body, and the outrider is trying to maneuver it

toward the chute, his expression drained of sport, his body pivoting his horse with every threatened feint of the white bull.

Gay is running across the bull's path. He doubles back and around the turning bull; the outrider's horse shields him for a moment and he drags Perce along the soft sand to the fence. Guido helps him lift Perce over it.

The crowd is standing, watching in silence. The grunted, growling breathing of the bull can be heard now. A cloud of gray dust hangs over the arena, but is already being carried away by the rising night breeze.

EIGHT

DARKNESS brightens the neon glare from the bars, and bluish vestigial light still glows along the mountain ridges. Cars are parked tightly against the bar fronts, one of which has been pushed in, its stucco face hanging agape. The crowd is thinner now and moving at promenade pace. The families are leaving in their cars and trucks. There are many small squads of cowboys moving in and out of the bars, with one girl to a squad. Unknowable conversations are going on in parked cars, between the freights, around unlit corners, between man and man and man and woman, some erupting in a shout and strange condemnations, or laughter and a reentry into the bars.

Roslyn is cradling her head in her arm in the front seat of the car. Her face is tired from weeping and she is still breathing shakily in the aftermath of a sobbing spell.

Gay calls her name from the window opposite. He has a wryness in his look, knowing she is displeased with him. "Come on, honey, we're gonna have some drinks." The hurt in her face makes him open the door and he sits beside her.

Roslyn: "Is he still unconscious?"

Gay: "Probably, but it ain't noticeable." He turns his head and she follows his gaze through the rear window.

Perce, his head enormously wrapped in white bandage, is heatedly arguing with the rodeo judge behind the car. Guido is standing between them, blinking sleepily.

"He's arguing with the judge about who won the bull ride. You still mad at me?"

Her resentment gives way to relief at seeing Perce alive. Now she turns to Gay. "Why did you hit me?"

"I didn't hit you. You were gettin' in the way and I couldn't carry him, that's all."

"Your face looked different." She stares at him now, a question in her eyes. "You looked like you . . . could've killed me. I . . . know that look."

"Oh, come on, honey. I got a little mad 'cause you were gettin' me all tangled up. Let's have some drinks, come on now."

Roslyn, glancing back at Perce: "He still hasn't seen a doctor?" Gay turns his back to her impatiently. "He might have a concussion! I don't understand anything; a person could be dying and everybody just stands around. Don't you care?"

Gay returns to the seat beside her. With anger in his voice: "I just went in for that boy with a wild bull runnin' loose—what're you talkin' about? I'm damn lucky I'm sittin' here myself, don't you know that?"

"Yes. You did." She suddenly takes his hand, kisses it, and holds it to her cheek. "You did!" She kisses his face. "You're a dear, good man . . ."

Gay, holding her, wanting her to understand him: "Roslyn, honey . . ."

"It's like you scream and there's nothing coming out of your mouth, and everybody's going around, 'Hello, how are you, what a nice day,' and it's all great—and you're dying!" She struggles to control herself and smiles. "You really felt for him, didn't you?"

Gay shrugs. "I just thought I could get him out. So I did, that's all."

Roslyn, her face showing the striving to locate him and herself: "But if he'd died . . . you'd feel terrible, wouldn't you? I mean, for no reason like that?"

"Honey . . . we all got to go sometime, reason or no reason. Dyin's as natural as livin'; man who's too afraid to die is too afraid to live, far as I've ever seen. So there's nothin' to do but forget it, that's all. Seems to me."

Perce sticks his head into the car. The tape is still on his

nose, the bandage like a turban on his head. He is slightly high from the shock. Guido sticks his head in on the other side of the car.

Perce: "Hey, Roslyn! Did you see me?"

"Oh, you were wonderful, Perce! Get in and we'll take you back to—"

"Oh, no, we got to have some fun now!"

Gay: "Sure, come on!"

Roslyn hesitates, then: "Okay. How do you feel?"

"Like a bull kicked me."

Guido opens the door for her. Gay gets out on Perce's side of the car. As she emerges from the car she quietly asks Guido: "Is he really all right?"

"In two weeks he won't remember this—or you either. Why don't you give your sympathy where it's appreciated?"

Roslyn, pointedly but with a warm laugh: "Where's that?"

She walks past him; he follows. They meet Gay and Perce in front of the saloon.

Perce: "In we go!"

Gay has her arm as her escort; Perce is on her other side, his open hand wavering over her back but not touching her: he is recognizing Gay's proprietary rights. Guido walks behind them. They enter the crowded saloon and take seats around a table.

There is a feverish intensity in Perce's speech and in his eyes. As they sit, he calls over to the bartender: "Hey, whiskey! For eight people."

He gets into his chair. He is strangely happy, as though he had accomplished something necessary, some duty that has given him certain rights. He laughs, and talks without diffidence to Roslyn now. "Boy, I feel funny! That man give me some kind of injection? Whoo! I see the prettiest stars, Roslyn." He reaches for her hand and holds it. Gay, whose arm is over the back of Roslyn's chair, grins uncomfortably. Roslyn pats Perce's hand and then removes her own. Perce does not notice this, and again takes her hand. "I never seen stars before. You ever see stars, Gay? Damn bull had the whole milky way in that hoof!" Gay laughs. Guido smiles with a private satisfaction. Roslyn is torn between concern for his condition and a desire

to celebrate her relief that he is alive. "Say, was that you cryin' in the ambulance? Was that her, Gay?"

"Sure was."

Perce rises from his chair, fervently shaking her hand: "Well, I want to thank you, Roslyn."

A waiter puts two glasses of whiskey before each of them, and Perce raises his high.

Perce: "Now! Here's to my buddy, old elderly Gay!"

Roslyn: "Gay's not old!"

Perce: "And here's to old, elderly Pilot. And his five-dollar elderly airplane." They all have glasses raised. "And my friend, Roslyn! We're all buddies, ain't we, Gay?"

Gay grins to dilute the growing seriousness of Perce's meaning. "That's right."

The jukebox explodes with "Charley, My Boy."

Perce: "Then what're you gettin' mad at me for, buddy? Can I dance with her?"

Gay: "Sure! Roslyn, whyn't you dance with Perce?"

Roslyn: "Okay." She gets up and goes onto the dance area with Perce.

Guido: "Nothin' like being young, is there, Gay?"

"That's right. But you know what they say—there's some keeps gettin' younger all the time." He grins at Guido, who turns back to watch the dancers with a faintly skeptical smile. Perce is doing a flat-footed hicky step, and she is trying to fall into it with him. Half-kidding, he nevertheless seems to be caught by an old memory, as he moves with straight-backed dignity.

"My father used to dance like this." Now he twirls her around, and himself starts to circle her; a dizziness comes over him.

"What's the matter!"

"Whoo!"

She catches him as he stumbles. "C'mon, let's see the world." Taking her hand, he goes out a door in the rear of the saloon. She glances back to see Gay turning drunkenly in his chair, and she waves to him as she is pulled out through the back door.

They emerge behind the saloon. Trash, a mound of empty

liquor bottles and beer cans, broken cartons, are littered about, but a few yards off the desert stretches away in the moonlight. He looks up at the sky and then turns to her. Wordless, he starts to sit on the ground, taking her hand and drawing her down, too, and they sit side by side on the sprung seat of an abandoned, wheelless car. Now he smiles weakly at her.

"Nobody ever cried for me. Not for a long time, anyway . . ." Full of wordless speech, longing to make love to her and be loved by her, he takes her hand. "Gay's a great fella, ain't he?"

"Yes."

"I want to lie down. Okay?"

"Sure."

He lies in her lap, and suddenly covers his eyes. "Damn that bull!"

She smooths his forehead. Now he opens his eyes. "Just rest. You don't have to talk."

"I can't place you, floatin' around like this. You belong to Gay?"

"I don't know where I belong."

"Boy, that's me, too. How come you got so much trust in your eyes?"

"Do I?"

"Like you were just born."

"Oh, no!"

"I don't like to see the way they grind women up out here. Although a lot of them don't mind, do they?"

"Some do."

"Did you really cry for me before?"

"Well, you were hurt and I—" She breaks off, seeing the wondrous shake of his head. "Didn't anybody ever cry for you?"

"No stranger. Last April the twelfth, I got kicked so bad I was out all day and all night. I had a girl with me and two good buddies. I haven't seen her or them since."

"They left you alone?"

"Listen . . . let me ask you something . . . I can't talk to anybody, you know?" She waits for him to speak. "I . . . I don't understand how you're supposed to do."

"What do you mean?"

"Well, see, I never floated around till this last year. I ain't like Gay and Pilot, I got a good home. I did have, anyway. And one day my old man . . . we were out back and suddenly, *bam!* Down he went. Some damn fool hunters."

"They killed him?"

"Uh-huh. And . . . she changed."

"Who?"

"My mother. She was always so dignified . . . walked next to him like a saint. And pretty soon this man started comin' around, and she . . . she changed. Three months, they were married. Well, okay, but I told her, I says, 'Mama, you better get a paper from Mr. Brackett because I'm the oldest and Papa wanted me to have the ranch.' And sure enough, the wedding night he turns around and offers me wages. On my own father's place."

"What does *she* say?"

Shaking his head in an unrelieved agony, and with a mystical reaching in his tone: "I don't know; she don't *hear* me. She's all *changed around*. You know what I mean? It's like she don't remember me any more."

She nods, staring.

"What the hell you depend on? Do you know?"

"I don't know. Maybe . . ." She is facing the distant horizon, staring at her life. "Maybe all there really is is what happens next, just the next thing, and you're not supposed to remember anybody's promises."

"You could count on mine, Roslyn. I think I love you."

"You don't even know me."

"I don't care."

He raises his face to hers, but his eyes are suddenly pain-wracked, and he grips his head. "That damn bull!"

The back door suddenly swings open, throwing the light of the saloon on them. Gay comes out, walking unsteadily, blinking in the sudden darkness. He calls: "Roslyn?"

"Here we are!" She gets up with Perce.

Gay comes over, shepherding them toward the door. "Come on, now, I want you to meet my kids."

"Your kids here?"

"They come for the rodeo. I ain't seen them in a year. You oughta see the welcome they give me, Roslyn! Nearly knocked

me over." They go through the door and up a short corridor. "She's gonna be nineteen! She got so pretty! Just happen to be here for the rodeo, the both of them! That great?"

"Oh, I'm so glad for you, Gay!" They go into the saloon.

Gay, now drawing Roslyn by the hand, and she holding onto Perce's hand, come up to the crowded bar, where Guido is standing in a drunken swirl of his own. The air is muddy with smoke and jazz. Perce is blinking hard, trying to see. Roslyn watches him even as she attends to Gay.

Gay reaches Guido first. "Where are they?"

"Where are who?" Guido turns to him slowly.

"My kids! I told them I'd be back in a minute. You heard me tell them."

"Went out there." Guido points toward the door to the street, then looks appraisingly at Roslyn and Perce.

Gay looks hurt and angered, then pushes through the door and goes out. He looks about at the parked cars and the moving groups of people and the armed deputies, and he yells: "Gaylord! Gaylord?"

Now Roslyn comes out of the bar, helping Perce. Guido is with them, carrying a bottle. Their attention is instantly on Gay, except for Perce, who immediately lays his cheek on the car fender, embracing it.

"Rose-May! Gaylord! Gaylorrrrd?"

Guido comes up beside Gay, a muddled, advice-giving look on his face. Roslyn remains holding onto Perce.

Guido bays: "Gaylord! Here's your father!" He sways, pointing at Gay.

People are beginning to congest around them, some seriously curious, some giggling, some drunk. Roslyn remains with Perce just behind Gay and Guido, watching Gay, tears threatening her eyes.

"Gaylord, where you gone to? I told you I was comin' right back. You come here now!"

A woman, middle-aged, dressed like a farmer's wife, comes up to Gay. "Don't you worry, mister, you'll probably find them home."

Gay looks at her, at the security emanating from her sympathetic smile. He turns and climbs up onto the hood of the car; he is very drunk, and shaken. He looks over the crowded street

from this new elevation. Just below him Roslyn and Guido are looking up into his face, and he seems twice his normal size. Drunks mill around below, the bar lights blink crazily behind him, the armed deputies look on blankly from the doorways, and the jazz cacophony is flying around his ears like lightning. His hat askew, his eyes perplexed, and his need blazing on his face, he roars out: "Gaylord! *I know you hear me!*"

There is now a large crowd around the car, the faces of alien strangers. Gay bangs his fist on the roof of the car. "I know you hear me! Rose-May—you come out now!" He suddenly slips on the hood and rolls off onto the ground, flat on his back. Roslyn screams and runs to him, as the crowd roars with laughter; she quickly lifts up his head and kisses him.

"I'm sure they're looking for you, Gay. They must've thought you'd left." He stares dumbly at her. "Oh, poor Gay, poor Gay!" She hugs his head and rocks him, crouched beside him in the gutter.

NINE

THE car is speeding on the dark highway. Guido is driving, the dog asleep beside him. In the back seat Roslyn has one arm around the unconscious Perce, whose legs hang out a window, the other arm around Gay, asleep against her breast. Her eyes are closed.

Suddenly the car bumps up and down, and Guido is trying to bring it back on the highway. For an instant the headlights catch a figure scurrying off the road shoulder. The car swerves back onto the highway. Now a man rises from the roadside, brushes himself off, picks up his bundle, and walks impassively on. It is the Indian.

The ride is smooth again, and Roslyn has opened her eyes. She is drunk and exhausted, a feeling of powerlessness is on her. Guido has a vague look of joy on his face as he drives. She speaks in a helpless monotone, as in a dream: "Aren't you going too fast? Please, huh?"

"Don't worry, kid, I never kill anybody I know."

The speedometer is climbing toward eighty.

"A fellow smashed up my best girl friend. All they found were her gloves. Please, Guido. She was beautiful, with black hair. . . ."

"Say hello to me, Roslyn."

"Hello, Guido. Please, huh?"

His eyes are glazed and oddly relaxed, as though he were happy in some corner of his mind. "We're all blind bombardiers, Roslyn—we kill people we never even saw. I bombed nine cities. I sure must've broken a lot of dishes but I never saw them. Think of all the puppy dogs must've gone up, and mail carriers, eyeglasses . . . Boy! Y'know, droppin' a bomb is like tellin' a lie—makes everything so quiet afterwards. Pretty soon you don't hear anything, don't see anything. Not even your wife. The difference is that I *see* you. You're the first one I ever really *saw*."

"Please, Guido, don't kill us. . . ."

"How do you get to know somebody, kid? I can't make a landing. And I can't get up to God, either. Help me. I never said help me in my life. I don't *know* anybody. Will you give me a little time? Say yes. At least say hello Guido."

She can hear the murderous beating of wind against the car.

"Yes. Hello, Guido."

From over ninety the speedometer begins to descend.

"Hello, Roslyn."

Headlights hit the dark, unfinished house, illuminating the unfinished outside wall and the lumber and building materials lying around on the ground. Now the motor is shut off, but the lights remain on.

No one is moving inside the car. Guido, exhausted, stares at his house. The dog is asleep beside him. Now he opens the door and lumbers out of the car. He opens the rear door and blearily looks in.

Roslyn is sleeping, sitting upright. Perce is still asleep on her lap, his feet out the window; Gay is on the floor. Guido stares at her, full of longing and sorrow for himself. He looks down at Perce, then at Gay, and as though they were unbearably interfering he steps back from the car and walks into the darkness.

Loud hammer blows open Roslyn's eyes; Gay sits up. "Okay, I'll drive, I'll drive."

"We're here, Gay."

"Where?"

She sees something in the headlights through the windshield; carefully she slides from under Perce's head and out the door, and walks unsteadily from the car toward the house, mystified. She walks in the headlight beams; the hammer blows are a few feet away. Awe shows on her face.

Guido is drunkenly hammering a sheathing board to the unfinished wall of the house. It is on crooked, but he gives it a final pat of satisfaction, then goes to the lumber pile and takes off another board, nearly falling with that, and lays it up against the wall, trying to butt it up against the previously nailed board. He hammers, as in a dream, the kind of pleasure and pain that comes of being freed of early logic, yet being driven toward some always receding center.

Roslyn comes up to him, not daring to touch him. "Oh, I'm sorry, Guido. Guido? I'm so sorry." He continues dumbly hammering. "Won't you hit your hand, it's so dark? It's dark, Guido, look how dark it is." He hammers on. She almost turns, spreading her arms and looking skyward. "Look, it's all dark!" A sob breaks from her. "Please! Please stop!"

From nearby Gay calls angrily: "What the hell you stompin' the flowers for?"

Roslyn turns to Gay, who comes up to Guido and swings him around by the shoulder and bends to the ground. "You busted all the damn heliotropes!"

Gay is on his hands and knees now, trying to stand up the fallen flowers. Guido is looking down dumbly, the hammer in his hand.

Gay: "Look at that! Look at that, now!" He holds up a torn stem. "What in hell good is that, now?"

Roslyn: "He was trying to fix the house."

Rising unsteadily to his feet, Gay asks menacingly: "What call *he* got to fix the house?"

Roslyn: "Don't! Don't! Please, Gay! He . . . he's just trying to say hello. It's no crime to say hello."

From behind them they hear Perce crying out: "Who's doin' that?"

They turn to see Perce staggering into the headlight beams, trying to free his head and arms from yards of unraveling bandage flowing off his head. He is fighting it off like a clinging spider web, turning around and around to find its source.

"Who's doin' that?"

Roslyn hurries toward him. "Don't! Don't take it off!" She reaches him and tries to unwind his arms.

"Get it off. What's on me?"

"Stop tangling it. It's your bandage."

He stops struggling and looks at the bandage as though for the first time. "What for a bandage?"

Roslyn is starting to laugh despite her concern. A few yards away, Guido is quietly but deeply laughing, glassy-eyed. Gay is beginning to feel the laughter's infectiousness. Feeling a hysteria of laughter coming on, Roslyn tries to wind the bandage on again. "It's for your head."

Perce: "My—" He breaks off as he raises his hands and feels the bandage wrapped around his head. "I have this on all night?" He looks angrily at Guido and Gay, who are roaring now, and to them he says: "Who tied this on me?" He is trying to pull it off his head.

She tries to stop his hands. "The ambulance did it. Don't take it off."

Perce, unwinding and unwinding the bandage: "You leave me at a disadvantage all night? Who put it on? Gay, you . . ." He lunges toward Gay and trips on a board, and the whole pile of lumber topples on him with a great crash. Guido and Gay fall about, dying with hysteria.

Roslyn, between laughter and tears, tries to extricate Perce from the lumber. "Get him up. Gay, come here. Guido! Carry him. Please. He can't help himself." The men come to help her, and still laughing crazily they lift Perce and almost carry him to the door of the house. She goes inside ahead of them.

Looped in their arms, Perce demands: "Who put it on? Leave me at a disadvantage all night?" She and Guido get him through the door of the house. "Where's this? Let me alone. Where is this place?" He lies on a couch as Guido sprawls on his favorite chair, catching his breath.

Roslyn: "This is my house . . . or Guido's." She laughs. "Well, it's a house, anyway."

Perce closes his eyes. Suddenly the house is quiet. She covers Perce with an Indian blanket, and the touch stirs him to resistance. "No, Ma, don't, don't!" He turns his face away.

Now she stands and sees Gay sitting outside the door on the step. She goes down to him, starting to wipe the hair out of his eyes, and he takes her hand. A curious inwardness, a naked supplication has come into his face.

"Wish you'd met Gaylord, Rose-May. If I had a new kid now, I'd know just how to be with him, just how to do. I wasted these kids. I didn't know nothin'."

"Oh, no, I'm sure they love you, Gay. Go to sleep now."

He grasps her hand, preventing her from leaving. "Would you ever want a kid? With me?"

She pats his hand, starting to turn away. "Let me just turn the lights off in the car."

He raises up, struggling to get on his feet.

"Whyn't you sleep now . . ."

"I don't wanna sleep now!" He staggers to his feet, swaying before her. "I asked you a question! Did I ask you to turn the lights off in the car? What are you runnin' away from all the time?" With a wide gesture toward windows and walls that nearly tumbles him: "I never washed the windows for my wife even. Paint a fireplace! Plant all them damn heliotropes!"

He suddenly goes to the doorway and yells into the house: "What're they all doin' here? What're you bringin' them around for?"

"I didn't bring them, they just—"

"Where are you at? I don't know where you're at."

Trying not to offend him and still speak her truth, she embraces him. "I'm here, Gay. I'm with you. But . . . what if some day you turn around and suddenly you don't like me any more? Like before, when Perce got hurt, you started to give me a look. . . . I know that look and it scares me, Gay. 'Cause I couldn't ever stay with a stranger."

"Honey, I got a little mad. That don't mean I didn't like you. Didn't your papa ever spank you, and then take you up and give you a big kiss?" She is silent. "He did, didn't he?"

"He was never there long enough. And strangers spank for keeps." She suddenly presses herself against him and he embraces her. "Oh, love me, Gay! Love me!"

He raises her face and kisses her. She smiles brightly.

Roslyn: "Now we made up, okay?"

Gay: "Yes, okay, okay!" Laughing softly, he hugs her.

"You sleep now . . . you're tired. Sleep, darling."

"And tomorrow I'll show you what I can do. You'll see what living is."

She nods in agreement, gently pressing him to the doorway. He goes into the dark house, talking. "We'd make out. I could farm. Or run cattle, maybe. I'm a damn good man, Roslyn—best man you'll ever see. Show you tomorrow when we hit those mountains. Ain't many around can keep up with old Gay. You wait and see."

She hears the bed groaning, then silence. She walks unsteadily to the car, reaches in, and pushes the switch. The lights go off. Now she stands erect and looks up at the oblivious moon, a vast sadness stretching her body, a being lost, a woman whose life has forbidden her to forsake her loneliness. She cries out, but soft, to the sky: "Help!"

For a long time she stands there, given to the dreadful clouds crossing the stars, racing to nowhere.

TEN

A PLUME of dust is moving across the desert, following Gay's old but still serviceable truck. On the open bed, lashed to the back of the cab, is a drum of gasoline with a hand-cranking pump protruding from its top. It is bumping along over the sage, here and there crunching a whitened skeleton of winter-killed cattle.

Gay is driving; Roslyn beside him has the dog in her lap, its muzzle on her shoulder. Perce spits out the window. His nose is still taped. The sun narrows their eyes. They bump along, facing the desert before them.

Roslyn can feel the dog shivering. She looks at it, then turns to Gay. "Why is the dog shivering?"

"She'll do that up here."

Suddenly Guido's plane zooms down over the roof of the cab and they see it flying straight ahead of them a few feet off the ground toward the mountains, its wings waggling a greeting. They shout in surprise. Gay waves out the window and speeds up the truck. His face and Perce's gain excitement, the knitting together of action.

True night is covering the mountains; it is the end of twilight, when the purple light is turning blue. Splashes of stars are tumbling onto the sky. The mountains, secretive and massive, wait. At their foot, the campfire shimmers—the only moving thing in the world.

The four are sitting around the fire. Nearby stands the truck, and a little farther away the lashed plane, both flickered by moon and firelight like intruding monsters resting before an onslaught.

A hiatus in the talk. Guido is telling a story, unable to keep his eyes from Roslyn across the fire from him. She is putting away the last of the dried dishes into the tote box. Now she listens raptly. Gay is idly going through the dog's fur for fleas, and Perce waits for Guido's next word, full of respect for him.

Guido looks skyward. "That star is so far away that by the time its light hits the earth, it might not even be up there any more." He looks at Roslyn. "In other words, we can only see what something was, never what it is now."

Roslyn: "You sure know a lot, don't you, Pilot?" Perce shakes his head.

Guido: "Oh, astronomy's all in the library books. Nothin' to it but reading."

Roslyn looks up at the sky. "Still, it's wonderful to know things."

"You got something a lot more important."

"What?"

Guido, glancing up at the sky: "That big connection. You're really hooked in; whatever happens to anybody, it happens to you. That's a blessing."

Roslyn, laughing: "People say I'm just nervous."

"If there hadn't been some nervous people in the world, we'd still be eating each other."

Gay, suddenly clapping his hands as though to clean them: "Well, I don't know about you educated people, but us ignorant folks got to hit the sack."

He gets up; a certain tension between him and Guido has sharpened his movements.

Roslyn: "Why is the dog shivering?"

Gay looks at the dog, then glances toward the mountains. "Got a whiff of those horses, I guess. They must be close by, Guido."

Roslyn has stretched over to stroke the dog. Suddenly it bares its teeth and nearly snaps her hand. She leaps away, terrified.

Gay is instantly furious. "Hey, you damn fool! Come here!" The dog crawls to him on her belly and he slaps her.

Roslyn: "Oh, don't hit her, she didn't mean anything! The horses ever kick her or something?"

Guido: "It's not the horses she's afraid of." They all look at him. He has the compact look of one who is taking a stand. "It's us."

Gay: "What're you talkin' about now, Guido? I never mistreated this dog." His anger is sharpening now.

Guido, holding his position, pitched high: "Just common sense, Gay. She's been up here enough times to know what's going to happen. There's wild animals up there that'll be dead tomorrow night."

There is a flare of astonishment in Roslyn's face. But the men all assume she knows this and Guido goes right on. "How's she know she's not next? They're not as stupid as people, you know."

Gay unrolls Roslyn's bedroll beside the fire. "Here now, honey, you can keep yourself nice and warm by the fire."

Guido has busied himself with his bedroll. Perce, however, is caught by the look in her face.

And now Gay, looking up from her bedroll, finds that she has not moved, and a strange look of fright is on her face.

At last she turns to him. "You kill them?"

"No, no, we sell them to the dealer."

Roslyn, her voice small, incredulous, even as somewhere in her this news does not come as a surprise: "He kills them?"

Gay, with complete neutrality, as a fact: "They're what they

call chicken-feed horses—turn them into dog food. You know —what you buy in the store for the dog or the cat?"

She has begun to quiver. He goes to her and starts to take her hand kindly. "I thought you knew that. Everybody . . ."

She gently removes her hand from his, staring incomprehensibly into his face, turns, and walks into the darkness.

". . . knows that." He hesitates for a moment, then, as much to cover his embarrassment before Guido and Perce as anything else, he picks up her bedroll and starts after her. "Maybe you better sleep on the truck. In case something comes crawling around. . . ." He walks after her into the darkness.

He comes on her beside the truck, tosses the bedroll aboard, and smooths it out. She is staring wide-eyed, shaking slightly. He turns her to him. Slowly she raises her eyes to him. In her face we see the astonishment and the agony she feels as two contrasting ideas of him clash in her mind.

Gay: "Get some sleep now. Come on."

He starts to lift her aboard, but she gently stops him—gently enough to tell him how afraid of him she is. She is looking at him as though she had never seen him before.

"Honey, I just round them up. I sell them to the dealer. Always have."

But her stare is unbroken.

"No need to look at me that way, honey. Now you're looking at *me* like a stranger."

The imminent threat of her estrangement breaks his heart and he sweeps her into his arms with a muffled cry: "Honey!"

He holds her away so he can see her.

Roslyn: "I . . . I thought . . .

"What?"

"They were for riding, or . . ."

"Sure, they used to be—especially Christmas presents for kids. 'Cause they're small horses, you see, the kids loved them for Christmas. But"—he almost smiles—"kids ride motor scooters now. Used to breed them a lot, too; mustang puts a lot of stamina into a breed."

She is beginning to listen, to perceive a dilemma in which he too is caught.

"When I started, they used a lot of them I caught. There was

mustang blood pullin' all the plows in the West; they couldn't have settled here without somebody caught mustangs for them. It . . . it just got changed around, see? I'm doin' the same thing I ever did. It's just that they . . . they changed it around. There was no such thing as a can of dog food in those days. It . . . it was a good thing to do, honey, it was a man's work, and I know how to do it. And I wanted you to see what I can do." He smiles. "Aside from sittin' around the house and movin' furniture."

"But they kill them now."

He is silent, struggling for an answer.

"You . . . you know it's not right, don't you? You're just saying this, but you know."

Gay's own guilt has been touched, and he cannot carry it alone. "Honey, if I didn't do it, somebody would. They're up here hunting all the time."

"I don't care about others!"

"You ate that steak tonight, didn't you? And you—"

Roslyn claps her hands to her ears. "I don't care!"

"You've bought food for my dog, haven't you? What'd you think was in those cans?"

"I don't want to hear it!"

"Honey, nothin' can live unless something dies."

"Stop it!"

She clambers aboard the truck, climbs into the bedroll, turns on her side, and covers her eyes with her hands. He hesitates, then hoists onto the truck bed and sits next to her. He knows he has all but lost her; only her evident agony tells him that parting will not be easy for her. At last, talking to her hidden face: "Roslyn, we never kidded, you and I. I'm tellin' you I don't want to lose you. You got to help me a little bit, though. Because I can't put on that this is all as bad as you make it. All I know is—everything else is wages; up here I'm my own man. And that's why you liked me, isn't it?"

A silence grows.

"I liked you because you were kind."

"I haven't changed."

"Yes. You have. This changes it."

"Honey, a kind man can kill."

"No he can't!"

"Well, if it's bad, maybe you gotta take a little bad with the good or you'll go on the rest of your life runnin'."

She suddenly faces him, her eyes full of tears. "What's there to stop for? You're the same as everybody!"

She bursts into disappointed weeping, covering her face. In a moment he lays a hand on her. "Yes. Maybe we're all the same. Including you." She uncovers her face, starting to raise on her elbows indignantly. His voice is calm again. "We start out doin' something, meaning no harm, something that's naturally in us to do. And somewhere down the line it gets changed around into something bad. Like dancin' in a nightclub. You started out just wanting to dance, didn't you? And little by little it turns out that people ain't interested in how good you dance, they're gawkin' at you with something altogether different in their minds. And they turn it sour, don't they?" Memory dissolves her anger, and she lies back. "I could've looked down my nose at you, too—just a kid showin' herself off in nightclubs for so much a night. But I took my hat off to you. Because I know the difference."

Her eyes search his. He looks off at the dark mountains.

"This . . . this is how I dance, Roslyn. And if they made somethin' else out of it, well . . . I can't run the world any more than you could. I hunt these horses to keep myself free. That's all."

Roslyn: "You . . . take your hat off . . . to me?" He bends and kisses her on the lips. "You mean it, don't you! Oh, Gay!"

They hold each other in the silence. He comes down off the truck bed. With troubled eyes he leans down and holds his mouth on hers and she presses his shoulders down upon her.

He stands erect, touches her eyelids. He goes from her to the diminishing fire, sits on his bedroll, and takes off his shoes. Perce and Guido are in their bedrolls nearby. The dog comes and lies down, and Gay mutters: "Shame on you, you fool." He climbs into his bedroll.

Guido turns in his bedroll. "I could fly her back in the morning, if you want me to."

Gay simply looks at Guido with an instinctive, as yet unformed, suspicion.

Guido: "I was wondering how she agreed to come up here."

Perce flicks a cigarette into the fire. "She's got a lot of right.

If you come to think of it, it don't make too much sense for fifteen horses."

Gay sighs. "Don't worry yourselves about her now. She's comin' along fine."

He turns on his side. Beside him the dog lies with head on paws, the firelight flickering on its eyes. Its breathing is still short and rapid. Gay, to the dog, very softly: "You quiet down now. Everybody's showin' off."

No one moves. Beyond the circle of light the land is empty. The night is filled with the firelit eyes of the dog, which blink toward the mountains and the still unseen animals that are to die.

ELEVEN

The first rays of dawn are brightening the sky. Perce is on the truck bed, cranking gas from the drum into the plane. Guido is on top of the wing, holding the hose and peering into the tank.

Gay walks over to a mound partially covered with drift sand. He reaches down, grasps something, and pulls; a tarpaulin is peeled off, revealing a dozen truck tires. On the wing Guido raises his hand, peering into the tank, and calls: "Okay, hold it!"

Gay calls to them from the pile of tires: "Let's go, Perce, gimme a hand here!"

Perce hops off the truck, gets in behind the wheel, and backs to the tires. Guido clambers down off the wing, reaches into the open-sided cockpit, and draws out a shotgun pistol, which he proceeds to load from a box of shells.

Roslyn, who is rolling up the bedrolls and tying them, happens to look and sees the pistol in Guido's hand, hesitates, then returns to her job. The dog comes up to her. She smiles down at the animal, then with some initial fear reaches down and pats it. Happily she calls: "She's not snapping any more, Gay!"

Gay is just heaving a truck tire onto the bed of the truck

with Perce's help. He turns to her, smiling. "Things generally look a little different in the morning."

Guido calls from the plane: "I guess I'm ready, Gay!"

He is drawing out of the plane a shredded Air Force jacket whose lamb's-wool lining is visible through slits in the outside leather. He and Gay go to each wingtip and unlash the plane. Perce goes to the tail and unlashes it. Roslyn comes near and watches now. Perce now comes alongside her and stands. Gay walks back to the cockpit with Guido.

Gay: "How you want her?"

Guido looks up at the sky, holding a palm up to feel the breeze. He points: "That way."

Gay goes to the tail, lifts it, and swings the plane to face the direction of take-off. Then he walks along the plane to the propeller and waits. Guido is about to get into the cockpit.

Roslyn, as though to relieve the weirdly charged atmosphere, calls rather gaily to Guido: "Boy, that's some jacket! Little breezy, isn't it?"

Guido: "Went on a lot of missions in this thing. Wouldn't take a hundred dollars for it . . . bulletproof." They chuckle as he climbs in and sits. To Roslyn: "Glad you decided to stay with us. Probably never see this again in history, y'know."

Roslyn: "Take care, now."

Guido mutely thanks her for her solicitude. "Okay, boy, turn your partner and do-si-do! Switch off!"

Gay glances behind him to see if there is any obstruction to his back step, reaches up, turns the propeller several times. Guido slips his goggles on.

Guido: "Switch on! With feeling now!" They laugh. Gay turns the propeller until it is horizontal and pulls down hard, but the engine does not start. "And again! And let us pray." Gay with special care grasps the propeller, pulls down. The engine huffs and dies. "That's that damn car gas for ya. Okay, let's try her again."

Again Gay yanks down on the propeller. The engine smokes, huffs, and with a sudden resolution clatters up to a roar. Guido straps himself in, lays the pistol in his lap, and with a wave to them guns the engine. The plane moves away from them, gains speed, and takes the air. Now it wheels in air and comes

back, roaring over their heads and away toward the mountains. They turn with it.

The three squint against the prop blast. Gay is the first to move; he looks for an instant at Perce and Roslyn. They feel his glance. Without reason, they feel separated from him, and he smiles.

Gay: "Here we go." He turns toward the truck and starts to walk, Perce and Roslyn following him.

Guido lifts his goggles and looks up at the clear blue sky. His lips move as though in prayer. He lowers his goggles and looks down. The barrier face of the mountains suddenly passes under the plane. Now the sharp interior walls and steep valleys show, manless, half in shadow, with patches of grass here and there. A hidden secret world is opened. The plane flies just within the crests of the mountains, turning with the valleys, which Guido scans through the open-sided cockpit. Suddenly his head moves sharply.

Instantly he pulls the stick back; the plane abruptly climbs. Now he banks and turns, the plane shuddering on uneven steps of air. Now he checks his instruments and grasps the pistol in his right hand. With a glance over the side to aim himself, he presses the stick forward and dives.

The herd is coming up to him fast. Now the animals start to gallop along the wall of the valley. Guido flattens his dive and zooms in over the horses, his wingtips only yards from the valley walls. He pulls the stick back and the plane noses upward; he points the pistol down as he passes over the herd, and fires. With the shot the horses surge ahead even faster. He is conscious of having held his breath, of having felt a strange tremor in his engine at the moment of acceleration. With a sigh he flies toward the sky, turns tightly, lines himself up with the herd, and once more starts his dive.

The truck bumps along on the sage desert, but now it crosses a border where the sage and soil end and a prehistoric lake bed begins. It is a floor of clay, entirely bare, white, and flat as a table. Now the truck halts close to a little hummock bordering the lake bed.

Perce emerges as the engine is turned off. He looks around

as Roslyn comes down out of the cab. Gay comes from the other side of the truck and walks around to them where they stand scanning the lake bed. The silence is absolute. There is no wind.

Roslyn: "It's . . . like a dream!"

Set between mountain ranges the lake bed stretches about twenty-five miles wide and as long as the eye can see. Not a blade of grass or stone mars its absolutely flat surface, from which heat waves rise. In the distance it glistens like ice.

Perce: "I seen a picture of the moon once. Looked just like this."

Gay: "He'll be drivin' the horses out of that pass."

She and Perce look toward an opening in the mountain face perhaps a mile away. "Does anybody own this land?"

"Government, probably. Just call it God's country. Perce? Let's get that drum off."

Gay goes to the truck, hops onto the bed, and proceeds to unlash the gasoline drum. Perce stands on the ground and helps jimmy the drum to the edge of the truck. Now Gay hops down and both men let it down to the ground and roll it off to one side. Roslyn watches for a moment, then goes to the cab and leans in. The dog is quivering on the floor of the cab. She reaches toward it tentatively.

Gay goes to one of the tires; he draws a rope from inside it and experimentally circles it over his head and throws it.

Perce, seeing him occupied, walks over to the cab and looks in from the side opposite to that of Roslyn. She is pressing her face against the dog's. Then she reaches up to the rearview mirror, turns it to look at herself, sees Perce, and smiles.

He speaks as though voicing a premonition: "I'd be a little careful what I said to Gay. For a while out here."

Gay's face appears beside his. "Got to get the glasses."

Perce steps aside. Gay moves into the truck doorway, hardly looking at Roslyn, who now shakes dust out of her hair in the rearview mirror. He reaches behind the seat and draws out a large binocular case. Looking at her now, grinning, an uncertainty still in his eyes, he takes the binoculars out of the case and puts the glasses to his eyes. Perce is watching him. He holds the glasses up to his eyes for a long moment, looking toward the pass.

She steps over to Gay, forcing a bright tone: "See anything?"

Gay, putting the glasses on a tire on the truck bed: "Climb up, make yourself comfortable. He'll be awhile yet."

He gives her a boost. She mounts the truck bed. He climbs up and sits inside a pile of two tires, his legs hanging over the edge at the knees, his armpits supporting his trunk.

Gay: "Go ahead. It's comfortable."

She does as he did; Perce mounts onto the truck.

Roslyn: "It is comfortable! Try it, Perce."

Perce does the same. The three sit in silence as Gay again raises the glasses and looks through them.

Gay turns to her. "You lookin' real good today, honey. Maybe tonight we go down to Reno and dance, okay?"

"Okay."

"I'd of brought your umbrella for you but I didn't think of it."

"I'm all right. It's not too hot."

She reaches over and touches his knee reassuringly, for she sees his anxiety about her. Now she withdraws her hand, and scans the lake bed.

Gay, for a moment, continues looking at her profile. He has sensed the dampened quality of her feeling. He turns and glances at Perce, who is on his other side. Perce is staring toward the pass, clearly preoccupied.

For a moment Gay sits staring straight ahead; then he turns to her. "I forgot to tell you something last night."

She looks at him with quick interest.

"Lots of cow outfits use the pastures up in those mountains, and when they find the mustangs there they just shoot 'em and leave 'em for the buzzards. 'Cause they eat up all the good grass, see."

She nods that she understands, but he sees he has not pierced her dampened air, and he turns to Perce.

"You know that, don't you, Perce?"

"Huh? Oh sure, I know that."

"Whyn't you say so?"

"I just said so."

Gay raises the glasses. "Nothin' but misfit horses, that's all they are, honey."

He studies the pass through the glasses. Putting the glasses down, he turns to her with a warm memory in his eyes. "Wished you'd been here in the old days." Stretching an arm toward the pass: "They'd come pourin' out of those passes, three, four, five hundred at a time. And we'd build us a big corral out here and funnel them right in. Some of them were real beautiful animals, too. Made sweet riding horses."

For a moment she feels the breadth of his memories. "It must have been wonderful."

"Best life any man could've had."

"I wished I'd been here . . . then."

Perce: "I hear something."

Gay: "What?"

Perce: "Tick, tick, tick, tick, tick."

Gay: "It's my watch."

Roslyn: "Boy, it's quiet here! You can hear your skin against your clothes." She tries to laugh.

Gay, exhaling, relaxing in the tire: "Ayah!" He leans back, closing his eyes. Perce and Roslyn, in effect, are becoming joined by a viewpoint toward Gay, who at every moment seems to be gathered up by a quickening forward rhythm. They look at each other, forced, as it were, to an awareness of looking on him with the same eyes.

Perce: "I hear something!"

Gay listens. He raises the glasses, sees nothing, puts them down.

Gay: "What?"

Perce: "Engine, sounds like."

They listen.

Gay: "Where?"

Perce, indicating with an open hand the general direction of the pass: "Out that way."

Gay, after listening for a moment: "Too soon. He wouldn't be in the pass yet."

Roslyn: "Wait." She listens. "I hear it."

Gay strains to hear. Now a certain pique is noticeable in him because he can't hear it. "No—just your blood pumpin' in your head, is all."

Roslyn: "Ssh."

Gay watches her. Perce is also tensed to listen.

Gay: "I always had the best ears of anybody, so don't tell me you—"

Perce, suddenly pointing, and screwing up out of the tire to sit on its rim: "Isn't that him?"

The three look into the distant sky, Roslyn and Gay trying to locate the plane, at the same time wriggling out of the tires, to sit on the rims.

She suddenly cries out and points. "I see it! There! Look, Gay!"

Almost insulted, he scans the sky, then unwillingly raises the glasses and sees the mountain pass up close; flying out of it is the plane, tiny even in the glasses. He puts down the glasses, blinks his eyes hard. "He never worked this fast before. I'd've seen him but I didn't expect him so soon."

Perce: "I could see him glinting in the sun. It was the glint. That's why."

Gay seems to accept the apology. Now, very distantly, an explosion is heard.

Roslyn: "What's that?"

Gay: "He fired a shot."

She watches the pass with growing apprehension and fascination. Perce glances at her in concern, then back to the pass. They are all perspiring now in the warming sun.

Gay: "I've sat here waitin' two-three hours before he come out. That's why I didn't see him." Now, however, he glances at Perce and nods. "You got good eyes, though, boy." He raises the glasses again. Silence. They watch the pass. The sun is higher; heat waves rise around them like a transparent sea. Suddenly Gay straightens.

"There they come. One . . . two . . . three . . . four . . . five . . . six. I guess he'll go back for the others now."

Perce: "Give me a look, heh?"

Gay hands Perce the binoculars. "See the others yet?"

"No. There's . . . six. And a little colt."

Roslyn's flesh moves; she shifts the position of one hand to relax her tension.

Gay notices her shock without facing her, and he asks Perce: "You sure?"

"Ya. It's a spring foal."

Gay, watching the pass, can feel Roslyn's deepening stillness beside him.

Perce keeps the glasses up. "It's a colt, all right." He lowers the glasses and faces Gay. He speaks with finality, not quite accusing, but nevertheless with an implication of question as to what will be done with it: "It's a colt, Gay."

Gay, concerned, but with barely a look at Perce, takes the glasses. Perce turns to watch the pass again. Roslyn is staring at Gay's profile as though it were constantly changing in her mind. Now Gay lowers the glasses, faces her fully. He will not be condemned. "Want a look?"

He gives her the glasses. She hesitates, but then raises them to her eyes. The lenses find the herd, galloping in file, the colt bringing up the rear with its nose nearly touching its mare's tail. Now the plane dives down on them and they lift their heads and gallop faster. The image shakes, as her hands lose their steadiness, then flows out crazily as the strength goes out of her hands. She sits there, blind.

Gay stands, and raises the glasses again. She wipes her fingers over her eyes. Another shot is heard. She opens her eyes to look. Perce and Gay are fixed on the distant spectacle. She gets to her feet and hops down off the truck. Perce looks to her.

She is barely audible: "Maybe it's cooler in the truck." She walks to the cab and climbs in.

Gay and Perce remain on the truck bed, sitting on the tires again. Gay, with a glance, notes Perce's new uneasiness.

"It's all right. She's goin' to make it fine."

Perce makes no attempt to reply. A challenge has somehow grown up before him. Their posture and movements relax now.

Perce: "I thought you said there was fifteen. There's only six."

"Probably lost a few. That'll happen."

"Don't make much sense for six, does it?"

"Six is six. Better'n wages, ain't it?" Perce doesn't answer. "I said it's better than wages, ain't it?"

Perce, with damaged conviction, looking at his shoe soles: "I guess anything's better'n wages."

They sit in silence. Then Gay crosses his legs.

"Perce? We've just about cleaned 'em out up here, but if you're interested in some real money, there's a place about a

hundred miles northeast—Thighbone Mountain. I never bothered up there 'cause it's awful tough to get 'em out. You gotta horseback up in there. But I believe there must be five hundred on Thighbone. Maybe more." Perce is silent, staring at the pass. "There'd be *real* money. You could buy yourself some good stock, maybe even a little van—hit those rodeos in style."

Perce cannot look at him. His voice oddly quiet, he says: "I don't know, Gay. Tell you the truth, I don't even know about rodeos any more."

"I'm beginnin' to smell wages all over you, boy."

"I sure wish my old man hadn't of died. You never saw a prettier ranch."

"Fella, when you get through wishin', all there is is doin' a man's work. And there ain't much of that left in this country."

They are brought bolt upright by a ferocious snarling of the dog and Roslyn's screaming. Both of them leap off the truck bed as Roslyn jumps out of the cab, going backward. Gay rushes to the cab and sees the dog on the seat, its teeth bared, snarling.

Roslyn: "She was shaking so I—"

Gay reaches in and throws the dog out of the truck. With tail between its legs, it crawls back to him. He reaches in behind the seat, takes out a length of cord, ties it to the dog's collar, and lashes the dog to the bumper. The dog crawls under the truck in the shade and lies down. Gay now goes to Roslyn, who is quivering; he starts to put his arm around her.

Roslyn halts and looks up into his face as though he must do something to calm the animal immediately. "She's scared to death, Gay!"

"Well, even a dog can't have it just right *all* the time."

The ring of his voice meets the sharp sound of a shot close by. It turns him toward the sky, and he immediately starts toward the truck, walking sideways as he talks to her behind him. Perce, a few paces away, turns to look for the plane.

Gay: "Just roll with it, honey, and see how you make out just this once."

He gets to the truck and immediately reaches behind the seat and draws out two iron spikes and a short-handled sledgehammer.

Now he glances for an instant toward the plane, which is just completing a dive. It is much closer now, its wing dents visible. The horses are galloping straight toward the bare white lake bed, but they are still on the sage-dotted desert.

All business now, Gay walks past Perce, who is staring at Roslyn. She is looking toward the horses. "Give us a hand here, Perce."

Perce, his eyes grown dreamy and strangely inward, follows Gay, who hands him a spike. He props it up as Gay drives it into the ground, ties a rope to it, and then, after pacing off several yards, does the same with the second spike and ties a rope to that.

Now Gay leaves Perce, walks to the truck, and tosses the hammer in behind the cab. For an instant he glances at Roslyn. She is wide-eyed, staring off at the horses. Gay passes her again, unties the dog, leads it to one of the spikes and ties it there. The three stand in silence, watching the plane and the horses, which have reached the border of the white lake bed and have broken file, scattering right and left in order to remain on the familiar sage desert, frightened of crossing over into the strange, superheated air coming off the clay. Two of them have turned back toward the mountains and a flare of hope brightens Roslyn's face.

The plane lays over on one wing in a long climb and dives down, down on the horses within a yard of their heads. Guido has turned them, and now they break out onto the lake bed, re-forming their herded grouping. The plane now flies above the lake bed itself and is not climbing for another dive.

Gay takes Roslyn's arm and walks her quickly to the truck cab, but she resists entering. They stop.

"Up you go, honey."

Before she can speak he hoists her into the cab, slams the door, quickly puts his head in, turns her face to him, and kisses her lips. "Now you watch some real ropin'!" With great joy he steps away and leaps up onto the truck bed. Perce is still on the ground, indecisively standing there. "Git up there, Perce, let's see what you can do now!"

Perce feels the force of Gay's command, and also sees what is evidently Gay's victory—for Roslyn is sitting motionless in the cab. He leaps aboard the truck bed.

The plane is just touching down on the lake bed and taxiing toward the truck. The horses are now trotting only, but so far away they seem like specks of illusion.

As the plane comes in fast, Gay hands Perce the end of a webbing strap whose other end is buckled to the post at Gay's corner. Perce passes the strap across his back and buckles the end to the post at his corner, so that both men are held, if rather precariously, to the cab and cannot fall backward. Gay now turns to the pile of tires behind him and takes out a coil of rope from the top tire. This Perce does too, from the pile behind him. Both men heft their ropes, grasping them a foot behind the nooses, turning them until the twist is out of them and they hang limber.

The plane taxis up, and the motor stops as it comes between the two spikes driven into the ground. Guido jumps out of the cockpit and runs to one spike, then the other, lashing the ropes to the plane struts. The dog, leashed to one of the spikes, snarls at him but he brushes it off and ties the rope. With his goggles on his forehead, his face puffed with preoccupation, he trots over to the cab and jumps in behind the wheel. Without a glance at Roslyn he turns the key, starts the engine, puts the truck in gear, and roars off at top speed across the lake bed, peering ahead through the windshield.

"Grab hold now, we're gonna do a lot of fast turning."

She grasps the dashboard, excitement pumping into her face. The faded Air Force insignia on his shoulder is next to her face.

Through the windshield the open lake bed spreads before them. A mile off, two black dots are rapidly enlarging. Now their forms become clear: two horses standing, watching the oncoming truck, their ears stiffly raised in curiosity.

She turns to Guido. His goggles are still on his forehead; a look of zealous calculation is coming into his face. She is feeling that first heat of real terror, and turns to look forward, her hands grasping the dashboard tighter. The two horses, a hundred yards off now, their rib cages expanding and contracting, their nostrils spread, turn and gallop, keeping close together. Guido steers right up to the flying rear hooves of the horses. Now they wheel, and Guido turns sharply with them—the truck leaning dangerously—and works brake and gas pedal simultaneously. Now the horses run straight, and in doing so they sep-

arate from each other by a foot or two; Guido presses the truck into this space, which quickly widens, and he speeds even faster. Now there is one horse on each side of the truck, running abreast of the cab windows.

Roslyn looks at the horse running only a yard to one side of her. She could reach out and touch its eyes. It is a medium-size brown stallion, glistening with sweat. She hears the high screaming wheeze of its breathing, and the strangely gentle tacking of its unshod hooves on the hard lake bed. It is stretching out now, and its stricken eyes seem blind and agonized. Suddenly, from behind, a noose falls over its ears and hangs there askew.

On the truck bed, Perce is whipping his rope to make its noose fall over the stallion's ears.

Guido, unable to see him, yells to him past Roslyn's face, and he is calling with such urgency that he seems furious. "Go on, get him! Throw again, Perce!"

At this instant Roslyn sees the other horse beyond Guido's head as a noose falls cleanly down over its neck. Guido calls out the window on his side: "Attaboy, Gay!"

Up behind the cab, Gay and Perce squint against the wind tearing at their hatbrims and their shirts. Gay, having just lassoed his horse, is now letting go of the rope, his horse swerving off to the left, away from the truck. The rope stretches to its limit, then suddenly yanks the heavy truck tire off the top of the pile behind him. The horse feels the pull of the dragging tire and the suffocating squeeze of the noose, rears in air, and comes to a halt.

The truck has never slowed. Perce, who has coiled up his rope, circles it over his head and throws it. The noose falls over the stallion's head. Veering away to the right, it pulls a tire off from behind Perce.

Gay shouts with joy: "That's the way!"

Perce returns a grateful look and Gay stretches and claps him on the shoulder, laughing. They are suddenly joined.

Guido steers sharply to reverse the truck's direction; Roslyn is looking out the window at the stallion being forced to a halt by the dragging tire. Now it turns with lowered head to face the tire; now it raises up in the air, its forefeet flailing. Suddenly the truck speeds up again, changing direction.

Roslyn turns to Guido and yells: "Won't they choke?"

Guido: "We're comin' back in a minute."

They are speeding toward three rapidly enlarging specks; forms emerge; the three horses turn and run. Now a fourth, that of the colt, appears from behind the screening body of the mare. The colt runs with its nose in the mare's long, full tail.

Both men are twirling their lassos over their heads, leaning outward over the truck's sides. The sound of clattering hooves grows louder and louder in their ears. Gay's body absorbs the motion of the truck, his hands gently guide the rope, giving it form and life, and a startling pleasure shines in his eyes.

Perce is now above and a length behind the big mare and her colt. He is readying his noose, getting set. Suddenly Roslyn's head sticks out of the window of the cab, looking up at him pleadingly. She is almost within arm's length of the colt, which is galloping beside her. The fright and pain in her face surprise him. And Gay yells against the wind: "Get that horse!" Now Gay throws his noose at the horse on his side, and Perce throws his rope. It lands over the mare's head and she veers to the right, the colt changing course with her. He turns and watches the mare being halted by the dragging tire, the colt running almost rib to rib with her.

The one remaining horse is trotting away toward the brushy edge of the lake bed and the safety of the nearby hills. Guido sees it and speeds across the distance, and Gay lassos this horse a few yards before the sage border; once it is caught Guido circles back, leaving it bucking and flinging its heavily maned neck against the remorseless noose. Straight ahead in the far distance all of them see the stallion. While the other horses stand still, some of them with drooping heads, the stallion is flailing at the rope with his forefeet, charging toward the tire and snapping at it with his teeth.

Guido speeds toward him, glancing at Roslyn. "Now we tie them up so they don't choke. We'll pick them up tomorrow morning in the dealer's van."

She is staring at the approaching stallion, and when he has stopped the truck beside it he merely gets out with a rope in his hand without turning back to her.

Gay and Perce have hopped off and Guido joins them. They are thirty feet from the animal, sizing him up. His sweat has

blackened him, and he shines in the sun. Gay and Guido move toward him, spreading out. Their steps are quiet and all their movements small. The horse, seeing men for the first time, suddenly stamps down on the clay and, twisting his head, flies to one side. He is yanked off balance by the tire rope, and stumbles onto his shoulder and springs up again. His wind is screeching in his throttle now and blood is trickling from one nostril, and he is lowering his head to cough. The men advance, hefting their ropes.

Roslyn: "The others are his mares?"

Perce, who is still near the truck, turns quickly and sees Roslyn looking at him from the window. He nods. "That was his colt."

Gay: "Get on that tire, Perce!"

The command sends Perce running away to the tire, which is sliding behind the stallion; in air now, the animal comes down awkwardly on his hind feet and runs a length, and Perce jumps onto the tire, digging his heels into the clay and holding onto the rope.

The stallion faces them again, groaning for air. The men stand still. Now Gay twirls his noose over his head and the stallion makes an abortive charge at Perce, who scampers off the tire. As the stallion's profile for an instant presents itself to Gay, he flings his noose onto the ground; its right forefoot comes down as it runs past, and Gay jerks his rope and the fetlock is caught. Gay runs around the rear of the horse, flipping the rope over its back; on the other side he pulls in fast, and the right knee bends and the hoof is tight up against the stallion's ribs. Guido quickly throws and his noose sails over its face and behind its ears; with Perce holding the tire rope taut from the neck, Guido half knee-bends with his rope over his thighs and pulls, and the two nooses squeeze now from opposite directions. They are choking the stallion down. On the other side of the animal Gay wraps his rope around his arm and with all his power leans back. The stallion's trussed right hoof is drawing up tighter and tighter into its ribs, and slowly it leans down until its knee hits the ground. Without for an instant releasing the tautness of his rope, Gay comes toward the stallion, hand over hand on the nylon, and when he is two feet away—Guido and Perce are still leaning with all their weight on their throttle

nooses—he raises up one boot and, setting his heel on the stallion's shoulder, pushes so that the stallion rolls onto its right side. But as it falls its right hoof flies out, and the rope is yanked through Gay's glove. The men scatter as the stallion bursts up from the ground, running at them, springing high and twisting its body like a great fish springing out of water. Perce runs to the sliding tire and digs in; the animal is jerked about by the neck and stands there, hawking air.

For a moment they are still. Now Guido walks softly and picks up his rope and Gay gets his, which is still noosed to the fetlock. After a moment when nothing moves but the horse's expanding and contracting rib cage, Gay suddenly flips his rope into the air over the horse's back, running around its rear at the same time, and once again he pulls and bends up the right leg. Faster this time, he comes in hand over hand to the stallion while Guido and Perce choke him down, and when he is close he jerks his rope suddenly and the horse goes down onto one knee. Now, to their surprise, its nose slowly lowers and rests on the ground as though it were doing an obeisance, blood running out of its nostrils onto the clay, its wind blowing up little puffs of talc. Gay pushes it over with his boot, and before it hits the ground he flips his rope around the left front fetlock. He knots both forefeet together and cuts the excess rope, stands away from the free hind feet, then delicately approaches, and with one movement wraps them together and draws them to the forefeet.

They have not heard her talking; Roslyn has come out of the truck and she is talking quietly. Only now in the quiet Perce senses her there and turns. She is smiling and her eyes are larger than life. "Why are you killing them? Gay?" She begins to move toward the three men when a drumming in the ground turns them. The stallion has broken out of the truss and his hind feet are flailing free, his head beating the ground. Gay rushes to the tire and pulls his head flat against the earth. "Grab this, Perce!"

Perce takes the rope from him. Now he runs to Guido and grabs his rope, and circling behind the horse he twirls the noose over his head. The hind hooves are cracking against the forehooves and Gay knows the rope around the forefeet may tear. He throws and nooses both hind hooves together, comes

around toward the head, and is drawing the hind legs up tight when he sees her hands.

She is pulling his rope, trying to get it away from him, and she is strangely smiling, calling into his face: "Okay, you won—you won, Gay!"

"Get away, that horse is wild!"

"Oh, Gay, darling—Gay!"

Gay yanks his rope and swings his arm at the same time—for she is coming at him with her smile, and her fists are hitting his arm—and she goes flying backward and falls.

Perce is in front of Gay. "Hey!"

For an instant they face each other.

Gay: "Get on that tire."

"No need to hit her."

"Get on that tire, Perce. Don't say anything to me. Just get on that tire and hold this horse!"

On the lake bed's silence they hear her sobs. They see her, all three turning now as she walks toward the truck, weeping into her hands.

Perce goes to the tire and holds the neck rope taut. Gay trusses the stallion tight, four hooves together. Now Perce stands. None of them looks toward the truck. Gay lights a cigarette. They wipe the sweat off their faces. Her sobs come to them softly through the air. The three men and the stallion on the ground suck air. The horse coughs. Guido looks down at it, noting the old scars on its shoulders and quarters. One ear is bitten off at the tip. "Boy, this son of a bitch must've kicked the shit out of every stud in Nevada."

Perce sees now that Roslyn's muffled weeping has entered Gay, who stares down at the trussed stallion. "I guess comin' up here the first time like her, there might not seem much sense to it at that, for only six horses. Not knowin' how it used to be." An ironic, nearly bitter flicker of a grin passes over Gay's lips. "I never thought of it, but I guess the fewer you kill the worse it looks."

He raises his eyes toward the distance, and the two other men know his vision, the picture in his mind of the hundreds that once poured out of these passes. Gay glances down at the stallion once more. An embarrassment, almost a shyness, has crept over him as he turns to them. Even his stance seems suddenly awkward and not quite his own.

"What you say we give her this herd?"

Guido laughs; he does not believe it. But Perce reaches thankfully to grasp Gay's arm, when he sees Roslyn coming up behind them.

Gay faces her and his offer is dying in his throat at the sight of her eyes, the unbelievable distance in them, a coldness that seems to reach into her soul.

Roslyn: "How much do you want for them? I'll pay you."

The tendons stiffen in Gay's neck. With his eyes narrowed, he seems like a man being drenched.

"I'll give you two hundred dollars. Is that enough?"

"Let's get on the truck." Gay is walking past her.

Perce almost leaps after him. "But Gay! You were just sayin' you'd give them to her."

Gay slows to a halt and thinks. The hurt is in his eyes like burning smoke. "I did think of that. But I sell to dealers only. All they're lookin' to buy is the horse."

Without moving toward him, her indignation still in her voice, Roslyn states as a fact: "I didn't mean to insult you, Gay."

"No insult. I was just wondering who you think you been talkin' to since we met, that's all."

He walks to the truck and hops aboard. In silence the others take their places, Guido behind the wheel with her beside him, and Perce on the back with Gay.

Guido starts the engine and drives slowly toward the next horse they must tie up. He feels the waves of anger emanating from her. The silence between them gnaws at him. "Brother, what a day."

She does not speak or look at him.

"I nearly hit the side of that mountain before. Cylinder cut out just at the bottom of a dive. That's the closest I ever come, I tell you."

She does not move. For a moment he can only glance at her in alarm, for she is evidently close to a state of shock.

"I . . . I know how you feel. I really do. . . ."

She is beginning to rock from side to side. Her alarm seems to require him to speak. "Took me a while to get used to it myself. Tell you the truth, the only part of it I ever liked is the

flying. Truthfully . . . you don't know me. I used to be afraid of too many things. I had to force myself. Because you can't run away from life, and life is cruel sometimes. . . ."

She claps her hands to her ears, a groan coming through her clenched teeth. It frightens him.

"Maybe you ought to wait in the plane. You want to? Look, I know how you feel but I can't stop it now. I know him. There'd be hell to pay!"

She looks at him directly, with a challenging contempt.

He suddenly senses a path for himself, a realization shows on his face, an excitement of a new kind.

"Listen, you want me to stop this?"

Her eyes open wide in surprise.

"You're through with Gay now, right?" She seems perplexed and he presses on against his own faltering. "Well, tell me. He doesn't know what you're all about, Roslyn, he'll never know. Come back with me; give me a week, two weeks. I'll teach you things you never knew. Let me show you what I am. You don't know me. What do you say? Give me a reason and I'll stop it. There'll be hell to pay, but you give me a reason and I'll do it!"

A power of contemptuous indignation has been rising in her, but he has seen nothing but what seemed to be her excitement at his offer. And when her voice strikes at him now, he almost leaps in surprise.

"A *reason*! You! Sensitive fella? So full of feelings? So sad about your wife, and crying to me about the bombs you dropped and the people you killed. *You* have to get something to be human? You were never sad for anybody in your life, Guido! You only know the sad words! You could blow up the whole world, and all you'd ever feel is sorry for *yourself*!"

A scream has entered her voice and it chills him. He stops the truck near the mare and colt and gets out. Guido seems transfixed as he walks around the truck to join Gay and Perce, who are hopping off the back. He moves up close to Gay, looks at the mare, and says in a peculiarly intimate, comradely way: "Let's get the old lady, come on."

"She's fifteen if she's a day." Gay uncoils his rope, hefting it loose. The mare stands with her head stretched toward them, getting their scent. "Probably wouldn't last the winter."

Perce sees Roslyn turning away from the sight of the mare

with a crazed look in her eyes. As Gay and Guido move toward the animal, the colt makes a bleating cry and runs a few yards and tumbles, rolling over and over, then springs up and runs back and collides with the mare, which does not budge.

Gay calls back over his shoulder, "Perce!"

Perce walks slowly to the tire and sits on it, grasping the rope.

The mare circles to keep Guido and Gay in front of her. They are easier in their movements with her than with the stallion; she moves more weightily because she is heavier and her foal is constantly in her way. They approach her with small movements to position themselves for the throw, and she observes them through her terrified eyes, but there is a waiting quality about her, an absence of fury. The foal makes a pass toward her teats, and then, as though remembering, jerks up its head to watch the approaching men.

Now Gay halts. He is on one side of the mare, Guido in front of her. He tosses a noose behind her forefeet. Guido shouts and rushes at her face, and she backs into the noose which Gay pulls tight and, running behind her, yanks to trip her to her knees. Guido walks up beside her and pushes her and she falls to earth. Gay lashes her four feet together and drops his rope. Perce lets go his rope, draws up his knees, and rests his arms on them, looking into the distance. The foal walks to him and sniffs the ground a yard from his hand.

Gay takes out his cigarettes. Guido blows his nose. They are standing with their backs to the truck. The three sense Roslyn's eyes on them, and this knowledge is like a raging sea on which they ride, falling and rising within themselves, yet outwardly even more relaxed than if all were calm under them.

Gay inhales, and Perce knows now that he is gathering himself to turn about and go back to the truck to resume the roping of the remaining horses. The hurt is deepening in Gay's face and this somber look of loss, this groping for his pride, is dangerous. "We can rope the others on the way back. What you reckon this mare weighs?"

In Guido's eyes the emptiness is like a lake as he surveys the mare's body.

Now Perce slowly turns. Roslyn is looking skyward through the windshield and he knows she can hear this. "There's hardly beer money in it for six, Gay."

Gay's eyes remain defiantly fixed on Guido's profile as he waits for the figures and Perce says no more.

Now Guido looks at him. "She might be six hundred pounds."

Gay: "The two browns be about four hundred, I'd say."

Guido: "Just about, ya."

"Must be five hundred on the stallion, anyway."

"A little lighter, I'd say. Call it nineteen hundred—two thousand pounds altogether."

"How's that come out, now?"

Guido looks up in the air, figuring. "Well, six cents a pound, that's —" He figures with silent, moving lips.

In the momentary silence they hear Roslyn's sobs fully pouring out of her. Gay and Guido keep their eyes on each other.

"Be about hundred and ten, hundred and twenty dollars, Gay."

"Okay, how you want to cut it?"

"Any way you like. . . . I'll take fifty for myself and the plane."

"Okay. I guess I oughta have about forty for the truck and me. That'd give you twenty-five, Perce—that all right?"

Perce, staring at the mare, seems not to have heard.

"Perce?"

"You fellas take it. I just went along for the ride, anyway."

Perce turns so sharply that the other two start. They see Roslyn walking. She is heading across the open lake bed.

"Roslyn!" Gay takes a step, and halts himself.

She has swerved about. Her shadow sketches toward them. Forty yards away, she screams, her body writhing, bending over as though to catapult her hatred.

"You liars! All of you!" Clenching her fists, she screams toward their faces: "*Liars!*"

Unnerved, Gay flinches.

"Man! Big man! You're only living when you can watch something die! Kill everything, that's all you want! Why don't you just kill yourselves and be happy?"

She runs toward them, but stops as though afraid, and says directly toward Gay: "You. With your God's country. Freedom!" She screams into his face: "*I hate you!*"

Unable to bear it, Gay mutters: "We've had it now, Roslyn."

"You sure did—more than *you'll* ever know. But you didn't want it. Nobody does. I pity you all." Looking from one to another and beyond them to imagined others: "You know everything except what it feels like to be alive. You're three dear, sweet dead men."

"*She's crazy!*"

The weird resonance of Guido's cry turns them all to him. His eyes seem peeled back, fanatical, as though he had been seized from within by a pair of jaws which were devouring him as he stands there. His head and hands are shaking, he seems about to fly off the ground at her, and he goes onto his toes and down and up again. "They're all crazy!" Now he moves away from Gay and back again, flinging his words toward Roslyn and beyond her toward the sky. "You try not to believe it. Because you need them. You need them but they're crazy!" Tears spurt out of his eyes onto his cheeks, but his ferocity is undiminished. "You struggle, you build, you try, you turn yourself inside out for them, but nothing's ever enough! It's never a deal, something's always missing. It's gotta be perfect or they put the spurs to you! We ask them too much—and we tell them too little. I know—I got the marks!" He hits his chest with his fist, heaving for breath; the veins are standing out on his neck. Suddenly he looks down at the ground dizzily. He walks away and after a few yards he stops, throwing his head back, trying to catch his breath. She, exhausted, looking at nothing, bends over and seems to crumple, sitting on the ground, weeping quietly. Perce is looking at her through the corner of his eye. Gay walks around the prostrate mare, goes to the truck, and climbs onto the back. Perce goes over to her as though to help her up, but she gets to her feet, the talc caked on her jeans, and walks weakly toward the truck and gets in. Perce comes around and gets behind the wheel beside her. Now Guido returns, staring at the ground as though he had puzzled himself. He hops aboard. The truck starts away.

A blasted look is on Gay's face, as though he had been beaten in a fistfight in a cause he only half-believed. Squinting against the wind, his eyes hover on the high mountains, full of wish, almost expecting the sight of the hundreds, the full herds

clambering into the open, the big horses and the sweet mares that gentled so quickly, the natural singlefooters, the smooth gallopers that just swept the ground under them, hardly touching it. . . .

TWELVE

THE clinking of Guido's wrench is the only sound; all else is silence. He finishes screwing in his number-four spark plug, unclips a wire, lays his wrench on number five, and screws it out. His flashlight tucked under his arm illuminates his hands. He is whistling under his breath, strangely energized, glancing quickly now and then at the others and brimming over with some private hope of his own.

A few yards from him Gay stands staring out at the sky's starry arch, seeing nothing. A sense of mourning flows from his very stance; he has his hands on his hips as though he must support his back. He seems exhausted.

Squatting on his heels, Perce is motionless, smoking. He is ten yards from Gay, and yet he can feel his mood. Off to his left, in the cab of the truck, Roslyn is resting her head against the doorframe, staring out over Perce's head toward a trussed horse lying on its side. As night deepens, only its darker mass is visible, and it never moves. Roslyn closes her eyes and seems to sleep.

Gay calls over to Guido: "How long you gonna be with that?"

"No time at all now." Guido's voice is high and crisp. He scrapes carbon from the plug's electrode and blows out the chips.

Roslyn sees Perce standing up. He walks over to her and stands. In the moonlight his face seems bonier and hard. His voice is close to a whisper, yet loud enough to avoid any air of conspiracy. "I'd turn them loose. If you wanted."

"No, don't fight."

"He got himself up so high he can't get down now." He

looks over toward Gay, who is standing with his back to them. She feels in Perce his impatient love for the older man, and she knows his uncertainty about what to do.

"It doesn't matter, anyway." She looks toward the trussed horse. "It's all a joke—how easy they agree to die! It's like a dream, look, it doesn't even move. Is it sleeping?"

"Might be, sure."

"Couldn't they leave the colt here?"

"Wouldn't stay. Follow the truck right into town. Probably drop on the way in."

He turns and leans against the door, looking with her toward the dark shape of the trussed horse. "I wish I'd met you a long time ago. Save me a lot of broken bones."

She turns to him, then reaches out and touches his arm.

He faces her. "I'd just about gave up—expectin' anything." He comes in closer to her, taking a breath. "I'd cut them loose for you."

They hear Guido's voice and turn quickly, seeing Gay going to him at the engine. Guido hands him the flashlight, which he shines on a spark plug in Guido's hand. Holding it up close to his eyes, Guido passes a feeler gauge between the electrode and the ground pin, then knocks the ground pin to lessen the gap and measures it again. They can hear his voice and his quiet laugh.

Guido: "Buck up, boy. Before you know it you'll be up to your neck in girls again."

Gay is annoyed, wanting to be off as quickly as possible.

But Guido goes on: "I just been thinking . . . I don't know how we got so stupid. The world's full of mountains . . . Colorado, Montana, Canada, even Mexico; and where there's mountains there's got to be horses. Probably we couldn't clean them all out till we're too stiff to walk. Now if we worked awhile, and I'd even sell my house—I don't know what I was keepin' it for anyway—and put everything into a good plane . . . we could get this thing on a business basis."

Gay shifts onto one hip, a deepening disgust and anger rising into his face.

Guido: "Why, we never even watered the horses before we weighed them in! We could put fifty pounds on just these five if we let them drink. We just been foolin' around with it."

Impatiently indicating for him to resume working on the spark plug, Gay hardly moves his lips. "I want to get out of here, come on."

As he screws the spark plug into the engine, Guido's confidence seems to flow. "With a good plane we could fly into Reno from anywhere—check in at the Mapes, have us a time, and off we go again! Boy, we wouldn't need anybody in this world!" He has taken the flashlight, and waits for Gay's reply.

Gay's face is flushed as though he were exerting himself to lift something. At last he bursts out in a pained voice: "Why don't you shut up, Guido?" Guido straightens in shock at the rumble of disgust he hears. "Just shut up, will you?"

But Guido smiles directly into Gay's threatening gaze. "Meet you at the dealer's in the morning; get his winch truck if we're early. Six o'clock, okay?"

Gay's non-reply is his agreement, and Guido moves away along the wing, goes to the cockpit, and climbs in. Gay stands before the propeller. "Okay, give her a twist—switch off!"

For a moment Gay seems not to have heard. His eyes are sightless, inward-looking. Roslyn and Perce can see him standing there.

"Turn her over, boy, huh?"

Gay faces the plane, reaches up, turns the propeller. The engine clicks like a clock being wound. Gay seems to be moving in slow motion, pulling the blade down, then gradually raising his arms and pulling it down again, priming the cylinders.

Perce walks along the length of the truck and Roslyn turns to watch him. He disappears around the back of it. She looks at the plane again.

Guido: "Okay! Switch on!"

Gay positions himself more carefully. The propeller is horizontal. He lays both hands on the blade, swings his right leg across his left, and quickly pulls and hops away as the engine clatters up to a puffing roar. He walks backward along the wing until he clears it. Guido motions from the cockpit for him to watch out for the dog, which is still tied to a stake under the wing. Gay motions for Guido to take off.

The engine's roar increases and the propeller becomes a wheel in the moonlight. The plane bucks forward and back against the grip of the wheel brakes as Guido warms the engine.

In the cockpit Guido is focusing the flashlight on his gauges. Now the engine roars up to its peak.

Roslyn turns quickly, seeing Perce getting in behind the wheel beside her. He starts the truck engine. She looks through the windshield toward Gay, who is now holding the dog's body down as the wing of the plane passes over it. The truck is suddenly in motion as the plane taxis away in the direction of the moon. She involuntarily grabs Perce's arm to stop him, but he now switches on the headlights and swerves the truck toward the trussed horse. Roslyn leans out the window and sees the plane taxiing off into the darkness, and Gay turning from it and finding the truck gone. He swings about, looks toward her, and starts to run. The truck's brakes squeal and it skids to a halt beside the trussed horse; Perce leaps out and runs to it, with an open clasp knife in his hand. He leans over the horse's belly and cuts the rope around its hooves, and it starts scrambling to stand up. He rushes to the tire and cuts the rope; the horse, on its feet, trots away for a few yards and stands stiffly. Perce starts to run after it and shoo it off but he sees Gay bearing down on him and hears his roaring voice. He jumps into the truck, grinds it into gear, and jams the gas pedal to the floor. The wheels spin for an instant and it jerks and roars away.

A wordless command bellows from Gay's furious face. He rushes toward the horse, which now trots, not very fast. The rope is trailing from its neck and he reaches down for it, but the animal's sense of him speeds it into a canter. Gay lunges for the rope and falls, and the horse clatters off into the darkness. He gets to his feet, turns in a circle. The headlights of the truck are impossibly distant now. He runs toward them. Tears are on his cheeks and angry calls come from his throat, but more than anger is his clear frustration, as though above all his hand had been forced from his grip on his life and he had been made smaller.

The truck halts beside another horse. Perce leaps out, cuts it loose, and rushes back into the truck and speeds it away. A wave of guilt passes over Roslyn's face now. She scans the lake bed for a sign of Gay. In her uncertainty she turns to Perce. His mildness has vanished and he seems inspired, a wild, rebellious joy on his face.

* * *

Guido has taxied close to the edge of the lake bed. For a moment he sits slumped on the torn cushions, staring out at nothing, wanting the engine's roar to enter and overwhelm his mind. He cuts the throttle; the plane slows, and he turns it about to face the wind. Far across the lake bed the mountain face gleams in the moonlight as though covered with snow; the white clay stretching away before him is luminescent with a greenish-silvery light that does not brighten the air but clings to the ground like a heavy gas. He has nowhere to go and no reason to move; the threat of total emptiness angers him. He guns the engine and the plane hurries. As he starts to press the stick forward to raise the tail and climb, his eye catches the truck's moving headlights; but he realizes that, oddly, it is not moving toward the sage desert and the homeward direction. Airborne, he flattens the trajectory of the plane, banks sharply, leans out the side of the cockpit a man's height above the earth. A horse is just crossing the headlight beams below—a horse running free. He pushes the stick forward, settling himself to watch the ground coming up beneath him, striving to remember where each horse was tethered, envisioning the crash should he hit one as he comes in to land.

A mile away the headlight beams pick up the stallion's form. Roslyn looks out and as it nears she cries out: "Oh, Perce! I don't know!" He glances at her surprised, perplexed, and brakes the truck.

The trussed stallion, ears cocked to the truck's sound, arches up his head. Perce runs to the tire. The stallion yanks it as he saws the rope. Roslyn runs out of the cab, glancing about guiltily for a sign of Gay. Suddenly the rope parts. The stallion, free, kicks up his rear legs, rushes past them, and turns about. Perce pulls her out of the way and yells wordlessly to scare off the beast. Before the reality of the freed stallion, Roslyn feels an ecstatic, terrified conviction. Almost unaware of her own voice, she cries out: "Go! Go home! Go home!"

Perce runs toward the stallion, which turns and gallops away, his neck rope trailing. Breathless, they watch him for a moment, then run to the truck. Roslyn gets into the cab. Perce halts, scanning the glowing lake bed, calculates the location of the two remaining horses, and hurries into the truck.

From the open cockpit of the taxiing plane Guido methodically keeps turning his eyes across the breadth of the lake bed, swinging the plane in wide arcs. Now two specks of light move very far away. He guns the plane toward them.

The headlights are larger in Gay's eyes. He has changed direction with their every movement, and now, impossibly distant, he still runs mechanically, anesthetized by his impotence. A tacking sound stops him instantly.

Trying to control his wheezing breath, wiping sweat from his eyes, be turns about slowly, listening. The moon is glowing and the lake bed seems bright, but night begins a few inches off the ground. His heart is surging in his chest, a pulse beating in his eyes. Again a shadow moves. He widens his eyes to be sure. He slowly sits down on his heels and makes himself small. A shadow moves again. He senses its direction now; surprisingly, it is not headed for the mountains. He turns toward the center of the lake bed. Gradually his eyes perceive the black forms of the mare and colt far off under the moon. Now he turns back toward the moving form. The tacking sound is closer now.

Silently he rises and moves toward the trussed mare, keeping his mouth wide open to let his breath escape without sound. He sees the colt getting to its feet now and lengthens his steps, keeping his head down. He halts at the sudden jagged sound of the mare's snickering. Off to his left, the stallion's form moves closer to her, and it stands over her trussed form. Gay sees its neck stretching down to her. He is moving again, crouching low, and now he runs. The stallion's head shoots up and it backs and stands, listening. The moon makes a yellow disk of one eye as Gay comes in from the side and grasps its neck rope in both gloved hands. The horse bares its teeth and gouges for his shoulder, and he slips his hands farther down along the rope, murmuring to it, but it suddenly swerves and gallops. Gay wraps the rope around his arm and runs behind, trying to dig in his heels. A quick burst of force yanks him about and he falls. He is being dragged on his side, the talc blinding him. The rope suddenly slackens; he scrambles to his feet and the shoulder of the horse hits the side of his head as it gallops past, and he is pulled to the ground again. He sits up, swinging his boots around in front of him, seeking the clay

with his heels. The stallion coughs and wheels, and for a moment stands facing him where he sits. The noose, he knows, is not tight enough to make it wheeze as it does, and he again wraps the rope around his arm, digging his heels in and preparing in his mind to roll away if it should charge him there. The stallion backs, experimentally it seems, testing his weight on the rope.

Gay starts sidling toward the mare. She is a length away. He reaches her without taking his eyes from the stallion, and feels with his elbow for the shape of her, trying to sense how far he must move to reach her neck rope and the tire. At his touch she shudders; he feels her quarter, and sidles so that she is between him and the stallion, which is restive on its hooves but not pulling hard any more. Gay gets his heels under him and creeps sideways toward the mare's neck. Now he has her neck rope under his arm. He becomes still. He will have to unwrap the rope to tie it to the mare's noose.

The stallion eyes him, gasping. Gay murmurs to him across the mare's neck: "Whoa now, whoa now, whoa now . . ." He begins to unwrap his arm, always keeping both hands around the rope. The stallion's head rises, and Gay stops moving. He knows the movement of the rope is vibrating into the stallion's body and can set him going again. After a moment, he again moves his arm to uncoil the rope. The mare suddenly blows out a high snicker, and the stallion flings its head into the air; Gay is yanked toward him over the mare's body. He goes with the force and lets it carry him to his feet; he leaps for the stallion's neck to pull the noose tight with both hands and the animal gallops, kicking out its hind legs, but Gay can feel it trembling and its power weakening. He hangs from the noose, pulling it down with all his force, the backs of his thighs being pounded by the horse's knees.

The stallion halts. Gay hangs his full weight from the tightening noose. The stallion's neck lowers and his shaking knees start to buckle. Gay yanks again, a short scream escaping his throat as a broken, thin cry vibrates in the stallion's head. Gay hears an engine. He yanks again, raising his feet off the ground, pulling the stallion's head lower. The headlight beams hit his face and burn his eyes. He hears the brakes squealing and the doors opening.

On both Roslyn's and Perce's faces is a look of near awe. The stallion is motionless, groaning against the asphyxiating noose. And yet between it and Gay hanging from its neck there is a strange relation, an aura of understanding; it is as though the vanquished beast belonged to Gay now, however this came to be, and that it knew this even as it would not come to earth.

Perce picks up the rope end and lashes it to the truck bumper. "Okay, let him go!"

Gay springs away from the horse, which tucks in its head and walks slowly and halts.

Swaying on his feet, Gay moves to the truck and lies over the hood, his arms outstretched.

He slowly opens his cramped hands. Roslyn does not approach him. She watches him from her distance, as Perce does, and she seems to soften under the power of his struggle. A wonder is rising in her eyes. She takes a step toward him, but Perce reaches out quickly and stops her. She sees fear in Perce's face, and she becomes afraid not so much of Gay's violence as of having done a thing which now she cannot comprehend.

The plane engine is heard, and in a moment it comes to a halt nearby. The engine is cut; Guido leaps out and runs toward Gay. Seeing him heaving for breath and the stallion tied, he laughs toward Perce and bends over Gay to give him a quick hug.

"You held him! Good boy! We'll get them all back tomorrow! Get your wind now, just get your wind now. . . ." He warmly pats Gay's back.

Gay is still sucking air, his trunk bent over the truck hood, his eyes staring at the stallion. Guido grips his shoulder. "Don't you worry, boy—we ain't through here. Not by a long shot! We're only starting! I'll go up to Thighbone Mountain with you—hear? There's five thousand dollars up there, but we gotta work at it. We'll *horseback* in up there! And there's more, there's more—but we gotta work at it! 'Cause we don't need nobody in this world, Gay—and I guess you know it now, don't you?" Toward Roslyn: "To hell with them all!"

Gay, oblivious of Guido, is staring at the mustang, his cheek pressed against the truck hood. His eyes seem to be peering toward a far point, and about him is a stillness, as though he

were alone here. He straightens, slipping a hand into his pocket.

Guido reaches to him: "Come on, I'll fly you back. They can take the—" He breaks off, seeing a clasp knife opening in Gay's hand. When he looks again into his face he sees tears in his eyes, and he is bewildered and, for the moment, silent.

Gay walks straight at him as though he did not see him, and Guido, stepping out of his path, asks: "What are—?" But Gay has bent to the rope at the bumper and is cutting it, his hand shaking. Guido grabs at his hand and holds it, and understands enough to raise a panic in his eyes as he stands pressed close to his friend. Gay's caked lips move; in a cracked whisper, looking into Guido's face but blind to him: "It's all finished."

"What the hell'd you catch him for?"

"Just . . . done it. Don't like nobody makin' up my mind for me, that's all."

A tremor seems to go through his body, and his brows tense together as though he would weep in anger. He weakly presses Guido to move aside, but Guido holds his wrist.

"I'll go with you to Thighbone!"

Gay shakes his head. He looks beyond Guido to the darkened hills, and anger hardens his face and straightens him. "God damn them all! They changed it. Changed it all around. They smeared it all over with blood, turned it into shit and money just like everything else. You know that. I know that. It's just ropin' a dream now." He slips his wrist out of Guido's grasp. "Find some other way to know you're alive . . . if they got another way, any more." He turns to the rope and leans his weight on the knife; the rope, cut, falls to the ground.

For a moment, the stallion does not move. With the pressure off the noose it stretches its neck and, taking a step to the side, almost stumbles to the ground, rights itself, and walks. Then it halts, stands unsteadily, and goes away. Gay walks over to the mare and cuts her hoof ropes and then the rope to the tire; she weightily clambers up and trots away, the foal following with its nose in her flying tail.

The four stand listening to the fading sound of the hooves. Gay, closing his knife and slipping it into his pocket, walks from Guido, looking at no one, absorbed in himself.

Their eyes follow him as he goes by and gets into the truck behind the wheel, exhausted, silent. For a moment he stares ahead through the windshield. Roslyn is on the opposite side of the truck now, looking across the empty seat at him. In this moment it is unknown what he will do, and she does not move. He turns to her, his loneliness in his eyes. "Drive you back . . . if you want."

Hesitant and afraid of him still, she gets into the seat, but not close to him. Her open stare is full of his pain and his loss.

Perce has come up to her window. "I'm pleased to have met you, Roslyn."

Roslyn: "Don't hurt yourself any more, will you?"

He thanks her with his eyes. "If you ever feel like droppin' a card, my address is just Black River . . . California."

Gay starts the engine and turns to Guido, who is on his side of the truck. "See you around. Give you a call in a couple days."

Guido, his eyes sharpened with resentment, laughs. "Where'll you be? Some gas station, polishing windshields?"

"You got me there, Pilot." Gay turns forward and starts the truck rolling.

Guido jumps onto the running board, laughing and yelling at him: "Or making change in the supermarket!"

Guido jumps off, and makes a megaphone of his hands, furiously calling: "Try the laundromat—they might need a fella to load the machines!"

But the truck is moving away, and his need is wide; he cries out, his fist in the air: "Gay! Where you goin'?"

He has come to a halt, angry and lost. Perce stands there, tears flowing into his eyes.

Gay drives in silence, exhausted. Roslyn is still a distance from him on the seat. Now she turns to him, not knowing his feeling. They seem like strangers for a moment.

"I'll leave tomorrow." She is asking, but he remains silent. "Okay?" He drives on. "You'll never believe it, but I didn't mean to harm you. . . . I honor you. You're a brave man."

He is silent.

"You don't like me any more. Do you?"

Now she turns forward. Her voice wavers. Everything seems to be moving away from her.

"But you know something? For a minute, when those horses galloped away, it was almost like I gave them back their life. And all of a sudden I got a feeling—it's crazy!—I suddenly thought, 'He must love me, or how would I dare do this?' Because I always just ran away when I couldn't stand it. Gay—for a minute you made me not afraid. And it was like my life flew into my body. For the first time."

He sees the dog in the headlight beams, tied to one of the stakes, and halts the truck.

She opens her door, but turns back to him as though she cannot leave. And suddenly she cries out, desperately: "Oh, Gay, what is there? Do you know? What is there that stays?"

He turns to her for the first time. There are tears in his eyes. He draws her to him and kisses her. She is weeping with joy, trying to see through his eyes into him.

Gay: "God knows. Everything I ever see was comin' or goin' away. Same as you. Maybe the only thing is . . . the knowin'. 'Cause I know you now, Roslyn, I do know you. Maybe that's all the peace there is or can be. I never bothered to battle a woman before. And it was peaceful, but a lot like huggin' the air. This time, I thought I'd lay my hand on the air again—but it feels like I touched the whole world. I bless you, girl."

She flies to his face, kissing him passionately. The dog barks outside. She runs out of the cab to it, and it greets her joyfully. She unties it and claps her hands to make it follow. The dog leaps onto the truck bed and she reenters the cab, her face infused with an overflowing love. He starts the truck and they drive. Suddenly, with the quick rapture of her vision: "If . . . if we weren't afraid! Gay? And there could be a child. And we could make it brave. One person in the world who would be brave from the beginning! I was scared to last night. But I'm not so much now. Are you?"

He clasps her close to his hip. He drives. The love between them is viable, holding them a little above the earth. The headlights pick up clumps of sage now, and the ride is bumpy.

Roslyn: "How do you find your way back in the dark?"

Gay nods, indicating the sky before them: "Just head for

that big star straight on. The highway's under it; take us right home."

She raises her eyes to the star through the streaks and dust of the windshield. The sound of Guido's plane roars in and away, invisible overhead. The truck's headlights gradually disappear, and with them all sound. Now there is only the sky full of stars, and absolute silence.

CHRONOLOGY

NOTE ON THE TEXTS

NOTES

Chronology

1915 Born Arthur Asher Miller on October 17 in New York City, the second child of Isadore and Gittel ("Gussie") Barnett Miller. (Father emigrated at the age of six from Eastern Europe and joined his parents and six siblings in New York City, where his father Shmuel owned a clothing business on the Lower East Side. As a young man he established his own highly successful business, the Miltex Coat and Suit Company, in Manhattan's garment district. Mother, born in the United States to immigrant parents, is a former schoolteacher. Their first child, Kermit, was born three years before Miller.) Family lives in a sixth-floor apartment at 45 West 110th Street, with a view of Central Park.

1916–28 At age six Miller begins attending P.S. 24 on West 111th Street. Sister Joan is born in 1922. Miller celebrates his bar mitzvah in 1928.

1929 Stock market crash devastates family finances and threatens the solvency of Miltex. Family moves to Gravesend in Brooklyn, living in a small house at 1350 Third Street where Miller shares a bedroom with his recently widowed maternal grandfather. Attends James Madison High School on Bedford Avenue.

1930–32 Brother Kermit begins attending New York University in the fall of 1930, while Miller transfers to Abraham Lincoln High School on Ocean Parkway. Works for Miltex in the summer of 1931, carrying samples for salesmen as they make their rounds. In the fall Kermit quits NYU to work full-time for Miltex. Miller makes deliveries for a local bakery before school, then takes new job driving a delivery truck for an auto-supply store.

1933–34 Graduates high school in June 1933. After working at Miltex in the summer, he finds a job paying $15 a week as stock clerk at the Chadick-Delameter auto-parts warehouse at 10th Avenue and West 63rd Street in Manhattan. Reads *Crime and Punishment* during his commute from Brooklyn. Applies unsuccessfully to the University of

Michigan. Enrolls in classes in history and chemistry at City College of New York's night school but stops attending after two weeks. Writes to the University of Michigan and asks that his application be reconsidered and is accepted on a probationary basis provided he prove his ability to pay tuition, room, and board. Matriculates at University of Michigan in Ann Arbor in fall 1934. Rooms with fellow New Yorker Charles Bleich in a private home.

1935 Works as reporter on school newspaper, the *Michigan Daily*; does well enough in his courses that the university rescinds his probationary status and offers him a loan to help cover expenses. Hitchhikes home for summer break. In the fall lives in rooming house off-campus. Takes creative writing course and continues to write for *Michigan Daily*, covering organizing efforts of the United Auto Workers and interviewing UAW leader Walter Reuther.

1936 Meets first-year student Mary Grace Slattery and becomes romantically involved with her. In six days writes his first play, *No Villain*, which wins $250 Hopwood Award from the university. Writes "In Memoriam," short story about a salesman; attempts to adapt it for the stage but abandons the effort. Miltex closes in the summer. Miller revises *No Villain* and submits new version, entitled *They Too Arise*, to a student playwriting contest sponsored by the Theatre Guild. Attends performance on Broadway of Ibsen's *A Doll's House* during his winter break and is deeply impressed.

1937 Enrolls in playwriting seminar with Professor Kenneth Rowe. Awarded $1,250 scholarship when *They Too Arise* wins Theatre Guild competition; the play is staged on campus and then in Detroit. Miller writes *Honors at Dawn*, which wins the Hopwood Award. Meets Norman Rosten, who has come to the university on a Theatre Guild scholarship to study with Kenneth Rowe. Interviews prisoners at nearby Jackson State Penitentiary and uses the material as the basis of play eventually entitled *The Great Disobedience*.

1938 Completes *The Great Disobedience* in March. Graduates from University of Michigan in June and returns to New York City, living in the family home in Brooklyn. Writes new version of *They Too Arise* entitled *The Grass Still Grows*, which after an enthusiastic response at the literary

agency Leland Hayward and Company is sent to Broadway producers. Miller is hired by the Federal Theatre and Writers Project and moves into a studio apartment on East 74th Street in Manhattan, but is then let go when the Project is forced to cut back.

1939 Writes tragedy about the Aztecs' encounter with Cortez called "The Montezuma Play," "The Children of the Sun," and ultimately *The Golden Years.* Collaborates with Norman Rosten on one-act play *Listen, My Children* and *You're Next!*, satire of the House Committee on Un-American Activities, which had investigated the Federal Theatre Project. Radio play *William Ireland's Confession* is performed on CBS on October 19.

1940 Miller marries Mary Slattery in a Catholic ceremony in her hometown in Ohio on August 5; tells parents about the marriage after the fact. The couple return to New York and move into a Brooklyn Heights apartment. In September, Miller sails alone to South America on a two-week trip to research *The Half-Bridge*, a play set on a merchant ship.

1941 Starts writing novel "The Man Who Had All the Luck" and receives modest advance from Atlantic Monthly Press; when he submits a partial manuscript, it is rejected by the publisher. Travels alone to North Carolina and sketches out ideas and stories for plays.

1942–43 Begins working the night shift at the Brooklyn Navy Yard. Finishes "The Man Who Had All the Luck" and sends it to Doubleday, Doran, which rejects it. Writes radio plays that are aired on the NBC Dupont Cavalcade of America. Quits job at Brooklyn Navy Yard when he is hired to write *The Story of G.I. Joe*, film adaptation of Ernie Pyle's *Here Is Your War.*

1944 Interviews soldiers at army training camps for *The Story of G.I. Joe* but is fired before script is completed and receives no writing credit on the film; uses material in a book of reportage, *Situation Normal . . .* , published by Harper. Adapts "The Man Who Had All the Luck" into a play and an early version is included in anthology *Cross-Section: A Collection of New American Writing.* Daughter Jane born September 7. *The Man Who Had All the Luck*, directed by Joseph Fields, opens at the Forrest Theatre on

November 23 to unfavorable reviews and closes after four performances.

1945 One-act play *That They May Win* is included in anthology *Best One-Act Plays of 1944*. Writes *Focus*, novel about anti-Semitism, which is published by Reynal & Hitchcock and becomes a commercial success.

1946 Completes play *All My Sons*. After Leland Hayward Agency is bought out by MCA, Miller is assigned to Katherine Brown, who will represent him for the next four decades. Harold Clurman, formerly of the Group Theatre, reads *All My Sons* and agrees to produce it, with Elia Kazan directing.

1947 After trial runs in New Haven and Boston, *All My Sons* opens on Broadway on January 29 and runs for 328 performances; book version is published by Reynal & Hitchcock. Miller buys farmhouse in Roxbury, Connecticut. Works for one week in a Queens factory assembling boxes as "a moral act of solidarity with those who had failed in life." *All My Sons* is named best new play of the 1946–47 season by the New York Drama Critics Circle; Miller and Kazan receive Antoinette Perry ("Tony") Awards for their work on the play. Son Robert is born on May 31. Moves in June to converted stable house at 31 Grace Court in Brooklyn Heights, living in upper floors and renting out two apartments in the building. Publishes essay in *The New York Times* arguing for a subsidized theater that "would lay upon all work and works the standards of art, and not primarily the standards of business men." Declines offer to write the screenplay for Alfred Hitchcock's *Rope*. Works on plays "Plenty Good Times" and *Death of a Salesman*. Max Sorensen, leader of the Catholic War Veterans, denounces *All My Sons* as Communist "propaganda," and the War Department prevents it from being staged in the American-occupied Germany. *All My Sons* is performed in the Netherlands and Poland.

1948 Miller travels to Europe for the first time, visiting Italy, Greece, and France. *Focus* is banned by the principal of DeWitt Clinton High School in New York on grounds that it is offensive to Roman Catholics. Film version of *All My Sons*, directed by Irving Reis and starring Edward G. Robinson and Burt Lancaster, is released. Dramatic sequence written by Miller is read at American Salute to

the Jewish State rally at the Polo Grounds in New York City. *All My Sons* is produced in London and is warmly received, with one critic calling it "the best serious play that America has sent us for some time." Miller completes *Death of a Salesman* and Kazan agrees to direct it. Revises play based on suggestions by Kazan, but does not use revised version after producer Kermit Bloomgarden expresses strong preference for original version. *All My Sons* is staged in Moscow and is not well received.

1949 After successful trial run in Philadelphia, *Death of a Salesman* opens on Broadway on February 10 and runs for 742 performances. Miller publishes essay "Tragedy and the Common Man" in *The New York Times* in February and another essay about tragedy and *Death of a Salesman* in the *New York Herald-Tribune* the following month. Attends Cultural and Scientific Conference for World Peace in New York City, a gathering criticized by anti-Communist liberals who claim it is too sympathetic to Communism, and chairs panel on the arts whose members include Dmitri Shostakovich, Aaron Copland, and Clifford Odets. *Death of a Salesman* is named best new play of the 1948–49 season by the New York Drama Critics Circle and is awarded Pulitzer Prize, Donaldson Award, and Antoinette Perry Award; London staging is met with an enthusiastic reception. Continues working on "Plenty Good Times"; "The Hook," a screenplay about union corruption on the Brooklyn waterfront; and an adaptation of Ibsen's *An Enemy of the People*, using a literal translation provided by Lars Nordenson, a Swedish businessman who is financing the production. *Death of a Salesman* is published in book form in America and England and becomes first play offered as a selection of the Book of the Month Club.

1950–51 *Death of a Salesman* tours the U.S. and is staged in Vienna, Copenhagen, Düsseldorf, and other European cities. Short story "It Takes a Thief," first published in *Collier's* three years earlier, is adapted for television and broadcast on NBC Cameo Theatre. Adaptation of *An Enemy of the People* opens on Broadway on December 28, 1950, and runs for 36 performances. Travels with Kazan to Los Angeles to seek studio backing for "The Hook." Meets actress Marilyn Monroe. Columbia Pictures expresses

interest in "The Hook," but Miller withdraws screenplay after studio executive Harry Cohn asks him to revise script along anti-Communist lines. Writes to Monroe, and they begin corresponding. Buys house at 155 Willow Street in Brooklyn Heights and moves family there. Reads passages from "The Third Play," a work-in-progress with origins in "Plenty Good Times," to friends. Film of *Death of a Salesman*, directed by Laslo Benedek and starring Frederic March, is released.

1952 Miller's relations with Kazan deteriorate after Kazan testifies before the House Committee on Un-American Activities on April 10 and names associates he knew to be members of the Communist Party. Miller begins researching and writing play about 17th-century Salem witch trials and works on it throughout the summer. Writes several pages of dialogue based on his job at the auto-parts warehouse that will later be developed into *A Memory of Two Mondays.*

1953–54 *The Crucible* opens on Broadway on January 22, 1953, to mixed reviews and runs for 197 performances; it is also staged in London, and in Paris in Michel Aymé's French adaptation, *Les Sorcières de Salem*, starring Yves Montand and Simone Signoret. When he is invited to Brussels for the Belgian premiere of the play, Miller's passport application is rejected by the State Department "under regulations denying passports to people believed to be supporting the Communist movement."

1955 Miller becomes romantically involved with Marilyn Monroe. Writes one-act version of *A View from the Bridge*, drawing on Brooklyn waterfront research for "The Hook." Works on screenplay for film about juvenile gangs in Brooklyn to be made in cooperation with the city government. After a summer tryout on Cape Cod and trial runs in New Haven and Boston, *A View from the Bridge: Two One-Act Plays* (*Bridge* and *A Memory of Two Mondays*) opens on Broadway on September 29 and runs for 149 performances. Miller separates from wife in October and moves into the Chelsea Hotel in Manhattan. City authorities cancel the gang film project after Miller is denounced as "a veteran backer of Communist causes" by the *New York World-Telegram.*

1956 Settles with wife on terms of divorce in February, and then spends six weeks near Reno to establish residency for a Nevada divorce. Works on "The Third Play" as well as a two-act version of *A View from the Bridge* and the introduction to his *Collected Plays.* Visits Los Angeles to see Monroe, who is filming *Bus Stop.* Granted divorce in June. Receives honorary Doctorate of Humane Letters from the University of Michigan. Appears before House Committee on Un-American Activities on June 21 in hearing ostensibly related to his passport application. In his testimony Miller admits to having attended meetings with Communist writers in 1947, but he refuses to identify others at these meetings and denies ever having submitted himself to "Communist discipline." Marries Marilyn Monroe in civil ceremony in White Plains, New York, on June 29 and in a Jewish ceremony in Katonah on July 1. Miller is cited for contempt by Congress on July 10. Travels to England with Monroe for honeymoon, where she films *The Prince and the Showgirl* with Laurence Olivier. Returns briefly to New York and writes short story "The Misfits, or Chicken Feed: The Last Frontier of the Quixotic Cowboy." Goes back to London for premiere in October of expanded *A View from the Bridge*, directed by Peter Brook. (Production is staged under the aegis of a private club after the censor refuses to license public performances because of the play's references to homosexuality.)

1957 Miller is convicted of contempt of Congress in federal district court in Washington, D.C., on May 31 after a six-day trial and is sentenced on July 19 to one-month suspended jail term and a $500 fine. Moves with Monroe from 2 Sutton Place to apartment on East 57th Street; also spends time at rented house in Amagansett, Long Island. Monroe has miscarriage in early August. *Arthur Miller's Collected Plays* published. *Les Sorcières de Salem*, film adaptation of *The Crucible* starring Yves Montand and Simone Signoret and with a screenplay by Jean-Paul Sartre, is released in France. *Death of a Salesman* is staged in Moscow. Miller begins adapting "The Misfits" into a screenplay intended as a vehicle for Monroe.

1958 Buys farm at 323 Tophet Road in Roxbury. Contacts Frank Lloyd Wright to design new house on the site but declines Wright's proposed plan and instead renovates existing

18th-century farmhouse; buys property adjoining the farm. Completes screenplay of *The Misfits.* Named a member of the National Institute of Arts and Letters. U.S. Court of Appeals for the District of Columbia overturns Miller's conviction for contempt of Congress in August. Miller continues work on "The Third Play" and writes essay "My Wife Marilyn" for *Life* magazine. Monroe suffers another miscarriage.

1959–60 Miller is awarded Gold Medal for Drama from the National Institute of Arts and Letters. Sends completed screenplay of *The Misfits* to John Huston, who agrees to direct the film. Travels with Monroe to Los Angeles, where she is filming *Let's Make Love.* Miller goes to Ireland to work with John Huston on *The Misfits*, but soon returns to California at Monroe's request. Works on rewrites of the *Let's Make Love* script. Monroe has an affair with co-star Yves Montand; Miller returns to Connecticut. They agree to divorce but defer public announcement of their breakup and travel to Reno, Nevada, in July 1960 for location shooting for *The Misfits.* Miller meets Ingeborg (Inge) Morath, an Austrian-born photographer sent by the Magnum agency to document the production. In late August, Miller takes Monroe, who is in a fragile mental state and dependent on barbiturates, to Los Angeles to be hospitalized. Returns to New York and moves out of the 57th Street apartment; divorce plans are announced on November 11.

1961 Monroe is granted divorce in Juarez, Mexico, on January 24. Novelization of *The Misfits* by Miller is published shortly before the film is released on February 1. Mother dies on March 6. Miller discovers that *Death of a Salesman* has been filmed in the Soviet Union without his permission. *Uno Sguardo del Ponte*, opera of *A View from the Bridge* by Renzo Rossellini, premieres in Rome and is staged in several European cities; Robert Ward's opera of *The Crucible* is staged in the fall and wins a Pulitzer Prize the following year. Short story "I Don't Need You Anymore" is included in *Prize Stories 1961: The O. Henry Awards.* Filming begins in Brooklyn and Paris for screen version of *A View from the Bridge*, directed by Sidney Lumet with screenplay by Norman Rosten.

1962 One-hour television adaptation of *Focus* is broadcast on NBC. Film of *A View from the Bridge* released in the U.S. in late January. Miller marries Inge Morath in Connecticut on February 17 and the couple depart for honeymoon in Europe. New production of *The Crucible* with essayistic passages read from the stage is presented in Boston. Marilyn Monroe dies from an overdose of barbiturates on August 5. Miller continues working on "The Third Play," now entitled *After the Fall.* Daughter Rebecca Augusta born September 15. (A son, Daniel, is later born with Down Syndrome and is raised in an institution for the mentally disabled.)

1963 As *After the Fall* is planned for production in the inaugural season of the Lincoln Center Repertory Theater, Miller works with director Elia Kazan for the first time since the early 1950s. Writes children's book *Jane's Blanket* for daughter Jane. Joins 47 other playwrights in refusing to allow their plays to be performed in South African theaters enforcing apartheid. *Death of a Salesman* staged as part of the inaugural season of the Guthrie Theater in Minneapolis.

1964 *After the Fall*, starring Jason Robards, premieres on January 23 and runs for 208 performances; among those attending the gala opening are Lady Bird Johnson, Adlai Stevenson, and Ralph Bunche. The play attracts controversy because of its presumed autobiographical elements, particularly concerning Miller's marriage to Monroe. Miller travels to Europe with Morath in February. Writes for the *New York Herald-Tribune* about trial in Frankfurt of former SS men who had served at Auschwitz. Returns home and completes draft of play *Incident at Vichy* in three weeks. Film rights for *After the Fall* bought by Carlo Ponti, Ira Steiner, and MGM; Miller works on script but then withdraws from the project because of differences with producers about the screenplay and casting. Makes cuts in *After the Fall* seven months into its run. Directed by Harold Clurman for the Lincoln Center Repertory Company, *Incident at Vichy* premieres on December 3 and runs for 32 performances.

1965 Miller travels to the Soviet Union and Poland. Elected president of PEN International at its annual conference

and serves four years in the position. Participates in demonstrations against the Vietnam War and antiwar teach-in at the University of Michigan, and refuses invitation from President Johnson to attend signing of the federal Arts and Humanities Act because "the occasion is so darkened by the Vietnam tragedy that I could not join it with clear conscience" (will maintain his antiwar activism for the duration of the conflict).

1966–67 While in England for production of *Incident at Vichy*, Miller falls ill with hepatitis and is hospitalized for two weeks. Television version of *Death of a Salesman* is broadcast on CBS on May 8, 1966, with Lee J. Cobb and Mildred Dunnock reprising their roles from the original Broadway production; adaptation of *An Enemy of the People* is broadcast by National Educational Television. Publishes story collection *I Don't Need You Anymore*. Travels to Abidjan, Ivory Coast, for PEN International conference in July 1967.

1968 *The Price* opens on Broadway on February 7 and runs for 429 performances. Harold Clurman publishes essay "The Merits of Mr. Miller" in *The New York Times* in response to negative assessment of Miller's career by critic Alfred Bermel. Campaigns for Democratic presidential candidate Eugene McCarthy and attends Democratic Party convention in Chicago as delegate from Roxbury. Travels to the Soviet Union and visits Czechoslovakia after Soviet invasion. *The Price* is staged in Tel Aviv.

1969 London production of *The Price* opens in March. Miller refuses to have his work published in Greece as a protest against the Greek military regime. One-act play *The Reason Why* filmed for television at Miller's Roxbury farm. Signs letter condemning the expulsion of Alexander Solzhenitsyn from the Soviet Writers' Union. *In Russia*, the first of several travel books illustrated with photographs by Morath, is published.

1970–71 Miller receives Creative Arts Award from Brandeis University. Russian television production of *The Price* is canceled and Miller's works are banned in the Soviet Union. American television productions of *A Memory of Two Mondays* and *The Price* are broadcast in February 1971.

1972–74 Miller is a delegate to the Democratic National Convention in Miami. After trial run in Washington, *The Creation of the World and Other Business*, comic adaptation of the Book of Genesis, opens in New York on November 30, 1972, and closes after 20 performances. Miller serves as writer-in-residence at University of Michigan. Adapts *The Creation of the World and Other Business* into a musical, *Up from Paradise*, which he directs and plays the onstage role of narrator in a production at the University of Michigan. Writes editorial of support for Soviet physicist Andrei Sakharov's six-day hunger strike in 1974 and criticizes the Nixon administration's silence about Sakharov and other dissidents as a "message . . . that the United States is a moral nullity." Becomes active supporter of Peter Reilly, a teenager from Canaan, Connecticut, who had been convicted of manslaughter in the killing of his mother; believing that Reilly had been coerced into confessing, Miller raises money for Reilly's legal fees and eventually hires a detective to investigate the case. Television version of *After the Fall*, starring Christopher Plummer, is broadcast on NBC on December 10, 1974.

1975–76 *Death of a Salesman*, starring George C. Scott, Teresa Wright, and Harvey Keitel, is revived on Broadway in June 1975 and runs for 71 performances. Persuades *The New York Times* to publish a series of articles about the Peter Reilly case. Appears before Senate subcommittee in November to advocate American pressure on governments that violate human rights and the freedom to publish, emphasizing the situation in Czechoslovakia. Peter Reilly is granted a new trial on March 26, 1976, and the charges against him are dismissed in November (he is fully exonerated in 1977).

1977 *The Archbishop's Ceiling* has world premiere on April 23 at the Kennedy Center in Washington; the play's scheduled New York run is canceled by its producers. *Up from Paradise* is also staged at the Kennedy Center. *In the Country*, with photographs by Morath, is published.

1978 Miller's version of *An Enemy of the People* is filmed, directed by George Schaefer and starring Steve McQueen, but film never receives wide release. Miller speaks in front of Soviet mission in New York protesting the trials of

dissidents Alexander Ginzburg and Anatoli Shcharansky. Visits China with Morath in November. *The Theatre Essays of Arthur Miller* is published. Hour-long comedy *Fame* is broadcast on NBC on November 30.

1979 *Chinese Encounters*, with photographs by Morath, is published. *The Price* is revived in New York in a successful off-Broadway run, then moves to Broadway; it is also staged at the Spoleto Festival USA in Charleston. Miller accepts offer to write television adaptation of *Playing for Time*, a memoir by Fania Fenelon, who had been forced to play in an orchestra of female prisoners at Auschwitz, and defends controversial casting of Vanessa Redgrave, a supporter of the Palestine Liberation Organization, in the lead role. *Arthur Miller on Home Ground*, documentary by Harry Rasky, is released in November.

1980 Version of *The American Clock* premieres at the Spoleto USA festival. After Miller extensively revises the play, the London production by the National Theatre receives Olivier Award for the season's best new play, but the Broadway production, with his sister Joan playing Rose Baum, closes after 12 performances in November. *Playing for Time* is broadcast on CBS on September 30. Miller is hospitalized in December after breaking his leg.

1981 Attends inauguration of French president François Mitterrand. Second volume of *Collected Plays* is published. First New York performance of *Up From Paradise* is staged at the Whitney Museum. Two-act version of *A View from the Bridge* is revived at the Long Wharf Theater in New Haven.

1982 Monologue *I Think About You a Great Deal*, written as a tribute to imprisoned Czech playwright Vaclav Havel, whom Miller had met in the 1960s, is performed at the International Theatre Festival in Avignon, France. Program of two one-act plays, *Elegy for a Lady* and *Some Kind of Love Story*, runs for six weeks at the Long Wharf.

1983 First Broadway production of the two-act *A View from the Bridge* opens on February 3 and runs for 149 performances. Miller agrees to direct a production of *Death of a Salesman* in Beijing and visits China with Morath from March to May; while they are away, a fire at their Roxbury house destroys many of his papers and possessions.

1984 Receives honorary doctorate from the University of Hartford. Broadway revival of *Death of a Salesman* starring Dustin Hoffman is well received and runs for 185 performances. *Salesman in Beijing* published in June. *After the Fall* is revived in New York in October. Miller threatens legal action against avant-garde troupe The Wooster Group for performing a segment of *The Crucible* without permission in their production *L.S.D.*; the troupe closes the play. Receives Kennedy Center Honors for lifetime achievement in the arts.

1985 Under the aegis of PEN, travels with British playwright Harold Pinter to Istanbul for five days in March to conduct inquiries into human-rights abuses and censorship in Turkey. Film of *Death of a Salesman*, starring Dustin Hoffman and directed by Volker Schlöndorff, is screened at the Venice Film Festival in September and is broadcast on CBS; *Private Conversations*, Christian Blackwood's documentary about the making of the film, is shown at the New York Film Festival. *The Archbishop's Ceiling* premieres in England. Miller visits the U.S.S.R. to meet with Soviet writers.

1986 Stage adaptation of *Playing for Time* premieres at theater festival in Edinburgh. Miller travels to the U.S.S.R. in October for a conference in Kyrgyzstan and meets Soviet leader Mikhail Gorbachev at the Kremlin.

1987–88 *All My Sons* is broadcast on the Public Broadcasting System's American Playhouse. *Danger: Memory!*, program of the one-act plays *Clara* and *I Can't Remember Anything*, opens at Lincoln Center in New York. London revival of the two-act *A View from the Bridge* runs for six months. *The Golden Years* is broadcast by the BBC as a radio play. Autobiography *Timebends* is published. *The American Clock* is revived for a run at the Williamstown Theater Festival.

1989 Miller's original screenplay *Everybody Wins* enters production, directed by Karel Reisz and starring Nick Nolte and Debra Winger. Arthur Miller Centre for American Studies is established at the University of East Anglia, under the directorship of Christopher Bigsby. *The Crucible* is revived at the Long Wharf in New Haven.

1990 *Everybody Wins* is released. Miller travels to Prague for Czech productions of *The Archbishop's Ceiling* and *The*

Crucible. The Archbishop's Ceiling is performed for the first time in New York. *After the Fall* is revived in London at the Royal National Theatre. Miller travels to South Africa to interview Nelson Mandela for the BBC.

1991 *Clara* is broadcast on the Arts & Entertainment network. *The Ride Down Mt. Morgan* premieres in London in the fall. *The Crucible* is staged in New York as the inaugural offering of the National Actors Theater.

1992 *The Price* is revived on Broadway and runs for 46 performances. One-act version of *The Last Yankee* staged in East Hampton, N.Y. Miller works on "Gellburg," play that will eventually be staged as *Broken Glass.* Directs production of *Death of a Salesman* in Stockholm.

1993 Full-length version of *The Last Yankee* premieres in New York and a production is mounted in London. *The American Clock* is broadcast on the TNT network. Miller receives National Medal of Arts.

1994 *Broken Glass* premieres at the Long Wharf in New Haven in March, starring Ron Silver (soon replaced by David Dukes), Amy Irving, and Ron Rifkin, with Miller revising the play during the production in preparation for its April 24 opening on Broadway; play earns Tony Award nomination for best play, and runs for 73 performances. Miller continues to work on the play for its London staging, and once again wins an Olivier Award for the best new play of the season. With Peter Reilly, becomes involved in the case of Richard Lapointe, a brain-damaged Connecticut man sentenced to life after confessing to the rape and murder of an 88-year-old woman. Oxford University names Miller to a one-year appointment as Professor of Contemporary Theatre.

1995 One-act *The Ryan Interview* is staged in May in New York. Film version of *The Crucible*, with screenplay by Miller, directed by Nicholas Hytner, and starring Daniel Day-Lewis and Winona Ryder, begins shooting; son Robert is one of the producers and daughter Rebecca is the production's still photographer. PEN American Center organizes tribute to Miller on the occasion of his 80th birthday. *Homely Girl: A Life*, collection of three short stories, is published by Viking.

1996 *The Ride Down Mt. Morgan* has its American premiere at the Williamstown Theatre Festival. *Broken Glass* is broadcast on PBS's Masterpiece Theater on October 20, directed by David Thacker; Thacker's revival of *Death of a Salesman* is mounted at the Royal National Theatre. Film version of *The Crucible* is released in November, and Miller's screenplay is published by Penguin. Daughter Rebecca and Daniel Day-Lewis are married.

1997 Screenplay of *The Crucible* receives Academy Award nomination. Roundabout Theater Company revives *All My Sons* in New York, in a production that soon moves to Broadway. Signature Theater Company in New York begins season-long Miller retrospective, staging revivals of *The Last Yankee* and *The American Clock.*

1998 Miller receives Berlin Prize fellowship by the American Academy in Berlin. *Mr. Peters' Connections* premieres as part of the Signature Theater's retrospective. Revised version of *The Ride Down Mt. Morgan*, starring Patrick Stewart, is staged in New York at the Public Theater.

1999 *Death of a Salesman*, starring Brian Dennehy and Elizabeth Franz, is revived on Broadway, runs for 274 performances, and wins four Tony Awards; Miller also receives a lifetime achievement award. William Bolcom's opera of *A View from the Bridge*, with libretto by Miller and Arnold Weinstein, is performed by the Lyric Opera of Chicago in October. *The Price* is revived on Broadway in November and runs for 128 performances.

2000 *The Ride Down Mt. Morgan* is staged on Broadway, with Patrick Stewart reprising his role in the Public Theater production, and runs for 121 performances. In Los Angeles, *The Man Who Had All the Luck* has its first American staging since 1944. *Mr. Peters' Connections* premieres in London, where the National Theatre revives *All My Sons. Echoes Down the Corridor: Collected Essays 1944–2001* is published.

2001 Miller's one-act *Untitled* is performed as a prelude to a staging of Havel's *Vanek Plays* in New York. *On Politics and the Art of Acting* is published. Film adaptation of *Focus*, directed by Neil Slavin and starring William H. Macy and Laura Dern, is released in the fall. At National Book

Awards ceremony in November Miller receives Medal for Distinguished Contribution to American Literature.

2002 Inge Morath dies of lymphoma on January 30. *The Crucible* is revived on Broadway in a production starring Liam Neeson and Laura Linney that runs for 101 performances; *The Man Who Had All the Luck* is also revived on Broadway for 62 performances. Miller meets painter Agnes Barley, who becomes his companion. *Resurrection Blues* premieres in August at the Guthrie Theater. Bolcom's *A View from the Bridge* is performed at the Metropolitan Opera in New York. Gail Levin's documentary *Making "The Misfits"* is broadcast on PBS in October.

2003 Miller completes *Finishing the Picture.* Brother Kermit dies on October 17.

2004 *After the Fall* is revived on Broadway and runs for 53 performances. *Finishing the Picture* has world premiere at the Goodman Theater in Chicago.

2005 Arthur Miller dies of congestive heart failure in Roxbury on February 10 and is buried in the Roxbury Central Cemetery.

Note on the Texts

This volume contains Arthur Miller's plays *The Man Who Had All the Luck* (1944, revised 1989); *All My Sons* (1947); *Death of a Salesman* (1949); *The Crucible* (1953); *A Memory of Two Mondays* (1955); and *A View from the Bridge*, in both one-act (1955) and two-act (1956) versions. It also includes Miller's adaptation of Ibsen's *An Enemy of the People*, first performed in 1950, and his novella *The Misfits* (1961).

In 1943, Miller began adapting his unpublished novel "The Man Who Had All the Luck" into a play. An early version was published in the anthology *Cross-Section: A Collection of New American Writing* (1943). The play closed after four performances at the Forrest Theatre in November 1944. Although stung by the poor reception of his first play to run on Broadway, he continued to work on *The Man Who Had All the Luck*, particularly its ending, which he claimed in 1989 that he'd "rewritten twenty times over the last half century." The revised version of the play was published in London by Methuen in 1989 in *The Golden Years and The Man Who Had All the Luck*, which is the text printed here. This version of the play was the basis for the 1990 staging of the play in London, the first since its 1944 Broadway premiere.

In writing his plays, Miller usually completed numerous drafts before arriving at a version that he deemed suitable to take the stage. For *All My Sons*, for example, he wrote six drafts (totaling some 700 pages) before the play was staged. After a play's initial run, he would continue to make changes that would be incorporated into separate book publications, actors' editions (in pamphlets published by Dramatists Play Service), and, ultimately, in the two volumes comprising the collected edition of his plays (the first volume published in 1957, the second in 1981). In the present volume, the texts of *All My Sons*, *Death of a Salesman*, *The Crucible*, *A Memory of Two Mondays*, and the two-act version of *A View from the Bridge* are taken from *Arthur Miller's Collected Plays* (New York: Viking, 1957); *Collected Plays, Volume II* (New York: Viking, 1981) contains the text printed here of *The Misfits*, an adaptation of his screenplay first published to coincide with the release of the film early in 1961.

The texts of Miller's adaptation of Ibsen's *An Enemy of the People* and the one-act version of *A View from the Bridge*, neither of which are included in Miller's two-volume *Collected Plays*, are taken from their first book publications: *Arthur Miller's Adaptation of* An Enemy

of the People *by Henrik Ibsen* (New York: Viking, 1951) and *A View from the Bridge: Two One-Act Plays* (New York: Viking, 1955). The Ibsen adaptation was aided by a literal translation from the Norwegian provided by Lars Nordenson, a Swedish businessman who financed the play's Broadway production in 1950. The one-act version of *A View from the Bridge* is included here because it is different enough from the expanded version to be considered a separate work in its own right, and not simply a version of the play superseded by revisions subsequently made by Miller.

This volume presents the texts of the original printings chosen for inclusion here, but it does not attempt to reproduce nontextual features of their typographic design. The texts are presented without change, except for the correction of typographical errors. Spelling, punctuation, and capitalization are often expressive features and are not altered, even when inconsistent or irregular. The following is a list of typographical errors corrected, cited by page and line number: 2.20, *Falk's*; 7.33, Mr David Falk; 8.19, For; 15.6, *J.B.*; 19.14, hesistates; 22.32, TO; 25.30, I'm,; 26.11, *himself*; 30.22, (*Laughs..*); 31.26–30 done? [] when you're young; 36.3, FALK'*s*; 37.9, *bannister*; 40.1, J.B.; 42.7, J.B..; 53.19, mean; 56.34, AUGIE; 69.19, *David*; 70.1, man; 71.29, *J.B.*; 71.30, DAVE; 72.5, *Gus*; 183.28, kitchen; 228.31, *Watch this.*; 247.13, *Let me think about it.* He glances at his watch.; 251.22, *graps*; 263.23, rascist; 268.28, musn't; 269.7, *That*; 290.4, that; 344.19, HAWTHORNE; 382.35, *Paris*; 414.22, send; 480.32, mater; 486.6, 'That; 583.5, EDDIE:; 600.35, besides; 704.16, smoothes; 723.34, in pass; 724.1, Perse; 748.1, There.

Notes

In the notes below, the reference numbers denote page and line of this volume (the line count includes chapter headings). No note is made for material included in standard desk-reference books such as Webster's *Collegiate*, *Biographical*, and *Geographical* dictionaries. For further information on Miller's life and works, see S. K. Bhatia, *Arthur Miller* (London: Heinemann, 1985); Christopher Bigby, ed., *The Cambridge Companion to Arthur Miller* (Cambridge: Cambridge University Press, 1997); Neil Carson, *Arthur Miller* (New York: Grove, 1982); Robert W. Corrigan, ed., *Arthur Miller: A Collection of Critical Essays* (Englewood, NJ: Prentice-Hall, 1969); Martin Gottfried, *Arthur Miller: A Life* (London: Faber & Faber, 2003), published in the U.S. as *Arthur Miller: His Life and Work* (New York: Da Capo, 2004); Mel Gussow, *Conversations with Arthur Miller* (London: Nick Hern Books, 2002); Alice Griffin, *Understanding Arthur Miller* (Columbia, SC: University of South Carolina Press, 1996); Robert A. Martin, *Arthur Miller: New Perspectives* (Englewood, NJ: Prentice-Hall, 1982); Arthur Miller, *Timebends: A Life* (New York: Grove, 1987); Benjamin Nelson, *Arthur Miller: Portrait of a Playwright* (New York: McKay, 1970); Matthew C. Roudané, ed., *Conversations with Arthur Miller* (Jackson, MS: University Press of Mississippi, 1987); Dennis Welland, *Miller: The Playwright* (London: Methuen, 1979).

THE MAN WHO HAD ALL THE LUCK

Original cast:

J.B. Feller	Forrest Orr
David Beeves	Karl Swenson
Shory	Grover Burgess
Aunt Belle	Agnes Scott Yost
Patterson Beeves	Jack Sheehan
Amos Beeves	Dudley Sadler
Hester Falk	Eugenia Rawls
Gustav Eberson	Herbert Berghof
Dan Dibble	Sydney Grant
Augie Belfast	Lawrence Fletcher

Director: Joseph Fields. Producer: Herbert H. Harris. Premiered at the Forrest Theatre, New York, on November 23, 1944.

The text of the play printed here was revised for publication in 1989; the character Andrew Falk was not part of the 1944 production, and a character named Harry Bucks does not appear in the final revised version.

ALL MY SONS

Original cast:

Dr. Jim Bayliss	John McGovern
Joe Keller	Ed Begley
Frank Lubey	Dudley Sadler
Sue Bayliss	Peggy Meredith
Lydia Lubey	Hope Cameron
Chris Keller	Arthur Kennedy
Bert	Eugene Steiner
Kate Keller	Beth Merrill
Ann Deever	Lois Wheeler
George Deever	Karl Malden

Director: Elia Kazan. Producers: Harold Clurman, Elia Kazan, and Walter Fried, in association with Herbert H. Harris. Premiered at the Coronet Theatre, New York, on January 29, 1947.

90.25 a movie] *Happy Land* (1943), film starring Don Ameche about a small-town pharmacist coming to terms with his son's death in World War II.

DEATH OF A SALESMAN

Original cast:

Willy Loman	Lee J. Cobb
Linda	Mildred Dunnock
Biff	Arthur Kennedy
Happy	Cameron Mitchell
Bernard	Don Keefer
The Woman	Winnifred Cushing
Charley	Howard Smith
Uncle Ben	Thomas Chalmers
Howard Wagner	Alan Hewitt
Jenny	Ann Driscoll
Stanley	Tom Pedi
Miss Forsythe	Constance Ford
Letta	Hope Cameron

Director: Elia Kazan. Producers: Kermit Bloomgarden and Walter Fried. Premiered at the Morosco Theatre, New York, on February 10, 1949.

AN ENEMY OF THE PEOPLE

Original cast:

Morten Kiil	Art Smith
Billing	Michael Strong
Mrs. Stockmann	Florence Eldridge

Peter Stockmann	Morris Carnovsky
Hovstad	Martin Brooks
Dr. Stockmann	Frederic March
Morten	Ralph Robertson
Ejlif	Richard Trask
Captain Horster	Ralph Dunn
Petra	Anna Minot
Aslaksen	Fred Stewart
The Drunk	Lou Gilbert

Townspeople: Lulla Adler, Barbara Ames, Paul Fitzpatrick, James Karen, Michael Lewin, Salem Ludwig, Gene Lyons, John Marley, Arnold Schulman, Robert Simon, Rod Steiger

Director: Robert Lewis. Prodcuer: Lars Nordenson. Premiered at the Broadhurst Theatre in New York on December 28, 1950.

THE CRUCIBLE

Original cast:

Reverend Parris	Fred Stewart
Betty Parris	Janet Alexander
Tituba	Jacqueline Andre
Abigail Williams	Madeleine Sherwood
Susanna Walcott	Barbara Stanton
Mrs. Ann Putnam	Jane Hoffman
Thomas Putnam	Raymond Bramley
Mercy Lewis	Dorothy Jolliffe
Mary Warren	Jennie Egan
John Proctor	Arthur Kennedy
Rebecca Nurse	Jean Adair
Giles Corey	Joseph Sweeney
Reverend John Hale	E. G. Marshall
Elizabeth Proctor	Beatrice Straight
Francis Nurse	Graham Velsey
Ezekiel Cheever	Don McHenry
Marshal Herrick	George Mitchell
Judge Hathorne	Philip Coolidge
Deputy Governor Danforth	Walter Hampden
Sarah Good	Adele Fortin
Hopkins	Donald Mayre

Director: Jed Harris. Producer: Kermit Bloomgarden. Premiered at the Martin Beck Theatre on January 22, 1953.

378.8–9 In nomine . . . infernos.] In the name of God and of His Son, go to hell.

416.30–31 "Do that which . . . thee."] Cf. Tobit 4:23 in the Apocrypha; the admonition to young Tobias is spoken by his father.

A MEMORY OF TWO MONDAYS

Original cast:

Bert	Leo Penn
Raymond	David Clarke
Agnes	Eileen Heckart
Patricia	Gloria Marlowe
Gus	J. Carrol Naish
Jim	Russell Collins
Kenneth	Biff McGuire
Larry	Van Heflin
Frank	Jack Warden
Jerry	Richard Davalos
William	Antony Vorno
Tom	Curt Conway
Mechanic	Tom Pedi
Mister Eagle	Ralph Bell

Director: Martin Ritt. Producers: Kermit Bloomgarden, Robert Whitehead, and Roger L. Stevens. Premiered at the Coronet Theatre on September 29, 1955.

466.18–21 "Courage, brother! . . . Right."] From "Trust in God and Do the Right," by Scottish clergyman Norman Macleod (1812–1872).

468.19–20 The minstrel . . . death] From "The Minstrel Boy," by Irish poet Thomas Moore (1779–1852).

A VIEW FROM THE BRIDGE

Original cast:

Louis	David Clarke
Mike	Tom Pedi
Alfieri	J. Carrol Naish
Eddie	Van Heflin
Catherine	Gloria Marlowe
Beatrice	Eileen Heckart
Marco	Jack Warden
Tony	Antony Vorno
Rodolpho	Richard Davalos
First Immigration Officer	Curt Conway
Second Immigration Officer	Ralph Bell
Mr. Lipari	Russell Collins
Mrs. Lipari	Anne Driscoll
Two "Submarines"	Leo Penn, Milton Carney

Director: Martin Ritt. Producers: Kermit Bloomgarden, Robert Whitehead, and Roger L. Stevens. Premiered at the Coronet Theatre on September 29, 1955.

510.37 and 571.36–572.1 Frankie Yale] Gangster murdered in his car in Brooklyn on July 1, 1928.

Library of Congress Cataloging-in-Publication Data

Miller, Arthur, 1915–2005.
[Plays. Selections]
Collected plays, 1944–1961 / Arthur Miller.
p. cm.—(The Library of America ; 163)
Contents: The man who had all the luck (1944) — All my sons (1947) — Death of a salesman (1949) — An enemy of the people (adaptation, 1951) — The crucible (1953) — A memory of two Mondays (1955) — A view from the bridge (one act version, 1955) — A view from the bridge (two act version, 1956) — The misfits (1961)
Includes bibliographical references.
ISBN 1–931082–91–X (alk. paper)
I. Title: The man who had all the luck. II. Title: All my sons. III. Title: Death of a salesman. IV. Title: An enemy of the people. V. Title: The crucible. VI. Title: A memory of two Mondays. VII. Title: A view from the bridge (one act version). VIII. Title: A view from the bridge (two act version). IX. Title: The misfits. X. Title. XI. Series.

PS3525.I5156A6 2006
812′.52—dc22 2005049442

THE LIBRARY OF AMERICA SERIES

The Library of America fosters appreciation and pride in America's literary heritage by publishing, and keeping permanently in print, authoritative editions of America's best and most significant writing. An independent nonprofit organization, it was founded in 1979 with seed money from the National Endowment for the Humanities and the Ford Foundation.

1. Herman Melville, *Typee, Omoo, Mardi* (1982)
2. Nathaniel Hawthorne, *Tales and Sketches* (1982)
3. Walt Whitman, *Poetry and Prose* (1982)
4. Harriet Beecher Stowe, *Three Novels* (1982)
5. Mark Twain, *Mississippi Writings* (1982)
6. Jack London, *Novels and Stories* (1982)
7. Jack London, *Novels and Social Writings* (1982)
8. William Dean Howells, *Novels 1875–1886* (1982)
9. Herman Melville, *Redburn, White-Jacket, Moby-Dick* (1983)
10. Nathaniel Hawthorne, *Collected Novels* (1983)
11. Francis Parkman, *France and England in North America*, vol. I (1983)
12. Francis Parkman, *France and England in North America*, vol. II (1983)
13. Henry James, *Novels 1871–1880* (1983)
14. Henry Adams, *Novels, Mont Saint Michel, The Education* (1983)
15. Ralph Waldo Emerson, *Essays and Lectures* (1983)
16. Washington Irving, *History, Tales and Sketches* (1983)
17. Thomas Jefferson, *Writings* (1984)
18. Stephen Crane, *Prose and Poetry* (1984)
19. Edgar Allan Poe, *Poetry and Tales* (1984)
20. Edgar Allan Poe, *Essays and Reviews* (1984)
21. Mark Twain, *The Innocents Abroad, Roughing It* (1984)
22. Henry James, *Literary Criticism: Essays, American & English Writers* (1984)
23. Henry James, *Literary Criticism: European Writers & The Prefaces* (1984)
24. Herman Melville, *Pierre, Israel Potter, The Confidence-Man, Tales & Billy Budd* (1985)
25. William Faulkner, *Novels 1930–1935* (1985)
26. James Fenimore Cooper, *The Leatherstocking Tales*, vol. I (1985)
27. James Fenimore Cooper, *The Leatherstocking Tales*, vol. II (1985)
28. Henry David Thoreau, *A Week, Walden, The Maine Woods, Cape Cod* (1985)
29. Henry James, *Novels 1881–1886* (1985)
30. Edith Wharton, *Novels* (1986)
31. Henry Adams, *History of the U.S. during the Administrations of Jefferson* (1986)
32. Henry Adams, *History of the U.S. during the Administrations of Madison* (1986)
33. Frank Norris, *Novels and Essays* (1986)
34. W.E.B. Du Bois, *Writings* (1986)
35. Willa Cather, *Early Novels and Stories* (1987)
36. Theodore Dreiser, *Sister Carrie, Jennie Gerhardt, Twelve Men* (1987)

37A. Benjamin Franklin, *Silence Dogood, The Busy-Body, & Early Writings* (1987)
37B. Benjamin Franklin, *Autobiography, Poor Richard, & Later Writings* (1987)

38. William James, *Writings 1902–1910* (1987)
39. Flannery O'Connor, *Collected Works* (1988)
40. Eugene O'Neill, *Complete Plays 1913–1920* (1988)
41. Eugene O'Neill, *Complete Plays 1920–1931* (1988)
42. Eugene O'Neill, *Complete Plays 1932–1943* (1988)
43. Henry James, *Novels 1886–1890* (1989)
44. William Dean Howells, *Novels 1886–1888* (1989)
45. Abraham Lincoln, *Speeches and Writings 1832–1858* (1989)
46. Abraham Lincoln, *Speeches and Writings 1859–1865* (1989)
47. Edith Wharton, *Novellas and Other Writings* (1990)
48. William Faulkner, *Novels 1936–1940* (1990)
49. Willa Cather, *Later Novels* (1990)
50. Ulysses S. Grant, *Memoirs and Selected Letters* (1990)

51. William Tecumseh Sherman, *Memoirs* (1990)
52. Washington Irving, *Bracebridge Hall, Tales of a Traveller, The Alhambra* (1991)
53. Francis Parkman, *The Oregon Trail, The Conspiracy of Pontiac* (1991)
54. James Fenimore Cooper, *Sea Tales: The Pilot, The Red Rover* (1991)
55. Richard Wright, *Early Works* (1991)
56. Richard Wright, *Later Works* (1991)
57. Willa Cather, *Stories, Poems, and Other Writings* (1992)
58. William James, *Writings 1878–1899* (1992)
59. Sinclair Lewis, *Main Street & Babbitt* (1992)
60. Mark Twain, *Collected Tales, Sketches, Speeches, & Essays 1852–1890* (1992)
61. Mark Twain, *Collected Tales, Sketches, Speeches, & Essays 1891–1910* (1992)
62. *The Debate on the Constitution: Part One* (1993)
63. *The Debate on the Constitution: Part Two* (1993)
64. Henry James, *Collected Travel Writings: Great Britain & America* (1993)
65. Henry James, *Collected Travel Writings: The Continent* (1993)
66. *American Poetry: The Nineteenth Century,* Vol. 1 (1993)
67. *American Poetry: The Nineteenth Century,* Vol. 2 (1993)
68. Frederick Douglass, *Autobiographies* (1994)
69. Sarah Orne Jewett, *Novels and Stories* (1994)
70. Ralph Waldo Emerson, *Collected Poems and Translations* (1994)
71. Mark Twain, *Historical Romances* (1994)
72. John Steinbeck, *Novels and Stories 1932–1937* (1994)
73. William Faulkner, *Novels 1942–1954* (1994)
74. Zora Neale Hurston, *Novels and Stories* (1995)
75. Zora Neale Hurston, *Folklore, Memoirs, and Other Writings* (1995)
76. Thomas Paine, *Collected Writings* (1995)
77. *Reporting World War II: American Journalism 1938–1944* (1995)
78. *Reporting World War II: American Journalism 1944–1946* (1995)
79. Raymond Chandler, *Stories and Early Novels* (1995)
80. Raymond Chandler, *Later Novels and Other Writings* (1995)
81. Robert Frost, *Collected Poems, Prose, & Plays* (1995)
82. Henry James, *Complete Stories 1892–1898* (1996)
83. Henry James, *Complete Stories 1898–1910* (1996)
84. William Bartram, *Travels and Other Writings* (1996)
85. John Dos Passos, *U.S.A.* (1996)
86. John Steinbeck, *The Grapes of Wrath and Other Writings 1936–1941* (1996)
87. Vladimir Nabokov, *Novels and Memoirs 1941–1951* (1996)
88. Vladimir Nabokov, *Novels 1955–1962* (1996)
89. Vladimir Nabokov, *Novels 1969–1974* (1996)
90. James Thurber, *Writings and Drawings* (1996)
91. George Washington, *Writings* (1997)
92. John Muir, *Nature Writings* (1997)
93. Nathanael West, *Novels and Other Writings* (1997)
94. *Crime Novels: American Noir of the 1930s and 40s* (1997)
95. *Crime Novels: American Noir of the 1950s* (1997)
96. Wallace Stevens, *Collected Poetry and Prose* (1997)
97. James Baldwin, *Early Novels and Stories* (1998)
98. James Baldwin, *Collected Essays* (1998)
99. Gertrude Stein, *Writings 1903–1932* (1998)
100. Gertrude Stein, *Writings 1932–1946* (1998)
101. Eudora Welty, *Complete Novels* (1998)
102. Eudora Welty, *Stories, Essays, & Memoir* (1998)
103. Charles Brockden Brown, *Three Gothic Novels* (1998)
104. *Reporting Vietnam: American Journalism 1959–1969* (1998)
105. *Reporting Vietnam: American Journalism 1969–1975* (1998)
106. Henry James, *Complete Stories 1874–1884* (1999)
107. Henry James, *Complete Stories 1884–1891* (1999)

108. *American Sermons: The Pilgrims to Martin Luther King Jr.* (1999)
109. James Madison, *Writings* (1999)
110. Dashiell Hammett, *Complete Novels* (1999)
111. Henry James, *Complete Stories 1864–1874* (1999)
112. William Faulkner, *Novels 1957–1962* (1999)
113. John James Audubon, *Writings & Drawings* (1999)
114. *Slave Narratives* (2000)
115. *American Poetry: The Twentieth Century*, Vol. 1 (2000)
116. *American Poetry: The Twentieth Century*, Vol. 2 (2000)
117. F. Scott Fitzgerald, *Novels and Stories 1920–1922* (2000)
118. Henry Wadsworth Longfellow, *Poems and Other Writings* (2000)
119. Tennessee Williams, *Plays 1937–1955* (2000)
120. Tennessee Williams, *Plays 1957–1980* (2000)
121. Edith Wharton, *Collected Stories 1891–1910* (2001)
122. Edith Wharton, *Collected Stories 1911–1937* (2001)
123. *The American Revolution: Writings from the War of Independence* (2001)
124. Henry David Thoreau, *Collected Essays and Poems* (2001)
125. Dashiell Hammett, *Crime Stories and Other Writings* (2001)
126. Dawn Powell, *Novels 1930–1942* (2001)
127. Dawn Powell, *Novels 1944–1962* (2001)
128. Carson McCullers, *Complete Novels* (2001)
129. Alexander Hamilton, *Writings* (2001)
130. Mark Twain, *The Gilded Age and Later Novels* (2002)
131. Charles W. Chesnutt, *Stories, Novels, and Essays* (2002)
132. John Steinbeck, *Novels 1942–1952* (2002)
133. Sinclair Lewis, *Arrowsmith, Elmer Gantry, Dodsworth* (2002)
134. Paul Bowles, *The Sheltering Sky, Let It Come Down, The Spider's House* (2002)
135. Paul Bowles, *Collected Stories & Later Writings* (2002)
136. Kate Chopin, *Complete Novels & Stories* (2002)
137. *Reporting Civil Rights: American Journalism 1941–1963* (2003)
138. *Reporting Civil Rights: American Journalism 1963–1973* (2003)
139. Henry James, *Novels 1896–1899* (2003)
140. Theodore Dreiser, *An American Tragedy* (2003)
141. Saul Bellow, *Novels 1944–1953* (2003)
142. John Dos Passos, *Novels 1920–1925* (2003)
143. John Dos Passos, *Travel Books and Other Writings* (2003)
144. Ezra Pound, *Poems and Translations* (2003)
145. James Weldon Johnson, *Writings* (2004)
146. Washington Irving, *Three Western Narratives* (2004)
147. Alexis de Tocqueville, *Democracy in America* (2004)
148. James T. Farrell, *Studs Lonigan: A Trilogy* (2004)
149. Isaac Bashevis Singer, *Collected Stories I* (2004)
150. Isaac Bashevis Singer, *Collected Stories II* (2004)
151. Isaac Bashevis Singer, *Collected Stories III* (2004)
152. Kaufman & Co., *Broadway Comedies* (2004)
153. Theodore Roosevelt, *The Rough Riders, An Autobiography* (2004)
154. Theodore Roosevelt, *Letters and Speeches* (2004)
155. H. P. Lovecraft, *Tales* (2005)
156. Louisa May Alcott, *Little Women, Little Men, Jo's Boys* (2005)
157. Philip Roth, *Novels & Stories 1959–1962* (2005)
158. Philip Roth, *Novels 1967–1972* (2005)
159. James Agee, *Let Us Now Praise Famous Men, A Death in the Family* (2005)
160. James Agee, *Film Writing & Selected Journalism* (2005)
161. Richard Henry Dana, Jr., *Two Years Before the Mast & Other Voyages* (2005)
162. Henry James, *Novels 1901–1902* (2006)
163. Arthur Miller, *Collected Plays 1944–1961* (2006)
164. William Faulkner, *Novels 1926–1929* (2006)

This book is set in 10 point Linotron Galliard, a face designed for photocomposition by Matthew Carter and based on the sixteenth-century face Granjon. The paper is acid-free Domtar Literary Opaque and meets the requirements for permanence of the American National Standards Institute. The binding material is Brillianta, a woven rayon cloth made by Van Heek-Scholco Textielfabrieken, Holland. Composition by Dedicated Business Services. Printing by Malloy Incorporated. Binding by Dekker Bookbinding. Designed by Bruce Campbell.